J.R. Morell

Bradshaw´s Pedestrian Route-Book for Switzerland, Chamouni, and the Italian Lakes

Salzwasser

J.R. Morell

Bradshaw´s Pedestrian Route-Book for Switzerland, Chamouni, and the Italian Lakes

1. Auflage | ISBN: 978-3-84604-790-3

Erscheinungsort: Frankfurt, Deutschland

Erscheinungsjahr: 2020

Salzwasser Verlag GmbH

Reprint of the original, first published in 1870.

BRADSHAW'S PEDESTRIAN ROUTE-BOOK

FOR

SWITZERLAND,

CHAMOUNI,. AND THE ITALIAN LAKES;

WITH AN

HOTEL AND PENSION GUIDE,

AND DESCRIPTIONS OF ALL THE BEST CENTRES FOR EXCURSIONS, &c.

EDITED BY J. R. MORELL.

CONTAINING ALL THE PRINCIPAL CENTRES OF SWISS EXCURSIONS
(WITH THE EXCURSIONS),
AND ALL THE PRINCIPAL PEDESTRIAN ROUTES TO THOSE CENTRES IN
ALPHABETICAL ORDER.

ACCOMPANIED BY A KEY MAP AND PLANS.

LONDON:
W. J. ADAMS (BRADSHAW'S GUIDE OFFICE), 59, FLEET STREET, E.C.;
MANCHESTER:
BRADSHAW AND BLACKLOCK, ALBERT SQUARE.
1870.

PREFACE.

There are many good Hand-books on Switzerland, in several European languages. The topography, geology, natural and political history of that interesting country have been carefully studied and graphically described by competent observers, especially English and German.

Several of these works, however, are voluminous and expensive, and contain details on points of no special interest to the mass of travellers. Others again, professing to be more popular, shorter, and cheaper, are either too meagre in information or confused from their brevity. It has appeared, therefore, that there might yet be room for a work aiming, at least, at a combination of full practical information within a moderate portable form, and at a union of clearness with conciseness.

Two other special objects have been kept in view in the present Hand-book. 1st. A fund and an arrangement of facts, adapted to a shorter or a longer stay in Switzerland. For this purpose the writer has been careful to single out the great centres, with their excursions, and all useful information about the accommodation they afford. 2nd. The majority of our modern Hand-books have adhered so closely to the lines of railroad, and to the old exhausted centres, that they have bestowed very little attention or space on the numerous delightful districts, affording charming pedestrian or equestrian excursions, among the green Alps (e. g. of Appenzell), out of the beaten track. Railways may change and be superseded by other systems, but the everlasting mountains will not rapidly pass away. Switzerland is intersected in all directions by excellent turnpike roads, which are destined to remain and endure in such a mountainous country, and which open up scenes of endless sylvan and pastoral beauty to those who are weary of the bustle and high prices of Chamouni or Interlaken. In fact, the lower level routes of Switzerland are, in certain cases, scarcely less interesting than those on a higher level, and lead to districts of peculiar charms, like the Münsterthal, Simmenthal, and Entlibuch.

When, however, it has appeared desirable, useful railway information has been added, for the benefit of those who have not much time at command. But it is apprehended, the best Guide for those will always be "*Bradshaw's Continental;*" while the present work contains the mileage of all the principal turnpike and pedestrian routes in Switzerland, arranged in alphabetical order, and with a fulness not found, we think, in any other English Guide.

In fact, the principal intention that has guided the preparation of this work has been general practical utility and clearness. To this end a partially new system has been adopted. The approaches to Switzerland and main arteries through that country, consisting partly of railways, are classed under the letters A, B, C, D, E, and F. To assist the traveller, these arteries are marked on a key map, by which he finds out at once the Cantons through which the arteries pass. He then looks to the Cantons, and finds in each of them all the principal centres in them, with their excursions in alphabetical order. At the end of these Cantons the traveller will find all the Pedestrian Routes, from their main centre to the other parts of Switzerland.

These Routes, with their mileage, are a special feature of the work, and can be consulted by themselves, without reference to the rest of the work, as their numbers run in alphabetical and numerical order, according to the place in the alphabet occupied by the Canton to which they belong. Thus, the Routes of Aarau begin as Nos. 1, 2, 3, &c., and those of Zurich terminate the series as Routes 305 and 306. To facilitate his search an Index of Cantons and Routes is added at the end.

It is proposed and hoped that, by the means here presented, the traveller will put his finger at once on all he wants, and will be able to steer himself in most cases, without the aid of professional guides, simply availing himself in certain cases of the assistance of a little boy, or, at most, of a porter. If the writer is not disappointed in his expectations, the book will be a useful source of economy, both of time and money, and, it may be added, worry, by enabling the traveller to dispense with many annoying appendages.

It is only necessary to add, that when hotels are classed as dear, this does not condemn them, because a book intended for a great number, is bound to supply information for those of slender means in search of cheaper quarters.

Lastly, the Editor will be thankful if travellers or hotel-keepers will point out any inaccuracies they observe in the prices marked in the work.

NOTICE.—A perfectly novel feature of this work is presented in the account of the remains of ancient lake habitations found recently in Switzerland, a brief Guide to which is offered in the Appendix.

CONTENTS

INDEX OF CANTONS.

INDEX OF ROUTES.

At all times and in all seasons this Alpine scenery, when visible, is overpowering, worshipful, and beautiful. Thus, when winter covers the low as well as high lands with its silver mantle of purity, often dazzling like fields of diamonds in the light of the sun, the blue, breezy waters of the lakes take a deeper azure or emerald, reflecting the thousand peaks around them in their crystal mirror.

Again, what can be grander than night in the great mountain solitudes. The music of the torrents, the sighing of the night wind, the unearthly mingled lights of morn and dawn, above all the holy tenderness of the sunset and sunlight tints, defy the pencil or brush and exceed language and poetry.

Travellers who have tarried as all should in such a sphere, and revelled in its mysteries and beauties, have told us much of the magic of the cloud scenery and the great atmospheric ocean seen above with its mirage and its illuminations, its fireworks and its fairy palaces. Great naturalists have told us how they have lived a life, and come down new and better men, after their communings with the Great Spirit and his wonders, upon ice-fields where they kiss the clouds. But poetry and art have never compassed the depth or pourtrayed the enchantment that accompanies these airy regions and bathes them so to speak in a flood of glory. Nor can any know, save those who have felt it, the enthusiasm and the reverence inspired by such scenes. It is impossible for a sound-minded man to view them and not improve. It is like communing with childhood or thoughts of the dead, a sacred sphere rich in innocence, purity, and peace.

The Alps, situated between 43° and 48° of north latitude, are placed at an almost equal distance from the Equator and the North Pole, and almost in the same latitude as the Caucasus, covering about the same amount of ground. They dominate and make Europe, determining its water basins and channels, and they thus seem upraised by a special decree of Providence to give beauty, fertility, and health to this the most important division of our earth.

The extreme limits of Switzerland consist to the west of a point half a league from Chancy on the Rhine (Canton of Geneva), long. 23° 37', and to the eastward of the Piz Clavalatsch (8,510 ft.) in the Grisons, situated between the Münsterthal and the Würmser Joch, long. 28° 9' 25".* The latitudinal limits are 45' 48' to the south, at Monte Cavallasca in Tessin, and 47° 48' 30" to the north, at the foot of the Hohe Rand in Schaffhausen.

The greatest diagonal breadth is 47½ German geographical miles, and the extreme breadth 30 German geographical miles, or 46 Swiss leagues.

According to the researches of General Dufour the area of Switzerland consists of 724₁₀⁹ German geographical miles, making 1,732₁₀ Swiss square leagues or 11,085,440 Swiss jucharts.†

* Ferro Island, 17° 39' 37" west of Greenwich is the first meridian of the Germans.

<pre>
      23° 37'   23° 49' 25"
      17° 39' 37"   17° 39' 37"
      ___________   ___________
       5° 57' 23" East of Greenwich,   10° 9' 45" East of Greenwich.
       West limit of Switzerland.   East limit of Switzerland.
</pre>

† 1 juchart=40,000 square Swiss feet; 1 Swiss league=6,400 jucharts; 1 geographical square German mile=2·39 Swiss square leagues; the Swiss foot=3 decimetres. the Ruthe (Rod)=3 metres; Swiss league= 6,000 feet or 4,000 metres; the juchart of 400 square Ruthen, or Rods=40,000 square feet = 36 French acres or 140,805 Prussian morgens. 1 Swiss league=2·983 English miles or nearly 3 English miles; 1 Swiss arpent or juchart=0·9 English acres, 9-10 of an acre nearly; 1 German mile= 4·602 English miles or nearly 4½ miles; 23·19 Swiss leagues form a geographical degree, or 1,460,000 of the natural longitude.

INTRODUCTION.

Δόξα ἐν ὑψίστοις Θεῷ.—LUKE ii. 14.

WHEN after a monotonous, perhaps tedious, transit across the fertile plains of France, or even the more diversified mediocrity of Germany, the Alps stand forth suddenly to view in their mantle of snowy grandeur, a mixture of delight and awe takes possession of the spectator. Perhaps refreshment is after all the dominant feeling they evoke, resembling the comfort brought to the mind of the African traveller at the sight of water, and in some degree the moral rapture inspired by the towers of Jerusalem in the Old Crusader, or that more ancient joy expressed by Xenophon's gallant ten thousand, when Θάλασσα, Θάλασσα (the sea, the sea) resounded through the war-worn host.

Reverence unites with refreshment in calling forth the gratitude of the traveller, and he feels a kind of worship for those "mountains whence our help cometh."

There is much in reason and in fact to justify these sentiments. Mountains have ever been the seat of health and the home of freedom. High thoughts and deeds have frequently emanated from these altitudes. The corruption and the vanities of the cities of the plain drop away as you rise into this purer region, when man, communing with the great forces of nature, partakes in a measure and for a time in the dignity and majesty of the eternal and the infinite, and learns to see all things, himself included, from a higher level. The mountains, like the sea, are the proper province of reverence, mystery, and worship, nor is it easy to meet a scoffer, born and bred among such venerable scenery. Our Lord himself loved the mountains, and retired frequently to them to pray. All the great events of sacred history are connected with the uplands, or the sparkling, ever-shining waters of the lake and fountain, which take their rise and their beauty from the powers of the air, wreathing the mountain's brow in their garlands of mist and mystery.

Great is the distance from which the Alps can be viewed, though perhaps not equal to the space over which the eye ranges from the supreme summits of the chain. Their fantastic and dim outline greets the traveller even at 120 miles on the side of Salzburg and Bavaria, but it is the nearer, clearer, though still distant view that produces the most overpowering effect. Who does not remember the Oberland chain seen from Berne or Neuchâtel, and above all Monte Rosa from Turin. From the towers of St. Marc's at Venice, and from the Cathedral dome of Milan, the eye takes in grand distant views of the Southern chain; while in Bavaria the Peissenberg in the Schwarzwald, the Feldberg, the tower called the Frauenthurm at Munich, and many other points, give an equally imposing view of the Northern chain. Unequalled also is the view from the Weissenstein, near Solothurn, the eye takes in an Alpine panorama of 280 miles in extent, perhaps in some respects the sublimest that is afforded on our globe.

The waters of Switzerland :—

1. The Rhone basin to the lake of Geneva drains 96 square German miles, and has a length of 24 German miles, draining (including the lake of Geneva) 112 square German miles, or 268 Swiss square leagues (one-sixth of Switzerland).

2. The Rhine basin to Bâle drains 523 square German miles (one-fourth of Switzerland), or 1,250 square Swiss leagues, with a length of 48 German miles, or 74 Swiss leagues.

3. The Inn basin drains 22 square German miles or 52 Swiss leagues ($\frac{1}{15}$ of the area of the republic).

4. The Swiss tributaries of the Po basin drain 68 square German miles or 162 square Swiss leagues (one-eleventh of the surface of the country).

Of subordinate tributaries three rising in Switzerland and falling into the Rhine deserve notice :—

The Aar to its confluence at Coblentz (Confluentia) in Aargau, drains 316 square miles, with a length of 37 German miles.

2. The Reuss basin drains 160 square German miles, with a length of 20·9 square German miles.

3. The Limmat drains 43·7 square German miles, with a length of 18·9 to its junction with the Aar.

Of the lakes we have to notice :—

1. In Rhone basin, the Lake of Geneva—Height, 1,154 to 1,160 feet above the sea ; area, 11¼ square German miles or 26¾ square Swiss leagues ; depth, 1,154 feet.

2. In the Rhine basin, Lake of Constance (Boden See)—Area, 9½ square German miles, or 22¼ square Swiss leagues ; depth, 856 feet.

3. In tributary basins to the Rhine : (a) Limmat forms Lake of Zurich—Area, 1½ square geographical miles ; depth, 600 feet. (b) Reuss forms Lake of Lucerne—Area, $1\frac{7}{10}$ square German miles ; depth, 800 feet. (c) Aar forms Lake of Brienz—Area, ¼ square geographical mile ; depth, 2,000 feet. Also, Lake of Thun—Area, ¾ square German miles or 2 square Swiss leagues ; depth, 728 feet.

4. Thiele forms Lake of Neuchatel—Area, $4\frac{4}{5}$ square German miles or 10¼ square Swiss leagues ; depth, 400 feet. Also, Lake of Biel or Bienne—Area, ¼ square German miles or 1¾ square Swiss leagues ; depth, 217 feet.

5. Tessin tributary of the Po forms Lago Maggiore—Area, 3¾ square German geographical miles or 8¾ Swiss square leagues ; depth, 2,465 feet.

Subordinate tertiary lakes will be noticed in the separate Cantons.

As a summary of this bird's eye view of the country it will be convenient to remember that :

1. The proportion of ground covered with everlasting snow and glaciers is $\frac{1}{18}$ or $\frac{1}{130}$.

2. Pasture land, 3,968,000 jucharts.

3. Forests, 1,980,000 jucharts (712,800 hectares or 309½ square Swiss leagues).

4. Agricultural area,* 1,615,000 Swiss jucharts.

5. Lakes, 38 square German miles.

---

* The Swiss Home Department estimates the surface of vineyard in Switzerland at 77,000 jucharts (12 square Swiss leagues or 69,300 acres).

LENGTH OF PRINCIPAL GLACIERS.*

Name and Place.	Feet.		Leagues.
Findelen Glacier	17,200	....	1
Ditto, with its Firnmulde, (or Névé basin)	38,000	....	2½
Mortiratsch Grisons	24,600	....	1½
Ditto, with Firnmulde............................	30,200	.... almost	2
Glacier des Bois, Chamouni	21,600	....	1½
Ditto, with Firnmulde	43,000	....	2¾
Aar Gletscher, Bern............................	24,600	....	1½
Ditto, with Firnmulde............................	49,250	....	3
Görner Gletscher, Valais	33,860	....	2
Ditto, with Firnmulde............................	46,800	....	3
Great Aletsch Valais Glacier..................	60,000	....	3¾
Ditto, with its Firnmulde........................	80,000	....	5

The latter is probably the longest glacier in the world. As regards surface that of the Aar glacier has been estimated at 9,600,000 square metres, and that of its Firnmulde at 8,000,000. The Mortiratsch Glacier has an area of 12,000,000 square metres, the Görner Glacier, with its 9 Firnmulde, 50,000,000 square metres, and the Aletsch Glacier, 110,000,000 square metres. (1 metre=3·29 feet).

HEIGHT OF WATERFALLS.

	Feet.
The principal falls are those of	
The Rhine at Schaffhausen	70
Aar at Handeck...	260
Tosa, in Val Formazza..	500
Staubbach. Lauterbrunnen	900
Reichenbach. Meyringen. Main fall	300
Giesbach. Brienz .... (including its 7 falls.)	1,100
Falls less known but worth notice:—	
Turtmann Fall. Valais	80
Seerenbach, above Lake Wallenstadt...	1,400
Baierbach „ „	600
The Linth, formed by several torrents. At the Todi Falls in 2 leagues to the Pantenbrücke	3,000

* *Explanation of Glacier Terms.*

Moulins or vertical shafts in the ice enlarged by the action of falling water melted on the glacier's surface. Two or three other glacier terms occurring in the work may need explanation. These are, Seracs, Névé, Bergschrund, Couloir, and Moraine:—*Seracs*, a term introduced by De Saussure, express névé when cut into huge square blocks by transverse crevasses. *Névé* is in the higher region, masses of snow after being partially thawed and then congealed being converted into glacier ice. It is transition snow. The Germans call it *Firn*. A peculiar kind of crevasse called in German, *Bergschrund*, forming the separation between the fields of névé that partake more or less of the downward motion of the glacier, and the upper snow slopes that remain attached to the rocky skeleton of the mountain. A Bergschrund is often 30 feet wide, and a serious difficulty in ascensions. *Couloirs*, are the channels of ice, snow, or stone avalanches grooved in the rock. *Moraines* medial are piles of stones carried down glaciers by their slow downward movement. Lateral Moraines are deposited at the side by the same movement. Grooved and scolloped rocks as near the Grimsel, &c., often show the presence of ancient glaciers which have thus scraped them with their moraines and blocks of stone. Avalanches are of three kinds,—snow, ice, and stone. The snow avalanches are very dangerous in early spring and winter, stone and ice in summer when the sun acquires power. An extensive avalanche may bury villages, and snaps large fir trees like reeds.

HEIGHT OF WATERFALLS—Continued.

	Feet.
At Thierfehd makes a fall of	400
The Schreyenbach, or Fissmatt, tributary of the Linth	400
The Sernf, another tributary of the Linth, falls in 2½ leagues	2,370
Near Schwenden makes a leap of	780
The Niederenbach, a tributary of the Sernf, falls over the Staffelwand	1,000
The Reuss falls in 1 league	1,000
The Saane, at Gsteig, makes a beautiful fall of	300
The Pletschbach. Lauterbrunnen	900
Buffalora Fall. Tessin, a tributary of the Ticino	200
Nant d'Arpenaz, in the valley of the Arve. Savoy	800

Feet above the Sea.		Feet above the Sea.	
The Rhine at Tavatsch is	4,375	The Aar at its source is	5,854
At Dissentis	3,557	At Grimsel	5,778
At Trons	2,654	At Handeck	4,421
At Reichenau	1,850	At Guttannen	3,253
At Ragatz	1,545	At Meiringen	1,852
At Schaffhausen	1,208	At Berne	1,560

The Alps proper occupy three-fourths of the surface, and the plateaux and Jura one-fourth of the surface of Switzerland.*

It may be useful to bear in mind the following facts:—

The twelve highest summits of the Alps are—

	Feet.		Feet.
Mont Blanc	14,809	Dent Blanche	13,421
Monte Rosa	14,284 or 14,429	Cima di Jazzi	13,240
Mischabelhörner	14,020	Finsteraarhorn	13,160
Matterhorn, or Mont Cervin	13,848	Lyskamm	13,074
Weisshorn	13,900	Zinal Rothhorn	13,065
Monte Cristallo	13,545	Distelhorn	12,966

The highest passes are—

	Feet.
1. The Weissthor, under Monte Rosa, and Cima di Jazzi, from Valais to Italy	11,138
2. Forcola di Mezzodi, from Bondo in Bergell to Val Codera in Valtellina	11,021
3. Col du Géant, from Chamouni to Courmajeur	10,553
4. St. Theodule, from Zermatt to Italy. Breuil	10,284

The Flora of Switzerland contains 3,000 phanerogamic, and 3,000 cryptogamic plants, and is relatively the richest on the European continent.

It occupies seven regions or zones from the plains to 12,700 feet, at which elevation a lichen was found near the summit of the Jungfrau, and hence called Umbilicaria Virginis-Schär.

The first, or Campestral zone, from the plain to 2,500 feet. The position makes a great difference in all the zones, and the southern or Italian slope in this zone produces oranges, lemons, and almost a tropical vegetation.

* The geology of Switzerland requires a special chapter in the Appendix.

The first and second, or hill zones, have much in common with the vegetation of South Germany. They are characterised by a great number of orchideæ, ranunculaceæ, rosaceæ, synantheriæ, scrophulariæ, &c.

The third, or Mountain Region, extends from 2,500 to 4,000 feet. It has many plants of the hill region, but the vine does not reach so high. It contains 600 kinds of plants, including the populus nigra to 4,400 feet, and the populus tremula, yet higher. The ash (fraxinus excelsior) vanishes at 3,000 feet; aconite, saxifraga, aizoon, to 8,000 feet. Crocus, vernus, longiflorus, &c., belong to this zone.

The fourth, or Subalpine Region, from 4,000 to 5,500 feet, contains among trees chiefly firs. The weisstanne (silver fir) ceases at 5,000 feet. This zone has 450 species.

The fifth, or Upper Alpine Region, to 7,000 feet, has 400 species, mostly remarkable for greater beauty and fragrance. They are mostly perennial, and few cryptogamic plants appear among them. Pinus pumilo exists largely, and Juniperas-nana and sabina. Myosotis alpestris, gentiana purpurea, achillea moschata abound. Of the coniferæ the arve (pinus cembra) reaches highest and nearest to the snow. Its normal elevation is near 6,350 feet, but it rises near Stelvio (Grisons) 7,883 feet. It does not occur much under 4,000 feet. The larch (pinus larix) rises to 7,108 feet. The rothtanne (pinus abies p. picea du roi) is the commonest fir tree in the Alps, rises commonly to 5,500 feet, and in the Engadin to 6,500 or 7,000 feet. Pinus sylvestris, called dähle, rises to 6,000 feet, but only as a dwarf species the pinus mughus scop or p. pumillio. The weisstanne, or edeltanne (pinus picea) only occurs in northern Switzerland, and not above 5,000 feet. The pinus strobus reaches 5,500 feet. The beech (fagus sylvatica) occurs mostly between 1,200 and 2,800 feet, sometimes at 5,000. The populus tremula reaches 5,000 feet; the birch (betula alba) 6,000 feet on Gneiss and Glimmerschiefer. The rhododendron flourishes splendidly at 5,000 to 7,000 feet, and the writer has plunged joyously in its gay bushes on the glorious slopes of Montanvert and Col de Balme. It is in fine flower at that height in July and August.

The sixth, or Subnival Region, lies between 7,000 and 8,500 feet. It has 230 plants, without any trees. Gentiana glacialis is found on the very ice. Saxifrages and mosses are numerous.

The seventh, or Snow Region, reaches up to the summits. Ranunculus glacialis was found at 1,000 feet on the Schreckhorn. Gentiana imbricata, saxifraga bryoides, and acaulis; and among mosses, anoectangium lapponicum frequently occur in this zone.

Fauna.—Von Tschudi divides Swiss animals into three classes: 1—those inhabiting the mountain region up to 4,000 feet; 2—those reaching to 7,000 feet; 3—those reaching to 14,000 feet. Of vertebrata, excluding domestic animals, there are 427 kinds (half of these belong to the mountain zone); of amphibia, 32 kinds; of mammalia, 46 kinds; of fish, 42 kinds; of articulata there are 5,000 kinds. Among the 4,600 insects are arachnidae, 300 kinds; crustacea, 50 kinds. Of beetles there are 1,500 kinds; but in one and the same region only 20 kinds. Of butterflies, 800 kinds; between 7,000 and 8,000 feet, butterflies only afford 20 kinds.

The most interesting mammalia are chamois* and steinbocks. Of the former 300 or 400 are shot yearly. Average weight in autumn, 100lb. Some old bucks live to 30 years. Latin name for them, capra rupicapra. Live in herds of 5 to 20, formerly of 60. Steinbock (capra ibex), remarkable for horns 2½ feet long, now almost disappeared, except among the Graian Alps of Piedmont. Marmots

---

* The chamois ranges to 12,000 feet.

(arctomys marmota-schreb) are 1½ feet long, and weigh 6 to 10lb. In autumn their flesh is sweet and good to eat. Bears* and wolves† are now very rare. Of birds the most remarkable is the lammergeyer (falco barbatus). A full-grown bird is 4½ feet long, measuring 9 to 10 feet from the tips of the wings, and 12 to 16, but rarely 20lb. weight. Of reptiles the commonest are the common adder (ringelnatter), (coluber natrix), of a steel-blue colour, 4 to 6 feet long, called ringed-snake in English, quite harmless, and used sometimes as food. On the south slope of the Alps the viper (vipera redii), 3 feet long and poisonous, also the hochnatter (vipera berus), found up to 7,600 feet.

Of fishes. there are 42 kinds, 36 in the Rhine, 27 in the Rhone, and 17 in the Tessin basins. The salmon is the dominant species of which the salmo sular is the largest and finest kind, salmo lacustris, salmo lavis, salmo salvelinus, rotheli, salmo umbla, salmo maraena are varieties of this species.

The brienzling is the S. albula, seven inches long, in the lakes of Brienz, Lucern, and Zurich, and much valued for its delicate flavour.

Of carps, there are 17 kinds, the largest weighing 8lbs.

CLIMATE OF SWITZERLAND.

The climate‡ is generally very healthy, and except in the high Alps, temperate.

Place.	Height in Feet.	Mean Summer Heat. Degrees. Reaumur.		Mean Winter Cold. Degrees.		Annual Mean. Degrees.
Locarno	641	...	...	...	...	10·98
Bâle	817	...	14·4	...	0·4	7·9
Aarau	1,127	...	...	...	...	7·8
Geneva	1,165	...	14·9	...	0·5	7·92
Zurich	1,268	...	14·66	...	0·96	7·087
Lucern	1,350	...	16·0	...	3·57	8·0
Solothurn	1,371	...	14·0	...	6·0	8·0
Glarus	1,397	...	12·67	...	...	7·0
Bern	1,600	...	11·9	...	1·16	7·1
Masschlins	1,780	...	...	...	...	8·918
Chur	1,844	...	15·0	...	0·1	7·65
St. Gallen	2,081	...	13·19	...	3·31	6·7
Bühler, in Appenzell	2,567	...	15·0	...	0·6	7·0
Chaux de Fonds	3,045	...	...	...	...	6·1
Zermatt	5,000	...	12·48	...	3·7	4·4
Hospice of St. Gothard	6,443	...	5·0	...	5·0	0·93
St. Bernard	7,610	...	...	...	...	1·1
Vincent's hutte on Monte Rosa	9,234	...	2·08	...	8·96	3·74
Summit of Monte Rosa	14,284	...	7·52	...	13·7	10·4

* The bear is the Ursus Arctos or brown bear found chiefly in the Grisons, Tessin, and Upper Valais. It occurs at 9,000 feet. Bears are not so rare as wolves.

† The wolf (Canis Lupus) is almost extinct, except in a corner of the Canton de Vaud and a few other places.

‡ The most settled weather for excursions is generally in August and September, but the flora of Switzerland is most glorious in June, and some expeditions are safer in the early summer (when a thick bed of snow bridges many dangers) than later. Winter expeditions even have special charms. See " Kohl's Ascent of the Rothhorn and visit to Rosenlaui in his Alpen Reisen, 1851."

ANTHROPOLOGY.

The population of Switzerland consists of 2½ millions. Taking language as t
test of derivation, there are of

German, speaking Swiss	....	1,681,000=7-10th
French,	„	„	....	540,000
Italian,	„	„	....	129,300
Rhæto Romance	...	....	42,000

Divided, as regards religious distinction, the Swiss census gives a return of
Protestants, 1,417,754; Catholics, 971.846.

The following table gives an exact picture of the area and population of t
Cantons, of which the largest is the Grisons, with 125 square German miles, and t
smallest Zug, with only 4. Switzerland contains 3,058 parishes, of which 29 conta
5,000 inhabitants. It contains an average population of 3,300 to the square Germ
mile, but as much of the land is covered with snow, rock, and ice, if we deduct 1-6
of the land as uninhabitable, the result obtained is 3,960 per square German mi
Bâle and Geneva are the most populous Cantons, and according to our last calcul
tion the proportion per square mile exceeds that of Prussia 1-5th, and of
Germany 1-14th.

Canton.	Area, square German miles.		Swiss square leagues.		Swiss jucharts Area.		Populatio
Aargau	25·3	...	60 5	...	387,200	...	199,8
Appenzell	7·5	...	17·9	...	114,560	...	54,8
Bâle	8·6	...	20·2	...	129,280	...	77,5
Bern	123·	...	294·	...	1,881,600	...	458,3
Fribourg	29·7	...	71·1	...	455,040	...	99,8
Geneva	5·2	...	12·4	...	79,360	...	64,1
Glarus	12·5	...	29 8	...	190,720	...	30,2
Grisons	125·	...	301·	...	1,926,400	...	89,8
Lucern	22·6	...	54·	...	345,600	...	132,8
Neuchâtel	14·5	...	34·7	...	222,080	...	70,7
Saint Gallen	36·7	...	87·	...	561,920	...	169,6
Schaffhausen	5·6	...	13·3	...	85,120	...	35,3
Schwyz	16·7	...	40·	...	256,000	...	44,1
Solothurn	13·7	...	32·8	...	209,920	...	69,6
Tessin	53·6	...	128·	...	819,200	...	117,7
Thurgau	18·1	...	43·2	...	276,480	...	88,9
Unterwalden	13·4	...	32·	...	204,800	...	25,1
Uri	19·7	...	47·	...	300,800	...	14,5
Valais	80·3	...	192·	...	1,228,800	...	88,5
Vaud	57·7	...	137·	...	881,920	..	199,5
Zug	4·4	...	10·4	...	66,560	...	17,4
Zurich	30·2	...	72·2	...	462,080	...	250,6
Totals	724·9	...	1732·1	...	11,085,446	...	2,392,7

The following principal cities of the Republic have more than 1,000 inhabitan

City.	Population.	City.	Populatic
Geneva	45,000	Lausanne	22,700
Bâle	27,000	Chaux de Fonds	12,638
Zurich	35,000	Saint Gallen	11,234
Bern	33,500	Lucerne	10,238

Of the smaller towns of note,

Fribourg has	9,065	Thun	8,820
Neuchâtel	7,727	Zug	3,300
Schaffhausen	7,700	Sitten	2,926
Schwyz	5,432	Altorf	2,112
Vevay	5,200	Bellinzona	1,926
Lugano	5,142	Stans	1,877
Glarus	4,082	Appenzell	1,516

The following additional statistics may be found useful :—

	Francs.
The national income is	15,686,000
The budget of expenses	15,206,000
Balance	480,000
The debt is	661,742 fr.

The President of the Confederation receives 8,700 fr. a year (£348). The whole expenses of the Canton of Glarus amount to 2,875 fr. The Finance Minister receives 350 fr. The Canton Landamman 700 fr., &c. Happy land, where standing armies and sinecures are not considered necessaries or luxuries.

Swiss National militia :—

Infantry—29 battalions of the line	59,114
Do. 45 companies of rifles	5,232
Total Infantry	64,346
Cavalry—Dragoons 1,485 ; guides 204	1,689
Artillery—40 companies	6,897
Engineers	1,016
Hospital service	156
Grand total	74,095
Active Militia Reserve	42,660
Landwehr	46,188
	162,943

The Artillery consists of 35 batteries of cannon from 6 to 12 pounders, 3 howitzer batteries, 4 mountain gun batteries, 8 rocket batteries, giving 50 batteries and 274 guns.

Europe groans under the weight of standing armies and is riddled with taxes to keep up this general misery, while Switzerland for little cost maintains a highly respectable force equal to any emergencies. An immediate comparison will make our folly evident :—

	Switzerland.	Wurtemburg and Darmstadt.
Population	2,390,000	2,590,000
Cost of army	3,500,000 fr	4,800,000 fl. or 10,270,000 fr.
Strength of army	140,000 men.	36,000 men.

The imports in 1857 were worth 1,031,815 fr.   Exports 5,163,697 fr.

Commerce and industry are now in a very flourishing state, the principal branches of manufacture being Cotton, Silk, and Lace, also Watch-making.

Switzerland is a Sovereign Republic in which the people enjoy universal suffrage, and are represented in a Diet by 120 deputies or one to 20,000 voters. It is the best educated country in Europe,[*] education being compulsory and universal.

OBSERVATIONS.—(MEANING OF CERTAIN NAMES.)

Alp—Mountain pasture.	Joch—Col, Neck.
Bach—Stream.	Lawi—Avalanche.
Bec, Becca—Peak.	Matt—Mayen.
Eck or Egg (Scheweck)—Watershed.	Mayen—Hay Châlets.
Firn—Snow Field.	Platte—Plateau.
Fluh—Rock.	Senne—Châlet.
Gletscher—Glacier (vadret in the Grisons.)	Staffel—Terrace.
Grat—Ridge.	Thal—Valley.
Horn—Rocky point. In Savoy, Aiguille. In Grisons and Tessin, Piz.	

ABBREVIATIONS USED IN THIS WORK.

Ft., feet; h., hour; l., leagues; m., minute; sq. l., square leagues.

HINTS TO TOURISTS.

To those who like unsophisticated characters, primitive simplicity in manners, and picturesque costumes, many parts of the Grisons, like the Tyrol, offer special attractions. In most parts of West Switzerland, except the Ormonds, Upper Simmenthal, and a few favoured spots, the costumes, honesty, and charm of ideal Swiss and mountain life have long departed. The decline of the latter virtue was even regretted in the last century by native poets, and referred to the inroads of French frivolity, lusts, and fashions, and since then matters have not improved. The French Revolution, with its withering results, passed across the country, and since then English tourists, though doing much for the country, have lavished their gold, and thereby helped to banish simple tastes and frugal habits. The picturesque has departed from its people, and its cities, Geneva and Zurich, stand forth patent bran new specimens of centralization, formalism, and bad taste, and when a fine old town like Glarus, with its quaint cottages, is burnt down, it rises from its ashes bereft of charm, a staring stone town with unæsthetic uniform streets drawn as straight as a cord. Interlaken, in a paradise of beauty, is invaded and occupied by crinoline, patent boots, and kid gloves. Chamouni is a fashionable watering place; the engine whirls by the azure lake and venerable walls of Chillon, and manufactories smoken and blacken the skies and streams of the most pastoral scenes.

Yet there is even here much to redeem. Switzerland has advanced in wealth and welfare if she has lost in simplicity, and it is well that it is so accessible that even fashionable loungers in the Paris boulevards are found tripping in ball costume over the Glaciers. And there are many spots, even now, free from the inroads of publicity and corruption. In certain remote parts the slowness and complacency of the bucolic mind are quite touching. Beginning with the Ormonds district, above

* The facts in the Introduction are chiefly derived from Berlepsch's *Schweizerkunde*; K. G. P. Kolb's *Hand-buch der Vergleichenden Statistik*; D. Völter's *Deutschland*; and Meyer's *Physik der Schweiz*.

Bex, it is still possible to obtain a draught of milk there without paying for it, and to meet with sons not ashamed of their fathers.   In the Upper Simmenthal you can earn golden opinions, with silver or copper, or even less, and live in an Eden of peace, among primeval men, for next to nothing.   There are corners of Unterwalden and Uri where the women are not too civilized to wear their mother's dress, where men are valued for what they are and not for what they have, where they still believe in *Tell*, and have not yet forgotten to pray.   But the lateral valleys of the Rhone, the Italian valleys south of Monte Rosa, and the Grisons, are the special seat of noble virtues, unaffected natural politeness, powerful natures in mind and body not broken down by contact with another order of things.   Bears, wolves, bouquetins, vultures, and other strong natures of a lower scale to man, are found in these parts and add to their attractions.   Thus, even the morale of man is not yet a dead level in the Alps, nor are Alpine beasts and plants the tame things of our plains.

Thus, according to the object, taste, and time of the visitor, Switzerland offers a number of centres for irradiating into the country and becoming acquainted with it and its people.   Thus, to the man who seeks the crowd, and, like Kohl, finds as much pleasure in studying man as scenery, Interlaken, Grindelwald, the Æggisch-horn, Champery, Chamouni, the Giessbach Hotel, the Grimsel, Stachelberg, Mon-treux, Zermatt, and the Riffelberg afford all he can desire.

Again, to the seeker after quiet pastoral homes in a primitive district, beautiful as a dream,—the Ormonds Dessus, Les Iles, La Tine, Val d'Anniviers, Gressonay Alagna, Val Mastalone, Sixt, Engelberg, in Unterwalden, Lenk, in the Upper Sim-menthal, Campfer, Pontresina, in the Upper Engadin, Davos and the Prattigau, in the Grisons and Inner Rhoden, Appenzell, are a fitting centre.   In the Ormonds are the best rifle shots in Switzerland.   The district has splendid trout streams.   In Val d'Anniviers you have a poor hearty population, who are nomadic, amidst a settled civilization, and have many houses to live in, though in straightened circum-stances.   The Gressonay and Alagna people are a charming idyl, free, equal, humble, pious, and manly, and as handsome as they are virtuous; crime being unknown among them.   Their description in Mr. King's work is quite enchanting, as that of their fairy-like valleys, with their ultramarine streams and pools.   Of Engelberg it is enough to say that *Kohl* in his travels describes the whole of Unter-walden as an Eden, in which view *Berlepsch* coincides; the people are still the sons of Arnold of Melchthal and of Winkelried.   Schwing feste (wrestling matches) yet flourish among them, and they have many of the sterling qualities of the best Swiss days.   Engelberg is a paradise of beauty and verdure, and the very home of cheese and butter, and such acceptable cheer to mountain appetites.

It is the practice in many Guide Books to mark out certain rapid galloping tours, by which Switzerland may be done in breathless haste, by a kind of race against time. We propose a more reasonable method of exploring its beauties by pointing out the best mountain centres for innumerable delightful excursions.   These are as follow:

In the Canton of Berne.—1. Mürren, above Lauterbrunnen.   2. Schienige Platte, between Interlaken and Lauterbrunnen, on the heights (grand views, good inns). 3. Kandersteg.   4. Giessbach Hotel.   5. Rosenlaui Baths (excellent hotel and centre.) 6. Jungfrau or Belle Vue Hotels, on the Wengeren Alp.   The above are in a very frequented district.   More retirement and simplicity will be found in the Simmenthal and Wildstrubel at Zweisimmen (Bär. Inn).   7. Saanen (Inn, Bär Landhaus).   8. Lenk (Inns: Krone, Stern, Bär).   9. Gsteig (Bär).

In the Canton de Vaud.—A number of choice pensions, with moderate prices, occur above Vevay, Montreux, Bex, and Aigle. They will be noticed at those places. We only mention here the choicest spots on the borders of Berne. 1. Montbovon (Hotel and Pension du Jaman). 2. La Tine (Bear Inn). wild glen in Canton Fribourg. 3. Pres d'Avent (Auberge l'Union). 4. Col de Pillon (Hotel Diablerets, Pension, 5*fr.* per day). 5. Vers l'Eglise (Cerf-Pension, 3*fr.* 50*c.*) 6. La Comballaz (Lys-Pension, 5*fr.*) 7. Sepey-Ormond (Etoile Hotel de Ville, Pensions, 3*fr.* 50*c.*)

In the Canton de Valais.—1. At Champery (Pension Dent du Midi, 4*fr.* 50*c.*) 2. Val d'Illiez (Pension Repos, 4*fr.* 50*c.*) 3. Evolena (Hotel Dent Blanche.) 4. Bella Tola Hotel, Pension, 4*fr.* 5. Weisshorn Hotel, Graben Alp, Tourtman Thal. 6. Riffelberg Hotel. 7. Bell Alp Hotel. 8. Æggischhorn Hotel, near Aletsch Glacier. [In the Italian valleys, good quarters at Macugnaga, Alagna, Gressonay, and Breuil.]

Unterwalden (Canton.)—1. Engelberg (Pensions Catani, Muller). 2. Hotel Rossli, at Hergiswyl. 3. H. Blättli, at the Klimsenhorn (Pilatus). 4. Stauz (several Pensions).

Uri (Canton).—1. Seelisberg, excellent Pension above Tellen Platte.

Schwyz (Canton.)—1. Gersau (Hotel and Pension, Muller).

Grisons.—1. St. Moritz (Pensions: Fuller, Bavier, Kreuz). 2. Pontresina (Hotel Kreuz). 3. Samaden (Hotel Bernina, Krone). 4. Poschiavo (Hotel La Croce). 5. La Prese (Bath Hotel). 6. Davos (Hotel Zum Strela, Pension, 4*fr.*) 7. Seewis (Pension Scesa Plana, 4*fr.*)

Tessin Lugano (Pension at the Hotel du Parc, 8 to 9 *fr.* in summer; in winter, the best season here, 5 or 6*fr.*)

Savoy and Chamouni.—1. Sixt (Pension des Cascades). 2. Chamouni (Pension Mont Blanc). 3. Châlet Auberges, on the Breven, Mont Anvert, and La Flegere.

Solothurn.—On the Weissenstein, an excellent hotel, with the most extensive panoramic view in Europe.

Further particulars will be found in each Canton, but let the visitor remember that if he wish to stay some time in a choice Canton, he can very commonly make arrangements for pension or lodgings in some clean cottage or châlet at a much cheaper rate. This is indeed the only way truly to enjoy and appreciate all the beauty and grandeur of the country.

We add a few words on attire, luggage, and diet.

Dress should be neither too hot nor too light, because of the great extremes and sudden transitions of mountain climate. Flannel is the best attire. For wraps, nothing are better than plaids. As waterproof, siphonias (pocket) are light and useful. To travellers proposing ascents and mountain bivouacs, thick long woollen Jersey shirts are a useful addition, answering the purpose of a blanket.

For head gear, it is well to have a light cap, and a straw hat or wide-awake. These can be exchanged according to position or circumstances. An umbrella, *à la Gamp*, will be useful in sunny ascents and corners, to infirm heads. Alpine club boots (genuine) and snow gaiters are desirable for ascents. Woollen socks do not blister on the march, especially if soaped outside.

LUGGAGE.—All heavy luggage should be kept at or sent to some convenient centre. This can be safely done by the public conveyances. For pedestrians, the less impedimenta the better. The pack, or light courier bag, should not weigh more than six to eight kilogrammes, containing at least one shirt, a pair of socks, a flannel waistcoat, and a siphonia [brush, slipper, &c.]*

ACCOUTREMENTS.—Every pedestrian should have an Alpine stock or Alpine pole. Adventurous climbers should bring their own from England. An ice axe, good English rope, fixed, when used, to a strong belt and ring of English make, are essential. The want of secure accoutrements may lead to broken ropes and necks, as at the accident on Mont Cervin, in 1865. A blue veil or spectacles are essential on the snow.

Scientific amateurs should at least take a good compass, a geological hammer, a thermometer (self-registering, Casella's, Hatton Garden, the best), and an aneroid, or if possible, a mountain barometer. Casella's Hypsometrical Apparatus is very desirable, and will be doubly useful, as it can, if needful, help to warm your tea or soup.

FOOD AND DRINK.—Take some tea with you as many cannot bear much unmixed mountain milk. Professor Forbes found cold tea in a bottle the best restorative. Do not drink much water or brandy in ascents, they render the pedestrian helpless. A little Beaujolais wine may be taken with advantage. Some good biscuits, a tin of preserved meat, and a cake or two of chocolate are desirable on ascents, as you may often be benighted.

Good guides are essential in difficult ascents. To prevent deception, apply to the most respectable hotel keepers—a list of the best will appear in this work—(see Appendix). The chief dangers in ascents are avalanche couloirs and falling stones. To avoid the former, start early before the sun loosens and melts the ground. To avoid the latter be guided by your guide. No crevasses are dangerous with a good guide and rope.

PRELIMINARY INFORMATION.

In point of access, Switzerland may be primarily divided into two broad sections, east and west; and secondarily into two northern and southern sub-divisions.

To the west it is attacked by the three main arteries of railroads, bringing the traveller to Bâle, Neuchatel, and Geneva; and to the east by the railroads that convey the traveller from Germany to Friedrichshafen and Lindau, on the Lake of Constance.

But there are subordinate, though highly important approaches on the side of Germany and Italy to the north and south, by the Schwarzwald and Schaffhausen, and by the Splugen and Simplon. Thus, it is important and even necessary to know the seven main arteries by which the great mass of travellers are conveyed to Switzerland from all points of the compass. Yet, to the great mass of English travellers for whom this Guide Book is especially intended, there are only three arteries that are essentially necessary to be known, because it is by these that at least three-fourths of our countrymen approach the Great Uplands of Europe. These arteries are to the west of Switzerland, and lead the traveller either to Bâle, Neuchatel, or Geneva. Of these three routes, that by Bâle still continues in some

* Notwithstanding certain Guide Books, let not the manly pedestrian encumber himself with mittens, hot water bottles, cotton masks for his face, several pairs or expansion gloves to save his precious hands from friction, and other appendages contained in the knapsack of poor Albert Smith's young friend on the Tête Noire.

respects the most important, because it admits of two modes of access through France or Germany. Thus the traveller has the option to reach Bâle either through Paris and the branch of the Strasbourg railway which takes him thither, or through Belgium and Germany by the Antwerp and Rhenish lines, or by Calais, Brussels, and Luxembourg.

Of the other main arteries followed usually by Englishmen, Neuchatel and Geneva; it is almost needless to say that the more direct and convenient access to them is through Paris. Further information respecting these routes is furnished in *Bradshaw's Continental Railway Guide*, and need not be repeated here. It will have been sufficient to have pointed out in general terms the most convenient approaches to the different sides of Switzerland. Our distribution of routes will be guided by the same principle, and considering that this Guide is intended for Englishmen, we shall arrange it according to the convenience of travellers proceeding from the north, and especially from the side of England.

Thus, as Bâle is the most usual and frequented point of access on the Swiss border, we shall commence our survey on that side, and conduct the traveller in the first instance from Bâle to Berne, and the scenery of the north-west Alps. Our second main route will carry us on to Lucerne to its Lake, and to the Uri, Unterwalden Districts, and then we shall pass south to Neuchatel and Geneva, and follow the routes of Chamouni and the Valais, thus exhausting west Switzerland before we attack the east in the Grisons and Glarus, which the English traveller reaches most easily from Lucerne.

It will be seen by a comparison of this statement with the map, that three-fifths of the splendid scenery chiefly attractive to the tourist lie in the three great Cantons of Berne, Valais, and Grisons, to which may be added Chamouni, in Savoy. If, therefore, the traveller be in search of a point of interest on some route, it is in all cases more than probable that they will be found under the head of one or other of these great Cantons.

The special feature of this Guide being its adaptation to the pedestrian, we shall as a general rule avoid all particulars relating to the Swiss railroads, which can be obtained in *Bradshaw's Continental Railway Guide*. (It may be useful to know that in almost all inhabited parts of Switzerland there is an Electric Telegraph office; invariable charge for the telegram of a certain number of words, 1*fr.*)

Thus in the case of our first main route through Bâle, dropping the particulars of uninteresting and unimportant stations on the route to Olten and Berne, we shall supply the tourist with varied and useful information respecting the Cantons and the whole tract of country through which he is passing. This will have the advantage of giving the traveller the fullest information relating to the whole of the Confederation in proportion as he approaches its several parts.

As regards Routes * for the pedestrian these will be found attached to every principal centre through which the traveller passes. They are arranged in alphabetical order to prevent the necessity of having recourse to an index, and thus for example, if the traveller wishes to know the route and distances on foot from Bâle to Solothurn he has only to look for the latter place under the letter S in the list of routes attached to the Canton of Bâle, and he learns immediately all the particulars required.

In short to use the present volume let the traveller—1. determine his approach to Switzerland by one of the main arteries of Continental Railways from the North-west. 2. Let him ascertain from the map the Canton to which or through which it leads him. 3. Let him ascertain all interesting information respecting such Cantons, arranged under the name of places in alphabetical order. 4. Let him refer to the list of pedestrian routes at the end of each Canton through which he passes in order to find the distances required to any place he seeks.

It is apprehended and hoped that in this manner the traveller will find to his hand the fullest amount of useful and authentic information arranged in the most systematic manner, almost dispensing with an index, and so clearly arranged that he can hardly go wrong.

It has been our particular aim to avoid leading the traveller too much in leading strings as has been too much the custom in our ordinary guide books. Supplying the traveller with the fullest possible information, we prefer after that to leave him a little to his own discretion and independence of action, knowing from personal experience the misery of having always to drudge along the beaten tract without deviation, and to see a certain number of sights in a certain time, because your guide or guide book prescribe it to you.

We thus point out and fully describe everything of the greatest interest in all parts of the country, and give an exact itinerary and mileage of all the principal and even subordinate pedestrian excursions, but we prefer to leave the suggestions of the days and hours and routes employed to the convenience and preference of travellers. It is to be inferred that one man has more time and another less, that one has a preference for escalading peaks and passes, and another a love of quiet enjoyment of breezy lakes, grassy uplands, and trout streams. thus one will pause when another will pass, and giving the exact pedestrian distances to all points of interest we leave it to the choice of the traveller to tarry or hurry through the majesty and marvels of this unrivalled scenery, which can never be truly appreciated or enjoyed unless we sometimes resolve to rest upon our staff in some favoured spot, and making it our centre, penetrate its mysteries and familiarise ourselves with its beauties. (A few tours are marked out in the Appendix for those who like leading strings).

In pursuance of this plan, and carrying out this principle, we have singled out and dwelt with emphasis on all points that have appeared to us from intimate personal knowledge the most favoured centres.

After giving this preliminary information, we shall take the gentle reader by the hand and introduce him to the grand scenery, the sight of which is to reward him for all his exertions. Supposing him to arrive either from Paris or Germany, we commence our Pilgrim's Progress with

MAIN ROUTE I. (A)

THROUGH BÂLE, AND THENCE BY RAIL TO BERNE AND THE OBERLAND.

Before we pass to a survey of the Canton and City of Bâle, we shall, for the convenience of the reader, furnish him with the following useful practical information :—

The Baden Railway Station at Bâle is at little Bâle, ten minutes from the bridge over the Rhine.

The French and Central Swiss Railway Stations are close to each other, in the principal part of the town.

Fares from Bâle by rail to—	1st cl. Fr.	c.		2nd cl. Fr.	c.		3rd cl. Fr.	c.
Antwerp, by Cologne	86	55	......	...		......	...	
Berne	11	10	......	7	80	......	5	60
Brussels, by Cologne	85	35	......	...		......	...	
Brussels, by Thionville	62	35	......	47	50	......	...	
Coire	23	90	......	16	60	......	11	65
Frankfort ....florins	16	42	......	11	21	......	..	
Fribourg (Swiss)	14	60	......	10	25	......	7	35
Geneva	27	10	......	19	15	......	13	85
Heidelberg ....florins	10	24	......	7	6	......	4	33
Lausanne	21	35	......	15	0	......	10	75
London	136	55	......	...		......	...	
Lucerne	9	85	......	6	95	......	5	0
Lyons	47	80	......	35	85	......	26	30
Manheim ....florins	13	24	......	9	9	......	...	
Mayence	38	30	......	28	15	......	...	
Neuchatel	14	5	......	10	0	......	...	
Ostend, by Cologne	96	35	......	...		......	...	
Paris, by Mulhouse	59	70	......	44	0	......	32	50
Schaffhausen	11	60	......	7	95	......	5	25
Strasburg	16	0	......	12	0	......	7	80
Thun	14	25	......	10	0	......	7	20
Vevay	23	35	......	16	40	......	11	75
Zurich	10	20	......	7	5	......	4	80

Omnibuses in Bâle. Fares from the French and Central Swiss Stations, 75 centimes. 50lbs. luggage carried free. From the Baden line Station to the French and Central Swiss Stations, 1fr. Carriages, ¼ an hour, 1 to 2 persons, 80c.; above 2 persons, 1fr. 20c. By the hour, 2fr.; above 2 persons, 3fr. From the hotel to the station (4 persons allowed), 1½fr.; each article of luggage, 25c. Fiacre from one station to the other, 2fr.; each trunk, 30c. A carriage with one horse, 12 to 14fr. per day; with two horses, 20 to 25fr. By the Valley of Moutiers, a carriage with one horse, 35fr.; with 2 horses, 60 to 65fr.

While engaged with financial details, it may be useful to inform the traveller that the Swiss currency consists of francs and centimes as in France; but in passing from Switzerland to France, remember that Swiss francs lose in value on crossing the border.

To travellers coming from Germany, it is important to recollect that the gulden or florin of South Germany is equal to 2fr. 20c. (2s)., and the Kreutzer to 2 centimes.

One Swiss league = 4,800 metres. In a plain district, a good walker easily does six kilometres in an hour (3 miles 5 furlongs).*

German	mile =	6,400	metres.
Austrian	„ =	7,586·472	„
Bavarian	„ =	7,425·786	„
Baden	„ =	8,888·900	„

*1 mil = 4 fur 213 yds. 1 ft, 11½ in.   6 kil. = 3 mls. 5 fur, 181 yds. 2 ft. 6 in.

BRADSHAW'S

PEDESTRIAN ROUTE BOOK FOR SWITZERLAND.

Our first Main Route (marked A in the Map) brings us to Bâle, and thence to Berne and the Bernese Oberland,

.. We shall therefore commence with a survey of the

CANTON OF BÂLE.

LIMITS.—This Canton is limited to the N. by the river Rhine, by the Grand Duchy of Baden, and by the Canton of Aargau; to the N.E. by the latter; to the S.E. and the S. by those of Solothurn and Berne; to the S.W. and the W. it borders on the last-named canton; and to the N.W. its limit is France.

. AREA, SOIL, AND CLIMATE.—The area of this Canton of Bâle comprises only 23½ square Swiss leagues (0 38 + 8 square German miles, or 458 square kilometres'.

Except in its north-western part, it is encompassed by a chain of mountains, whose ramifications form several valleys in its interior, of varying extent, and mostly watered by rivulets. In the lowland and valleys the climate is generally very mild, which occasions an earlier ripening of crops and vegetation than happens in several even of the southern cantons of Switzerland.

MOUNTAINS.—All the mountains in this canton, including those that limit and also those that intersect it, belong alike to the Jura, the great calcareous chain of Switzerland, forming its almost unbroken frontier towards France from the Rhine in the Canton of Bâle, where it approaches the Black Forest and the Vosges to the Canton of Geneva, beyond which its outlines shade away into the plains of Southern France, towards Savoy. The highest summits of the Jura, in the Canton of Bâle, are the Schaffmatt and the higher and lower Hauenstein.

RIVERS.—The Rhine is the only navigable river in this canton. It also receives all the others that flow through the district; the Wiese falls into the Rhine on the German or right bank; the Ergolz, which has its source on the Schaffmatt, flows into it near Augst; the Birse, taking its rise near Pierre Pertuis, in the Canton of Berne, joins the Rhine near Bâle; and the Birsig, which rises in the Leimenthal, after passing through the capital of the canton, falls into the Rhine at the port of Bâle. The canton contains a number of other streams and torrents not entitled to special notice, but it does not possess a single lake.

CROPS, INDUSTRY, &c.—This canton is well stocked with cattle, horses, and fishes. It yields wine, cereals, fruits, vegetables, &c. Its hills and slopes are clothed with fine forests, and offer limestone and sandstone quarries, marl, and springs of mineral water. Several manufactures are carried on with much success in the Canton of Bâle, especially large paper mills, riband, silk stuffs, cotton and woollen factories, considerable dyeing works, iron forges, wire works, &c.

THERMAL WATERS AND COLD BATHS.— The baths of Bubendorf, near the village of the same name, 4 leagues (12 miles) from Bâle, are in high repute; its waters are said to be very salutary, and present a great analogy to those of Pfeffers baths in St. Gallen. But the old and new baths of Schauenburg are even more frequented than those of Bubendorf.

POPULATION AND RELIGION. — This canton contains, according to a recent census, in the division called the stadt or town, 29,555 inhabitants, and in the country or land 47,830 inhabitants, giving for the canton (Basel stadt and Basel land united) 77,385 persons. Thirty years ago the population was 45,000, of whom 4,000 were Roman Catholics. At present the Protestants number 62,901, and the Catholics 14,560.

EDUCATIONAL AND CHARITABLE INSTITUTIONS.— These are for the most part established in the capital, and will be described under that head. The elementary schools in the villages are reckoned to be among the best in Switzerland.

SURVEY OF THE CANTON.

Divided in 1832 into town and country, Basel stadt and Basel land.

BÂLE (CITY.)

HOTELS.—Hotel de la Croix Blanche, kept by Mr. A. Gubler. Fine situation on the banks of the Rhine, and close to the German Railway station. Hotel de la Cigogne, situated near to the Rhine; moderate charges; Mr. J. Klein Weber, proprietor. The Black Bear Hotel, close to the German Railway station; patronised by English travellers; reasonable; English spoken. Hotel du Sauvage (Wild Man), the nearest to the Cathedral, Diligence Office, and the Swiss, French, and German Railway termini. Hotel Euler, large and well situated hotel, near the French and Swiss Railway station. Hotel Suisse, E. Merian, proprietor; situated near the springs on the Promenade, opposite the French and Swiss Railway stations. Hotel des Trois Rois.

Bâle is built on both banks of the Rhine, whose green waters lave its ancient walls. An uncovered bridge, 600 feet in length, unites the two parts of the town called respectively the great and the little town (Gross and Klein Basel), of which the population amounts now to 31,000, while about 1830 it was only 16,000.

The important position of Basel, on the bend of the Rhine, where it turns N. towards the German Ocean, had, at an early period, attracted the attention of the Romans, who built a city, Augusta Rauracorum, now Augst, at the junction of the Ergolz. This city (Augusta Rauracorum) was one of the chief places of ancient Helvetia. Frequent destructions at the hands of the barbarians who invaded the Roman empire caused its removal to its present site, and thus arose Basilea, which ultimately became a large and important emporium. Basel was one of the most powerful German imperial cities, and is now the most commercial town of Switzerland, so as to have earned the name of the " Swiss Millionaire City."

It is the only town on the upper Rhine that spreads its walls on both banks of the dark green river. The finest view of Bâle is obtained from the bridge. To the right the eye takes in Klein Basel (Little Bâle), consisting mostly of straight, regularly built streets, while to the left the principal part of the town presents itself, surrounded by walls and ditches. The streets in this latter and older part of Bâle are for the most part narrow and tortuous, producing rather a gloomy impression, like most of the ancient imperial and free cities of Germany. But this effect is a good deal redeemed by the quaintness of several of the old buildings with their queer, original turrets, and above all by the charm of the scenery that everywhere greets the traveller who steps upon the free and favoured soil of Switzerland. The glancing, shining Rhine, and inviting peeps of the neighbouring uplands, already lead the wayfarer to anticipate some of the magical beauties that will open upon him as he passes into the heart of the country.

The *Cathedral* of Bâle is built of red sandstone, and was formerly the chapter house of the ancient bishopric of Bâle; accordingly it is rich in historical associations. It is supposed that a fortress existed on its site in the time of the Romans, and this conclusion appears to be borne out by the remains of sepulchres and coins that have been found at this spot.

The Church, which was in the Byzantine style, was built by the emperor, Henry VI., from 1010 to 1019, was partly destroyed by an earthquake in 1356, and restored in the Gothic style. The grotesque figures that adorn or disfigure the capitols, and were used as ornaments in the middle ages, date from the former construction. Above the gate of St. Gall to the north is a large, round, or rose w.ndow, called "the wheel of happiness." The façade, with its lofty, elegant towers (one 250 feet high), and the three great gates, are of the 16th century. On this side of the church the most remarkable sculptures are—an equestrian statue of St. George with the Dragon; St. Martin dividing his cloak; a king (either Henry I. or Conrad II), with his wife and dau.hter; and above, the Holy Virgin, with Henry II and St. Cunegonde, or the Empress Helena. The two cloisters behind the church are rich in tombs of the 16th and 17th centuries, including those of the reformers, Œcolampadius and Grynäus. In the interior of the church are to be remarked—the pulpit, of a single piece, in the shape of a Gothic cup; it is of the date of 1486; the baptismal fonts, of the same date, adorned with Gothic foliage and figures; the sarcophagus of the Empress Anna, Empress of Rudolph, of Habsburg, with her sons, Hartmann and Charles (died 1276); two sculptures in relief of the 16th century, one representing the apostles and the other some martyrs. The new stained glasses (the four evangelists, Moses, David, Peter, and Paul) are the work of the painter, Grell, of Paris. In an adjacent building was held the celebrated council, and in the salle of the council and the chapel of St. Nicholas is a collection of the middle ages (curator, Prof. Wakernagel); it contains remains of plastic art, paintings, arms, and objects of all ages. It is open on Sundays at 10½ a.m.; on other days it may be seen on feeing the guardian of the church. Catalogues, 20 cents. Close by are the Reading Rooms, built in 1855 (library of 60,000 books), with a good collection of French, English, and German books. Strangers, presented by a member, enjoy its advantages for a month. To the east is the statue of Œcolampadius. The Museum deserves special notice. It stands in a very narrow street on the site of the old convent of the Augustines, but it contains more valuable artistic productions. To the right of the entrance is the library (Professor Gerlach, curator), open every day from 1 to 3, containing 80,000 printed volumes and 4,000 MSS. It contains interesting letters of Reuchlin, Erasmus, and the reformers of the 16th century, also the Acts of the Council of Bâle. At the entrance of the building are the Amphitheatre, the Chymical Laboratory, and the Cabinet of Natural Philosophy. On the first storey the Aula and the collections of Natural History. In the Aula are the portraits of celebrated professors of the university, Œneas Sylvius, Coelius Secundus Curio; of the reformers, Œcolampadius and John Micon; of the noted geographers, Sebastian Münster; of the anatomists, Andrew Vesalis, Felix Platter, Grynäus, Buxdorf, Zwinger, Bernouilli, &c., and more recent ones of Vinet, de Wette, Gerlach, Wackernagel, Peter Merian, Hagenbach, Schönbein, &c.

The collection of Natural History is open, gratis, on Sunday, from 10½ a.m. to 12 noon, and Wednesday from 2 to 4 p m.; other days for a fee. Professor Merian, curator. It has rare specimens, especially of birds from the Gold Coast and South America. The collection of petrifactions from the Jura is almost complete. On the upper storey are antiquities and works of art. The collection of Antiquities (under Prof. W. Vischer) is divided into special rooms. The cabinet of Antiquities contains Greek, Roman, Celtic, and German remains, and has improved by the acquisition of the collection Schmid bought in 1852, and containing objects found at Angst. It has also remains of lacustrine habitations, objects proceeding from the treasury of the old church at Bâle, &c. To see the collection of coins you must apply to the curator. The Ethnographic collection, which may be viewed in the same manner, contains very curious Mexican antiquities, arms, and other objects of American nations, Egyptian mummies, East Indian idols, &c *Works of Art:* These consist of paintings and drawings of Holbein and other masters, from the 15th century down to our time. They may be viewed, with the portfolios containing engravings and drawings, from 1 to 4 p.m. on Thursdays; on other days for a fee. The curators are, Professors Wackernagel and Falkeisen.

The First Room contains pictures of Hans Holbein, Junior (Nos. 1 to 86); of Albert Durer, &c. (from No. 132 to 134). The finest pictures have now been photographed by order of the commission of the museum. The engravings comprise many of ancient date. Two portfolios consist of landscapes in water colours, by Samuel Birmann. The Praise of Folly, by Erasmus, with valuable drawings of Holbein, deserve to be noticed. The oil paintings are in a large salle, lighted from above, and divided into five parts. Its contents are described in a printed catalogue, price 60 cents.

The principal pictures are:

1. In the salle of Holbein, the 36 pictures of Holbein, Junior, especially (No. 25) the Passion, for which Maximilian, Elector of Bavaria, offered 30,000 florins' worth of salt; (No. 18) the Dead Christ, painted, it is said, from the corpse of a Jew drowned in the Rhine in 1521. Three portraits of Erasmus (Nos. 15 to 17); of the printer, Frobène (No. 33); of Doctor Amerbach (No. 12); the family of Holbein (No. 19), one of his best pictures.

2. Old German School; M. Schongauer's Adoration of the Magi (No. 55); Peter Breugel, Senior's St. John Preaching in the Wilderness (No. 94); Louis Cranach

(Nos. 73 to 75); three very old paintings by the door (Nos. 96 to 98).

3. The Swiss Room contains in particular a good painting of the Schréckhorn, by Calamé, a living artist of Geneva (No. 136); a painting of horses, by Koller (No. 139); the interior of St. Marc's at Venice, by Aurele Robert (No. 137); H. Hess' the Battle of St. Jacques, fought by the Swiss near Bâle (No. 100); and three good paintings of Alb. Landerer, Miville, and L. Burckhardt (Nos. 127, 112, and 123).

4. The Fourth Room has a portrait of the Anabaptist, David Jovis (No. 187); Stückelberger's painting of a Fête of the Blessed Virgin in the Sabine Mountain (No. 132); good pictures by D. Teniers, the Lute Player (No. 174); a Madonna of John van Mabuse (No. 162); a Dead Christ, by P. Tyssens (No. 181); Macbeth and the Witches, by J. Koch (No. 209).

The Fifth Room has the Collection Birmann. Among the pictures notice (No. 287) the Dream of Joseph, H. Swanefeld: the Adoration of the Magi, J. de Mabuse (No. 282); the Smoker of D. Teniers (No. 291); Landscapes of Poussin (Nos. 263 to 265); a Nativity, Ann. Caracci (No. 267); cartoons for a Church at Munich, by Cornelius; other cartoons of Schnorr.

The Anatomical Collection in the University building at the Rheinsprung (curator, Prof. Jung). The new missionary establishment before the Spahlenthor contains a good ethnographical collection of arms, dresses, &c., from India and Africa. There are many private collections in Bâle, but they are only accessible to persons recommended to the proprietors.

Other public buildings are—the Arsenal, with the once gilt coat of mail of Charles the Bold. The Fish Market fountain, in the Gothic style. The Industrie Hall, to the left of the Rhine Bridge, used as an exhibition of works of industry; entrance free. The noted painting of the Dance of Death, to commemorate the plague of 1439, no longer exists. Behind the

Minster is a terrace called the Pfalz, raised 75 feet above the Rhine. The other buildings deserving notice are the Rathaus of 1508 and the new church of St. Elizabeth. Bâle has numerous manufactories, and is the centre of great commercial activity, and a great shipping place for the Rhine navigation. Its confectionary forms a considerable item in the export trade. The people of Bâle city are noted for their speculative character in commercial transactions, for their conservative politics, and rigorous, almost puritanical, orthodoxy; in all this contrasting with the country of Bâle, which is essentially radical in politics. The town of Bâle is a great centre of Protestant missionary institutions and life, as well as of charitable establishments, several of which are to be found in the vicinity, such as Beuggen, St. Crischona, Riehen. &c. The University has always possessed celebrated professors, but is only attended by few students. The present population of Bâle is 31,000 souls.

In front of the gate called the Aeschthor is the monument of St. James, in honour of the Swiss who fell in the battle in 1444, from which circumstance the wine grown in this neighbourhood is called Swiss blood (Schweizerblut). * Three parishes are united with Bâle to form the division called Bâle city.

Basel land, or Bâle country, contains 7⅔ German square miles (421 square kilometres) and 51,773 inhabitants, of whom the greater part are Protestants, the Catholics amounting to 10,000.

Arlesheim is 1½ leagues (4½ miles) from Bâle, and is in general repute on account of its splendid position. It contains what is called the finest English garden in Switzerland, and the ruins of the Castle of Birseick. †

Augst, 2 leagues (6 miles) from Bâle, is on the site of the ancient Augusta Rauracorum; it still exhibits some traces of Roman remains.

Huningen, formerly a French fortress, was destroyed by the Austrians, at the end of the war against Napoleon I. It is three-quarters of a league from Bâle, and half way to it used to be a monument to General Abatucci, now also destroyed. ‡

Riehen is a pretty village, situated on the right bank of the Rhine, and embellished by several elegant country residences of the more opulent citizens of Bâle. The House of Correction is situated here.

St. Crischona offers a magnificent view from different points near the Church.

St. Margaret.—On a slight elevation, near this place, you obtain a sight of the battlefields of St. Joseph, and of Dornach and Friedligen on the opposite bank of the Rhine. The general view obtained from this eminence is charming. The remaining towns and villages of the canton that deserve notice are—

Schweizerhall.

Sissach, 5¾ leagues (17½ miles) from Bâle.

Waldenburg, 5¾ leagues (17½ miles) from Bâle.

---

* The battle was fought August 25th, 1444, and deserves to be compared with Thermopylæ, for it consisted of an engagement between 1,200 Swiss and 30,000 French led by the Dauphin. So gallant was the resistance of the handful of mountaineers that only 10 survived, while 8,000 of the French were stretched dead on the field. History shows few examples of heroism equal to that displayed by the Swiss on this occasion.

† Near this, the valley of the Birse, with ruins of Reichenstein, the Pfeffingerfluh, with the ruins of the Castles of Tschapperhein. Klus Monchsberg, and Pfeffingen. To the left is Dornach, with the ruins of a castle. It was here that, July 22, 1499, 6,000 Swiss beat 15,000 Austrians, and obliged Maximilian I. to conclude peace. A Capuchin Convent, with painting of Brandmüller and Bone House. The mathematician, Maupertius, is buried here.

‡ Liestahl, 3 leagues (9 miles) from Bâle, is the seat of the Government of Bâle Country (Basel Land).

EXCURSION TO VAL MOUTIER (MUNSTERTHAL).

From Bâle, post road of 19 l. (57 m.) A post cart travels it twice a day, in ten hours. Best way to see Val Moutier: take post to Delemont, proceed thence on foot. Corandelin has good forges, and produces good scythes. Near it "Falls of the Anabaptist." Here begins Val Moutier, a split in the limestone rocks presenting fantastic shapes, and clothed with dark forests. At La Roche are waterworks. At Moutier Granval (Inns—Stagg; Crown) in a fine basin. Country cultivated, and cleared by St. Germain. Interesting collection of minerals, by Dr. Moschard. On a hill a castle and priory. After passing another defile is Court, in smiling meadows. Mallerey (Inn—Lion d'Or). Tavannes, in German Dachsfelden (Inn—Crown). Three roads meet here. 1. To Bellelay (3 leagues) ; to Unde-veller and Malettes (2½ leagues). 2. To Saignelegier (4½ leagues); and the third to Pierri Pertuis; a natural tunnel, with a Roman inscription " Numini augustorum via facta per Titum Du (nuium) Paternum IL vir (um) Col. Helvet." At Sonceboz an inn, the Crown. At Frinvillier, fine view of the Alps.

More distant excursions from Bâle may be made to the Baths of Badenweiler (by rail and omnibus (2 hours). Frohburg (2 hours), a water (?) cure establishment, with a view over the Alps. Langenbruck (2,209 feet above the sea) and Kilchzimmer (2,800 feet), 3½ leagues (10½ miles), very pure air.

An agreeable pedestrian tour may be made by the Upper Hauenstein. Take the rail from Bâle to Liesthal; then proceed by carriage or on foot (a post cart every day, 6½ a.m. and 6 p.m.) by the valley of Frenken, to the saline baths of Bubendorf, ¾ league (2¼ miles), situated near the Château of Wildenstein, in fine country, and well kept (painted windows). One league further, Höllstein. By Nieder and Oberdorf (1 hour), to Waldenburg, a little town in a romantic district, with the ruins of a castle. Ascending (1½ hours), you reach the Baths of Langenbruck, on the Col of the Pass of Ober-Hauenstein (2,254 feet). Fine view. Interesting petrifactions. Descent to Holdenbach (½ hour). A little before reaching it turn to the right, at the foot of the mountain, and near Wolfgang (½ hour), to the right, in the valley of Mumliswyl. In it are situated the very picturesque ruins of Falkenstein. Quarter of an hour further is Balstal. Pass on by Clus (with iron foundries), to Oensingen, on the high road. To the right, in 3½ hours, is Solothurn ; to the left (3½ hours), Olten.

To reach Porrentruy from Bâle you pass through Aesch, Lauffen, and Delemont. Aesch (2¾ leagues) is on the frontiers of Bâle and Berne, in an interesting, hilly country. Castle of Angernstein, in a forest. Near a saw mill, Grellingen. A pretty path leads to Neuhusli, and by the Passwang, to Bastal, near the fine ruins of Neu-Falkenstein. By the village of Zwingen, the valley of Lussel, the ruins of Thierstein, and the Château of Ramstein, you come (2½ leagues) to Lauffen (hotel Du Soleil). Another defile brings you to Soyhiere, a French-speaking village, by the ruins of Vorburg, to Delemont (3⅝ leagues). Hotel de l'Ours. 2,100 Catholic inhabitants in the valley of the Birse. Remains of a Roman bath. Once a Catholic bishopric. Three roads lead hence :—1. To Moutier (10¼ leagues) and Bienne. To the S.W. by La Roche and Saignelegier (6¼ leagues); and third by St. Arsanne and the foot of Mont Terrible to Porrentruy. Hotel de l'Ours. Well-built town. 3,500 Catholics. Fine view from Château. Good picture in the Church of St. Stephen. Distance, 14¼ leagues (42¾ miles). To Delemont every day, a post cart, 2fr., 4¼ hours. Thence to Porrentruy, 1fr. From Bâle, 9fr. 20c. Posts twice a day, by Delle (French frontier), to Befort, 7½ leagues (22½ miles), in 3½ hours. 4fr. 20c. Once to Bellefontaine, 5½ leagues (16½ miles), in 4 hours. 3fr. 45c. Once to Montbeliard, France, 6 leagues (18 miles), in 3 hours. 3fr. Once to Saignelegier, 8 leagues (24 miles), in 4¼ hours. 5fr. 20c., or 6fr. 40c. in the Coupét.

ITINERARY OF THE CANTON OF BÂLE.

Bâle to Aarau (see Nos. 3, 4, or 5). Aarberg, by Berne (see Nos. 32 and 53).

ROUTE 29.

BY BIENNE. 19 L. (57 m.)

	Leagues.	Miles.
Reinach	1	3
Aesch	¾	1½
Grelligen	1	3
Zwingen	1	3
Laufen	¾	2¼
Liesberg	2	6
Soyeres	1	3
Corandelin	1	3
La Roche	½	1½
Moutiers-Grandval	¾	2¼
Court	1½	3¾
Bevillard	½	1½
Mallerey	¾	1½
Reconvilliers	¾	2¼
Tavannes	½	1½
Sonceboz (1½ L. 42 m.)	1	3
La Reuchenette	1¼	3¾
Büzigen (Boujean)	1¼	3¾
Bienne (16½ L. 50¼ m.)	¼	1¼
Nydau	½	[illegible]
Belmont	½	[illegible]
St. Nicholas	½	[illegible]
Hermzingen	½	[illegible]
Bühl	½	[illegible]
Aarberg	¾	2¼
	19	**57**

ROUTE 30.

AARBERG, 8¼ L. (25¼ m.)

	Leagues.	Miles.
Olten (No. 3)	7¾	23¾
Aarberg	½	1½
	8¼	**25¼**

Aigle, by Berne (Nos. 32 and 54), or by Aarberg (Nos. 29 and 262).

Altdorf, by Lucerne (No. 89 and 147).

Altstaetten, by Zurich (No. 44 and 196) and St. Gallen (No. 180).

Appenzell, by Zurich (No. 44 and 28).

Art, by Aarau (Nos. 3, 4, or 5 and 17), and Zug (No. 281).

ROUTE 31.

BADEN, 12¼ L. (36¾ m.)

	Leagues.	Miles.
Frick (No. 4)	6¼	18¾
Hornussen	1½	4½
Effingen	1	3
Bözberg	1	3
Brugg (10¾ L, 32¼ m.)	½	1½
Königsfelden	¼	1½
Geblstorf	¼	1½
Unterwell	¼	1½
Weil	¼	1½
Baden	¼	1½
	12¼	**36¾**

Bellinzona, by Berne (Nos. 32 and 73 or 74) and Sion (No. 236), or by Lucerne (Nos. 89 and 147) and Altdorf (No. 229).

ROUTE 32.

BERNE (BY BALLSTALL) 19¼ L. (58¼ m.)

	Leagues.	Miles.
Rothaus	1¼	3¼
Liestal	1¼	5¼
Bubendorf	¼	1¼
Höllstein	1	3
Niederdorf	¼	1¼
Oberdorf	¼	1¼
Wallenburg	¼	¾
Langenbruck	1	3
St. Wolfgang	1¼	3¼
Ballstall	¼	1¼
Klus	¼	1¼
Durremühle (9½ L, 28¼ m.)	¼	1¼
Wietlisbach	1	3
Attiswyl	¼	2¼
Neuhaus	¼	[illegible]
Solothurn (12¼ L, 38¼ m.)	1¼	3¼
Lohn	1	3
Krayllingen	¼	1¼
Bätterkinden	¼	1¼
Fraubrunnen	1¼	3
Graffenried	¼	[illegible]
Jegistorf	¼	1¼
Urtenen	¼	1¼
Papiermühle	1¼	4¼
Berne	¼	2¼
	19¼	**58¼**

ROUTE 33.

BERNE, BY THE ANCIENT BISHOPRICK OF BÂLE, 23 L. (69 m.)

	Leagues.	Miles.
Aarberg (No. 29)	19	57
Berne (No. 53)	4	12
	23	**69**

Bex and Bulle, by Berne (Nos. 32, 58 and 54.)

Bienne (No. 29.)

Brugg (No. 31.)

ROUTE 34.

BURGDORF, 15¾ L. (47¼ m.)

	Leagues.	Miles.
Dürremühle (No. 53)	9¼	28¼
Aarwangen	¾	1¼
Butsberg	¾	2¼
Herzogenbuchsee	1	3
Oberönz	¼	¾
Senzberg	¼	1¼
Höchstetten	¼	1¼
St. Nicolas	¼	1¼
Oesberg	¼	¾
Kirchberg 14¾ L (44¼ m.)	1	3
Burgdorf	1	3
	[illegible]	**[illegible]**

From Aarwangen you can also pass by

	Leagues.	Miles.
Langenthal	1	3
Bleinbach	¾	2¼
Dörigen	½	1½
Rietwyl	1	3
Wynigen	1	3
Burgdorf	1½	3½

Chamouny, by (Berne Nos. 32 and 63).
Lausanne (No. 96) and Geneva (No. 95), or by Solothurn (Nos. 32 and 223).
Lausanne (No. 96) and Geneva (No. 95), or by Solothurn (Nos. 32 and 178).
Neuchâtel (No. 97) and Geneva (No. 95).

*ROUTE 35.

CHAUX DE FONDS, 20½ l. (61½ m.)

	Leagues.	Miles.
Sonceboz (see No. 29)	14	42
Corgémont	¾	2¼
Courtelary	1¼	3¾
St. Imier	1½	4½
Renan	1	3
Chaux de Fonds	2	6
	20½	61½

Chiavenna, by Zurich (Nos. 44 and 142).
Coire (Nos. 121, 122, or 123).
Coire, by Zurich (Nos. 44 and 142).
Einsiedeln, by Zurich (Nos. 44 and 299, or 300).
Engelberg, by Lucerne (Nos. 39 and 153).
Frauenfeld, by Schaffhausen (Nos. 41 and 190), or by Zurich (Nos. 44 and 245).
Fribourg, by Berne (Nos. 32 and 54), or by Aarberg (Nos. 79 and 80).
Gais, by Zurich (Nos. 44 and 196), and Saint Gallen (No. 186).
Geneva, by Berne or by Solothurn and Neuchâtel (see Chamouny).
Glarus, by Zurich (Nos 44 and 116).
Herisau, by Zurich (Nos. 44 and 301).

* Courtelary, 1,100 inhabitants, is a fine little town with an ancient castle, and the birth place of Nic. Beguelins, tutor of Frederic the Great. This valley is a nursery for tutors and governesses supplied throughout the face of the earth. St. Imier has 5,000 inhabitants and takes its name from a saint who lived here in the 7th century. The valley was cleared and cultivated by monks. The inhabitants make watches and lace. Near it, ruins of the castle of Erguel, fine waterfalls and caverns. Sonvillier is a great and rich village of watchmakers, with 2,900 inhabitants. The road ascends continually to Renan, 2,758 feet above the sea. Two roads hence to Chaux de Fonds. Common post road followed by the diligence, once a day goes by the Bas Monsieur. The road now usually followed is by le Convers to the railway station (trains 4 times a day from St. Imier) and hence by rail to Chaux de Fonds. (See Canton of Neuchâtel.

ROUTE 36.

HOFWYL, 17½ l. (51½ m.)

	Leagues.	Miles.
Kirchberg (No. 34)	14½	44½
Am Sand (No. 6)	2	6
Hofwyl	½	1½
	17½	51½

ROUTE 37.

LAUFFENBURG, 6¾ l. (20½ m.)

	Leagues.	Miles.
Stein (No. 4)	5¼	15¾
Lauffenburg	1½	4½
	6¾	20½

Lausanne, by Berne (Nos. 32 or 63), or by Solothurn (Nos. 32 and 223).
Locarno, by Lucerne (No. 39 and 147), Altdorf (No. 229), and Bellinzona (No. 232).

ROUTE 38.

LOCLE, 22½ l. (67½ m.)

	Leagues.	Miles.
Chaux de Fonds (No. 35)	20½	61½
Au Locle	2	6
	22½	67½

Loesch (Baths), by Berne (Nos. 32 and 65), or by Solothurn (Nos. 32 and 227), and Sion (No. 268).

ROUTE 39.

LUCERNE, 17½ l. (53½ m.)

	Leagues.	Miles.
Aarberg (No. 30)	8¼	25¼
Lucerne	9¼	27¾
	17½	53½

Lugano, by Lucerne (Nos. 39 and 147).
Altdorf (No. 229), and Bellinzona (No. 283), or by Berne (Nos. 32 and 73, or 74), Sion (No. 236), and Bellinzona (No. 283).
Mendrisio, by Lucerne (Nos. 39 and 147), Altdorf (No. 229), and Bellinzona (No. 285), or by Berne (Nos. 32 and 73, or 74), Sion (No. 236), and Bellinzona (No. 285).
Morat, Morges, and Moudon, by Solothurn (Nos. 32 and 223), or by Berne (Nos. 32 and 63).

ROUTE 40.

NEUCHÂTEL, 25 l. (75 m.)

	Leagues.	Miles.
Aarberg (No. 29)	19	57
Walperswyl	½	1½
Treiten	1	3
Siselen		2¼
Anet (Ins)		2¼
Champion (Gampelen)		1½
Au Pont de Thiele		1¼
Montmirail		¾
Saint Blaise		¾
Neuchâtel	1½	3¾
	25	75

Or by Berne (No. 32 and 70).
Orbe by Neuchâtel (Nos. 40 and 97), or by Berne (Nos. 32 and 71).
Peyerne, by Solothurn (No. 32 and 223), or by Berne Nos. 32 and 77).
Pfeffers (Baths), by Zurich (Nos. 44 and 304).
Righi (Mount), by Aarau (Nos. 14 or 5, and 17) and Zug (No. 294)
Saint Gallen, by Zurich (Nos. 44 and 196).

ROUTE 41.

SCHAFFHAUSEN, 17¾ L. (53¼ m.)

	Leagues.	Miles.
Lauffenburg (No. 37)	6¾	20¼
Hauenstein	1¼	3¾
Waldshut	1¾	5¼
Tiengen	2	6
Lauchingen	1	3
Gysslingen	½	1½
Erzingen	1	3
Neuhaus	1½	4½
Schaffhausen	2	6
	17¾	53¼

Schwyz, by Lucerne (Nos. 39 and 161).

ROUTE 42.

SEMPACH, 14¼ l. (42¾ m.)

	Leagues.	Miles.
Aarburg (No. 30)	8¾	25¾
Sursee (No. 11)	4¾	14¼
Sempach (No. 15)	1¼	4¾
	14¾	42¾

Sion, by Berne (Nos. 32 and 73 or 74), or by Solothurn (Nos. 32 and 227).

ROUTE 43.

SOLOTHURN, 12¾ l. (26¼ m.)

(See No. 32).

Stanz (see Unterwalden).
Thun, by Berne (Nos. 32 and 55).
Trogen, by Zurich (Nos. 44 and 196), and Saint Gallen (No. 193).
Unterwalden, by Lucerne (Nos. 39 and 153).
Vevay, by Berne (Nos. 32 and 54), or by Aarberg (No. 39 and 262).
Winterthur, by Zurich (Nos. 44 and 301).
Yverdun, by Neuchâtel (Nos 40 and 97), or by Berne (Nos. 32 and 77).
Zug, by Aarau (Nos. 3, 4, or 5 and 17).

ROUTE 44.

ZURICH 16¼ l. (48¾ m.)

	Leagues.	Miles.
Baden (see No. 31)	12¼	36¾
Zurich (see No. 17)	4	12
	16¼	48¾

CANTON OF SOLOTHURN (SOLEURE).

The rail from Bâle to Berne, and almost every part of Switzerland, brings you to the great central junction at Olten, where all change carriages. Olten is in the Canton of Solothurn, contiguous to Bâle, which we must proceed to notice.

LIMITS.—North Bâle, E. Aargau, S. and W. Berne. Two little districts called Leimenthal belong to Solothurn, and are entirely cut off from it by the Canton of Bâle, touching France and Berne on all other points.

AREA, SOIL, CLIMATE.—Surface of the Canton, 33½ square Swiss leagues (785 square kilometres). It has but few plains, consisting chiefly of mountains, hills, and valleys. The soil is not exactly fertile, except certain districts, which are very productive. The climate is generally very healthy.

MOUNTAINS.—The Jura, with its ramifications, traverses the entire Canton from S.W. to N.E.; its highest summits are the Weissenstein and Hasenmatt. The view from these summits is magnificent, extending over a great part of the highest Alps, the whole central table land, and the Jura chain.

RIVERS AND RIVULETS.—1. The Aar flows through the whole Canton, from the little village of Staad, on its S.W. frontier, to that of Wöschnau, on the N.E. border. 2. The Dunneren, rising at the Weissenstein, above the village of Welschenrohr; it runs N.E. to Ballstall, where it unites with the Limmern and the Steinbach; thence it flows E. to pass La Klus, where it turns again N.E., and ultimately joins the Aar near Olten. 3. The Lusel takes its rise at the Vogelberg, in the Canton of Bâle, winds through the valleys of Beinwyl and Thierstein, and enters the Canton of Berne at the village of Rohr. 4. The Emmen, coming from the Canton of Berne, only flows through a corner of the centre of Solothurn, and falls into the Aar near Lauterbach, at a little distance from the town of Solothurn.

RIVULETS.—Very numerous in this Canton on account of the limestone formation. The principal are the Limmern and the Steinbach, the Erlisbach forming the frontier on the side of Aargau; the Siggern and Limpach on the side of Berne in certain places.

AGRICULTURAL AND INDUSTRIAL PRODUCTIONS.—This Canton is rich in horned cattle and horses of a good race. It has fewer sheep and pigs and not many goats. Poultry, bees, fish, and game are very abundant. It raises all kinds of cereals, hemp, flax, vegetables, potatoes, &c., fruit, and a little wine. It has fine meadows and forests; it yields iron ore, marble, limestone, sandstone, gypsum, coal, and mineral springs. The industrial productions consist chiefly in glass, pottery, paper, prints, cotton stuffs, tobacco.

HOT SPRINGS, &c.—The most frequented are at Attisholz, Ammansegg, near Solothurn (town); those of Lostorf, near Olten, of Fluh, near Mariastein, in the Leimenthal, and of Meltingen, near Thierstein, are less visited.

POPULATION AND RELIGION.—The population of the Canton of Soleure is 59,624, of whom about 9,604 are of the Protestant confession, and the rest Roman Catholics.

ABBEYS AND CONVENTS.—The Canton contains two chapters of canons, one at Solothurn, the other at Schönenwerth; three convents of nuns, and four monasteries, which are at Solothurn, Olten, and Marienstein.

EDUCATIONAL AND CHARITABLE INSTITUTIONS.—The schools have been on a very good footing for more than a generation. Superior education is given in the college and lycée of Solothurn, of which we shall speak shortly, as well as of the charitable institutions in the capital of the Canton.

SURVEY OF THE CANTON.

Dornach, near the road from Bâle to Dèlemont and Porrentruy, has the ruins of a castle, and is the place where (July 22nd, 1499) a battle was fought, in which 6,000 Swiss defeated 15,000 Austrians, and forced the emperor Maximilian I. to conclude peace. On the field of battle is an ossuary, or bone-house, as at Morat. In the church of the village of Dornach Brugg is the tomb of Maupertius. At the Capuchin Convent is an altar-piece by Brandmüller.

Hasenmatt, The—See Solothurn.

Olten is the central station for the railways of Bâle, Zurich, Berne, and Geneva, and frequented in the summer by thousands of strangers, who, however, mostly only pass through it without stopping. You change carriages here in almost any case, and whatever be your destination. The starting place for Bâle and Zurich is at the north end of the station; that for Lucerne, Berne, Solothurn, and Geneva the south end. Good restaurant; stoppage, a quarter of an hour. Olten contains a manufactory of locomotives for the Central Swiss line. The little town of Olten is five minutes' from the station (Hotel Von Arx, la Tour, and the Croissant), was founded by the Romans (Ultinum), sustained a siege against the Bernese in 1382, and is now one of the most industrial places in the Canton. Fine views are obtained at Säli Schlössli (three-quarters of an hour), at the Galgenhölzli (three-quarters of an hour), and the baths of Lostorf (one hour).

Solothurn the capital (in French, Soleure, the Solodurum of the Romans).

Hotels. — Couronne, good; Latour Rouge. *Cafés.*—De la Poste; Du Commerce, &c. Trains, 6 a-day, to Bâle, Berne, and Zurich; 5 a-day to Neuchâtel and Geneva; 4 a-day to Lucerne. After Treves, Solothurn is the oldest town N. of the Alps, and now the residence of the Bishop of Bâle. Built on the slope of the

Jura, it is divided by the Aar into two parts, united by two wooden bridges. The town is charmingly situated, a tranquil cheap residence, slow to those who only live for theatres, noise, show, and vanity, but with much to interest thinking men, who have a useful companion always with them in a well stored mind and intellectual tastes.

PUBLIC EDIFICES: The Cathedral or Collegiate Church of St. Urs (Ours) was built by Pisoni, of Locarno, in 1762 to 1773. Its architecture is in the Modern Italian style; the façade in particular is handsome and in good taste. A broad staircase of 33 steps, adorned on both sides with fine fountains, leads up to the three principal doors. This front elevation and its commanding position give it an imposing appearance, and it is justly regarded as one of the finest ecclesiastical buildings in Switzerland. Connoisseurs complain that the nave is rather small. This church contains several fine paintings by Domenico Corvi. The former Jesuit Church has also a fine altar piece. The Tour de l'Horloge, almost in the centre of the town, is of great antiquity, if not Roman it is at least Burgundian. The Hotel de Ville contains some Roman inscriptions, and a gallery of portraits of the avoyers or chief magistrates of the state, and two fine rooms, one with a plaster relief of Nicholas von der Flue, by Pancrace Eggeuschwyler. The Arsenal is very interesting on account of its trophies, including 900 sets of armour of the middle ages, &c., most of them taken from the Austrians and Burgundians in the great Swiss victories of the 14th and 15th centuries. The former palace of the Ambassador of France was turned into barracks by the French republican troops when they invaded Switzerland in 1798. Other buildings are the Theatre, the Civil Hospital, the Orphanage, and the House of Correction. The three latter buildings are in the Faubourg, on the banks of the Aar. The Prison, in the same Faubourg, is not only noticeable on account of its architecture and arrangement, but also for its well ventilated and lighted cells, strength and security, combined with humanity.

EDUCATION AND CHARITIES. — The Lyceum, the Gymnasium, the Orphan School, and several elementary schools. The town Library contains Roman antiquities found on the spot. At the Orphanage is the geological collection of the naturalist, Hugi. It was at Solothurn that the Polish patriot, Kosciusko, died in 1817. His heart was buried at Zuchwil and his body at Cracow. There is a collection of medals at M. Amiet's.

WALKS.—To the Kreutzacker—Hernesbuhl with shady alleys of trees, and watered by the Aar. In 1313, when Solothurn was besieged by the Austrians, the bridge broke under them at this place, and hundreds of knights were on the point of drowning if the magnanimous Swiss of the of the town had not saved them in boats, disregarding every other feeling, save a noble humanity. They afterwards released them without a ransom. This has no parallel in Pagan, and few in Christian times; but it was gracefully acknowledged. Leopold touched with this sublime generosity, raised the siege, and presented the city with a banner, still kept in the Church. To the hermitage of St. Verena ½ l. (1½ m.) by various roads; the most pleasant, a path along a little stream which makes several picturesque cascades. The Verenathal, is a charming valley 20 minutes long, filled with groves and chapels and other sanctuaries of devotion. You can strike off by the Nesselboden Alp to the Weissenstein Road. Carriages up that mountain with two horses 20fr. and a pourboire. The château of Waldegg ½ L (1½ m.); the baths of Attishölz and of Ammannsegg 1 L. (3 m.) the Hohlberg, &c., are other points to visit.

EXCURSIONS.—The Weissenstein (3,950 feet) 2½ hours by the road, 1½ by the path. It is 2,682 feet above Solothurn. The road goes by Langendorf and Oberdorf; where it divides into two, one going to the left to the posterior Weissenstein, and the other to the right to the anterior Weissenstein, where is now a good hotel, where many persons stay days and weeks to enjoy the fresh air, and one of the most perfect panoramic views in the world. The eye embraces not only all the central table land of Switzerland, 16 l. (48 m.) wide, but it follows for 130 l. (390 m.) an almost uninterrupted series of snowy peaks and glaciers, extending from the Tyrol to Mont Blanc. Pension, 4½ to 6*fr.* per day. The view is still more extensive from the Roethefluh ½ l. (1½ m.) from the hotel, and especially from the Hasenmatt 4,476 f. above the sea, and 3,192 f. above the town of Solothurn. The view towards the Alps is the same as from Weissenstein, but you see more of Burgundy and Alsace. A path leads from the Hasenmatt to Court in the Munsterthal, passing by Chaluat. Another path leads from Weissenstein to Munster in three hours, by the village of Gansbrunnen, advancing thence to Bâle, you can diverge near the Aesch (on the Birse) to see Dornach. (See further back.)

ROUTES OF SOLOTHURN.

Solothurn to Aarau, rail (or No. 16.)

ROUTE 216.
AARBERG, 6 l. (18 m.)

	Leagues.	Miles.
Läussligen	¾	2¼
Leuzigen	¾	2¼
Arch	½	1½
Rutti	½	1½
Buren	½	1½
Dozigen	½	1½
Buetigen	¾	2¼
Lyss	1	3
Aarberg	¾	2¼
	6	18

Bellinzona, by Lucerne (Nos. 162 and 147), and Altdorf (No. 229).

Berne (No. 75).

Bex, by Berne (Nos. 75 and 58), (or by Moudon (Nos. 225 and 247).

ROUTE 217.
AARBOURG, 7¾ l. (23¼ m.)

	Leagues.	Miles.
Olten, rail or (No. 16)	7	21
Aarbourg	¾	2¼
	7¾	23¼

Aigle, by Berne (No. 75 or 54), or by Moudon (No. 225 or 227).

Altdorf, by Lucerne (Nos. 162 and 147).

Altstaetten, by Aarau (Nos. 16 and 18), Zurich (No. 196), and Saint Gallen (No. 180).

Appenzell, same Routes as far a Zurich, and thence by (No. 188).

Art, by Aarau (Nos. 16 and 17), and Zug (No. 281).

Baden, by Aarau (Nos. 16 and 2), Bale (No. 82).

ROUTE 218.
BIENNE, 4¼ l. (12¾ m.)

	Leagues.	Miles.
Bellach	½	1½
Selzach	½	1½
Bet-lach	¼	¾
Gränchen	½	1½
Längnau	½	1½
Pieterlen or Perle	½	1½
Bozingen (Boujean) 3¾ L (11¼ m.)	1	3
Bienne	½	1½
	4¼	12¾

Brougg, by Aarau (Nos. 16 and 7.)

Bulle, by Berne (Nos. 75 and 54), or by Aarberg (Nos. 216 and 80), and Fribourg (No. 54.)

ROUTE 219.
BURGDORF, 4¼ l. (12¾ m.)

	Leagues.	Miles.
Lohn	1	3
Bätterkinden	½	1½
Uzenstorf	¾	2¼
Kirchberg	1	3
Burgdorf	1	3
	4¼	12¾

Chamouny, by Neuchâtel (No. 178 and 97), and Geneva (No. 95), or by Berne (No 75 and 63), Lausanne (No. 96) and Geneva (No. 95).

ROUTE 220.
CHAUX DE FONDS, 12¾ l. (38¾ m.)

	Leagues.	Miles.
Bozingen (No. 218)	3¾	11¼
Renchenette	1¾	3¾
Sonceboz	1¼	3¾
Chaux de Fonds (No. 35)	6¼	19¾
	12¾	38¾

Chiavenna, by Aarau (No 16 and 18), Zurich (No. 142) and Chur (No. 121, 122, 123), or by Lucerne (No. 162 and 162), Schwytz (No. 134) and Chur (No. 1 1, 122, 123).

Chur, by Aarau (No. 16 and 18) and Zurich (No. 142), or by Lucerne (No. 162 and 161) and Schwytz (No. 134).

Einsiedeln, by Lucerne (No. 162 and 152).

Engelberg, by Lucerne (No. 162 and 153).

Frauenfeld, by Aarau (No. 16 and 18) and Zurich (No. 245.)

ROUTE 221.

FRIBOURG, by **BERNE** (No. 75 and 54), or by **AARBERG**, 12½ L. (37½ m.)

	Leagues.	Miles.
Aarberg (No. 216)	6	18
Bargen	¾	¾
Kalnach	¾	1½
Fraschels	¾	1½
Kerzers (Chiêtre)	½	1½
Morat (9½ l., 28½ m.)	1¾	5¼
Munchwyler (Villars)	½	1½
Courtepin	1	3
Fribourg	1½	4½
	12½	37½

Gais, by Aarau (Nos. 16 and 18), Zurich (No. 190), St. Gallen (No. 186).

Geneva, by Neuchâtel (No. 178 and 97), or by Berne (No 75 and 63) and Lausanne (No. 96).

Glarus, by Aarau (No. 16 and 18) and Zurich (No. 116).

Herisau, by Aarau (No. 16 and 18) and Zurich (No. 301).

ROUTE 222.

HOFWYL, 5¼ l. (15¾ m.)

	Leagues.	Miles.
Urtenen (No. 75)	4½	13½
Am Sand	¾	¾
Hofwyl	½	1½
	5¼	15¾

Lauffenbourg, by Aarau (Nos. 16 and 10).

ROUTE 223.

LAUSANNE, by **BERNE** (Nos. 75 and 63), or by **MORAT**, 21 L. (63 m.)

	Leagues.	Miles.
Morat (No. 221)	9½	28½
Faoug	½	2¼
Avenches	½	2¼
Domdidier	½	1½
Dompierre	½	1½
Corcelle	½	1½
Payerne, 13 l. (39 m.)	½	1½
Lausanne No. 63	8	24
	21	63

Locarno, by Lucerne (Nos. 162 and 147), Altdorf (No. 229), and Bellinzona (No. 232). The Simplon road may also be taken.

ROUTE 224.

LOCLE, 14¾ l. (44¼ m.)

	Leagues.	Miles.
Chaux de Fonds (No. 220)	12¾	38¼
Aux Eplatures	¾	1½
Sur le Crêt	½	1½
Au Locle	1	3
	14¾	44¼

Loesch (Baths), by Berne (Nos. 75 and 65) or by Sion (Nos. 227 and 268).

Lucerne (No. 162).

Lugano, by Lucerne (No. 162 and 147), Altdorf No. 229), and Bellinzona (No. 233). Or by the Simplon.

Mendrisio, by Lucerne (Nos. 162 and 147), Altdorf (No. 229), and Bellinzona (No. 235). The Simplon Route can also be taken.

Morat (No. 221)

Morges, by Lausanne (No. 223 and 96).

ROUTE 225.

MOUDON, 17 l. (51 m.)

	Leagues.	Miles.
Payerne (No. 223)	13	39
Moudon (No. 63)	4	12
	17	51

Neuchâtel (No. 178).

Orbe, by Neuchâtel (Nos. 178 and 97), or by Berne (Nos. 75 and 71).

Payerne (No. 228)

Pfeffers (Baths), by Aarau (Nos. 16 and 1º) and Zurich (No. 304).

Righi (The) by Aarau (Nos. 16 and 17) and Zug (No. 294), or by Lucerne (Nos. 162 and 158, or 159).

Saint Gallen, by Aarau (Nos. 16 and 18) and Zurich (No. 196).

Schaffhausen, by Aarau (No. 16 and 14).

Schwyz, by Lucerne (Nos. 162 and 161)).

ROUTE 226.

SEMPACH, 14 l. (42 m.)

	Leagues.	Miles.
Olten (No. 16)	7	21
Aarberg	¾	2¼
Sursec (No. 11)	4¾	14¼
Eich	1	3
Sempach	½	1½
	14	42

ROUTE 227.

SION, by **BERNE** (No. 75 and 73 or 74) or by **MOUDON**, 36½ L. (109½ m.)

	Leagues.	Miles.
Moudon (No. 225)	17	51
Carrouge	1½	4½
Mezières	½	1½
Essertes	½	1½
Chexbres	2	6
Vevay	1	3
Aigle (No. 54)	3¾	11¼
Bex	1½	4½
Sion (No. 77)	8¾	26¼
	36½	109½

Stanz, see Unterwalden.

Thun, by Berne (Nos 75 and 55).

Trogen, by Aarau (Nos. 16 and 18).

Zurich (No. 196) and Saint Gallen (No. 193).

Unterwalden, by Lucerne (Nos 162 and 153), or by Berne (No. 75), Thun, and the Brunig (Nos. 55 and 76).

Vevay, by Berne (Nos. 75 and 54), or by Moudon (Nos 225 and 227).

Winterthur, by Aarau (Nos. 16 and 18), and Zurich No. 301).

ROUTE 228.

Yverdun, 17¾ l. (53¼ m.)

	Leagues.	Miles.
Payerne (No. 223)	13	39
Yverdun (No. 77)	4¾	14¼
	17¾	53¼

Zug, by Aarau (Nos. 16 and 17).

Zurich, by Aarau (Nos. 16 and 18).

Zurzach, by Aarau (Nos. 16 and 17).

Strasburg, Frankfort, and the Rhine, and Paris, by Bâle.

Paris and Central France, by Neuchâtel.

Lyons, Southern France, Turin, and Genoa, by Geneva.

Austria, Bavaria, and Eastern Germany, by Olten, Winterthur, and Romanshorn, or Rorschach, over the Lake of Constance to Friedrichshafen, and Lindau.

Milan and Italy in general, by Altdorf, or by the Simplon.

After leaving Olten (see *Bradshaw's Continental Guide*) and its Great Central Station, our main route A soon brings us by rail to the Canton of Berne.

CANTON OF BERNE.

LIMITS.—The outline of the canton of Berne is so irregular that it is rather difficult to determine its frontiers with complete accuracy. In general terms, however, it may be described as being bounded to the east, by the Cantons of Uri, of Unterwalden, of Lucerne, of Argovie, of Solothurn, and of Bâle; to the south by the Canton of Valais; to the west by Fribourg and Neuchâtel, and to the north by France and the Canton of Solothurn.

SURFACE, SOIL AND CLIMATE. — The area of the Canton of Berne exceeds that of any other in Switzerland (except the Grisons), and embraces a surface of 326¼ square Swiss leagues (128 German square miles, 6,889 square kilometres). The surface of the soil presents a very various character, a large portion of the

Canton consisting of valleys bounded by hills of various but mostly moderate elevation, rising gradually till they culminate in the colossal peaks and eternal glaciers of the Oberland, in the south. It is evident that in these higher regions the climate must be severe, but it becomes more genial in proportion as you recede from the higher Alps, and in the lower districts it is very mild and suitable to all kinds of crops.

MOUNTAINS.—The highest Alpine chain (after that of Monte Rosa and Cervin), forms the southern boundary of this Canton, separating it from that of the Valais, and running in a north-easterly and south-westerly direction. This chain, known popularly as the northern Oberland, or Bernese Alps, contains the largest glaciers and some of the highest summits in Switzerland, including the Jungfrau, Eiger, Finsteraarhorn, Schreckhorn, Wetterhorn, Tschingel, and many others, rising far above the line of perpetual snow and giving birth to numberless streams. These giant mountains diminish gradually in elevation, and ultimately sink into gentle outliers and ramifications extending into the heart of the Canton. The Jura, a range distinct from the Alps, traverses the Canton of Berne, in the north. Its highest summit in this part is the Chasseral.

LAKES, RIVERS, AND RIVULETS. 1. LAKES.—The lake of Brienz is situated in the Oberland, and enclosed by the Alps; its greatest length from north-east to south-west is 3 leagues (or 9 English miles), and its width a league or 3 miles. This lake yields a large kind of trout, called in the country Brienzling, and usually eaten after being salted and potted.

The lake of Thun is only ½ a league (1½ mile) from that of Brienz, with which it communicates by means of the river Aar, the main stream that supplies both sheets of water. The lake of Thun stretches from the south-east to the north-west, having an extreme length of 5 leagues (or 15 miles) and a width of ½ a league (1½ miles); it is remarkably well stocked with fish.

The lake of Bienne having a length of 3 leagues (9 miles), and a width of 1 league (3 miles), is situated almost at the foot of the Chasseral. It yields also a large number of fish, and contains the island of St. Pierre, celebrated as the residence of Rousseau. This lake communicates to the south-west with that of Neuchâtel, by the river Thiele, which after passing through both lakes, falls ultimately into the Aar. The Thiele and both these lakes which are fed by it, afford an uninterrupted navigation from Yverdun to the Rhine, and are much used for the water transport of wine, colonial produce and other exports and imports.

The small mountain lakes or tarns of Amsoldingen, Seedorf and Guerzensee are too insignificant to require a separate notice.

RIVERS.—Navigable rivers. The Aar takes it source in the two glaciers of that name (Aar-Gletscher) and in its course through the Canton receives the following tributaries, the Emmen, the Saane, and the Thiele, and falls into the Rhine, near Coblentz in the Canton of Aarau. The Thiele or Ziel rises in the Jura, feeds the lake of Neuchâtel, and only assumes that name on issuing from the lake in its onward course to supply that of Bienne, which forms the limit of the two Cantons of Neuchâtel and Berne. Soon after issuing from the lake of Bienne, the Thiele falls into the Aar.

Non-navigable rivers: (a) The Emmen, or Great Emmen, rises among the mountains of the Entlibuch, in the Canton of Lucerne, waters the Emmenthal, and flows on through Burgdorf and Kirchberg to the Aar, which it joins near Solothurn. Generally speaking, the water is very low in this stream, but a few hours suffice to con-vert it into an impetuous and destructive torrent. (b) The Saane (Sarine) rises near Sanetsch, on the borders of Valais, and after flowing through the Canton of Fribourg it unites with the Singin (Sense) near Laupen, and both streams soon after fall into the Aar near Wyleroltigen. (c) The Kander rises at the Gemmi, and on reaching Einigen receives the Simmen, when their united waters fall into the lake of Thun, between Einigen and Gwatt. The Singin (Sense) is partly supplied from the Schwarz-see, or Black Lake, and partly from the Ganterisch. The Simmen rises in the valley of Iffigen, the Suze flows through the valley of Saint Imier, and the Birse through the valley of Moutiers. It would be useless and tedious to enumerate the multitude of smaller streams that water this large and fertile Canton.

RIVULETS.—Their name is legion, and cannot of course enter into the limits of this work. Several will be noticed in connection with the cascades that they form so liberally in the Oberland.

THE SOIL, CROPS, AND MANUFACTURES. —The Canton of Berne is very rich in horned cattle, horses, and goats; sheep are less numerous, but swine particularly abundant. Bees receive considerable attention, and the Canton yields a moderate supply of poultry. Fish and game are fairly plentiful, especially chamois, hares, cock de bruyeres, &c. The Alpine pastures of the Oberland and other districts are excellent and celebrated. In the lowlands crops of cereals are largely raised, besides hemp, flax, potatoes, and various other vegetables. The yield of wine is limited. Many parts of the mountains are clothed with noble and extensive forests, especially of the fir tribe (coniferæ). The mineral produce of the soil consists in crystals, limestone, sandstone, gritstone, coal, iron ore, and mineral springs.

Certain districts of the Canton of Berne (especially the Emmenthal and Gessenay) are noted for the production of excellent cheeses. The chief articles manufactured in this Canton are good linens, different silk stuffs, floss silk and cotton, tape, printed calico, cloth, leather, paper, felt hats and straw hats of the best quality. A few water mills and forges are also in operation in different parts of the Canton.

MINERAL SPRINGS AND BATHS.—Bathing institutions are more numerous in this Canton than in any other. The following are the most frequented:—

1. The Aarzihle Baths, close to the city of Berne.

2. The Gurnigel Baths, 6 leagues or 18 miles from Berne, situated on the north-western slope of a mountain of that name, forming part of the Stockhorn ridge. The temperature of the water does not exceed 6° Reaumur (or 50° Fahrenheit). These waters are rather popular both for drinking and bathing.

3. The Baths of Weissburg, in the Lower Simmenthal, are situated 5 leagues (15 miles) from Thun; 4½ leagues (13½ miles) from Berne. The waters on issuing from the source have a temperature of 23' Reaumur (102° Fahrenheit), and are also used alike for drinking and bathing.

4. The Baths of Blumenstein almost at the foot of the Stockhorn, 4½ leagues (13½ miles) from Berne. The temperature of these waters at their source is 8½° Reaumur (57½° Fahrenheit); they hold in solution both iron and magnesia. At a ½ of a league or ¾ of a mile from Blumenstein is the cascade of Fallbach.

5. The Baths of Engistein, on the high road, up the Emmenthal, 2 leagues (6 miles) from Berne, and those of the Rüttihubel, ½ a league (1½ mile) further on. Both these springs are ferruginous, but the latter are inferior to the former.

6. The Baths of Thalgut, 3 leagues (9 miles) from Berne. On the way you pass by Guerzensee, which offers some magnificent views.

7. The Lochbad and Sommernaus, ¾ of a league (¾ of a mile) from Burgdorf, and 4¼ leagues (12¾ miles) from Berne. Both these baths are situated in a highly romantic and picturesque district.

8. The Limpach is 1 league (3 miles) from Thun, and we might swell this list with the names of many other less noted baths occuring in different parts of the Canton.

POPULATION AND RELIGION.—The present population of this Canton is 460,000 inhabitants. Thirty years ago it had only 291,200, of whom 229,000 occupied the ancient territory of the Canton, and 62,000 the newly added parts, ceded to it after the Treaty of Paris. In the latter portion, which belongs chiefly to the bishoprick of Bâle, there are 58,319 Catholics, the rest of the population are Protestants.

WEIGHTS AND MEASURES.—The currency is now same as in France. As regards weights, the quintal is = 100lbs., and the lb. = 34 lots, or = 520·131 grammes, French measure, and about 1lb. English measure. One Bernese foot equals 29·32ſ French centimetres or nearly an English foot. The brach = 54·171 centimetres (or 1¾ feet.) The mütt (grain measure) is divided into 12 measures; mäs of 4 emins (or imi). Each measure or mäs = 14,011 litres (or 28lbs). The saum, a liquid measure, contains 100 pots, and 1 pot = 1,671 litres (or 3,346 pints).

SURVEY OF THE CANTON.

Berne (city) being the capital and heart of the Confederation, is an active centre for railways. It is on the Central Swiss Line, communicating through Olten with Bâle, Zurich, and Lucerne, by seven trains a-day, with Neuchâtel and Geneva by five trains, and Thun (for the Oberland) by four trains, and with Fribourg and Lausanne by three trains.

Direct tickets and fares to the following places :—

	Kind of Train.	1st cl.		2nd cl.		3rd cl.	
		f.	c.	f.	c.	f.	c.
Aix-la-Chapelle	ord.	79	55	58	95	...	
Antwerp	exp.	99	35	81	30	...	
Baden-Baden (available for ten days)	{ ,,	29	95	20	8	...	
	{ ord.	27	5	18	90	12	75
Bâle	ord	11	10	7	80	5	60
Berlin	exp.	133	20	92	10	...	
Bienne	ord.	3	75	2	65	1	90
Bonn (for six days)	,,	67	40	49	90	...	
Brussels	exp.	98	15	80	10	...	
Carlsruhe (for ten days)	{ ,,	32	60	24	65	...	
	{ ord.	29	20	20	30	13	85
Coblenz (five days)	,,	61	0	45	10	...	
Chur	,,	27	45	19	15	13	10
Cologne (five days)	,,	69	95	51	85	...	
Dresden	exp.	123	10	87	45	...	
Frankfort (10 days)	,,	47	55	32	80	...	
Geneva	ord.	16	85	11	75	8	45
Heidelberg (ten days)	{ exp	38	40	26	65	...	
	{ ord.	34	0	23	65	...	
Lausanne	,,	10	25	7	20	5	15
London	exp.	153	80	135	75	...	
Lucerne	ord.	12	5	8	50	6	10
Mayence (five days)	,,	51	5	37	60	...	
Munich (six days)	{ exp.	51	50	35	95	...	
	{ ord	47	10	32	95	...	
Neuchâtel	,,	6	75	4	85	3	50
Olten	,,	7	5	4	95	3	35
Ostend	exp.	109	15	91	10	...	
Paris, Verrieres	ord	62	15	47	0	35	25
Paris, by Rheims, (available one month)	{ ,,	63	80	47	75	...	
Romanshorn	,,	22	50	15	75	11	25
Rorschach	,,	24	40	17	10	12	20
Saint Gallen	,,	22	60	15	85	11	30
Schaffhausen	,,	16	50	11	55	8	25
Solothurn	,,	5	65	3	95	2	85
Strassurg (one month)	,,	28	75	21	45	...	
Stuttgardt (three days)	exp.	42	45	29	30	...	
Thun	ord	3	15	2	20	1	60
Vevay	,,	12	25	8	60	6	15
Zurich	,,	13	75	9	65	6	90

VOITURES DE PLACE, AT BERNE.—2 persons in the town, 40c ; 3 or 4 persons, 80c.; ¼ hour for 1 or 2 persons, 80c.; 3 or 4 persons, 1fr. 20c.; every ¼ of an hour more, 40c ; 3 or 4 persons, 60c.; from or to station with trunk, 60c.; by the day, 2 persons, 12fr.; 3 or 4 persons, 18fr.; by night, double fares.

SURVEY OF THE CANTON.

Berne, the capital of the Canton, and of the Swiss Confederation, built on a peninsula formed by the river Aar. Present population, 29,000, increase in 30 years, 9,000 or 4.

HOTELS.—Bernerhof Hotel—first-class hotel, delightfully situated, commands a full view of the Alps. Hotel de Belle Vue, commanding a splendid view of the "Alpes de Oberland;" comfort and excellent accommodation. Hotel du Faucon, situated in the finest part of the town; a very good house, excellent *cuisine*, moderate charges. De l'Europe; Schweizerhof; Du Maure; Singe; Cigogne; Baer; Des Marechaux.

Berne may be pronounced, next to Geneva, the handsomest and largest town in Switzerland. It stands on a hill on the left bank of the Aar, at an elevation of 1,708 feet above the Mediterranean. A handsome bridge of freestone unites both banks of the river, built by Müller of Altdorf in 1844, of granite from Hasli, cost 1½ million francs. The bridge has only one arch of 156 feet, length 426 feet, width 40 feet. It is a colossal work and its appearance is very fine. The architecture of the town is quaint and novel, but pleasing in its general effect, and generally regular in design. Three principal and parallel streets, communicating by several cross streets, represent the general plan on which it is constructed, and intersect the town from the Gate of Solothurn to the Belfry Tower. The only exceptional part of Berne, called the Matte, is situated to the S. E. at the foot of the hill, and close to the Aar. The central one of the three parallel streets, previously noticed, runs in almost a straight line from the Gate of Solothurn to that of Morat, and thus forms the principal thoroughfare of the city. Most of the houses bordering this, and many of those in the lateral streets, are still built on arcades, affording complete shelter to the foot passenger. A stream, confined in a bed of masonry, flows through many of the streets, and feeds several handsome and copious fountains, which adorn and refresh the city. Berne has 19 principal streets and 3 squares: 1, that of the Arsenal, or of the wood market, cutting the city transversely from the Orphan House to the Upper Graben ; 2, that of the Great Granary, also contained between the Lower Graben and the Guard House ; 3, and lastly, the Cathedral Platz, or Close, facing the prison

Porch, and surrounded by other substantial buildings.

PUBLIC BUILDINGS.—The Cathedral, which formerly bore the name of Church of St. Vincent, is a beautiful monument of the architecture of the 15th century. It was commenced in 1421, and only completed in 1502, built either by Mathias Oensiger or by Mathias Heinz, son of the architect who, with Erwin of Steinbach, built the Cathedral of Strasburg. On the north side, near the high gallery, is the statue of the architect, at the spot where he fell and was killed. In the choir are the tomb of Berthold von Zähringen, and six tablets of black marble raised to the memory of 18 Swiss officers, who fell in 1799, fighting the French then engaged in "enforcing liberty on Switzerland." The stalls of the Chapter were the work of Rüsch and Seewagen. The organ is by Hans, and has 3,294 pipes and 66 stops. Mendel is the organist. In the Sacristy are many valuables taken from Charles the Bold by the Swiss at the battles of Morat and Grandson. Fee, ½ fr. Its general effect is much admired, but the traveller's attention is particularly directed to the gateway and the choir; the former is adorned with a great number of stone sculptures, by Kung, and ornaments, and the latter with handsome stained glass windows. Both are curious as specimens of the anti-papal spirit that prevailed at Berne before the Reformation. The length of the nave is 160 feet, and the height of the tower to the beginning of the roof 175 feet. This tower is very handsome, and is surrounded by a gallery which commands splendid and widely extended views. The large bell of this tower weighs 203 quintals, without its adjuncts. A Roman Catholic Church, in a florid style, and adorned with marble, has been lately erected in the N. of the town. It has some very fine paintings.

The Church of the Holy Ghost, or of the Hospital, presents a strong contrast to the Cathedral, or its modern architecture in the Italian or French style. It was built in 1622.

The Hotel de Ville deserves notice as the place of assembly of the Great Council; it also contains some remarkable pictures. Among the other public buildings we may notice the Assembly Room of the Diet; Bernerhof, built on the plan of M. M. Kubli and Fred Stadler (374 feet long, 160 wide) at the cost of 2 million francs, it has fine stained glass windows; the Hotel of the Stift; the Mint; the Corn Exchange; the Building of the University, founded in in 1834, and attended on the average by 150 to 180 students; the Gymnasium, or Grammar School; the Public Library, open every day, rich in Swiss works and valuable MSS., and its Museum*; the Chief Hospital and that of the island, which are the two finest and largest public buildings in the city; the two Orphanages; the Arsenal; the Barracks; the Riding School, &c., &c..

BUILDINGS DEVOTED TO AMUSEMENT OR TO THE CORPORATION.—The Music Hall contains a theatre and a handsome café. The New Casino, or Concert Room, is a handsome building in the modern style, containing, besides a concert room, a ball room, and several salons, decorated with much taste and elegance. Attached to it are also a very good café and restaurant. Another building, formerly connected with the Guilds, or trades, was called the Thirteen Abbeys, a term employed to

[* In the Bernerhof. Admission free from 8 to 4. Contains already some good pictures, especially two by Calamé of Geneva; 1. The Handeck Fall, No. 140; 2. The Alpbach, No. 141; 3. A Châlet, by Diday, No. 134; the Valley of Lauterbrunnen, No. 147; Charles Girardet's Battle of Morat. No. 110; Curious pictures of Reinhard, &c. The Museum of Natural History (open, Tuesday and Saturday, 3 to 5 p.m., Sundays. 10 a.m. to 12 noon) has a good collection of Fauna, especially of the Alps, including vultures, eagles, bouquetins, lynxes bears, and the faithful dog, Barry, of St. Bernard (stuffed), who saved the lives of 14 persons. There is also a collection of Swiss antiquities of the middle ages, with the moveable altar of Charles the Bold, and other collections of various interest.]

describe those mediæval corporations which included the tanners, shoemakers, the golden lion, the weavers, the blacksmiths, the carpenters, the bakers, the butchers, the merchants, the boatmen, that of the monkey, the moor, and the gentlemen.

EDUCATIONAL, SCIENTIFIC, AND CHARITABLE INSTITUTIONS.—The University, or former Academy, is divided into an upper and a lower department. In the upper department lectures are delivered on philosophy, history, mathematics, natural science, and philology; in the lower department, theology, law, medicine, and the veterinary art are taught. To this department are attached an anatomical museum and a veterinary school. The other educational establishments of Berne consist of the Gymnasium; the Elementary School; the Latin School, and that of Mutual Instruction (the Lancasterian); the Academy of Design; the Gallery of Antiques, containing many casts in plaister of Paris; the School of Gymnastic Exercises directed by Mr. Clias, and the Ladies' School under the direction of Professor Meissner.

The Public Library contains upwards and a fine collection of medals and of of 30,000 volumes, a number of MSS., Roman antiquities. There are several other libraries, including that of the Preachers, of Medical Sciences, of the Students, &c., and some valuable collections, especially the Museum of Natural History, especially rich Swiss Fauna, the Botanical Garden, the collections of Professors Studer and Meissner, the Swiss numismatic collection of Dr. Isenschmid and Mr. Sprungli, and the collection of Celtic and other antiquities.

Berne possesses a Society for researches into Swiss History, a Medical Association, a Natural History Association, as well as musical and artistic societies.

Among the numerous charitable institutions those deserving special notice are the Orphan Asylum, that of the island; the Great Hospital; the Hospital for the Insane and the Incurable (about 2½ miles from Berne); the Poor-house, for the relief of the indigent, including an almshouse for superannuated servants; the Musshafen, for the support of poor students; several savings' banks, &c.

Berne has long and justly enjoyed a high reputation as a centre of Swiss art. Its painters and artists have been particularly distinguished for their works in water colours, representing Swiss scenery. Among the most distinguished names we may notice Mr. Lory, Weibel, Lafond, Löhrer, and more recently Diday, Dietler, &c.

COMMERCE AND MANUFACTURES.—The preparation of local produce is the chief branch of industry at Berne, including especially cheese and wine. There are, however, some *bona fide* manufactories in the town, particularly straw hats, floss silk, millinery, jewellery, cloth, saltpetre, and powder mills. A fair is held twice a year at Berne, at Easter and in the autumn; it lasts each time a fortnight.

CURIOSITIES.—There are two ditches or fosses outside the walls, one called that of the stags, and the other of the bears. The former is outside the gate of Morat. There used to be two ditches here containing stags, and gymnastic exercises used to be carried on here in summer. The foss of the bears* is close to the Aarberg gate, it is deep and protected by a parapet which enables the visitor to view, in safety, the bears which are supported by a special fund devoted to the purpose. Bouquetins used to be kept in a small foss near this gate.

BERNESE ALPS.—The district called in

* A "civis romanus" was eaten up here lately, apparently to the satisfaction of the Bernese, who did not interfere with the indulgence of the appetite of their favourite bear.

German the Oberland,* is the grandest mass of mountains in the Alps, after the Chamouny, and Monte Rosa districts, and contains the largest fields of ice (glaciers) in the whole range.

' It will be convenient here to give a summary sketch of the whole district, which is principally formed of a high snowy range, running east and west, irradiating branch chains, and intersected by the main artery of the Aar and its tributaries. The main chain commences at the Grimsel Pass to the east, where it joins the the chain of St. Gothard, runs west in a long series of lofty peaks to the Gemmi Pass to the west, rises again to high summits in the Wildstrubel district, and sinks into the Canton of Fribourg beyond the Saane. The main artery of the Aar waters the Hasli valley, forms the Brienz lake, receives the Lütchinen near Interlaken, supplies the lake of Thun, which receives the Kander, turns N.W. and enters the Rhine, near Baden in Aarau. The N.W. valleys of Hasli, Grindelwald, Lauterbrunnen, the Kander, Simmen and Saane are the chief intersections of these uplands and offer the finest centres. The main chain presents the following conspicuous summits, beginning from the Grimsel.

* Fixed Rates of guides and porters in the Oberland. —Guides are bound to carry 15lbs. of luggage. Rate of pay, 6 to 8 *fr.* per day. A regular day's journey, 24 miles (8 leagues). On dismissing a guide he is entitled to 6 *fr.* for a day, for each day of 8 leagues (taking the nearest way home). Over 4 leagues (12 miles) extra day's work reckons as ½ a day, being more reasonable than the red tape regime of the schoolmaster's office in Downing Street. Trinkgeld is optional with the traveller if pleased. Guides may use as porters, to aid them, young men without license, but the latter must be subject to the regulations. For the high Alps extra charges are made. The guide and hotel keeper are responsible for the porters whom they recommend. Porters 6 *fr.* per day, and the same to return. On the beaten track of large parties, guides are not wanted. In many places little boys will do the work and carry your pack cheaply. Beggary used to be a great nuisance here; it is now diminished. Still it is well to have a few coppers in your pocket, and not refuse all the frantic attention as horn-blowing, nosegays, and bad singing offered you. In cases of imposition British decision of manner and good nature, beat down opposition and get through anything.

1. The Finsteraarhorn 13,160 French ft., 14,028 English ft.
2. Schreckhörner, east peak, 12,563 French ft., 13,914 English ft., west peak, 12,359 English ft.
3. Wetterhörner 11,412 French ft. (Hasli Jungfrau) 12,149 English ft.
4. Jungfrau, 12,827 French ft., 13,761 English ft.
5. Mönch, 12,666 French ft. (Kleiner Eiger) 13,438 English ft.
6. Silberhorn, 11,360 French ft., 12,106 English ft.
7. Eiger, 12,240 French ft., 13,045 English ft.
8. Lauteraarhörner, 10,719.
9. Breithorn, 11,610.
10. Mittagshorn, 11,966.
11. Aletschhorn, 12,874 French ft., 13,803 English ft.
12. Tschingelhorn, 11,000.
13. Altels, 11,187.
14. Groshorn, 11,582.
15. Blumlis Alp or Frau, 11,298 French ft., 12,041 English ft.
16. Wildstrubelhörner, 10,000 French ft., 10,715 English ft.
17. Oldenhorn, 9,644.

The great Aletsch glacier running S. into the Valais is 5 leagues (15 miles) long and covers 116 million square metres.

As regards the ascents of the highest peaks and glacier passes of the Oberland, the following may be useful:—

1. The Finsteraarhorn (height 4,275 metres) is best ascended from the Æggischhorn (see Canton of Valais). You must sleep at the Faulberg or under the Rothhorn. The ascent takes 10 hours. The summit, 20 paces in width, can only be reached from the south-west. View wild and extremely grand. Guides 40 to 50 *fr.*

2. Schreckhorn.—A long day from the Grimsel (4,080 metres.) Consists of two peaks. Highest ascended first in 1861. Ascent takes 4½ hours; descent the same. View unique from its central position.

3. Jungfrau.—First climbed 1803. Best ascended from Æggischhorn. Sleep at Faulberg (4h. 30m.) It takes four hours then to Roththal Col, and two more to the top of Jungfrau (4,167 metres) 70 ft. long 50 wide. View superb. Can be ascended from Wengeren Alp by the Guggi Glacier, the Schreckhorn and the Silberlucke.

4. Silberhorn. — First ascended 1863, (3,690 metres) by the little Scheideck, the

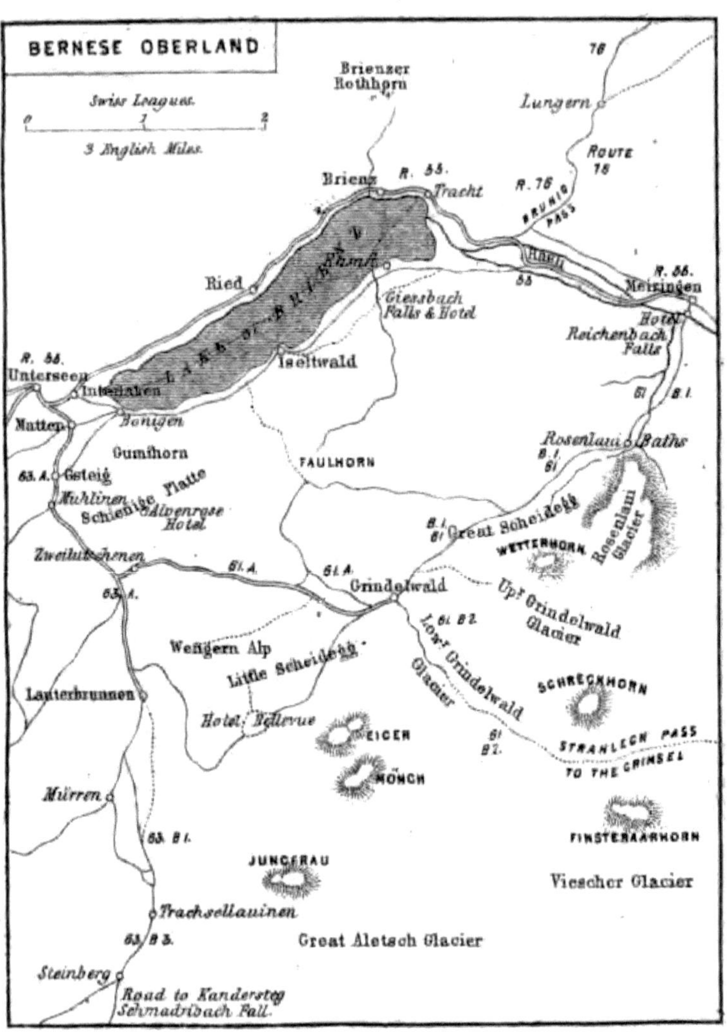

BERNESE OBERLAND
Swiss Leagues.
0   1   2
3 English Miles.
Brienzer Rothhorn
Lungern
76
ROUTE 76
R. 55.
Brienz
Tracht
R. 76
BRUNIG PASS
HAIL
55
R. 55.
Meiringen
Hotel Reichenbach Falls
Ried
Giessbach Falls & Hotel
Rhine
LAKE OF BRIENZ
Iseltwald
R. 55.
Unterseen
Interlaken
Bonigen
Matten
Gumihorn
Rosenlaui Baths
B. 1.
51
FAULHORN
B. 1.
Gsteig
Schienige Platte
Alpenrose Hotel
Muhlinen
B. 1.
51 Great Scheidegg
Rosenlaui Glacier
WETTERHORN
Zweilutschnen
51. A.
51. A.
Grindelwald
Up.r Grindelwald Glacier
51 B2.
53. A.
SCHRECKHORN
Wengern Alp
Lowr Grindelwald Glacier
Little Scheidegg
Hotel Bellevue
EIGER
51
B2.
STRAHLECK PASS
Lauterbrunnen
MÖNCH
TO THE GRIMSEL
Murren
FINSTERAARHORN
53. B1.
JUNGFRAU
Viescher Glacier
Trachsellauinen
53. B3.
Great Aletsch Glacier
Steinberg
Road to Kandersteg
Schmadribach Fall.

Eiger and Mönch Glaciers, and the North slope of the Jungfrau.

5. Aletschhorn. — (See Æggischhorn; Canton of Valais.)

6. Wetterhorn, chief summit (3,703 metres), climbed first 1843. It is usual to sleep at the Gleckstein. Can be also ascended from Rosenlaui (12h. ascent, 5½h. descent.) Summit very narrow, steep and slippery. View sublime.

7. The Mönch (4,096 metres) one of the most difficult mountains in the chain, ascended first 1863; from Faulberg in 9h. and descended in 6h. 45m. to Æggischhorn.

8. Eiger (3,973 ft.), a hard ascent first made in 1861.

9. Great Doldenhorn, near Kandersteg (3,647 metres), difficult and dangerous; first made in 1863. Ascent 9h., descent 5h. 20m. Admirable view.

10. Weisse Frau (3,661 metres), second peak of Blumlis Alp which has seven summits, equally dangerous, 15h. to 16h. required.

11. Altels, near the Gemmi (3,631 metres). Ice-axe, and ropes wanted. Ascent, 6h.; descent, 3h. View very grand.

12. Diablerets (10,113 feet), has been ascended from the Châlets of Creux de Champ. Admirable view. Descent to Gsteig 6h.

Other ascents will be noticed as we transport the reader to the different districts of the Oberland. The principal high glacier passes are the following:—

1. From Lauterbrunnen to the Æggischhorn, by the Lauwinenthor (3,600 metres), between the Jungfrau and the Gletscherhorn. Difficult and dangerous. Discovered by Professor Tyndall, 1860, 19 hours.

2. From the Wengeren Alp to the Æggischhorn, by the Jungfraujoch, between the Eiger and Mönch. Discovered 1862; 9 hours' difficult ascent from Wengeren (3,382 metres high). Descent by Aletsch glacier, easy; 6h. 30m.

3. From Wengeren Alp to Æggischhorn, by Eigerjoch. Discovered, 1859, by Alpine Club (3,747 metres). Have to sleep at Trugberg (cavern bivouac). Time, a day and night to Æggischhorn.

4. From Grindelwald to Æggischhorn, by Mönchjoch. Discovered, 1859, by Mr. Hudson, &c., 15 hours. You can pass the night at Zœsenberg Châlet, or at Eigerhöhle (a cavern). The pass is between the Mönch and the Vieschergrat. Ascent, 9 hours; descent 7½ to Æggischhorn Hotel. [A more difficult path leads over the Trugberg Glacier.]

5. Grindelwald to Æggischhorn, by Viescherjoch, discovered, 1862, by Mr. Stephens, is more difficult and less grand than No. 4.

6. Grindelwald to Grimsel, by Finsteraarjoch. Discovered 1862. Shorter but harder route than the Strahleck. The Joch is 4h. 30m. from the Kastenstein, a grotto where you sleep. Pass takes two days.

7. Grindelwald to Grimsel, by Lauteraarjoch, 15 to 17 hours (3,156 metres), between the Schreckhorn and the Berglistock. Sleep at blocks of rock called Gleckstein, 4h. 30m. from Grindelwald. Ascent thence to Joch, 6h. 30m. Descent from Joch to Grimsel. 6h. 30m.

8. Grimsel to Æggischhorn, by the Oberaarjoch, 12 to 13 hours. A hard day's work (3,238 metres). Ascent, 7 hours, by Oberaar Glacier. Descent by névé of Viescher Glacier, to base of Rothhorn, 2 hours. By a difficult pass called Auf der Trift, 2 hours, to Merjelen Alp Châlets, 2h. 30m.; or to Viesch, 2 hours more.

9. Meiringen to Engelberg, by the joch, 10h. 30m. Mule path. Hotel Pension at Engstlen Alp. Joch (2,208 metres). Ascent begins at Hof, 1 hour. Engstlen, 5h. 45m. Pastures. Schwingfest, July 26. To Col by Wunderbrunnen (intermittent spring), 1h. 20m. Descent to Trubsee, 45m. Two paths thence to Engelberg; longest a mule path in 2h. 30m.

10. Meiringen to Sarnen, by Melchthal, 9h. 30m. (see Unterwalden).

The best guides in the Oberland are the Laueners of Lauterbrunnen; at Grindelwald, Christian Almer, P. Bohren, and the two Michels; at Meiringen, Melchior Anderegg and Gaspar Platter.

Blumlis Alp.—See *Frau.*

BRIENZ.—HOTELS: Croix Blanche; L'Ours (both good, but the former somewhat fallen off).

Boats to the Gies-bach, 3*fr.*, stopping 1 hour; there and back, 4 to 5*fr.* To Iseltwald, 6*fr.*

Post Car, twice a day, over the Brunig to Lungern; good private carriages.

	Carriage with 1 horse.	2 horses.
To Meiringen (carriage returning empty)	7*fr.*	13*fr.*
There and back, stopping 3 hours	8	15
Interlaken and back, stopping 2 hours	8	18
Saddle horse to the Rothhorn for the day	15	0

Brienz consists of three villages, Dorf, Tracht, and Kienholz. Population, 2,300. Boatmen are noted for their songs (in glees). Black vipers occur in the debris behind Kienholz. For ascent of Rothhorn, see *Rothhorn.*

Brienz, distant from Berne 43½ miles, from Interlaken 9½, from Meiringen 9 miles, is situated at the head or north end of the lake of the same name, and at the foot of a mountain called the Brienzer-Grat. Its principal occupation is sculpture on wood (carvings). Noted establishment of the Brothers Wirth. The only object worth noting in the village is the Church, which is one of the most ancient in the Canton of Berne; but the female peasantry of this neighbourhood are celebrated for their Swiss songs and ranz des vaches. They may often be heard on the water as they row their boats, enlivening their work with the popular airs; and it is an additional charm to the traveller, provided they be genuine, if he engage them to conduct him to the falls of the Muhlbach and the Giessbach, which presents a magical spectacle, especially about noon. Brienz is on the road from Berne, over the Brunig, to Unterwalden. A steamboat plies on this lake (three times a-day) to Giessbach, 50c.; (fare in row boat, 3*fr.,*) summer and winter, and enables the traveller, at his ease, to enjoy the charming and varied scenery of both banks of the lake. The present population of Brienz, consisting of 1,800 souls, carry on a considerable trade in cheeses. Brienz (the lake of) is a narrow basin, from ¼ to ¾ of a league (1½ to 2¼ miles) in width, and from 3 to 3½ leagues (9 to 10½ miles) in length, open to the east and west, but shut into the north and south by two uniform ridges of mountains of middling height, and without a break. At its upper angle it receives the Aar, to the south-west the Lütschenen; between its two extremities several considerable streams, such as the Mühlibach, near Brienz, and the Giessbach, opposite that village, not to mention many others. Its greatest depth near the mouth of the Giessbach is, according to Saussure, 500 feet. Other earlier measurements give it 175, and even 350 fathoms, and according to some accounts it is in certain parts unfathomable. Its navigation is perfectly safe, though steep rocks render the landing difficult in certain places.*

The Lake of Brienz is not reckoned so fishy as that of Thun, but it has a good number; pike of some pounds weight are caught in it, also trout, gwiniad, a great many eels, char, and other kinds. The briensling is fished in autumn, and used to be so abundant that 14,000 were sometimes taken in a single net. Now it is rare to take 1,000 or 1,200 at a draught.

It appears that this lake and the Aar were formerly frequented by beavers, as well as the Reuss, the Limmat, &c. A few swans visited the lake in 1726-7, a very rare phenomenon.

It is usual to visit the Giessbach fall from Brienz or Interlaken by crossing the lake in a boat. For a description of the fall see *Giesslach.*

Biel or *Bienne.* Principal Inns: The Crown; Croix Blanche; Jura. It is an ancient town at the foot of the Jura, a

* According to some the Lake of Brienz is 1,751 feet above the sea, 500 feet deep by the Giessbach, and 2,100 feet in the deepest part. It is 30 feet above the Lake of Thun.—*Murray's Handbook*, p. 94 (1843); *Dr. H. A. Daniel's Deutschland.*

mile from the lake, and surrounded with old walls and towers. Its population is now 6,000 inhabitants, mostly Protestants, and of industrious habits, but speaking vile German. (Interesting pile works on lake.)

The lake is 3 l. (9 m.) long, and 1 l. (3 m.) broad, almost at the foot of the Chasseral, the highest point of the Jura. The lake is well stocked with fish, and contains the island of St. Pierre, once inhabited by J. J. Rousseau.

Chasseral (The), a high summit of the Jura, above Bienne, 4,986 ft. above the sea, 3,616 ft. above the lake, can be easily ascended from Bienne, and affords a glorious distant view of the Alps, embracing even the chain of Mont Blanc. A carriage-way leads within one hour of the top. The distance from Bienne to the summit is four hours.

Burgdorf.—See *Plateau of Berne.*

Dauben See.—A wild mountain lake on the summit of the Gemmi pass, ¼ of a German league in length (¾ of a mile), its black waters contrasting finely with the glittering sun slopes surrounding it.

Diablerets, or *Teufelshorner,* the dividing ridge of the Cantons of Berne and Valais, about the Wildstrubel (10,113 feet).—See *Wildstrubel.*

Œschinen, a beautiful small mountain lake near Kandersteg.—See *Kandersteg.*

Eiger.—See *Bernese Alps.*

Eselsrucken.—See *Scheideck.*

Emmenthal.—A fine productive valley in the N. E. part of the Canton, contains Langnau, 7 leagues (21 miles) from Berne. The district is noted for cheese.

The *Faulhorn,** a mountain situated be-

*The Faulhorn can be reached by 8 different paths; but only 3 of these are much frequented. Berlepsch says the easiest way is from the Scheidegg, but the prettiest from the Giessbach. Joanne is of opinion that the latter is the best way up.

1. Distance from the great Scheidegg to the top 3½ to 4 hours, by sloping pastures.

2. From Grindelwald way steep at first, distance 5 leagues (15 miles).

3. From Giessbach, 5 leagues. Road not to be taken without a guide. There is a dangerous path up from Sengg on the lake of Brienz, another safer from the Schienige Platte.

The inn is of stone, and is not so well conducted latterly. A poor chamber, 3 fr.; very scanty supper, 3½ fr.; coffee, 2 fr.; attendance, 1 fr.

The near view of the Bernese Alps is grand in the extreme from this point, from which the Finsteraarhorn and the Schreckhörner in particular are seen to advantage.

tween Grindelwald and the lake of Brienz, may be visited from both, and commands a very fine view of the Oberland main chain. It has a small inn on the top, and the ascent from Grindelwald (5 hours) is easy and safe, but that from the Giessbach side (14 miles) is described as even dangerous. The road from Grindelwald passes by the Bach Alp and a small lake 1,000 ft. above the summit. The inn is only tenanted for four months in the summer. A circuitous road leads in two hours to the Great Sheideck. The height of the Faulhorn is 8,674 ft. above the sea.

Falchernbach.—A fall of 200 feet, near Meiringen.—See *Hasli.*

Finsteraarhorn (The).—See *Bernese Alps.*

Frau, or *Blumlis Alp.*—A mountain near Kandersteg, 11,298 feet high.

Frutigen, a large village in the Kander valley, 4¾ l. (14¼ m.) from Thun, was noted for its excellent hotel, which led many travellers to prefer it to Kandersteg when the inn used formerly to be objectionable. Frutigen was burnt down and rebuilt a few years ago (1826–7). The Adler and Helvetia are both good hotels.

Furcka.—See *Grimsel.*

Gemmi.—This is the most frequented pass in the western Bernese Alps. Its elevation is 7,086 feet. The distance from Kandersteg to Leuk in the Valais is 5 L (15 m.) Near the top of the pass is the small Dauben Lake; the descent on the Valais side consists of a zig-zag path cut down the face of a tremendous precipice, and commanding a magnificent view of the Pennine Alps. It is not safe to ride down this descent, as fatal accidents have occurred from this imprudence. The Altels, 11,187 feet high, rises a little to the left of the pass. A small inn at Schwarenbach, half way up, has been made the scene of an imaginary murder.

Giessbach.—This waterfall, though not the grandest, is one of the most beautiful in Switzerland. The sound of its rushing waters is distinctly heard at Brienz which a rapid row of 25 minutes brings you to the spot where the torrent leaps into the lake over a rock 20 feet in height. Landing, and climbing up a steep path, a few minutes bring you within view of the principal cascades, which descend in the form of steps over several ridges of rock. These cascades are 7 in number, and being enclosed in a verdant frame of fir trees, and generally supplied with a good volume of water, they are thought quite to equal if not surpass in beauty, the noted Reichenbach Fall, near Meiringen.

The second fall from below is considered the finest. Trees of various kinds adorn the banks of these lovely cascades, and you may even see the cherry growing freely in the neighbouring pastures. Grey rocks pierce through the dark mass of verdure that overhangs the streams, and in its interstices admits a magical play of light on the animated waters. Bridges and seats have added to the convenience and comfort of the traveller, who can devote a day in lounging about this romantic spot. Over the upper fall the water leaps in an arch-like mass, leaving a free passage underneath and behind, where you can enjoy the luxury of a shower bath in the most charming of dressing rooms.

The same torrent, the Giessbach, which descends from the Faulhorn, makes another waterfall higher up, and well worth a visit, at the distance of 2½ l. (7½ m.) from the lake. It is in a charming valley called Im Bottchen, by the pastures of Axalp. The stream falls over two rocks of 80 and 400 feet into a deep hollow, which it fills with spray and foam.

Two excellent Hotels, rather dear, with Café, Restaurant, and with abundant accommodation have been erected near the Giessbach, from which the Faulhorn may be reached in 5 hours. The falls are lighted up at night with Bengal lights. One *fr.* per head. Pension, 6 to 10*fr.* per day.

Grimsel.—The Hospice of the Grimsel situated not far from the top of the pass of that name, is in a convenient situation for visiting some of the higest peaks and noblest glaciers of the Oberland.

The Hotel is now well conducted and comfortable. It was also in high repute in the time of Vater Zybach, who, unfortunately, came to grief in consequence of setting fire to the old hospice, which was largely insured.

The following objects may be conveniently approached from this centre:—

1. *The Ober Aar Glacier* which descends steeply into the valley; the extremity has only a slope of 15°, but near the Kastenhorn 40°. The Glacier has four regions. 1, the Glacier Region; 2, the Krusten Region; 3, the Firn Region; 4, the Snow Region.

2. * *The Unter Aar Glacier.*—The Ober and Unter Aar streams are divided by the Zinkenstock. The Unter Aar Glacier is also called Vorder Aar or Lauter Aar Glacier. It is reached by the Aarenboden, the Spitalbuhl, Bärenbuhl, and Trübtenbach.

3. † *The Rhone Glacier.* — Ascending from the Hospice you reach to Ober Gestelen in the Canton of Valais, and thence turning to the left you arrive in a ¼ of a league (¾ of a mile) at the Meyenwand, thence to the Rhone Glacier in 1½ league (4½ miles.)

From the Rhone Glacier you can pass over the Furcka to Realp in the Canton of Uri. (See Routes Nos. 55 c. 7).

4. *The Strahleck.* — This pass takes a journey of 14h. from Grindewald to the Grimsel. Tyndall says, "that he had never seen anything finer than the view from the summit. I had no idea that the Strahleck was so fine a pass." You pass up by the Mattenberg and down between the Aar Glacier.

5. *The Æggischorn in the Valais,* by the Ober Aar Joch, a difficult pass. (See among the Routes 55 c. 6.)

Ascents may be made to the Little and Great—

1. *Sidelhorn,* easy of access, without much snow, with a grand view. Ascent 3 hours, (2,766 metres.)

* Kohl's Alpen-Reisen.
† Kohl Ubi Supra.

2. *The Schreckhorn.* — The summit is very difficult to reach from the south-east. The Lauteraarhorn can be reached more easily.

The top of the Schreckorn is so very sharp that you can only reach it by crawling on hands and feet. The whole ridge to the Abschwung is called the Lauteraarhorner. The Great Lauteraarhorn is 10,719 ft. high.

The Finsteraarhorn. — The best approach to the summit which consists of Hornblende, is from the Walcher Grat near the Strahleck pass. The summit consists of a wave-shaped ridge, free of ice, about 20 steps long. It is surrounded by 17 horns above 10,000ft., to which scientific names have been lately given.

Grindelwald. — The carriage road from Interlaken to Grindelwald passes through Zweilutschenen, where the two branches of this tributary of the Aar unite; following the Schwarz Lutschenen brings the traveller to his destination through Burglauienen. From Grindelwald to Interlaken, 9 miles. Principal Hotels: Hotel et Pension du Glacier, the Golden Eagle, the Bear, and the Boar. The church stands on an eminence whose base is washed by the Lutschenen, which is fed by the Aar glaciers. Most of the cottages are scattered over the valley, which contains a population of above 2,000 souls, and extends from N.E. to S.W., 4 leagues or 12 miles, with a width of hardly 1½ miles or half a league. Measured from the eminence by the church, its elevation above the Mediterranean is 3,150 French feet. Its situation is particularly favourable as a centre for surveying the principal glaciers and mountains of the Oberland chain, including the Wetterhorn, the Eiger, the Schreckhorn, the Mönch, the Jungfrau, and the Finsteraarhorn, also the two glaciers of Grindelwald (upper and lower). The upper or great glacier is situated between the Wetterhorn and the Mettenberg; the lower glacier is between the latter and the Eiger, and they are both separated by the rocks of the Schreckhorn. They can be approached and explored with equal facility, and are only 3 miles from the hotels.

This is the home of celebrated guides, such as: 1. Peter Bohren, 44 years old, called the Glacier Wolf, the hero of a hundred ascents. 2. Christian Almer, 34 years, firm, brave, and sensible. Christian Michel, 50 years, very well for the glaciers. Peter Michel, his brother, 38 years, a brave man. John Baumann and Ulrich Kaufmann. These are the most in request. They speak French and English. Other good guides, Ulrich Wengen. Christian Bohren, Peter Schlegel, Peter Rubi, Christian Jostl, Christian Hertsch, Christian Bleuler, Rodolph Boss, Peter Baumann, and others. From Grindelwald to the Faulhorn, 5 L. (15 m.), 1 horse for one day 15 *fr.* To Lauterbrunnen by the Wengeren Alp, 6 l., (18 m.) Down the Lutschenen Thal to Interlaken, 3¼ L. (14½ m.) To Meiringen by the Scheidegg, 7 L. (21 m.)

Great changes have taken place in these glaciers within the last 700 or 800 years. In the 11th century rich pastures are supposed to have extended all the way over to the Valais, affording ample nourishment to cattle, and easy access to man in spots now covered with vast and almost impassable fields of ice. This valley of Grindelwald presents on all hands admirable points of view, and delightful excursions which it would be too long to enumerate.

We shall confine our notice to the most usual and eligible excursions from this centre. The first is over the Wengeren Alp to Lauterbrunnen; the second over the Sheideck to the Haslithal, by the Reichenbach Falls and Rosenlaui Glacier to the Handeck Aar Falls and the Grimsel; the third up the Faulhorn, a mountain above the village, commanding an admirable view of the Oberland range.

The road over the Wengeren Alp is easy of access, and brings the traveller in close propinquity to the majestic chain of the Eiger, Mönch, and Jungfrau, from which an almost constant succession of avalanches descend in summer. On the top of the Wengeren Alp an hotel has been erected for the convenience of tourists. From the top of the ridge the eye plunges into both valleys (Grindelwald and Lauterbrunnen) and takes in a succession views unrivalled in grandeur. The road passes at the foot of Mount Eiger, through Lauterbrunnen, Scheideck, and Itramen Alp, to Lauterbrunnen. The distance is 7 or 8 leagues, 21 to 24 miles. The height of the Wengeren Alp is 4,910 feet above the lake of Lucerne, 6,284 feet above the Mediterranean.

[Ascending from Grindelwald you pass Moosgarlen, Wergisthal, and Alpiglen (a châlet with coffee, cream, and strawberries). Proceed by a few *pinus cembras* to the little Scheidegg, hotel Bellevue (6,284 ft.) Rooms, 2 *fr.*; Dinner, 3 *fr.*; Breakfast, 1½ *fr.*; Service, 75 *c.*; Candles 50 *c.* Avalanches from Eiger are well seen here. Lauberhorn and Tschuggen are directly opposite. The Eiger was scaled n 1858, by a Mr. Harrington, a Scotchman, but his guide could not reach the top with him. M. Porges, of Vienna, July 27th, 1861, had to cut, with his guide, 1,420 steps in the ice; overtaken by the darkness, had to stay on the ice all night, with 4° to 5° Reaumur of cold. Hotel Bellevue, 4½ leagues (13½ miles). Le Moine, or Der Mönch, was climbed, it is said for the first time, June 12th, 1855, by a Wallach princess, Kozloff Massalsky, ca led Dora D'Istria, a fact not admitted by certain Alpine clubbists, to whose pride it is rather hurting. On to Wengeren Alps, hotel Jungfrau, is always full (5,800 feet high), same prices as at Little Scheidegg. First Sunday in August, a Schwingfest. For a close view, especially of the Jungfrau, this is the finest point, only separated from it by Trumletenthal; avalanches frequently seen hence. Mornings and evenings here are superb, and the Morgenglühen or rose tint on the ice is seen here to perfection. Avalanches best seen at noon. Jungfrau first ascended in 1812, since frequently, especially from the Ægulschhorn in the Valais (see Canton of Valais). N. W. point of the Jungfrau, is the Stellifluh, highest point, the Black Monk (Schwarz Mönch). The western vertical wall is called Rothe Brett (red plank). Two lower terraces. Silberhorn ascended, 1863 (11,359 ft.), and Schnechorn are most beautiful in shape. 3 leagues (9 miles) down to Lauterbrunnen, by Gurmischbühl and Wiggibort, with a fine lake view. Then follow Schiltwald (fine echo). Wengeren (4,611 ft.), with a fine view of Lauterbrunnen valley, Schilthorn, Sulegg. Pletschbach, and Murren. Thence over the Lutschenen to Lauterbrunnen,]

For an account of the road over the Scheideck to the valley of Hasli, see under Scheideck, p. 35.

The ascent of the Faulhorn is strongly recommended to all who have a moderate share of health, and wish thoroughly to enjoy the mountains, For a description of the Faulhorn and the view from its summit. see Faulhorn.

Gsteig.—See *Wildstrubel.*

Handeck (The Falls of the).—The finest waterfall in Switzerland, formed by the Aar, here joined by the Ærlenbach, distant 5¼ L. (15¾ m.) from Meiringen, and 2 L. (6 m.) from the hospice of the Grimsel.

It has now a moderate inn with 15 beds, at 1½ *fr.*, and otherwise immoderate prices.

About 200 feet beyond the Châlet of the Handeck a path leads to the left through a wood of fir-trees to the brink of a deep gorge watered by the Aar, and the eye rests at length on the noted cataract, which can also be reached in less time and by an easier route from the châlet on the immediate bank of the stream, giving the traveller the opportunity of seeing the falls from above and below. The morning about 9 or 10, and at latest 11, is the most favourable time for viewing the falls. Standing on a rocky eminence you see to the right the Aar rushing over the precipice in large waves covered with foam, while to the left the Aerlenbach eddies along in joyous haste to throw its waters in mid-air into a common embrace with the majestic flood of the main stream. When lighted up by the sun a rainbow plays in magic colours across the hell of waters. It is fruitless to attempt a description of the rush, the roar, the darkness of the abyss, down which the maddened waters rush to the depth of 200 feet. Suffice it to say that the scenery of these falls is the perfection of the sublime. The pitchy horrors of the basin into which the foaming waters are precipitated have never been penetrated by man, though a bold painter, named Wolf, once attempted to descend into it by means of ropes, and he actually reached a giddy point from which he was able to take a beautiful sketch—but now very rare—in which he introduced himself in the shape of a wolf.

Harder (The).—Precipitous grassy slopes north-west of Interlaken, rising above the north side of the Bödeli, and commanding delightful views. The ascent, and especially descent, of the dry, slippery grass requires caution, as fatal accidents have happened there from neglect of caution.

Hasli (*Valley of*) runs from S. E. to N. W., is 10 l. (30 m.) in length, and is divided into the upper and lower Hasli-thal. The former (upper) extends for 7 l. (21 m.) from the Grimsel to Meiringen; and the second (lower) is 3 l. (9 m.) in length from Meiringen to the Lake of Brienz. It is watered throughout its length by the Aar, and is inhabited by a people distinguished by some advantageous peculiarities over the other Alpine populations, both in point of idiom as well as fine physical development, besides certain other points. If we must trust certain traditions and old popular songs, besides a register preserved on the spot, the people of Hasli are of Scandinavian origin. Flying to escape a famine that raged in Sweden in the 5th century, their ancestors, led by a man named Hatis, a native of Hasle (a town in Sweden), after having long wandered over various countries reached at length this district of the Oberland and settled there.

From an eminence situated behind the church of Meiringen, you command almost the entire valley, offering magnificent and varied views. Close at hand descend the 7 cascades of the Reichenbach, of which the upper fall is only ¾ of a mile from the village. The stream that supplies the upper waterfall falls over a vertical rock 300 feet in height, and has a width of 30. The sound occasioned by the fall resembles thunder, and the spectacle presented by it, especially at sunrise, is sublime in its beauty, particularly in summer and towards the solstice. The best point to see the Reichenbach to advantage is from the Aar bridge, on the side of Meiringen. Viewed from this spot the falls are often seen spanned by a glorious rainbow of the most brilliant colours. The lower fall is not so high but very beautiful; this fall is seen in its perfection in the evening. Two other cascades in this part of the valley deserve some notice, 1st, the Falcherubach, which makes a fall of 200 feet a little below Meiringen; 2nd, the Alpbach, which is seen on the ridge of mountains bounding the valley to the east. There are others but they are of minor importance.

Above Meiringen the valley closes in, and is ultimately almost blocked up by the Kirchet. This mountain must be climbed to reach Hasli im Grund, where the road forks, giving off one branch that leads to the hamlet of Wyler, while the direct road continues to the Grimsel. After passing this spot a road striking off to the left leads to the Gentelthal, and by the Joch or Col to Engelberg. Another road turning to the right leads to the Nesselthal and to the Gadmenthal, and over Mount Susten to Wasen, in the Canton of Uri. Not far from this first fork on the Grimsel road a second is encountered on the right, consisting of a branch road that leads to the valley of Urbach, which is commanded by the Great Urbach, also called the Gauli Glacier. All these roads present striking and delightful scenery. Equally grand is the road up to the Grimsel, of which the following is a brief outline:—

From Meiringen to Guttannen are 3 l. (9 m.); thence 1½ l. (4½ m.) take you to the Châlet of Handeck. On reaching this point the ear is greeted with the sound of the great Aar waterfall, which rushes over a precipice of 200 feet into a rocky abyss. This magnificent scene must be viewed under several aspects to obtain a just idea of it (see Handeck). From the Handeck there is a continual rise of 2 l. (6 m.) to the hospice of the Grimsel.* In order to reach it several bridges have to be passed, and while crossing the last one, another fine fall of the Aar meets the eye. The whole of this district presents the picture

* The Grimsel Hospice is still an old dreary stone building, with small rooms, first-class company and prices, though rebuilt of late years. Little room and bed, 2 fr. Dinner (or rather supper) without wine, 3 fr. Breakfast, with bad coffee, 1½ fr. Service according to Berleysch indifferent. Height above the sea, 5,730 feet.

of complete desolation, but notwithstanding the presence of a quantity of snow on the top of the pass even in the heat of summer, many hundred beasts of burden cross over it every week. The elevation of the pass half a league (1½ m.) above the hospice is 6,570 feet above the Mediterranean. From the Galenstock and Furcka, points not very remote from the Grimsel, the view embraces the whole southern chain of the Valais to Mont Blanc.

Several excursions can be made from the Hospice of the Grimsel, for instance, to the Siedelhorn and the Lauteraarhorn; the road leading to the latter takes you, after a climb of 3 hours, to the Abschwung, a point whence the Finsteraarhorn and the Schreckhorn can be seen close at hand, and in all their majesty. The vicinity of the Zinkenstock is noted for its crystals. From the Grimsel it is easy to visit the Rhone Glacier, and to descend by the Rhone to Viesch, whence the traveller can diverge to the Æggischhorn, or go on to Visp and visit Zermatt and Saas. Other travellers may be disposed to diverge from the Grimsel in the direction of the Lake of Lucerne, which it is quite easy to reach at Alpnach on a fine summer's day, starting at early dawn and making the passage over the Brunig, which is quite easy and presents charming scenery.

Guttannen (Inn—Bear), a village in the valley of Hasli, the last inhabited spot towards the Grimsel Pass. It stands on both banks of the Aar, which are united by a bridge of 24 feet in length. After having suffered two destructive fires (in 1803 and 1812) it has been rebuilt on a better plan, and contains a good parsonage and inn. Guttannen is 1,040 feet above the valley Im Grund; its population in 1817 was 50 families or households, much reduced by fire and pillage during the French war. So narrow is the valley in this part that in winter the length of the day during which the village enjoys sunlight is little more than 1 or 1½ hours.

Hofwyl, the celebrated educational institution of Fellenberg, is distant —m. from Berne, and deserves a visit.

Interlaken (Interlacus) is situated as implied by its name between the lakes of Thun and Brienz, at the distance of about 3 miles from the former and close to the latter. Its central position and vicinity to the most interesting scenery of the Oberland have long contributed in rendering it a favourite resort of tourists, which has led to the usual result of increasing the comforts and raising the prices.

The principal hotels are noticed below.

Interlaken offers also an abundance of lodgings and pensions.

Interlaken originated in the convent founded in the middle ages on the fertile isthmus formed by the deposits of the Lütschenen, and filling up a space of 3 miles between the lakes, which were once united. The soil of this little plain, called Bödeli, is celebrated for its fertility, and the view of the Jungfrau seen up the opening of the Lütschenen valley is perhaps unique in the Alps for artistic effect and grouping. The principal point, however, that makes Interlaken so favourite and desirable a residence is the central nature of its position for making excursions through the finest parts of Switzerland; as will appear by the following survey of routes from this centre.

1. From Interlaken, by following the Aar up the stream you reach the Grimsel, the Canton of Valais, and the Italian lakes.

2. By following the Aar down the stream you reach the foot of the Jura, France, and Bâle in an easy day, or even part of a day.

3. By Brienz you reach the Brunig, the oldest Swiss Canton, Unterwalden, the Lake of Lucerne, and if you wish to extend your excursions, the Lakes of Zurich and Constance, the high lands of Appenzell and the Grisons.

4. Returning to Thun you reach the Gemmi Pass by the Kanderthal, and cut thus into the Valais, the Rhonethal, and hence to the charming banks of Lake Leman and to Savoy and Chamouny.

Interlaken is almost equidistant from the west end of Switzerland at Geneva, and from the N.E. end where the Rhine falls into the Lake of Constance, and about the same distance separates it from Bâle to the N.W. and Lugano to the S.E.

A pleasant tour may be made from Interlaken by going to Brienz, up the Hasli, back to Grindelwald, and Lauterbrunnen; then up the Kander or over the Gemmi or by the Siebenthal.

The following are pretty villages near Interlaken, Aarmühle, Matten, Wilderwyl, Mühlinen, Gsteig, Bönigen, Ringgenberg, and Golzwyl. Pleasant walks may be made to Goldey, Vogtsruh, the rock of Wageren, the forests of Matten Ey, the ruins of the Castle of Weissenau, Unspunnen, and Ringgenberg.

Other longer walks may be made to Matten and Bönigen; at the former are springs that used to supply the convent. Passing to the latter you advance through large plantations of flax and hemp. The Stockberg has a cavern which the mythology of the country once peopled with dwarfs. From Bönigen is a fine view of the lake of Brienz, and the Suleck and Iselten Grat. Bönigen is a pretty village, with a fine healthy population.—(Kohl's *Alpen Reisen.*—Wyss' voyage dans l'Oberland Bernois.)

The finest view near Interlaken is from the Gumihorn, above Breitlauenen to the left on the Lauterbrunnen Road. This and a neighbouring point, Schienige Platte, are said to have finer views than the Faulhorn. Alpen Rose Hotel, at the Schienige Platte, is good. (Prices: Rooms, 2*fr.*; Breakfast, 1½*fr.*; Dinner, 3*fr.*; attendance, 75c.) Distance from Interlaken, 3½ hours (can be ridden).

HOTELS.—Grand Victoria, opposite the Jungfrau; beautiful new house, opened 1st April, 1870; Edward Ruchti, proprietor. Hotel and Pension des Alpes, very good, and deservedly recommended. Jungfrau, situated on the finest promenade; recommended to English travellers; comfortable and clean. Oberland, well conducted; café and restaurant also very well conducted. Belle Vue, Herman Rimps, proprietor; excellent second-class hotel; well situated. Kurhaus and Hotel Jungfraublick, exceptionally situated near the finest promenades and the Park; extensive view over the splendid Valley of Interlaken. Belvedere, J. Staehli-Muller, proprietor; well situated; reading and conversation rooms; moderate charges.

Tariff for Carriages:

	One horse. Francs.	Two horses. Francs.
To Lauterbrunnen, stay two hours.	8	15
If you stay longer	10	20
Neuhaus—each person	1	2
Each box.......... 25 *cents.*		
Grindelwald, same day back	12	22
Two days	20	40
If a whole day be employed	17	30
To Lauterbrunnen and Grindelwald, for the day	16	28
Two days	20	40
Lauterbrunnen and Grindelwald (taking the horses over the Wengeren Alp) one day	20	40
Two days	25	50
Lauterbrunnen (taking horses to Murren, round to Grindelwald and back) to Interlaken, in two days	25	50
Faulhorn and back, two days	30	60
Schienige Platte, one day	13	20
Brienz and back, stay two hours	8	15
Meiringen and back, one day	16	28
Two days	20	40
Sending back carriage empty	17	30
Kandersteg	25	45
Thun	15	25
Lungeren direct	20	35
Do. by Meiringen	23	43
Wimmis	10	20

Rates by distance and hour.—

	One horse. Francs.	Two horses. Francs.
1 league, with one horse	3	6
2 " "	4½	9
3 " "	5½	11
4 " "	6	12

Saddle Horses—Per day, 11 francs; 10 francs for every extra horse. Donkeys—One hour 1½ francs; every extra hour, 1 franc. In no case more than 6 francs per day.

Before penetrating into the higher parts of the Oberland the traveller will do well to visit some of the delightful scenery close to the lakes. Among these may be specified the Aar island, the Hohbuhl, the ruins of the castle of Unspunnen, the presbytery of Ringgenberg, &c. These are in the immediate vicinity of Interlaken. Longer excursions can be made to the Hohgaut, distant about 4 leagues or 12 miles, and which can be reached by an excellent road. The view from the summit is magnificent. Another expedition can be made to the Rothenfluh, 3 miles beyond where you arrive at two beautiful cascades, the Bellenbach and the Sansbach; situated near the hamlet of Eisenfluh, 2½ l. (7½ m.) from Interlaken. Another point worth visiting is the Suleck, 9 miles (3 leagues), &c., &c.

Among the excursions on the neighbouring lakes, should be specially noticed the Giessbach by the Lake of Brienz (see under that head), and the Beatenberg or mountain of St. Beatus, reported to have been established by this disciple of St. Peter who converted the Swiss, and died there in 112. The view from the cavern (Beatenhöhle) is superb.

Iselbogen, a hamlet in the Hasli valley.—See *Hasli.*

Itramen, a hamlet near Grindelwald.—See *Grindelwald.*

Im Grund (Hasli), a village situated in the Hasli valley above a rocky barrier, the Kirchet crossing it near the Grimsel, through which the Aar has worked its way in a deep chasm.

Jungfrau (The).—See *Bernese Alps.*

Kander (The), a tributary of the Aar, now conducted into the lake of Thun. It rises near the Gemmi and waters the romantic Kanderthal.

Kalchenberge, a cavern of chamois hunters N. of the Abschwung.

Kandersteg, a charmingly situated mountain village at the foot of the Gemmi, 5 l. (7 hours) from Lenk, 7 L. (21 m.) from Thun, and near glorious scenery surrounding the Blumlis Alp, besides the fine wild district of the Wildstrubel and about the head of the Saane. Its principal hotels are the Ours and the Victoria, which are superior to the old inn once in great disrepute. Kandersteg, which is enlarged since the writer's first visit in 1831, is 3,280 feet above the sea, contains 700 inhabitants, and is 7 l. (21 m.) from Thun. From this centre, delightful excursions can be made to the following points:—1. To the valley of Œschinen, with a charming blue lake at the foot of the Blumlis Alp, and surrounded by glaciers, precipices, and waterfalls. Distance, 3 m. English. 2. To the Gasterenthal, 7 hours from Kandersteg. The head of the valley is closed by the magnificent Kander Glacier. By pursuing this route you reach the head of the Lauterbrunnen valley by the Tschingel Glacier, at the back of the Frau or Blumlis Alp. The journey is not dangerous though fatiguing, and the distance a good day's march. 3. From Kandersteg you also diverge to the Rawyl Pass leading to Sion in the Valais.

Langnau.—See *Plateau of Berne*.

Lauterbrunnen (Hotel: The Steinbock; Pension of the Staubbach), considered as a separate district, is bounded to the S. by the Sheideck of the Wengeren Alp and its prolongation, including the Laubhorn, the Thunertschruggen, and the Männlichen. This ridge is also sometimes called the Wergisthalgrat and Itramen. The outer Eiger separates the valleys of Lauterbrunnen and Grindelwald. The inner Eiger, with the Mönch and Jungfrau, are their continuation; the Grosshorn, the Breithorn, and the Tschingelhorn separate Lauterbrunnen from the upper Valais. To the W. it is shut in by the Tschingel Glacier, the Rothe Zähne (red teeth), the pass of the Furgge and the Hundfluh (dog's rock), and Schilthorn, on to the Sausgrat. To the N. it is bounded by the Eisenfluh, Vogelfluh, and Eiseck mountains. The length of the main valley from Zweylutschinen to Trachsellauenen, at the foot of the Hauri, is 3½ l. (10½ m.), 1 from Zweylutschenen to the church, 1½ to Stechelberg, and 1 to the old abandoned iron mines of Trachsellauenen. The valley is nowhere more than ¾ of a mile in width, often much less. Its direction is from S. W. to N. E., its area 16 Swiss square leagues (144 square miles), and it was made into a separate parish in 1487. Previously it was attached to the parish of Gsteig under the name of *St. Andreas ad fontes limpidos (Teutonice lauter brunnen).* The climate in winter is very cold, with frequent north winds, but in summer the heat is almost insupportable. The morning sun only illumines the valley at 7 a.m. in summer and at 12 in winter. The only fruit produced consists of apples and pears. There are no oaks, very few walnut trees, not many beech trees, and only a few bushes of holly; but maple, lime trees, and ash are numerous and have a fine growth. Copses of alder and willow grow on the banks of the Lütschenen. The valley contains 30 or 40 forests of fir trees; and a few scattered pines (pin alvier) grow on the Steinberg. The valley does not produce much corn, and the principal yield of vegetables consists of turnips, carrots, potatoes, and cabbage. A good deal of flax and hemp is raised. As but few of the glaciers run down into the valley the slopes of the hills are on all sides covered with beautiful pastures, decorated with many and various flowers, and enriched with medicinal plants.

High above the valley of Lauterbrunnen and immediately under the Jungfrau is the wild, almost inaccessible valley of Rotothal, long viewed with dismay by the inhabitants as the abode of evil spirits, and of the wild huntsman and his shadowy pack. This sequestered ravine was visited twice, and carefully examined by the naturalist, Hugi, who has thus added much valuable matter to our imperfect knowledge of the botany and geology of the Jung frau. His attempt to scale the Sattel was a failure, and even Tyndall pronounced it impossible to reach the Valais from this side.

Hugi pronounces the structure of the Jungfrau to be the same as that of the whole mass of the Alps under similar circumstances. The Strata (beginning below) offer the following gradations:—

1. The deeply seated basis of granite and gneiss.

2. Immediately above it, the calcareous stratum rising to the grauwacke.

3. The intermediate grauwacke formation.

4. Above it the cretaceous and liassic beds.

5 Finally, the topmost stratum of granite, in which the limestone reappears on the Jungfrau.

The principal plants gathered in this wild and elevated district, are:—1. Of the cryptogamic class. 2. Sphaeria confluens and lecanora miniata Hoffm. Of algæ there was not a vestige, and the only moss was the oxytropis, occurring on the rocks at 10,000 feet. Artemisia spicata is frequent: it is used as well as a mutellina, by chamois hunters as an infusion in cholica. Gnaphalium leontopodium was rarer. The beautiful red flowers of the arctia pennina Gaud, and of the bright white A. Helvetica Gaud, presented a charming appearance. Saxifraga coespitosa, and muscoides occurred, also primula pedemontana. A remarkable variety of achillea moschata was found. Other plants were, the saxifraga oppositifolia and rosacea Gaud, geum reptans, myosotis, alpestris, ranuncu'us glacialis, androsace villosa L, asteralpinus, agrostia rupestris, cardamine resedifolia, erigeron hirsutum festuca violacea, sesleria sphaerocephala var and coerulescens Gaud, &c., &c.

There is little doubt, formerly, that the verdure extended much higher. Tradition ascribes the earliest population to a colony from the Lötschthal, in the Canton de Valais, and a chapel is said formerly to have existed on the Wengeren Alp, whence a road between the Eiger and Mönch is supposed to have led into the Valais. At that period the Blumlis Alp and even the Jungfrau are reported to have been covered with grass.

At the beginning of 1811 the valley contained 116 households and 499 souls. Wengeren had 99 families and 449 persons, the whole district reckoned 1,238 persons and has now increased to 1,800. In 1817 the number of cows in the valley in winter was 800; in 1783 the total of cattle was, in summer, 608 cows, 27 horses, 1,000 sheep, 400 goats, and a multitude of pigs. The best Alps or pastures in the valley are 11 in number, viz.:—The Pletschen, Winteregg, Schilt, Sevinen, Busen, Steinberg, Wengeren, Spütinen, Breitlauinen, Hohen-

alp, and Stufenstein. Their animal produce was, from 1780 to 90, about 50,000 fr., or £2,500, most of it belonging to other parishes, such as Unterseen. The church and parsonage of Lauterbrunnen have not much pretension. The windows of the former are of good stained glass, and the date of 1492 has been traced on an inscription.

Lauterbrunnen has more cascades than any other valley in Switzerland, or perhaps the world. The principal falls are 20 in number, and of these the Staubbach deserves the first place, to which we shall devote a special notice at a future page. With regard to the others we have to remark that the Weiss or White Lütschenen, which is peopled by excellent trout, and pours a large body of water through the centre of the valley, sometimes rushing angrily over rocky rapids, at others gliding smoothly over a sandy bed, shaded by willows and alder bushes, is formed by the junction of two streams, the Sevilütschenen and the Steinbergslütschinen, both of which make superb cascades. The former, near Rufigraben, and the houses of Stechelberg is particularly remarkable. Issuing from a dark ravine the stream makes two consecutive leaps, often spanned by a glorious rainbow. Among the other falls may be noticed the Mürrenbach, Schiltwaldbach, and Trümmelbach, besides a pretty fall called the Mättelibach. A pleasant walk of little more than 1 l. (3 m. English) from the village leads to the Trümmelbach, which receives the waters of three glaciers of the Jungfrau. Another charming afternoon excursion leads, after a walk of 2 l. (6 m.), to Steinhalde, near Hunnenfluh, near which is the fall of Mättelibach. The path passes over lovely flowery meadows, and offers most graceful points of view, taking in the following cascades: the Greifenbach, Fluhbach, Lauibach, Herrenbächlein, Küpferbächlein, Staubbach, Buchibach, and Spissbach, which stand out clear like silver bands over the vast rocky curtain to the right.

The most interesting points to visit from

Lauterbrunnen are three in number (without reckoning the Staubbach, which is close at hand). 1. The Winteregg, with its view of the Jungfrau, which has been compared to th t of Mont Blanc from the Breven. 2. The upper Staubbach Fall, near the source of the stream in the Alp or pasture of Pletschen, from which you command a glorious view of the Jungfrau, Silberhorn, and Lower Eiger. 3. The Schmadribach Fall, at the head of the valley near Trachsellauenen. The upper Staubbach will be noticed with the principal fall of that name, and we shall confine our present attention to Nos. 1 and 2. The road to the Winteregg is the same as that which leads to the Pletschen Alp. The easiest access is from Zweylutschenen, through the village of Eisenfluh, to Mürren,* by the Sansalp and Suleck. The

Winteregg is above the rocky screen, over which the Pletschbach falls, forming the lower cascade of Staubbach.

Facing you is presented the Wengeren Alp, rising a league above the valley, with the pretty valley of Wengeren on a grassy slope. Above this again rises another terrace formed by the Wengberg and peaks of the Tschuggen. Straight above the lower summits tower aloft the mighty masses of the Jungfrau and Eiger, looking like columns of white marble, in the great temple consecrated to the Almighty. Seldom has the traveller to wait long before his ear is greeted by the thunder of avalanches from the precipices of the Jungfrau, which he can watch in peace and safety reclining on the bushes of alpine roses (rhododendra) that clothe the slopes above the Staubbach. The Winteregg is only five miles from Lauterbunnen. The expedition to the Schmadribach is rather more extensive.

As far as Stechelberg the valley is mostly level, but from that point it rises rapidly after the junction of the lateral valley of Fangfluh leading to the right to the Büttlosa. Following the Steinberg-Lütschinen you come opposite to a few houses called Schwendi, under the towering peaks of Ellstal and Spitehorn. The valley becomes narrower and is strewed with vast masses of granite. At Sichellauenen you meet the gneiss, and at Indermatten you see the old works opened in the schist strata stretching under the Jungfrau and Mönch to obtain the iron ore contained in it. We can only rapidly notice the most interesting objects that claim attention before the falls are reached.

Four great terraces rise from the head of the valley to the glacier of Tschingel. Sichellauenen is the first, Trachsellauenen* is the second, a bank of rock called Nadel

---

* At Mürren is the Hotel du Silberhorn, well spoken of, 2½ L. (7½ m.) reached on foot or horseback. Grand view of the Jungfrau, Mönch and Eiger, to the left, the Gspaltenhorn, Gletscherhorn, &c., to the right, 30 or 40 châlets, blackened by age, scattered over the meadows. Children have to go down here twice a week to school at Lauterbrunnen. In winter, snow is from 10 to 12 feet deep.—Excursions can be made from Mürren to the following places:—1. The Schilthorn, 4½ L (13½ m., 9,128 ft.) a good guide and good legs wanted A new path has been made. Horses to be had at the Inn, at Mürren, can be taken to the foot of the little Schilthorn. Grand view, comprising to the right, the Blumli Alp, the Doldenhorn, Altels, Wildstrubel, Niesen. Thun, Berne, and the Jura in the blue distance 2. From Mürren an interesting excursion can be made to the Sefinenthal, by the Sefinenfurke to the Kienthal and Frutigen in the Kanderthal. The road presents scenes of the highest romantic interest. and even grandeur. The distances are as follows· Mürren to Gimmelwald ½ 1 (1½ m., 4,254 ft.): to the Sefinenthal ½ 1. (½ m), by the Sefinenfurke to the Kienthal 1½ L (5½ m.), and several deviations may be made in the Kienthal. Thus you can visit the Dundengrat 3 L (9 m.), and on to the Œschinen Lake, near Kandersteg 1½ L (4½ m.) You can descend the Kienthal to Tschingel and the Falls of Dünden (1 L 3 m.), by the Scharmachthal 1 1 (3 m.). to Reichenbach in the Kanderthal, and on to Thun The Sefinenfurke and Kienthal are surrounded by lofty peaks, and give the tourist magnificent views of many of them, such as the Wildfrau (10,042 ft). the vast snow fields of the Blumlis Alp (11,298 ft.). the Tschingelhorn (11,021 ft.) From the Sefinenthal you can return to the valley of Lauterbrunnen, by Stechelberg.

* At Trachsellauenen is a decent house for refreshments, and passable quarters, before starting for an excursion to the Tschingel and Kander Glaciers, or on through the Gasterenthal to Kandersteg.

the third, and the Steinberg* the fourth. As you advance you see the remains of extensive avalanches at Staiensteinlauine, which threaten soon to destroy some fine pastures below. Three-quarters of a mile beyond Trachsellauenen you come to the Hauri and Nadel, two bulwarks of the Steinberg. At this spot, 2 to 3 l. (6 to 9 m.) from the parish church, mines were worked from 1782 to 1805 by a company at Berne. The yield consisted of argentiferous lead, but, though carried on with skill and energy, the product did not give sufficient encouragement to continue them. Passing thence through the wild valley of Ammerten, alongside of the raging torrent of Thalbach, the traveller reaches the châlet of Steinberg, whence, crossing the Krummbach, he soon after approaches the Schmadribach, which offers one of the grandest sights in the Alps.

This fall consists of a main stream with an accompaniment of many side rivulets, descending from the snowy heights above and rushing over a steep rocky declivity into a great basin situated amidst a chaos of rocky fragments. The best spot to see it is from the Châlet of Bohenmoos, in the midst of the woods. Above is seen the shining snowy peak of the Breithorn, below and through the woods of fir-trees, appear the boiling waters of the bach rushing after the great cascade to disappear among the shady recesses of the forest.

Lenk (An der).—See *Wilustrubel.*

Meiringen.—See *Hasli.*

Neuhaus.—At the east end of the lake of Thun, 2½ miles from Unterseen ; this is the landing place of the steamers on the lake.

Niesen.—A mountain near Thun. See its description under *Thun.*

Nydau.—See Plateau of *Berne.*

Peter's (St.)—Island in the lake of Biel, inhabited by Rousseau in 1765, half a

league in circumference, and offering charming views. It is 2 l. (6 m.) from Biel.

Plateau (The) or high level of the Canton of Berne, extending from Bulle to Berne, filled with flourishing villages and signs of industry and prosperity. It forms a remarkable and pleasant contrast to the Oberland or Highlands of Berne. The principal places on this table land are :—

Laupen, noted for a battle in 1339.

Burgdorf, an industrious place and great centre of railroads, where Pestalozzi founded his first establishment. Near it is Lueg, with a fine view from an eminence in the plain.

Lü‘zelflüh, is the place where Albert Bitziers, a popular historian, lived as pastor.

Langnau is one of the richest and finest villages in the Canton in the Langenthal.

Aarwangen, Aarburg, Hojwyl, Büren, and *Tannen,* noted for its cheeses, are other boroughs in this fertile district, which is, perhaps, the most populous and prosperous in Switzerland.

Pletschbach.—A waterfall near *Lauterbrunnen.*

Rawyl.—A pass in the Western Bernese Alps between Sion in the Valais and Thun. This pass can be reached from Thun by the Simmenthal, which you leave at Lattenbach, 10 miles from Thun. From Lattenbach you cross the Grimmi (5,580 ft.), descend to the Fermal Thal, and arrive at An der Lenk, near the source of the Simmen, whence you ascend the Rawyl (7,960 ft.), and reach Sion in 10 hours.

You can also go from Thun to Lenk, leave Frutigen, and passing up the Engstligen Thal to Adelboden. This Pass may also be reached from Kandersteg. The view of the Pennine Chain from the Rawyl is very sublime. Nor is the pass dangerous, except in one place on the Valais side.

---

* At the Steinberg Châlet is the best place to sleep (rough quarters) ere you cross the Peters Grat to Loetschen Thal (Kippel) in the Canton de Valais.—(See that Canton under Loesch.)

D

*Reichenbach (The Falls of).**—Situated close to Meiringen in the valley of Hasli, and near the road leading over the Great Scheideck from Grindelwald are among the finest in the Oberland. In the S.W. of the valley, near the Zwirgi, the Reichenbach makes its first and highest leap. Particularly in June, and seen from the bridge it often offers the gorgeous spectacle of an iris colouring the foam of its waters. The stream makes 6 or 7 leaps, each of which has a special charm. In the case of the upper fall, it is formed by a rock of 200 or 300 feet, standing out on each side of a central niche, down which the waters madly plunge. The diameter of the stream is about 25 feet, and after heavy rain, nearly 40. The cascade near Bögelein is distinguished by its impetuosity, and the scenery by its wild and sublimely romantic character. The last cascade but one (penultimate) is the most graceful of all. The stream bursts through a chaos of rocks, clothed with various foliage, it is here bisected by a rocky island, and the divided waters rush to meet each other below in an angry and foaming collision, covering rocks, woods, and the abyss below with a watery avalanche and a cloud of spray. One of the falls tumbles over four terraces, another near the Fachshütte is still more remarkable, being divided into 3 jets. The rocks are here whitened with foam, and one of the streams breaks forth at right angles to the main fall. This cascade may be reckoned the third, if not in beauty, at least in strangeness and originality.

Rosenlaui (The Baths of),† in German,

Rosenlauibad—The baths of Rosenlaui are situated ¾ of a mile from the direct road from Grindelwald, over the Great Scheideck, to Meiringen. They were restored in 1793-4, and consisted till the fire, of two wooden buildings, one the bath house, the other the inn. They are situated in a dark gorge, shaded by a thick wood, on the banks of the Reichenbach. The baths have been principally frequented by people of the country, and are supplied by a source of water holding sulphur in solution. Crossing the Reichenbach a walk of one hour takes the traveller to the Glacier of Rosenlaui, long noted as the bluest and fairest in the Alps. It descends a valley between the Wellhorn, the Stellihorn, and the Engelhorn, and it is adorned with a multitude of pyramids and crevasses of a beautiful azure blue. Some dispute has existed about the name, one writer inferring that the glacier has invaded pastures once noted for their flowers, while another more probable opinion refers the name to the colouring given to

paces from it issues a spring that has already done wonders in cures. Mine host sells Alpine plants with names attached, at 4 to 30 *fr.*—Close at hand is the fine Schwarzbach Fall.

Excursions (horse or foot)—1. To the Tschingel, 3 hours (7,155 ft.), complete view of the Hasli, of the Alps to Grimsel, of those of Unterwalden and the Pilatus. 2. To the Garren, 3 hours. (7,487 ft.), 2 hours on horseback, 1 on foot; view still more extensive than from the Tschingeln. 3. To the Wildgerest, 4 hours, (8,904 ft.) the last hour on foot, the view equal to that from the Faulhorn.—View from the Schwarzhorn (9,020 ft.) is grander than that from the Faulhorn. The Glacier of Rosenlaui is the greatest attraction, being perfectly lovely especially, in winter by moonlight. You approach it over a great moraine of granite blocks, with interspersed Alpine roses, and lofty firs mask the ice till you are close upon it. The glacier which discharges the Weissbach is (4,658 ft.) high, descends from the névés accumulated between the Dossen Well and Gateillhorna, and joins below the Gaul Glacier. The Rosenlaui Glacier is among the first for unsullied beauty and purity. It has no medial moraine and its crevasses are of a brilliant azure. Unfortunately its popularity has led to the adoption of devices by the natives to extract money, detracting from the enjoyment of the delicious scenery. Funnels have been cut in the ice, cannons are fired for the echo, and children pester you with posies, chamois, crystals, et id genus omne.

---

* There are now two hotels close to the fifth of the Reichenbach Falls.—Hotel des Alpes, and Hotel Reichenbach.

† The hotel which was burnt in 1869 has been rebuilt by M. Brunner, a well known botanist. It has pretty rooms at 1½ to 2 *fr.*; attendance, 50 c. Pension (without wine) 5 *fr.* a day. but it is obligatory to remain, or if you go before, to pay the pension of one week. A bath, 1 *fr.* 30 c. The hotel and its fare are good. John Zurflue, a noted carver in wood, is there throughout the year. The position of the hotel is exceptionally beautiful. A hundred

....se ice and snow slopes by the setting sun. The valley in which the Rosenlaui Glacier is situated is 4,500 feet above the sea, but it presents a deep depression between the towering masses of the Wetterhorn, Wellhorn, and Engelhorns that rise 7,000 to 8,000 feet above it. The Engelhorns are said to have derived their name from a certain resemblance to angels' wings that was thought to be traceable in their shape. The Wellhorn forms a part of the Wetterhorn, and between the two exists a chasm or great rocky gate filled up by the Rosenlaui Glacier, direct south from Rosenlauibad. At Grindelwald and Rosenlaui the shortest day is only half-an-hour long, and even this length is only procured by the southern openings opposite to each. The waters of the Rosenlaui Glacier flow off in a chasm, 200 feet deep, and only 2 or 3 feet wide, ¼ l. (¾ m.) in length. This rent in the rock has probably been worn by the water, and is crossed by a bridge near the glacier. The intensity of the blue observed in the latter is said to increase in winter, but diminishes and even disappears by moonlight.*

Rothkorn (The).—The highest point of the Brienz Grat (7,715 feet), rising behind Brienz, and separating that lake from the Entlibuch. The summit may be reached in 4 or 5 hours from Brienz, and presents a glorious panoramic view of snowy pics, glaciers, lakes, and plains. The winter view is, according to Kohl. particularly fine, affording occasionally very uncommon and brilliant atmospheric appearances. The clumps of fir on the hill side are frequented in winter by chamois, and especially by eagles.†

Saanetsch.—See *Wildstrubel.*

Scheideck (Pass of).—This is the direct route from Grindelwald to Meiringen, in the valley of Hasli. Its highest ridge, called the Eselsrucken, or Ass's Back, is 6,045 Swiss feet above the Mediterranean.

The road over this pass, which is easy of access, presents some delightful scenery. From the Eselsrucken, which is 2 l. from Grindelwald, the traveller enjoys a grand view of the Wetterhorn, to which you approach quite close on crossing the Rossalp. From the top of the ridge to the foot, at the Châlet of Schwarzwaldalp, the distance is 1½ l. (4½ m.), and another league (3 m.) brings you to Rosenlauibad. Near a bridge you cross on this part of the road a delightful view is presented of the Glacier of Rosenlaui, which is noted for the beauty of its blue pinnacles and crevasses. From Rosenlaui 1½ l. (4½ m.) bring you to a rock called Zwirgi or Twirgi, whence you descry the valley of Hasli, and ½ l. (2½ m.) further you reach Meiringen, passing close to the falls of Reichenbach.

Schmadribach.—See under *Lauterbrunnen.*

Schwarenbach.—See *Gemmi* and *Wildstrubel.*

Simmenthal, a valley watered by the Simmen, which joins the Aar at Thun, and rises on the borders of the Canton of Vaud. The tourist can pass by this route through some fine scenery into the upper part of the Canton de Vaud, near Bex, and into the lower Valais. This valley, which is 13 l. (39 m.) long, and rarely ½ m. wide, is interesting from its luxuriant pastures, celebrated for their yield of cheese and its excellent cattle. A fine waterfall formed by the Simmen adds to its attractions. The principal crops in the valley are hemp and flax, and the only manufacture is the preparation of woollen stuffs.

The Simmenthal offers the pleasantest pedestrian route from the Oberland to Vevay and Lake Leman. The road from Thun passes along the Kander by the Castle of Strättlingen to Brodhäsi, 2½ l. (7½ m.) Thence to Latterbach, opposite the Diemstigthal, and on to Erlenbach, with a good inn (Crown), full of picturesque Bernese houses. Stockhorn easily ascended hence in 3 to 4 hours; guide not essential. Proceeding you arrive at Weissenburg, with a ruined castle (Hotel de la Poste). 1½ l. (4½ m.); ½ l. (2½ m.) to the right the baths of Weissenburg, in a rocky chink like Pfäffers. The springs are saline and gypseous. Old bath can hold 300 persons. Hotel du Bain is recommended. Next we come to Simmeneck by a road now shut in by mountains. In

* Kohl's Alpenreisen, v. 1, p. 247.

† Kohl op. cit.

2 L. (6 m.) is Boltingen (2,560 feet), with 2,000 inhabitants: colossal Bernese houses, with enormous roofs; ¼ L. (⅓ m.) a road strikes off by Kin» to the valley of Jaun, Canton of Friburg, leading to Gruyeres and Bulle. The Simmen valley narrows. You pass Weissenbach, Garstatt, and Laubegg to Zweisimmen (3,017 feet). District capital with 2,000 inhabitants (Hotels—Bear and Crown); there the little Simmen falls into the main stream. To the left is the O-ersimmenthal, with a good carriage road; at bottom the Rasli Glacier. To the right the Great Simmen leads into a peopled district. St. Stephen's, Amseligrat, Matten, the Fenne'thal; above it the Albriathorn (8,518 feet), 2¼ l (8¼ m.) Further on is An der Lenk, with a sulphurous source. Hohlich (Hotels—Crown, Star, Bear), a village of 2,800 scattered over the valley; a tale of the valour of its women is attached to this place. At Rothenbach branch to Rawyl Pass, to Sion in the Valais. In 2 hours you reach the end of the Ober Simmenthal, with one of the finest waterfalls in Switzerland. The Simmen rushes from a rock called Seeh«rn, but this spot called Siebenbrunnen is seldom visited. From Zweisimmen main road takes you by Saanen Moser (2 l.) to Gessenay or Saanen. District capital, 2,629 inhabitants (Hotels—Landhaus, Bear). A renowned cheese, the Vacherin, is made here. The wooden houses surrounded with galleries have texts of scripture painted on them. The population, especially the women, are handsome. Hence by the Saanetsch Pass to Sion and Col de Pillon to Bex. Near the ruins of the Château de Vanel you enter the Canton de Vaud. 2¼ l further is Château d'Oex (Hotels—Bear, dear; Maison de Ville). Crossing the Saane you come to the Pré et les Moulins, from which there is a pass by la Mossetta and les Mosses into Ormond's dessus. 3 L. (9 m.) To the left is the Pension Henchoz. Proceeding by Rossinieres, La Tine, a romantically situated village, round Mont Cullan, you come to Montbovon (Hotel de Jaman Cross), from which two routes take you to Vevay.

1. By Gruyeres, Bulle, round Moleson, and by Châlet St. Denis.

2. By the Plan de Jaman, 1 l, to the Grand Châlet, Plan de Jaman. The Col is 4,651 feet; above it rises the Dent de Jaman. 5,783 feet, whose view has been called a dream of beauty by Byron. You see the whole Lake of Geneva to the Jura, and the Alps to the Dent du Midi. Many paths lead down from these sunny heights, fragrant with Alp roses and narcissus, one by *En avant*, with a good inn. and Chernex, turning right to Vevay, left to Montreux. (See Canton of Vaud.)

Staubbach (The), the highest waterfall in Switzerland, and probably in Europe, situated close to Lauterbrunnen, deserves a separate notice on many accounts. There are in fact two Staubbachs, an upper and a lower fall, formed by the Pletschbach, but the lower is the principal fall, and makes one distinct leap of 925 feet into the valley, over a screen of rock called the Pletschberg.

Two special features deserve notice in this (the lower) fall, and give it a distinct character. Half the stream falls perpendicularly, and would reach the bottom without a break were it not that the rock retires underneath it, suffering the water to take a leap through the air, striking half-way down a rocky projection, which shivers it into a thousand flashing jets before it reaches the basin of blackish rock scooped out at the bottom by the constant action of the water. The second column, separated from the other at the top of the fall, is carried impetuously clear off the rock, and scattered far and wide as foam and water dust, giving rise to the name of the cascade. When a strong wind prevails the whole mass (both columns) of water are swept wide of their course, and descend far and wide in a silvery shower. The most favourable spot for viewing the fall is the Furen, near the cascade of the Lauibach, at 9 or 10 o'clock in the morning. It is essential that the fall should be lighted up by the sun (in summer from 7 to 12 o'clock), which often presents the spectator with the magical effect of the rainbow.

The basin at the foot of the fall is a short ¼ l. (¼ m.) from the old inn, and is reached by following the left bank of the stream under the shade of willow and alder trees, leaving to the right the road that goes higher up the valley. Arrived at the rocky basin the visitor is surrounded with a luminous and aqueous atmosphere of scintillating bubbles that gather round his head and clothes like a nimbus.

The upper fall is reached by following the road from Lauterbrunnen to Mürren, crossing some pastures, following the Greifenbach, crossing it, then the Flühbachli, the Lauibach, the Herrenbachlein, and entering the forest of Pfrundwald. From the Herrenbachlein a path leads to the left over some rocks of decomposed schist to the upper cascade. This upper Staubbach forms three splendid arcs of dustlike water descending over a rock, which, leaving a cavern underneath, enables the visitor to see the silvery masses of the Jungfrau and Silberhorn across the valley through the transparent veil of the aqueous atmosphere. The Iris is often seen to hover over this fall displaying its prismatic glories in a scene of enchantment.

Stockhorn (The).—A mountain near Thun.—See *Thun.*

St·ahleck (The).—A pass only practicable for good mountaineers, leading from Grindelwald past the Mettenberg, near the great Glacier of Grindelwald, by the foot of the Schreckhorn and Finsteraarhorn and the Ober Aar Glacier to Grimsel. The pass is 10,500 feet high, and offers views of the grandest possible description. Distance, 14 hours. Requires a rope and veil.

Strahlhorner.—A ridge S. of the Ober Aar Glacier, near the Grimsel.

Thierberg, a mountain above Finster Aar Glacier, opposite the Abschwung, a buttress of the Schreckhorn, and near the Zinkenstock.

Tisch (The), Table, a great granite block perched on the Unter Aar Glacier, near the Abschwung.

Tschingel.—Horn and Glacier, head of valley of Lauterbrunnen.—See *Lauterbrunnen.*

Thun.

Rail: Central Swiss, four trains per day from and to Berne; time, one hour. Fares: 1st class, 3 *fr.* 15 *c.*; 2nd class, 2 *fr.* 20 *c.*; 3rd class, 1 *fr.* 60 *c* Return Tickets: 1st class, 5 *fr.*; 2nd class, 3 *fr.* 50 *c.*; 3rd class, 2 *fr.* 55 *c.*

Steamers to Neuhaus twice a day, in 1¼ hours: 1st class, 2 *fr.*; 2nd class, 1 *fr.*

Omnibus and Post Cars from Neuhaus to Interlaken: 1 *fr.*, each box, 25 *c.*

HOTELS.—Hotel Belle Vue; well conducted and agreeably situated, with very extensive grounds, and every convenience. Hotel and Pension Baumgarten; exceedingly good and delightfully situated,

Fares by Rail from Thun to

	1st class.		2nd class.		3rd class.	
	fr.	*c.*	*fr.*	*c.*	*fr.*	*c.*
Bâle	14	25	10	0	7	20
Berlin ....exp	136	70	94	60	0	0
Chur	30	60	21	40	15	85
Cologne	75	50	54	45	0	0
Frankfort	50	65	34	95	0	0
Geneva	20	8	15	95	10	5
Heidelberg ....exp	41	55	28	85	0	0
Lausanne	13	40	9	40	6	75
Lucerne	15	20	10	70	7	70
Neuchatel	9	90	7	5	5	10
Paris	68	20	51	25	38	10
Romanshorn	25	65	17	95	12	85
Rorschach	27	55	19	30	13	80
Schaffhausen	19	65	13	75	9	85
Vevay	15	40	10	30	7	75
Zurich	16	90	11	85	8	50

Post Cars once a day to Frutigen, 4¼ l. in 3 hours, 3 *fr.* 70 *c.*; to Zweisimmen, 8¼ l., Saanen, 11¼ l. in 8¼ hours, 10 *fr.* 60 *c.* Seven times a day by Thurneu and Belp to Berne, and by Kiesen to Burgdorf, 9¼ l. in 4¼ hours.

This little town, which may be considered the key to the Oberland, is built on the Aar, near the W. end of the lake of Thun, and is 16½ m. from Berne. Its present population is 3,400 inhabitants. It is usual to proceed from Berne to Thun by rail, the transit occupying 1 hour. The old carriage road passes through Muri, Munsingen, Wichtrach, Kiesen, &c., villages pleasantly situated and inhabited by a contented population in a fertile country. As you approach Thun the view improves, and the Oberland Chain rises grandly into view. Thun derives its name from the Celtic word *Dunum,* meaning hill or sandhill, a name recurring in Maldon (Camalodunum), Dunkirk, Bonny Dundee, Dundreary, and sundry other well known places or persons. The town of Thun is ¼ l. ($\frac{3}{4}$ m.) in length. The Aar on issuing from the lake forms two branches, creating an island just above the town. In this island is the quarter called Belliz, bisected by one street named Rosengarten. The river is crossed by two bridges. Two gateways form the entrance to these bridges, and a third occurs on the side of Berne, while through a fourth, called Laui, you pass out to the pretty walks on the Grüselberg.

In 1817 Thun contained 228 houses, 55 other buildings, and only 1,300 inhabitants. Within its district outside the walls there were 113 buildings and 300 inhabitants. At the end of the 18th century the citizens consisted of 68 families and 1,024 persons. The town consists of one principal street leading through a good sized square and on to the Sinnebrücke. The castle with its four towers and the church, formerly dedicated to Saint Maurice, stand on a hill to the E. The castle and the old walls are attributed to Berchtold V., Duke of Zähringen. Thun is rather an old-fashioned town with narrow irregular streets, but its vicinity offers striking points of view, especially the platform or cemetery near the church, and the castle, from which you obtain a delightful prospect of the town, the lake, the Niesen, and the Stockhorn. A pleasing walk leads along the Aar to Scherzlingen and Schadau. At the former, which was founded by Rodolph of Stättlingen, king of Burgundy, is an old factory. The Schadau is charmingly situated on the lake, here bordered by a pretty wood.

The road to Thierchen, a village 2¼ m. from Thun, passes by the plain of Alment, where is the school for artillery and engineering of the Swiss Confederation. Reviews of artillery on a large scale are often held at this place, and have been witnessed by the writer during a stay of 3 or 4 months which he made in the vicinity of Thun. On the road to Schwabis, which you take by turning to the left near the Berne Gate, at Thun, you enjoy some fine views, and reach the spot where Professor Tralles traced in 1788 a line of 6,464,013 feet as the base of his trigonometrical and geodesic survey of the heights of the Oberland Chain.

The two most interesting excursions from Thun are to the Niesen and Stockhorn. (a) The Niesen forms an immense pyramidal mass, 7,340 French feet above the sea, and 5,564 feet above the lake of Thun. The view from its summit is very extensive and magnificent. A small inn at the top. To reach it you take the road from Thun to Muhlenen, 3 L (9 m.), from which the mountain can be ascended in 4 or 5 hours. The route may be varied by returning into the Simmenthal, first to Wimmis, 2⅓ l. (8¼ m.), thence through Latterbach to Erlenbach, 1¼ L (3¾ m.) From this latter place a safe and easy path leads to the top of the Stockhorn. (b) Stockhorn (The): The summit of this mountain is shaped like a truncated cone of rock, is 6,767 feet above the Mediterranean, and 4,987 feet above the lake. The view here is as fine, and even more extensive to the west, than that from the Niesen. From the Stockhorn you can return to Thun by the Baths of Blumenstein, near which are the falls of Fallbach. The path by this route is considerably steeper, and those who wish to avoid it can fall back to Erlenbach and drop into the road to Berne by the baths of Weissenbourg or those of Gurnigel (3 or 4 hours from Erlenbach). At Erlenbach, Hotel de la Couronne.

Unterseen.—This little town, as its name denotes, is situated between the lakes of Thun and Brienz, which tradition, as well as the appearance of the country, show to have been once united. The interval consists of a level (the Bödeli) intersected by the Aar, and often ravaged by inundations of the Lutschenen, descending from Grindelwald and Lauterbrunnen. The security of the district has, however, been increased by digging new channels for the stream.

Unterseen is an ancient parish, once subject to Austria (from 1298 to 1393). Its old castle was burnt in 1470, and the town destroyed (except one house) the following year. It was rebuilt in the form of a square, but its suburbs exceed it in size. Of these the Spielmatt is built on an island in the Aar, and Aarmühle, the second, is partly built on another island. The houses of Goldey stand to the left, at the foot of the Harder, a rocky and woody eminence. The Aar flows along peacefully till it encounters a wear at Hohbühl, which impedes navigation between the two lakes. A street with numerous shops leads to two bridges that conduct you to the left bank of the Aar, and along the fine road of Höheweg to Interlaken. This is the best road in the country, and is much frequented. To the right appears the gorge of the Lutschenen leading up to the Jungfrau, on the other side beyond the shining Aar rises the dark rock of Harder, whilst the road on either hand is shaded by high hazle nut trees.

Near Unterseen at the village of Aar-mühle (called Rameli in the patois of the district) is an establishment for Molken Kur or whey cure, conducted for some years by Dr. Ebersold. The situation and fine air no doubt contributed to give efficacy to the treatment which was procured from the neighbouring herds of cows and goats that supply the whey.

The following excursions can be made from Unterseen or Interlaken, for they are in point of fact one place, occupying the alluvial level between the lakes of Thun and Brienz, called the Bödeli:—

1. To Interlaken ¼ l. (¾ m.), thence to Hohbühl ½ l. (1½ m.); to Goldschwyl ¾ l. (2¼ m.); to Ringgenberg 1 l. (3 m.); to Gsteig ¾ l. (2¼ m.); to Gsteigwyler 1 l. (3 m.); to the Castle of Unspunnen and to Wilderschwyl ¾ l. (2¼ m.); to the hill of Sattler Hübeli ¼ l. (¾ m.); to the Rugen or Galgen Hubel ½ l. (1¼ m.); to Oberbleiki on the Harder 1¼ l. (3¾ m.); to the Waldegg on the side of the Beatenberg and the Lake of Thun 2½ l. (7½ m.) or 3 l. (9 m.); to Wypenum, at the point where the Aar joins the lake ¾ l. (2¼ m.)

The Rugen or woody hill with pleasant walks and rustic seats, is only 1 l. (3 m.) from Unterseen and Interlaken.

The following are longer excursions:—
(a) Unterseen to Habkeren 2 l. (6 m.) hard climbing; thence to Polhöchst 3 l. (9 m.); thence to Wydegg ½ l. (1½ m.); and thence to the Hohgant 2 l. (6 m.) Another way from Polhöchst leads from the pastures

of Hagletsch ½ l. (1½ m.); to Hohgant 1½ l. (4½ m.) This latter ascent is more laborious, but the neighbourhood was reported to be frequented by chamois till within a recent period.

(b) Unterseen to Saxeten 2½ l. (7½ m.); thence to the Sulegg, 2½ l. (7½ m.), offering very fine views.

(c) From Unterseen to Saxeten again, 2½ l. (7½ m.); thence to the Rotheck, to the ridge Abendberg above Leissigen 2½ l. (7½ m.), commanding a grand view. A pleasanter way from Unterseen leads through Inner bergli 3 l. (9 m.) This way is said however to be rather difficult if not dangerous, at least for ladies.

(d) From Unterseen to Gsteig ¾ l. (2¼ m.); thence to the Alp pastures of Breitlaninen 1½ l. (4½ m.), from which you enjoy a superb view of the valleys of Interlaken and Lauterbrunnen, besides taking in the snowy pics surrounding the district of Grindelwald.

The roads along both banks of the Lake of Thun, from Thun to Unterseen present delightful views.

Thun (Lake of) is 1 l. (3 m. English) in width at Merlingen, and its length 5 l. (15 m.), while its greatest depth is 120 fathoms (720 feet). Its general direction is in the first instance to the S. E., but it turns rather eastward at the Nase. The lake is exceedingly well stocked with fish, of which there are said to be 14 species, one (the Aalbock) being thought to be peculiar to it.

On entering the lake from Thun the mountains seen near at hand are the Engel, the Dreyspitz, the Hundshörner, First, Schwalmeren, Schnabelhörner, and Suleck.

To the right the river Kander, descending from Kandersteg, after receiving the Simmen, used to pass behind the hill of Strättligen and fall into the Aar at Hervi-berg, occasioning frequent devastation in the plain near Thun. To obviate this a canal was made by order of the government of Berne, on the plan of the engineer Samuel Jenner, and opened in 1714 to

...henberg, a ridge near the Unter Aar (Finster?) and Lauteraarhorn, whose prolongations are buttresses, called Grumenberg and Erzberglein, covered with snow.

Zinkenstock, a mountain near the Grimsel, noted for its fine view and crystals.

Zweylutschenen, a hamlet at the spot where the Schwarzlutschenen from Grindelwald meets the Weisslutschenen from Lauterbrunnen. It is 2 l. (6 m.) from Interlaken; 1 l. (3 m.) from Lauterbrunnen, and

Zweysimmen, a village at the entrance of the Obersimmenthal.—See *Wildstrubel*.

Zwirgi, or *Twirgi*, a rock on the Great Scheideck, ¾ L. (2¼ m.) from Meiringen, near the Reichenbach fall.

ROUTES FROM BERNE.

Berne to Aarau and Aarbourg (No. 6).

ROUTE 53.

Aarberg, 4 L (12 m.)

	Leagues.	Miles.
Neubruck	½	1½
Ortschwaben	1	3
Maykirch	½	1½
Friensberg	½	2½
Seedorf	½	1½
Aarberg	½	2½
	4	12

ROUTE 54.

Aigle, by Saanen (No. 72 or 55 b 6), 20¼ L. (6"¼ m.)

	Leagues.	Miles.
Wangen	1¼	3¾
Neueneck	1¼	4¼
Wunnewyl	½	1½
Schmitte	½	1½
Mariahilf	1	3
Fribourg (5½ L)	1	3
Villars	1	3
Poisieux	1	3
Avry	2	6
Vuippens	¾	2¼
Bulle (11½ L)	1	1½
Vuidens	½	1½
Vauruz	½	1½
Semsale	1½	4½
Chatel St. Denis	1	3
Vevay (17 L)	2	6
La Tour de Peilz	¼	¾
Clarens	½	1½
Villeneuve	1	3
Renaz	½	1½
Roche	½	1½
Aigle	1	3
	20¼	62¼

ROUTE 52.

Berne to Altdorf, by Lucerne (Nos. 60, 62, 63 and 147 (or by Mount Susten, 32½ L. (98 m.))

	Leagues.	Miles.
Muri		
Allmendingen		
Rubigen		
Munsingen		
Nieder Wichtrach		
Ober Wichtrach		
Kiesen		
Heimberg		
Thun (5 leagues)		
Untersern (by lake)	5	15
Interlaken		
Brienz (by lake)	3	
Wyler Brücke	1	
Unter die Heide	1	
Meiringen	1	
Hasli im Grund	1	
Muhlithal	1	
Gadmen	2	
Top of the Susten	3½	10½
Wasen	4	12
Weyler		
Meitschlingen		
Im Ried		
Am Steg		
Sillinen		
Klus	1	3
Ernsted	1½	
Altdorf	1½	4½
	32½	98½

ROUTE 55 (b 1).

Thun to Bulle by the Simmenthal, 20½ L. (63 m.)

	h.	m.
Gwatt	0	45
Brodhusi	0	15
Latterbach	0	45
Erlenbach (3 h. from Thun)	0	30
Em oldingen	0	35
Wyler	0	25
Weissenburg (4¾ l. from Thun)	0	25
Hotel: Post.		
Wustenbach	0	15
Boltigen	0	45
Hotel: Bär.		
Reidenbach	0	20
Weissenbach	0	20
Laubeck Castle	0	20
Zweisimmen (12¾ leagues from Thun)	0	45
(Hotels: Bär; Krone).		
To Saanen	2	30
Schlundi Bridge	1	0
Col Schlundi	0	15
Schoenried	0	30
Saanen (Ge-senny) 11¾ l. 34 m from Thun)	0	30
Hotels: Grosses Landhaus Bär.		
Saanen to Bulle (¾ L, 27¼ m.)		
Vanel	0	30
Rougemont (Rothenburg)	0	15
Hotel: Le Croix.		

ROUTE 55 (b 1)—Continued.

	h.	m.
Flendon	0	35
Château d'Oex	1	0
Au Pré	0	15
Aux Moulins	0	16
La Tine (Gorge)	0	35
Auberge L'Ours.		
Montbovon	0	35
Albeuve	1	10
Neirivue	0	15
Villars sous Mont	0	20
Heney	0	50
Eparny	0	10
La Tour de Trême	0	30
Bulle	0	15

SECONDARY ROUTES FROM THE SIMMENTHAL.

ROUTE 55 (b 2.)

FROM ZWEISIMMEN TO LENK AND THE RHAZLI GLACIER. To Lenk, 2h. 30m. in 3h. From Lenk to the Sept Fontaines and back 4 to 5 h.

	h.	m.
Bettelried	0	20
St. Stephan	0	30
Matten	0	10
Boden	0	30
Lenk	0	30
Hotels Krone, Stern, Bär)		
To Simmen Falls	1	15
To Sept Fontaines (there and back)	4	0
To Rhæzi Glacier from Sept Fontaines	3	0

ROUTE 55 (b 3).

FROM LENK TO GSTEIG, 4h. 45m.

	h.	m.
Châlets of Ober Staffel	2	30
Col of Truttlisberg	1	0
Laueren (to Gsteig, 2h. 30m.)	1	15
Ascent to Col de Chrinen	1	30
Descent to Gsteig	1	0

ROUTE 55 (b 4).

FROM SAANEN TO BEX, by the Col de Pillon and the Col de la Croix, 9h. 45m. to 10h.

	h.	m.
Getaad	0	30
Lauibach Bridge	0	30
Ledi	0	30
Gsteig (2h. 30m. from Saanen)	0	40
Hotels: Ours; Wurstein.		
Col de Pillon	1	30
Grande Meille	0	15
Pillon	0	15
Les Plans	0	30
Les Iles	0	10
Châlets des Mazots Col de la Croix	1	0
Two roads hence to Bex (By A). Taveyannaz, la Croix, & Grion	3	30
(B) By the other side of the Grionne valley	3	0

ROUTE 55 (b 5).

FROM SAANEN TO AIGLE, by the Col de Pillon, 10h. 30m. Carriage road from Saanen to Gsteig, 2h. 30m. Mule path from Gsteig to the Hotel des Diablerets, 3 h. Good carriage road from the Hotel to Aigle 5 hours descent, 6 hours ascent). For one horse from Hotel des Diablerets to Gsteig, 8 fr.

	h.	m.
To Col du Pillon (see Route 55, b 4)	4	0
Descent to the Hotel des Diablerets	1	0
Ascent to it	1	30
Room, 1 fr. 50 c.; breakfast, 1 fr. 50 c.; pension, 5 fr.		
Vers l'Eglise	0	30
Pension Cerf, 3 fr. 50 c.		
Moulin de Galesè	6	30
Aigrement	0	45
Combaz to Sepey	0	30
Sepey to Comballaz	2	30

ROUTE 55 (b 6).

CHATEAU D'OEX TO AIGLE, BEX, AND TO VILLENEUVE

(A) To Aigle, by les Mosses, 7h. 45m. Mule paths to Comballaz. Carriage road from Comballaz to Aigle.

	h.	m.
Le Pré	0	15
Le Devant	1	0
Steep ascent	0	45
Descent to Hotel de la Lecherette	0	30
Les Mosses	0	25
La Comballaz	0	50
Pension of Lys, 5 fr. a-day.		
Sepey	1	30
Hotel Etoile; Hotel de Ville. Pensions, 3 fr. 50 c.		
Aigle	2	30

ROUTE 55 (b 6).

(B) SAANEN TO VILLENEUVE, by the Col de Chande. Foot path, 5 to 6 hours.

	h.	m.
Sarine Bridge	0	15
Ratevel	0	30
Les Crosets	0	40
Les Crêtes	0	15
Lovanchy	0	35
Châlets en Chandes	0	25
Col de Chande	0	15
Planardray	1	30
Villeneuve	2	30

ROUTE 55 (b 7).

FROM MONTBOVON (see Route 55, b 1) TO VEVAY AND MONTREUX, by the Col de la Dent de Jaman, 6h. 45m. to 7h., to Vevay. Horse to the Col, 10 frs.; to Vevey or Montreux, 20 fr.

	h.	m.
Bridge on the Hongryn	0	45
En Alliere (Inn: Croix-Noire)	0	30
Châlets of Plan de Jaman (3 hours from Montbovon & Col de Jaman	1	30
(Top of Dent de Jaman, 1h. 30m.)		

ROUTE 55 (b 7).—Continued.

	h.	m.
Mont d'Avent / Pres d'Avent }	1	15
Auberge l'Union.		
Vevay	2	45
To Montreux	3	0

(See Canton of Vaud, Vevay Excursions, and Routes.)

ROUTE 55 (c 1).

BRIENZ TO THE GRIMSEL.

To Meiringen, a diligence in 1h. 45m. (1 fr. 25 c.)

	h.	m.
Tracht	0	15
Kienholz	0	15
Meiringen	1	45
Hotels: Wilder Mann; Krone; Bär —Pensions.		
Over Kirchet (through Im Grund Valley to Hof) }	1	15
Hotel: Im Hof.		
Aar Bridge	1	0
Urweid Schlafplatte	0	15
Spreitbach Bridge	0	30
Guttannen (3h. 15m. from Meiringen) }	0	15
Hotel: Hirsch.		
Schwarzenbrunnen Bridge	0	25
Handeck Kehren (Handeck Falls)	1	0
Erlenbach Bridge	0	15
Handeck Châlet (5t. 10m. from Meiringen) }	0	10
Hotel:		
Hellenplatte	0	15
Buegelein	0	10
Aar Bridge	0	15
Boechlibach	0	20
Roeterisboden	0	15
Sommerloch	0	25
Spitallam	0	15
Hospice of Grimsel (2 h. from Handeck); (7h. 30m. from Meiringen) }	0	30
Hotel. 50 beds, 2 fr.; supper, 3 fr.; Breakfast, 1 fr. 50 c.		
37½ miles from Berne.		

ROUTE 55 (c 2).

Brienz to Sarnen and Lucerne by the Brunig (No 76).

ROUTE 55 (c 3).

Meiringen to Sarnen, by the Melchthal (No. 352, b 7.)

ROUTE 55 (c 4).

Meiringen to Engelberg, by the Joch (No. 352, c 6), and Bernese Alps, p 19).

ROUTE 55 (c 5).

Meiringen to Wasen (No. 55 a).

ROUTE 55 (c 6).

THE GRIMSEL.

To Viesch or the Ægischhorn, by the Ober Aar Joch, 12 or 13 h. Difficult, good guide wanted.

	h.	m.
End of Ober Aar Glacier	2	30
Ober Aar Joch	3	0
Down to Grimsel	4	0
Descent to Nevé, head of Viesch Glacier, difficult passage }	2	0
Auf der Trift	3	0
Châlets of Märjelen Alp	2	30
Viesch	2	0

ROUTE 55 (c 7).

THE GRIMSEL TO REALP IN URI, by the Furka (6 h.)

	Miles.
Meyenwand / Rhone Glacier }	4½
By the Furka (Small cheap Inn, 20 beds.)	
Châlets of Siedelnalp and Eimeten-alp to Realp }	16½
(Hotel des Alps and Capuchin Convent.)	

To Altstaetten by Zurich (Nos. 79 and 196), and St. Gallen (No 180).

Appenzell by Zurich (Nos. 79 and 28.)

Art by Zug (Nos. 78 and 281.)

ROUTE 56.

BERNE TO BADEN, 19 L. (57 m.)

	Miles.
Morgenthal (No. 6)	28½
Rotherist	5½
Saffenwyl	3
Köliken	2
Entfelden	1
Suhr	1½
Hunzenschwyl	2
Lenzbourg	2½
Ottmarsingen	1½
Wollenschwyl	3
Meilingen	
Baden	4½
	——
	57

ROUTE 57.

Bâle (Nos. 32 or 23).

Bellinzona, by Sion (Nos. 73, 74, or 236), or by Altdorf (Nos. 55 and 229), or by Lucerne (Nos. 66, 67, or 68 and ·47), and Altdorf (No. 229), or by the Oberland and Saint Gothard, 45¼ l. or (137½ m.)

	Miles.
Wasen (No. 55)	84½
St. Joseph	
Göschenen	
The Devil's Bridge	
Andermatt	

ROUTE 57—Continued.

	Miles.
The Hospital	2½
Top of St. Gothard	6½
Airolo	5½
Stavedno	1½
Protta	1½
Ambri Sopra	1½
Fless	1
Aldacio	¾
Faido	3¼
Chischiogna	¾
Giornico	5½
Bodio	1½
Poleggio	1½
Osogna	3¾
Ciaciano	3
Torracia	2¼
Arbedo	3
Bellinzona	¾
	137½

ROUTE 58.

Bex, 22¼ l. (66¾ m.)

	Miles.
Aigle (No. 54)	62¼
Bex	4½
	66¾

ROUTE 59.

Bienne, 6 l. (18 m.)

	Miles.
Aarberg (No. 53)	1¾
Buhl	2¼
Hermringen	
St. Nicholas	
Belmont	
Nydau	
Bienne or Biel	
	18

To Brougg (No. 197).

Bulle (No. 54).

ROUTE 60.

Burgdorf, 12¾ m.

	Miles.
Papiermühle	2¼
Sand	3
Hindelbank	3
Motschwyl	1½
Rohrmoos	1½
Burgdorf	1½
	12¾

Chamouny, by Lausanne (Nos. 63 and 96) and Geneva (No. 95).

ROUTE 61.

Chaux de Fonds, 10½ l. (31½ m.)

	Miles.
Bienne, or Biel (No. 59)	6
Bötzingen	1½
La Reuchenette	3½
Sonceboz	3
Corgemont	2½
Courtelary	2½
Saint Imier	3½
Renans	3
Chaux de Fonds	5½
	31½

or by Neuchâtel (Nos. 70 and 169).

Chiavenna, by Zurich (Nos. 79 and 142) and Chur (Nos. 121, 122, or 123).

Chur, by Zurich (Nos. 79 and 142), or by Thun and Lucerne (No. 76), and the lake from Alpnach, and on by rail from Lucerne.

Einsiedeln, by Lucerne (Nos. 66 and 67, or 68 and 152).

Engelberg, by Lucerne (Nos. 66, 67, or 68, and 153), or by the Brunig (No. 76), or from Meiringen (No. 55 a).

Frauenfeld, by Zurich (Nos. 79 and 245).

Fribourg (No. 54).

Gais, by Zurich (Nos. 79 and 196), and St. Gallen (No. 186).

Geneva, by Lausanne (Nos. 63 and 96).

Glarus, by Zurich (Nos. 79 and 116).

ROUTE 61 (a).

Grindelwald, 46¼ miles.

	Miles.
Thun	16½
Across the lake to Neuhaus	15
To Unterseen	2½
Zweylutschenen	6
Grindelwald	6
	46¼

ROUTE 61 (b 1).

Grindelwald to Meiringen, by the Great Scheidegg, 6h. 30m. to 7h. Mule path.

	h.	m.
Upper Grindelwald Glacier	1	0
Bergelbach	0	30
Col of Great Scheidegg (inn), 3h. up from 2h. down to Grindelwald }	1	0
Alpiglen Châlets	0	30
Reichenbach Bridge	0	20
Schwarzwald (inn)	0	15
two paths hence, best by the		
Right bank of the Reichenbach	0	45
to the Baths of Rosenlaui, 1h. 45m. from Scheidegg (Inn - Steinbock)		
By Breitenmatt to bage	0	35
Zwirgi	0	45
Schwændi	0	25
Willigen	0	15
Meiringen	0	25
(2h. down, 3h. up to Rosenlaui.)		

ROUTE 61 (b 2).

GRINDELWALD TO THE GRIMSEL, by the Strahleck, 14h. to 15h., 10h. on the glacier. 5 to 6 L in a direct line.

	h.	m.
Bænisegg	3	0
To the glacier	0	30
To the foot of the Strahleck	2	0
Climbing up the rocks	2	0
To the Col	0	30
From Col to Finsteraar Glacier	0	45
To the Abschwung ...2h. 30m. or	3	0
To Grimsel—on the glacier	3	0
on the mountain side..	1	0

Grindelwald to the Grimsel, by Meiringen and the Handeck, No. 61. 8 b 1 to Meiringen, and No. 55 e 1 from Meiringen to the Grimsel.

Zurich, by Zurich (Nos. 79 and 301).

ROUTE 62.
HOFWYL, 4½ miles.

	Miles:
Sand	3½
Hofwyl	1½
	——
	6½

Another route passes by Reichenbach.

ROUTE 62 (a 2).
KANDERSTEG.

	Miles.
Thun	16½
Gwatt	2½
Wyler	^
Mühlenen	3½
Frutigen	4½
Kandersteg	9
	——
	39

ROUTE 62 (b 1).

FROM FRUTIGEN TO ADELBODEN AND AN DER LENK, 7h. To Adelboden, cars; thence a mule path.

	h.	m.
Adelboden	3	30
Hotel: Bär.		
Col of Hahnenmoos	2	15
Descent to An der Lenk	1	15
A detour may be made by Gellubach to the Upper Col of Hahnenmoos and by Amerten and Sept Fontaines to Lenk	5	0

ROUTE 62 (b 2).

KANDERSTEG TO LAUTERBRUNNEN, by the Dunden grat and the Sefinen Furke, 14 to 15h. Foot path. Guides, Kunzi of Seiden (Gasterenthal).

	h.	m.
Œschinen Lake	1	15
Ober Œschinenalp	1	15
Dundengrat	1	45
Short difficult cut to Sefinen Furke or safer way to Ober Dundalp	1	30
Kienthal Unter do.	0	45

ROUTE 62 (b 2 — Continued).

	h.	m.
Tschingel Châlets	0	45
Kienthal (car road from Tschingel).	1	0
(hence to Mühlenen, 2h.)		
From Tschingel, by Durrenberg-alp, to the Sefinen Furke	2	0
Descent to Châlet of Boganggenalp		
To Oberbergalp, and in 3 or 4h. ascending to Stechelberg.	3	0
Lauterbrunnen	1	30

From Oberbergalp you can reach Gimmelwald and Mauren by the Schiltthal.

(For the route from Kandersteg. by the Gasterenthal, to Lauterbrunnen Route 63, 2 b 3.)

Lauffenbourg, by Aarau (Nos. 6 and 10).

ROUTE 63.
LAUSANNE, 16⅔ L. (50¼ m.)

	Miles.
Payerne (No. 77)	26½
Marnand	4½
Hennies	1½
Lucens	3
Moudon	3
Bressonaz	1½
Montpreveyre	4½
The Croisettes	3½
Lausanne	2½
	——
	50¼

ROUTE 63 (a).
LAUTERBRUNNEN, 43½ miles.

	Miles.
Unterseen (No 61a)	34½
Zweilutschenen	6
Lauterbrunnen	3
	——
	43½

ROUTE 63 (b 1.)

FROM LAUTERBRUNNEN TO THE SCHMADRIBACH AND STEINBERG, 1h. 40m. to 4h. to go. 6h. there and back.

	h.	m.
Stechelberg	1	15
Sichellauinnen	0	30
Trachsellauenen	0	30
Nadel	0	15
Ammerten	0	30
Laeger (Châlet)	0	20
To see the Schmadribach.		
From Ammerten to Steinberg Chalet	1	30

ROUTE 63 (b 2.)

LAUTERBRUNNEN TO KIPPEL in the Loetschenthal (Valais) by the Loetschenthal Grat, 11 hours) Glacier pass. Guide wanted.

	h.	m.
To Steinberg (63 2 b 1)	4	0
To the Moraines of the Kander Glacier when you leave the part to Kandersteg	1	40

ROUTE 62 (b 2)—Continued.

	h.	m.
Ascent to Col of the Leœtschen-thal Grat }	2	30
Descent to Telli Glacier	1	0
Chalets of Telli	1	15
Wyssenried	0	20
Wyler	0	45
Kippel	0	10

ROUTE 63 (b 3.)

LAUTERBRUNNEN TO KANDERSTEG by the Gasterenthal, 11h. 30m. 6h. over the ice. Guide wanted. Sleep at Steinberg.

	h.	m.
Ober Steinberg Châlet (63 b 1)	4	0
By Tschingel Glacier to Tschingel Trift }	0	40
Upper Tschingel Glacier	1	30
Tschingel Joch	0	30
Alpetli; issue of Kander Glacier	1	30
Gasterenthal	1	0
Im Selden	1	0
Kandersteg	2	0

ROUTE 64.

LOCARNO BY SION (No. 73 or 74 and 236), and Bellinzona (No. 232) or by Altdorf (Nos. 55 and 229) or by Lucerne (No. 66, 67, or 68 and 147). Altdorf (No. 229) and Bellinzona (No. 232), or by the St. Gothard, 50¾ L. (152¼ m.).

	Miles.
Airolo (No. 57)	105
Nant	¾
Fusio	6½
Prato	7½
Covergno	4½
Bignasco	3
Someo	4½
Coglio	4½
Maggio	6½
Avegno	6½
Locarno	7½
	152¼

Locle, by Neuchatel (Nos. 70 and 175).

ROUTE 65.

LOESCH (BATHS), 18½ L. (54¾ m.)

	Miles.
Thun (No. 55)	15
Gwatt	2½
Wyler	3
Mühlenen	3½
Frutigen (69 a 2)	4½
Kandersteg (69 a 2)	8
Schwarenbach over the Gemmi	9
Loesch	8¼
	54¾

Another road passes through Sion (Nos. 73 or 74 and 276).

ROUTE 66.

LUCERNE, BY ZOFINGEN, 19½ L. (56½ m.)

	Miles.
Rotherist (No. 56)	3½
Zofingen	[illegible]
Reiden	[illegible]
Dagmersellen	[illegible]
St. Erhard	[illegible]
Sursee	[illegible]
Oberkirch	[illegible]
Notwyl	[illegible]
Neukirch	[illegible]
Emmenbrucke	[illegible]
Lucerne	[illegible]
	56½

ROUTE 67.

LUCERNE, BY THE ENTLIBUCH, 19½ L. (56½ m.)

	Miles.
Gumligen	[illegible]
Rüfenach	[illegible]
Worb	[illegible]
Rychigen	[illegible]
Ried	[illegible]
Hochstätten	[illegible]
Signau	[illegible]
Langnau	[illegible]
Trubschachen	[illegible]
Escholzmatt	[illegible]
Emmenbrucke	[illegible]
Shupfen or Schupfheim	[illegible]
Hasli	[illegible]
Entlibuch	[illegible]
Wohlhausen	[illegible]
Wertenstein	[illegible]
Schachen	[illegible]
Malters	[illegible]
St. Just	[illegible]
Littau	[illegible]
Lucerne	[illegible]

ROUTE 68.

LUCERNE, by Burgdorf, 16½ L. (49½ m.)

	Miles.
Burgdorf (No. 60)	[illegible]
Eggerdingen	[illegible]
Waltringen	[illegible]
Durrenroth	[illegible]
Huttwyl	[illegible]
Huswyl	[illegible]
Zell	[illegible]
Gettnau	[illegible]
Ettiswyl	[illegible]
Sursee	[illegible]
Lucerne (No. 66)	[illegible]

ROUTE 69.

LUGANO, by Sion, or by Lucerne and Altdorf, and afterwards Bellinzona (No. 235), see Locarno; or by St. Gothard, 51¼ L. (154½ m.)

	Miles.
Bellinzona (No. 57)	137½
Giubiasco	¾
Cadenazzo	3½
Bironico	3½
Taverna Sotto	3
Lugano	6
	154½

Mendrisio, by Sion, or by Lucerne and Altdorf, and then Bellinzona (No. 235), see Locarno.

Morat (No. 77).

Morges, by Lausanne (Nos. 63 and 96).

Moudon (No. 63).

ROUTE 70.

NEUCHATEL, 30 miles.

	Miles.
Aarberg (No. 53)	12
Neuchatel (No. 40)	18
	30

ROUTE 71.

ORBE, 15¼ L. (46¼ m.)

	Miles.
Yverdun (No. 77)	40¼
Treycovagnes	1½
Succevaz	1½
Mathoud	¾
Orbe	2¼
	46¼

Payerne (No. 77).

Pfeffers Baths, by Zurich (Nos. 79 and 304).

Rigi (Mount), by Lucerne (Nos. 66, 67, or 158, or 159).

ROUTE 72.

SAANEN (GESSENAY), 15¼ L. (45¼ m.)

	Leagues.	Miles.
Thun (No. 55)	5	15
Gwatt	½	2½
Glutsch	¼	1¼
Wimmis	1¼	3½
Latterbach	½	1½
Erlenbach	½	1½
Ringoldingen	½	1½
Weissenburg	¾	2½
Oberwyl	½	1½
Wustenbach		
Eichstalden		
Boltigen		
Weissenbach	½	1½
Zweysimmen, 12¾ L. (38¼ m.)	1¼	3½
Reichenstein	¾	2¼
Auf die Möser	½	1½
Kannenried	½	1½
Auf der Halden	¼	¾
Saanen	½	1½
	15¼	45¼

Saint Gallen, by Zurich (Nos. 79 and 193.)

Schaffhausen (Nos. 197).

Scheideck Pass.

	Miles.
Thun (No. 55)	16½
Over the Lake to Unterseen and Grindelwald (No. 61 a)	27
	43½
Grindelwald to the Eselsrucken (top of Scheideck)	6
	49½

Schwytz, by Lucerne (Nos. 66, 67, 68, and 161.)

ROUTE 73.

SION, by the Ravil Pass, 23¼ L. (70¼ m.)

	Miles.
Zweysimmen	38½
Blankenbourg	1½
Matten	3
Lenk	2½
Top of the Ravil Pass	14½
Agent	6
Sion	5½
	70¼

ROUTE 74.

SION, by the Main Road, 31 L. (93 m.)

	Miles.
Bex (No. 58)	66½
St. Maurice	1½
Pissevache	3¼
Martigny	3
Chataz	3
Saxon	3½
Riddes	2
St. Pierre	1½
Ardon	1½
Vetro	1½
Sion	4½
	93

ROUTE 75.

SOLOTHURN, 6¼ L. (19¼ m.)

	Miles.
Papiermühle	2¼
Urtenen	3¼
Jägistorf	1½
Graffenried	1½
Fraubrunnen	
Bätterkinden	3¼
Lohn	3
Solothurn	3
	19¼

Stanz (see Unterwalden).

Thun (No. 55).

Trogen, by Zurich (Nos. 79 and 193), and Saint Gallen (No. 193).

ROUTE 76.

UNTERWALDEN, by Lucerne (Nos. 66, 67, 68 & 153), or by the Brunig, 22¼ l. (68¼ m.)

	Miles.
Brienz, over the Brunig (No. 55)	41¼
Lungeren	9
Gieswyl	4¼
Sachselen	3
Sarnen	1¼
Alpnach or Stanz	9
	68¼

Vevay (No. 54); or by the Simmenthal to Saanen (No. 72), and thence over the Col de Jaman (No. 55, b 1, and b 7); or by Bulle (No. 278).

Winterthur, by Zurich, rail or road (Nos. 79 and 301).

ROUTE 77.

YVERDUN, 13½ l. (40½ m.)

	Leagues.	Miles.
Bethlehem	¾	2¼
Riedern	½	1½
Kappelen	½	1½
Allenluften	1	3
Gummenen	½	1½
Gempenach	¾	2¼
Morat, 5¼ l. (15¾ m.)	1½	3¾
Faoug		2¼
Avenches		2¼
Domdidier	½	1½
Dompierre		1½
Corcelles	½	1½
Payerne, 2¾ l. (26¼ m.)		1½
Cugy	½	1½
Montet		1½
La Chable	1	3
Cheiry	¾	2¼
Yvonant	¾	1½
Cheseaux	1	3
Yverdun	½	1½
	13½	40½

ROUTE 78.

ZUG, 24¼ l. (72¾ m.)

	Leagues.	Miles.
Lenzburg (No. 56)	15¾	47¼
Zug (No. 17)	8½	25½
	24¼	72¾

ROUTE 79.

ZURICH, 23 l. (69 m.)

	Leagues.	Miles.
Baden (No. 56)	19	57
Zurich (No. 18)	4	12
	23	69

or by rail.

Zurzach (No. 197).

Austria, Bavaria, and East Germany, by Schaffhausen or Romanshorn, Friedrichshafen and Lindau.

The Rhine, Strasburg, and Frankfort, by Bâle.

Lyons, Turin, and Genoa, by Geneva.

Paris, by Bâle or Neuchâtel.

Milan and Italy, by the Simplon or St. Gothard.

Soon after leaving Olten you enter the

CANTON OF AARGAU

by our second main approach to the Swiss Highlands at Lucerne.

LIMITS OF AARGAU.—This Canton borders to the E. on those of Zurich and Zug, to the S. on that of Lucerne, to the W. on the Cantons of Berne, Solothurn and Bâle, and to the N. its limit is the Rhine, separating it from the Grand Duchy of Baden.

AREA, SOIL AND CLIMATE.—The Canton of Aargau embraces a surface of 69¾ German square leagues, (1,405 square kilometres). It is intersected by ridges of low mountains and hills, generally cultivated with considerable care, and forming a number of vallies, which are mostly irrigated by streams throughout their length. Plains of a considerable extent also cover a portion of the surface of the Canton, which is one of the flattest in the Confederation. The climate of this canton is generally mild, and adapted to almost every kind of crop, proper to the temperate districts of Europe.

MOUNTAINS.—This territory is crossed from the W. to the E. by a portion of the Jura chain, forming in fact the diameter of the Canton. The most elevated points in the ridge are the Wasser-Fluh (2,880 ft.), and the Gyssli-Fluh or Gysula-Fluh (2,720 ft. above the Mediterranean). Both these summits are immediately in front of the town of Aarau, and offer delightful views. The elevations that occur in the S.E. of Canton, and following a direction from N. to S. are mere continuations of Mount Albis, sinking gradually into undulations.

LAKES, RIVERS AND RIVULETS.—The only lake in this canton is that of Hallwyl. It is not extensive, but well stocked with a certain kind of crab, and also with a species of salmon (salmo albula) which is held in high esteem, and called in the country Hägling.

RIVERS.—The river Rhine forms the north frontier of this Canton throughout its length, and receives at Coblentz (confluentia), the Aar, already increased at Windisch, by the Reuss, and at Vogelsang, by the Limmat.

RIVULETS.—With one exception all the rivulets in this Canton derive their source from the Canton of Lucerne, and fall into the Aar. We can only notice the principal amongst them which are, the Wigger, near Aarburg; the Suhr, below Aarau, having previously received the tributary waters of the Wina; the Aa formed by the water issuing from lake Halliwyl and the Bunz near Wildegg.

PRODUCTIONS OF THE SOIL AND INDUSTRY.—The principal live stock bred in that Canton consist of swine. Horned cattle and sheep receive less attention, and are fewer in number. Game is somewhat scarce, but the rivers and streams are well stocked with fish. Large crops of cereals and grass are raised on the fertile plains of this Canton, which yields a fair supply wine, besides vegetables, fruit, hemp, flax, and rape, but very little wood. In point of minerals, some iron is found in this district (on the Hungerberg, facing Aarau), alabaster occurs (close to the road leading to the Frickthal, by the Staffelberg), limestone, gypsum, marl, and turf are also found in different parts of the Canton. A number of springs of mineral and saline waters in the Sulzthal (the valley of Sulz); but they are not abundant enough to be a source of profit. In regard to manufactures, a good amount of silken and cotton goods are made in the Canton, besides oil of vitriol, plaited straw, leather, cutlery, &c.

HOT SPRINGS AND COLD BATHS.—The most noted and valued hot springs in the Canton occur at Baden and Schinznach, which are constantly frequented by a great number of Swiss and of foreigners. The cold baths of Leerau, Schwarzenberg, and Niederwyl do not attract much attention.

POPULATION AND RELIGION.—The last census of the population gives 199,720 inhabitants, of whom 107,194 are Protestants and 91,095 Catholics. Thirty years ago the population consisted of 143,749 souls, distributed in 276 towns, boroughs, villages, hamlets, &c. There are 48 Protestant and 70 Catholic parishes. The Jews have synagogues at Endigen and Lengnau, in the district of Zurzach, where they enjoy perfect toleration.

ABBEYS AND CONVENTS.—The former consist of the Abbey of Wettingen of the Cistercian Order, and that of Muri of the Benedictine Order. At Baden and at Bremgarten are convents of Capuchin monks, and at Fahr, Gnadenthal, Hermetswyl, and Baden are convents of nuns. These convents are now secularized.

SCIENTIFIC, CHARITABLE, AND EDUCATIONAL ESTABLISHMENTS.—The Cantonal Library deserves special attention, besides that of the town of Zofingen, as well as the Patriotic Society for the promotion of arts and sciences (Gesellschaft der Vaterländische Kultur), connected with the Natural History Society. We may also notice the Medical Society, the Cantonal School at Aargau, and the Establishment for Young Ladies in the ancient abbey of Olsberg. There is, moreover, in every district of the Canton a secondary school, and at Lenzburg a normal school for schoolmasters.

SURVEY OF THE CANTON.

Aarau (the capital). The principal hotels of Aarau are the Savage, Ox, and Cigogne. Restaurant at the station. The town is situated in a fine position on the right bank of the Aar, which is crossed by a suspension bridge, erected 1851. It contains about 5,100 inhabitants, Protestants as well as Catholics, who worship in one and the same building. Aarau is built with tolerable regularity, and most of its streets are watered throughout their length by pretty clear streams. The new suburb is particularly well-built, containing a handsome platz or square, the arsenal, and the cantonal school, in which the public library is situated, besides several other handsome public buildings. The town-house, remarkable for its size and for the simplicity of its architecture, also adorns the new suburb. Pleasant walks are afforded by the Rampart to the west and by the Balünenweg to the east of the town, presenting agreeable views, extending over pretty gardens and meadows along the banks of the Rhine to the cultivated slopes and vineyards that clothe the outliers of the Jura. The eye of the visitor dwells with pleasure on the rocky outline of that fine limestone chain, forming a picturesque background to the rich champain country stretched at his feet. The principal cantonal establishments of Aargau are found in the capital. These consist chiefly in—1st, the Cantonal School; 2nd, the Cantonal Library of 60,000 volumes, containing the large collection of MSS. that belonged to the family, Zurlauben, so interesting in its connection with Swiss history; 3rd, the Society for the promotion of Art and Agriculture, previously mentioned. The latter association holds a meeting every week, and some of its members meet together every evening in the salle of the Cantonal School. Any stranger introduced by a member is most kindly received, finds congenial society, and a good supply of papers and periodicals. There are several good collections of minerals at Aarau, especially that of M. Meyer. Aarau has long been noted for good paintings and artists, and for able makers of mathematical instruments. The names of M. M. Schenermann and Essor have been distinguished in these departments. Aarau has some manufactures that stand in good repute, especially those of Herzog and Comp, and of the brothers Heviose. Their cotton goods and calico prints have been thought to rival English articles.

Aarburg, is a small town 1 l. (3 m.) from Zofingen and 32 l. (10 m.) from Aarau, on the roads to Berne and Lucerne, and since the introduction of railway communication it has risen to some importance as the junction of several Swiss lines. Its principal inn is the Crown. Besides the railway traffic there is a good deal of activity in the transit trade on the Aar, which consists chiefly in the shipment of wine and salt. Besides these causes of animation, Aarburg has manufactures of cotton and copper works. The fortress of Aarburg, built on a rock, affording a fine view, is the only one in Switzerland, but is untenable in the present advanced state of the art of war.

Baden is a little town situated on the left bank of the Limmat, which is crossed by a handsome wooden and covered bridge. Its distance from Zurich is 4 l. (12 m.). and from Aarau, 5½ l. (16½ m. It contains about 1,500 Catholic inhabitants, and its principal hotels are the Station Hotel and the Café of the Telegraph. In the town, the Balance, Linden, and Lion. Baden contains a well organised secondary school, an old parish church with a chapter of canons, a convent of Capuchin monks and another of Capuchin nuns, now secularized, and a hospital founded by Queen Agnes. The Hotel de Ville deserves a visit, because it answered for many years the purpose of an assembly place for the Diet of the Confederation, and also because the Congress met here in 1714, which put an end to the War of Succession in Spain. Baden is also the seat of the correctional and reformatory establishment of the Canton of Aargau. Close to the town, on the Stein, are the ruins of an ancient fortress, supposed to be of an era even anterior to the occupation of Helvetia by the Romans. This fortress was used as a stronghold by the Austrians in 1315, and in 1386 when they marched against the Swiss, and lost the battles of Morgarten and of Sempach. In 1415, it was burnt by the confederates; but it was rebuilt in the 17th century by the

Baden. It was ultimately destroyed in 1712 by the Zurichers and Bernese. A quarter of a league ($\frac{3}{4}$ of a mile) from the town are the Baths of Baden, lining both banks of the Limmat. Those called the Great Baths are on the left bank, and the Little Baths are on the right bank of the river. The former are visited by the more opulent classes of all countries, while the Little Baths are chiefly frequented by operatives and peasants. A new bridge has been lately constructed, facilitating the communication between the two banks. Both the Large and Little Baths are private peoperty. At the former there are seven hotels:—The Stadthof, the Hinterhof, the Crow, the Ox, the Tun, the Bear, and the Flower; all of them containing baths varying in number and quality. The Little Baths have only four hotels containing baths. There are also free public baths (Freibäder) on both banks, and charitable institutions (verpflegungs-anstalten) for the use of the sick. The meadow (die Matte), the stone (der Stein), the farm (das Bauerngut), and the hermitage are pleasant walks; occasional balls, dramatic representations, and other amusements add to the attractions of the place.

Brougg (Bruck) a small town of about 1,200 inhabitants, situated on the Aar, on the high roads to Zurzach and Bâle 3½ l. (10½ m.) from Aarau. Its principal inns are the Horse and the Maison Rouge. The river is at this place reduced to a narrow channel by high rocks rising on both banks, and supporting a bridge 65 ft. in length. The tower called the Black Tower, which stands on ...he entrance of the bridge, is considered by many persons as a Roman work, but it is of later origin, and has been probably built with masonry obtained from the remains of the ancient Vindonissa. This little town has often suffered from fires, which have probably given a black colouring to its walls. An antique head, of excellent workmanship, placed in the middle of the wall, about the middle of the tower, is considered by some to be

the head of Nero, and by others as that of Tiberius. On a hill near the town, called now the Botzberg and anciently Vocatius, a very fine view is obtained.

Habsburg, (the Castle of) the cradle of the Imperial dynasty now reigning in Austria, is at present the property of the Canton. Its only existing remains consist of a few mouldering walls, covered with moss, from which the eye passes with pleasure to feast on the fine country spread at the foot of the mountain, presenting some rich and diversified scenery. The back-ground of the picture is formed by a grand chain of mountains, whose glistening snowy summits and colossal glaciers command all the other ridges to the southward. Turning to the N. and at the foot of the mountain of Habsburg, vulgarily called Wulpesburg or Wulpisburg, you descend to the high road from Aarau to Brugg.

Königsfelden: now cantonal property, and consisting of a hospital and lunatic asylum. It was here that on the 1st of May, 1308, the Emperor Albert I. was assassinated by his nephew John, Duke of Suabia, and his fellow conspirators. Two years later, a convent of Minims and another of Franciscan nuns, of the Order of St. Clara, were founded here. Queen Agnes, the daughter of the murdered emperor, took the veil at this very place. Her cell is still shown there, and the altar of the church now stands on the exact spot where the emperor was assassinated. The stained glass windows in the choir are beautiful productions of mediæval art. One of the curiosities of the place consists in the crypt, serving as a burial place for various princes; and some remains of Roman architecture claim the attention of the antiquary at this place

Lenzburg: Principal inns, the Loew and the Krone. This pretty town con tains about 2,000 inhabitants, and situated at the foot of a hill crowned l a castle still inhabited, and in a go state of repair. This castle was ancien the abode of the Counts of Lenzburg, and affords a splendid and a very extensive view. The town contains a large and handsome town-house, several well-built private houses, cotton stuff manufactories, and a very superior bleaching establishment, belonging formerly to M. Hunerwadel. Lenzburg possesses besides some well-organised schools, a choral institution. directed for some time by M. M. T. Pfeiffer, the founder of a method of teaching singing on the Pestalozzian system. At Lenzburg is also held the monthly meeting of all the medical men of this Canton. The Staufberg; close to the town, offers some charming views.

Rheinfelden and Lauffenburg, in the Frickthal, were formerly two forest towns. The former contains 1,500, and the latter 800 inhabitants. They stand on the banks of the Rhine 7 l. (21 m) from Aarau. They are of some note in a historical point of view, but they offer no special attraction to the traveller in the present day. The most interesting object in the district is the fall or rapid in the Rhine, near the bridge of Lauffenburg, to which we may add the ruins of the Castle of Habsburg, on a hill near the same town. Under the bridge of Rheinfelden there is a dangerous whirlpool called the Höllenharken (or hooks of hell). The principal inns at Rheinfelden are the Schiff and the Drei Könige, and at Lauffenburg, the Schinznach (the baths of), $3\frac{1}{4}$ l. from Brugg, and $2\frac{3}{4}$ l. ($7\frac{1}{2}$ m.) from Aarau, are among the most noted in Switzerland. The interior arrangements of the establishment have long been noted for their excellence, and have had a large share in contributing to the popularity of these baths, which are frequented in the summer by a large number of foreigners, and of Swiss of different class and profession. It was at this place that was founded in 1760, the Helvetic Society, which was afterwards transferred to Olten, and thence to Zofingen.

Wildegg (the Château of), to the east of Aarau, 2 l. (6 m.), is private property, lately in the hands of a Colonel Effinger. It is situated at the foot of a small mountain, on the road from Brugg to Zurzach. The celebrated calico print manufactory of M. M. Laue and Co., situated at the foot of this hill, occupies a very picturesque position. A path ascending this elevation, leads eastward to the château of Brounegg, once the property of Colonel Hünerwadel, of Lenzburg, offering a superb view over some of the finest districts of Switzerland. Continuing to the N. along the same ridge, you arrive in $\frac{3}{4}$ l. ($2\frac{1}{4}$ m.) at the Castle of Habsburg. Windisch, on a height commanding the confluence of the Reuss, the Limmat, and the Aar. This little village stands near the site of the famous Vindonissa, a Roman city, situated on the borders of Helvetia, and forming for 500 years, a bulwark against the tribes of Germany. From the presbytery your eye takes in the whole vast area once covered by this flourishing city, an area now containing the villages of Fahrwïndisch, of Gebistorf, of Königsfelden, and of Altenburg, and the town of Brugg. Roman antiquities are frequently found at this place, and at a spot named Berlisgruben occur the ruins of an amphitheatre. The first bishop in Helvetia established the see of Vindonissa, in the 6th century; but, at the time of the destruction of that city, in 595, this see was transferred to Constance by Childebert II., King of Austrasia. Zofingen, is a pretty little town of 1,700 inhabitants, on the high road to Lucerne, and distant $4\frac{1}{2}$ l. ($13\frac{1}{2}$ m.) from Aarau. Its principal inns are the Rössli and the Ochs. The library of this town is deserving of attention, containing a great number of valuable classical works and MSS., among others the correspondence of several Swiss reformers. It possesses also a collection of medals and of natural history, as well as a work called the Malerbuch (or painter's book). This is a kind of album founded and continued by a society of Swiss artists, which like the Helvetic Society, meets every year in this town

Besides these curiosities, Zofingen has an excellent secondary school, and manufactories of silk, of cotton velvet, of linen, stuff, and of cotton. The town-house deserves to be noticed, and also the shooting ground (Schützen haus), which ought to be a special attraction to the fire-eating lawyers of the Devil's Own Volunteers.

Zurzach is a borough of about 800 inhabitants, celebrated for its two annual fairs, which are admitted to be the most frequented in Switzerland. The spring-fair begins on the Saturday preceding Pentecost; and the autumn fair on the Saturday preceding the festival of Saint Verena. Both fairs last about a fortnight. Zurzach contains two churches, one for the Protestants and the other for the Catholics; in the latter is the tomb of Saint Verena, whom tradition reports to have accompanied the Theban legion. Zurzach has, moreover, a chapter of canons and a secondary school, lately established. At the time of the fair the canons have been wont to practise hospitality, and the custom has been followed by many private persons. The canons hold a table d'hôte, and house strangers during those seasons when the town is frequented by a multitude of strangers. The principal inns here are the Sword and the Wheel. The distance from Zurzach to Schaffhausen is 6½ l. (19½ m.), and to Aarau 7¼ l. (21¾ m).

ROUTES FROM AARAU.

To Aarberg, by Berne (Nos. 6 and 53), or by Solothurn (Nos. 16 and 216).

ROUTE 1.
AARBURG, 3 l. (9 m.)

	Leagues.	Miles.
Wöschnau	¼	¾
Schönenwerth	¼	1½
Gretsenbach	¼	¾
Däniken	¼	¾
Stärkirch	¼	1½
Olten (2¼ L)	¼	1½
Aarburg	¾	2¼
	3	9

Aigle, by Berne (Nos. 6 and 54).

Altdorf, by Lucerne (Nos. 11, 12, or 13, and 147).

Altstaetten, by Zurich (Nos. 18 and 196) and Gallen (No. 180).

Appenzell, by Zurich (Nos. 18 and 28).

Art, by Zug (Nos. 17 and 281).

ROUTE 2.
BADEN, 5 l. (15 m.)

	Leagues.	Miles.
Buch	¼	¾
Huntzenschwyl	¾	2¼
Lenzburg (2 L)	1	3
Ottmarsingen	½	1½
Wollenschwyl	¾	2¼
Mellingen	½	¾
Baden	1¼	4½
	5	15

ROUTE 3.
BÂLE, 10 l. (30 m.)

	Leagues.	Miles.
Olten (No. 1)	2¼	6¾
Trimpach	½	1½
Hauenstein	¾	2¼
Läufelfingen	½	1½
Buckten	¼	¾
Rümlingen	½	1½
Diepflingen	½	1¼
Durnen	¼	¾
Sissach	¼	¾
Lausen	¾	2¼
Liestahl	½	1½
Rothaus	1¾	5¼
Bâle	1¼	3¾
	10	30

ROUTE 4.
BÂLE, by the Frickthal, 9 l. (27 m.)

	Leagues.	Miles.
Kuttingen	¾	2¼
Asp	¾	2¼
Deutschburen	¼	¾
Herznach	¼	¾
Uecken	¼	¾
Frick	½	1½
Eicken	½	1½
Stein, 3¾ L (10¾ m.)	½	1½
Mumpf	¼	¾
Möhlin	1	3
Rheinfelden	1	3
Augst	1¼	3¾
Bâle	1¼	5¼
	9	27

ROUTE 5.

BÂLE, by the Schaffmatt, a horse-path and footpath, 8½ L (25½ m.)

	Leagues.	Miles.
Erlisbach	¾	2¼
The Schafmatt to the summit, with a very fine view	1	3
Oltingen....................................	½	1½
Weisecke	⅓	1
Teguau	¼	¾
Sissach	1¼	3¾
Bâle (see No. 3)	4¼	12¾
	8½	25½

Bellinzona, by Lucerne (Nos. 11, 12, or 13, and No. 147), and Altdorf (No. 229).

ROUTE 6.

BERNE, 19½ L. (58½ m.)

	Leagues.	Miles.
Aarburg (No. 1)	3	9
Morgenthal	2	6
By Entfelden	¾	2¼
Köllken..................................	½	1½
Saffenwyl	¾	2¼
Rothrist	1¼	3¾
Morgenthal	1¾	5¼
Wynau	½	1½
Kalte-Herberge	½	1½
Butzberg	1	3
Herzogenbuchsee..................	1	3
Oberönz................................	¼	¾
Seeberg	½	1½
Höchstetten	½	1½
St. Nicholas	⅓	1
Oeschberg............................	¼	¾
Kirchberg, 10¾ l. (30¾ m.) ...	1	3
Hindelbank	1	3
Sand, 12¾ l. (37¾ m.)............	1	3
Papeterie	1	3
Berne	¾	2¼
	19½	58½

Bex, by Berne (Nos. 6 and 58).

Bienne, by Solothurn (Nos. 16 and 218)

ROUTE 7

BRUGG, 3½ L. (10½ m.)

	Leagues.	Miles.
Rohr	½	1½
Rupperschwyl	¾	2¼
Wildegg.................................	¾	2¼
Holderbank	¼	¾
Schinzuach (Baths)	½	1½
Brugg....................................	¾	2¼
	3½	10½

Bulle, by Berne (Nos. 6 and 54).

ROUTE 8.

BURGDORF, 11¼ L (35¼ m.)

	Leagues.	Miles.
Kirchberg (No. 6)	10¼	32¼
Burgdorf	1	3
	11¼	35¼

Chamouny, by Solothurn (Nos. 16 and 223), Lausanne (No. 96), and Geneva (No. 95), or by Berne (Nos. 6 and 63), Lausanne (No. 96), and Geneva (No. 95.)

Chaux de Fonds, by Solothurn (Nos. 16 and 220), or by Berne (Nos. 6 and 70), and Neuchâtel (No 169).

Chiavenna, by Zurich (Nos 18 and 142), and Coire (Nos. 121 and 122, or 123).

Coire, by Zurich (Nos. 18 and 142).

Einsiedeln (Nos. 18 and 227, or 300).

Engelberg, by Lucerne (Nos. 11 and 12, or 13, and 153).

Frauenfeld, by Zurich (Nos. 18 and 245).

Fribourg, by Berne (Nos. 6 and 54).

Gais, by Zurich (Nos. 18 and 196), and Saint Gallen (No. 186).

Geneva, by Solothurn (Nos. 16 and 223), and Lausanne (No. 96), or by Berne (Nos. 6 and 63), and Lausanne (No. 96).

Glaris, by Zurich (Nos. 18 and 116).

Herisau, by Zurich (Nos. 18 and 301).

ROUTE 9.

HOFWYL, 13¼ L (39¾ m.)

	Leagues.	Miles.
Sand (No. 6)...........................	12¾	38¼
Hofwyl	½	1½
	13¼	39¾

ROUTE 10.

LAUFFENBURG, 5¾ L (17¼ m.)

	Leagues.	Miles.
Stein (No. 4)...........................	3¾	11¼
Lauffenburg	2	6
	5¾	17¼

Lausanne, by Berne (Nos. 6 and 63), or by Solothurn (Nos. 16 and 223).

Locarno, by Lucerne (Nos. 11 and 12, or 13 and 147) Altdorf (No. 229), and Bellinzona (No. 232).

Locle, by Solothurn (No. 224).

Or by Berne (Nos. 6 and 70), and Neuchâtel (No. 175).

Loeïch the baths of, by Berne (Nos. 6 and 65) or by Solothurn (Nos. 16 and 221), and Sion (No. 266).

ROUTE 11.
LUCERNE 13 l. (39 m.)

	Leagues.	Miles.
Aarburg (see No. 1)	3	9
Zofingen	1	3
Reiden	1¼	3¾
Dagmersellen	¾	2¼
Saint-Erhard	1¼	3¾
Sursee	1¼	3¾
Oberkirch	¾	2¼
Nottiwyl	½	1½
Neukirch	1¼	3¾
Emmenbrücke	1¼	3¾
Lucerne	¾	2¼
	13	39

ROUTE 12.
LUCERNE by Münster, 9¾ l. (29¼ m.)

	Leagues.	Miles.
Suhr	¾	2¼
Gränichen	½	1½
Kulm	1	3
Reinach	1¼	4½
Münster	1½	4½
Neudorf	¾	2¼
Hildisried	1	3
Rothenburg	1¾	5¼
Lucerne	1	3
	9¾	29¼

ROUTE 13.
LUCERNE by Schöftland, 10½ l. (31½ m.)

	Leagues.	Miles.
Suhr	¾	2¼
Entfelden	½	1½
Schöftland	1½	3½
Moosleerau	1¼	3½
Triengen	½	1½
Büren	½	1½
Sursee	1	3
Lucerne (see No. 11)		
	5¾	17¼

Lugano, by Lucerne (Nos. 11, 12, 13, and 147) Altdorf (No. 229), and Bellinzona (No. 233).

Mendrisio, by Lucerne and Altdorf (Nos. as above), and Bellinzona (No. 235).

Morat, by Solothurn (Nos. 16 and 221.

Morges, by Solothurn (Nos. 16 and 223).

Moudon, by Solothurn (Nos. 16 and 225). The three latter towns may also be reached through Berne.

Neuchâtel, by Solothurn (Nos. 16 and 178), or by Berne (Nos. and 70)

Orbe, by Solothurn (Nos. 16 and 178), and Neuchâtel, (No. 92), or by Berne (Nos. 6 and 71).

Fayerne, by Solothurn (Nos. 16 and 223), or by Berne (Nos. 6 and 77),

Pfeffers (Baths). by Zurich (Nos. 18 and 304).
Righi (Mount), by Zug (Nos. 17 and 294).
Saint-Gallen, by Zurich (No. 18 and 196.)

ROUTE 14.
SCHAFFHAUSEN, 13¼ l. (40¼ m.)

	Leagues.	Miles.
Brugg (see No. 7)	3½	10½
Rein	½	1½
Stilli (a creek of the Aar)	½	¾
Wurelingen	¾	2¼
Tägerfelden	1	3
Zurzach (creek on the Aar, 7½ 22 m. from Aarau)	1	3
Reinheim	½	1½
Dangstetten	½	1½
Berchtelbohl	½	1½
Erzingen	2¼	6¾
Neuhaus	¾	2¼
Schaffhausen	2¼	6¾
	13¼	40¼

Schwytz, by Lucerne (Nos. 11 and 12, or 13, and 161).

ROUTE 15.
SEMPACH, 7¼ l. (21½ m.)

	Leagues.	Miles.
Sursee (No. 13)	5¼	17¼
Eich	1	3
Sempach	½	1½
	7¼	21½

Sion, by Berne (Nos. 6 and 73, or 74), or by Solothurn (Nos. 16 and 227).

ROUTE 16.
SOLOTHURN, 9¼ l. (27½ m.)

	Leagues.	Miles.
Olten (No. 1)	2¼	6¾
Wangen	½	1½
Hägendorf	¾	2¼
Egerkingen	¾	2¼
Oberbuchsiten	½	1½
Oensingen	¾	2¼
Dürremuhle	¾	2¼
Wietlisbach	1	3
Attiswyl	½	1½
Neuhaus	½	1½
Solothurn	1¼	3¾
	9¼	27½

Stanz (see Unterwalden).

Thun, by Berne (Nos. 6 and 55).

Trogen, by Zurich (Nos. 18 and 196), and to Saint Gallen (No. 193).

Unterwalden, by Lucerne (Nos. 11, 12, 13 and 153).

Vevay, by Berne (Nos. 6 and 54), or by Solothurn (Nos. 16 and 227).

Winterthur, by Zurich (No. 18 and 196.)

Yverdun, by Solothurn (Nos. 16 and 228), or by Berne (Nos. 7 and 77).

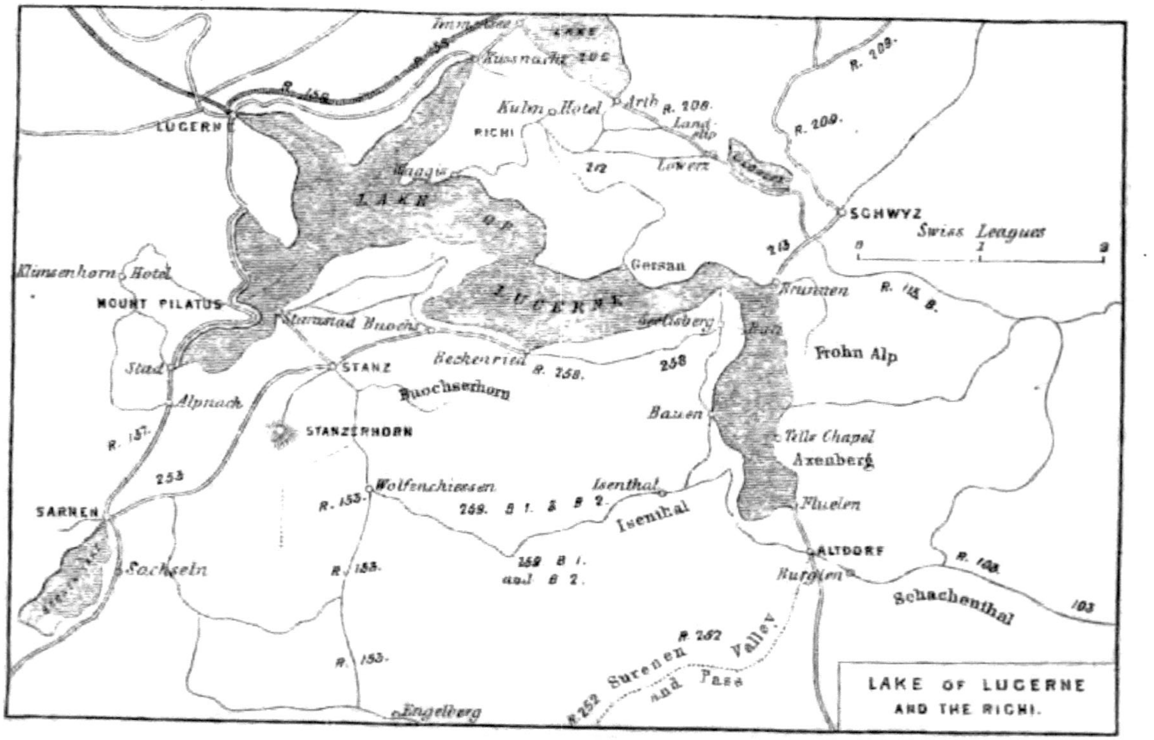

LAKE OF LUCERNE AND THE RICHI.
LUCERN
MOUNT PILATUS
Klunsenhorn Hotel
Stad
Alpnach
R. 157.
253
SARNEN
Sachseln
STANZ
STANZERHORN
Buochserhorn
Stanstad Buochs
Beckenried R. 258.
Wolfenchiessen
R. 153.
R. 153.
R. 153.
Engelberg
R. 252 Surenen Valley and Pass
R. 252
258. B 1. & B 2.
159 B 1. and B 2.
Isenthal
Isenthal
Bauen
Telle Chapel
Axenberg
Fluelen
ALTDORF
Rurglen
Schachenthal
103
R. 102.
R. 114 B.
Frohn Alp
Krumten
Seelisberg
258
Gersan
LUCERNE
LAKE
Q. P.
Maggis
Kulm Hotel
RICHI
Arth R. 208.
Landstip
212
Lowerz
Lowerz
213
SCHWYZ
Swiss Leagues
0   1   2   3
Kussnacht R. 208
Immensee
LAKE
R. 156
R. 208.
R. 209.
R. 209.

ROUTE 17.

Zug, 10½ l. (31½ m.)

	Leagues.	Miles.
Lenzburg (No. 2)	2	6
Hendschiken	¾	2¼
Vilmergen	1	3
Bülisacker	½	1½
Boswyl	¾	2¼
Wyli	¾	2¼
Muri	½	1½
Langdorf	¼	¾
Benzschwyl	½	
Wollischwyl	½	1½
Rustenschwyl	½	
Au	½	1½
Sinsbrucke	½	1½
St. Wolfgang	½	1½
Cham	½	1½
Zug	1	3
	10½	31½

ROUTE 18.

Zurich, 9 L. (27 m.)

	Leagues.	Miles.
Baden (No. 2)	5	15
Dietikon	2	6
Schleren	¾	2¼
Altstätten	½	1½
Zurich	¾	2¼
	9	27

Zurzach (No. 14).
Strasburg, Paris, Frankfort, and the Rhine district through Bâle by rail.

SECOND MAIN ROUTE B.

The second of the usual grand routes by which the English traveller approaches the finest scenery of the High Alps from Bâle is the line from Olten to Lucerne.

The first part of this main route takes him to the Canton of Aargau, from which he passes to that of Lucerne, which we have now to consider. The railway, its stations, distances, and fares from Olten to Lucerne, will be found most correctly in *Bradshaw's Continental Guide*.

If the traveller proceeds by rail from Bâle to Lucerne let him remember that he will have to change carriages at the great central junction of Olten. Fare from Bâle to Lucerne, 1st class, 9*fr.* 85*c.*; 2nd class, 6*fr.* 95*c.*; 3rd class, 5*fr.* There are five trains per day. In the morning a swift *1st and 2nd class train in 3¼ hours. Ordinary trains, 4¼ to 4½ hours.*

After passing Zofingen (see Canton Aargau) the traveller soon enters the

CANTON OF LUCERNE.

This canton borders to the N. on that of Aargau; to the E. on the same and on the cantons of Zug and Schwyz; to the S.E. it touches Unterwalden; to the S. its frontiers are formed by the Bernese Oberland; and to the W. it is limited by the Bernese Lowlands.

AREA, SOIL, AND CLIMATE.—The area of this Canton covers 72½ Swiss square leagues (1,501 square kilometres). It contains few plains, but many cultivated hills and fine valleys, generally watered by copious streams. The south-east part of the Canton, and more particularly the district known as the Entlibuch, includes several mountains of considerable elevation, but generally clothed with fine pastures. The climate is tolerably moderate in the Canton of Lucerne, and is suitable to most kinds of crops.

MOUNTAINS. — None of the colossal mountains whose summits reach the regions of eternal snows, are found within the limits of this Canton. The highest points are the Pilatus, on the frontier of Unterwalden, 6,565 feet high, and the Napf, on the frontiers of Berne.

LAKES, RIVERS, AND RIVULETS.— (*a*) Lakes: The Lake of Lucerne, or of the four cantons (in German, Vierwaldstätter see), has a length of 9 l. (27 m.) from Lucerne to Fluelen; its greatest breadth from Kussnacht to Alpnach is 5 l. (15 m.), but in no other part exceeds 1 l. (3 m.) Its depth is very considerable (800 feet near its head). Its waters bathe the shores of four cantons—1, Lucerne; 2, Uri; 3, Schwyz; 4, Unterwalden. It is situated almost in the centre of Switzerland, fed principally by the Reuss from St. Gothard, which, issuing from it at the town of Lucerne, pours its rapid, dark blue waters into the Aar. This lake is well stocked with excellent fish. Its banks have been the seat of the great achieve ments in the early heroic age of Swiss history, and were the cradle of Tell and the men of Rütli, sung by Schiller, and enshrined in the hearts of their country-men. Thus, historically, this district is the most interesting in Switzerland.

2. The Lake of Sempach, also called Lake of Sursee, 3 l. (9 m.) north-west of Lucerne. Its length is 3 l., its breadth only ½ l.; it is extremely well supplied with fish, yielding in particular a special kind of fish called balles, or aalbock (salmo lavaretus), besides very large crabs. It discharges its waters into the Suhr.

3. The Lake of Baldegg, also known as the Lake of Heidegg; its length is only ½ l., and its width ¼ l. It is also very well stocked with fish, and communicates with the Lake of Hallwyl, in Aargau, by means of the Aa. Several other little lakes un-deserving of attention occur in this canton.

(b) Rivers: 1. The Reuss is formed of three branches, the first issuing from the lake of Luzendro, situated on the Saint Gothard; the second from that of Ober-alp; and the third from the foot of the Furcka. These branches unite in the val-ley of Urseren, and their united waters roll through the great valley of Uri to fall into the lake of Lucerne, on issuing from which, the Reuss receives ½ l. (1½ m.) below Lucerne, the Wald-Emmen, and a little further the Lorez. Between Honau and Dietwyl the Reuss passes into the Canton of Zug.

2. The Little or Wald-Emmen: It takes its source in the Canton of Unter-walden; it is gradually swollen by the accession of a great number of torrents and rivulets, such as the Kragenbach, the Weiss Emmen, the Entle, the Fontane, the Rumlig, &c.; it waters the whole Entlibuch, and falls ultimately into the Reuss.

3. The Entli: This impetuous torrent is formed by the confluence of several streams. It gives its name to the Entli-buch, and falls near a village so called, *into the Wald-Emmen.*

4. The Suhr, formed by waters dis-charged from the lake of Sursee, only flows through a small portion of the Can-ton of Lucerne, which it leaves below Triengen, passing into the Canton of Aargau.

5. The Wigger, takes its source in a small lake between Menznau and Wolf-hausen, it is subsequently increased by the accession of the Lutheren and many other rivulets, and also leaves the terri-tory of Lucerne below Adelboden, where it passes into the Canton of Aargau. The Wigger and the Suhr are strictly speak-ing nothing more than large streams.

(c) Rivulets: These are very numerous in this Canton, but the principal have just been mentioned.

AGRICULTURAL AND INDUSTRIAL PRO-DUCTIONS.—This Canton is very rich in horned cattle, sheep, goats, and pigs; fish, poultry, and game abound, includ-ing among the latter, the hare, marten, fox, wood cock, grouse, the pheasant, the white and red partridge, &c. The soil is generally fertile in the Canton of Lucerne, and its produce exceeds the consumption, comprising all kinds of cereals, forage, hemp, flax, potatoes, &c. It yields excellent fruit and a little wine. Some districts are covered with fine forests, and several springs of mineral water have been found in the Canton. The mineral productions are not very valuable, including only some limestone quarries, and building stone of different descriptions. Manufacturing industry has not made much way in this Canton, and consists only in the preparation of hemp, flax, and cotton, and the manu-facture of goods from these materials.

THERMAL WATERS. BATHS. — The baths of Knutwyl are the most frequented; after which may be named those of Augs-tholz, Ybenmoos, Russwyl, Luthern, and Salwyden.

POPULATION AND RELIGION.—This Can-ton contains 130,000 inhabitants, mostly of the Catholic religion.

ABBEYS AND CONVENTS.—Chapter of canons at Lucerne and Beromunster ; the Cistercian abbey of Saint Urban, the convents of Cordeliers at Lucerne and Wertenstein ; those of Capuchins at Lucerne, at Sursee, and Schupfen. There are also convents of Cistercian nuns at Rothansen and Eschenbach, and a convent of Sisters of St. Ann at Steinbruch. The town of Lucerne possesses a seminary.

ESTABLISHMENTS OF PUBLIC EDUCATION ; SCIENTIFIC, AND CHARITABLE INSTITUTIONS.—Much attention has been bestowed on the promotion of elementary education in this Canton. The town of Lucerne contains several institutions for a superior class of instruction.

The town library at Lucerne and that of St. Urban deserve notice. Other institutions are noticed under the head of the town of Lucerne.

SURVEY OF THE CANTON OF LUCERNE.

The Emmenthal is a valley 8 l. long, watered by the Emmen, and renowned for its cheese. At the top the character is Alpine, but lower down the scenery is softer and richer. It yields crops of flax and a good breed of horses. Its population is hearty, vigorous, and intelligent ; noted as good wrestlers and in all gymnastic sports. The women have a handsome costume. It has immense magazines of cheese. The principal place in the valley is Langnau, in the Canton of Berne, 13 l. (6 fr. 70 c. posting) ; from Lucerne.

Entlibuch : This valley is noted for its inhabitants, whose lively sallies, love of old customs, and gymnastic sports, have made them popular. The village of Entlibuch 2,252 feet above the sea, has two inns (Hotel du Port, Trois Rois). Distance from Lucerne, 6¼ l. in 3¾ hours. Fares by post, 3 fr. 20 c.

WRESTLING FETES.—At Enetegg, on the 29th June, contest between wrestlers of Romoosen and Dopfischwand and the men of Hasli. Second Sunday in August, on the Sörenberg between those of Brienz, Obwalden, and Entlibuch. The same day on the Scheidegg between those of Hasli and of Schupfheim. First Sunday in September at Entlibuch, 29th September at Wyttenbach, and Sunday after at Schüpferberg.

TOWN OF LUCERNE.

HOTELS.—Lucerne, kept by M. Chevrier Rufenacht, opened on the 1st January, 1866 ; fine situation. Beau Rivage, a newly established hotel, fitted up with comfort. Swan, kept by H. Hæfil ; first-rate hotel for families and single gentlemen ; highly recommended. Hotel d'Angleterre, Mr. Reber, proprietor ; an admirably conducted establishment ; well recommended. Hotel des Balances, kept by Mr. G. Brindschadler ; recommended to English travellers. Schweizerhof—view from its windows superb : this is a first-rate house, one of the best in Switzerland. Rigi, G. Regli, proprietor ; a very good hotel ; moderate charges. Hotel et Pension de Belle Vue ; new and well situated hotel, with a large garden, recommended to families. Grand Hotel National, opened on the 15th of June ; new hotel, one of the largest and finest in Switzerland, 50 balconies overlooking the Lake of the Four Cantons ; comfort combined with moderate charges ; recommended. Adler ; Hirsch ; Post ; Kreuz.

PENSIONS.—Kaufmann, Seeburg, Pietzker, Sonnenburg, Aeschmann.

RESTAURANTS and CAFES.—Café du Lac, at the landing place ; Café du Theatre, near the Railway station ; Café Regazzoni at the bridge over the Reuss ; Café des Alpes.

BATHS.—The improved Turkish Baths, near the Schweizerhof hotel, are conducted by Dr. Bruu, resident physician. Hot at Lindenhof ; douches and restaurants. At Lowengarten Baths of the Lake, above the church, 30 cents.

Tivoli and Seeburg. On the river a new establishment at Nöllithor and St Karli. Railroads, same station, both lines.

1. Central Swiss: Berne, Geneva, and Bâle; 2. North East line: Zurich, Constance, Bavaria, and Wurtemburg, 4 to 5 trains per day.

FARES.	1st class.		2nd class.		3rd class.	
	fr.	c.	fr.	c.	fr.	c.
Lucerne to Antwerp exp..	97	95...	80	30...		...
Baden Baden (for 10 days)..	2×	70...	20			...
Bâle	9	85...	6	95...	5	...
Berlin	181	80...	91	5...		...
Berne	12	5...	8	50...	6	10
Brussels	96	75...	79	10...		...
Coire	22	6'...	15	90...		...
Cologne	68	55...	50	80...		...
Geneva	28	5...	19	85...	14	35
Heidelberg	82	75...	22	80...	15	33
Lausanne	22	30...	15	70...	11	25
London	152	40...	134	75...		...
Munich	39	50...	27	60...		...
Paris	70	5...	52	40...		...
Strasbourg	27	35...	20	40...		...
Thun	15	2'...	10	70...		...
Vevey	24	30...	17	10...	12	25
Zurich	6	50...	4	55...	3	25

RATES OF POSTING.

	Time. Hours.		Fare inside. fr.	c.
Lucerne to Airolo	23¼	......	17	10
Andermatt	17¼	......	11	10
Bellinzona	35¼	......	27	20
Brienz	11¾	......	7	60
Hergyswyl (Mount Pilatus)	1	......	...	80
Lugano	...	......	31	40
Milan	56	......	41	80
Meiringen	14¾	......	9	10
Einsiedeln	12	......	7	50
Sarnen	5¼	......	2	30
Schwyz	7	......	3	70
Stanz	2	......	1	55

Lucerne, with a population of 11,500 Catholics, stands on the lake of the same name at the point where the Reuss issues from its crystal basin. It is therefore the key to the forest cantons, the ancient stronghold of Swiss freedom and the kernel of the republic. The position of the town is particularly beautiful, and few places in Switzerland have such, and so many interesting excursions in their neighbourhood. Accordingly, Lucerne is a favourite centre and summer halting place for tourists.

It is divided into two unequal parts by the rapid Reuss, crossed by two covered bridges for pedestrians and an open bridge for carriages. It is the fourth Swiss city in size, and the residence of the Papal Nuncio.

From the quay, by the Schweizerhof, the eye takes in to the left the Righi and the Schilt;. in front, farther off, the Faulen, Ross stock, and Axen, above the chapel of Tell; still further, the Tödt (distance, 33 miles), only visible in fine weather. Nearer, rising above the lake, are the Seelisberg; behind it, the Oberhauen; still nearer, the Buochserhorn and Bürgenstock. In the distance, to the right, rise the snowy summits above the valley of Engelberg, especially the Sättelistock. the Righidal stock, and the Wallen stöcke. Then, nearer to the right, the half-circle is completed by the Stanzerhorn, the mountains of Kerns and Melchthal, and Pilatus, with its two hotels.

Among the public buildings must be noticed the Cathedral Church of St. Leger (or Leodagarius), a French saint of Autun in Merovingian times, rebuilt in 1633 after a fire, except its two towers, one of which is 250 feet high; and has the date 1406. The altar-piece of the high altar, Christ on the Mount of Olives, is by Lanfranc. Other objects of interest are the carved stalls, stained glass, richly gilt altars, wood relief, sculpture of "the death of Mary," of the 16th century, repaired in 1861 by Muller de Wyl, and the great organ, the finest in Switzerland. It was repaired in 1862 by Haas de Laufenburg, has 90 stops, and is so well adapted to the church that the voices and tones of the chaunt seem to descend like an anthem of angels from on high. Every evening at 6 p.m. there is a concert with the organ; the entrance, 1fr. The church is surrounded by a campo santo in the Italian style. The view of the lake from the church is delightful.

Other churches are that of St. Peter, or of the Franciscans of the 13th century;

the former Jesuit college; the Jesuits' Church, with a fine altar-piece; the town house (stadthaus); the arsenal, containing flags, swords, morgensterns, and other weapons of Burgundy, Suabia, &c.; eight horns, given to the Lucerners by Charlemagne; and the cuirasse of Leopold II., Duke of Austria, killed at Sempach in 1386. Fee, ½fr. to 1fr.

The Wasserthurm is said to have been used as a lighthouse to guide boatmen on the lake, which gave the name to the town (lucerna, a lamp). Lucerne has a hospital, orphanage, theatre, and casino.

The Museum, near the Post-office, contains the cantonal library of 60,000 volumes (many valuable MSS., &c., bearing on local history) and the Cabinet of Natural History (minerals from St. Gothard, good). Not far off is the town library of 10,000 books, being founded by the historian, Felix de Balthazar, with curious ancient national plays used in Lent; engravings by Frey; the Chronicle of Diebold Schilling, on parchment, adorned with drawings. The archives of the city, dating from the 12th century, comprise the armorial seal of Charles the Bold, taken at the Battle of Granson. The Cabinet of Medals has 7,000 pieces, mostly Papal coins.

A curious bas-relief, by General Pfyffer, has long been exhibited at Lucerne, showing the forest and neighbouring cantons to the extent of 180 square Swiss leagues, and executed with considerable skill on a plan 22½ feet long and 12 feet wide.

Lucerne has a Lyceum and Gymnase with excellent professors of classics, history, mathematics, pilosophy, theology and law. It has a public school of design, an academy of music and several elementary schools. In the Faubourg of Weggis is the great panorama of the Righi, painted by Henry Keller, of Zurich, it is 24 feet in length. Other panoramas of M. Meyer, giving the morning on Righi, the evening on Pilatus (entrance 1 *fr.*) Staufer's museum of Alpine animals (entrance 1 *fr.*) can be also seen in this part of the town.

Lucerne possesses a number of literary, artistic, and charitable institutions, especially the Literary Society, with a fine Library, that of Artists, that of Music, &c. The great hospital, that of Incurables, and of the Prebends; the Orphanage in the Faubourg St. Jacques, a Savings' Bank, the establishment for poor workmen, that of work for the poor, providing occupation for every person in the town or country.

CURIOSITIES.—Lucerne has been noted for its three covered bridges — 1. The Bridge of Hof, (removed 1852) joining the town and the Cathedral, and passing over a corner of the lake. Its length was 1,380 feet, being the longest in Switzerland. It had 238 pictures of subjects from the Bible, and of very inferior execution. 2. The Chapel Bridge (Kapellenbrücke) is 1,000 feet long, crossing the Reuss at the spot where it issues from the lake. It is ornamented by 144 pictures representing the heroic events of Swiss history, and scenes from the lives of patrons of the city, St. Maurice and St. Leger. 3. The Mühlen or Sprener Bridge also across the Reuss is 300 feet long, and has thirty-six paintings copied by Meglinger from the "Dance of Death," at Bâle.

Another and certainly the greatest lion at Lucerne, is the Monument of Swiss fidelity, commemorating the Swiss guard who fell in defence of Louis XVI. on the 10th August, 1792. It is in the garden of General Pfyffer, at the foot of the Wesemlin; its idea was conceived by Colonel Pfyffer, all Switzerland subscribed to the work, and its execution was entrusted to the great Thorwaldsen, who conceived the design and made the model from which the artist, Lucas Ahorn, of Constance, sculptured the present monument out of a great block of granite. The monument consists of a colossal lion couchant, his side pierced by a spear, spreading his paw out to defend a shield with the fleur de lys. It is 28½ feet long, 18 feet high, and the grotto is 44 feet wide. It has the inscription "Helvetiorum fidei ac virtuti," and underneath the name of the Swiss officers who fell August 10th, 1792. By the side is a Chapel with the inscription "Invictis pax," in which a Requiem Mass is every year said, August 10th.

EXCURSIONS AND VIEWS NEAR LUCERNE. — Allenwinden and Gutsch, a country house and summer châlet, with a fine view to the east of the town. 2. To the Wesemlin near the Capuchin Convent. 3. Pretty walks to Meggenheim the chapel of St. Charles, the Mohrenthal, the villages of Kriens, of Horw and of Winkel $\frac{3}{4}$ l. (2$\frac{1}{4}$ m.) By Adligenschwyl and Udligenschwyl to the Cross of St. Michael, called the little Righi 2,520 feet 3 l. (9 m.) Thence return in half an hour to Roth, and back to Lucerne by rail at Ebikon Station. Near Lucerne the traveller who has a little leisure will enjoy gentle strolls to the neighbouring hills of Ober, Wartenflue de Homberg, Sonnenberg, Uttenberg, Blattenberg, and especially Dietschenberg, a short league from the town. All these points offer magnificent views. Between the Sonnenberg and the Blattenberg you see the Rengloch, a canal cut in the rock, by which the waters of the upper stream of the Kriens are drained into the Emmen. Opposite Sonnenberg in a S. direction is the Schattenberg, and on its slope Schauensee Castle, built in 1586, with a splendid view $\frac{3}{4}$ l. (2$\frac{1}{4}$ m.) from Lucerne. Herrgottswaid is a pilgrimage on the slope of Pilatus. By Scharmoos 1$\frac{1}{2}$ hour from Schauensee you have a view over most of the canton, and reach Schwarzenberg, Wurzenegg, and the Eigenthal, a delightful valley with a trout stream, are worth a visit on this side.

SURVEY OF THE LAKE OF LUCERNE.

Steam boats five times a day, from Lucerne to Fluelen, in 2$\frac{3}{4}$ hours; three times a day to Kussnacht, 1$fr.$ 50c.; three times a day to Alpnach, by Stansstad. Diminution of one-third on return tickets. [Steamers infested by hotel touters. This pest should be rigidly shunned by the traveller].

Of all Swiss lakes, that of Lucerne is the most picturesque, from its irregularity and contrast of savage grandeur, with charming woodland and soft fertility. Its banks are also hallowed as the home of Tell and the men of Grutli, names immortal as the heroes of Thermopylæ and Salamis. The lake consists of seven basins, extending in all directions. The four northern basins form almost a cross, and the southern four are at right angles. The southern and deepest basin is called the Uri lake; its banks are wall-like rocks, rising steep from its margin, and giving it a character of majesty and danger. The next basin, to the west, is that of Gersau or Brunnen. At its west end, two capes approach and appear to bar all passage, the narrows are only $\frac{1}{4}$ l. in width. After passing it you enter the cross, of which the north-east arm is the Kussnacht lake, 2 l. (6 m.) in length; while the south-west is that of Stansstadt, joining the Alpnach lake by a very narrow strait; lastly, the north-west forms the lake of Lucerne proper. The greatest depth of the lake is 1,070 feet, its mean height, 1,348 feet above the sea; it covers 93$\frac{1}{2}$ square kilometres (66 square miles). It is animated by the transit of many sailing and row boats and of 10 steamboats. It is much exposed to sudden squalls, especially when the Föhn decends the valley of the Reuss, in Uri, driving the waves before it, and being interrupted by the mountains it drives the water in the Buochs lake, to the east, and forms frequent tempests in the corner about Brunnen.

The temperature of the water varies with the basins. At a depth of from 500 to 600 feet it is of 4° to 5° Reaumur, while in summer the surface water reaches 16° to 22° Reaumur. It has never been quite frozen. Its waters are limpid and of a dark green.

Excursions on the lake may be made

(by steamer).—1, to Hergiswyl, Stanztad or Stansstadt and the lake of Alpnach, in Unterwalden. Starting from Lucerne you coast along the right bank of the lake, passing in succession the pretty island called Inseli, the charming district of Tribschen and the picturesque farms of Stuz, St. Nicholas, Krämerstein, and Kästenenbaum, after which you reach the promontory of Spisseneck, and thence proceed to Hergiswyl. Between this promontory and the village of Ener-Horw, the lake forms a little basin which advances as far as the village of Winkel, situated at its northern extremity. Near this spot may be seen some caverns, dug in the calcareous rock, remarkable for their deligthful coolness. A pretty path leads from this village to that of Hergiswyl, situated at the foot of a spur of Mount Pilatus, called the Rengg; another path leads over this spur, to Alpnach, to Kerns, and to Sarnen. On the heights of Rengg you enjoy a superb view. The passage over the lake, from Hergiswyl to Stansstad, which is opposite, is only ½l. (1½ m.) in width, and from Stanztad the distance is only ¾l. by land, to Stanz. It was in the Council Chamber of the latter city that the pious hermit, Nicholas von der Flue, reconciled, in December, 1481, the members of the Swiss Diet, when implicated in a quarrel which might have broken up the union of the republic. The hotel de Ville, at Stanz, contains several portraits of ancient magistrates of eminence, and particularly a fine painting, by Volmar, representing Nicholas or Klaus von der Flue, bidding adieu to his family. The church at Stanz, which is built on an eminence, is very handsome, and decorated in the interior by columns of a greyish black marble, obtained from a neigbouring quarry. Over a fountain, built of the same marble, is a statue of Arnold von Winkelried, the national hero, who, in 1386, at the battle of Sempach, sacrificed his life to save his country from Austrian oppression. In a neighbouring meadow, the house is still pointed out in which he dwelt, and which now or lately belonged to the Traxler family.

Half a league separates Stanz from Lotsloch, situated on the Alpnach lake, near a fine cascade formed by the Melchbacha. At this place there are also paper works and a sulphur spring. Above this Melch or Mehlbach rises to the left the Rotzberg, which commands a magnificent view near the ruins of the ancient castle of the bailiff, Wolfenschiessen, which was razed to the ground by the first champions of Swiss liberty. Above these ruins, on the slope of the Muterschwanderberg, you can visit the Dragon's Cavern (Drachenhöhle) to which a legend is attached, and giving its name to the valley of Drachenriedt.—See Canton of Unterwalden.

2. Second Excursion : From Lucerne or Stanztad to the Grütli or Rütli, Tellsplatte and Fluelen. You must cross almost the entire length of this beautiful lake to visit these hallowed spots of the heroic age of Swiss history. The usual way is to proceed direct by boat from Lucerne to the head of the lake. Having arrived at Kreutzrichter you are at about the widest part of the lake, with grand views in all directions. Going S.W. you soon reach Wäggis, the landing place for the ascent of the Righi on this side. Proceeding you leave to the left the villages of Lutzelan and of Vintznau, and on the right the steep slopes of Mytenstein and of Weispleneck, and after passing through the narrows previously noticed formed by the Nasen, you enter the Middle Lake, extending west and east, and almost entirely surrounded by high mountains. On the right bank you see the little town of Buochs, on the south bank the villages of Ridli, Beckenried, and Emmetten, on the northern the pretty village of Gersau, embowered in fruit trees, on the slope of the Rigi range, and lastly on the Eastern shore Brunnen. Opposite Brunnen is the port of Freif, where is an inn which has often proved

refuge to boatmen in this stormy part of the lake. Here is another strait in the lake, after which it takes a bend to the south. Immediately after passing through the straits you see to the right a singular rock of a pyramidal shape, called the Witenstein, and not far thence, the Grütli or Rütli, at the foot of the Seelisberg. This spot, the Rütli, the sanc'uary of Swiss freedom is a green grassy slope, tolerably elevated, and planted with fruit trees. Near a house three sources of fresh water gush forth, and are looked on as sacred by the country people, because they think that they point out the spot where (Nov. 17, 1307) the first Swiss confederates, Werner Stauffacher, of Schwyz, Arnold an der Halden, of Melchthal, in Unterwalden, and Walter Furst, of Attinghausen, in Uri, took a common oath to deliver their country from the tyrants who oppressed it. On the 25th June, 1313, this oath was renewed on the same spot by the three primitive cantons, after they had conquered and established their freedom, and it was repeated in 1713 by 360 deputies from the Cantons of Uri, Schwyz, vnd Unterwalden. Immediately above the Grütli is the village of Seelisberg, with the pension of Sonnenberg, commanding a view of almost the entire lake of Uri. The house is new and handsome, with a garden and terrace above the precipice, and enjoying a glorious view. Pension, 4 to 6*fr.* per day. Season, May to October. [Excursions from Seelisberg to the little lake of Seeli in a sublime country; to the Schwandfluh; to the old castle of Beroldingen, thence to Huven by a steep but beautiful path, and on by boat to the Tellenplatte. From the pension you can ascend the Seelisberger-Kulm or Nieder Bauen (5,933 ft.) offering views rivalling those from the Rigi, 3 l. (9 m.) Fee to guide, 3 fr.]

Not far hence is the mountain of Axenberg, rich in springs; height above the lake, 5,340 feet. Its slopes descend almost sheer into the lake to the depth of 600 feet under the surface. On the shore,

near this spot, which is very dangerous in stormy weather for little boats, stands forth the rock called Tell's Platten, or Tell's Spring; and it was here, according to the perpetual and authentic tradition of the people, that William Tell jumped from the boat when led away as a prisoner by the bailiff Gessler, his chains were removed to let him assist in managing the boat, which was in danger of perishing. In making the daring leap, he is recorded to have kicked off the boat, and thus escaped the tyrant. Thirty years after his death, his fellow citizens built a chapel in this place to his honour, and since that time the spot is known as Tell's Kapelle. The façade of the little temple, which fronts the lake, is open, and its interior is decorated with several paintings, depicting the principal events in the life of this illustrious man. The view of the opposite bank from Tellen-Platte is extremely picturesque, including the Isenthal, the Rothstock, Surenen and Seelisberg mountains, the village of Bauen; and at the back of the picture, the glacier of Geschenen. The distance from the Grütli to Tell's Chapel is 1½ l. (4½ m). Embarking again, you coast along under the vertical rocks of the Axenberg, and passing the spot where the Milchbach joins the lake, arrive in ¾ of an hour at Fluelen.

Fluelen, which will be noticed under the Canton of Uri, is the great emporium and landing place at this end of the lake, on the high road to the St. Gothard, and thence to Italy. From Fluelen to Altdorf is ½ l. (1½ m.), by a pretty valley covered with fine meadows. Of the other spots noticed in this excursion on the lake, Brunnen, Gersau, and Wäggis will be described under the Canton of Schwyz, and Buochs under that of Unterwalden.

Munster, or Bero-Munster, 4 l. (12 m.) from Lucerne, is situated in a charming and fertile country. It is one of the prettiest towns in Switzerland, regularly built, and consisting of straight broad streets. The church and some buildings situated on an eminence have a picturesque effect, and the whole place presents the appearance of an amphitheatre of a very graceful aspect. A certain count Bero of Lenzburg founded here in the 9th century a collegiate chapter, consisting in the present day of a provost, 19 canons, and 14 chaplains. The Church to which they are attached was repaired and decorated afresh in 1776; it contains the tomb of the founder, Bero, and stalls ornamented with beautiful sculptures in wood. But the point which gives special interest to Bero-Munster'is the fact that it had the first printing press set up in Switzerland, established there in the latter half of the 15th century, by the Canon Elias,. of Lauffen. Some works still exist that have issued from this press, and are looked upon as typographical curiosities. Ulrich Gering, who taught the art to Bero-Munster, was the first who made it known in France, where he carried on his profession at Paris.

MOUNT PILATUS.—This colossal mass is the highest summit in the canton, being 5,760 feet above the lake and 7,080 feet above the sea. Ancient documents prove that formerly it bore the appellation of Frackmund, Fract-Mont, or Mons-Fractus, on account of its rugged, broken slopes and precipitous escarpments on the north and east sides. In fine weather its summit is generally capped by a small cloud, from which some derive its name of Pilatus, or Mons Pileatus; when this cloud is wanting rain is anticipated. The Pilatus is crowned by seven peaks, the Esel, Oberhaupt, Band, Tomlishorn, Gemsmättli, Widderfeld, and Knappstein. These peaks, though not far distant from the Alpine pastures of Brundlen-Alp, of Tomlis, Matt, Treyen, Hastelen, and Oberalp, are rather difficult to approach. Six roads or paths lead up from Lucerne to Pilatus; the easiest is by Alpnach towards the Tomlishorn. The distance is 5 l.: to Eigenthal, by Kriens and Herrgottswald, 2½ l. (7½ m.); thence to the *Chálet of Gantersey*, on the Brundlen-

Alp, 1¼ l. (3¾ m.); and thence from 1 l. to 2 l. to the peaks of the Esel, Gemsmättli, Widderfeld, and Knappstein. The views discovered from these summits are perfectly magnificent, and even more extensive than from the Righi culm, because 1,000 feet higher and 4 l. (12 m.) nearer to the Bernese Alps.

2. The best Lucerne route is by Horw ½ l., and Winkel to Hergiswyl, ¾ l. Hotel Rössli, on the banks of the lake, with a fine view. It is usual to procure guides and horses here. The ascent is first through farms and meadows, 1 l. (3 m.), to the inn of Brünneli (good bier, 20c. the glass); five minutes higher up you reach a bench under the fir-trees, commanding a grand view of the lake and surrounding mountains; ½ l. (1½ m.) further is Alp Altengschwend; ¼ l. Alp Frankmünd, a good resting-place. The house of Klimsenhorn and a chapel are seen in a hollow. Ascending by a steep path, with a fine lake view, you come to (1½ l.) the Hotel Blättler on the Klimsenhorn (5,900 feet above the sea), recently erected. It is a comfortable place, with 80 good beds in two houses, and 40 well-kept rooms. Pure wines. Moderate prices. Deserves high recommendation. Very lively in the evening. The host, Blättler, of Rozloch, spent 25,000*fr.* to make the road up to this point and on to the Chriesiloch and Esel. Post every day. Five minutes to the Klimsenhorn (6,150 feet), 700 feet higher than Righi, by a good path. Grand views, north and east; splendid *sun-sets*.

From the Klimsenhorn you can ascend the Esel in 35 minutes. Good nailed shoes but no guides are wanted, except by persons subject to giddiness (1*fr.*) Chaise *a porteur* up and back (4*fr.*) Horses can only go to the Chriesiloch (22 minutes). Iron chains have been placed at awkward places where timid climbers might be frightened. The Chriesiloch is a dark cavern through which you pass on ladders, and on issuing from it enjoy a delightful surprise with the whole Bernese chain and its glittering glaciers standing out in t view before you. Nothing equal to it can be seen on the Righi. Following a long ridge (8 minutes) deep crevasses are seen, in which the snow never melts. At length you reach the Hotel de Bellevue. Ascent from Alpnach, 4 hours; descent, 3½ hours. Five minutes to top of the Esel (6,532 feet). On the summit is a wooden pavilion.

Independently of its grand view the Pilatus is very interesting in itself in its wilderness of rocks and its legends.

From the Klimsenhorn to the Tomlishorn (45 minutes), view still wider than from the Esel. The other peaks are avoided as too difficult.

At Brundlen Alp, 1 l. (3 m.) from the Klimsenhorn, are several matters of interest, including a tarn, which was supposed to have no bottom. Little fogs frequently arise over this tarn; if they rise to the peaks they are dissipated, but if they adhere to the sides of the rocks, they become condensed, and form a large chain, which developes into a tempest that descends on the town of Lucerne. This phenomenon, inexplicable in an unscientific age, gave birth to various mysterious stories about the mountain. The people believed, and perhaps still believe, that the Roman prefect, Pontius Pilate, tormented by the remorse of his conscience, wandered to this spot and threw himself into the lake; that when any one ventured to approach, his furious spirit issued from the water, and only returned to it after chastising the country with a dreadful tempest. This belief held such sway over the popular mind, that in the 14th century, the government of Lucerne expressly forbade strangers to approach the lake. At length, however, M. Muller, curate and dean of Lucerne, in 1585, succeeded in undeceiving the people. Accompanied by some persons, he went to the spot, conjured the spirit and his accompanying furies, but in vain did he evoke them and insult them; nothing came. Lastly, to remove the prejudice that the pond was bottomless, he caused several of his followers to walk through the shal-

lower part. Two other curiosities exist near Brundlen Alp : St. Dominick's Cave (Dominikloch) and the Moon Cave (Mondloch). The former is 800 feet above the pasture; the latter, in the face of the rock, was only explored as late as 1814, by a Chamois hunter, named Ignatius Matt, who was let down 306 feet by a rope, and found it 90 feet high, 28 broad, and 120 deep. Some rocks at the beginning of it were thought to be a statue of St. Dominick, others thought them the work of Roman soldiers. The Mondloch is more accessible. Out of it issues a stream so remarkably cold that, even in summer, the mercury descends to 8 degrees below freezing point. Rare echo at this place.

Righi.—Most of this mountain being in the canton of Schwyz, see under that canton.

St. Urbain, a monastery of the Cistercian Order, 10 l. (30 m.` from Lucerne, remarkable for its fine architecture and vast size. The church, surmounted by two very lofty towers, is magnificently decorated in the interior, contains some good paintings and some very remarkable wood carvings. This abbey possesses an interesting library. The religious of St. Urbain's have always been distinguished for the urbanity with which they receive strangers.

Sempach (Inns—The Cross, the Eagle) is a little, unimportant town, situated on the east bank of the lake of that name, 8 l. (9 m.) from Lucerne. It is only noticeable on account of its association with the battle so glorious in the annals of Swiss heroism. The town is thinly peopled, badly built, and ¼ of a league from the S.W. end of the lake. At ⅓ l. (1½ m.) to the N.W., on the slope of the hill, is the site of the famous battle, in which the Confederates gained that great victory over the Austrians which secured their liberty. It occurred the 9th July, 1386. Duke Leopold, of Austria, attacked, with a force six times their strength, a small Swiss army corps of only 1,400 men, of whom 400 were furnished by Lucerne,

900 by Uri, Schwyz, and Unterwalden, and 100 from Glaris, Zug, Gersau, and the Entlibuch. The close and bristling ranks of the Austrians presented an impenetrable barrier of spears to the daring attack of the Swiss, whose valour was on the point of yielding to the weight of superior numbers and weapons, when Arnold Von Winkelried, a farmer of Unterwalden, devoted himself to death for his country. Issuing alone from the ranks of the Swiss, he sprang upon the enemy, seized with his two arms as many lances as he could grasp, and, drawing them upon his dauntless breast, he beat them down by the weight of his falling body. The Swiss, taking advantage of the opening thus made, darted in, passing over the body of the hero, and penetrating into the enemy's ranks made terrible havoc of their broken multitude. 656 knights, who fought on foot, bit the dust, among them Duke Leopold himself. The field of battle was moreover covered with the bodies of some thousands of squires and attendants. The Swiss, on their side, had to deplore the death of 200 of their brave men; almost all their leaders were killed on that bloody day. On the spot where the action took place a chapel has been built, in which the anniversary of the victory is celebrated every year. On the height where the little Swiss force took up its position the eye embraces a charming view.

Sursee (Hotel du Soleil) is a very ancient little town, at the north of the lake of Sempach; its town house is in the Burgundian style. There is a fine view from the chapel Maria Zell, ½ l. (1½ m.) off. The rail from Bâle to Lucerne follows the banks of this lake which is 1,560 ft. above the sea, tolerably deep and surrounded by an amphitheatre of hills. *Wäggis*. Landing place for the ascent of the Righi from the lake. Great place for the practice of extortion and the exercise of the importunity of sham guides, porters *et id genus omne*, who should be dispensed with and dismissed by a few

decided words, and a look which tells them that *Civis Romanus Sum*. Hotel, Golden Lion, in a bower of verdure, rooms 1½ to 2*fr.*; breakfast, 1¼*fr.*; Hotel and Pension Concordia; Pension Waldis; Pension Gehrig, well kept, cool, and pleasant.

Boats.—To Lucerne, 1st class, 1*fr.* 70*c.*; 2nd, 60*c.* To Gersau, 1st class, 1*fr.* 50*c.*; 2nd, 70*c.* To Brunnen, 1st class, 2*fr.*; 2nd, 1*fr.* To Fluelen, 1st class, 13*fr.* 10*c.*; 2nd, 1*fr.* 60*c.*

Wäggis is a choice spot sheltered from the north, presenting a flourishing growth of chesnuts, figs, almonds, and other southern trees, bearing good fruit. These slopes of Righi are rather exposed to landslips and a considerable piece of ground (80 arpents) was thus lost, with 31 houses that were cast into the lake.

For the road from Wäggis to the Righi see Canton of Schwyz.

Boats on the lake at Lucerne usual fare, 75*c.* per hour, the same for a boatman, total 1*fr.* 50*c.*

PEDESTRIAN ROUTES OF THE CANTON OF LUCERNE.

Lucerne to Aarau, see Nos. 11, 12, and 13.
Arberg. by Berne, (Nos. 66, 67, 68, and 53.)
Arbourg, see No. 11.
Aigle, by Berne (Nos. 66, 67, or 68, and 54).

ROUTE 147.
ALTDORF, 9¼ l. (28¼ m.)

	Leagues.	Miles.
Over the lake by steamer to Fluelen	9	27
Altdorf	¼	1¼
	9¼	28¼

Altstaetten, by Zurich (Nos. 160 and 196), and St. Gallen (No. 180).
Appenzell, by Schwyz (Nos. 161 and 26).

ROUTE 148.
ART 4¼ l. (13¼ m.)

	Leagues.	Miles.
By land passing by Meggen and Morlischachen or by lake to Küssnacht	3	9
By the Chemin Creux (scene of Gessler's death) to Immensee	¼	½
By the lake of Zug to Art	1	3¾
	4¼	

ROUTE 149.

BADEN, 13¾ l. (41¼ m.)

	Leagues.	Miles.
Sihr (See No. 12)	9	27
Huntzenschwyl, 9¾ l. (29¼ m.)	¾	2¼
Baden, (See No. 2.)	4	12
	13¾	41

ROUTE 150.

By BREMGARTEN, 12¼ l. (36¾ m.)

	Leagues.	Miles.
Ebikon	1	3
Dieriken	½	1½
Roth	½	1½
Geisliker-Brücke	¾	2¼
Klein-Dietwyl	¾	2¼
Ruti	½	1½
Sins	¾	2¼
Russek	¾	2¼
Muhlau	½	1½
Mehrischwanden	1	3
Bremgarten	2	6
Göslikon	¾	2¼
Mellingen	1	3
Baden	1½	4½
	12¼	36¾

Bâle (See No. 39).

Bellinzona, by Altdorf (See Nos. 147 and 229).

Berne (Nos. 66, 67, or 68).

Bex, by Berne (Nos. 66, 67, 68, and 58), or Thun, and the Simmenthal (No. 55 and 56).

Bienne, by Solothurn (Nos. 162 and 228).

ROUTE 151.

BROUGG, 12¼ l. (36¾ m.)

	Leagues.	Miles.
Hunzischwyl (See No. 149).	9¾	29¼
Wildegg	1	3
Holderbank	¼	¾
Schinznach (Baths)	½	1½
Brougg	¾	2¼
	12¼	36¾

Bulle, by Berne (Nos. 66, 67, or 68 and 54).

Burgdorf (No. 68.)

Chamouni, by Berne (Nos. 66, 67, or 68 and 63), Lausanne (No. 96), and Geneva (No. 95).

Chaux-de-Fonds, by Berne (Nos. 66 and 67, or 68 and 61), or by Berne (Nos. 66 and 67, or 68 and 70), and Neuchâtel (No. 169), or by Solothurn (Nos. 162 and 220).

Chiavenna, by Altdorf (Nos. 147 and 256).

...z (Nos. 161 and 134).

ROUTE 152.

EINSIEDELN, 8½ l. (25½ m.)

	Leagues.	Miles.
Art (No. 142)	4½	13½
By Ober-Art or by the Goldau landslip to Steiner-berg	1	3
Ecce-Homo	¾	2¼
Sattel	¼	¾
Rother Thurm	½	1½
Einsiedeln	1½	4½
	8½	25½

ROUTE 153.

ENGELBERG, 6¾ l. (20¼ m.)

	Leagues.	Miles.
Winkel	1	3
By the lake to Stanzstad	1	3
Stanz, 2¼ l., (7½ m.)	½	1½
Dellenwyl	1	3
Wolfenschiessen	¼	¾
Dörfli	¼	¾
Grafenort	¾	2¼
Engelberg	2	6
	6¾	20¼

Frauenfeld, by Zurich (Nos. 160 and 245).

Fribourg. by Berne (Nos. 66, 67. or 68 and 54).

Gais, by Zurich (Nos. 160 and 196), and Saint Gallen (No. 186).

Geneva, by Berne (Nos. 66, 67, or 68 and 63), and Lausanne (No. 96).

Glarus, by Schwyz (Nos. 151 and 113).

ROUTE 154.

HERISAU, 23¾ l. (71¼ m.)

	Leagues.	Miles.
By Zurich (Nos. 160 and 301), or by Einsiedeln (No. 152)	8½	25½
Liechtensteig (No. 21)	10¾	32¼
Brunnadern	1½	4½
Degersheim	1½	4½
Herisau	1½	4½
	23¾	71¼

ROUTE 155.

HOFWYL, 19¾ l. (59¼ m.)

	Leagues.	Miles.
Zofingen (No. 11)	9¼	27¾
Zum Rotherist	½	1½
Morgenthal, 11¼ l. (34½ m.)	1¾	5¼
Am Sand (No. 6)	7¾	23¼
Hofwyl	½	1½
	19¾	59¼

Or by Burgdorf and thence by Am Sand to Hofwyl.

Lauffenburg, by Aarau (Nos. 11, 12, or 13 and 10).

Lausanne, by Berne (Nos. 66, 67, or 68 and 63).

Locarno, by Altdorf (Nos. 147 and 229), and Bellinzona (No. 232).

Locle, by Berne (Nos 66, 67, or 68 and 70), and Neuchâtel (No. 175), or by Solothurn (Nos. 162 and 224).

ROUTE 156.

LOESCH BATHS, by Berne (Nos. 66, 67, or 68 and 74), and Sion (No. 268), or by Thun, 33¼ L (99¼ m.)

	Leagues.	Miles.
Thun (No 163)	20	60
Loesch (Nos. 65 and —)	13¼	39¼
	33¼	99¼

Lugano, by Altdorf (Nos. 147 and 229), and Bellinzona (No. 233).

Mendrisio, by Altdorf (Nos. 147 and 229), and Bellinzona (No. 235).

ROUTE 157.

MEIRINGEN, in the Bernese Oberland, 10¼ L. (30¾ m.)

	Leagues.	Miles.
Winkel	1	3
By the lake to Alpnach	2	6
Kägiswyl	1¼	3¾
Sarnen	½	1½
Sachseln	½	1½
Giswyl	1	3
Lungern	1½	4½
Over the Brunig to Meiringen	2½	7½
	10¼	30¾

Morat, Morges, and Moudon, by Berne (Nos. 66, 67, or 68 and 70).

Orbe, by Berne (Nos. 66, 67, or 68, and 71.)

Payerne, by Berne (Nos. 66, 67 or 68, and 77).

Pfeffers, by Zug (Nos. 165 and 292), or by Zurich (Nos. 160 and 304).

ROUTE 158.

RIGHI (The), by Küssnacht, 5½ L. (16½ m.)

	Leagues.	Miles.
Küsnacht, by land or water	3	9
By Seeboden to the Righi Staffel	2	6
To Righi Kulm	½	1½
	5½	16½

ROUTE 159.

By WAGGIS, 5¾ L. (17¼ m.)

	Leagues.	Miles.
Over the lake to Wäggis	2¼	5½
To the Cold Baths on the Righi	2¼	7½
To Righi Kulm	¼	2¼
	5¾	17¼

ROUTE 160.

To SAINT GALLEN, 24 L (72 m.)

	Leagues.	Miles.
Ebikon	1	3
Dieriken	½	1½
Woth	½	1½
Honau, 2½ (7½ m.)	½	1½
St. Wolfgang	1½	4½
Knonau	1¼	3¾
Rifferschwyl	¾	2¼
Inn on the Albis (fine view)	1½	4½
Adlischwyl	1	3
Wollishofen	½	1½
Zurich, 10 L. (30 m.)	1	3
Schwammendingen	1	3
Wallisellen	¼	¾
Rieden	¼	¾
Basserstorf	¾	2¼
Breite	¾	2¼
Töss	¾	2¼
Winterthur, 14 L. (42 m.)	¾	2¼
Räterschen	¾	2¼
Elg	1¼	3¾
Aadorf	½	1½
Dutwyl	½	1½
Munchwyl	1	3
Wyl	¾	2¼
Buren	1½	4½
Niederwyl	¾	2¼
Gossau	¾	2¼
Krazernbrücke	1¼	3¾
St Gallen	1	3
	24	72

Schaffhausen, by Zurich (Nos. 160 and 200) or R see Zurich (town) and Schaffhausen (town).

ROUTE 161.

SCHWYZ, 7 L. (21 m.)

	Leagues.	Miles.
Over the lake to Brunnen	6	18
Schwyz	1	3
	7	21

Sion, by Berne (Nos. 66, 67, or 68 and 73 or 74).

ROUTE 162.

SOLOTHURN, 17 L. (51 m.)

	Leagues.	Miles.
Morgenthal (No. 155)	11½	34½
Wynau	½	¾
Kalteherberg	½	1½
Buzberg	1	3
Herzogenbuchsee	1	3
Ober-Oens	½	¾
Aeschi	½	1½
Eziken	[illegible]	[illegible]
Subiken	½	1
Zuchwyl	[illegible]	[illegible]
Solothurn	½	[illegible]
	17	51

ROUTE 163.

STANZ, see Unterwalden.

Thun, by Berne (Nos. 66, 67, or 68 and 55), or by the Entlibuch, 20 L. (60 m.)

	Leagues.	Miles.
Escholzmatt (No. 67)..........	10	30
Marbach....................	2¾	8½
Tschangnau	1⅛	3¾
Suderen	1⅞	5½
Schwarzenegg	¾	2½
Steffisburg...................	2⅜	7⅜
Thun	1	3
	20	60

	Leagues.	Miles.
Or Thun, by Meiringen (See No. 157).................	10¼	30¼
Brienz	3	9
Interlaken...................	3	9
Thun	5	15
	21¼	63¼

ROUTE 164.

TROGEN, by Saint Gallen (Nos. 160 and 193), or by Herisau 27¾ L. (83¼ m.).

	Leagues.	Miles.
Herisau (See No. 154)	23¾	71¼
St. Gallen	2	6
Speicher.....................	1	3
Trogen	1	3
	27¾	83¼

Unterwalden, that is, Stanz and Stanzstad (No. 153).

Alpnach, Sarnen, and Sachseln (No. 157).

Vevay, by Berne (Nos. 66, 67, or 68 and 54), or by Thun (No. 163B), and the Simmenthal (No. 55).

Winterthur (Icil under Zurich town), or post road (No. 160).

Yverdun, by Berne (Nos. 66, 67, 68, and 77).

ROUTE 165.

ZUG, 5¼ L (15¼ m.)

	Leagues.	Miles.
Honau (No. 160)	2¾	7½
Holzhäuser	1¼	3¾
Cham	¾	1½
Zug............................	1	3
	5¼	15¼

Zurich (No. 160).

Zurzach, by Zurich (Nos. 160, and 305 or 306), or by Baden (Nos. 150 and 306).

Suabia, Bavaria, and North Germany, by Zurich.

...urg, Paris, Frankfort and the Rhine, by Bâle.

...y, Piedmont, and the South of France, by ... and Geneva.

Italy, by Altdorf.

CANTON OF UNTERWALDEN.

Crossing the Lake of Lucerne to it south bank, we enter the Canton of Unter walden, described by Kohl and Berlepsc as a perfect gem, filled throughout wit. charming pastures, rich sylvan scenery, and lovely nooks of verdure. North limits Lucerne and the lake ; west, the Canton of Lucerne ; south, Berne ; east, the Canton of Uri.

AREA, SOIL, AND CLIMATE.—The surface of Unterwalden is 37 square Swiss leagues. Surrounded and intersected by high mountains, its interior consists of several valleys, of which, however, only two principal ones open on the lake of the Four Cantons, i. e., those of Alpnach and Engelberg, both running north and south. The climate is mild in the northern and western parts of the Canton, but severe on the southern uplands, though generally very healthy.

MOUNTAINS.—Some of the mountains of Unterwalden reach the region of perpetual snow. The highest is the Titlis, on the borders of the valley of Engelberg, of the Bernese Oberland and of Uri. Its summit, called the Nollen, is 10,117 feet above the Mediterranean, and 8,749 above the Lake of Lucerne. To the north of the Titlis are the Surenen mountains, separating Unterwalden from Uri. The pass over these mountains known as Sureneneck, is 7,215 feet above the Mediterranean, and though the ridge and path over it be only a few feet wide it is much used by the inhabitants of both cantons. It affords magnificent views of the neighbouring mountains. To the west of Titlis extends a range of mountains separating Unterwalden from the Bernese Oberland. Its first summit is the Joch, then the Geisberg, thirdly the Brunig pass to Hasli (3,579 feet), over which a new road has been lately made. Paths used chiefly by shepherds lead from the two former summits to Hasli ; but the Brunig road by Lungern to Meiringen 3 l. (9 m.), and Brienz is one of the most frequented in

Switzerland. From the Wetterhorn, a peak of the Brunig (5,895 feet), a singularly wild and interesting view of the surrounding mountains is obtained. The Nesselstock may be viewed as the last remarkable mountain in the west of the Canton, and forms the link with another chain, running north as far as the Pilatus. The most conspicuous points of the latter chain are the Bläth-Eck, the Glaubenstock, Feuerstein, &c. In the interior of the Canton, the other noticeable mountains are the Engelberg, Rothstock, Wallistock, Biesen, Bürgenstock, &c.

LAKES, RIVERS, AND RIVULETS.—
(a) Lakes : 1. The Lake of Lucerne and that of Alpnach, the latter a bay, in fact, of the former, whose clear glassy mirror reflects the beauty of the surrounding scenery. It is 1½ L long (4½ m.) and ½ L (1½ m.) wide.

2. The Lake of Sarnen is of the same length and ½ L (2½ m.) wide.

3. The Lake of Lungern, reduced lately by drainage, once 1 L (3 m.) long, ½ L (½ m.) wide. These three lakes communicate by means of the river Aa, which drains them all. This Canton has other little lakes, such as those of Melch, Engstlen, Trübi, &c.

(b) 1. Rivers : The Aa in Unterwalden (Nid Walden). This torrent issues from the Surenen ridge, flows through the Engelberg valley, receives the waters of lake Trübi and other streams, and falls into the Lake of Lucerne. near St. Anthons.

2. The Aa of Unterwalden, Ob dem Walden, receives the waters of Lungeren and Sarnen lakes, and flows into that of Alpnach.

3. The Melch, issues from the lake of that name, flows through the Melch valley, and unites with the Aa of Ob dem Walden, below Sarnen.

(c) Rivulets : The Tätschbach and Erlenbach in the valley of Engelberg ; the Mehlbach near the Rozloch ; the Upper Schieren and the Lower Schieren, besides many other torrents.

AGRICULTURAL AND INDUSTRIAL PRODUCTIONS. — This Canton breeds large herds of cattle, many horses, goats, sheep, pigs, and much poultry. Game is abundant, such as chamois, marmottes, hares, woodcocks, &c., as well as fish. The surface of the ground is covered with superb pastures and vast forests, but it does not yield much corn, hemp, or flax, not even enough potatoes and vegetables for home consumption. On the other hand it produces a large yield of fruit and chestnuts. The minerals consist of marble, lime, slate, and some mineral waters. Dairy produce and cotton are the only things prepared by the inhabitants.

BATHS, SPRINGS, &c.—The Kalte Bad 1½ L from Alpnach, 1½ L (3½ m.) above Schieren, is the only Bath frequented by the neighbouring people.

POPULATION, &c.—The population of the two divisions of Unterwalden is 25,200; of whom in Ob Walden 13,800 ; in Nid Walden 11,400; total, 25,200. They are all Catholic, primitive in their habits, honest and faithful in character, and very democratic in their local form of government.

RELIGIOUS ESTABLISHMENTS. — The Abbey of Engelberg of the Benedictines ; two Capuchin convents and two nunneries.

PUBLIC INSTITUTIONS, CHARITIES, &c.—Education cannot be so advanced as in the plains of more level districts. The time of the population for half the year is nearly absorbed in tending cattle, and attending to the dairy. But if simplicity, honesty, and loyalty in character are trifles as valuable as facility in reading, writing, and summing, the true hearted people of this Canton may be pronounced very highly cultivated. Many of the women are very pretty, the men are broad shouldered, powerful wrestlers, and it is only on the high roads crowded with strangers that corruption has made an entrance among them.

A College is attached to the Abbe Einsiedeln, which is almost more as promoting education than all the parishes of the Canton.

The Library of the Abbey will be described presently.—There are no general charitable institutions in this Canton, each commune being obliged to support its own poor; many parishes have little hospitals of their own.

Since 150 this Canton has been divided into two parts: Upper Unterwalden (Ob Wald) and Lower Unterwalden (Nid Wald). Their boundaries are marked by the Titlis, whence the line runs to Blum Alp, and passes by the forest of Kernwald. Each district is independent, but the two combine to form one Swiss Canton. It follows from the division that Unterwalden has two capitals, Sarnen of Ob Wald and Stanz of Nid Wald. The population is thus distributed: Ob Wald 13,798 inhabitants, Nid Wald 11,337. Total area of both parts 12½ square German miles. As regards the capitals, the population of Sarnen 3,300, Stanz 2,000.

SURVEY OF THE CANTON.

Alpnach.—It has been seen that the two main valleys of this Canton are those (1) of Alpnach and (2) of Engelberg; the former in Nid Wald, the second in Ob Wald. The steamboat, which leaves Lucerne three times a-day (2*fr.*), takes you to Alpnach Gstad, whence the post proceeds by Sarnen and Lungern to Brienz, 11¾ l. (35¼ m.) in 9 hours; fare, 7 *fr.* 60*c.* Fare to Meiringen, 9*fr.* 10*c.* From Brienz you can proceed by steamer to Interlaken, and on to Thun by steamer on the Lake of Thun. Fare from Lucerne to Interlaken, 9*fr.* 60*c.* Alpnach Gstad is 1½ l. from Hergyswyl (see Canton of Lucerne). An omnibus takes you hence to Sarnen. It is necessary to keep a good eye on your luggage, as the crowd of tourists encumbering this place in the summer have brought in their train the usual accompaniments of over-reaching, greed and thieving, forming a sad *contrast to* the usual character of *people of this Canton.* At the landing *Hotel and Pension Pilate.* Fare of

a horse to Pilatus, 12*fr.*, and 1*fr.* for trinkgeld. Ascent and descent the same day, 18*fr.* Stopping a night on the top. retaining the horse, 20*fr.*

From Alpnach Gstad to Alpnach, ½ l. (1½ m.) Hotels: the Sun; the Key. Alpnach contains a Church of rather heavy architecture, with an inscription in letters of gold. Its expenses were met by clearing a great forest on Pilatus, and bringing down the timber by a wood course 40,000 feet long, passing over rocks and precipices. The stations and distances between Alpnach and Brienz, passing the Brunig, will be found in the itinerary to this canton.

Brunig.—Height of the Col, 3,135 feet. A fine new road over the pass. Pedestrians can shorten the way by following the old road and the telegraph line. Below the summit is the Hotel Brunig, said to have good bier at 60*c.* Descending to Hasli you pass near some remarkable peaks—the Tschingelhorn (7,190 feet), with the cascade of the Wandelbach; the Wandelhorn (5,210 feet); the Axalphorn (7,050 feet); and a fine waterfall, the Ottschibach.

Beckenried, 1,360 inhabitants. Landing place for travellers from the St. Gothard or Schwyz, wishing to reach Sarnen, Stanz, the Brunig, and Brienz, without going to Lucerne. Hotel du Soleil, with pension (prices moderate); the Moon; the Star. Furnished apartments, with good beds, *chez Feller-Bucher.* Steamer to Lucerne, 1st class, 2*fr.* 30*c.*; 2nd class, 1*fr.* 20*c.* To Wäggis, 1st class, 1*fr.* 20*c.*; 2nd class, 60*c.* To Gersau, 1st class, 70*c.*; 2nd class, 50*c.* To Fluelen, 1st class, 2*fr.* 30*c.*; 2nd class, 1*fr.* 20*c.*

Beckenried, at the foot of the Spiessberg, is a good point for ascending the Seelisberg. Carriage road, 1 l. (3 m.) to Emmatten. Thence on foot through woods, 1½ l. (4½ m.) A post twice a-day from Beckenried to Buochs, 4*c.* To Stanz, 2 l. (6 m.), 95*c.* Carriage to Engelberg and back, 15*fr.*

Buochs is a large, handsome village, giving its name to the middle basin of the Lake of Lucerne. Distance from Stanz, 1 l. (3 m.) This was the birthplace of the celebrated painter, Warsch. who, though old and blind, was pitifully butchered by the French in 1791. when they at length overcame the heroic resistance of the inhabitants, and, with their usual moderation. reduced everything to chaos and ashes. Such was their fury that they spared neither age nor sex, and made a complete ruin of the place.

The neighbouring mountains are the Stollen (5,521 feet). the Bauen (6.535 feet), the Musen Alp, the Buochserhorn, and the Stanzerhorn.

Engelberg (Valley of) is 3.180 feet above the sea in its upper part. and 1.800 feet above the Lake of Lucerne: it is watered by the Aa, 2 l. (6 m.) in length. and $\frac{1}{2}$ l. (1½ m.) broad. Surrounded on all sides by colossal mountains. whose summits exceed the line of perpetual snow. this valley has only a single issue, or rather it can only be entered by a defile to the north-west. The Aa, contracted in a narrow pass by the Welli and the Selistock, flows through this defile into the valley of Unterwalden or Stanz, and thence into the Lake of Lucerne. Vegetation, though vigorous in this valley, is limited to the grasses of the pastures and Alpine plants, for it does not yield cereals or fruit trees.

Till 1798, the inhabitants of this valley were subject to the Abbot, but since that period they enjoy the same independence as the other inhabitants in this Canton. The abbey of Engelberg co si s of several buildings handsomely and substantially built, it was founded at the end of the 11th century, by Conrad of S lts aburen, and was subsequently handsom y ndlowed by various knights and nobles. Among the abbots of a recent date Leger Salzmann, of Lucerne, deserves honourable mention; not only the monastery but the people of the valley owing to him many useful institutions; thus he founded the college of the abbey, and a good school in the village of Engelberg. The library of the Monastery, though pillaged by the French, contains 10,000 vols., with 200 rare *works of typography* emanating from some of the earliest presses. Near the abbey is a fine dairy giving a rich produce to the monks. and not far off the Erlenbach issues from 20 sources, while $\frac{1}{4}$ l. (2¼ m.) further is the superb cascade of the Tätschbach, presenting a sublime scene. especially in the morning. The village of Engelberg. consisting principally of scattered habitations. reckons 1.400 inhabitants. Pension Catani and Pension Müller, with good trout, fresh butter. excellent cows' and goats' milk. Hotel de Engelberg (pension everywhere 4 to 5 fr. per day). A pleasant excursion may be made to the valley of Horbis. to the "End of Water" an important basin. surrounded by snowy summits: the Rizhidalstock, the Sättelistock, the Weisstock and the Gemsispiel (7.600 feet), others to Gerschni Alp, $\frac{1}{2}$ l. (1½ m.): to Engstlen Alp, 4 l. (12 m.); to Schwandli Alp, 1 l. (3 m.); but especially to the Titlis, covered with an icy mantle, 175 feet thick, 8 hours from Engelberg; a guide is desirable, but there is no danger. It is a good place to sleep at the Upper Trubsee Alp. Fee to the guide, 10 fr. Good shoes, provisions, and a veil are desirable. It was first ascended by a monk, in 1739. From Engelberg to Gerschni Alp, (1½ m.), from thence to Lower Trubsee Alp, 1¼ l. (4½ m.), then to the Upper Trubsee Alp, 1 l. (3 m.); a horse can ascend thus far the mountains, which presents bright pastures and a shining lake, surrounded by glaciers. To the Bitzistock an easy ascent of $\frac{1}{2}$ an hour. Throughout the summer these uplands are covered with 1,000 head of cattle. Thence you go up easily, but over ice and snow, in the northern or summit presenting fine views. The view, especially to the south, is extremely grand: 1st the Glacier of Weneden, above it the Sustenhorn (10,830 feet); whence descends the great Susten Glacier; to the left the Steinen Glacier; above the latter the Galenstock (10,073 feet); to the right the Diechterhorn (9,930 feet). Far off the Monte Leone, above the Simplon, the Viescherhorner, the Finsteraarhorn, and many other peaks of

Oberland, which look quite different on this side, including the Jungfrau, Monch, Eiger, &c. Nearer at hand you have the Hangendhorn (10,140 feet), the Fossenhorn (9.648 feet), and the Engelhörner above the Rosenlaui Glacier. To the E. you see the Spitzlihorn (10,522 feet), and remoter the Grisons chain, with the Piz Alv and Six Madem above the Hinter Rhein. Still further appear the Adula group, the medals and Piz Beverin, and nearer the Bristenstock an infinite number of peaks fill up the intermediate part of the picture which embraces the Tödi, Glarnisch and Säntis. The Righi looks like a mole hill. You can even see South Germany. The return must be made before the snow is softened.

Various roads may be taken to reach Engelberg. From Sarnen you can pass by Storeg, but the distance is 7 or 8 l., while it is only 4¼ l. (12¾ m.) by the road in our itinerary.

From Engelberg, paths lead into the Cantons of Uri and Berne. To Altdorf, in Uri you cross the Surenick, 9 l. (27 m.) You pass over beautiful meadows to the Horbisthal ¾ l. (2¼ m.) By the Tätschbatch fall you advance through savage scenery to the Cheesery of Herrenhüti ½ l. (1½ m.) The valley of Surenen opens like a crevace 1½ l. (4½ m.) to Blackalp; a steep path with fine views leads to Surenenalp; waterfall of Stierenbach; on over snowfields to the Col de Surenen (7,110 ft.) a narrow pass; precipices on both sides; fine view of the Reuss and St. Gothard road; the valley of Maderan, and snowy peaks; Windgälle; Scheerhorn, &c, all round, 1¼ l. (3¾ m.). Sliding over snowfields, you descend to Waldnacht Alp, 1 l. (3 m.). In an hour, an easier road takes you between Hockfluh and Bockischlund; waterfall, of the Waldnacht; on to Ruhshhausen, 1 l. (3 m.). A short but not very safe cut by Hochweg. The best way by Attinghausen, ½ l. (1½ m.). Near is the house of Walter Furst, a hero of the *Grutli*, ½ l. (1½ m.) over the Reuss, with *fine lake views, to Altdorf.*

2. Another route from Engelberg to Meiringen, passing by the two Trubsee Alps, to the Joch, Engstlen Alp, and into valley of Gentelen, 12 l. (36 m.). This road takes you by the Engstlen lake, ½ l. long, and ¼ l. wide, and the Gadmenfluh. An avalanche from this side laid waste the whole of Gentelthal in 1860. The distances are as follow:—From Engelberg to Upper Trubsee, 9 m.; to the Joch (6,905 feet) ½ l. (1½ m.). Pass into the Canton of Berne. To Engstlen Alp, by a source that flows from 8 a.m. to 4 p.m., ½ l. (1½ m.); to Gentelthal, ¾ l. (2¼ m.); Meiringen, 2½ l. (7½ m.) You reach the Haslithal at the village of Hof.

Another path leads over the Juchli to the Melchthal. The way is bad, and wants good shoes, provisions, and a pole. Distance, 6 l. (18 m.). Very fine view from the steep ascent. The Col (6,691 feet) is narrow and covered with moss. Sometimes chamois are seen here. Road easy to find if you follow the Melchthal, containing the house of another hero of the Grütli, in the village of Melchthal. A difficult pass leads hence to the Gentelthal over the Tannlialp. From Melchthal to Sarnen you go through a forest, 1½ l. (4½ m.).

Kerns.—A pretty village, with a large well-built church (1 l., 3 m., from Sachseln; 1¾ l. from Sarnen). It can be reached by the lake in three-quarters of an hour, and on by the road from Alpnach to Stans. Its position is charming, in a verdant valley, watered by the Aa, and surrounded by smiling meadows and orchards. The interior of the church contains five fine altar pieces by Wursch. It is here that the shepherds of Obwald hold an annual schwing fest (August 1st). From Kerns to Stans there are 2 l. (6 m.), passing by Weissöhrli and Aennenmoos.

Lungern (*Inns*—Zum Brunig; Löwe; fair, but dear), picturesquely situated in the valley above Sarnen, near the fall of the Dunderbach, 200 feet high. This village is on the road over the Brunig, and stood formerly on the shore of the lake of Lungern, which having been drained in 1836 has been much reduced, thus diminishing the beauty of the scenery without being of much service in any way. The level has been lowered 120 feet. Near Lungern are some curiosities, especially to the West, the Giswylerstock presenting twisted strata, interesting to geologists. Lungern is 3¼ l., or 9¾ m. from Sarnen, and 8 l., or 24 m. from Lucerne.

Sachselen is three quarters of an hour from Sarnen, by the lake. It is a fine village, situated at the foot of a mountain of the same name, on the Brunig road, containing a splendid Church, decorated with columns of fine black marble, and containing the tomb of brother Nicholas von der Flue; his figure sculptured on the sepulchral stone is considered to be a fine work of art, and his tomb attracts, every year, a great number of pilgrims, as his memory is held in great veneration as well as his relics which are kept there. A pretty path leads hence, with varied and pleasing views, to a wild solitude on the height called Rauft, and to Flueli, a place which gave its name to Nicholas and his family, whose real name was Löwenbragger. Two houses are still pointed out, one as his birth-place, the other as his residence. In the valley of Melchthal, under Flueli, are also seen the chapel and hermitage of this pious man, who, after leaving his family, lived here a solitary life, of austerity and contemplation, till his death, March 21st, 1487. He is proved to have lived for 18 years with no other nourishment than the monthly communion he was in the habit of receiving. His life was one of great purity, self-denial, and innocence; and he appears to have been one of those exceptional characters that sometimes appear in history, free from many of the weaknesses of their race, and exhibiting virtues as rare as they are admirable. The valley of Melchthal was also the home of another Swiss hero, Arnold an der Halden—one of the three men of Grütli, the founders of Swiss liberty. The family of Arnold is extinct, but that of

Nicholas is said still to exist, and a curé of Sachselen, in 1829, was a descendant of the holy man.

Sarnen (Hotels: Schlussel, Adler, Sarnerhof) is the capital of Ob Wald, in the Alpnach valley, on the road to Brunig (½ m. from Sachseln). It stands in a smiling situation at the point where the Aa issues from the lake of Sarnen, it is the residence of the cantonal authorities, and the legislative assembly of Unterwalden meets there every year on the last Sunday in April.

PUBLIC BUILDINGS. — The Hotel de Ville is decorated with the portraits of the Landamman and of Nicholas von der Flue, the latter painted by Wursch. The Arsenal is built on the site of the castle of the Austrian bailiffs, destroyed in 1318, by the liberators of Switzerland. The parish Church has a fine organ. This town contains a Convent of Capuchins and a nunnery.

[Excursions from Sarnen to Sachseln, Kern, and Engelberg (see those places.)]

Stanz (capital of Nid Walden). — Reached by steamer, through Stansstad, from Lucerne, water passage (¾ hour) three times a-day. Post through Acheregg to Stanz (1½ hour), 1fr. 95c. Hotels at Stanz: The Angel, good; the Crown, not good; Hotel, and Pension Mettweg, out of the town, in meadows by the new road, 30 rooms; whey and milk cure. Pension Breit, a pretty house with an extensive view. Pension Langenstein, in a fine country. Pension Christen, on the Rossberg, 400 feet above the lake.—This town is the capital, and seat of the Nid Walden government—population, 2,000—and stands at the foot of the Stansberg, in a valley covered with fruit trees. Some description of the town has been already given under the head Lake of Lucerne (see Canton of Lucerne), leaving little more to be added. The Church was the scene of a horrible massacre, in 1728, by the French, when near 100 of the population, men women and children, who had taken refuge there, were brutally massacred with the priest at the foot of the altar. On the *Place* is a statue of Arnold von Winkelried; near the town is his house, which has been repaired; and the Arsenal contains the breastplate he wore at the battle of Sempach. Stanz is the residence of the painter Deschwanden, and of the statuary Kaiser; and contains a telegraph. From the Capuchin Convent, a fine view is obtained.

Excursions.—Numerous pleasant walks and fine views occur on all sides of Stanz, among which may be noticed visits to the Rozberg, and the Buochserhorn, distant 1¼ l. (3¾ m.). Rozberg has been noticed under the Canton of Lucerne. At Oedweil, or Drachenriedt, is a cavern, which, according to an ancient tradition, served as the retreat of an enormous dragon, killed in 1250, by Strutt de Winkelried. Fine views are obtained near the marble quarry of Kniri, and near Bergli, a country house at the base of the Burgenstock. Excursions may also be made to the Stanzerhorn (5,874 feet), 2 l. (6 m.) by the Blum-Alp, a good châlet, where night quarters may be obtained. Guide, 3 to 4*fr.* The Buochserhorn is not so well adapted for a visit (5,570 feet).

Engelberg can be easily visited from Stanz, distance, 2½ l. (7½ m.), passing by Wolfenschiessen. The Knight of Wolfenschiessen was here killed, in 1307, by Conrad Baumgartner, when the former attempted to insult his wife. In the Church are kept the relics of Conrad Schenber, grandson of Nicholas von der Flue, a pious anchoret. There are also pictures representing his life. To the left, by Gigefluh, you can pass into Uri, between Hoch Briesen and the Kaiserstuhl. To the right is the Gumenberg. After this the valley narrows, you pass a fine waterfall, the Fallenbach, and to the left is the village of Alzellen, where Baumgartner killed the bailiff of Wolfenschiessen. 1½ l. from Stanz is Grafeunt, a chapel, and a few houses with an inn (where good omelettes are prepared.)

Hence 1½ l. through the forest. Little huts occur along the road, made of trunks of trees, where the traveller can rest. The pastures about here are admirable, indeed, among the best in Switzerland.

Stanzstad, ¾ l. (2¼ m.) from Stanz, is a village with a good port, and an emporium for goods on the lake of Lucerne. It was completely burnt by the French, September 9th, 1798. On the banks of the lake is an old tower, which probably once served the purpose of a lighthouse. Opposite Stanzstad is Hergiswyl, of which notice has been taken in the account of the Canton of Lucerne. The hotels at Stanzstad are the Winkelried and Freihoff, near the bridge. The Schlüssel and Rössli are little inns. We must here notice the engagement with the French, which took place here in 1798, and is equal in heroism to the great events of Greek and Roman history. In that year, 1798, a part of Switzerland adopted the new ideas of progress and civilisation so successfully propagated by French bayonets, and proclaimed the Helvetic Republic, but the blessings of the new constitution were rejected by the smaller cantons. Hereupon the French Directory marched French troops into the country to promote the welfare of the country. But the men of Unterwalden, proud of their independence, which had lasted five centuries, and had been upheld by men like Tell and Winkelried, prepared to make an energetic resistance to the new-fangled ideas of freedom, hatched by the Reign of Terror. The French, 16,000 men strong, under General Shauenburg, tried to disembark near Stanzstad, but from the 3rd to the 7th September all their efforts were repulsed, for this little tribe of shepherds had become a band of heroes. Desperate combats took place on this occasion, recalling the times of Leonidas and Horatius Cocles; but the French managed to enter the valley of Alpnach by a rapid march, and valour had at length to yield to numbers. Women and young girls fell fighting near their fathers and brothers, emulating the Maid of Saragossa. There were scarcely 2,000 opposed to 16,000. At length all succumbed. The massacre and pillage were dreadful. The whole country was a waste, and the great and good Pestalozzi used his benevolent efforts to gather round him and succour the vagrant orphans left behind the strife. A general subscription, raised throughout Switzerland, came to his assistance.

ROUTES FROM STANZ.

To Aarau, by Lucerne (Nos. 153, 11, 12, or 13).
Aarberg, by Lucerne (Nos. 153 and 66, 67 or 68), and Berne (No. 53).
Aarberg, by Lucerne (Nos. 153 and 11).
Aigle, by Lucerne (Nos. 153 and 66, 67, or 68), and Berne (No. 54). (See also No. 256).

ROUTE 251.
ALTDORF, 8 L. (24 m.)

	Leagues.	Miles.
Buochs	1¼	3¾
Over the lake to Fluelen ...	6¼	18¾
Altdorf	½	1¾
	8	24

Altstaetten, by Schwyz (Nos. 213 and 191), and Saint Gallen (No. 18).
Appenzell, by Schwyz (Nos. 213 and 26).
Art, by Schwyz (Nos. 213 and 208).
Baden, by Lucerne (Nos. 153 and 149, or 150)
Bâle, by Lucerne (Nos. 153 and 39).
Bellinzona by Altdorf (Nos. 251 and 229).
Berne, by Lucerne (Nos. 153 and 66, 67, or 68).
Bex and Bulle, by Lucerne (Nos. 153 and 66, 67, or 68), and Berne, (Nos. 54 and 58).
Bienne, by Lucerne (Nos. as before), and Berne (No. 59), or by Lucerne (Nos. 153 and 162), and Solothurn (No. 218).
Brougg, by Lucerne (Nos. 153 and 151).
Burgdorf, by Lucerne (Nos. 153 and 68).
Chamouni, by Lucerne (Nos. 153 and 66, 67, or 68), and Berne (No. 63), Lausanne (No. 96), and Geneva (No 95).
Chaux de Fonds, by Lucerne (Nos. 153 and 66, 67 or 68), and Berne (No. 61).
Chiavenna, by Altdorf (Nos. 251 and 256).
Coire, by Schwyz (Nos. 213 and 134).
Einsiedeln, by Schwyz (Nos. 213 and 209).

ROUTE 252.
ENGELBERG, 4¼ L. (12¾ m.)

	Leagues.	Miles.
Dellenwyl	1	3
Wolfenschiessen	½	½
Dörfli		
Grafenort		2¼
Engelberg	2	6
	4¼	12¾

ROUTE 252 (b 1.)
ENGELBERG TO ALTDORF, by the Surenen Pass, 7h. 30m. Mule and foot path.

	h	m.
Cascade of Toetschlach	0	45
Châlets of Herrenhütti	0	30
Breakfast provided.		
By Cascade of Aa	0	50
Châlets and Chapel of Blackenalp...	0	15
By Surenenalp to Surenen Joch	1	30
Descent to Châlets of Waldnacht...	1	0
The Gorge of the Böckischlund	0	30
Rübshausen	1	0
Attinghausen	0	30
Altdorf	0	25

ROUTE 252 (b 2.)
ENGELBERG TO AMSTEG (8h. 20m.) As far as Rübshausen, same road as b 1.

	h	m.
Erstfelden (Village) and Falls of Fulenbach	0	30
Reuss Bridge	0	15
Amsteg	1	15

ROUTE 252 (b 3).
ENGELBERG TO WASEN, by the Grassen Joch (8h., 55m.) Pass discovered, 1864. Guide wanted.

	h.	m.
Ascent to Col of Grassen (45 minutes on the Glacier)	4	30
Descent easier	3	45

ROUTE 252 (b 4).
ENGELBERG TO SARNEN, by the Storegg (4h. 30m.)

	h.	m.
Nunalp	0	45
Lautersie	0	30
Storegg Joch to Fluhli (1,740 metres)	2	15
Rauft to Fluhli	0	15
Fluhli to Sarnen	0	45

ROUTE 252 (b 5).
ENGELBERG TO SARNEN, by the Jochli (7h.)

	h.	m.
To Storegg path (Fork)	0	45
Ascent	1	45
Over Col of Jochli to Melchthal (2,170 metres high)	2	0
Melchthal to Rauft	1	30
Rauft to Fluhli	0	15
Flühli	0	45

ROUTE 252 (b 6).
ENGELBERG TO MEIRINGEN, by the Joch (10h. 30m.) Mule path. (See Bernese Alps). High Level Passes

ROUTE 252 (b 7).

SARNEN TO MEIRINGEN, by the Melchthal (10h.)

	h.	m.
To Melchthal. by Rauft (the hermitage of Nicholas von der Flue) ...	2	45
Or by Kerns (carriage road)	2	0
[At Melchthal a good hotel : Kaplanel.]		
An Alp Châlets and Chapel.............	1	0
Melchsee	0	15
Lanbergrat (2 2⋅1 metres)	1	0
Châlets of Mæris	2	0
Haslibergor Mœgis Alp (fine view) to Ruti..	0	20
Ruti to Meiringen	0	40

[A path leads up from Engelberg to Melchsee in 6h. 10m. by the Tanneband, 2,039 metres high.]

Frauenfeld, by Lucerne (Nos. 153 and 160), and Zurich (No. 245).

Friburg, by Lucerne (Nos. 153 and 66, 67, or 68), and Berne (No. 54).

Gais, by Schwyz (Nos. 213 and 191), and Saint Gallen (No. 186), or by Lucerne (Nos. 153 and 160); Zurich (No. 196), and St. Gallen (No. 186).

Geneva, by Lucerne (Nos. 153, and 66, 67, or 68), Berne (No. 63) and Lausanne (No. 96).

Glarus, by Schwyz (Nos. 213 and 113).

Herisau, by Schwyz (Nos. 213 and 210).

Hofwyl, by Lucerne (Nos. 153 and 68), and from Burgdorf, by the Sand to Hofwyl.

Lauffenburg, by Lucerne (Nos. 153, 11, 12, or 13), and Aarau (No. 10).

Lausanne, by Lucerne (Nos. 153, 66, 67, or 68), and Berne (No. 63).

Locarno, by Altdorf (Nos. 251 and 229), and Bellinzona (No. 232).

Locle (to the), by Lucerne (Nos. 153, 66, 67, or 68), Berne (No. 70), and Neuchâtel (No. 175).

ROUTE 253.

LOESCH (Baths), 29⅓ l. (88½ m.)

	Leagues.		Miles.
Æennenmoos	1	......	3
Kerns...	1	......	3
Sarnen	½	......	1½
Sachseln	½	......	1½
Giswyl	1	......	3
Lungern..................................	1½	......	4½
Over the Brunig to Meiringen	3	......	9
Unter die Heide ....,.......	1	......	3
Wyler-Brücke	1	......	3
Brienz...................................	1	......	3
By lake to Interlaken..........	3	......	9
Unterseen 14⅔ l. (44¼ m.) ...	⅓	......	⅔
Over lake of Thun to Spiez	3	......	9
Wyler....................................	⅓	......	⅓
Loesch (No. 65)	11¼	......	34½
	29⅓		88½

Or by Lucerne (Nos. 153 and 66, 67 or 68), Berne (No. 74), and Sion (No. 268).
Lucerne (N

Lugano, by Altdorf (Nos. 251 and 229), an Bellinzona (No. 233).

Mendrisio, by Altdorf (Nos. 251 and 229), and Bellinzona (No. 235).

Morat, Morges, and Moudon, by Lucerne (Nos. 153 and 66, 67 or 64), and Berne (Nos. 77 and 63).

Neuchâtel, by Lucerne (Nos. 153, 66, 67, or 68), and Berne (No. 70).

Orbe, by Lucerne (Nos. 153 and 66, 67 or 68), and Berne (No. 71).

Payerne, by Lucerne (Nos. 153 and 66, 67 or 68) and Berne (No. 63).

Pfeffers (Bath), by Schwyz (Nos. 213 and 113), and Glarus (No. 111).

Righi (The), by Schwyz (Nos. 213 and 212).

Saint Gallen, by Schwyz (Nos. 213 and 191).

Schaffhausen, by Lucerne (Nos. 153 and 160), Zurich (No. 200), Schwyz, No. 213)

ROUTE 254.

SION, 33½ l. (100½ m.)

	Leagues.		Miles.
Loesch (Baths, No. 253)...	26¼	......	79¼
Waren	1¼	......	4¼
Salgesch	1	......	3
Sierre..................................	1½	......	4½
St. Leonard	2	......	6
Sion....................................	1	......	3
	33½		100½

Or by Lucerne (Nos. 153 and 66, 67 or 68), and Berne No. 74).

Solothurn, by Lucerne (Nos. 153 and 162).

ROUTE 255.

THUN, 17¼ l. (51¾ m.)

	Leagues.		Miles.
Unterseen (see No. 253)...	11¾	......	35¼
By lake to Thun	5½	......	16½
	17¼		51¾

Trogen, by Schwyz (No. 213 and 191), and Saint Gallen (No. 193).

Vevay, by Lucerne (Nos. 153, 66 and 67, or 68), and Berne (No. 54).

ROUTE 256.

	Leagues.		Miles.
Or by Thun, 53¼ m. (No 255)	17⅔	......	53¼
The Simmenthal to Zweysimmen (Nos. 55, b 4, b 5)	10⅔	......	32¼
Saanen (Gessenay)	1¼	......	3⅔
Over the Col de Pillon Pass by Château d'Oex to Les Iles	4	......	12
Aigle (No. 55, b5)	4¼	......	13¼
By rail to Vevay	4¼	......	13½
	42¼		128½

Or by Gessenay and Plan de Jaman (Nos 55, b 7).

Winterthur by Lucerne (Nos 153 and 160).

Yverdun, by Lucerne (Nos. 153, 66, 67 or 68) and Berne (No. 77).

Zug, by Lucerne (Nos. 153 and 165).
Zurich, by Lucerne (Nos. 153 and 160).
Zurzach, by Lucerne (Nos. 153 and 151) and Brougg
    (No. 197).
Strasburg, Carlsruhe, Mannheim, Frankfort, and
    the Rhine by Lucerne and Bâle.
Bavaria and Austria, by Lucerne, Zug, Zurich,
    Romanshorn, and Friedrichhafen.
Turin, Lyons, South France, by Lucerne, Berne,
    Lausanne, and Geneva.
Milan, and all Italy, by Altdorf and Bellinzona.

Bordering on Unterwalden, and with it and Schwyz, the cradle of Swiss freedom, and the home of Tell, we come to this Canton at the head of the Lake of Lucerne. Its northern limit is the Canton of Schwyz; to the east it has the Cantons of Glarus and Grisons; to the south, Tessin, and to the west, Unterwalden, Berne, and Valais.

AREA, SOIL, AND CLIMATE.—Surface, 56½ square Swiss leagues. The Canton consists of one main valley, 14 l. (42 m.) in length, from the source of the Reuss, to its entrance into the Lake of Lucerne, and of about ten lateral valleys, rising from the Reuss Thal to the highest Swiss Alps, which completely surround Uri with their snowy and icy walls. The flanks of the mountains are mostly very scarped so that there is little cultivable land.

1. The first lateral valley on the side of Schwyz, from which it is separated by the Frohnalp, is that of Sissigen or Sessiken. It begins at the village of that name, situated on the right bank of the Lake of Lucerne, and rises east, to a ridge of mountains blocking all further passage; to the south, it is bounded by the rugged, savage-looking Axenberg, whose spurs stand out in the lake, with the Tellen Platte, of which mention has been made under the Canton of Lucerne.

2. Opposite the Axenberg, and on the other side of the lake is the entrance of the Valley of Isi or Isen (Isenthal), rising south-west to Engelberg. This valley is closed by the Glacier of Geschenen and is watered by a stream of the same name issuing from it. The Isenthal is not much visited, but presents fine wild scenery.

3. A quarter of a league (¾ m.) east of Altdorf, *begins the valley of* Schächen.

Length, 4 l. (12 m.) A tolerable path leads by this valley over the Klausenberg, into that of the Linth, in Glarus. The formidable Glacier of the Scheerhorn, at the bottom the Schächen valley, gives birth to an impetuous torrent of the same name, and flowing through it. At the west entrance of the valley is Bürglen, the birth-place of Tell.*

4. The principal, or Reuss, valley runs due south from Altdorf, presenting sublimely savage scenes in its upper part, whilst lower down, the basin becomes very fertile, especially the east side of the Reuss, in the direction of Fluelen, where the ground becomes even rather marshy, and hence unhealthy.

5. Four leagues (12 m.) from Altdorf, near Amsteg, the Maderanerthal, or Gerstelenthal, opens between the Renchenberg and the Bristenstock, watered throughout by the Gerstelen torrent. Its length is 6 l. (18 m.), and its end is blocked up by the Glaciers of the Husifura, Schuechorn, Clariden Grat, and Tödi. A single track, used mostly by Chamois hunters, leads over these glaciers to the Sand Alp and Pantenbrücke, in the Canton of Glarus (which see).

6—7. Two other valleys issue from the Maderanerthal, running south; they are the Etzli and Rubleten valleys. The first opens above Bristen, 1 l. (3 m.) from

* Bürglen must be viewed with an interest akin to that felt for the birth-place of all greatness. Mythical theories have now done their worst, and the strong sense of nature still teaches men to cling with unswerving affection to the homes of the true-hearted and high-minded. Unfortunately bad taste sometimes abuses this tendency to perpetuate true greatness. The Châlet of Tell has been turned into an inn. The splendid view from its balcony does not reconcile us to this desecration. At the side of the Hotel is the Chapel of Tell, built 1522, with frescoes representing events in his life. The spot is still shown where Tell (dying nobly as he had lived) was drowned, trying to save the life of a child, carried off by the waters of the Schächen. Above Bürglen rise the summits of the Gubel-töcke, Seewellgrat, the Waldnacht Alp, the savage Uri, Rothstock, &c. A shady road leads to Altdorf, distant 1 l. (1½ m.) by the sacred forest, or Bannwald, mentioned by Schiller in his tragedy of Wilhelm Tell.

Amsteg, and extends, retaining a considerable width, to the Crispalt and Kreuzlistock, whose ramifications, in fact, include the valley, while it is bordered throughout by their glaciers. A road passes up the Etzlithal, over the Kreuzli pass into a little and very elevated valley, surrounded by glaciers, and called the Strinn Valley: proceeding hence, the path continues by the side of the valley, and leads ultimately to Tavätsch, on the Vorder Rhein, in the Canton of Grisons (which see). The other, or Rubleten Valley, bordering to the east on the Canton of Grisons, gives its name to the upper district of the Maderanerthal. Ascending the Reuss valley from Amsteg, you arrive at Wasen, where an ancient entrenchment is seen, thrown up by the men of Uri to defend themselves against the Bernese.

To the west of this entrenchment opens the Mayen valley, 4 to 5 l. (12 to 15 m.) long, closed in by the Susten-Scheideck to the north, and blocked to the north by the Urazhorn, and to the south by the Sustenhorn. The two latter supply the water of the Mayenbach, which makes some fine leaps in its course through the valley. A bridle-path leads from Wasen by the Mayenthal over the Susten, to Gadmen, 11 l. (33 m.), and to Meiringen, 14 l. (42 m.)

8. Ascending the Reuss, and passing the Devil's Bridge, you come to the Urserenthal, through the Urner Loch, and out of the Urserenthal issue other lateral valleys, closed in by precipices of great height. These lateral valleys are the Ober and Unter-Alpthals. From the Ober-Alpthal, which stretches to the north-east, and is watered by one branch of the Reuss, a road leads to St. Giacomo, in the Vorder Rheinthal, Grisons (see that Canton). The Lower Alpthal stretches south-east along the frontiers of the Grisons, and is blocked up by the *Stella* and Petersberg. At the confluence *of the two highest sources* of the Reuss, *and near the Hospital*, the main valley forks again, forming two others corresponding to the two incipient sources of the Reuss. One extends almost due south, and the road that follows it passes along the second source of the Reuss, and proceeds by narrow passes, between the Blauberg, the Prosa, the Hunereck, and the Lucendro, to Val Tremola, in Tessin. (See that Canton.) The other initial Reuss valley runs south-west, is larger than the former, and everywhere encompassed by glaciers. It leads up to the Furka, over which pass a road leads into the Canton de Valais (which see).

The entire Canton of Uri is in the midst of the high Swiss Alps, and is almost entirely on the north and west slope of St. Gothard.

In the elevated valleys near the glaciers, the climate is naturally cold and severe; but in the districts exposed to the south wind, called Föhn, it is remarkably mild, and near Altdorf the finest fruits and vegetables come to maturity and ripen even precociously.

MOUNTAINS. — From the great knot around the St. Gothard, other ridges are detached, crossing and intersecting the Canton in all directions, their ramifications forming its different valleys. Most of the mountains in this Canton attain an elevation of from 4 to 10,000 feet; as it would be impossible to specify them all we shall confine ourselves to notice the highest points, including the Galenstock (9,930 feet), the Mutterhorn (8,450 feet), the St. Gothard, or properly, the Punta della Fibia (8,410 feet), the Scheerhorn (10,071 feet), the Bristenstock (8,165 feet), the Sustenhorn (10,768 feet), the Spizliberg (9,285 feet), the Furka (top of pass, 7,795 feet), the Prosa (7,850 feet), the Axenberg 5,340 feet), besides many others.

LAKES, RIVERS, AND RIVULETS.—(a), Lakes: 1. The lake of Lucerne (see Canton of Lucerne). 2. The lake of Oberalp (Oberalpsee) situated near the Canton of Grisons, ¼ l. in circumference, well stocked with fish. 3. The lake of Seelisberg.

There are many mountain tarns of which we cannot give a special notice.

(*b*) Rivers: The Reuss is in fact the only river of the Canton, and is formed by the confluence of three streams, of which the first descends from the east slope of the Furka, and the second issues from lake Lucendro on St. Gothard. Below Hospital, a village on St. Gothard, these streams unite and receive near Urseren a third tributary coming from the lake of Oberalp. From Urseren to Amsteg the Reuss dashes and thunders in its rocky bed for 4 l. (12 m.), descending in that space 2,500 feet, and forming therefore almost one succession of cascades. Below Amsteg the current becomes gentler and the river falls into the lake of Lucerne at Fluelen, after having passed through the principal valley of Uri. It receives in its course almost all the waters flowing from the mountains of this Canton, and it yields the fisherman salmon, eels, trout, and many other kinds of excellent fish.

(*c*) Rivulets: The streams of this Canton are almost numberless, being mostly furious torrents often the occasion of great ravages. Those deserving special notice are the Schächenbach, proceeding in part from the waters flowing from the Glacier of the Scheerhorn and partly from a source issuing from the Tismar. It receives, subsequently, all the torrents pouring into the valley of Schächen, through which it flows, forming several cascades, of which the most beautiful is known by the name of Stäubi, and it ultimately falls into the Reuss opposite Attinghausen. It was in the waters of this torrent that, according to tradition, William Tell was drowned in 1354, ending his noble life with a worthy death by seeking to save a child carried away by its waters. The Gerstelen, or Gerstenach, is a stream rising in the Glacier of Husifura, situated at the top of the Valley of Maderan; running throughout this valley, it receives all the waters that pour into it, and joins the Reuss at Amsteg. The Mayenbach is formed by the waters flowing from the Stemberg,

Susten, Urazhorn, and other nigh alps above the Mayenthal, through which it runs, and taking up all the other waters of the valley, it pours into the Reuss near Wasen. The Schreienbach and the Fleisbach issue from the inner valley of Schächen and flow into the canton of Glarus. The Sisiken and the Isi' fall into the lake of Lucerne.

AGRICULTURAL AND INDUSTRIAL PRODUCTIONS.—Uri is rich in large cattle, and is supposed formerly to have had a breed of wild cattle, whence its name, and the head of the ox on its cantonal flag. The canton has few horses, goats, sheep, and pigs. Fish and game, on the other hand, are abundant, large flocks of wild ducks coming to the lakes from the southward. Chamois, marmottes, hares, &c., are found in considerable numbers. The soil is covered with pine forests and pastures; there are not many crops of cereals, but potatoes, fruit trees, hemp and flax grow abundantly in parts of the main valley. The mineral treasures consist of crystals, garnets, amethysts, marble, gypsum and slate. The inhabitants are chiefly herdsmen or gardeners, and their industry is confined to the production of cheeses; those of Urseren being reckoned among the best in Switzerland.

THERMAL WATERS.—The Canton has only one mineral spring, the Baths of Unterschächen.

POPULATION AND RELIGION.—The population being only 14,800, gives only the proportion of 14 per square kilometre (in the Grisons it is only 13 per square kilometre). The Canton has only 20 parishes. They are exclusively Roman Catholics. The men of Uri are laconic, dreamy, reserved, rather slow, and stolid, like all shepherd races, but, on the other hand, loyal, benevolent, and hospitable, brave in danger and resigned in misfortunes. The government is entirely democratic, like that of Unterwalden. It meets in the open air the first Sunday in May, with the landamman, or chief magistrate, at its head. It then advances with an armed escort, drum, and trumpet, and, with the cantonal flag of Uri, showing the head of a wild ox (the *bos urus*), under which their ancestors fought. They then ,proceed to acts of sovereignty, vote the taxes, and appoint the principal functionaries.

ABBEYS AND CONVENTS. — Besides a Benedictine Abbey at Seedorf, near the confluence of the Reuss with the Lake of Lucerne, there is a Convent of Capuchin monks, and another of Capuchin nuns at Altdorf.

EDUCATION ESTABLISHMENTS AND CHARITIES.—Secular education is somewhat behind in this Canton, owing to the pastoral habits of the people; yet, strange to say, they are moral, faithful, and orderly. There is no library in the Canton, which must be a dreadful calamity in this age of book-worms, and each parish supports its poor. It does not appear that there are workhouses or casual wards.

SURVEY OF THE CANTON.

Altdorf, capital of the Canton, 2,400 inhabitants. Hotels: Aigle, good; table d'hôte, 3*fr.*, with wine; rooms, 1*fr.* to 1½*fr.*; breakfast, 1*fr.*; vins d'asti; Goldener Schlüssel; post and telegraph office; carriages with one and two horses; Lion. William Tell, small, moderate. Altdorf has been several times burnt; the last time, 1779. It has a parish Church; a Hotel de Ville; the Capuchin Convent, with a fine view; and an old tower, on the spot where this stubborn, unenlightened people will persist in believing, in defiance of spectacled critics and composers of heavy folios in Germany, that Tell's son stood when the apple was shot from his head by his father at the distance of 100 paces.

The Church contains a fine organ and some pictures by Vandyke, Caracci, &c. The exterior walls of the old tower are painted over with grotesque pictures representing scenes in the life of Tell, whose statue decorates the town fountain. Altdorf is the residence of an eminent painter, *Muheim.*

EXCURSIONS.—We are now in the classic land of Swiss history, and it would be almost sacrilege to visit it without going to Burglen in the Schächenthal, ½l. (1½ m.), the birth-place and home of Tell. Schiller's play is the best guide to this district, and let the traveller carefully avoid captious mythical theories, emanating mostly from men of the plain, who, unable to conceive of grandeur in human nature, seek to level all heroism to their own prose, by explaining it away as they cannot explain it to themselves. Another excursion to the Riedemthal (1 l.) Pass of the Klausen to Stachelberg in Glarus, and by Surenen to Engelberg in Unterwalden; only one day to go and return.

Mountains surrounding Altdorf: Balmistock (7,462 feet), Hohe Faulen (7,705 feet), Sittliserhorn (7,548 feet). The ruins of Schweinsberg; the echo on the Rinachfluh, left of the road; Erstfelden, at the entrance of the valley of that name, with the Joch-Glesschen and Spannörter, make an interesting two hours' tour, including Attinghausen, the birth-place of Walter Fürst.

Other points near Altdorf: Tellen Platte and Grütli (see Canton of Lucerne).

Amsteg...................}	See St. Gothard.
Andermatt ....}	
Attinghausen ....}	See Altdorf.
Burglen...................}	
Devil's Bridge	
Hospital	
Lucendro	
Realp..................... }	See St. Gothard.
Urner Loch	
Urseren...................	
Wasen	

The St. Gothard pass is undoubtedly one of the finest lower passages in the Alps. Almost all the principal points of interest in Uri are in the main valley of the Reuss, followed by this route. The first part of the road from Altdorf to Amsteg does not afford any special interest. Amsteg, 1,160 feet high (Hotels: White Cross, chez Inder Gand; good

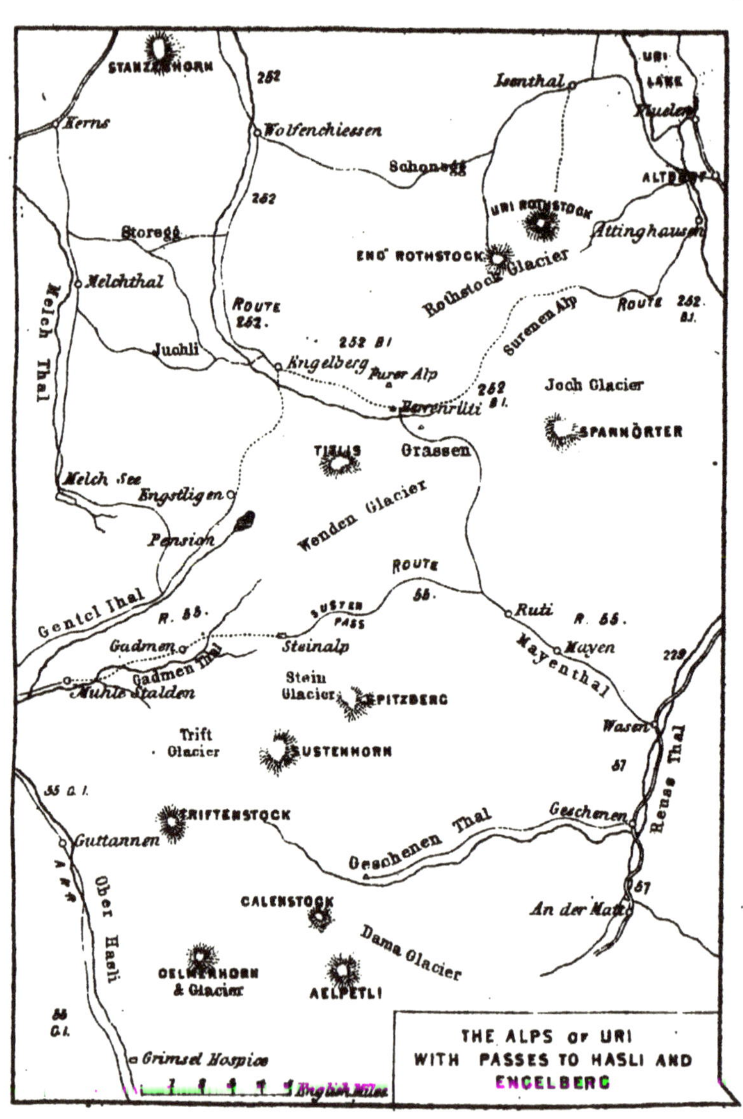

STANZERHORN
Kerns
Wolfenchiessen
Schonegg
Isenthal
URI LAKE
Fluelen
ALTDORF
252
252
Storegg
Melchthal
URI ROTHSTOCK
ENG. ROTHSTOCK
Rothstock Glacier
Attinghausen
Melch Thal
ROUTE 252
Juchli
Engelberg
Purer Alp
Surenen Alp
ROUTE 252. 81.
252 81
252 81
Horchrütti
Joch Glacier
SPANNÖRTER
Melch See
TITLIS
Grassen
Engstligen
Pension
Wenden Glacier
ROUTE 55
Gentel Thal
R. 55.
SUSTEN PASS
Ruti
R. 55.
Gadmen
Steinalp
Mayen
Mayenthal
228
Gadmen Thal
Muhlestalden
Stein Glacier
SPITZBERG
Wasen
Trift Glacier
SUSTENHORN
57
55 Gl.
TRIFTENSTOCK
Geschenen Thal
Geschenen
Reuss Thal
Guttannen
An der Matt
57
Aar
Ober Hasli
CALENSTOCK
Dama Glacier
55 Gl.
OELWENHORN & Glacier
AELPETLI
Grimsel Hospice
English Miles
THE ALPS OF URI
WITH PASSES TO HASLI AND
ENGELBERG

people; not dear; good trout; stay, 3*fr.*; breakfast, 1*fr.* Star, cheap) is at the foot of the Bristenstock, an interesting but difficult mountain to ascend, surrounded by precipices, where it is easy to lose your way.

Amsteg is at the entrance of the Maderanerthal, and may be made a centre for pleasant excursions, especially to the Arniberg Alps. Distance from Altdorf, 1½ l. (4½ m.) Ascending from Amsteg to Wasen you pass several waterfalls and some bridges boldly placed on the side of precipitous rocks flanking the Reuss, such as the Fellibrücke, the Pfaffensprung, and the Schönebrücke. To the Pfaffenbrücke is attached a legend which relates how once upon a time a monk carrying off a fair damsel, and being pursued, on reaching this spot, leaped the chasm as his only means of rescue. Up to this point the waterfalls are of no particular importance, if we except the Fellibach; but beyond the Schönebrucke they become frequent and imposing. First to the left you see the Rohrbach, dashing down from a very high rock, and the Reuss, of which you seldom lose sight, pours its waters with much impetuosity over its rocky bed, and emits a thundering roar as it passes from fall to fall. Before arriving at Geschenen, you see the entrance of the valley so called, the cascade of the Geschenen torrent which falls into the Reuss. At the top of the Geschenenthal may be descried the Lochberg Glacier, and in a valley, running N. from the foot of that glacier is a cavern, once noted for crystals called sand balm. A little way above Geschenen is the large Brücke or Häderli-brücke; here commences the terrible defile or gorge called the Schœllinen, which is traversed by the road, sometimes on one and sometimes on the other side of the stream, over which three bridges have been made with great daring. At the middle or Tanzebein Bridge is the limit of the districts of Uri and Urseren. The last of the three is the Devil's Bridge (Teufelsbrücke), consisting of a single

arch of 75 feet in width, resting on two naked and perpendicular rock buttresses. It is considered a master-piece of architectural skill, and is the work of an Italian engineer. The Reuss passes under this bridge at a depth of more than 200 feet, sending up a cloud of vapour from its fall, wetting the traveller as he crosses. A little farther on you reach the Devil's Mountain (Teufel's Berg) through which you pass by means of a cutting, called the Urner Loch, 220 feet long, 15 broad, 12 high, bringing you to the romantic, verdant Urserenthal. The Urner Loch was made in 1707, by a clever engineer of the Val Mazzva, named Pietro Morattini, the expenses being paid by the four parishes of the Urserenthal. The traveller is delighted on issuing from the Devil's Bridge district to find himself in the pastoral Vale of Urseren, which contains four villages, Andermatt or Urseren, Hospital, Zum-Dorf, and Realp. The first of these villages is 4,446 feet above the Mediterranean, the last 4,733 feet. Notwithstanding the elevated position of the Urserenthal, it has very good vegetation, though the only trees are the fir and the birch. Formerly the entire valley was covered with wood.

From the Urner Loch, 1¼ l. (¾ m.) brings you to Andermatt, the principal village of the Urseren valley, with a population of 600 inhabitants. Inns: Hotel and Pension Gothard chez de Christen: 40 rooms at from 1 to 2 fr. Breakfast, 1½*fr.* Excellent honey. Table d'hôte, 3 fr. Pension, 5*fr.* per day. Good trout and vino d'Asti. Carriages for Fluelen, the Furka, and Oberalp. Three Kings: Post, cheap table d'hôte; Sun. Andermatt is 4,438 ft. above the sea, at the foot of the Kirchberg. In the middle ages it was completely destroyed by an avalanche. Its inhabitants were almost reduced to beggary by the wars consequent on the great French Revolution. The church is served by four Capuchins. A good collection of minerals at Müller's and Nagel's. An ornithological collection at Nagel's.

Many excursions can be made from this spot as centre. Oberalp and its lake, 2 l. (6 m.) On Badus, 9,022 ft. (a guide required) with a view of the Oberland, Tessin, and Grisons Alps. To the Fibbia, 2½ l. (7½ m.) From Andermatt you can diverge by the Furka Pass to the Grimsel. *

Half-a-league (1½ m.) from Andermatt is Hospital, and 2½ l. (7½ m.) thence the Hospice of St. Gothard. Though the country passed through in this part of the journey be savage and arid, it is less shut in than the district from Schoellenen to the Urner Loch. Near the hospice is a substantial inn, built of stone to resist the weather. To the left above it is the hospice, which receives yearly 11,000 to 12,000 persons, and distributes 20,000 rations of bread, soup, and coffee. The expenses are supported by the Cantons and voluntary contributions. As Berlepsch justly remarks, an extraordinary resignation and love of humanity are required to remain in such a spot during nine months continual and dreadful winter weather, often cut off from all human aid and intercourse for days together, merely with the view to help the unfortunate with funds, hardly raised and scarcely sufficient. Alms if anywhere well bestowed are so here. The hospice is not a convent, but directed only by a chaplain who also makes meteorological observations on the spot. The old hospice, built in 1431, was destroyed by an avalanche in 1715, and again burnt by the civilizing French in 1799.

Mount St. Gothard is not a summit but a depression among summits. The surrounding points are the Prossa (9,241 feet), the Gospis (8,700 feet), the Sasso di San Gotardo (8,429 feet), Schipsiers (7,782 feet), Lucendro, or Pizzo di Vinet (9,109 feet), and Fibbia (8,441 feet). The ascent of most of them is easy. The easiest is the Fibbia, from the hospice; it has a fine panoramic view. ¾ l. (2¼ m.) from the hospice, is the lake of Lucendro (5,412 feet), one source of the Reuss.

The descent from St. Gothard to Tessin, through Val Lavinia, is delightful; after the desolation of the Reuss, flowers and southern vegetation greet the eye on all sides, as descending by the slopes of the Fibbia you pass through the Val Tremola, to the Val Leventina. The descent to Airolo is 1½ hour, on horseback 1 hour, and the ascent 3 hours. The Val Leventina is 13 l. (39 m.) long. (See Canton of Tessin.)

The road over St. Gothard is much exposed to avalanches, but easy-minded travellers do not scruple to cross it in sledges even in winter.

PEDESTRIAN ITINERARY FROM ALTDORF.

To Aarau, by Lucerne (Nos. 147 and 11, 12 or 13).

Aarberg, by Lucerne (Nos. 147 and 66, 67 or 68) and Berne (No. 53), or by Susten, Thun, and Berne (Nos. 55 and 58).

Aarburg, by Lucerne (Nos. 147 and 11).

Aigle, by Lucerne (Nos. 147 and 66, 67 or 68) and Berne (No. 54), or by Sien (No. 261, 262).

Altstaetten, by Glarus (Nos. 103 and 104).

Appenzell, by Glarus (Nos. 103 and 105).

Art, by Schwyz (Nos. 207 and 208).

Baden, by Lucerne (Nos. 147 and 149, or 150).

Bâle, by Lucerne (No. 147 and 39).

Bellinzona (No. 229).

Berne (No. 55), or by Lucerne (Nos. 147 and 66, 67 or 68).

Bex and Bulle, by Lucerne (Nos. 147 and 66, 67 or 68) and Berne (Nos. 54 and 58), or by Sion (Nos. 261, 74, 58, and 54).

Bienne, by Lucerne (Nos. 147, 66, 67, or 68) and Berne (No. 59),

Brougg, by Lucerne (Nos. 147 and 151).

---

* Realp is ¾ h. from Hospenthal. (Comfortable new inn: Hotel des Alpes.) The hamlet is 246 ft. above Hospenthal, and 5,034 above the sea. Passing the head of the interesting Muttenthal, you advance to the Furka by treeless slopes, covered however with a profusion of Alpine plants. Three hours take you to the top (7,792 ft.), with a decent inn, recently erected, from which the Galenstock and Mutthorn can be ascended. Western descent of Furka steep to the Rhone Glacier; in 2 l. (6 m.) you reach the *Rhon Gletscher* Inn, recently opened and comfortably *kept at the junction of the road to the* Grimsel *and down the Valais.—See* Canton of Valais.

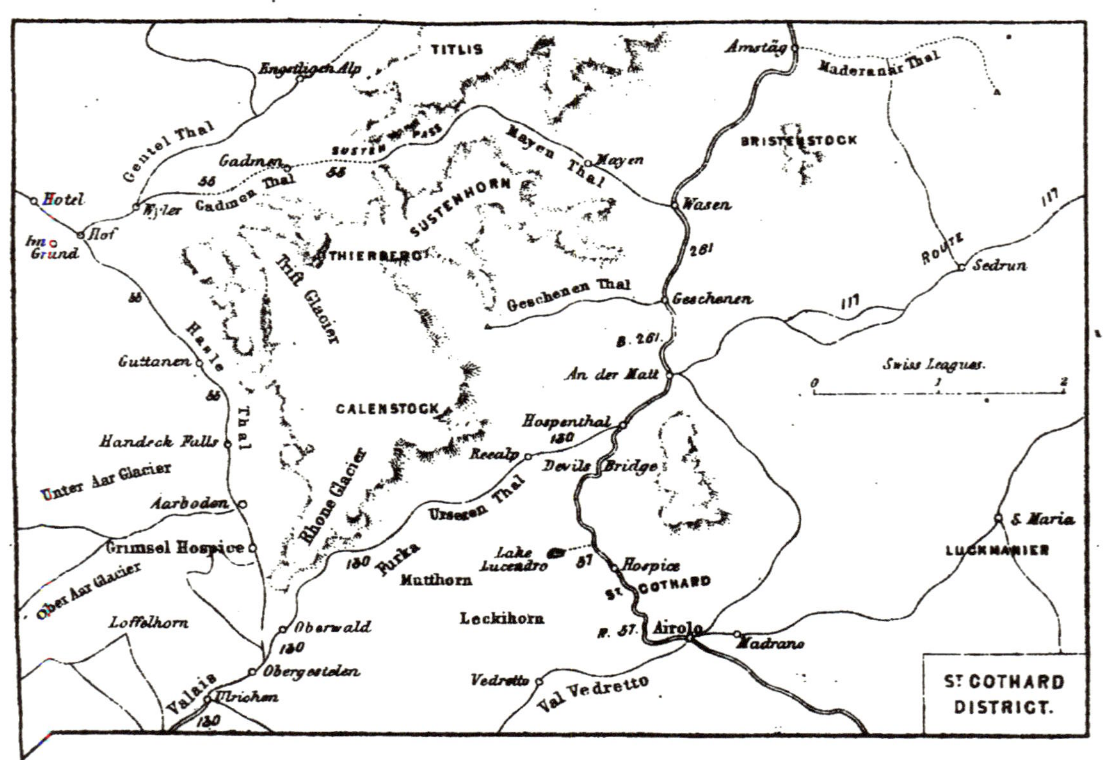

ST GOTHARD DISTRICT.
TITLIS
Engstligen Alp
Gentel Thal
Gadmen
55
Wyler Gadmen Thal
55
Hotel
Hof
Inn Grund
55
Hasle Thal
Guttanen
55
Handeck Falls
Unter Aar Glacier
Aarboden
Grimsel Hospice
Ober Aar Glacier
Loffelhorn
SUSTEN PASS
Mayen Thal
Mayen
SUSTENHORN
THIERBERG
Trift Glacier
CALENSTOCK
Rhone Glacier
Geschenen Thal
Geschenen
B. 261
An der Matt
Hospenthal
130
Reealp
Devils Bridge
Urseren Thal
130
Furka
Mutthorn
Lake Lucendro
57
Leckihorn
Oberwald
130
Obergestelen
Valais
Ulrichen
130
Vedretto
Val Vedretto
Amstäg
Maderanar Thal
BRISTENSTOCK
Wasen
281
ROUTE
117
Sedrun
117
Swiss Leagues.
0   1   2
Hospice
ST GOTHARD
R. 57. Airolo
Madrano
S. Maria
LUCKMANIER

Burgdorf, by Lucerne (Nos. 147 and 68).

Chamouni, by Lucerne (Nos. 147 and 66, 67 or 68) and Berne (No. 63), Lausanne (No. 96), and Geneva (No. 95), or by Sion (No. 261 and 265).

Chaux de Fonds, by Lucerne (Nos. 147 and 66, 67 or 68) and Berne (No. 61), or from Berne, by Neuchâtel (Nos. 70 and 169).

ROUTE 256.

CHIAVENNA, 40½ L. (121½ m.)

	Leagues.	Miles.
Iláns (No. 117)	21	63
Peiden	1½	4½
Furth	½	1½
St. Martin	½	1½
St. Anne	½	1½
Vals	½	1½
Hinter Rhein	2½	7½
The Hospice of St. Bernardin	3	9
Piano di San Giacomo	1½	4½
Misocco or Misox	1	3
Soazza	½	1½
Chiavenna (No. 122)	7½	22½
	40½	121½

Coire (No. 117).

Einsiedeln, by Schwyz (Nos. 207 and 209).

ROUTE 257.

ENGELBERG, 12¼ L. (36¾ m.)

	Leagues.	Miles.
Fluelen	½	1½
Over the lake to Buochs	6¼	18¾
Stanz	1¼	3¾
Engelberg (No. 252)	4¼	12¾
	12¼	36¾

ROUTE 258.

Or 10¼ L. (30¾ m.)

	Leagues.	Miles.
Fluelen	½	1½
Over the lake to Brunnen	1	3
Seelisberg	1	3
Beckenried	1½	4½
Buochs	1	3
Stanz	1¼	3¾
Engelberg (No. 252)	4¼	12¾
	10½	31½

ROUTE 259 (a).

Or, 9 L. (27 m.)

	Leagues.	Miles.
Attinghausen	½	1½
Over the Surenen Pass to Engelberg	8½	25½
	9	27

ROUTE 259 (b 1).

ALTDORF TO ENGELBERG by the Isenthal and Uri Rothstock. Difficult Route. Good guide, Joseph Imfanger, of Isenthal. Best to sleep at the Châlets of Musenalp or Oberalp. 12h. 30m. Two routes, 1, by Great Isenthal (easiest); 2, by Little Isenthal. Altdorf to Isenthal, 2½ hours.

	h.	m.
Negenalp	1	30
Musenalp	1	0
Top of Kessel	2	30
Rothstock (2,932 metres)	1	30
Descent to Mittalgraetli	1	0
By dangerous glacier of Blumlisalp firn to Plankenalp	4	0
By Engelberg	2	0

ROUTE 259 (b 2).

To ENGELBERG from ISENTHAL, by the ROTHGRÄTLI, 9h. 30m.

	h.	m.
Isenthal	2	15
Sankt Jacob	0	45
Oberalp (night quarters)	2	0
By glacier to Rothgrätli	2	30
To Engelberg by Horbisthal	4	0

Frauenfeld, by Schwyz (Nos. 207 and 215), and Zurich (No. 245).

Friburg, by Lucerne (Nos. 147 and 66, 67, or 68), and Berne (No. 54), or by Sion (Nos. 261 and 74, 58 and 54).

Gais, by Schwyz (Nos. 207 and 191), and Saint Gallen (No. 186).

Geneva, by Lucerne (Nos. 147, 66, 67, or 68). Berne (No. 63), and Lausanne (No. 97), or by Sion (Nos. 261 and 98).

Glarus (No. 103).

Herisau, by Schwyz (Nos. 207 and 210).

Hofwyl, by Lucerne (Nos. 147, 68), and from Bergdorf, by the Sand to Hofwyl.

Lauffenburg, by Lucerne (Nos. 147, 11, 12, or 13), and Aarau (No. 10).

Lausanne, by Lucerne (Nos. 147, 66, 67, or 68), and Berne (No. 63), or by Sion (Nos. 261 and 267).

Locarno, by Bellinzona (Nos. 229 and 232).

Locle (To the), by Lucerne (Nos. 147, 66, 67, or 68), Berne (No. 70), and Neuchâtel (No. 175).

Neuchâtel, by Lucerne (Nos. 147, 66, 67, or 68) and Berne (No. 70).

Orbe, by Lucerne (Nos. 147 and 66, 67 or 68), and Berne (No. 71).

Payerne, by Lucerne (Nos. 147 and 66, 67 or 68) and Berne (No. 77).

Pfeffers (Bath) by Glarus (Nos. 103 and 111).

Righi (The) by Schwyz (Nos. 207 and 62).

Saint Gallen, by Glarus (Nos. 103 and 112).

Schaffhausen, by Schwyz (Nos. 207 and 215), Zurich (No. 200).

Schwyz (No. 207).

ROUTE 260.

LOESCH (Baths) 32¼ l. (96¼ m.)

	Leagues.	Miles.
Wasen (see No. 229)	5	15
Andermatt (No. 57)	2	6
Loesch (No. 130)	25¼	77¼
	32¼	98¼

Lugano, by Bellinzona (Nos. 229 and 233).

Lucerne (See No. 147).

Mendrisio, by Bellinzona (Nos. 229 and 235).

Morat, Morges and Moudon, by Lucerne (Nos. 147 and 66, 67 or 63), and Berne (Nos. 77 and 63).

ROUTE 261.

SION, 34¼ l. (73½ m.)

	Leagues.	Miles
Wasen (No. 229)	5	15
St. Joseph	¼	¾
Göschenen	½	2¼
Devil's Bridge	½	2¼
Andermatt	¼	¾
Loesch (Town, No. 130)	23¼	69¾
Sion, (No. 135)	4¼	12¼
	34¼	103¼

Or by Lucerne (Nos. 147 and 66, 67 or 68), and Berne (No. 74)

Solothurn, by Lucerne (No. 147 and 162).

Stanz, see Unterwalden.

ROUTE 261.

ALTDORF to STANZ, by ISENTHAL and SCHONEGG, 9h. 30m. Footpath.

ISENTHAL by land 2¼ h., by boat from THUN, 2h. 30m. FLUELEN, 30m.

	h.	m.
Boat to Isleten Path to Blanen	1	30
Schartiberg Chapel (Frutt)	0	30
Join land route from Altdorf (by Seedorf:		
Isenthal (Inn, Joseph Imfanger good guide. Oberhauenstein may be ascended, 3 to 4 h., 2,120 metres)	0	30
By Great Isenthal to Sanct Jacob	0	45
Schonegg Pass (1,925 metres)	1	30
Oberrickenbach	1	0
Wolfenschiessen	0	45
Stanz	1	45

Thun (see No. 55), or by Lucerne (Nos. 147 and 66, 67 or 68), and Berne (No. 55).

Trogen, by Glarus (Nos. 203 and 112), and Saint Gallen (No 193).

Unterwalden (No. 251)

Vevay, by Lucerne (Nos. 147, 66, 67, or 68) and Berne (No. 54), or by Sion (Nos. 261 and 262).

Winterthur, by Schwys (Nos. 207 and 215), and Zurich (No. 3...)

Yverdun, by L... 147, 66, 67, or 68 and Berne N...

Zug. by Schwyz (Nos. 207 and 214.

Zurich, by Schwyz (No. 2 7 and 215).

Zurzach, oy Schwyz (Nos. 207 and 215), and Zurich (Nos. 305 or 306.

Bavaria and Austria, by Lucerne or Schwyz, Zurich, Romanshorn, and Friedrichshafen.

Baden and the Rhine, by Lucerne and Bâle.

Strasburg and Paris, by Lucerne and Bâle.

Turin, Lyons, and South France, by Lucerne, Berne and Geneva.

Milan and Italy, by the St. Gothard and Bellinzona.

The link between Lucerne and East Switzerland is the Canton of Zug, and before we leave this centre, we must give a passing notice of this, the smallest Canton of the Republic.

CANTON OF ZUG.

The branch of the Zurich rail takes the traveller now from Lucerne into the Canton, and direct to the city of Zug. You can also reach Zug by steamer. 1st, to Küssnacht on the lake of Lucerne, thence by the Hollow Way and Tell's Chapel to Itramen See, and on by steamer to Zug, over the Lake of Zug. (Five trains a-day, 1hr. 47min. Fares, 6fr. 50c., 4fr. 55c., and 3fr. 25c.)

LIMITS.— North, Zurich; east, Zurich and Schwyz; south, Schwyz; west Lucerne and Aarau.

AREA, SOIL, AND CLIMATE.—This is the smallest Swiss Canton; its surface is only 10 square Swiss leagues (239 square kilometres), and consists partly of plains, stretching principally west and north of the Lake of Zug, and partly of mountains, none of which exceed 5,000 feet, and generally covered with verdure to their summits. The climate of Zug is mild and healthy, and the soil generally fertile.

MOUNTAINS.—The most remarkable are the Ruffiberg, part of whose base extends along the east bank of the lake of Zug; the Zugerberg, rising behind the town of Zug; a branch of the Hohe-Rohnen, prolonged from east to west, and shading off gradually into the district of Baar.

LAKES, RIVERS, AND STREAMS.—(*a*) Lakes: The lake of Zug bathes the foot of the Righi on the south, it extends thence for the length of about 4 l. (12 m.) to Cham; its mean breadth is 1 l. (3 m.), and its depth 200 fathoms, or 1,200 feet. Near the Chapel of St. Adrian, at the foot of the Righi, and 180 to 200 feet near the town of Zug. This lake is extremely well stocked with fish, receives a number of streams, and discharges its waters into the Lorze, equally well-stocked with fish. Among the numerous species of fish with which the Lake of Zug is peopled, a very delicate trout is called on the spot Rötheli (salmo salvelinus), or red trout. The lake yields a great number of carp, some of them weighing 90 ℔., as well as pike of 50 ℔. The banks and country near the lake of Zug present some of the most graceful scenery in the republic. Most travellers, ascending the Righi, do well to visit Zug, and quiet English families will find a stay and strolls and sails near Zug, sweet in the present and a joy for the memory. For those passing some time there, it will be useful to add that the prevailing winds are the south, or Föhn, and Arbis, or north-west, but little or no danger need be apprehended from them. The barks of the country are, however, rather frail, and admit of improvement. 2. The lake Ægeri, 1 l. (3 m.) long, and ½ l. (1½ m.) wide, is to the east of Zug, with which it communicates by the Lorze, and its romantic position in the midst of grassy uplands renders it deserving of a visit. 3. The Feister Lake, near Menzigen, is very small.

(*b*) Rivers: The Reuss forms the west limit of Zug towards Aargau. 2. The Sihl forms the north-east limit of Zug towards Zurich. 3. The Lorze, or Loreze, issues from the Ægeri lake and waters the fertile district of Baar; falls into the lake of Zug, and issues from it at Cham. It leaves the Canton of Zug near the Convent of Trauenthal, and joins the Reuss in the Canton of Zurich. (*c*) Streams, numerous, but *none of any importance*.

AGRICULTURAL AND MANUFACTURED PRODUCTIONS.—Cattle are bred in this Canton, also goats and pigs, and much care is bestowed on bees. Fish is very abundant. Zug has excellent and rich meadowlands, and pastures, and fine forests. There are crops of hemp and flax, and a little wine is made; but it yields a large quantity of excellent fruit of a more hardy sort, including walnuts and chesnuts, and especially apples and cherries, from the former of which they prepare cider, while from the cherries they distil superior cherry brandy, or kirchenwasser. Freestone quarries occur in Zug, also tracts of turf, used for fuel, and one mineral spring. Agriculture forms the chief occupation of the inhabitants, but some cotton and silk mills exist in the Canton, and paper mills occur at Cham and Baar. The inhabitants of the circles of Ægeri and Mensingen, dwelling mostly in the uplands, are chiefly engaged in pastoral pursuits.

THERMAL SPRINGS.—The only mineral waters are at Walterschweil, but they are not much frequented.

POPULATION AND RELIGION.—The present population is 19,608, all Roman Catholics except 618, who are Protestants. In 1817 the population was 13,738. A German patois is the language.

ABBEYS, CONVENTS, &c.—At Zug is a Capuchin monastery and a convent for Franciscan nuns, and at Frauenthal is a Cistercian convent for nuns.

EDUCATIONAL INSTITUTIONS, CHARITIES.—Education is much more advanced in this than in any other purely democratic cantons. Zug has a gymnasium, a public school, and a girls' school, taught by nuns. The Educational Institute in their convent is so well conducted, and the methods used and instruction given there are so good, that girls of a better class, and even of a different religion, are sent to it.

Each parish is compelled to take care of its poor and infirm; some of the parishes possess hospitals, and the three co-

contribute to the support of the poor by frequent alms. An insurance office has existed for many years in this spirited little Canton, of which the people are intelligent, gay, and industrious.

SURVEY OF THE CANTON.

Cham, a little castle at the head of the lake, on the Zurich side, commanding the best view of this fine sheet of water.

Immensee,* landing-place of the steamer for those going to Lucerne or to the Righi, by Kussnacht. The lakes of Zug and Lucerne are here separated by a narrow isthmus, and the road passing from Immensee on the Zug lake to Kussnacht, on that of Lucerne, goes by the Chapel of Tell, built on the spot where the hero, after escaping from the boat at Tellen Platte, is said to have anticipated Gessler, and shot him dead with his unerring dart (see Canton of Schwys, Kussnacht).

Morgarten.—Small though its territory, and few the number of its people, the Canton and men of Zug shine bright in history, and prove again in later times, as in the earlier days of Greece, that greatness of heart and virtue of action are not to be limited or controlled by material magnitude or multitude. Hero souls and stalwart arms have gone forth from the hills of Zug and proved again what free and freedom-loving citizens, especially if buttressed by God's everlasting bastions, can do for the sacred cause of home and fatherland. May the lesson never be forgotten by the brave Switzers in this age of much talk and writing, but of feeble will and muscles.

3½ l. from Zug, and on the eastern bank

* From Immensee a road leads to Righi Kulm; distance, 3½ l. (10½ m.) This is the shortest route. Zurich morning train arrives at Zug at 10; steamer on Lake of Zug brings you to Immensee at 11½ a.m.; 1 p.m. Zurich train brings you to Immensee at 4 p.m ; rather late to ascend the Kulm This latter train is best suited to the long June days. To ascend you pass the Chapel of Tell, where there are two hotels, the Oak and the Lily. Hence in 1¾ l. (5½ m) to the *Alp of Seeboden, where you fall into the road that ascends from Kussnacht.*

of the Lake of Ægeri, a small mound attracts the eye of the wayfarer. It is the tumulus of Morgarten raised to commemorate a great and glorious victory of the Swiss over the Austrians. A little chapel stands at St. Jacques, in which, on the 16th November, Divine Service is celebrated in memory of the heroes who fell in the battle. ½ l. (1½ m.) from the chapel is the scene of the action thus described in history.

Duke Leopold of Austria resolved to punish the men of Grütli for having thrown off the oppressive yoke of his father. With a large army, in which were many knights and nobles, he advanced to punish them. Unterwalden was surrounded by an armed force commanded by Count Otho, of Strasburg, the governor of Lucerne, and others. But the main body marched on under the duke from Ægeri by Morgarten, bringing boats full of ropes to hang the Swiss chiefs. To oppose the host the Confederates had 1,300 men; 400 of Unterwalden, and 300 of Uri had joined those of Schwyz. Posted on the slope called Sattel, they stood firm awaiting the enemy, who, in serried array, their armour flashing in the rising sun, advanced to attack them. Near the little plateau of Haselmott the Swiss rushed upon them with loud shouts; 50 men of Schwyz rolled down immense rocks on the Austrians, and, rushing on the enemy out of the fog, spread terror and havoc in their track. Henry Hospenthal and the sons of old Reding of Bibereck headed these glorious men of Schwyz. The enemy was crowded between the defile and Lake Ægeri, and soon fell in crowds under the halberts and battleaxes of the stalwart mountaineers. It was with difficulty that even Duke Leopold escaped. The next day the conquerors crossed the lake and defeated the Austrian party from Lucerne, and Strasburg was so frightened that he ran off and did not dare to face the Swiss. The Confederates, after this great victory, renewed their oath to die one for all and all for one, and not to make any engagements with any foreign power. At Morgarten they had beaten fifteen times their own number. The battle was fought November 15th, 1315. Though the heroes of Morgarten were men of Uri, Schwyz, and Unterwalden only, for Zug did not join the Confederacy till 1353, yet, as we shall see soon, they performed deeds of prowess worthy to stand beside the proudest annals of any country. (See Canton of Tessin, Giarnico.)

Oberwald, a pretty village on the lake of Zug, to which you arrive by a delightful walk.

Zug, the capital of the Canton, is a quiet, little, ancient town, on the slope of the mountain of Zug, rising from the eastern shore of the blue lake. Chief Hotels, The Ox, the Stag, the Löwe. Population, 3,800—in 1830, 2,800. The situation of Zug is smiling and charming. The north end of the town is approached by a long, ill paved, and ill built suburb, but the interior of the place is fair enough, presenting tolerably wide streets and respectable houses, as well as public squares, especially that by the lake, offering a very fine view.

PUBLIC EDIFICES. — Among the churches are those of St. Oswald, and of the Capuchins, both of which are adorned with paintings of Caracci. The parish church of St. Michael, is situated above the town, and has some Altar pieces by John Brandeberg, a celebrated painter, of Zug. The Hotel de Ville, contains some fine stained glass windows, by Michael Müller, of Zug, who was in high repute in the 16th century. Another curiosity, at Zug, is a topographical chart of the canton, by Colonel Landwing, held in much esteem on account of its exactness. In the Arsenal are preserved many banners and arms, trophies of early victories in the glorious ages of Swiss history. The most interesting object in the collection is the flag, stained with the blood of Peter Kolin, who died while bravely defending it, with a handful of followers, against eight times *their number of Italians*, at the battle of Arbedo, 1422.—(See Canton of Tessin.)

EDUCATIONAL, SCIENTIFIC, AND CHARITABLE INSTITUTIONS.—1. The gymnasium. 2. The town library, founded in the 14th century. The library of the Capuchin fathers, probably the richest in historical MSS. of all the Swiss monastic libraries.

Zug being almost at the foot of the Righi is unfortunately infested with the tormentors of travellers, in the shape of guides, hotel agents, horse dealers, *et id genus omne*, who effectually thwart the impressions of the sublime and beautiful, and interfere with the peace of visitors. It is well to escape from them at once by a peremptory announcement that you have formed your engagements, or that you are stationary for some days.

WALKS NEAR ZUG.—At the Menzingerberg, 1½ L. (2¼ m.) from Zug, is a hydropathic institution called Schönbrunn (2,360 feet high), conducted by Dr. Hegglin, and commanding a fine view over the Hochwacht. Near the church of St. Michael, and from the tower of St. Oswald's and the Capuchin church, you enjoy beautiful views of the lake and surrounding country. But by ascending the Kanisthal (912 feet above the lake), a hill above the town of very easy access, you obtain a more extensive and varied prospect. Charming walks may be taken on all sides of Zug. That to Oberweil has been already noticed, and the numerous excursions on the lake are quite delightful. Thus you can reach Chain by a water passage of 1 l. (3 m.) Another château, opposite Zug, is also 1 l. distant by water. Immensee is 2 l. (6 m.) and can be visited in order to view the glorious spot, hallowed by the unfailing memory and affection of a grateful people, where the dart of Tell put an end to the tyranny of Gessler. From Immensee to Kussnacht is ½ l. (1½ m.) Steamboats ply in summer 3 times a-day from Zug to Immensee and Arth.

HISTORICAL NOTICE.—In the year 1433 some works were undertaken at Zug with the view to help in draining the lake.

The result was that two streets of the town gave way and sank into the waters of the lake. But this accident was by no means unforeseen, and the greater part of the inhabitants had time to escape, carrying off their goods with them. There were about thirty, however, who being sturdy conservatives, unwilling to listen to all representations, and stubbornly opposed to reform, would not abandon their hearths and homes. These illustrious thirty became the victims of their own obstinacy, and were drowned in the lake under the ruins of their houses.

ROUTES OF ZUG.

Aarau (No. 17).

Aarberg, by Aarau (Nos. 17 and 16) and Solothurn (No. 216), or by Berne (Nos. 78 and 53).

Aarbourg, by Aarau (Nos. 17 and 1).

Aigle, by Lucerne (Nos. 165, 66, 67 or 68) and Berne (No. 54), or directly by Berne (Nos. 78 and 58), or by Thun (No. 255), and the Simmenthal (No. 55).

Altdorf, by Schwyz (Nos. 214, 207).

Altstaetten, by St. Gallen (Nos. 195 and 180).

Appenzell, by St. Gallen (Nos. 195 and 25).

ROUTE 281.

ART, by the lake, 3 l. (12 m.)

ROUTE 282.

BADEN, 9 l. (27 m.)

	Leagues.		Miles.
Cham	1		3
Sins	1		3
Russek	½		1½
Muhlan	½		1½
Mehrischwanden	1		3
Breniggarten	2		6
Gorliken	¾		2¼
Meiliken	1		3
Baden	1½		4½
	9		27

ROUTE 283.

BÂLE, 21¼ l. (63¾ m.)

	Leagues.		Miles.
Baden (No. 282)	9		27
Frick No. 31)	6		18
Bâle (No. 4)	6¼		18¾
	21¼		63¾

Or 19 l. (57 m.)

	Leagues.		Miles.
Aarau (No. 17)	10		30
Bâle (No. 4)	9		27
	19		57

Bellinzona, by Schwyz (Nos. 214 and 207), and Altdorf (No. 229).

Berne (No. 78), or by Thun (No. 255).

Bex, by Berne (Nos. 78, 54, and 58), or by Thun (No. 255), and the Simmenthal.

Bienne, by Aarau (Nos. 17 and 16), and Solothurn (No. 218), or by Berne (Nos. 78 and 59).

ROUTE 285.

BROUGG, 11 l. (33 m.)

	Leagues.		Miles.
Baden (No. 282)	9		27
Brougg (No. 31)	2		6
	11		33

Bulle, by Berne (Nos. 78 and 54), or by Thun (No. 255), and the Simmenthal (No. 55).

Burgdorf, by Lucerne (No. 165 and 68).

Chamouni, by Berne (Nos 78 and 63), Lausanne (No. 96), and Geneva (No. 93), or by Thun (No. 255), the Simmenthal (No. 55), Rail from Aigle to Martigny and over the Col de Balme or Tête Noire (see Canton of Geneva, Chamouni, and No 265).

Chaux de Fonds, by rail from Lucerne to Olten and Neuchâtel, or by Berne (Nos. 78 and 70), and Neuchâtel (No. 169).

Chiavenna, by Chur (Nos. 236 and 121, 122 or 123)

ROUTE 286.

CHUR, 25¾ l. (77¼ m.)

	Leagues.		Miles.
Allen Winden	1		3
Lorzentobebel and Brugg ...	½		1½
Aegero	¼		¾
Ober Aegoro	½		1½
Sulmatten	½		1½
Sattel, 3¾ l. (11¼ m.)	¾		2¼
Rothenthurm	¼		1¼
Altmatt	1		3
Schindellegi	1½		4½
Richtenschwyl	1		3
Pfäffikon	1½		4½
Altendorf	1½		3½
Lachen 10½ l. (31½ m.)	½		1½
Galgemen	½		1½
Siebenen	¼		¾
Schubelbach	¼		¾
Richenburg	1		3
Bilten	¼		¾
Urner Bad	½		1½
Wesen	½		1½
Over the lake or by rail to Wollenstadt	4		12
Berschis	¾		2¼
Halbmell	¾		2¼
Sargans	1½		4½
Ragaz	1		3
Untere-Zollbrucke	1½		3½
Carried forward	23		69

ROUTE 286—(Continued.)

	Leagues.	Miles.
Brought forward	23	69
Obere-Zollbrücke	¼	...
Zeara	¼	2¼
Klein-Rufihaus	¼	2¼
Gross Rufihaus	¼	¾
Magnus	½	1½
Cham	¼	¾
	25½	77½

ROUTE 287.

Or, 23¼ L. (69¾ m.)

	Leagues.	Miles.
Baar	¼	2¼
Sohlbrücke	¾	2¼
Horgen	1¼	5¼
Wädenschwyl	1	3
Richtenschwyl, 5 L. (15 m.)	¾	2¼
Pfäffikon	1¼	4¼
Altendorf	1¼	3¾
Lachen	¼	¾
Cham (No. 286)	15¼	45¼
	23¼	69¾

See also No. 141.

ROUTE 288.

Einsiedeln, 5¾ L. (17¼ m.)

	Leagues.	Miles.
No. 286)	3¾	11¼
...eln	2	6
	5¾	17¼

...berg, by Lucerne (Nos. 165 and 163).
...enfeld, by Zurich (Nos 295, 296, and 245).
...bourg, by Berne (Nos. 78 and 54).
...als. by St. Gallen (Nos. 195 and 186).
...eneva, by Berne (Nos. 78 and 63, and Lausanne (No. 96), or by Lucerne, Thun (No. 255), and the Simmenthal (No. 72) and to Vevay and thence by rail or boat.
Glarus (No. 115).

ROUTE 289.

Herisau, 22 L. (66 m.)

	Leagues.	Miles.
Einsiedeln (No. 288)	5¾	17¼
Herisau (No. 183)	16¼	48¾
	22	66

ROUTE 290.

Or, 19½ L. (58½ m.)

	Leagues.	Miles.
Zurich (No. 295)	5½	16½
Herisau (No. 301)	14	42
	19½	58½

ROUTE 291.

Hofwyl, 20½ L. (61½ m.)

	Leagues.	Miles.
Lucerne No. 165)	5½	15½
Burgdorf (No. 68)	12½	36½
Rohrmoos	¼	1¼
Mötschwyl	¼	1¼
Hindelbank	½	1½
Sand	1	3
Hofwyl	½	1½
	20½	61½

Lauffenburg, by Aaran (Nos. 17 and 10).
Lausanne, by Aaran (Nos. 17 and 16) and Solothurn (No. 553), or by Berne (Nos. 78 and 63).
Locarno, by Schwyz (Nos. 214 and 207), Altdorf (No. 220) and Bellinzona (No. 232).
Locle, by Aarau (Nos. 17 and 16), and Solothurn (No. 224), or by Berne (Nos. 78 and 70) and Neuchâtel (No. 1.5).
Loesch (Baths) by Lucerne (Nos. 165 and 156), or by Berne (Nos. 72 and 65, or Nos. 78 and 74) and Sion (No. 268).
Lucerne (No. 165).
Lugano, by Schwyz (Nos. 214 and 207), Altdorf No. 229), and Bellinzona (No. 233).
Mendrisio, by Schwyz (Nos. 214 and 207), Altdorf (No. 229), and Bellinzona (No. 235).
Morat, Morges, and Moudon, by rail to Olten, and rail or road to Solothurn (No. 223), or by Berne (Nos. 78 and 63).
Neuchâtel, by rail to Olten and the junction at Herzogenbuchsee, or by road to Solothurn (No. 171) or by Berne (Nos 78 and 70).
Orbe, by rail to Olten; rail or road to Solothurn (No. 178) and Neuchâtel (No. 97), or by Berne (Nos. 78 and 70).
Payerne, by Berne (Nos 78 and 77), or by Olten, rail, and Solothurn, rail and road (No. 223).

ROUTE 292.

Pfeffers (Baths), 24 L. (72 m).

	Leagues.	Miles.
Lachen (No. 286)	10¼	30¼
Galgenenen	¼	1¼
Schubelbach	¼	1¼
Richenburg	1	3
Bilten	¼	¾
Urner-Bad	¼	1¼
Ziegelbrücke	¼	1¼
Wesen	¼	1¼
Rail or boat on lake to Wallenstadt	4	12
Berschis	¾	2¼
Hallemüll	¾	2¼
Sargans	1¼	4¼
Ragaz	1	3
Valens	1¼	4¼
Pfeffers		
	24	72

ROUTE 293.

Or, 24½ L. (73½ m.)

	Leagues.	Miles.
Glarus (No. 215)	12¼	36¾
Pfeffers (No. 111)	12¼	36¾
	24½	73½

ROUTE 294.

Righi (The), 6 L. (18 m.)

	Leagues.	Miles.
By lake to Art	3	9
To Hospice of Righi	2½	7½
Righi Kulm	¼	1½
	6	18

Saint Gallen (No. 195), or Zurich (Nos. 295 or 296 and 196).

Schaffhausen, by Zurich (Nos. 295, 296, and 200).

Schwyz (No. 214).

Sion, by Berne (Nos. 78 and 73 or 74). or Thun (No. 255) and the Rawil Pass (Nos. 72 and 73).

Solothurn, by Olten, rail, or by Aarau, road (Nos. 17 and 16).

Stanz, see Unterwalden.

Thun, by Lucerne (Nos. 165 and 163) or (Nos. 253 and 255), or by Berne, rail or road (Nos. 78 and 55).

Trogen, by St. Gallen (Nos. 195 and 193).

Unterwalden, by Lucerne (Nos. 165 and 153).

Vevay, by Berne (Nos. 78 or 54), or by Lucerne, Thun, the Simmenthal, and Dent de Jaman (Nos. 253 and 255 or Nos 72.)

Winterthur, by Zurich (Nos 295, 296, and 301).

Yverdun, by rail to Olten, or road to Aarau (Nos. 17 and 16), Solothurn (No. 178), Neuchatel (No. 97), and the Lake Steamers, or by Berne (Nos. 78 and 77).

ROUTE 295.

Zurich, 5½ L. (16½ m.)

	Leagues.	Miles.
Baar	½	2¼
Kappel	¾	2¼
Hausen	½	1½
Inn on the Albis	1	3
Adlischwyl	1	3
Wollishofen	½	1½
Zurich	1	3
	5½	16½

Or, 6½ L. (19½ m.)

	Leagues.	Miles.
Baar	¾	2¼
Sihlbrücke	¾	2¼
Horgen	1½	5¼
Oberrieden	¼	1¼
Thalwyl	¼	1¼
Ruslikon	¼	1¼
Küchberg	¼	1¼
Wollishofen	¼	2¼
Zurich	1	3
	6½	19½

ROUTE 297

Zurzach, 13½ L. (40½ m.)

	Leagues.	Miles.
Baden (No. 282)	9	27
Zurzach (No. 306)	4½	13½
	13½	40½

Bavaria, Austria, and East Germany, by Zurich and Schaffhausen or Romanshorn, and Lindau.

The Rhine, Francfort, and Paris by Lucerne, Olten, and Bâle.

Turin, Lyons, and Genoa by Olten, Berne, and Geneva.

Milan and Italy by Schwyz and Altdorf.

Few travellers proceed to Lucerne without visiting the Righi, which in some respects commands the most remarkable panoramic view, especially of Alpine scenery. As the Righi lies principally within the borders of Schwyz, our attention is therefore next directed to that Canton.

CANTON OF SCHWYZ.

Northern limit, Glarus; southern, the Lake of Lucerne and Canton of Uri; western, the Cantons of Lucerne, Zurich, and Zug; northern, Zurich and St. Gallen.

AREA, SOIL, AND CLIMATE.—The area of this canton comprises 31⅓ Swiss leagues (908 kilometres). It has few plains, consisting essentially of mountains and valleys; the climate varies according to the altitude and aspect, &c.; it is rather mild in the principal valley of Schwyz.

MOUNTAINS.--This Canton, though completely intersected by mountains, does not contain one covered with perpetual snow. The highest points are the Righi (5,555 feet), the Rossberg, also called Ruffiberg, the Engelstock, the Haggen, or Hacken (height of the inn, 4,470 feet), the Mythen (5,858 feet), the Pragel, the Fallenfluh, the Schonbücherberg, and the Frohnalp.

LAKES, RIVERS, AND RIVULETS.—(a) 1. The Lake of Lucerne (see Canton of Lucerne). 2. The Lake of Zug (see Canton of Zug). 3. The Lake of Zurich (see Canton of Zurich). 4. Lake of Lowertz, a pretty sheet of water, 1 l. (3 m.) long, ½ l. (1½ m.) wide, is very well stocked with fish; it discharges its waters by a rivulet, called Severn, into the Muotta. Two little islands, formerly inhabited by hermits, rise above its waters, and the largest of them still preserves the remains of the Castle of Schwanau, destroyed by the Swiss in 1308.

(*b*) Rivers: 1. The Linth, forming the frontier of Schwyz, on the side of St. Gallen. 2. The Muotta, an impetuous torrent formed by a multitude of streams issuing from the head of the valley of Muotta, flows through the valley of Schuz, and falls into the Lake of Lucerne near Brunnen. 3. The Sihl originates in the Thalbach and other little streams in the valley of Sihl; it leaves the Canton of Schwyz below Schindelegi, passing into that of Zurich. 4. The Alpfluss takes its rise in a remote part of the Alpthal, passes in front of Einsiedeln, and, after receiving the Biber, near Bennau, flows into the Sihl. 5. The Aafluss, formed by several streams in the valley of Wergi, flows into the Lake of Zurich, near Nu len.

(*c*) Rivulets: Schwyz contains a great number of small streams, of which the most considerable are the Severn, Biber, Bibi, Thalbach, Aabach, &c.

AGRICULTURAL AND INDUSTRIAL PRODUCTIONS.—The horned cattle and horses bred in this Canton are of a fine breed; there are fewer sheep and goats. Game is not so abundant as fish. The ground is covered with splendid meadows, magnificent mountain pastures, and fine forests. It yields good crops of fruit, vegetables, potatoes, and a little wine. The useful mineral productions are gypsum, marble, and coal. Silk and cotton stuffs are chiefly manufactured at Gersau. Cheese and butter are produced in good quantity and of good quality.

THERMAL WATERS, BATHS.—There are none of any importance.

POPULATION AND RELIGION.—45,000 inhabitants, all Roman Catholics.

MONASTERIES AND CONVENTS.—The Abbey of Einsiedeln (Nôtre Dame des Hermites), of the Benedictine order, whose abbot has the title of prince; the Convent of Dominicanesses, at Schwyz; the Franciscan Nuns' Convent, in the Muotta valley; the Chapter of Ladies of St. Benedict at Auw; the Capuchin Convents at Schwyz and at Art; and the Hospice of Capuchins on the Righi.

PUBLIC SCIENCE, AND CHARITIES.—Education has received more attention latterly. Schwyz and Einsiedeln possess schools and colleges. The Monastery of Einsiedeln has a library well furnished with books, &c.; very rich in MSS.; also a collection of objects of natural history. At Schwyz there is a very interesting and complete cabinet of medals. There is no general charity, but each parish is obliged to succour its own poor, and the religious communities deserve an honourable mention on account of the charity they practice.

SURVEY OF THE CANTON.

Egeri.—See Morgarten.

Art, 2 l. (6 m.) from Schwyz. The road from Schwyz passes first to Seven, ½ l. (1½ m.); thence to Lowertz, 1 l. (3 m.); and on over the landslip of Goldeu, ¾ l. (1½ m.). *Inns.*—Black Eagle; Hotel de la Clef stands at the south end of the Lake of Zug, and at the foot of the Rossberg, surrounded by fine meadows and orchards. All travellers going up the Righi on this side land here arriving from Zug. (In summer a steamer runs three times a day from Zug to Arth.) It was between Art and Lowertz that took place the dreadful landslip of the Gnipenspiz, September 2, 1806. In a few minutes this part of the Rossberg slipped down and covered the smiling valley of Goldau with its fragments, destroying instantaneously the three villages of Goldau, Busingen, and Röthen. The waters of the lake being driven back, rushed up to Seven, doing considerable mischief. 457 persons perished in this catastrophe; 14 were disinterred alive, though for the most part badly wounded. The whole district is now a chaos of rock and desolation. A foot and bridle path leads along the lake from Arth to Zug. It passes the villages of St. Adrian, Walchweil, Ottersweil, Oberweil, and St. Karli. The distance is 3 l. (9 m.); the water passage is preferable. To the Hospice of the Righi, from Arth, 3 l.; to the Righi Culm, 4 l. (12 m.)

Brunnen.—Hotel du Cheval Blanc, first-class hotel, well situated, comfortable and clean. Post carts twice a-day for Schwyz, 1 l. (3 m.), 70c.; Einsiedeln, 6¾ l. (20¼ m.), 4fr. 40c.; once a-day, at 8 a.m., to Arth, 2fr. 40c. Steamer to Fluelen, 1st class, 1fr. 50c.; 2nd class, 70c. To Gersau, 1st class, 70c.; 2nd class, 50c. To Lucerne, 1st class, 3fr. 10c.; 2nd class, 1fr. 60c. To Waggis, 1st class, 2fr.; 2nd class, 1fr.

Here again prepare to encounter the Swiss plague of cochers and boatmen. A boat to Treil (whence you ascend to Seelisberg), 1½ fr.

Observe rather grotesque frescoes of the early confederates, &c. in the hospice on the quay. Another of Swen and Swito, the legendary founders of Schwyz. A good painting in the Chapel of Henry.

EXCURSIONS.—Güsch, hill above Brunnen, with fine lake view. 2. To the Stoss pension (4fr. per day), 2 l. (6 m.) Take a boy for guide, view still finer from Frohnalpstock (5,430 feet, 4,100 above the lake), 1½ l. (4½ m.) from Stoss. 3. Boat excursion to Mythenstock, an isolated block of rock, with the inscription "Dem Sänger Tell's, Friederich Schiller, die Urkantonen, 1860." No worthier monument could be raised to the great poet. 4. ½ l. (1½ m.) S., still boating, on to the Grütli (see Canton of Lucerne). 5. Across to Triel and up to Seelisberg (see Lake of Lucerne, under Canton of Lucerne.)

Einsiedeln, 2,800 feet above the sea. Hotels: Peacock and Three Kings; both good. Great number of minor hotels for pilgrims. Post five times a-day between *Biberbuch and Einsiedeln*. This is one of the most celebrated pilgrimages in Europe, and obtains an equal place with St. Jago de Compestella in Spain, and Loretto in Italy. A special object of veneration is the miraculous image of the Virgin which it possesses. The convent is now occupied by 60 Benedictines and 20 lay brothers. The façade is 414 feet long, and has two high towers. The interior is overloaded with decorations and gilding. In the midst is the black marble chapel of the Virgin, in which is kept the miraculous image, of black wood, sculptured and covered with gold and diamonds. An ostensorium, weighing 10lb., is preserved in the treasury of the abbey. The convent library, kept in good order, contains 32,000 volumes, principally on history, also MSS. of the 8th to the 12th centuries, including one of great value, called the Regionator Einsiedliensis, representing the description of Rome in the 10th century. There are, moreover, a cabinet of minerals and a gratuitous school, in which Latin and several sciences are taught. The grand square in front of the convent is full of booths, in which medals, prayer books, &c., are sold. Mr. Banziger's printing office requires for this work alone several dozen presses and 400 workmen. The number of annual pilgrims is 150,000; in 1861 it was 200,000. The great day is September 24, the anniversary of the consecration of the church by the angels.

The Abbey was founded by Count Eberhard, of Hohenzollern, to whom the Emperor Otho granted, in 946, a great tract of land covered with forest. By degrees the abbey was enriched by numerous donations till, in 1274, the abbot was made a prince of the empire. At the time of Zwingli it was abandoned by the monks from 1520 to 1525, and remained almost deserted, but, in the latter year, Blaarer, the abbot, succeeded in collecting a few monks again. In 1798, when the French entered Switzerland and marked their progress by havoc and license, the abbey was threatened with entire dissolution. It was pillaged twice, and the sacred chapel irretrievably ruined. The exiled Benedictines returned in 1802, bringing back the miraculous image which they reported that they had saved, and they have somewhat recovered in prosperity since those disastrous times.

The road from Schwyz to the Lake of Zurich passes by Einsiedeln, and another route leads by St. Just, Ober and Under Ægeri, to Zug. From Einsiedeln you can also proceed by some footpaths to the valley of the Muotta, but they pass over very steep mountains and require some care.

Gersau.—Hotel and pension Müller, with baths on the lake. Inns: Sonne and Krone. This charming little solitude formed a kind of pocket republic till the French revolution, escaping the blessings of courts, taxes, parliaments, and politics. It governed itself, and all the people being relations of course there were no quarrels. Its population is 1,700, and a mule path leads hence to the Righi. A kind of goat track leads to Brunnen, and Gersau, with its quaint Swiss houses and fragrant orchards,* hangs suspended above the deep green lake, on the rugged flank of the Righi ridge, which is not a very agreeable vicinity, as it is decidedly addicted to landslips, like its neighbours, the Rossberg; still, with this little variety to give animation to so quiet a place, a summer's stay at Gersau has been thought delightful by many a wandering Briton in search of that ease difficult to be obtained so long as he carries his fidgetty self with him. Down to 1820 Gersau would have been a paradise for the vagabonds of our casual wards, as all vagrants were given a free asylum for three days (robbers included), with plenty of good cheer and laughter,

* A few years ago Gersau was quite one of those Swiss idyls alluded to in the Introduction; quaint old houses, primitive manners, honest prices, &c., coupled with the beauty of the lake and views, made it an Eden. The writer has not heard if it has "fallen," but landslips are common thereabouts. A charming walk of 2½ hours leads along the lake from Gersau to Wäggis, passing by Fitznau, 1½ hour from Gersau.

and no interruption allowed; but the fourth day they were bound to depart. Gersau being in those days inaccessible to Smith, Jones, and Robinson, it is said that its good people never had occasion to regret their hospitality. Steam-boat to Lucerne, 1st class, 2*fr.*; 2nd class, 1*fr.* 30*c.* To Fluelen, 1st class, 2*fr.*; 2nd class, 1*fr.* To Wäggis, 1st class, 1*fr.* 50*c.*; 2nd class, 70*c.*

Righi (The).—Five excellent paths lead to the summit of this noted mountain.

1. From Kussnacht: This path passes by the Seeboden, crosses rich pastures, ascends some steep pinches, and takes you to the Righi Staffel, 2 l. (6 m.). Thence to the Righi Kulm, there are ½ to ¾ of a league (1½ to 2¼ miles).

2. From Art: This ascent is mostly easy, and takes you in two hours to the Hospice of the Righi, whence you arrive by the Staffel to the Kulm.

3. From Lowerz: This is the best route. There are 4 l. (12 m.) to the Hospice, and 5 l. (15 m.) to the Kulm. This is the usual route by which the herds are driven up to the different pastures on the mountain.

4. From Gersau: This path is less followed than the others. It passes by the Hochfluh and Schneealp to the Righi Scheidegg, and on to the Hospice, 3 l. (9 m.) This is described as the longest but most beautiful of the paths leading to the Righi. At the Righi Scheidegg, near the east end of the mountain, is a large hotel, with a fine view, with good accommodation, where many Swiss families live en pension, paying 4½ to 5½*fr.* per day. This would be a very suitable centre for a naturalist wishing to explore the mountain. One hour thence to the Klösterli or Maria zum Schnee, and on to the Kulm, in 1½ hour. Average time of walk from Gersau to Kulm, 5 hours.

5. The Wäggis ascent is through fine meadows, pastures, and forests, to Hohenstein, thence to the Kaltenbad, 1½ l. (4½ m.), and thence to the Staffel and Kulm, in 1½ hour.

The base of this isolated mountain (the Righi) has a circumference of 10 L (20 m.): its foot is bathed by the Lake of Lucerne to the west and south, and by those of Zug and Lowerz to the north and north-east. The intervening space between these two last Lakes, from Goldart to Lowerz, is covered by the remains of the Gnipen-pitz, which fell from the Rossberg, at the beginning of this century. The north-west end of this mountain flattens down by degrees towards Küssnacht and Immensee, and its south-east end, towards the valley between Brunnen and Schwyz. The Righi is almost entirely within the territory of Schwyz, only a corner of it belonging to Lucerne. The frontier line passes from the promontory of Obere-Nasen, crosses the Vitznauerstock to Dosen, thence follows a north-west direction along the ridge, and descends over the Seeboden to the village of Greppen. No mountain in Switzerland has been altogether so much visited as the Righi, nor does any point equally accessible present such varied views, especially of lake scenery. The old hotel on Righi Kulm dates from 1816. The other at the Staffel is ½ a league (1½ m.) lower down, where all the different roads meet that lead to the summit. Four other inns are scattered about the mountain, which has a Capuchin Hospice near Maria zum Schnee, and a chapel dedicated to St. Michael. A new hotel was opened in 1856, at Righi Kulm, belonging to the same proprietor as the old one, and though the two houses receive above 200 travellers, they are found insufficient, and often overcrowded. The establishments are altogether good, and properly conducted. Prices, those of the best hotels. Table d'hôte ¾ of an hour after sun-set. Sun-rise is the great sight from the summit if it be clear. The eye ranges to the distance of 75 miles, taking in mountains above Bregenz on the Lake of Constance on one side, and the Jura above Geneva on the other. Fourteen cantons can be descried from the Kulm. 12 lakes of different sizes, 100 square miles of territory in Northern Switzerland, the Finsteraarhorn (17 L), the Jungfrau (13 L), the Glärnisch (104 L), the Titlis (9 L), &c. At all times and in all seasons mountain scenery is grand: when the peaks stand forth in mystery amidst rolling thunderclouds like the spectres of a giant race; when the distant church and convent bells reach up through the mist like unearthly harmony: when the moon silvers the world of lakes stretched round you; in the majesty of sun-set and in the tenderness of dawn. The view is generally more misty throughout the day. The Alpine horn rouses the visitor half an hour before sun-rise. The hotels are 60 or 70 feet below the summit, but the Righi has other summits besides the Kuhm. These are first: the Schild, the Dosen, and the Fitznauerstock to the south; the Schneealp and Hochfluh to the south-east; the Horrick and Schwendi to the east. Practicable paths lead to all these summits, which command varied and splendid views. The Righi is covered with a vigorous vegetation in all parts except its north side, which is rocky towards the Lake of Zug. Everywhere else it is carpeted with beautiful verdure, has many rare Alpine plants and charming forests. It has 150 châlets, more than 3,000 cows, and a multitude of sheep and goats, which browse there throughout the summer; the middle zone is woody, and the base covered with rich meadows and fine orchards, giving excellent fruit to the eleven towns and villages that surround it.

CURIOSITIES OF MOUNT RIGHI.—The Chapel of Notre Dame des Neiges (Kapelle unserer lieben Frau zum Schnee) is near the Capuchin Hospice, the fathers being obliged to pass the winter on the mou tain. Every Sunday, the herdsmen a shepherds on the Righi, come to hear m there, and on July 22nd (St. Mary M; dalene's day), its dedication is celebra by a fête, terminating in a wrestl match. Above the hospice is a gro with stalactites, known as the Br..lerb

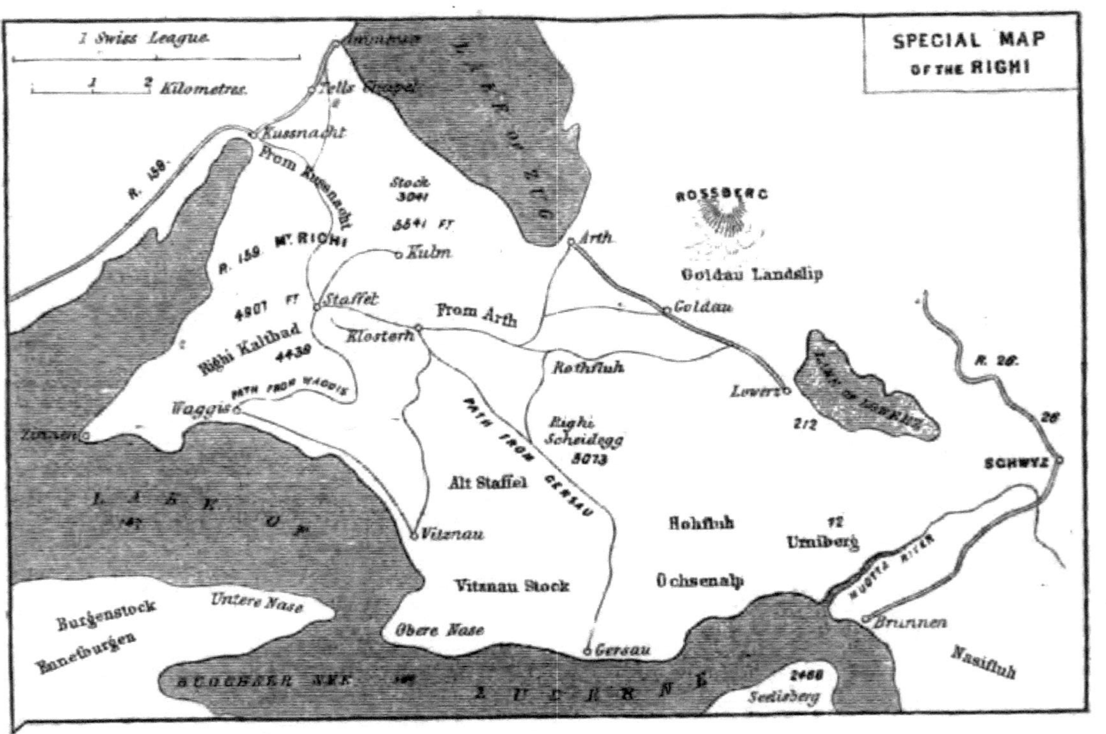

SPECIAL MAP
OF THE RIGHI
1 Swiss League.
1   2 Kilometres.
LAKE OF ZUG
ROSSBERG
Goldau Landslip
Amsteg
Tells Chapel
Kussnacht
From Kussnacht
Stock 3041
3541 FT
MT. RIGHI
R. 158.
R. 159.
Kubn
Arth
Goldau
4907 FT
Staffel
From Arth
Righi Kaltbad 4439
Klosterh
Rothfluh
LAKE OF LOWERZ
212
Lowerz
R. 26.
26
Waggis
PATH FROM WAGGIS
Righi Scheidegg 5073
SCHWYZ
Zinnen
Alt Staffel
PATH FROM GERSAU
LAKE OF
Vitznau
Hohfluh
Umiberg
12
MUOTTA RIVER
Vitznau Stock
Ochsenalp
Untere Nase
Burgenstock
Ennetburgen
Obere Nase
Gersau
Brunnen
Nasifluh
BUOCHSER SEE
LUCERNE
2468
Seelisberg

Still higher above the Hospice, between the Staffel and Kulm, is another cavern known as the Kessis-bodenloch. It is deep, and has an issue on the north side of the mountain. The Chapel of St. Michael, at Kaltenbad, is served by a chaplain, whom the shepherds have the right to appoint. Every year, August 18th, the day of St. Lawrence, they celebrate the anniversay of their patron, with a fête and wrestling match. Tradition relates that this chapel owes its origin to the times of the Emperor Albert, when three sisters fled hither and hid themselves for the rest of their lives, to escape the amorous pursuit of the Austrian bailiffs. Hence the name Schwesternbrunnen given to the stream and inn at Kaltenbad. The waters of this stream are reported to be very salutary. Near is the Känzseli (little pulpit), with a very fine view. Several paths lead hence to the Schild, the First, to Waggis, and by a stair-case in the rock to Küssnacht.

Sattel.—A village on the road from Biberbruck and Rotherhorn, by the lake Ægeri, Morgarten. Distance from Biberbruck, 2¼ l. (6¾ m.) The road leads thence past the Ægeri Lake, under the Rossberg, ½ l. (1½ m.) leaving to the right the Chapel of Ecce Homo, surrounded by fine substantial peasants' houses. From this part of the road the traveller enjoys a good view of the Lake of Lowers; of the landslip of Goldau; of the Righi, and of the Lake of Uri (the upper basin of the Lake of Lucerne). In ½ l. (1½ m.) he reaches Steinen (see further on), greeting as he advances the bright pleasant appearance of the town of Schwyz; the peaks of the Mythen, and the mountains of the Muotta Valley. [A path leads over the landslip of Goldau to Arth, and thence on to the Righi.]

Schwyz. — Hotels: Hediger, Pension Jütz. Capital of the Canton, with 5,700 Catholic inhabitants: at the base of the Mythen (one of its points 5,586, the other 5,856 feet). This place has few curiosities to detain the visitors, who chiefly pass or stay there in order to ascend the Mythen. In the town-house are 43 portraits of landammans; and among the archives the original treaty made among the first Swiss Confederates. In the Council Chamber is a sculptured ceiling. The Arsenal contains many ancient banners. The Cathedral was built in 1769, by voluntary subscriptions. The town contains a hospital, seminary, and two convents. But undoubtedly the greatest curiosity at Schwyz is the cabinet of medals, of which mention has been already made. It was established in 1772, by Chevalier J. R. Hedlinger, who in his day was noted as a very skilful engraver. In the Cathedral Church, the pulpit is supported by four figures, who are supposed to represent Luther, Calvin, Zwingli, and Melancthon. A plan in relief of the Muottathal is to be seen at the dyer's Schindler (a fee demanded).

Excursions near Schwyz. Above Schwyz rises the Mythen, which may also be ascended from the side of Einsiedeln. Path from Schwyz, ¼ l. (¾ m.) to Rickenbach, then a path 1½ l. (4 m.) to the passage of Holzegg. At the Chălet of "Hasli and Holz" are refreshments. Near Holzegg begins a new road cut in the rock, 8,500 feet long, 4 feet broad, safe and convenient for ladies. To the top, 48 windings or bends, ¾ l. (2¼ m.) After ascending (½ l.) you come to a schreen of rock, once the terror of those who ascended the Mythen. They were obliged to scramble up by a difficult path over the rocks. Now there is no difficulty. In 10 minutes you are on the top, which is 6 feet broad, and 40 feet long. On each side you look straight down to the depth of 1,000 feet; wherever there is danger, palings have been placed. A wooden cross stands on the summit. Those ascending the Mythen from Einsiedeln pass by Alpthal (1½ l.) Inn, the Ross, then by a bridle path (1½ l.) to the Hacken (an inn), 4,679 feet, and thence, bearing to the left, to Holzegg (1¼ l.), and from Holzegg to the Mythen, ¾ l. (2¼ m.) All the paths can be found without a guide. A guide, acting as porter

4*fr.*; one horse from Schwyz to Holsegg, 8*fr.*; to return, 6*fr.* The Mythen is divided into Great and Little. Its elegant pyramidal form is easily distinguished from the surrounding mountains. It was formerly richly clothed with forests, destroyed by a fire, August, 1800, which lasted 15 days. The view embraces a district 80 l. in diameter.

2. From Schwyz there is a pleasant excursion over the Pragel, by the valley of Wäggi, to Rapperschwyl, whence you reach Zurich by steamer.

The Pragel Pass was the scene of two days' desperate fighting between the French and Russians in 1799.

A great part of this route will be described under the Canton of Glarus.

The first part of the route from Schwyz is by the fertile Muotta Thal, affording picturesque views of châlets and forests. From Schwyz to Ibach, ¾ l. (2¼ m.), thence to Ober Schönenbach (20 min.) on to Hinter Iberg, 1½ l. with a grand view. Hence passing some fine rocks, a hamlet (Ried) with good bier, and a waterfall Gstübt Bach, you march up the narrow Muotta Thal to Muotta. Hotel du Cerf, rustic, but good, with good trout, furnished with a saw mill for dividing wood for musical *stringed* instruments. The convent of nuns of St. Joseph was founded 1280, and is built entirely of wood. Suwarow stopped here in his retreat. Difficult paths lead h nce to the valley of Schachen, in Uri, and others to the valley of Riemstalden and Sissigen on the banks of the lake of Lucerne.

From Muotta you advance to the Col, where General Suwarow retired before Lecourbe and his French division. A guide is wanted over the Col (2½ hours) to Richisau, a great place for cheeses, in a charming situation, with a whey cure and a fine view over the Kloenthal and the lake. On the top of the Pragel Pass you have to the left the Glarnish, Reiseltstock, Pfannenstock, and the Silberen; *to the right the Wannenstock,* the Fluh-

berig, and the Drusberg. Near the top a road branches off to the valley of Wäggis. At Richisau you must sleep on hay—no great hardship to philosophic temperaments. Below Richisau an excursion may be made into the Valley of Rossmatt with a superb view of the Glaciers of the Glarnish and Reiselstock (2 l.) from Voranen, where are two mountain inns, with cheeseries and 60 cows. On the road you pass the Deyenstock and Rautispitz (7,031 feet) two points easily reached without a guide. You pass hence to the Kloensi and down the Klonthal to Glarus (see Canton of Glarus), good road. Distance, 10½ l. (31½ m.) Seven hours from Weber's of Netstal's inn at Vorauen to Muotta.

Steinen, 1 l. from Schwyz was the residence of Werner Stauffacher, one of the heroes of Grütli (Hotel du Rossli.) On the site of his house stands a little chapel raised in 1,400, its walls covered with grotesque frescoes. The road leading hither passes by Seven, where are baths. Another road leads from Steinen to Zurich, passing over the Sattel. (See further back Sattel.)

PEDESTRIAN ITINERARY FROM SCHWYZ.

From Schwyz to Aarau, by Lucerne (Nos. 161, 11, 12 or 13.

Aarberg, by Lucerne (Nos. 161 and 66, 67 or 68), and Berne (No. 53).

Aarberg by Lucerne (Nos. 161 and 11.)

Aigle, by Lucerne (Nos. 161 and 66, 67 or 68), and Berne (No. 54).

ROUTE 207.

ALTDORF* 5 l. (15 m.)

	Leagues.	Miles.
Brunnen	1	3
Over the lake to Fluelen	3¼	10¼
Altdorf	¼	1¼
	5	15

Altstaetten, by Saint Gallen (Nos. 191 and 180), or by Appenzell (Nos. 26 and 19).

Appenzell (No. 26).

* A road is in process of construction along the east side of the lake.

ROUTE 208.

Art, 2⅘ l. (8¼ m.)

	Leagues.	Miles.
Seven	¼	¾
Lowerz	1	3
Art	1¼	4½
	2⅘	8¼

Baden, by Zurich (Nos. 215 and 18).

Bâle, by Lucerne (Nos. 161 and 39).

Bellinzona, by Altdorf (Nos. 207 and 229).

Berne, by Lucerne Nos. 161 and 66, 67 or 68).

Bex, by Lucerne (Nos. 161 and 66, 67 or 68) and Berne (No. 58), or by Unterwalden and Thun.

Bienne, by Lucerne (Nos. as above) and Berne (No. 59). or by Lucerne (Nos. 161 and 162) and Solothurn (No. 218).

Brougg, by Zurich (Nos. 215 and 298).

Bulle, by Lucerne (Nos. 161, 66, 67, and 68), and Berne (No. 54), or by Meyringen, Thun and the Simmenthal.

Burgdorf, by Lucerne (Nos. 161 and 68).

Chamouni, by Lucerne (Nos. 161 and 66, 67 or 68, and Berne (No. 61); Lausanne (No. 96) and Geneva (No. 95), or by Thun and the Simmenthal, as before, to Aigle, and thence by rail to Martigny and over the Tête Noire or Col de Balme.—See Cantons of Valais, Martigny, and Canton of Geneva, Chamouni.

Chaux de Fonds, by Lucerne (Nos. 161 and 66, 67, or 68) and Berne (No. 61), or by Lucerne (Nos. 161 and 162) and Solothurn (No. 220).

Chiavenna, by Chur (Nos. 134 and 121; 122 or 123).

Chur (No. 134).

ROUTE 209.

Einsiedeln, 4 l. (12 m.)

	Leagues.	Miles.
Seewen	½	1½
Steinen	½	1½
Sattel	1	3
Rothen Thurm, 2⅘ l. (7¼ m.)	¾	1½
Einsiedeln	1¼	4½
	4	12

Engelberg, by Stanz (Nos. 213 and 252).

Frauenfeld, by Zurich (No. 215 and 196) and Winterthur (No. 245).

Fribourg, by Lucerne (Nos. 161 and 66, 67, or 68) and Berne (No. 54).

Gais, by St. Gallen (Nos. 191 and 186).

Geneva, by Lucerne (Nos. 161, 66, 67, or 68); Berne (No. 63) and Lausanne (No. 96), or by Thun and the Simmenthal.

ROUTE 210.

Herisau, 22¼ l. (60¾ m.)

	Leagues.	Miles.
Einsiedeln (No. 209)	4	12
Herisau (No. 183)	18¼	54¾
	22¼	66¾

ROUTE 211.

Hofwyl, 22¼ l. (66¾ m

	Leagues.	Miles.
Lucerne (No. 161)	7	22½
Burgdorf (No. 68)	12¼	36¾
Am Sand (No. 60)	2⅔	7¾
	22¼	66¾

Lauffenburg, by Zurich (Nos. 215 and 303).

Lausanne, by Lucerne (Nos. 161, 66, 67 or 68), and Berne (No. 63), or by Thun and the Simmenthal ubi supra.

Locarno and Lugano, by Altdorf (No. 207 and 229), and Bellinzona (No. 232 and 233).

Locle by Lucerne (No. 161 and 66, 67 or 68), Berne (No. 70), and Neuchâtel (No. 175), or by Lucerne (No. 161 and 162), and Solothurn (No. 224).

Loesch (Baths) by Lucerne (Nos. 161 and 66, 67 or 68) and Berne (No. 65); or by Berne (Nos. 66, 67, or 68; 73 or 74) and Sion (No. 268).

Lucerne (No. 161).

Mendrisio, by Altdorf (Nos. 207 and 229) and Bellinzona (No. 235).

Morat, Morges, and Moudon, by Lucerne (Nos 161, 66, 67, or 68) and Berne (No. 63).

Neuchâtel, by Lucerne (Nos. 161 and 66, 67 or 68, and Berne (No. 70); or by Lucerne (Nos. 161 and 162) and Solothurn (No. 178).

Orbe, by Lucerne (Nos. 161 and 66; 67 or 68) and Berne (No. 71).

Payerne, by Lausanne (Nos. 161 and 66; 67 or 68 and Berne (No. 77).

Pfeffers (Baths), by Glarus (Nos. 113 and 111); or by Zurich (215 and 304).

ROUTE 212

Righi (The) 5½ l. (16½ m.)

	Leagues.	Miles.
Seewen	½	1½
Lowerz	1	3
Over the Goldau Landslip to Righi Hospice	3	9
To Righi Kulm	1	3
	5½	16½

St. Gallen (No. 191).

Schaffhausen, by Zurich (Nos. 215 and 200).

Sion, by Altdorf (Nos. 207 and 261); or by Lucerne, Nos. 161 and 66, 67 or 68) and Berne (Nos. 73 or 74); or by Thun and the Simmenthal (Nos. 213).

Solothurn, by Lucerne (Nos. 161 and 162).

Stanz.—See Unterwalden.

Thun, by Stanz (Nos. 213 and 255); or by Lucerne (Nos. 161 and 66, 67 or 68) and Berne (No. 55).
Trogen, by St. Gallen (Nos. 191 and 193).

ROUTE 213.

UNTERWALDEN (to the nearest point to Stanz) 5¼ l. (15¾ m)

	Leagues.	Miles.
Brunnen	1	3
By the Lake to Buochs	3	9
Stanz	1¼	3¾
	5¼	15¾

Vevay, by Lucerne (Nos. 161 and 66; 67 or 68) and Berne (No. 54); or by Thun (Nos. 215 and 253), and the Simmenthal.
Winterthur, by Zurich, rail (or Nos. 215 and 196).
Yverdun, by Lucerne (Nos. 161, 66, 67, or 68) and Berne (No. 77).

ROUTE 214.

Zug 5¾ l. (17¼ m.)

	Leagues.	Miles.
Art (No. 208)..........................	2¾	8¼
By Lake, to Zug	3	9
	5¾	17¼

ROUTE 215.

Zurich, 10¼ l (30¾ m)

	Leagues.	Miles.
Rothen-Thurm (No. 209) ...	2½	7½
Schendellegi	2½	7½
Bokenbad	1½	4½
Horgen (hence by Steamer if preferred)	½	1½
Obervleden	½	1½
Thalwyl..............................	½	1½
Ruschlikon	½	1½
Kiichberg	¼	¾
Wollishofen	¼	2¼
Zurich	1	3
	10¼	30¾

Zurzach, by Zurich (Nos. 215 and 305, or 306)
To Bavaria, Austria, and North Germany, by St. Gallen, Romanshorn, or Rorschach.—(See St. Gallen city)
Suabia and the Rhine, by Zurich and Schaffhausen or Lucerne, Olten, and Bale. - See Schaffhausen, Zurich, Lucerne, and Bâle (cities).
Strasburg, Paris, and the Rhine by Bâle.
Lyons and Turin by Berne and Geneva.
Milan and Italy, by Altdorf and Bellinzona.

The third C main approach to the High Alps is from Paris to Neuchâtel, by *Pontarlier* (*see Bradshaw's Continental Railway Guide.*) This is probably the shortest and easiest way from London to the Pennine and Valaisan Alps, and to the south side of the Bernese chain. The railroad from Paris passes Dijon, Salnis, and Pontarlier. From Dijon to Neuchâtel, by Salnis, is open throughout. The time consumed on the road from Paris to Neuchâtel is 13½ hours. There are direct through carriages to Berne. (For rail on from Neuchâtel, see Neuchâtel.)

Portarlier is the last French town on the frontier of Switzerland, at the foot of the Jura. Soon after passing it the railroad enters the

CANTON OF NEUCHÂTEL,

Is bounded on the E. by the Canton of Berne and the lake of Neuchâtel; S. by the same lake and the Canton de Vaud; W. by France; and N. by France and the Canton of Berne.

AREA, SOIL, AND CLIMATE.—The Canton of Neuchâtel has a surface of 36¼ square leagues (102¾ square miles), and consists exclusively of valley and of hills (the Jura range), which, with a few exceptions, are cultivated to their very summits; nevertheless this cultivation is much more considerable on the S.E. slope and on the side of the Jura facing the lake. The climate is so hot that its vines produce wine of excellent quality. In the high valleys, and those situated among the mountains and on the heights generally, the climate is severe, cold, and unfavourable to crops. The limestone rocks in the uplands are often very precipitous and quite bare of vegetation.

MOUNTAINS.—The Jura runs throughout the Canton, it also fills it up from the frontier of France to the Cantons of Vaud and Berne. It does not, however, present any very remarkable elevation, the Chaumont, near Neuchâtel (town), being one of the highest points.

LAKES AND RIVERS.—(a) Lakes: The Lake of Neuchâtel forms the frontier of the Canton on the side of Fribourg. Its length from Yverdun to the spot where the Thiele issues from it is 9 l. (27 m.), whilst its greatest width, from Neuchâtel to Cudrefin, is only 2 l. (6 m.), and its depth is about 300 feet. The narrowest part is in the south-west, where it belongs to the Canton de Vaud. Marshes which exist at both ends of the lake, lead to the supposition that it was once larger; it probably formed a single sheet of water extending from Diesse to the Jolimont, and was united with the Lake of Bienne, as well as probably with that of Morat. Its height above the Mediterranean is 1,340 feet, and above the Lake of Geneva 186 feet. The Lake of Neuchâtel receives the waters of the Broye, the Orbe, the Reuse, and the Seyon, and it discharges its waters by the Thiele into the Lake of Bienne. Among the numerous fish that inhabit its waters, the Ombre Chevaliers deserve special notice, on account of the delicacy of their flesh. 2. Lake of Bienne (See Canton of Berne. 3 to 5. Three other little mountain tarns occur in the neighbourhood of La Brevine. They hardly deserve notice.

(b) Rivers: The Thiele, or Zihl, unites the Lake of Neuchâtel with that of Bienne, and forms the frontier of the Cantons of Neuchâtel and of Berne. The Thiele is the only navigable river of the Canton. The others are, properly speaking, only torrents, such as—1. The Seyon, which has a very impetuous current, often causing great ravages; it takes its source in the Val de Ruz and passes before Valangin, thence it proceeds among precipices and rocks to the town of Neuchâtel, where it joins the lake. 2. The Reuse, of which the principal source is near St. Sulpice, and in the mountains bordering the S.E. of the Canton. It passes through the Val de Travers and the little town of Boudry to the lake. 3. The Doubs forms to the N.W. the frontier of Neuchâtel on the side of France.

AGRICULTURAL AND INDUSTRIAL PRODUCTIONS.—This Canton is rich in horned cattle, but has few horses, donkeys being chiefly used on the steep uplands. Little

game occurs but fish are very abundant. The crops of cereals do not suffice for the consumption of the inhabitants, but flax and hemp are largely raised, and a little fruit. The valleys and mountains are generally clothed with rich pastures and fine forests; but the chief produce of the Canton is wine. The vintages are very abundant, yielding both red and white wines of good quality. The finest wines are grown at Hauterive, Peseux, Corcelles, Auvernier, Cortaillod, St. Aubin, Vaumarcus, and almost all on the south-east slope of the Jura. The mineral kingdom is tolerably rich yielding a good kind of limestone, marl, gypsum, coal, and tufa: it also offers asphalt, stalactites, and many mineral springs. But what contributes specially to the prosperity of this Canton, is the different branches of manufacturing and mechanical industry carried on here with much success. The principal of these branches are watch making, physical and mathematical instruments, lace making, cotton prints, paper mills, liquors and cheese. Industry appears to have centred specially at Locle, Chaux de Fonds, and Val Travers, the most sterile districts of the Canton. Many thousand watch makers and lace makers live in these parts. Lace is made from a few sous to a Napoleon. The value produced yearly is estimated at one and a half million francs. The number of watches made yearly in these districts is estimated at from 130,000 to 140,000, and the manufacture of prints occupies a large number of operatives. *Absinthe*, made originally from mountain plants (but sadly adulterated in France) is in high repute and largely exported.

THERMAL SPRINGS, &c.—The most frequented mineral springs are at la Brevine, aux Ponts, at Brot, and at Motiers. Their waters are sulphurous and ferruginous.

POPULATION AND RELIGION.—Present population, 87,000, of the Gaug Indian race, seven-ninths Protestants and all French speaking. The Roman Catholics are four chiefly at the capital, at Landeron, Cressieres, and at Lignieres.

EDUCATIONAL AND SCIENTIFIC INSTITUTIONS.—Except in the capital, each parish has to look after and support the education of its own people, as ought to be the case in England and as was proposed by the Royal Commission of 1860. In many places elementary education is excellent, but it is nowhere better than at the capital. Locle and Chaux de Fonds have also good schools. There are also excellent, superior, and secondary schools for both sexes, much frequented by foreigners coming to learn French, which is here spoken in great purity. Scientific institutions are confined to the capital, which has produced or developed many able naturalists of even European reputation, such as Desor and Agassiz.

INSPECTION OF THE CANTON.

Brenet (Aux.) is a village in a valley of the same name, separated from France by the Doubs. At 1 l. (3 m.) from Brenets, you reach the Saut du Doubs, in a very wild position, and so called because the river here leaps over a rock 80 feet high. Half a league (1½ m.) from Brenets is also la Caverne de Toficnè, remarkable for its extraordinary echo.

Brot, a village in the Post Road to France, situated in the Val de Travers.

Chaux de Fonds (Hotels: Fleur de Lys; Hotel Struver; Guillaume Tell; Balance; Hotel de France), the largest and finest *village* in Switzerland, with 17,000 inhabitants, who boast that they set the time for the whole civilized world. It is 3,075 feet above the Mediterranean, and 1735 feet above the Lake of Neuchâtel, situated on a spur of the Jura, and filling for 2 l. (6 m.) a grassy valley, without trees. In 1834, it had only 6,300 inhabitants, now, though called a village, it has theatres, a casino, clubs, gas works, a telegraph, and other privileges or drawbacks of our civilization. *It has a Church of an oval form, several good streets with handsome houses and*

an unexampled prosperity, owing to the watchmaking, a branch of industry introduced almost accidentally in 1679, by an ingenious young man, Jean Richard, developed largely here, and at Locle, which, even in 1741, furnished 200 to 300 watches a year, among which were the best chronometers of the age. J. Droz and H. Droz were much noted in their day for making writing, drawing, and playing automata. In watchmaking, division of labour is carried to the minutest details, and the workmen labour at home. A good deal of lace is also made here.

Fares, by rail to Neuchâtel, 1st class, 3*fr.* 75*c.*; 2nd class, 2*fr.* 70*c.*; 3rd class, 2*fr.* 2*c.* Every day, a post car by les Ponte, 6½ l. (19½ m.) 4*fr.* 25*c.* The line of rail from Neuchâtel is remarkable and interesting, with many tunnels, and made at great expense, and with much labour.

Locle (Hotels le Grand Frederic), 1 L (3 m.), from Chaux de Fonds, trains five times a-day, in 23 min., with which it is connected by an almost uninterrupted succession of houses. The Post Road is 2 l. (6 m.) through Eplatures and le Cret du Locle. Population, 9,000, the first watchmakers in the world. Houses scattered, watered by the Bied; very curious subterranean mills. Waters of the Bied shut in a canal cut in a rock for 1,000 feet, turn, when they fall 100 feet over a precipice, three mills, adventurously placed, vertically under one another. Near the mills, in the Roche Fendon, where you look into France. You can here descend the Doubs, in boats (an interesting trip), and visit the spot at the French douane, where the Doubs disappears. Near it is (¼ h.) the Saut du Doubs. Excursion there and back, to Locle, 6*fr.* for 4 persons. Post cars from Locle to Brenet, four times a-day, 1¼ l. (3¾ m.), half an hour, 80*c.* Thence once a day to Morteem and Besançon. From Locle, three times a-day, To Ponte 2¼ l. (6¾ m.) in 1½ hour, 1*fr.* 45*c.*, and to Couvet, the Verrieres rail.

Neuchâtel, capital of the Canton, on

W. bank of lake, at foot of Chaumont (Latin, Neocomnum; German, Neuenburg), 10.100 inhabitants, described by most English guides as in rather tame scenery, but by Berlepsch as deliciously situated. The fact is, that anywhere but in Switzerland, its position would be called enchanting. The fort Novum Castrum, built in the 5th century was enlarged in the 12th, and became the nucleus of the town. (Hotels: Bellevue, 1st class; Des Alps and Du Commerce; then three by the lake, Faucon Hotel du Lac; Du Vaisseau; Du Soleil). Trains to Verviers; to Chaux de Fonds and Locle; to Lausanne and Geneva; to Bâle and Berne.

Post cars every day, once, Aux Ponts, 4½ l. (13½ m.) 2*fr.* 80c.; once a-day to Dombresson, 3½ l. (12¾ m.), in 2 hours, 2*fr.* 10c.; once a-day to Inns, 3¼ l. (9¾ m.), and Aarberg, 3⅛ l. (9⅜ m.)

The inhabitants of Neuchâtel have often shewn a princely munificence in improving the town, especially the channel of the Seyon. The streets are generally clean and the neighbourhood is adorned by pretty villas. Some of the houses in the town are very substantial.

PUBLIC EDIFICES.—The Cathedral, at the top of the town, built in the 12th century. Near is the château of the same date, seat of the government (since 1848, when the sovereignty of Prussia ceased, it is republican), with 13 portraits of counts and countesses of Neuchâtel. The Hotel de Ville; l'Hopital des Bourgeois, built by a munificent citizen, David de Pury; the Orphanage; the House of Correction; the Hospital Pourtalès, served by Sœurs Grises; the Great Hospital, &c. Many of these are fine, large, well-built institutions, due to the patriotism and philanthropy of generous natives like M. M. David de Pury and J. L. de Pourtalès.

EDUCATION AND SCIENTIFIC INSTITUTIONS.—The College and Gymnase, the former with chairs for classics and law. Distinguished *men, like Agassiz,* have been professors in the Gymnase. Good natural history collection. Neuchâtel has also three elementary schools, three ladies' schools, and several private pensionnals, &c. Near the Gymnase a statue of David Pury, by David d'Angers, in 1855. There are two libraries—the Town Library and the Library of Ecclesiastics. The Town Hall was built in 1784. The Museum contains a good collection by Swiss artists; admission, 1*fr.* Best pictures: Sun-rise on Monte Rosa, by Calamé of Geneva; Lake of Wallenstadt, by Meuron; Huguenots attacked at prayer in a cavern, by Ch. Girardet; Glacier of Rosenlaui, by Calamé, &c. In a supplementary building is an excellent collection of Alpine animals, with fine illustrations of the Reinecke Fuchs, by Kaulbach.

WALKS.—The Cathedral Terrace, a charming shady walk to Cret, above the lake; views beautiful. Slopes of vineyards all round the town, surrounded by stone walls, 10 feet high, that often block out the view. Other pleasant walks: (*a*) Villa Rochette; (*b*) Maisons Belvaux; (*c*) up the Chaumont, 3,608 feet, with grand view of the Bernese Alps.

Sagne (Valley of the), with a village of that name, is 4 l. (12 m.) long, and consists of the Sagne and des Ponts valleys. It contains much peat and a mineral spring. It runs on to the south-east as far as the mountain de la Tourne, whose summit, called la Tablette, offers a most superb view of the Lake of Neuchâtel, with the Alps beyond; very accessible.

Travers (Val de) is reached by the high road to France from Neuchâtel. After passing the village of Brot you reach a gorge called La Clusette, and not far thence the Creux du Vent, so called from a sort of whirlwind which revolves continually among the high vertical sides of some rocks, forming half a circle. At La Combe, near Travers, asphalt is found, and near Couvet are iron mines.

Valengin, 1 l. (3 m.) from Neuchâtel, is reached by Le Plan and Pierrabot, great erratic block, the rock of offence of geologists. You follow the bed of the Seyon. From Valengin you reach the heights of Les Loges, 1½ l. (4½ m.), with a pleasing view over 22 villages in the Val de Ruz. From Loges to Chaux de Fonds is 1½ l. (4½ m.)

PEDESTRIAN ROUTES OF THE CANTON OF NEUCHÂTEL.

Aarau, by Solothurn (Nos. 178 and 16), or by Berne (Nos. 70 and 6).

Aarberg (No. 40).

Aarbourg (to Olten, and thence to Aarbourg).

Aigle, by Lausanne (Nos. 173 or 174 and 267), and Vevay (Nos. 54).

Altdorf, by Berne (Nos. 66, 67, and 68, or 70), and Lucerne (No. 147), or by Solothurn (Nos. 178 162), and Lucerne (No. 147).

Altstaetten, by Solothurn (Nos. 178 and 16), Aarau (No. 18), Zurich (No. 196), and Saint Gallen (No. 180), or by Berne (No 70), and thence by Zurich and Saint Gallen (the routes as the preceding ones).

Appenzell, by Solothurn (Nos. 178 and 16), Aarau (No. 18), and Zurich (No. 28).

Art, by Berne (Nos. 70 and 78), and Zug (No. 281).

ROUTE 166.

AVENCHES, 4½ l. (13½ m.)

	Leagues.	Miles.
By the lake to Port St. Alban	2	6
Delley	½	1½
St. Aubin, 3 l. (9 m.)	¼	1¼
Domdidier, 4 l. (12 m.)	1	3
Avenches	½	1½
	4½	13½

Baden, by Solothurn (Nos. 178 and 16), and Aarau (No. 2).

Bâle (No. 40), or by Aarberg (Nos. 40 and 29).

Bellinzona, by Lausanne (Nos. 173 or 174 and 267), and Sion (Nos. 236).

Berne (No. 70).

Bex, by Lausanne (rail under Lausanne), or Nos. 173, 174, and 267), Aigle (No. 54), and Bex (No 54).

ROUTE 167.

BIENNE, 8 l. (24 m.)

	Leagues.	Miles.
Aarberg (No. 40)	6	18
Bienne (No. 29)	2	6
	8	24

ROUTE 168.

By NEUVEVILLE, 6 l. (18 m.)

	Leagues.	Miles.
St. Blaise	1¼	3¾
Cornaux	⅓	1
Cressier	⅓	1
La Neuveville	⅔	2
Gléresse (Ligerz)	¾	2¼
Twann	½	1½
Alfermé	¾	2¼
Vigneule	¾	2¼
Bienne	½	1½
	6	18

Brougg, by Solothurn (Nos. 178 and 16), and Aarau (No. 7).

Bulle, by Fribourg (Nos. 170 or 171 and 54).

Burgdorf, by Berne (Nos. 70 and 60).

Chamouni, by Geneva (Nos. 97 and 95).

ROUTE 169.

CHAUX DE FONDS, 4½ l. (13½ m.)

	Leagues.	Miles.
Vallengin	1	3
Bandeviller	½	1½
Aux Loges	1¼	4½
Chaux de Fonds	1½	4½
	4½	13½

Chiavenna, by Lausanne (Nos. 173 or 174 and 267) Sion (No. 236), and Bellinzona (Nos. 230).

Coire, by Solothurn (Nos. 178 and 16).

Aarau (No. 18) and Zurich (No. 142), or by Berne (Nos. 70 and 79), and Zurich (No. 142).

Einsiedeln, by Berne (Nos. 70, 66, 67, or 68) and Lucerne (Nos. 152), or by Solothurn (Nos. 178 and 162), and Lucerne (No. 152).

Engelberg (same routes as above), and from Lucerne (No. 153).

Frauenfeld, by Berne (Nos. 70 and 79) and Zurich (No. 245), or by Solothurn (Nos. 178 and 16), Aarau (No. 16), and Zurich (No. 245).

ROUTE 170.

FRIBOURG, by the lake, 7 l. (21 m.)

	Leagues.	Miles.
Domdidier (No. 166)	4	12
Grolley	1½	4½
Belfaux	½	1½
Fribourg	1	3
	7	21

ROUTE 171.

By MORAT, 12½ l. (37½ m.)

	Leagues.	Miles.
Aarberg (No. 40)	6	18
Fribourg (No. 80)	6½	19½
	12½	37½

ROUTE 172.

GAIS, 46¾ l. (140¼ m.)

	Leagues.	Miles.
Solothurn (No. 178)	12	36
Aarau (No 16)	9¾	27¾
Zurich (No. 18)	9	27
St. Gallen (No. 160)	14	42
Teufen	1¼	3¾
Bühler	½	2¼
Gais	¼	1¼
	46¾	140¼

Geneva (No. 97)

Glarus, by Solothurn (Nos. 178 and 162), Lucerne (No. 165), and Zug (No. 115), or by Berne (Nos. 70 and 29), and Zurich (No. 116).

Herisau, by Solothurn (Nos. 178 and 16), Aarau (No. 18), and Zurich (No. 301).

Kœfwyl, by Berne (Nos. 70 and 62).

Laufenbourg, by Solothurn (No. 178 and 16) and Aarau (No. 10).

ROUTE 173.

LAUSANNE (by rail), or 13¼ l. (39¾ m.)

	Leagues.	Miles.
Yverdun (No. 97)	6¼	19¼
Vallaires	1¼	3¾
Essertine	½	1¼
Vuarens	¾	2¼
Echallens	1	3
Assens	1	3
Cheseaux	¾	2¼
Lausanne	1¼	4¼
	13¼	39¾

ROUTE 174.

LAUSANNE, by ORBE, 16 l. (48 m.)

	Leagues.	Miles.
Yverdun (No. 97)	6¼	19¼
Treycovagnes		1¼
Succevaz		1½
Mathond		¾
Orbe		2¼
Lasarraz	2	6
Cossoney	1	3
Romanel	1½	4½
Preverenge	1	3
Lausanne	2	6
	16	48

Locarno, by Lausanne (Nos. 173 or 174, and 267), Sion (No. 236), and Bellinzona (No. 232).

ROUTE 175.

AU LOCLE, 6¼ l. (19½ m.)

	Leagues.	Miles.
Chaux de Fonds (No. 169)	4½	13½
Aux Eplatures	¼	1¼
Sur le Crèt	¼	1½
Locle	1	3
	6¼	19½

Loesch (Baths), by Lausanne (No. 173 or 174, and 267) and Sion (No. 268).

Lucerne, by Berne (Nos. 70, 66, 67 or 68).

Lugano, by Lausanne (Nos. 173 or 174, and 267), Sion (No. 236), and Bellinzona (No. 233).

Mendrisio, by Lausanne (Nos. 173 or 174, and 267), Sion (No. 236), and Bellinzona (No. 235).

Morat, by Aarberg (Nos. 40 and 80).

ROUTE 176.

MORGES, 14¼ L. (43¼ m.)

	Leagues.	Miles.
Yverdun (No. 97)	6¼	19¼
Treycovagnes	½	1½
Succevar	½	1½
Mathond	¼	¾
Orbe	¾	2¼
Lasarraz	2	6
Cossoney	1	3
Romanel	1½	4½
Preverenge	1	3
Morges	½	1½
	14¼	43¼

ROUTE 177.

MOUDON, 9¼ L. (27¾ m.)

	Leagues.	Miles.
St. Aubin (No. 166)	3	9
Dompierre	1¼	3¾
Corcelle	½	1½
Payerne	½	1½
Moudon (No. 63)	4	12
	9¼	27¾

Or by Aarberg (Nos. 40 and 262).

Orbe (See No. 97).

Payerne (No. 177), or by Aarberg (Nos. 40 and 262).

Pfeffers (Baths), by Solothurn (Nos. 178 and 16), Aarau (No. 18), and Zurich (No. 304).

Righi (The), by Berne (Nos. 70, 66, 67 or 68) and Lucerne (Nos. 158 and 159).

Saint Gallen, by Solothurn (Nos. 108 and 16), Aarau (No. 18), and Zurich (No. 160), or by Berne (No. 70 and 79) and Zurich (No. 160).

Schaffhausen, by Solothurn (Nos. 178 and 16) and Aarau (No. 14).

Schwyz, by Berne (No. 70, 66, 67 or 68) and Lucerne (No. 161).

Sion, by Lausanne (No. 173 or 174, and 267).

ROUTE 178.

SOLOTHURN, 12 L. (36 m.)

	Leagues.	Miles.
Aarberg (No. 40)	6	18
Solothurn (No. 92)	6	18
	12	36

Stanz see Unterwalden.

Thun, by Berne (Nos 70 and 55).

Trogen, by Solothurn or by Berne.

Zurich and Saint Gallen (routes to Saint Gallen, as above, and from Saint Gallen, No. 195).

Unterwalden by Berne (Nos. 70 and 76), or by Berne (Nos. 70, 66, 67 or 68), and Lucerne (No. 153).

Vevay, by Lausanne (Nos. 173 or 174 and 267).

Winterthur, by rail to Olten, or post road by Solothurn (Nos. 178 and 16), Aarau (No. 18) and Zurich (No. 1'0).

Yverdun (No. 47), and steamers (under Neuchâtel town and in *Bradshaw's Continental Railway Guide*).

Zug, by Solothurn (Nos. 178 and 16), and Aarau (No. 17), or by Berne (Nos. 70 and 78)

Zurich, by Berne (Nos 70 and 79), or by Solothurn (Nos. 178 or 16), and Aarau (No. 18).

Zurich, by Solothurn (Nos 178) and Aarau (No. 16).

Paris, by Pontarlier and Dijon, see introduction.

Lyons and South France, by Geneva.

Turin and Genoa, by Geneva.

Milan and the whole of Italy, by Lausanne and Sion.

Strasbourg, Francfort and the Rhine, by Bâle.

Suabia and North Germany, by Zurich, Winterthur, Schaffhausen or Romanshorn.

The line from Neuchâtel to Lausanne, and thence on by Vevay to Martiguy and the High Alps in the Rhone valley, skirts the lake and soon enters the

CANTON OF VAUD.

This Canton has a surface of 152½ square leagues (3,223 sq. kilometres) and consists of fertile slopes, hills, and in part of high Alps. The climate is generally healthy, mild, and even warm in the districts, bordering on the lake of Geneva ; but rather cold and severe in the uplands.

Mountains : Part of the Jura chain runs for the space of 12 l. (36 m.) through the W. side of the Canton, forming in fact the frontier towards France. The highest summits of this chain are the Dôle, Montendre, Mont Suchet, Chasseron, &c., but none of them reach the limit of perpetual snow. At the S.E. of the Canton occurs a loftier chain, being, in fact, the continuation of the Bernese Alps, and offering peaks like the Diablerets over 11,000 ft.; the Panneyrossaz, the Plan de Névé, and the Martinets, from which numerous glaciers descend, and *the Dent de Morcle (8,951 feet), which makes the terminus of this ridge at the* point where the Rhone has cut its way out of the Valais by the Gorge of St. Maurice. All these mountains are on the borders of the Cantons of Vaud and Valais, but do not belong exclusively to either. A third chain of mountains stretches from the Diablerets, N.W., to a beautiful district and strikes into the heart of the Canton. It rises in the Dent de Jaman to 4,572 feet, and to it belongs the Molesson in the Canton of Fribourg; it includes several high summits, such as the Tour d'Ay (6,815 feet), and the Tour de Mayen (7,188 feet), connected with this chain is the Jorat, which runs E. and W. through the Canton, rising above Vevay and Lausanne and terminating in the Jura, near Lasarraz. Its width is 3 l. (9 m.), and its height above the Lake of Geneva, near the Molesson, 2,000 feet, but only 1,700 feet in its middle part, where the high road passes from Lausanne to Berne.

LAKES, RIVERS, AND STREAMS. — (a) Lakes: The Lake of Geneva, or Lake Leman, bathes the whole southern boundary of the Canton in a semi-circular form from Villeneuve to Coppet. For a description of the lake see Canton of Geneva.

2. The Lake of Neuchatel belongs to the Canton de Vaud in three places, (a) on its E. bank, along the circle of Cudrefin, (b) further on again from Chieri to Yverdun, and (c) on the west bank from the latter place to Vaumarcus.

3. The Lake of Morat. About a third of this lake belongs to the Canton de Vaud, i.e., the S.W. extremity advancing into the district of Avenches.

4. The Lac de Joux, in a valley of that name, situated high up the Jura; its length is 2½ l. (7½ m.), its breadth ⅓ l. (1½ m.), and its depth, 150 feet. A visit to it forms a charming excursion through a delightful district. The lake is 1,900 feet above the Lake of Geneva.

5. The Lac de Bray, is on the Jorat, in a solitary valley, 2 l. (6 m.), N.W. of Vevay ; it is about ½ l. (1½ m.) long, and

10 minutes in width, with a depth of 100 feet. This little lake freezes every winter.

(*b*) Rivers: The Rhone forms the junction of the Cantons of Vaud and Valais from St. Maurice to Bouveret, where it flows into the Lake of Geneva.

2. The Venoge, rises at the village of Lille, increases as it flows for 6 l. (18 m.) through the Canton of Vaud, by the addition of the Veyron and several other streams and ultimately falls into the Lake of Geneva, near the ruins of the ancient Abbey of St. Sulpice.

3. The Sarine or Saane, coming from Sanetsch, enters the Canton of Vaud, near the Gessenay, and leaves it, after having flowed through it for the space of 4 l. (12 m.), ultimately entering the Canton of Fribourg, near Montbarron.

4. The Broye, whose source is above Semsales, in the Canton of Fribourg, passes through the district of Oron, where it receives four streams, reaches Mendon where the Merine flows into it, and then falls into the lake of Morat.

5. The Orbe, issues from the Lac des Rousses in Franche-Comté, supplies the lake of Joux, and disappears near the mill of Bonport. After passing under ground ½ l. (1½ m.) it reappears from under a rock, flows through the village of Valorbe, and decends (making several cascades) to the town of Orbe. There it changes name and under that of The Thiele it reaches the Lake of Neuchâtel.

(*c*) Rivu'ets: The principal rivulets in this Canton are the Vevayse, rising at the Molesson and flowing through a deep ravine from Châtel St. Denis to Vevay, where it falls into the Lake of Geneva. This torrent often occasions great devastation. The Aubonne is formed by several streams issuing from the Jura, and falls likewise, into the Lake of Geneva, near Allaman The Chendon rises at the village of Echelle, in the Canton of Fribourg, forms, in many parts. the frontier of the Canton of Vaud and Fribourg and *falls, ultimately, into the lake of Morat.*

AGRICULTURAL AND INDUSTRIAL PRODUCTIONS.—A large number of cattle, sheep, goats, and pigs are bred in this canton, but horses are less numerous. Game and fish are abundant. The yield of cereals is not sufficient for the consumption, but the growth of wines is very abundant. The most noted are those of La Côte, La Vaux, and Yvorne; the first grown on the slopes from Lausanne to Coppet; the second from Lausanne to Vevay; the third from near Aigle. Good fruit, even of southern climates, such as figs, almonds, and chesnuts, are grown in this Canton. Several districts are clothed with fine forests, and among minerals Vaud offers gypsum, marl, grès bleu, grey and yellow sandstones, very well fitted for building. Marble of different colors is found at Bex, St. Tryphon, Roche, and Ollen. Iron is abundant in the Jura, and coal mines (houille) occur in the Jorat Rock. Crystals occur in the romantic Ormond Valley, near Bex, where are celebrated salt mines. This Canton contains several mineral springs. The manufacturing industry is confined chiefly to iron, silk, and porcelain.

THERMAL WATERS.—These occur at Yverdun, Lallias, Estwier, Rolle, Henniez, St. Loup, near Lasarraz, and in other places. The waters of Yverdun are efficacious in cutaneous maladies, and those of Lallias have much analogy with the springs of Gurnigel, in the Canton of Berne. They are extensively used.

POPULATION AND RELIGION.— Present population, 213,000 ; in 1830, 150,000. Of these about 6,000 are Catholics, the rest Protestants.

EDUCATION, SCIENCE, CHARITIES. — Education has long been a prominent object in this Canton, where Pestalozzi first introduced his system. Each parish has at least one elementary school, several have more than one—the Canton has more than 620. In the towns of Avenches, Orbe, Rolle, Aigle, and Bex, Latin classes have been joined to these primary schools and Lausanne, Vevay, Moudon, Yverdun, Morges, Aubonne, and Payerne possess regular colleges. Indeed, ever since 1537 there has been at Lausanne an academy, latterly reorganised and enlarged, where the ancient and modern languages, mathematics, history, philosophy, physical scienc' law, chemistry, etc., are taught. The Ecoles de Charité, at Lausanne, also deserve a special notice. They were founded in 1726, by voluntary contributions, and being gradually developed, are now perfectly organised, receiving 200 poor children of both sexes, who are received gratuitously, and not only taught to read, write, and cypher, but instructed in the principles of religion, and of some useful trade, points discouraged by the new code of education in England. These schools are frequented by two classes of pupils. 1st. The externes, 160 in number, who are neither boarded nor fed by the school. 2nd. The 25 *internes*, who are entirely supported by it. If among the latter any child is found evincing superior talents, he is trained to be a schoolmaster, and as far back as 1830, 150 schoolmasters (called regents) had issued from this institution. The Ecoles de Charité are under a special board of management, whereas all the other schools of the Canton, as in general all that relates to public instruction, depend on the Academic Council, whose patriotic efforts are continually directed to perfect this important branch of public welfare, while, in great and enlightened England, the effort of Government appears to have been of late years to depreciate the entire framework of natural education, and to do all in its power to grind down the miserable pittance allowed for such an object to the lowest level consistent with meanness. Besides these establishments, there are in the Canton de Vaud a great number of private schools and pensionnats, where many foreigners come, especially to learn the French language. *Schools of this character are found in almost all the small towns.* The Pesta-

lozzian Institution at Yverdun is too generally known to require a special notice, but the same town has another very praiseworthy institution, well deserving notice, *i.e.*, the Deaf and Dumb Establishment, long directed by M. Naef, a man of great merit, coupled with much modesty, devoting superior talents, zeal, and much labour, with great success to the unfortunates deprived of two essential senses.

The Cantonal Library is in the building of the Academy at Lausanne, contains many excellent works and a great number of very interesting MSS.; the admission is free. In another part of the same building is the Bibliothèque des Etudiants, less volumnious than the previous one, but having a good collection of scientific books. Admission confined to the students. Other public libraries exist at Yverdun, at Morges, and at Vevay; they were in most cases founded by subscription. Many private individuals in this Canton have also good collections of books, medals, ornithology, minerals, and pictures.

Relief of the poor proceeds in this Canton from three sources, 1st the state; 2nd, the parish; 3rd, the Société de Bienfaisance. The Cantonal Hospital at Lausanne belongs to the first category; it contains 100 beds for the sick poor of the Canton, 40 for strangers, and 30 for incurables. The government, moreover, distribute 40,000 to 50,000 francs a-year to aid the poor in parishes that are unable to do so themselves. The towns of Lausanne, Moudon, Vevay, Payerne, Nyon, Yverdun, Montreux, Chateau d'Oex, &c., possess hospitals where patients are properly cared for. In districts where incomes are too poor to relieve the poor, a collection is made among the inhabitants and at church; this practice is peculiar to the pays d'en haut. There are in many towns of this Canton Sociétés de Bienfaisance, whose object is to succour the poor of all classes, natives as well as strangers, and especially to give them work. The English reader

carcely fail to be struck with these
lent arrangements, forming a re-
able contrast to the workhouses,
cted casual wards, and manufactur-
aisery, as well as juvenile depravity
own country. One of these benevo-
ocieties, called la Chambre des habi-
pauvres non-bourgeois, has existed
ausanne since 1760; it makes every
a collection in favour of its clients,
he proceeds of it amount to 5,000 or
francs. Societies of the same kind
at Yverdun, Morges, and Vevay.
lerman churches in this Canton, and
corporations of artisans have also
al charitable funds devoted to the
enance of their poor, but we do not
is yet of the abuses of burial clubs
nietness, though, perhaps, these may
rate even here with the advance of
ation. Among the institutions of
utility may be mentioned the Bible
y, the Agronomical Society, which
ng published a journal of agricul-
and general economy. Its central
ittee resides at Lausanne. A section
old society of emulation exists at
', where it has established a fund for
its (caisse), an institution that de-
imitation in other communities.
rt it is scarcely possible to do jus-
the public spirit of this Canton, or
liberality, good sense, and charity,
vhich the matters of vital social in-
are regarded and treated. It would
l if certain economists nearer home,
ave little head and less heart, would
icend to take a lesson from the most
ed country in Europe.

ECTION OF THE CANTON.

e, with 1,290 to 2,600 inhabitants,
ifle shots, stands at the entrance of
arming Ormond Valley, near the
f the Lake of Geneva, and not far
t. Maurice in the Canton de Valais,
vhich and Vevay it communicates
West Swiss Railway. (Hotels:
ia, handsome structure, good attend-

ance; Beau Site, near the station; Hotel
and Pension du Midi; Hotel du Nord;
Hotel de Ville). Charge for Cars—

	1 horse.	2 horse.
	fr.	fr.
To Yvorne	3	5
Villeneuve (Hotel: Byron)	6	10
Bex	6	10
Mo, they	6	10
The Salt Mines (round)	7	12
St. Maurice and Lavey	9	16
Chillon, Montreux, Claveus	9	16
Vevay	12	20
Pissevache	12	20
Comballaz	12	24
Diablerets	16	30
Champery	18	36

Rail fares from Aigle—

	1st class.		2nd class.		3rd class.	
	fr.	c.	fr.	c.	fr.	c.
To Bâle	25	50	17	90	12	85
Berne	14	40	10	10	7	25
Bex	0	90	0	70	0	50
Geneva	10	75	7	45	5	40
Lausanne	4	15	2	90	2	10
Lucerne	26	45	18	60	13	85
Martigny	3	40	2	85	1	70
Romanshorn	36	90	25	85	18	50
Schaffhausen	30	90	21	65	15	50
Sion	6	40	4	85	3	20
Thun	17	55	12	30	8	85
Vevay	2	20	1	50	1	5
Zurich	28	15	19	75	14	15

Aigle was an old Roman colony (Aquila).
All its houses are built of black marble.
The wine of Aigle is one of the most noted
in Switzerland.

WALKS NEAR AIGLE.—To the Clavel-
leire (20 minutes), fine view. To the
Cascades of Fontanney, ¼ hour. Drapel,
¼ hour, higher. On the left bank of the
Grande Eau le Fai, ½ hour. Plantour,
with a fine view and le signal, 20 minutes.
Yvorne, where the fine wine of that name
can be drunk at its source. St. Triphon,
with interesting ruins and a fine echo at
Dessous le Scex. To the Salines of Deven.

EXCURSIONS.—The Ormond valley (see
below). 2 hours to Leysin, a fine village
built of wood, and to Corbalet, with a
beautiful view. Sepey (see below), to
Pont de la Tine (1½ hour), a bridge over
a frightful abyss. Creux d'Enfer, 1 hour.
Aux Agites, 3 hours. The way is by
Yvorne, Corbeyrier, Barinea, Nombrlons.

and S·rzas, through savage rocky scenery leading to a glorions view suddenly bursting upon you (4,688 feet). A mountain tour to Bretaye, with the Châlets of Morgex, Cretaz, and Conches, from which you ascend the Chaux Ronde, with a fine view above the pastures of Perche, noted for its excellent cheese and primitive and original form of government. Near Bretaye the Chamossaire (6,505 feet) commands a magnificent view.

Aigle is at the entrance of the Ormond valley, one of the most attractive spots in Switzerland, from its splendid sylvan and Alpine scenery and simple uncorrupted population. The Ormond Valley leads up to the Upper Simmenthal (Canton of Berne) by les Iles and the Col de Pillon to Gessenay. There is a fine well made road to Sepey, from Sepey to Plans a bridle path, over the Col de Pillon the same, and at Gsteig a carriage road again.

The Vale of Ormond is an idyl, a corner of Eden, yet uneffaced amidst the dust, glare, and artifice of our modern world; there you meet poetry and the ideal as a reality, and the primitive simplicity of patriarchal life is found at two steps from rails, telegraphs, gas, cafés, and billiards. The valley is the perfection of the picturesque, and is occupied by a highland race, proud of its liberty, not ashamed to work, hospitable, simple, officions, a mixture of the good qualities of the German and French races without much alloy. Like the people of Val d'Anniviers, in the Valais, the men of Ormond are civilized Nomads, possessing 7 or 8 houses, and passing their time in migrations according to the season. When the supply of hay or the grass down below is exhausted, the Ormond peasantry migrate according to the time of year to other parts of the valley, where they have other houses. You may often meet these families on the move, the women carrying a cradle on their head, with milking utensils on their back, knitting as they go to their new abode. The *food of the people is as simple as their character.* Cheese, dairy produce, pota-

toes, smoked and very aged meat, hard as flint, cut with a hatchet, and soaked or steeped before eaten. Formerly their ovens were only heated twice a year, now more often. Avalanches, inundations, and landslips are frequent. Ormond is said to be a corruption of Aurimons, because the Grande Eau, or river of the valley, was said formerly to bring down gold sand in its current.

The following is the itinerary from Aigle to Gessenay:—From Aigle you ascend (1½ hour) to Fontaney, by Charvoni, with a fine cascade; hence, straight on through fine scenery, near Pont de la Tine, ½ l. (1½ m.) to Sepey, ½ l. (1½ m.) Chief place of Ormond Dessus. (Hotel des Alpes; Hotel Mont d'Or.) Rich country, picturesque position, and quaint old Swiss town, an admirable centre for numerous and delicious excursions. The people about here are the best rifle-shots in Switzerland. Above Sepey, ½ l. (1½ m.) to Comballaz (with an excellent pension De la Roche), and to the left the stream of Rionsettaz, descending from the high, marshy pastures of Des Mosses. Ruins of Aigremont, 1 l. (3 m.) At La Galese are the ruins of a fallen mountain. Grand Eau in a broader shady bed.

Vers l'Eglise, ½ l. (1½ m.), chief place of Ormond Dessus, a name appropriate to the simple primitive character of the whole district.

Plan des Isles, ½ l. (1½ m.) (Hotel des Diablerets, an excellent house, one of the highest in Europe, much frequented in summer on account of the fine fresh air.) Many houses are here scattered over the valley, which is quite idyllic, the *beau ideal* of the artist, with glancing trout streams, emerald pastures, and ancient forests. To the left appears the dentelated ridge of La Tornette (7,856 feet), and La Cape du Moine (7,237 feet); to the right the savage Diablerets and the Sexronge (9,644 feet). Botanists are advised to make an excursion to Mont Isenaux, presenting fine specimens of the Alpine flora. Hence over delicious prairies, called Les Iles, to a rocky basin,

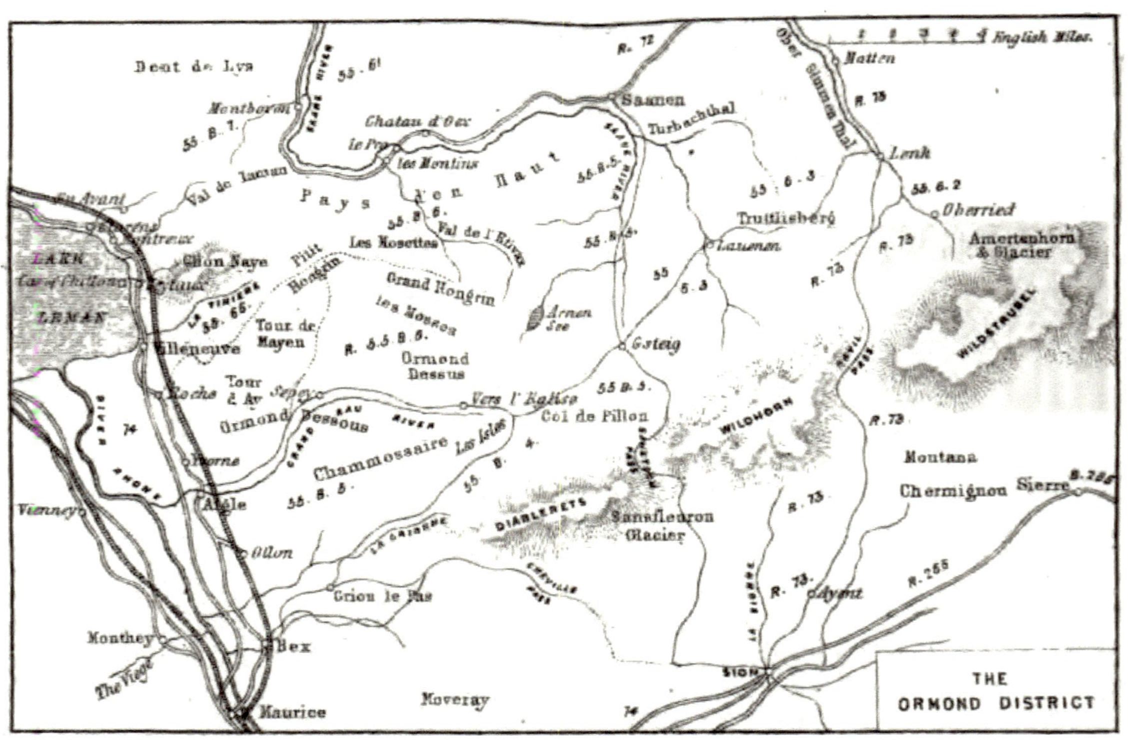
THE ORMOND DISTRICT
English Miles.
Dent de Lys
Ober Simmen Thal
Matten
Saanen
Turbachthal
Lenk
Chatau d'Oex
le Pre
les Montins
Truttlisberg
Oberried
Amertenhorn & Glacier
Pays d'en Haut
Val de Lauun
Montbovon
Val de l'Etivaz
Les Mosettes
Lauenan
WILDSTRUBEL
Au Avant
Montreux
Chion Naye
Filit Hongrin
Grand Hongrin
les Mosses
Arnen See
Gsteig
LAKE
Lac de Chillon
LEMAN
La Tiniere
Tour de Mayen
Ormond Dessus
WILDHORN
Montana
Villeneuve
Roche
Tour d'Ai
Sepey
Vers l'Eglise
Col de Fillon
Chermignou Sierre
Ormond Dessous
Chammossaire
Les Isles
DIABLERETS
Sanafleuron Glacier
Horne
Aigle
Ollon
Vienney
Grion le Pas
Ayent
Monthey
Bex
The Viege
Maurice
Moveray
SION
RHONE
GRAND EAU RIVER
SAANE RIVER
SAARE RIVER

Creux de Champs, surrounded on all sides by the naked rocks of the Diablerets. Following the rapid stream of the Dard, you reach, 1 l. (3 m.), the Col de Pillon (5,295 feet), forming the frontier of Vaud and Berne. Descending hence by the Reuschbach you reach Gsteig, and thence Gessenay or Saanen (see routes to this Canton and Canton of Berne, Simmenthal.)

Avenches belongs to this Canton, and is 2 l. from Morat, on the road from Payerne, on the Neuchâtel Lake, to Fribourg. (Hotels: Maison de Ville; Couronne.) It is on the site of the Roman town, Aventicum, which, in the time of Julius Cæsar, was the capital of Helvetia; and Tacitus calls it *caput gentis*. It is said to have flourished greatly under Vespasian and Titus. It was destroyed by the Allemani in 307, rebuilt, and destroyed a second time by the Huns in 447. In the 7th century it was an episcopal see. The present population is 1,600, though it once reckoned 60,000. The extent of the ancient city can be easily recognised, and there are traces of an amphitheatre and of other Roman constructions, including, near the town, a solitary Corinthian column and ruins of a Temple of Apollo. A good many of the Roman remains found at Avenches are in the museums of Geneva, Lausanne, and Berne. Now, however, there is a collection on the spot.

For conveyances from Morat, through Avenches, to Payerne, Neuchâtel, Berne, Lausanne, &c., see Morat, under Canton of Fribourg.

Bex, a fine little town, in a charming country on the borders of Valais, and on the rail from Lausanne to Sion. It is specially remarkable for its salt mines, the only ones in Switzerland, producing annually from 20,000 to 30,000 quintals of excellent salt. A single gallery of one of the mines runs for 4,000 feet under ground; and from the shaft of Bouillet, 667 feet deep, it is said the stars are visible in the day time. Bex is a great centre for excursions, and has in and all round the town many excellent and reasonable hotels and pensions, such as Hotel et Pension des Bains, exceedingly well situated and clean; moderate prices: recommended. Grand Hotel de Salines; Belle Vue; L'Union. At Bevieux, Pension Montchâlet.

To visit the mines, you must go to the Bureau des Mines at Fonderens, where you get a guide and lamp. To make the grand tour, takes ¾ hour and costs 5f. The salt baths are much frequented in summer. In the cemetery is the tomb of the naturalist Charpentier, (1855). Walks: To a fine cascade, ½ l. (1½ m.) not far from Devens, Valley of Grionne. Round and above Bex, are a number of pleasing points, on cool heights, surrounded by fine scenery, where pensions are established at fair prices. Of these, Grion deserves special notice on the way to Sion by the Pas de Cheville (see below). (Cheap Auberge of the Croix Blanche, and many pensions). Grion is a pretty village, on a high ground, amidst woods and pastures, 2¾ l. (8¼ m.) above Bex.

From Bex, you can ascend direct to Les Iles and the Col de Pillon without going to Aigle.

Another excursion, well worth making, is from Bex to Sion, by the Pas de Cheville, 12 l. (36 m.) Path for horses. Guide to the Col only wanted 20fr. From Bex to Bevieux, ¾ l. (2¼ m.); thence to Grion, 1 l. (3 m.); thence to the Châlets of Serniémin, to those of Solalex, pleasantly situated, ½ l. (1½ m.), and on by the Avecon and a stony road to Enzeindaz. Another group of Châlets in meadows, ½ l. (1½ m.) Hence ascend the Diablerets. Ascent safe, four hours. Two Guides required. Best Guide, Philippe Marletta. From Enzeindaz to Col de Cheville (6,207 feet), 1¾ l. (5¼ m.) Down by zig-zags, to the Châlets of Cheville, and leaving to the left the lake Derborence, ¾ l. (2¼ m); after this, pass a scene of terrible desolation, occasioned by frequent landslips from the Diablerets (that of 1714 the worst), which have given rise to the name Diablerets and many superstitious stories. It is here popular superstition represents the devil as leading the witches to his sabbaths, and that evil spirits lead astray the wanderer. You pass under the precipices of the Diablerets, leaving to the left the ridge of Fara (8,057 feet). Passing over meadows, with rocky fragments, come to a saw-mill, 2 l. (6 m.) On by a narrow valley, where the Lizerne flows in a crevasse, reminding you of the Viâ Mala. On to the Chapelle St. Bernard. Fine view, including Mont Blanc. Hence by the mountain and village of Avent to Vetroz. 2 l. (6 m.), and thence to Sion, 1⅓ l. (3¼ m.)

Chernex.—See Vevay.

En Avants.—See Vevay.

Chillon.—See Montreux.

Clarens.—See Montreux.

Coppet.—Station on the rail from Geneva to Lausanne, on the Lake of Geneva. The château belonged to a millionaire banker, of St. Gallen, Haegger, who afterwards died a beggar at Versailles (age of Louis XIV.). It afterwards belonged to Necker, and was inhabited, after 1804, by his celebrated daughter, Madame de Staël, who was there visited by a circle of literary stars; dispised, subsequently, by Napoleon I., she is buried in a mausoleum under shady trees.

Grandson, near Yverdun, on the Neuchâtel railway (Station), and by the lake. This, again, is classical Swiss ground, and worthy to compete with Marathon or Platæa. Charles the Bold, Duke of Burgundy, had taken the town and drowned its garrison in the lake. He was then attacked by the Confederates, 20,000 strong, and with such fury, that his entire army, 60,000 strong, was cut to pieces or took to flight. The booty amounted to three million crowns; and many trophies taken here, are still seen in the Swiss arsenals. Three great granite blocks have been raised to commemorate the battle.

Grandson has an old ivy-mantled castle, an old church, and a cigar manufactory.

Lausanne, capital of the Canton, in a charming position above the lake, and

about ⅓ l. (1½ m.) *Hotels.*—Hotel Gibbon, a first-rate house in every respect, highly recommended; proprietor, Mr. Ritter. Hotel Riche Mont, surrounded by large gardens; the situation of this house is one of great beauty: it commands a most extensive view of the Lake, and is a first-rate, quiet hotel, worthy of the highest recommendation. Hotel du Faucon, first-class establishment, situated in the finest part of the town; magnificent view. Hotel de Belle Vue, Herman Rimps, proprietor; excellent second-class hotel, well situated. Grande Pension Victoria, agreeably situated on the Clos Java, beautiful suburb near the town. Pensions at Mon Port, Madame Gandard; P. Chevalier Rue de la Caroline; P. Dugue, at Martheray; P. Frohlich, au Grand Chêne; P. Mansfeld, Baths; P. Givet et Meynior, en Georgette; P. Larguier. ditto; P. Cuerel, at Maupas, Café Morand, noted. *Carriages.*—Tariff: 1 carriage with 2 horses, by the day, 25*fr.*; 1 carriage with 1 horse, by the day, 15*fr.*; 1 carriage with 2 horses, first hour, 8*fr.*; the second hour, 4*fr.*; the third hour, 3*fr.* A carriage with 1 horse, first hour, 4*fr.*; second hour, 3*fr.*; third hour, 2*fr.*; carriage with 2 horses, for station or in the town, 8*fr.*; a carriage with 1 horse, for the station or in the town, 4*fr.* Bonnes mains to cochers are included. After the first hour you count by fractions of half an hour. Rail: Return tickets for the day, 20 per cent. reduction. Omnibuses from station to hotels, 50c. Boxes, 50c. 7 trains a-day to Geneva. To Paris direct, by Pontarlier and Vervieres. To Neuchâtel, Bienne, Soleure, Olten, Bâle, Lucerne, Zurich, Romanshorn, and the whole of German Switzerland, morning express trains changing carriages at Olten only. To Vevay 7 trains a-day; to Montreux, Villeneuve, Aigle, Bex, 6 trains a-day; To St. Maurice, Martigny, Sion, and the Simplon, 3 trains a-day. Direct tickets to Domo d'Ossola, Arona, Milan, and Geneva. Post-cars: To Moudon, 5 l. (15 m.), 2¾ hours, 4*fr.*, 3*fr.* 25c.; to Morat, 13½ l. (40½ m.), 7 hours, 10*fr.* 80c., 8*fr.* 75c.

Lausanne was the Losonium of the Romans; present population, 20,000 doubled in 30 years; on a slope of the Jorat, 450 feet above the lake, is built on three hills, above which rise the handsom

Cathedral and the mediæval château. The unevenness of the ground has given rise to numerous irregular, narrow, and winding, but clean streets. The quarters of St. François and St. Laurent are connected by a fine bridge built in 1840, called the Grand Pont. The town is becoming modernized and what some call embellished every year. The Place de François is cited as a paragon, and Bazaar Vaudois as a prodigy. Still it is admitted even by men of ultra progressive views that the older public buildings are the glory of Lausanne.

PUBLIC EDIFICES.—Among these especially the Cathedral, formerly the Church of Nôtre Dame. It is described by competent judges as a superb specimen of the Gothic and Burgundian styles of architecture, and as the handsomest church in Switzerland. From the palud (market) you ascend to the terrace of the Cathedral, which is open every day from 9 to 12 a.m. and 2 to 5 p.m., entrance gratis. It was begun in 1,000, consecrated in 1,275, by Pope Gregory X.; burnt several times in the 13th and 14th centuries, and rebuilt as often. It is 333 feet long and 143 feet wide. Its exterior does not correspond to the magnificence of the interior; the tower is only partly completed, but what exists shows the grand scale on which it was designed. The choir is surrounded by statues of the Apostles; the principal door is very simple, but the vaults are of the noblest proportions, and supported by above 1,000 columns. It contains the tombs of Pope Felix V. (1451); of bishops Guillaume de Monthonex (1406); of Haimon de Montfaucon (1517); of Baron Otho, of Grandson, who perished in a duel, employed as a judicial enquiry; of several foreign princes and counts; of Major Davel, a courageous defender of liberty and justice, decapitated by the Bernese Government, April 24th, 1723. When Calvin removed the gold and silver vessels of the Church, the worthy government of Berne seized them, and quietly appropriated them to the value of 2½ million francs. It was seized and used

afterwards to pay the French revolutionary expedition to Egypt, in which Bonaparte was defeated by Sir Sydney Smith. The Church of St. Francis is the spot where the Council of Bâle, after being transferred to Lausanne, held its last sittings (1449). The Church of St. Laurence was built in the beginning of the 18th century. Lausanne has a Catholic Church; hotel de ville, formerly the episcopal palace; an academy; a hospital; an arsenal; a mint; and a theatre.

EDUCATIONAL, SCIENTIFIC, AND OTHER INSTITUTIONS AND SOCIETIES.—These are the Academy. the College, the Gymnase, the Cantonal Library (46,000 books), the Cantonal Museum (with mineralogical, ethnological, numismatic, archæological, and other collections), containing objects found in ancient Italian and Sicilian cities, also curiosities belonging to Napoleon I., open Wednesday and Saturday, from 10 to 4, Sunday, from 11 to 2. Lausanne has several other useful institutions, such as the Blind Asylum, open from 9 to 12 and 2 to 5, an admirably conducted establishment; the Elementary Industrial Museum (Rue Chanorau 16), open to the public on Wednesdays and Saturdays, 12 to 3½ p.m., and on Sundays at the same hours as the other Museums. The Penitentiary is a real convict's palace, and must meet the approval of all at home who wish to pamper and coddle garotters et id genus omne. The charitable institutions have been noticed above.

The Musee-Arland, Place de la Riponne has some fine paintings. Among these may be noticed the Lake of Brienz, by Calamé; the Glacier of Rosenlaui, by Diday; water colour paintings by Kaisermann; Romans passing under the yoke, by Gleyre, &c. Open on Sundays and Thursdays from 11 a.m. to 2 p.m., apply to the Concierge.

Walks.—The neighbourhood of Lausanne is delightful, especially in May, when all nature looks like one garland. Pleasantest near walks: Mont Benon a fine shady walk on the Geneva road, view of Lake, reviews are held here; Promenade du Casino and Beausejour command fine views; 30 minutes from Lausanne, Belles Roches or Grandes Roches, view of Mont Blanc; north of Belle Roches, the Plaine du Loup, where Charles the Bold's army camped some weeks between the defeats of Grandson and Morat, in 1476; the farm called Les Cerises; the Châlet, ¼ L. (2¼ m.), above Lausanne; Vidy, with Roman remains of a road vulgarly called Estrada, and above all the Signal, 40 minutes from the town, with one of the finest lake views in Switzerland. The road to it is on foot, by the place and street St. François, the Place de la Palud, Rue de la Madeleine; Place di les Riponne, and the Chemin Neuf to la Barre. Here you pass through a tunnel. Hence by the Nouvelle route du Mont, above the valley of La Borde; following the road for 10 minutes, you see the pavilion, with refreshments on an eminence. You can return in 25 minutes by the pretty valley Des Eaux, and into the Route Neuve to the streets of St. Pierre and of Bourg. Or you can come back in 1 hour and 25 minutes by the forest of Sauvabelin (Sylva Belini), a forest consecrated by the Druids to *Bel* or *Baal* the God of Light. Pass the Château de Vennes, or Deaf and Dumb Asylum, near the Cemetery of la Sallaz, with the tomb of Kemble (1823) down by the Chemin du Calvaire, direct to Lausanne.

The walk to Ouchy is very pretty. Ouchy is the port of Lausanne. Hotels Beaurivage (luxurious), built 1859. Prices high. Anchor not very good. Omnibus to Lausanne, ½fr., with luggage, 1fr. Ouchy has a grand quay, forming a fine walk, with beautiful views. Villa and Park Haldimand bequeathed by will to the public, by its generous proprietor. It is a charming spot.

[Excursions from Lausanne; half a day to the Bois de Vernand, forest and charming valley; half a day to the Bois de Boveress; fine view of the Valais Chain; a whole day to the Tower of Gourze, by Rovereaz, Savigny and the heights. Back by Lutry].

Montreux.—Station on the Lausanne and Sion Railway. Beautiful sheltered position, rich graceful vine slopes, majestic mountains, the deep blue lake; a thousand charms have made this spot a great favourite, and have half spoiled it in certain respects. It is considered the healthiest parish in Europe. The whole district is dotted with pensions, among which and the hotels may be noticed: Hotel de l'Union and Hotel du Pont; Hotel de la Couronne. At Territet: Hotel des Alpes. At Veytaux, a charming village above Chillon, well known in its primitive times to the author: Hotel de Bonnivard, 5 or 6fr. a day. At Glion: Hotel du Righi Vaudois; Hotel du Midi, 4fr. a day. At Vernex: Hotel and Pension du Cygne, beautiful position. At Clarens: Hotel and Pension, J. J. Rousseau, 4 to 7fr. per day. Pensions at Montreux: P. Vautier, fashionable; P. Moser, charming situation and comfortable; P. Gabriel, near the church, described as rather puritanical. Beau Rivage: P. Bonport, P. Visinand, and P. Henchoz, cheap. At Territet: A l'Abri. At Veytaux, P. Masson Dessous, by the lake; P. Bonnivard. At Vernex, by the lake, P. Sans Souci; P. des Bains. Swimming school: P. Rollandais; P. de la Plaine de Montreux. Landing place of steamers: P. Germain; P. Lorieus; P. Roche, hydropathic cure; Higher up, P. Haut Riode; P. Moser. Between Vereux and Clarens: P. Clarenzia. At Clarens: P. Mury, good, cheap; P. de l'Ermitage, 5fr. per day; P. Bellerive, Blaser, Genton, &c., &c. At Baugy is the P. Pavillon, 3½ to 4fr, At Chailly: P. Benker, pleasantly situated, ¾l. (2¼ m.) from Vevay, 20 minutes from Clarens. At Brent: P. Dufour, 30 minutes from Clarens, 3½ to 4fr. English Church Service, on Sunday, at Hotel des Alpes, in rotation with Hotel Byron.

Several villages in charming positions are scattered round Montreux, including

Clarens, Vernex, Chernex, Glion, Collinges, Territet, and Veytaux. The whole district is known better than his native parish to the writer, as he spent years of his early life in this earthly paradise. The Church of Montreux is a very picturesque object. The whole country has been made classical by the pens of Byron and Rousseau. The Château of M. Dubochet, with delightful gardens, is on the site of the Bosquet de Julie at Clarens.

Walks near Montreux are endless and perfect. To Glion (Hotel du Midi, Hotel du Righi Vaudois; pension, 4 *fr* per day). The first vines in the Canton were planted here. Sonzier is said to be in a heavenly situation. Chatelan Castle, among vines above Vevay, has fine views. Château de Crêtes, above Clarens, is among fine chesnut trees.

Excursions, especially over the ridge of the Dent de Jaman towards the Simmenthal, lead to a delicious country, with views on all sides, beautiful as a dream.

All the glens and hills are intersected with paths, and the traveller will often do well to leave the beaten track and follow water courses or his own inclination. If he seek lovely scenery he cannot go wrong. Only let him avoid wood courses and beware of snakes. Excursions among many can be made to the Rochers de Naye (6,495 feet), four or five hours up, with glorious views, and crocuses and snowdrops in full summer by the side of snow. To Mont Cubly (3,630 feet). By Charnex, the Hotel Dufour, one hour from Clarens, the farms Chanlin and En Saumont, along the gorge of the bay of Clarens to the baths of Alliaz, hence to Mont Princemavauon to the Pleiaux or Pleyades (a châlet with refreshments) which the writer has seen white with narcissus in the early summer; return by the Château de Blonay to Chailly. At St. Legier is an agreeable pension with fine air. Excursions can also be made to the valleys of Ormond and Illiez. See *Aigle* (Canton of Vaud) and *Monthey* (Canton of Valais).

Close to Montreux by the Veytaux Chillon Station is the Château of Chillon on a rock over the deep blue waters of the lake. All the world knows Byron's Prisoner of Chillon. It is very ancient and was used as a state prison in 800. Conquered by Peter of Savoy in the 13th century, it received its present form then. The souterrains in the rock and the oubliettes are the most curious objects about it, and its most celebrated inmate was the unhappy Bonnivard, prior of St. Victor of Geneva, shut up by the Duke of Savoy, and set free by the Bernese, Feb. 1st, 1536. The marks worn by his footsteps in the rock are still pointed out. Hotel Byron, between Chillon and Villeneuve (ten minutes from each station), in a beautiful situation, has been in high repute.

Villeneuve (Hotel du Port) station and landing place for steamers, is in a rather unhealthy, marshy position. It was the Penniluens of the Romans, and near here was fought the battle between the Helvetians under Divico and the Romans under Lucius Crassus, B.C. 107, whose defeat is noticed with bitterness by Julius Cæsar. The wild pass of la Tiniere leads hence to Hongrin and on by the Col and Dent de Jaman, in 4½ hours to Monthovon. Omnibus from all the trains at Villeneuve to the Hotel Byron.

Morges. Railway Station. Lines branch here to Geneva, Lausanne, and Neuchâtel. Rich little town. Active port and trade. 3,600 inhabitants. (Hotel du Port; Couronne). Trades much in wine grown in the surrounding country (La Côte). Its castle is of the 12th century with four large towers. Morges has a fine arsenal worth a visit.

Nyon. Railway Station (Geneva and Lausanne line). Hotels: Couronne, Soleil, Ange. Founded by Julius Cæsar and called Julia Equestris, or Nensium. Castle of the 16th century. The terrace, ¼ l. (⅜ m.), affords a fine view, including Mont Blanc. Nyon and neighbourhood (at Prangins) were much resorted to by emigrants the time of the first French Revolution. Joseph Bonaparte and Voltaire resided there too. Bergerie, near it, belongs to Prince Napoleon, and has good shooting. From Nyon you ascend the Dôle in the Jura by Dappes. The view of the lake and Mont Blanc from the Dôle, especially at sun-rise, is very sublime.

Orbe (Verbigenum). Hotels: Guillaume Tell, Maison de Ville, Hotel de France. Ancient and picturesque town on the Orbe, a considerable place in Roman times, as proved by many Roman remains found there. In the middle ages, capital of Little Burgundy. Brunehild was here put to death with torture, at the age of 80, by Chlotaire I. Louis, Lothaire, and Charles le Gros here divided their empire. The castle is in ruins.

The first orthopedic establishment was founded here by M. Venel.

Vallorbe is a village situated in the valley of that name. The road offers on all points charming views, and passes from Yverdun by Traycovagnes, Succevaz, Mathoud, Valeirè, Ligneroles, and Balaigue, 3½ l. (10½ m.) To the last village it is fit for carriages, but after that it is necessary to proceed on foot up the valley of the Orbe, which offers even sublime scenery, and some great curiosities, among which especially the source of the Orbe, ¾ l. (2¼ m.), above the village of Vallorbe; this river, having disappeared at Bonport, and flowed for ½ l. (1½ m.) under ground, reappears in a basin of 17 to 18 feet wide, and 4 feet in depth, after which it descends by a succession of little falls to the town of Orbe. Other curiosities are the Grotto de Vallorbe; that of des Feès; that of Agi; the asphalt mines, near Orbe, Vallorbe, and Chavornay, &c.

Payerne (Paterniacum) (Hotels: Maison de Ville; Reine Berthe; Ours), is a very old town surrounded by walls, on the Broye and on the post road from Estavayer, on the lake opposite Neuchâtel to *Fribourg. Queen Berthe* and Rodolph of *Strättlingen* are buried here. Their re-

mains were placed in a marble monument, 1828. The people still venerate the charity of this noble man. General Jomini, the military historian, was born here.

Estavayer is a little town on the Lake of Neuchâtel, pleasantly situated in a fertile country. Ranz des Vaches, called Coraulés, and sung in the Romance language, are still heard here. (Hotels: Maison de Ville; Cerf.)

Payerne is 4½ l. (13½ m.) from Fribourg (see routes of Cantons of Fribourg and Neuchâtel).

Rolle, a station on the Geneva-Lausanne Railway. (Hotels: Tête Noire; Couronne.) Widest part of the Lake of Geneva, close under La Côte, producing a generous wine, 1,600 inhabitants. Near it, charming villas, Beaulieu, Fleur d'Œau, and Choisy. Above it, the Signal de Bougy, with a view of the whole length of the lake; and up La Côte, in the woods, a curious glacier cavern full of accumulations of frozen snow.

Vevay.—Hotel Senn; newly built; very comfortable; large garden; Pension in winter. Hotel des Trois Couronnes, kept by M. Schott and Co., close to the lake; one of the best inns in Switzerland. Grand Hotel; a first-class establishment, beautifully situated. Grand Hotel du Lac, Ed. Delajorn, proprietor; first-class hotel, well situated, and good accommodation. Café du Lac. Trains, five a-day to Lausanne; five to Geneva; five to Bex; three to Sion. Post cars every day to Chatel St. Denis, 2½ l. (7½ m.), and Bulle, 6¼ l. (20¼ m.); to Fribourg or Berne; to Montbovon, 10½ l. (31½ m.); and to Gessenay or Saanen, 16 l. (48 m.) Carriages, one horse, 12fr. to 15fr. per day. Boats by the hour, without a boatman, 1fr.; with a boatman. 2fr.

Pensions: Price from 4 to 8fr. per day. Pension Du Château, by Stocker; Maillard and Du Quay, above the town; Delessert; Du Quai; Turin; Chemenin Frederic. At Chardonne, ¾ hour above

Vevay, Bellevue. At Chexbres, 1 hour (1 fr. by post car); Signal; Directeur Graf.

There are Russian and English church services at Vevay. Good doctors are—Curchod, Montet, Dor (oculist), and Rossier (for children). Library, 11, Rue du Lac (Lesser), &c. Vevay, the Vibiscum of the Romans, 6,500 inhabitants (800 Catholics), is one of the most lively, charming, and popular of Swiss towns. The views it commands are delightful, and its climate is very mild in winter, being protected by the Jorat, on whose south slope the town is built. It stands on the Vevayse, has good straight streets, a fine place by the lake, 600 feet long and 400 feet broad, and many good public buildings and institutions, due to the public spirit of its inhabitants.

Public Edifices: Among these notice the Palais Communal Couvreu, by the lake, with fine gardens; open Monday, Thursday, and Friday, at 10 o'clock. The Dent d'Oche, in Savoy, and the Valais Alps are well seen here. The Hotel de Ville, the Halle aux Blés, and the Hospital. New quays are being built along the lake. The finest view is from the Church of St. Martin, above the town, with the tombs of Ludlow and Broughton, the regicides. The names of the mountains seen here are engraved on a stone table on the terrace. Cigars and Vaudois champagne are made here. The Abbaye des Vignerons is a decennial fête (last 1865), representing by mythological allegories and characters the Worship of the Bottle. Ceres, Bacchus, Silenus, etc., are generally personated by some of the most promising and well-favoured youth of the town. There are fauns, bacchantes, nymphs, etc., with much music, gaiety, and a great crowd of visitors.

Walks near: Along La Vaux, in all directions, affording charming pictures to artists. To the Château de Blonay, for centuries belonging to the family of that name. To the Château de Hauteville, ¾ l. (1½ m.)

Excursions: Above all to En Avant, over the Col de Jaman, to Montbovon, and up the Dent de Jaman, in a paradisaical country, with heavenly views. See Simmenthal. (Canton of Berne.)

La Tour de Peils is close to Vevay (a railway station), with an old castle of 1239, built by Peter of Savoy, round which the present house has gradually risen. Between it and Vevay is the Institution Sillig, and a flotilla of boats for the pupils.

Yverdun.—(Hotel de Londres; Croix Fédérale). The Roman Eburodunum, on the Orbe, at the south end of the Lake of Neuchâtel, which having retired, has left some marshes. Near here are traces of ancient lacustrine habitations. Population, 5,000. Yverdun has obtained a European reputation by the Pestalozzian system being first founded by its author, in the Château of the Dukes of Zähringen (built in the 12th century). The château contains Roman antiquities, a cabinet of natural history, etc. Yverdun is well built, and cheap as a residence. It has a hotel de ville, a hospital, and public gardens, with fine views of the lake and Jura. Rail and boat hence to Neuchâtel, etc. Trains to Geneva and Lausanne.

[Excursions near Yverdun. To the Chasseron, by Grandson, Grez, Fiez, etc., 3 l. (9 m.) Splendid view, but still finer from the Aiguille de Baume and the Suchet, 4 hours from Yverdun. From these two points you see all the lakes of western Switzerland, and have a fine view of the High Alps.]

ROUTES OF THE CANTON DE VAUD.

Lausanne to Aarau, by Berne (Nos. 63 and 6), or Soluthurn (Nos. 228 and 16), or rail to Olten.

ROUTE 276.

AARBERG, Rail through Berne, or Post road by Morat, 15 L (45 m)

	Leagues.	Miles.
Croix Blanche or Croisettes.	¾	2¼
Montpreveire	1¼	3¾
Cioals	1	3
Bressonaz	½	1½
Moudon, 4 L (12 m.)	½	1½
Lucens	1	3
Henniez	1	3
Marnans	½	1½
Payerne, 8 L (24 m.)	1½	4½
Corcelles	½	1½
Dompierre	½	1½
Domdidier	½	1½
Avenches	½	1½
Favorg	¾	2¼
Morat, 11½ L (34½ m.)	¾	2¼
Aarberg (No. 80)	3½	10½
	15	45

Aarberg, by Berne (Nos. 63 and 6), or by Solothurn (Nos. 223 and 16), to Olten, and thence to Aarberg.

Aigle, rail or road to Vevay (Nos. 267 and 54).

Altdorf, by Berne (Nos. 63 and 55), or by Berne (Nos. 63, 66, 67, or 68), and Lucerne (No 147), or by Bulle (No. 278), the Simmenthal (No. 72), to Thun, and thence to Unterwalden (Alpnach or Stanz, No. 76) and by lake to Fluelen.

Altstaetten, by Solothurn (Nos. 223 and 16), Aarau (No. 18), Zurich (No. 196), and St. Gallen (No 180), or rail to Olten, and thence to Zurich and St. Gallen.

Appenzell, same route as last, and then No. 25, or by Thun and Lucerne (Nos. 72, 76, and 281), to Zug, Zurich, and St. Gallen, the last part of the way from Zug by rail.

Art, by Solothurn (Nos. 223 and 16), Aarau (No. 17), and Zug (No. 281), or by Berne (Nos. 63 and 7*), and Zug (No. 281), or by Nos. 72, 76, and 281 through Thun as before.

Daden, by Berne (Nos. 63 and 56), or by Solothurn (Nos. 223 and 16), and Aarau (No. 2), or by rail all through.

Bâle, by Berne (Nos. 63 and 32), or by Aarberg (Nos. 276 and 29), or by rail throughout.

Bellinzona, by Sion (Nos. 267 and 236).

Berne (No. 63), or rail.

Bex, by Vevay (Nos. 267, 54, and 58), or rail

ROUTE 277.

BIENNE, 17 l. (51 m)

	Leagues.	Miles.
Aarberg (No. 276, or rail)	15	45
Buhl		2¼
Hermringen		
St. Nicholas		
Belmont		
Nydan		
Bienne		
	17	51

Brugg, by Berne (Nos. 63 and 197). or by Solothurn (Nos. 223 and 16), and Aarau (No. 7 or by rail,

ROUTE 278.

BULLE, 10½ l. (31½ m.)

	Leagues.	Miles.
Vevay (No. 267)	4	12
Châtel St. Denis	2	6
Semsale	1	3
Vauruz	1½	4½
Viridens	½	1½
Bulle	1½	4½
	10½	31½

Burgdorf, by Berne (Nos 63 and 60).

Chamouni, by Geneva (Nos. 96 and 95), or by rail to Martiguy, and thence over the Tête Noire (No. 265).

Chaux de Fonds, by Neuchâtel (rail), or road (Nos. 173, 174, and 169).

Chiavenna, by Sion (No. 267 and 236), and Bellinzona (No. 230).

Chur, by Solothurn (Nos. 223 and 16), Aarau (No. 18), and Zurich (No. 142), or by Berne (Nos 63 and 79), and Zurich (No. 142), or by Bulle (No. 278), Thun (No. 73), Lucerne (Nos. 255 and 253) and rail thence through Zurich.

Einsiedeln, by Berne (Nos. 63, 6*, 67, or 68), and Lucerne (Nos. 152), or Thun (Nos. 278, 73, or 255 and 253), through Brienz, and by the Brunig to Stanz, whence over the Lake of Lucerne to Brunnen.

Engelberg, same as last routes. The best by Thun and Brienz and over the Brunig, or from Hasli im Grund, Gadmen and the Susten Pass (No. 55).

Frauenfeld, by Solothurn (Nos 223 and 16); Aarau No 18) and Zurich No. 245); or by Berne (Nos. 63 and 79) and Zurich (No. 245); or by rail throughout.

ROUTE 279.

FRIBURG, 11½ L (34½ m.)

	Leagues.	Miles.
Croisettes	¾	2¼
Mount Preveire	1¼	3¾
Carouge	½	1½
Ecublens	½	1½
Rue	½	1½
Sivirier	1½	3¾
Romont	2	6
Chenens	1½	4½
Cottens	½	2¼
Neuruz	½	2
Villars	1	3
Friburg	1	3
	11½	34½

Another route passes by Payerne.

Gais, by Berne (Nos. 63 and 79), Zurich (No. 196) and St. Gallen (No. 186); or by Solothurn (Nos. 223 and 16), Aarau (No 18), Zurich (No. 196), and St. Gallen (No. 186); or by Thun (Nos. 253 and 72), Lucerne (No. 157) and on by rail.

Geneva (No. 96).

Glarus, by Berne (Nos. 63 and 79). Zurich (No. 116); or by Solothurn, Aarau, and Zurich (rail); or by Thun (Nos. 258 and 72), Lucerne (No. 157), and Schwyz (No 213) to Glarus (No. 113—A.B.)

Herisau, by Berne (Nos 63 and 79), and Zurich (No. 301); or by Solothurn (No. 223 and 16), Aarau (No. 18) and Zurich (No. 301).

Hofwyl, by Berne (Nos. 63 and 62).

Lauffenbourg, by Soluthurn (Nos. 223 and 16) and Aarau No. 10)

Locarno, by Sion (Nos 267 and 269); or by Sion (Nos. 267 and 235) and Bellinzona (No 232).

Locle, by Neuchâtel (Nos. 173 or 174 and 175).

Loesch (Baths), by Sion (Nos 262 and 268).

Lucerne, by Berne (Nos. 63 and 66, 67 or 68).

Lugano, by Sion (Nos. 267 and 270); or by Sion and Bellinzona.—(See those routes.)

Mendrisio, by Sion (Nos. 267 and 271).

Morat (No. 276).

Morges 2 l. (6 m.).

Moudon (No. 276).

Neuchâtel (Nos. 173 or 174).

Orbe (No. 174).

Payerne (No. 276).

Pfeffers (Baths), by Solothurn (Nos. 223 and 16), Aarau (No 18), and Zurich (No. 304); or by rail to Vevay, thence to Gessenay by Dent de Jaman (No. 55) or by Bulle (No. 278), to Thun by the Simmenthal (72), from Thun to Lucerne by the Brunig (76), and from Lucerne to Zurich by rail.

Righi (The), by Berne (Nos. 63, 66, 67, or 68), and Lucerne (Nos. 158 or 159).

Saint Gallen, by Solothurn (Nos. 223 and 16), Aarau, (No. 18), and Zurich (No. 196), or by Berne (Nos. 63 and 79), and Zurich (No. 196), or by the same routes as Pfeffers, as far as Zurich, and from Zurich, by rail, to St. Gallen.

Schaffhausen, by Solothurn (Nos. 223 and 16), and Aarau (No. 14), or by Berne (No. 63 and 197).

Schwyz, by Solothurn (Nos. 223 and 162), and Lucerne (No. 161), or by Berne (Nos. 63, 66, 67, or 68), and Lucerne (No. 161).

Sion (No. 267), or rail.

Solothurn (No 223).

Stanz. see Unterwalden.

Thun, by Berne (Nos. 63 and 55), or by Bulle (No. 268), or Vevay and Dent de Jaman (No. 72); the Simmenthal.

Trogen, by Solothurn (No. 223 and 16), Aarau (No. 18), Zurich (No. 196), and Saint Gallen (No. 193), or by Berne (Nos 63 and 79), Zurich (No. 196), and Saint Gallen (No. 193).

Unterwalden, by Berne (Nos. 63, 66, 67, and 68) and Lucerne (No. 153), or by Berne (Nos. 63 and 76), or by Bulle (No. 278); the Simmenthal (Nos. 55 and 72), Lucerne and the Brunig (No. 76).

Vevay, by rail or by road (No. 267).

Winterthur, by Solothurn (Nos. 223 and 16), Aarau (No. 18), and Zurich (No 301); or by Berne (Nos. 63 and 79), and Zurich (No. 501).

Yverdun (No. 174).

Zug, by Solothurn (Nos. 223 and 16), and Aarau (No. 17), or by Berne (Nos. 63 and 79), or by Bulle (No. 258); the Simmenthal (No. 72), Lucerne and the Brunig (No 76).

Zurich, by Solothurn (Nos. 223 and 16) and Aarau (No 18). or by Berne (Nos. 63 and 79), or by Bulle (No. 258); the Simmenthal (No. 72), and Lucerne (No. 76).

Zurzach, by Solothurn (Nos. 223 and 16), and Aarau No. 14), or by Berne (Nos. 63 and 197).

Paris, by Neuchâtel and Pontarlier, through Dijon, or by Geneva and Macon (rail).

Lyons, Turin, and Genoa by Geneva and the Victor Emanuel Railway to Mont Cenis (rail).

Strasburg, Frankfort. the Rhine, and North Germany by Bâle (rail).

Bavaria, Austria, and East Germany by Olten, Winterthur, and Romanshorn, or Schaffhausen (rail).

Milan and Italy, by Sion and the Simplon, or by Geneva and Mont Cenis (rail).

Many districts of the Canton de Vaud, especially near Vevay, Montreux, Bex, and Aigle, and more especially towards the source of the Sarine and the Upper Simmenthal, containing some of the most delightful pastoral scenery in Switzerland, take us into the Canton of Fribourg, which also forms the greater part of the eastern bank of the Lake of Neuchâtel, and must be noticed in this place before we proceed into the Canton de Valais.

CANTON OF FRIBOURG.

This canton is almost entirely encompassed by those of Berne and Vaud. It borders on the former to the east, and the latter forms its frontier to the south, west, and north. In the latter direction it even runs through the Canton of Vaud as far as the lake of Neuchâtel.

AREA, SOIL, AND CLIMATE.—The Canton of Fribourg has an area of 28 German square miles, 74½ Swiss square leagues, with a population of 100,000 souls. In its northern part it has many large fertile plains, but the southern portion of the Canton is throughout very mountainous and exposed to a severe climate, while in the north it is very mild. It may be observed in general that the climate of this Canton exhibits frequent and great variation at short distances.

MOUNTAINS.—The south of the Canton is intersected by two chains of mountains, of which one is a continuation of the Bernese Alps, and the other a part of the Jorat. These ridges gradually sink as they advance northwards, and at length terminate in the fertile plains near the lakes of Morat and Neuchâtel. The highest summit in this Canton is the Molesson, near Gruyeres; it does not exceed an altitude of 6,181 feet above the Mediterranean, and therefore does not reach the line of perpetual snow, which in the latitude of Switzerland is found to be about 8,000 feet.

LAKES AND RIVERS.—Lakes: The Lake of Neuchâtel, of which a description has been given under the Canton of that name. The Lake of Morat, which has an elevation of 1,344 feet above the Mediterranean, and a circumference of 5 l. (15 m.) The lake of Morat is extremely well stocked with fish, and formed by the Broye that unites it with the Lake of Neuchâtel, from which it is separated by a small mountain, called Vuilly, commanding a delightful prospect. The Schwarzsee (Black Lake), or lake of Omeina, is situated in a dismal and savage country, and is only 1½ l. (4½ m.) in circumference. Its pike and its red trout are highly esteemed. The waters of this lake are discharged by the river Singine.

RIVERS: The Sarine, or Saane, takes its source in the Glacier of Sanetsch, which is situated in the district of Gessenai, in the Canton of Berne, passes through the town of Fribourg, and falls into the Aar, near the village of Wyleroltigen. The Singine (Sense), which issues from the Schwarzsee, and partly from the Gantrisch, joins the Sarine, near Laupen. The Broye rises at Semsales, in the Canton of Fribourg, crosses part of this Canton, and of the Canton de Vaud, and after supplying the Lake of Morat, issues from it to fall into that of Neuchâtel. The Vevayse is an impetuous torrent, which, rising at Mont Molesson, falls into the *Lake of Geneva, near Vevay.*

CROPS AND INDUSTRY.—Fribourg is noted for its large herds of cattle and horses, of a strong and good breed. It also supports large flocks of sheep and goats, and a great many pigs; the sheep are in part of an improved breed. Poultry, game, and fish are found in considerable abundance. The Canton has good crops of cereals, hay, and fruit, and produces a little wine, besides flax, hemp, and tobacco. A good many large forests of timber trees are met with in different parts of the Canton, and among the mineral productions may be enumerated quarries of sandstone and tufa, coal pits, and mineral springs. The best cheeses in Switzerland, those of Gruyeres, are made in this Canton, which contains manufactures of plaited straw, glass (at the glass works of Semsales), and tobacco.

MINERAL SPRINGS AND BATHS.—The most frequented springs are at the Bains de Bonn (Aqua bona), in the district of Fribourg; the water of these springs contains sulphur and alum. The baths of Neigels, or Neigeln, are less visited than the former, though their waters are admitted to be equally efficacious.

POPULATION AND RELIGION. — This Canton has a population of 100,000 souls, being an increase of 30,000 in 30 years. Only 7,300 profess the Protestant religion, all the remainder being Catholics.

ABBEYS AND CONVENTS.—The religious communities of the Canton consists of 6 chapters of canons; 10 monasteries for men, and 9 convents of nuns. In the town of Fribourg alone there are 2 chapters of canons; 1 seminary; 4 convents for men, and 5 for nuns; the remaining chapters and monasteries are in other parts of the Canton.

EDUCATIONAL, SCIENTIFIC, AND CHARITABLE INSTITUTIONS. — For some years now the elementary schools of this Canton have been greatly perfected, with a zeal and intelligence worthy of admiration. So much is this the case that Mr. Barnard, in his work on education in Europe, published as long since as 1852, considers the primary girls' school of this Canton about the best in Switzerland; and another even earlier writer represents (in 1826) that the poor schools of Romont, of Gruyeres, of Morat, and that of Fribourg, directed by Pere Girard. were among the best in Switzerland. The Lyceum and Gymnasium in Fribourg offer instruction in classics, mathematics, physical science, theology, and jurisprudence.

Among the libraries may be noticed that of the Jesuits, before their expulsion in 1847; that of the Abbey of Hauterive; and several others belonging to communities and individuals.

Fribourg, Morat, and other towns in the Canton have hospitals that are extremely well managed. In the capital there are, moreover, a community of Sœurs Grises, and an Orphanage connected with the great hospital. Occupation is also provided for the poor, in a great manufactory, established with the view of destroying mendicity. This is a really philanthropic institution, and it would be very desirable for others to be founded on the same pattern.

The Economical Society deserves also to be noticed.

SURVEY OF THE CANTON OF FRIBOURG.

Bulle.—See Saane (Valley).

Fribourg, the capital. *Hotels.*— Grand Hotel de Fribourg, kept by Mr. T. Monney; a very good house, commanding a magnificent view of the Alps (Divine service). Zahringer Hof is one of the best and most pleasantly situated houses in Switzerland. Post-cars twice a-day to Bulle, 5¾ l. (17¼ m.), in 3¼ hours, 5fr. 60c., 3fr. 85c.; once a-day to Saanen or Gessenay, 15 l. (45 m.). 9fr. 45c.; twice to Morat, 3½ l. (10½ m.), in 2 hours, 2fr. 20c.; twice to Payerne, 4½ l. (12½ m.), in 2½ hours, 2fr. 70c. Is in the part of the canton called the Uechtland, is an unwalled town, built partly on the banks of the Sarine, which runs in the deep ravine, partly on the steep and rocky declivity above the river. It is remarkable, not only for its quaint and lofty houses, built on the very verge of the precipice, but also because part of the population speak French and part German. Its present population is 10.500, and its principal building a Church in the Gothic style, of which the tower, reaching an elevation of 365 feet, is the highest, and its organ the best in Switzerland, and one of the best in the world, made by Moser, having 7,800 pipes, the largest of 32 feet. It is played in summer at 4 30 p.m. and at nightfall. Fribourg is divided into two parts by the Sarine, the lower town, which is the smallest, being formerly united to the high, or principal quarter of the town, by three bridges, to which must now be added that triumph of art, the suspension bridge, spanning the ravine from cliff to cliff, 163 feet above the river and 941 feet in length, designed by the French engineer, Chaley. Four wire cables, 1,200 feet long, consisting each of 1,056 wires, supporting it. They are fastened deep in the rock and held by 128 anchors. A second bridge passes over the precipice of Gotteron, 154 feet high and 894 long; it was made in 1840.

The lower town consists of several small blocks of buildings along the river side, while the upper houses stands on a cliff of sand stone, rising precipitously from the river to the houses, and presenting in certain places almost a terrifying aspect. The town covers a large area, and it used to be surrounded with walls, flanked with towers. These have been destroyed since the Sonderbund war, in 1847. The ground covered by the town is of so uneven a nature that many of the streets are very winding and hilly, so that some of them can only be compared to a staircase, and cannot be even approached in a carriage. Owing to this cause certain parts of the town present singular piles of building, for example, the Rue de la Grande Fontaine, built on the vertical edge of a high rock, answers as a roof to the houses of the Little Rue du Court Chemin, which are excavated in the rock and the gate of the town called Porte de Bourguillon, seen from the lower town, looks like a castle in the air, because the eye does not take in the abyss over which it impends.

Fribourg contains several fine buildings, and reckons among the first in Switzerland in consideration of the number of its houses. The isolated position of some of the streets, the gardens, and even orchards contained within its area, give it an extraordinary appearance from whatever side it may be viewed.

PUBLIC BUILDINGS.—The Cathedral of St. Nicholas is a fine specimen of the architecture of the 13th century. It was begun in 1283, but the tower was only completed in 1452. Its ring of bells is the finest in Switzerland.

The old College of the Jesuits is a fine building (now converted into the cantonal school).

Its Church contains some good pictures. The hotel de ville is built on the site of the castle of the Duke of Zœhringen. The chancery, the old academy, latterly used as barracks, but somewhat decayed, are well-built. The new school-house behind the Cathedral deserves notice, having been built under the superintendence of Perè Girard, who, in connection with education, has so many claims on the gratitude of his countrymen.

EDUCATIONAL AND CHARITABLE INSTITUTIONS, &c.—The Lyceum and the Gymnasium used to be almost entirely under the direction of the Jesuits. This is no longer the case since their suppression in 1847. An important institution is the Boys' School, on the Lancasterian system, long under the direction of Pere Girard. The Orphan Girls' School and the Girls' Schools, directed by the Ursuline and Visitandine Nuns, are also deserving of notice.

Among the various industrial institutions the dyeing works of M.M. Kern, Guidi, and Co. were long noted as the *best in Switzerland for the red dye given to cotton.*

The sulphur steam bath of **Dr. Galè** is very remarkable, and the only one of its kind in Switzerland.

WALKS AND EXCURSIONS.—1. Walks: Within the town the best walk is to the Place des Tilleuls (Lime Tree Square); outside the old walls the Grandes Places and Tirage may be visited. The Palatinate, outside the Porte de Morat, is a pleasant walk, from which delightful views are enjoyed, but to see the country round Fribourg to the best advantage it is expedient to ascend the Cathedral tower, that of the old Jesuit Church, or the top of the Bourguillon gate. The Grand Tilleul, which is situated at about the centre of the town, recalls a warlike achievement highly honourable to the Swiss. The tree in question was planted on the 22nd June, 1476, the same day as the Battle of Morat, to commemorate the victory gained by the Confederates over the Burgundians under Charles the Bold. Subsequently, it was under the same tree that assembled, every Saturday evening, a kind of court of justice, known by the name of the Lime Tree Court (Linden-Gericht). The court decided the disputes between the peasantry who attended on market days.

The narrow valley of Gotteron,* close to the town, is remarkable on account of an aqueduct that has been cut through the rock, nearly 1,000 feet in length, and supplying one forge and several mills with water.

The Ponds are reservoirs outside the gate, called des Etangs; their water helps to preserve the cleanliness of the streets, and is of great use in the case of fires, but the continual pressure of this mass of water in the upper town causes an infiltration injurious to the houses standing in certain low quarters, rendering them damp and unhealthy.

2. Excursions to a distance:—
Madeleine ('The Hermitage of the) is 1 l. (3 m.) from Fribourg, and well worth

* This valley is spanned by another suspension bridge, erected in 1840.

a visit as a curiosity. An excavation of 400 feet carried into the rock on the bank of the Sarine contains a Church with a tower 80 feet in height, a kitchen, a cellar, and some chambers and vestibules. A man named Jean Dupré, of Gruyeres, with only one companion to assist him, undertook this trial of patience in 1670, and finished it in 10 years. He lost his life while attempting to assist some visitors across the river in 1708.

Gruyeres.—See Saane (Valley).

Molesson.—See Saane (Valley).

Mistelbach ('The), or the Petit a Mont de Veuilly, is situated opposite Morat, and commands a grand view, embracing the Lakes of Morat, Neuchâtel, and Bienne, with the charming country in their vicinity, and in the distance the sublime background of the High Alps.

Morat, called Murten in German, is reached from Fribourg through Courtepin and Villars, the distance being 3 l. (9 m.) The principal inns at Morat are the Couronne and the Croix Blanche, formerly the Aigle, the Couronne, and the Lion Rouge. Near this little town, which contains 2,000 inhabitants, and is the seat of a considerable transit trade, there used to be a small Chapel, called the Ossuaire, containing the bones of the Burgundians killed in the Battle of Morat, but it was destroyed by the French in 1798. A lime tree planted on the site of the chapel shows where it stood.

Neigles (The Bains de), at Garmiswyl, and the Baths of Bonn, are 2 l. (6 m.) from Fribourg.

Villars offers a fine view, similar to that from the Mistelbach, described above.

Saane Valley.—

The most interesting excursion in the Canton of Fribourg is up the Valley of the Saane, or Sarine, to the Molesson, and on to the Simmenthal.

Bulle is an ancient town 5¾ l. (17¼ m.) from Fribourg (2,379 feet above the sea), burnt down 1805. Hotels: Cheval Blanc; Hotel de Ville. Post, 2 a-day to Fribourg. Bulle is a great centre for trade in Gruyeres cheese.

The Molesson is easily ascended from Bulle. Passing an old convent, la part Dieu, secularised 1848, by two c. echo châlets, Châlet Neuf and Vieux,

on through fine cheese yielding pastures to top, which has no inn. View over S.W. Alps to Mont Blanc, almost all the Jura, the Lake of Geneva, Neuchâtel, Bienne, and Morat, &c

Tour de Trème, ¼ l. (¾ m) from Bulle, is a charmingly situated village. Hence 1 l (3 m.) to Gruyeres, quaint little town of European reputation, dear to after dinner loungers (2,555 feet). Castle founded in 436, walls 14 feet thick Pretty country.

Road hence leads by Enney and Albeuve to Montbovon, where it joins that of the Simmenthal. (See Canton of Berne under Simmenthal). For distances to Vevay from Bulle see routes at the end of Cantons of Fribourg, Berne, and Vaud.

ITINERARY FROM FRIBOURG.

To Aarau and Fribourg, by Berne (Nos. 54 and 6)
Aarberg (No. 80.)
Aigle (No. 54)
Altdorf, by Berne (Nos. 54 and 55), or by Berne (Nos. 54 and 66, 67 or 68), and Lucerne (No. 147).
Altstaetten, by Berne (Nos 54 and 79), Zurich (No. 196), and St. Gallen (No. 180).
Appenzell, by Berne (Nos. 54 and 79), and Zurich (No 28).
Art, by Berne (Nos. 54 and 78), and Zug (No. 28)).
Baden, by Berne (Nos. 54 and 56).

ROUTE 80.

BÂLE, 25¼ l. (75¼ m).

	Leagues.	Miles.
Courtepin	1½	4½
Villars (Munchwyler)	1	3
Morat, 3 l (9 m.)	¼	¾
Chietre (Kerzers)	1¼	5¼
Fräschels	½	1½
Kalnach	½	1½
Bargen	½	1½
Aarberg, 6¼ l. (19¼ m.)	½	½
Bâle (No. 29)	18¾	56¼
	25¼	75¼

Or to Bâle, by Berne (Nos. 54 and 32).
Bellinzona, by Sion (Nos. 89 or 90 and 236).
Berne (No. 54).

ROUTE 81.

BEX, 16¼ l. (49¼ m.)

	Leagues.	Miles.
Aigle (No. 54)	15	45
Bex	1¼	4½
	16¼	49½

ROUTE 82.

BIENNE, 8½ l. (25½ m.)

	Leagues.	Miles.
Aarberg (No. 80)	6½	19½
Bienne (No. 80)	2	6
	8½	25½

Brougg, by Berne (Nos. 54 and 6), and Aarau (No 7), or by Berne (Nos. 54 and 197).

Bulle (No. 54).

Burgdorf, by Berne (Nos. 54 and 60).

Chamouni, by Lausanne (Nos. 83 and 96 or 279), and Geneva (No. 95).

Chaux de Fonds, by Neuchâtel (Nos. 85 and 169).

Coire, by Berne (Nos. 54 and 79) and Zurich (No. 142.)

Einsiedeln, by Berne (Nos. 54 and 66, 67 or 68) and Lucerne (No. 152).

Engelberg, by Berne (Nos. 54 and 66, 67 or 68), and Lucerne (No. 153.)

Frauenfeld, by Berne (No. 54 and 79), and Zurich (No. 245).

Gais, by Berne (Nos. 54 and 79), Zurich (No. 196), and Saint Gallen (No. 186).

Geneva, by Lausanne (No. 83 or 96 or 279 and 96).

Glarus, by Berne (Nos. 54 and 79), and Zurich (No. 116).

Herisau, by Berne (Nos. 54 and 79), and Zurich (No. 301).

Hofwyl, by Berne (Nos. 54 and 62).

Lauffenbourg, by Berne (Nos. 54 and 6) and Aarau (No. 10).

ROUTE 83.

LAUSANNE, 12 l. (36 m).

	Leagues.	Miles.
Payerne (No. 93)	4	12
Lausanne (No. 63)	8	24
	12	36

For another route (No 279).

Locarno and Lugano by Sion. See Bellinzona, and thence (Nos. 232 and 233). To Locle, by Neuchâtel (Nos. 85 and 75).

Loesch (Baths of), by Sion (No. 89 or 90, and 268).

Lucerne, by Berne (Nos. 54, 66, 67, or 68).

Mendrisio, by Sion (Nos. 89 or 90) and Bellinzona (No. 235).

Morat (No. 80).

Morges, by Lausanne (Nos. 83 or 279 and 96).

ROUTE 84.

MOUDON, 8 l. (24 m.)

	Leagues.	Miles.
Payerne (No. 93)	4	12
Moudon (No. 63)	4	12
	8	24

ROUTE 85.

NEUCHÂTEL, 7 l. (21 m.)

	Leagues.	Miles.
Belfaux	1	3
Grolley	¾	1½
Domdidier	1½	4½
Saint Aubin	1	3
Delley	½	1½
Portalban	½	1½
Over the Lake to Neuchatel	2	6
	7	21

ROUTE 86.

BY MORAT, 12½ l. (37½ m.)

	Leagues.	Miles.
Aarberg (No. 80)	6½	19½
Neuchâtel (No. 80)	6	18
	12½	37½

ROUTE 87.

ORBE, 9½ l. (27½ m.)

	Leagues.	Miles.
Yverdun (No. 93)	8¾	26¼
Orbe (No. 71)	2	6
	10¾	32¼

Payerne (No. 93).

Pfeffers (Baths of), by Berne (Nos. 54 and 79) and Zurich (No. 304).

Righi (To the), by Berne (Nos. 54, 66, 67, or 68) and Lucerne (Nos. 158 or 159).

ROUTE 88.

SAANEN (GESSENAY), 15½ l. (46½ m.)

	Leagues.	Miles.
Bulle (No. 54)	5¾	17¼
Tour de Treême	½	1½
Gruyeres	¾	2¼
Heney	1¼	3¾
Villars	1¼	3¾
Albeuve	1	3
La Tine	1½	4½
Cave	½	1½
Chateau d'Oex	½	1½
Rougemont	1½	4½
Saanen	1	3
	15½	46½

Saint Gallen, by Berne (No. 54 and 79) and Zurich (No. 196).

Schaffhausen, by Berne (Nos. 54 and 6) and Aarau (Nos. 14, or 54 and 197).

Schwyz, by Berne (Nos. 54, 66, 67, or 68).

ROUTE 89.

SION, 25¼ l. (75¾ m.)

	Leagues.	Miles.
Bex (No. 81)	16¾	49¼
Sion (No. 75)	8½	26¼
	25¼	75¾

ROUTE 90.

By ZWEYSIMMEN, 20¾ l. (62¼ m.)

	Leagues.	Miles.
Martenbrach	1¼	3¾
Giffers	1¼	3¾
Plafeisn	1	3
Scwezzsec	2	6
Veltigen	3	9
Weissenbach	¼	¾
Garstadt	¼	¾
Zweysimmen	1	3
Sion (No.73)	10¾	32¼
	20¾	62¼

ROUTE 91.

SOLOTHURN, 12¼ l. (36¾ m).

	Leagues.	Miles.
Berne (No. 54)	5¾	17¼
Solothurn (No. 75)	6½	19½
	12¼	36¾

ROUTE 92.

By AARBERG, 12½ l. (37½ m.)

	Leagues.	Miles.
Aarberg (No. 80)	6¼	19½
Lyss	¾	2¼
Buetigen	1	3
Dotzigen	¾	2¼
Buren	½	1½
Rütli	½	1½
Arch	½	1½
Lenzingen	½	1½
Lüsslinger	¾	2¼
Solothurn	¾	2¼
	12½	37½

Stanz (Unterwalden).
Thun, by Berne (Nos. 54 and 55)
Trogen, by Berne (Nos. 54 and 79), Zurich (196) and St. Gallen (No. 193).
Unterwalden, by Berne (Nos. 54, 66, 67, or 68) and Lucerne (No. 153); or by Berne (No. 64 and 76).
Vevay (No. 54).
Winterthur, by Berne (Nos. 54 and 79) and Zurich (No. 501).

ROUTE 93.

YVERDUN, 8¾ l. (26¼ m.)

	Leagues.	Miles.
Pelfaux	1	3
Grolley	½	1½
Aux Echelles	¾	2¼
Montagnay	¾	2¼
Payerne (41)	1	3
Yverdun (No. 77)	4¾	14¼
	8¾	26¼

Zug, by Berne (No. 54 and 78).
Zurich, by Berne (Nos. 54 and 79).
Carslruhe, Francfort-on-the-Main, Strasburg and the Rhine, by Bienne or Berne and Bâle.
Southern France, as well as Turin, Genoa, and Italy, by Geneva.
Milan and Venetia, by Sion and Bellinzona, or by Altdorf and the St. Gothard.

CANTON OF VALAIS.

Our second grand route to the Alps (B) having taken us through the Canton de Vaud brings us to the Canton de Valais, which contains the highest summits, the finest scenery, and the largest glaciers in *Switzerland*.

Its northern frontiers are Berne and Vaud; to the west it has Savoy; to the south Piedmont and Italy; to the east Italy, Tessin, and Uri.

AREA, SOIL, AND CLIMATE.—The surface of this Canton is 216 square Swiss leagues, and consists of one main valley, and about 20 lateral valleys. The main valley begins at the Furka (4,266 feet), above the Lake of Geneva, and extends 35 l. (105 m.) to that lake. It is watered throughout by the Rhone. The lateral valleys, of which 16 are inhabited, rise to both sides of the main valley, to the two main walls of the Pennine Alps (S) and the Bernese Alps (N), where their ends are blocked up by enormous glaciers.

The climate is greatly varied in this Canton, the heat being sometimes almost insupportable in summer, while such is the cold in winter, that even the " arrowy " Rhone has been known to freeze. In the higher valleys, and especially near the glaciers, it is naturally colder than lower down, but the temperature is more constant and healthy in the higher districts. About Martigny, in the Rhone valley, the climate appears to be unhealthy, owing to marsh nuisances and the river vapours. Accordingly it is the very home of cretinism and goitres.

MOUNTAINS.—Two great chains of primitive mountains, both linked to the great Furka Gothard knot, extend northeast and south-west, along the Canton of Valais, which is thus enclosed between them. They gradually part from each other, and form the lateral valleys, by means of their ramifications. At St. Maurice they approximate again so closely that they scarcely suffer a passage for the Rhone, between the Dent de Morcle (8,951 feet) to the north, and the Dent du Midi (9,805 feet) to the south.

The most conspicuous peaks of the northern chain of the Valais are: the Galenstock (9,930 feet), the Sidelhorn (8,580 feet), one of the peaks of the Grimsel, the Viescherhörner (12,500) the Aletschhorn (12,950 feet), the Bietschorn (12,169 feet), the Altels (11,187 feet), the Breithorn (11,691 feet), the Tschingelhorn (11.021 feet), the Schilthorn (9,128 feet), the Doldemhorn (11,227 feet), and Diablerets (11,120 feet). In the southern chain the most conspicuous peaks are the Gries (7,336 feet), Monte Rosa (14.284 feet), Mont Cervin (13,795 feet), Weisshorn (13,900 feet). Mischabelhörner (14,108 feet), Dom (14,935 feet), Graffeneire (14,164 feet), Taschhorn (14,032 feet), and Dent Blanche (13,433 feet). Most of the mountains comprising these two chains send down vast glaciers, whence issue copious streams, watering and often devastating the adjacent valleys. The most remarkable glaciers in this Canton, and, in fact, in the entire chain of the Alps, are the great Aletsch Glacier, the Viescher and Rhône glaciers, to the north and east, and the Zmutt, Turtman, and Gietroz, with many others, in the south chain.

ASCENSIONS IN THE VALAIS.

NORTH CHAIN.

1. Aletschhorn —First time, 1860; 12 hours (4,207 metres) from Æggischhorn.

2. Bietschhorn (above Lotschthal).—12,969 feet; ascended 1859; 15 hours from Kippel.

3. Nesthorn (Gross).—12,593 feet; same position; unexplored.

SOUTH CHAIN.

4. Monte Rosa.—Nine peaks.

   1. Höchste Spitze.- 4,638 metres; 15,217 feet; ascended first, 1855.

   2. Nordend.—15,132 feet; ascended, 1861.

   3. Zumstein Spitze.—15,004 feet.

   4. Signal Kuppe.—14,961 feet; 4,561 metres; ascended, 1842.

   5. Parrot Spitze.—14,577 feet; ascended first, 1817.

   6. Ludwigshorn.—14,187 feet; ascended first. 1822.

   7. Balmenhorn.—13,927 feet.

   8. Vincent's Pyramid.—13,859 feet; ascended first, 1819.

   9. Schwarzhorn.—Ascension of Höchste Spitze 12 to 14 hours from Riffel.

5. Matterhorn.—4.482 metres; Several attempts to ascend it; two failed in 1861. In 1865 (July 14th), summit was reached by Lord F. Doug'as, Messrs. Hudson. Hadow. Whymper, Michael Croz, guide of Chamouni, and two Taugwalders, of Zermatt. On the descent Mr. Hadow slipped, knocked down Croz, and drew Hudson and Lord Douglas over a precipice of 4.000 feet. Whymper and the two Taugwalders are said to have been saved by the breaking of the rope. Only fragments of the bodies were found below. Mont Cervin, or the Matterhorn, was ascended a few days after by Carral Bich, Meyret and Gorrer, an Italian priest, and guides of Val Tournanche, in safety.

6 Dom, the highest of the Mischabelhörner. and the highest genuine Swiss mountain (Monte Rosa being Italian and Mont Blanc French), 14,935 feet; ascended first, 1861; 16 or 17 hours from Randa.

7. The Weisshorn.—14,804 feet; ascended by Prof. Tyndall, 1861; 20 hours from Randa, including bivouac at 9,000 feet.

8. Breithorn, ascended by Lord Minto and Sir J. Herschel; 13,685 feet; 3½ hours from Col di St. Theodule.

9. Lyskamm.—14,889 feet; ascended first, 1861; 8½ hours from Riffel Hotel.

10. Zwillinge, or Twins.—4,230 metres; 13,432 feet; 8 hours from Cour de Lys Châlet.

11. Combin (Grand).—14,164 feet; 2 hours from St. Pierre to the Châlets of Vassovey; 8 hours from Châlets of Vassovey to top; 10 hours from the Châlets of Corbassiere to the top; 7 hours from the top to Bourg St. Pierre; 9 hours to Hotel du Pont Monvoisin; 30fr. per guide; good guides at St. Pierre, the brothers Daniel and Emanuel Ballay, at Chable, Jean Faillet

LAKES. RIVERS, AND RIVULETS.—The Canton de Valais touches the Lake of Geneva at the place where the Rhone enters it. All its other lakes are tarns, like the Marjelensee at the Æggischhorn.

RIVERS: The Rhone is the only river of the Valais; its source is in the glacier of the same name. It flows through the main valley, 38 l. (114 m.) in length, receiving in its course more than 80 streams from the lateral valleys. and ultimately falls into the Lake of Geneva near Villeneuve. Though its current is very rapid it is well stocked with fish.

STREAMS AND TORRENS: It would be tiresome to enumerate all the streams of this canton. We shall therefore rest satisfied with mentioning the principal, such

a Glacier Table
The Matterhorn
Oberland Chalet
The Titlis
The Reichenbach Falls

as the Viège, the Salanze, the Trient, the Dranse, the Borque, the Navisanche, the Turtman, the Saltine, the Binne, the Egine, the Visp, on the left; and the Sionne, Dola, Loza, Masa, and others on the right bank.

AGRICULTURAL AND INDUSTRIAL PRODUCTIONS.—The Canton of Valais is rich in cattle, sheep, and goats, but its horses are not so numerous as mules. It contains a great abundance of game, such as chamois, deer, hares, foxes, marmottes, black cock, &c., also a few bears and wolves. The small lakes and the Rhone are full of fish. In the vegetable kingdom this Canton yields all kinds of cereals and excellent wine. The extreme, almost tropical, heat of some parts of the valley, especially near Sion, favours the growth of southern plants and fruit, including figs, oranges, almonds, chesnuts, &c. Splendid meadows, rich pastures, and noble forests of old trees of vast girth, complete the vegetable advantages of this Canton, which is not less favoured on the score of minerals, though the difficulty of working the ore has hitherto proved an impediment to any great development of these resources, for evidences exist of the presence of the precious metals, and traces have been found of copper, lead, and iron mines. Many crystals of large size are found near Naters, and the valley of Anniviers produces cobalt, out of which blue enamel is prepared at Sierre. Black marble is found near Sion, and alabaster, as well as talc, in other places lime, gypsum, and slate are very abundant, and the country yields coal and mineral sources. The manufactures are of little importance, being chiefly confined to the preparation of cheeses, blue enamel, and woollen or hempen stuffs.

THERMAL SPRINGS, &c.—The Valais contains 14 springs of mineral water, far the most noted and frequented being the Baths of Loesch (see further on).

POPULATION AND RELIGION.—The inhabitants amount to 96,800, almost entirely Roman Catholics. In the upper Valais bad German is spoken; in the lower bad French, being a patois mixture of French and Romance. The people are hardy, obstinate, very courageous, loyal, and faithful, when not corrupted by gold and strangers. Complaints have been made latterly of robbery and murder in some of the unfrequented parts. This has happened since the revolutionary troubles of 1847, but it is to be hoped that it is only a passing evil. At all events it is well to have a trusty guide and keep a good look out.

ABBEYS AND CONVENTS.—Chapters of Canons at Sion, St. Maurice, and St. Bernard; two Convents of Capuchins at Sion and St. Maurice; an Ursuline Nuns' Convent at Brieg; the Bernhardine Nuns at Colombay; and the Sœurs Grises at Sion.

EDUCATIONAL ESTABLISHMENTS AND CHARITIES.—There is an Episcopal Seminary at Sion; it is directed by the chapter of Sion. Another college exists at St. Maurice, whose professors are chosen among the canons of the chapter. Primary instruction is in a backward state in the rural districts. Education is generally backward, owing to the pastoral habits of the population.

Public libraries are wanting, but private collections exist of ancient documents, of minerals at the Great St. Bernard, of natural history in the College of St. Maurice, &c. The cantonal treasury only gives 1,200 Swiss francs to the poor, but there are seven hospitals with free admission for strangers as well as natives, and large endowments have even given them the means of affording outdoor relief. In many parishes there are besides this, communal bursaries for the assistance of the poor. Several of the religious confraternities have also sums specially appropriated to the relief of distressed members or of their children. One of these confraternities, that of St. Maurice, possesses even a hospital. The other hospitals are at Sion, Viège, Brieg, Martigny, St. Branchier, and Monthey. They are mostly directed by an ecclesiastic called rector.

The two philanthropic institutions of St. Bernard and of the Simplon deserve the most honourable mention. The latter is managed by two canons of the chapter of the Great St. Bernard and four lay brothers, whose praiseworthy occupation consists chiefly in rescuing unfortunate travellers from the snow storms, avalanches, and other mountain accidents.

SURVEY OF THE CANTON.

We shall adopt the clearest and most systematic treatment in our survey of this important Canton, by giving a list of the principal centres in the main Rhone valley, in alphabetical order, and appending to each centre the different connected excursions up the adjacent lateral valleys.

The scenery of this valley has only been duly appreciated within the last few years, but now that its beauties are known it is almost a greater favourite than any other, and with reason, for it contains probably the grandest scenery in the whole Alpine chain.

Æggischhorn.—See Viesch.
Anniviers (Val d').—See Sion.
Bagnes (Val de).— See Sion.
Barth·lemy (St.).—See Sion.
Bernard (St.).—See Martigny
Biona.—See Sion.
Breuil.—See Visp.
Brieg.—A quaint old town in Upper Valais, on the Rhone, at the foot of the Simplon Pass.

Hotels: Hotel de la Poste, or Three Kings; Hotel Anglais. Post twice a-day to Visp, 1⅞ l. in 1 hour (1*fr.* 40c., 1*fr.* 15c.); to Turtman, 4¾l. in 2½ hours (3*fr.* 70c., 3*fr.*; to Loesch, 5⅝ l. (4*fr.* 50c., 3*fr.*, 55c.); to Sierre, 7¼ l. in 4¼ hours (6*fr.* 10c., 4*fr.* 95c.) Departure for the Simplon every morning at 5½ o'clock, 23¼ l. (70½ m.) to Baveno, on Lake Maggiore.

Two-horse carriages to Sion, 40 to 50*fr.*; to Domo d' Ossola, 80 to 100*fr.* and 5*fr.* *trinkgeld;* to Baveno and Palanza, 120 to 140*fr.* and 8*fr.* trinkgeld; to Arona, 140 to 160*fr.* and 8 to 10*fr.* trinkgeld;

to Visp, 20*fr* and 1½*fr.* trinkgeld horse carriages taken to Vièg Additional horses taken to dra Simplon are at the charge of the

Brieg has 1,000 inhabitants. I capital of the district. Its shin roofs, and the green and yellow v cupolas of its churches, give i turesque appearance. Excursio be hence made to the Gorge of the to the Aletsch Glacier, by Bell / (with a horse, there and back i 10*fr.*), and on the Sparrhorn. Alp or Aletschbord is a good in Bell Alp. Not much visited when known will rival the Æggi from which it is 4 to 5 l. (12 t because the view hence is finer, a nearer to the Aletsch Glacier (6,0 The view commands Monte Leon the Mischabelhörner, the Dent the Matterhorn, the Weissho Prices the same as at the hotel Jungfrau. Hence, in 1½ hour, ascend the Sparrhorn or Bellhor feet), with a very fine panoram You have at your feet the upper the Glacier of Aletsch and that Good walkers can ascend he Aletschhorn, 12,950 feet, and con the same day. Guides, Anton Emanuel Ruppen, Moritz Jos Naters. Descent to Brieg in Ascent from Brieg, on horseback, Alp, 4 hours; horse and guide 10*f* geld; porter, 5*fr.* At Brieg con the ascent of the Simplon Pass, b justly considered a masterpiece gineering skill, but finished in les years (1801 to 1805). The Simpl begins properly at Geneva, foll lake to St. Gingoulph, then en Valais, which it almost entirely t to the extent of 43 l. (129 m.), metres, and leaves just below Gon posting stations have been est at St. Gingoulph, Vionaz, St. Martigny, Riddes, Sierre, T Viège, Brieg, and Simplon, and gence which regularly makes t

Cas of Spietz   Lake of Thun
Macugnaga Church   and Monte Rosa
BRIEG
Castle of Chillon
Visp Valley of Zermatt

ney in 6½ hours, from Brieg to Baveno, contribute to the convenience and animation of this road, the only pass from Switzerland to Italy adapted to heavy carriages. The road is about 25 feet wide throughout, and its incline, even in the steepest places, does not exceed 2½ feet per fathom (6 feet). The engineers were Gianella, of Milan, and Ceard, of Paris; 30,000 men were employed in its construction, and its expense amounted to 17,000,000*fr.* It was necessary to blow up 500,000 cubic fathoms of rock; to build 70,000 cubic fathoms of masonry; to remove 400,000 cubic fathoms of earth; and employ 1,750 quintals of powder on the work. 613 bridges had to be built, besides 8 galleries and 20 refuges. The distance from Glys, near Brieg, to Domo d'Ossola is 14 l. (42 m.), between which places there are 22 bridges, some of them thrown with the greatest daring over frightful chasms. The longest gallery is that of Gondo, 625 feet long. Above the sixth refuge is a miliary stone, marking the greatest height of the pass, 6,174 feet above the sea. Half a league further is the new hospice, and hence 3⅜ l. (11¼ m.) to a chapel beyond Gued and Ruden, marking the frontier of the Valais. The whole road presents the most charming variety of savage scenery, with imposing views of the snowy Bernese chain, as you rise from Brieg; awful chasms, near Gondo, through which the furious torrents rage, at apparently unfathomable depths; and further on, nearer Italy, the graceful outlines, sunny, smiling glens, southern vegetation, and emerald elysian meadows by the Tosa, that greet the delighted traveller as with a scene from Eden, as he passes the Crevola Bridge, and enters the beautiful valley of Domo d'Ossola.

The distances will be found in the Itinerary at the end of this Canton. The following are the principal stations on the Pass:—1. The Ganter Bridge, over the Ganter torrent, 2½ l. (7½ m.) Above the Bortlehorn and Furggenbaumhorn, 3 l. (9 m.) is Berisal, third refuge, with a little church. Passing under the Glyshorn, with a fine view of Gredetschorn, the Griesieghorn, and the Sparrenhorn, and above them of the Great Bernese Chain, you go through two galleries, the second the l'Eau-firoide, near a waterfall. To the left are seen the imposing masses of the Schönhorn and Monte Leone. By the third gallery is a fine waterfall, and the fourth gallery, finished in 1852, has 18 windows or portholes; soon after which you come to the summit of the pass. The hospice is inhabited by 6 or 8 Canons of St. Augustin, with servants, to help travellers. The expenses are 12,000*fr.* a year. It has room for 300 persons, who are received gratis, but it is usual to leave 5*fr.* (if possible) for bed, breakfast, and supper. You arrive next at the valley of Krummbach. In 2 leagues is the village of Simplon (4,341 feet), with the Hotel du Fletschhorn, well kept and moderate. Fine view of the Rossboden Glacier, with dark blue crevasses. The Fletschhorn should only be attempted by practised pedestrians (12,301 feet). From the village of Simplon you advance to Gsteig and the Gallery of Algaby, leaving to the right the Laquinthal. Passing through the gallery, 216 feet long, an eighth refuge, and crossing the Ponte Alto, over the Doveria, you reach the Gallery of Gondo, 19 feet wide, 15 high, with the inscription "Aeve Italo MDCCCV. Nap. imp." Issuing from the tunnel you cross the Alpine or Frossinone torrent, and reach Gondo with another hospice, the last place in the Valais. Near it gold mines at Zwischbergen. First Italian houses at San Marco. Passing the Gallery of Isola you find a good posthouse and softer vegetation. Advancing by Davedro and Val Cherasco you enter a picturesque but desert country, devastated by a tempest August 27th, 1834. Last gallery, Crevola, whence you reach the Toccia from Val Formazza, joining the Doveria, now crossed for the last time. You are now in the Val d'Ossola, near white marble quarries, whence the stone was taken for the Arc of Peace, at Milan. Several glens are passed before you reach Domo d' Ossola. This place, 13 l. (39 m.) from Brieg, is 8¼ l. (26¼ m.) to Baveno, on the Lago Maggiore. You are now in a new world. All is Italian, narrow streets, arcades, trades carried on in the streets, and all the usual habits of Italians. Best hotel, Post, now called Hotel de Ville. (Importunity of drivers and postilions to be resisted). From Domo d' Ossola the road passes down the Toccia Valley, a scene of peaceful sunny beauty, like a poet's dream. It leads through villas Ovesca, Valanzano, and Masone, leaving to the right the Val Anzasca, leading up to Monte Rosa at Macugnaga, 8½ l. (25½ m.) Near Borgo is a Roman miliary stone, with the inscription "Hic iter Cæsaris."

In 2⅓ l. from Domo d' Ossola you reach Vogogna (Crown Inn, good), with two ruined castles. Through Premosello, Corciago, and crossing the Toccia, through Migiandone (2½ l.), and Ornavasso (white cross), you pass marble quarries, used for the Milan Cathedral, and soon reach Gravellona (Hotel de l'Europe), whence the Lake of Orta (1½ hour) may be reached. The Strona joins the Toccia near here, and you gradually catch sight of Lago Maggiore as you approach Fariolo. In 3¼ l. (13½ m.) you are at Baveno (Hotel Bellevue), and if you prefer it you can take up your abode on Isola Madre (Hotel des Iles Borromees, elegant, but dear). Excursions hence to Monte Motterone and the Lago d'Orta. 4 l. (12 m.) further is Arona, whence rail to Milan and all Italy.

Champery.—See St. Maurice.
Cervin (Mont).—See Visp.
Einfisch.—See Anniviers.
Entremont (Val d').—See Martigny.
Evolena.—See Herens (Val d').
Fenetre (Col de).—See Martigny.
Heremence.—See Sion.
Herens.—See Sion.
Lax (40 minutes from Viesch, 4 hours *from Brieg*), in the Upper Valais. (Hotel *de la Croix*). The cheese of this district *is thought the best* in the country. Near

this spot is a grand circular view of the Alps, especially the Weisshorn, while the immediate foreground consists of delicious sylvan scenery, with gigantic chesnut and walnut trees. The absynthe shows its pale yellow leaves among the rocks, and the houses resemble those in the Grisons.

Loesch.—(Hotel de la Couronne, fair, cheap). An omnibus to the baths. Loesch stands like a mediæval town, picturesquely perched on a vine-covered hill. The Torrenthorn can be hence ascended, 4½ hours. The baths can be reached on foot (3 hours), the descent 2½ L (7½ m.) Opposite Loesch, on the left bank of the river, is the Illhorn, with a basin shaped like a crater, out of which in rainy weather rushes a furious torrent, making a grand waterfall. The pleasantest road from Loesch to Sion is along the right flank of the Rhone Valley, by Varen and Salgetsch (Sarquenens). It is at Loesch, 3 l. from Sierre (Terminus of the Ligne d'Italie Railway) that you start to reach the Baths of Loesch, and hence the Gemmi Pass, Kandersteg, and the Bernese Oberland. The waters of Loesch are considered the most beneficial in Switzerland, especially for the cure of cutaneous, gastric, and abdominal diseases. The water issues from twelve sources, generally almost in a boiling state, but the hottest spring is the Lorensquelle, in which Reaumur's thermometer marks 41½°. As a complete contrast to this the Liebfrauenbrunnen spring is of an icy coldness.

Remarks have often been made on the peculiar system of bathing in fashion at Loesch, differing from the practices usual in English watering places. But it appears that the arrangements are all quite proper, for the bathers, though of different sexes and meeting in the same large bath, are perfectly and properly dressed in long bathing habits. It is not unusual to see them taking coffee or playing at chess, &c., during the time they enjoy the bath, and it must be admitted that the indulgence of such pastimes much more reasonable and ethical than certain fancy balls and exhibitions, tolerated and admired in fashionable circles in the gay capitals of Europe.

These baths are greatly frequented in summer, though the elevated position, 4,404 feet above the sea, renders it necessary to bring warm clothing with you. Two other pieces of advice will be of use to the traveller. If possible provide yourself with a private servant, and get your own wine. The principal is called the New Bath, at the Promenade, with two basins, each capable of holding 35 persons, who often remain 4 to 5 hours consecutively in the water, and are seen occupied with the little floating tables, covered with books, papers, cards, &c. to pass the time. Visits are made there, religious disputes are forbidden, and all are admitted who conduct themselves properly. The second, or Wevra Bath, has 4 large basins, beside private or family baths. Then follow the Lorenz-quelle, the Alpen Bad, and the Zuricher Bad. All are opened from 4 to 10 a.m., and from 2 to 5 p.m. There are in all at Loesch, 20 springs, containing in particular sulphate of lime, magnesia, sodic oxide, and carbonate of lime.

It is usual to begin by taking a bath, lasting half an hour, and in three weeks to pass to longer baths of 4 hours in the morning, and some hours again in the afternoon. After the bath you go to bed for an hour.

Near the church is the monument of five Chasseurs of Chamois, crushed by an avalanche in 1839. Loesch Bads have a population of 550, and stands in a basin, surrounded by the Trubelu, Daubenhorn, Gemmi, Plattenhörner, and Maringhorn. Even in summer the sun sets behind the Gemmi at 5 p.m. The district has been much injured in former times by avalanches (especially 1719 and 1758), but the baths are now protected by strong walls and buttresses, and in the summer nothing of the kind occurs. The season *lasts from June to October.* The springs

of a saline gypsous nature were discovered in the 12th century.

Beautiful excursions may be made on all sides of Loesch, especially to

1. The Falls of the Dala, ½ l. (1½ m.) They are generally visited in the afternoon, when they are fully lighted up, and splendid iris is sometimes seen through the spray.

2. The Echelles, 1 l. (3 m.) The path thither leads through beautiful meadows to a wall-like rock, over which the inhabitants of the Alpine village of Albinen have to pass to reach their mountain home. The people, though carrying heavy loads, ascend and descend these ladders safely every day. Other excursions may be made to the Grottoes, ¼ l. (2 m.); to the heights of Foljiret, ½ l. (1½ m.); to the Châlets of Maing, ¾ l. (2¼ m.); to Clavines, on the Dala, near the Rinderhorn, 1 l. (3 m.); to the Glacier of Fluh, 2¾ l. (8¼ m.); to the Gouggerhoubel, 2½ l. (7½ m.) by the Pass du loup, or on horseback, by Chermignon, 1½ l. (4½ m.), with a fine view of the Rhone Valley, and 1 l. (3 m.) on to Gouggerhoubel; the Torrenthorn or Mainghorn (9,100 feet), 5 l. (15 m.) This is the Righi of the Canton de Valais, with the finest panoramic view in the whole country. The road to the summit from Loesch is very convenient, and even practicable for horses. Provisions, but no guide required. The Galmstock, ¼ l. from the Gouggerhoubel (7,580 feet) offers a fine view.

Loesch Baths are on the direct path to the Gemmi. The Gemmi itself is an enormous mass of rock, rising almost vertically above Loesch Baths and appearing to bar all progress. But a road that can be passed by horses as well as pedestrians was carried up the nearly vertical side of the mountain, by means of zig-zags, and takes you over to Kandersteg, in the Canton of Berne. It is perfectly safe to ascend, but the descent requires precaution if you ride, for in August, 1861, the Countess d'Arlincourt was dashed to pieces down the precipice, by not trusting to the instinct of her horse, and interfering with his movements. Above half-way up, the road passes through a kind of vault formed by the overhanging rock. This spot, called the Grandes Galleries, is 1,600 feet up the vertical side of the rock. An hour now brings you to the summit, from which the view of the southern chain bursts upon you with an almost overpowering effect. The mountains that stand forth with especial grandeur are the Mischabelhörner and the Weisshorn, ascended for the first time by Professor Tyndall and his guide, Bennen, of Laax, August 5th, 1861; also Mount Cervin, the awful scene of the accident to Lord Francis Douglas and his party, in July, 1865.

Some stone châlets are found at the top of the Pass which was opened in 1737 to 1741, by the two governments of Berne and Valais who caused the new road to be carried 10,000 feet, with 5 feet in width. The distances will be found in the Itinerary to the Canton of Berne. Half a league brings you from the summit to the Dauben Lake, and the highest point of the Gemmi (7,701 feet), with dirty, troubled, water issuing from the Lämmeren Glacier; the lake is ½ l. (1½ m.) long, 20 to 30 feet deep, and freezes three-fourths of the year.

The Daubenhorn rising to the left (8,865 feet), offers a very fine view. ¾ l. (2¼m.) from the Dauben See, you come to the Schwarenbach Inn (6,357 feet), and 3¼ hours further down, you come to Kandersteg. (See Canton of Berne.)

Loetschthal and *Loetschjoch.*—Berlepsch calls this a fine excursion for pedestrians, too little visited. It is the nearest access, in distance, from the Valais to the Oberland, and appears to have been more used at one time. The naturalist, Hugi, crossed this Pass about 35 years ago, and it has been occasionally attacked by sturdy Britons. The chief drawback appears to be *the entire want* of anything like decent *inns or accommodation in the Lotschthal. Hugi appears to have slept at the Stein-*

berg Châlet by the Schundbach Fall, and to have crossed the ridge, under the Shilthorn and near the Petersgrat, to Ferden, in the Löetschthal. He did not find any great impediments by the way, which has been subsequently followed by other Alpine climbers. The distance from Ferden to Gasteren, over the Löetschjoch (the easiest route is only about 4L, 12 m.), but part of the way is over snow and ice, with rough climbing. The primitive roughness of the people of the Loetschthal seems to have remained since the time of Hugi, who was viewed with some amazement and suspicion by these sequestered mountain sons. The Alpine Club may do well to take the hints and, in this district, for the present, to conceal their battery of thermometers, barometers, sympiesometers, and aneroids, for fear of passing for sorcerers and encountering a dip in the Märjelen Lake, if they avoid starving on the mean fare and fossilized food of the valley. Hence the advice of Berlepsch, "Prendre des provisions," and my advice, "Cacher ses instruments." You enter the Löetschthal, 2½ l. (7½ m.) from Visp, by a bridle path. After ascending the valley 1 l. (3 m.), amidst fine views, without a vestige of man or horse, you pass the Lonza, flowing from the Glaciers of Löstch and Telli, and reach the lone Chapel of Goppenstein, swept away almost yearly by avalanches, and rebuilt with determined perseverance by the natives. At Ferden, 1 l. (3 m.) further up, Berlepsch announces that there is bon vin à l'auberge. He adds that you can sleep at the Curé's, at Kippel, ¼ l. (¾ m.), and that the Curé's brother can be engaged as guide. The top of the valley is little visited, but Hugi, and English tourists have swept round these ways to the Aletsch Glacier, reaching the Æggischhorn or Bell Alp Hotel after a hard day's work. By going this route you avoid the uninteresting valley of the Rhone. From head of Löetschenthal, thence to Märjelen See, 19 m., almost all over ice and snow. But it is the easiest Glacier Pass in the Alps.

It passes Gletschenstaffel Châlets, ½ hour from end of Löetsch Glacier (6,175 f.)

Hugi describes the Löetschthal as the largest lateral valley in the Canton de Valais, towards the Bernese Alps, and 6 l. (Stunden) 18 m. in length. In the middle of it stands Kippel and a handsome parish church, like all those in the valley, such as Old Rechingen, Niederwalde, &c., which are expensively and often tastefully decorated, in this respect, corresponding to the handsome churches in the valleys south of Monte Rosa. Mr. King justly praises the people of the Italian valleys for the care and ornaments they bestow on the house of God. The same remark may extend to the poor people of the Löetschthal. It is surely well to find that, in this remote and ignorant corner, man can still think of something better than the passing hour and earthly interests, and show his appreciation of the comparative value of heavenly and earthly things, by the care he bestows on what appertains to the worship of God. The valley is also remarkable for a great number of small churches and chapels, but the villages are often constructed in a manner to expose them to avalanches, with narrow roofs and houses crowded together. At Biel, in 1828, half the village was thrown down by a hurricane and snow-storm and fifty-one men buried under the ruins. At Obergestelen, a similar accident occurred in 1720, and eighty-four men perished. Löetschthal has nine villages, inhabited by a lively people. The curate of Kippel is the only school-master of three villages in the lower valley, passing from village to village, while his vicar attends to the six villages in the upper valley.

To pass the Löetschloch to the Gasterenthal, you ascend to Kummenstafel 1 l. (3 m.) on to Stier Sturz by a steep, rocky path, up zig-zags to the Platten, pastures, with châlets and snow 1 l. (3 m.). In ½ l. (1½ m.) you reach the Col, 8,252 feet high, between the Balmhorn to the left and the Schildhorn to the right. From the Joch you command a grand view of the Gasterenthal, Kander Glacier, Mittelhorn, Löetsch Glacier, Doldenhorn, Blumlisalp, Nesthorn, Bietschorn, and the range between the Löetsch and the Rhone valley. The Nest and Bietschhorn can be ascended from Ferden and the Löetschthal. The latter mountain is in the best possible situation to command a view of the Southern or Pennine chain. It was once ascended, but on a misty day, by the Rev. Leslie Stephen. Distance from Kippel, up and back 15 hours, nine ascending and six returning. The ascent is by the Nest Glacier, and along a narrow rocky arrête.

Johann Zijler is named as a good guide. Height of Bietschorn, 12,969 feet.

The descent from the Löetschjoch to Gasteren is an affair of 2 l. (6 m.), passing the Châlet Im Gefäll, 1½ l. (4½ m.), and near a fine cascade to the Gasteren Châlets, ½ l. (1½ m.). From hence to Kandersteg is 1½ l. (4½ m.). From Kippel in the Löetschthal there is a pass only frequented by chamois hunters over the Birchfluh, by the Jägi and Ober Aletsch Glacier to Bell Alp.

Two or three other difficult passes, only fit for Alpine Clubmen and others who hang on to rocks with their eyelids, occur between Lauterbrunnen and the Löetschthal or Æggischhorn. 1. The Petersgrat and Lotschen Lucke to Æggischhorn, distance from Steinberg Châlet 35 miles. Pass, 10,500 feet high. 2. The Lawinen Thor was taken by Prof. Tyndall by the head of the Roththal. Height, 12,000 feet. 19 hours from Lauterbrunnon. A dangerous route requiring the aid of the Laueners and other men good and firm as guides.

Martigny.—There are two places of this name in the Lower Valais at the point where the Rhone, after receiving the Dranse from the Val de Bagnes, makes a bend to the north-west to fall into the Lake of Geneva. Martigny la Ville is ¼ of a league from Martigny le Bourg. Both are on the right bank of the Dranse.

Martigny contains some pretty good buildings, such as the Cathedral Church of St. Mary, with many Roman inscriptions. The presbytery and priory of St. Bernard furnishes eight canons to the Hospice of the Great St. Bernard, and two to that on the Simplon. At Martigny the principal Rhone Valley, or basin, attains its greatest width, and the climate in this district is heavy, intensely hot in summer, and unhealthy. Hence Martigny, like Aosta, is noted for goitres and cretinism, which are now ascertained to result, not so much from the use of glacier water, as from stagnant waters and the stagnant water.

air of shut-in valleys. Vines are cultivated with great success on the slopes surrounding Martigny, which produce the celebrated wines known by the names of Coquinpin and la Marque; the honey of this part of the Canton is also highly estimated.

From the Château de Batia, situated on a rock opposite the town, you enjoy a splendid view over the surrounding district, which was the scene of a dreadful devastation, June 16th, 1818. It happened that the Dranse was stopped in its course by a fall of a part of the Glacier of Chedroz, formed in the Valley of Bagnes, a lake ¼ of a league long (¾ m.), 400 feet wide, and 200 feet deep. The circumstance was well known, fears of a catastrophe were entertained, the cleverest engineer in Switzerland was employed to tunnel through the ice and thus help to drain the lake artificially. Valaisan workmen were engaged on this perilous work, exhibiting, it is said, a quiet devotion to duty and calm courage, difficult to equal and impossible to exceed. The calamity was thus deferred for a time and mitigated in the end. Yet it came at last, and may have been even accelerated by the subterranean works made to avert it. Suddenly the lake burst through its embankment, and its waters rushing down the valley with almost inconceivable impetuosity, swept everything before them till they reached the Rhone, causing frightful devastation throughout the valley. Forty persons perished in the flood, besides a number of cattle, the forest of Livounaire, 164 châlets, nearly 100 barns, 85 houses, many bridges and mills, with other buildings. The soil of the valley was covered with mud and gravel, and thus rendered sterile for some years, and in some places all vegetation was irretrievably destroyed.

Two valleys forking a little above Martigny bring their united waters to the Rhone. Of these the right-hand valley (called d'Entremont) leads by the noted pass of St. Bernard to Aosta, in Piedmont; while the other (Val de Bagnes), watered by the Dranse, affords another route over the Chedroz Glacier to Bionna, in the Val Pellina, distant 9 l. (27 m.) i. e. from Bagnes. A third route may be followed branching from Orsieres, on the St. Bernard road to Cormajeur, by Val Ferret, 8 l. (24 m.) Lastly, a fourth branches off from the principal road near the Bourg of Martigny, leads by the Val Forclaz to Trient, where it forks again, leading from Trient (a) by the Col de Balme (7,086 feet) to Chamouni, 7 l. (21 m.), and the other branch to the right leading from Trient (b), by the Tête Noire to Valorsine, 3 l. (9 m.)

We shall first consider the Val d'Entremont and the Great St. Bernard, which, notwithstanding ungenerous and ungrateful remarks even from eminent poets like Byron, must be pronounced one of the most philanthropic establishments in the world. The Pass of the Great St. Bernard separates the Val d'Entremont from that of Aosta, and even in the remotest times a road crossed over this ridge, facilitating the communication between the Valais and Piedmont. The present road is generally narrow, and above Liddes only practicable for pedestrians and mules, though the French army of the First Consul, Napoleon, managed, in 1800, to convey 60 cannon, at a great expense, and with some loss, over the pass.

The distance from Martigny by the Great St. Bernard to Aosta is 14 l. (42 m.) As far as St. Pierre, 5 l. (15 m.) from Martigny, and 3 l. (9 m.) from the Hospice, you can go in a char-a-banc, but above that point it is necessary to proceed on foot or on mule back.

From Martigny to Sembranchier, where the road to the Val de Bagnes branches, there are 2¼ l. (6¾ m.), but a shorter cut may be made on foot, saving a league, taking a path by Le Borgeau and Bovernier, by some houses called Les Valettes, and by Val Champeys, with a view of the small lake of that name. After Sembranchier, turning to the right, you enter the Val d'Entremont, which yields a little corn and has some cattle in its lower parts, but as you advance shows nothing but sterili y and sternness. You soon pass the ruins of a castle, large enough in 1444 to receive the Emperor Sigismund and 800 knights going to Italy. To the right is Mont Catogne, and in 1½ l. (4½ m.) you arrive at Orsieres (Hotel of the Alps); here, as before remarked, a road branches off by Col Ferret to Cormajeur. You now pass the ruins of Chatelard as you continue to advance up the Valley of Entremont, by many windings which can be cut off by pedestrians.

In the background appears the snowy ridge of Mont Velan, and, looking back, you have a fine view of Orsieres. Making several turns, and passing Fontaine dessous and Fontaine dessus, you arrive next at Liddes, 1½ l. (4½ m.) (Hotel d'Angleterre; Hotel de l'Union, said to be common inns with very high prices), 4,302 feet above the sea. Liddes is a well-built village, and has some cultivation round it. Advancing thence by other windings, you come to more Alpine scenery, and may still shorten your route, if a pedestrian, by cutting off corners of the winding bridle road. In 1½ l. (4½ m.) you come to the Bourg de St. Pierre, or St. Pierre Mont Jeux. (White Horse, White Cross, Breakfast of Napoleon, Inns). This is rather a dismal place, offering nothing remarkable except its Church, which is of the 11th century. The wall contains an inscription drawn up by Bishop Hugo of Geneva, and showing that the Saracens, who had advanced as far as that point, were stopped and driven back here. A Roman miliary pillar seen here is thought by some to be a column dedicated to the Emperor Constantine II. The only industrial occupation of the people of St. Pierre consists in the transit service over the Great St. Bernard. This is the best point from which to make the ascent of the Grand Combin. It is proper to add that the topography of the Combin is intricate, and scarcely to be understood without studying a correct map. The intricacy is increased by the fact that the Grand Combin is known in the Val de Bagnes by the name of Graffeneire, or Grafioneyre, while the name of Grand Combin is applied to an inferior summit on the west side of the Glacier de Corbassierè, to which the name of Petit Combin has been often given. A third summit, known as Dent du Midi, in certain districts of the Val d'Entremont, has received the name of Petit Combin from the inhabitants of the Val de Bagnes. Price for guides to Grand Combin. 30fr. The Grand Combin can be reached from Valorsey, which joins Val d'Entremont at St. Pierre, and also from the Val de Bagnes. These two valleys are here separated by two high ridges, nearly parallel to each other, and to those valleys, and both emanating from a short but very lofty transverse ridge. The southern extremity of the space, shut in between these three ridges, is a high and extensive table-land, full of an accumulation of névé, supplying the Glacier de Corbassiere, which flows down from it for several miles. This remote and savage glacier, though well worth a visit, is seldom trod by the foot of a visitor. Several paths connect the Entremont and Bagnes valleys in these parts. Another mountain, well worth a visit, and easily though seldom ascended, can be reached most conveniently from the road to St. Bernard, and even from the Hospice. This is Mont Velan, which is most easily attacked from Valorsey, or from the Cantine de Proz, at the spot where the carriage road to St. Bernard stops. André Dorsaz and Vierre Victor Morey, of St. Pierre, are mentioned as good guides to the Velan. Dorsaz demands 20fr. for the excursion. The view is said to be one of the finest in the Alps. The height of the Velan is 12,353 feet, and is reached in 6 hours from the Cantine. The Cantine de Proz is 1¼ l. (3¾ m.) from Bourg St. Pierre, and 5,550 feet above the sea. It is reached by a cutting in the rock, through a defile called Cherayre. After the Cantine, you continue by a bridle-path, passing the Glacier of Menouve, where a tunnel was commenced, intended to be 7,566 metres long, and to connect the Valais with Piedmont; but it has been discontinued for want of co-operation on the part of the Italian Government. We next reach the Defile of Marengo, a safe spot, once noted for avalanches, accidents, and snow-storms. The old Morgue that used to contain the bodies of those lost in the snow, is now nothing more than a bone or skeleton house, a relic of the past, as such events never occur now, at this point. You now ascend the valley called Vallée des Morts, and passing a bridge, reach, in 1¼ l. (3¾ m.), the Hospice of the Great St. Bernard, situated 7,609 feet above the sea, and founded in 962, by St. Bernard, of Meuthon.

Every traveller who arrives at the Hospice is hospitably sheltered and entertained, and those who are ill are nursed till well, without any fee being demanded. Nothing whatever is expected from the poor, and the rich are only welcome to give any donation they please. In times of snow-storms, and at dangerous seasons, the valets of the monastery, called maronniers, accompanied by the celebrated dogs, and often by two of the fathers, have been in the habit of scouring the country round the Hospice in search of half-frozen or buried wayfarers. Many have been thus brought to life, while the bodies of others from whom life had departed are exhibited in the Morgue near the Hospice. The genuine breed of St. Bernard dogs is extinct, the last of them being kept as a stuffed specimen in the Berne Museum. The present animals are mongrels. It is estimated that 16,000 to 19,000 persons pass the mountain annually, most of them stopping at the Hospice by the way. On some occasions, especially festivals, it has happened that 500 persons have been entertained at the Hospice at the same time.

The Monastery, which is a substantial stone building, with comfortable bed-*rooms for* lady and gentlemen visitors, *and a cheerful warm* refectory, where travellers are cheered with good fare, and the intelligent, courteous society of the fathers, stands on classical ground. For here stood once a Roman redoubt called Ostiolum, and a Roman temple existed formerly at the spot known as Place de Jupiter. The old Roman road which used to cross St. Bernard has been destroyed many ages ago; the avalanches and land-slips have completely obliterated it. The Monastery has a cabinet of coins and Roman Antiquities, containing curiosities found on the spot, such as statuettes; 300 Roman and 30 Greek medals, &c., &c. Abbé Lomon, a distinguished naturalist, has made a very rich collection of the flora of these mountains, particularly mosses. Careful meteorological observations are made here throughout the year, showing the following results:—Annual mean temperature, that of Spitsbergen, 75° N. lat; mean winter temperature, 9¼° centigr. below zero. In summer mean temperature about 9° centigr. above zero. Observation has proved that there are in the year 90 cloudy days. A clear sky rare. Snow, 9 months in the year. Rises to 7 or 8 feet in winter in low places; in others to 40 feet. The Monastery has a fine library; a cabinet of natural history; a votive tablet dedicated to Jupiter Penninus; the mausoleum of General Desaix, killed at the Battle of Marengo. This establishment is maintained at an expense of 80,000*fr.* a year, and has 80 beds always ready.

Excursions near.—To the Chenalette, free from snow, some weeks in the dog days; to the Mont Mort (8,813 feet), both easy to ascend. Plan de Jupiter is behind the lake, on the side of Italy, it gave the name of Mons. Jovis, still applied by the Savoyards, to St. Bernard. Celtic coins found here bear out Livy, who said that the Veragrians had a temple here. There was also a military station at this spot, mentioned in the Itinerary of Antoninus.

No passport wanted on the Italian frontier. The descent is rapid. Passing

La Vacherie, the Cantine of Fontainte (whence you can return to Martigny another way, by the Col de Fenêtre and Pains de Sucre, leading to Val Ferret and Sembranchier), you arrive at St. Remy, 1 l. (3 m.). Here is the Douane. Carriage, with 1 horse, to Aost ι, for 1 person. 10*fr.;* 2 persons. 14*fr.;* 3 persons 15 to 18*fr.* Thence there is a path by the Col de la Serena to Morgex and Cormayeur.

At St. Remy, southern luxuriant vegetation commences. In ½ l. (2¼ m.) St. Oyen, in ¼ l. (¼ m.), Etrouble, where you join the road to Col de Menouve, near Gignod, ½ l. (2¼ m.) the road branches off to Ollomont, by the Col de Fenêtre. Rich and pleasing vine-covered country. In 1½ l. (4½ m.) you reach Aosta (Hotel du Mont Blanc ; Crown or Post ; Ecu du Valais). This is an old Roman town, Civatas Augusta, Prætoria, founded by the Salasians, 1,100 years B.C.; conquered by the Romans, 28 years B.C.; destroyed and rebuilt by Augustus, in whose honour a triumphal arch was built, which is still standing, and has ten columns. There are also remains of Roman ramparts, of an amphitheatre, &c. Aosta is a bishopric, and has 6,500 inhabitants. The Cathedral deserves a visit; its portico has some good fres.oes, and on a pillar in the nave, Calvin's flight from Aosta is noticed. There is a fine town hall on the Place Carlo Alberto.

From Aosta, a post road of 13 l., leads to Ivrea. Thence rail to Turin and Genoa. From Aosta to Cormayeur are 9 l. (27 m.) Post road.

From Aosta to Evolena in Val d' Herens (Valais) a footpath.

The second principal valley debouching into Val d'Entremont, at Sembranchier, and watered by the principal branch of the Dranse is the Val de Bagnes. This takes you among some of the finest scenery in the Alps, but is not much frequented owing to want of good accommodation, though the people are courteous and hospitable, and less afflicted with cretinism than in the Entremont valley.

After leaving Sembranchier, the Val de Bagnes is for some leagues populous and animated. Passing through Villette, Chables, and Versegerè, you reach Chamsec, 2 l. (6 m.), where the high road ceases, then you cross the Dranse, which works several horizontal mills, and in ½ l. (1½ m.) you arrive at Lourtier, a poor place, and the last inhabited village in the valley. Travellers intending to proceed by the Col de Fenêtre to Aosta, must take a guide at Chables or at Champsec. Professional guides are not here met with. It is a matter of civility if they offer and they must be treated with consideration. They are often chamois hunters. The patois of the country is a very corrupt Romance, but in many parts the peasantry speak French with purity and even accuracy.

[Excursions may be made from Lourtier to Mont Gélé (9,321 feet) in 5 or 6 hours. Ascent rather arduous. View very fine over the Valais Alps, especially the Grand Combin. A path from Lourtier leads by the Col de Severen to Liapey, at the top of the Valley of Heremence.]

Above Lourtier the Val de Bagnes increases in sternness and sublimity. All fruit trees disappear, the Dranse dashes through the rocky barriers that break its waters into foam, and the mountains tower aloft, assuming fantastic and picturesque outlines. Those not intending to proceed to the Col de Fenêtre stop at the Pont de Mont Voisin, offering a fine view of Mont Pleureur (11,400 feet) and of the Glacier de Gétroz. But to those who have time to spare, half-a-day will be well repaid, if they visit the wild scenery at the head of the valley. "I know few more magnificent ice streams," says an Alpine writer, "than this of Chermontane, fed by numerous lateral tributaries, and bounded by noble summits, of which the principal are, the Pic d'Otemma (11,513 fee·), and the Pigne de l'Arolla (12,471 feet) on the north ; and the Trumma de Bones (11,149 feet), and Mont Gélé (11,539 feet), on the south ; while to the west, across the head of the Val de Bagnes, rise the Grand Combin (14,164 feet), and Mont Avril (10,961 feet), faced in the opposite direction by the Mont Collon (12,264 and 12,596, feet). The breadth of the Glacier de Chermontane averages three-fourths of a mile, and its length, according to the federal map, cannot be less than six miles."

From Pont de Mont Voisin to Chermontane d'en bas (Lower) is only a walk of 4 hours. You can pass the night at the Châlets of Torembec, if you have started in the morning from Martigny, 10 l. (30 m.) To the left is the Glacier of Breney, which, only forty years ago, stretched into the valley, and up the other side. Further on is the fine Glacier of Mont Durand, coming down from the Grand Combin. This is easily and safely passed in 7 minutes, when you reach the upper Châlets of Chermontane, at the foot of the large Glacier of Otemma (6,863 feet). Hence you ascend to the Col de Fenêtre (8,573) by the safest glacier pass in the Alps. The scenery is much more interesting than by the Great St. Bernard. The Col is easily reached in 4 hours from the Châlets of Torembec, and offers a perfectly magical view southward, embracing the Graian Alps, beyond Aosta, with the fine Glaciers of the Ruitor. Below appears the Val d'Ollomont, shut in by a serrated ridge. To the left Mont Gélé towers up almost perpendicularly to the height of 10,827 feet. To the right is Mont Avril (10,286 feet). The descent from the Col to the Châlets de Balme is steep but safe, and offers beautiful views of Val d'Ollomont. By Les Veaux, 1 l. (3 m.), and Ollomont, you descend, 1 l. (3 m.), to Valpelline, 4 l. (12 m.), from the Col, offering the glories and softness of Italian and subtropical vegetation within an easy walk of scenery that might rival the icy horrors of Greenland or the Poles. The vine here clusters in festoons round gay and picturesque *cottages; noble chesnuts give a deep and dreamy shade under the fires of an Italian* sun; and all is beauty, softness, and luxuriance. Unhappily, man does not help to complete the happy harmony of the picture. Cretins are numerous all the way hence to Aosta, and present a sad contrast to the symmetry of this paradisaical scenery. From Valpelline, by Roysan, to Aosta, there are 3 l. (9 m.)

[BRANCH ROUTES. — Before reaching the Col de Fenêtre, a path strikes off to the right and leads you over a steep rocky ridge, to the Glacier of Mont Durand, by which, towards the Grand Combin, an ice path takes you over the Col and Glacier de Sonadon, to the Valley of Valsorey and Bourg St. Pierre, on the road up Val d'Entremont to St. Bernard.]

Another path takes you over the ice from Chermontane and over the lower part of the Glacier d'Otemma, and leads you by the Glacier of the Crête Seche and over the Col (8,890 feet) to Perguis, in Val Pellina.

Maurice (Saint).—(Hotels, the Ecu de Valais; Restaurant at the Station.) Population, 1,300 inhabitants. This is a small tolerably well built-town, situated on the left bank of the Rhone, at the spot where this river escapes from the narrow gorge, between the Dent de Morcle and Dent du Midi. This position is, in fact, the key of the Valais, and might be easily defended, for the pass is so narrow that the Rhone and the road completely block it. Its importance was easily perceived by the great military leaders of Rome, and they kept a garrison there to hold the pass from the Pennine Valley to Helvetia. St. Maurice was then called Tarnaias or Tarnada, and later, Agaunum or Agaunus. It has been inferred, from the great number of sepulchral stones found at this spot, that the Romans had catacombs there. According to an ancient tradition, there must have been Christians at St. Maurice, as early as the year 58 of our era, *i.e.*, under the Emperor Nero, and the existing Church of St. Lawrence, is said to have been their first place of assembly. If this can be relied on, the Church is the most ancient Christian place of worship in Switzerland, and its extremely ancient architecture gives some countenance to the belief. At St. Maurice, a Chapel is also pointed out as the spot where some officers of the Theban legion suffered martyrdom, September 22nd, 302, for refusing to abjure Christianity. They were first buried in the catacombs, but their bones were subsequently removed to the church of the Abbey, built in memory of them. The name of St. Maurice, adopted by the town and the abbey, was that of the leader of the Theban legion. In 517, Sigismund, King of Burgundy, bestowed large funds on the abbey, in expiation for the murder of his son. The Church is almost entirely paved with sepulchral Roman stones, but the inscriptions are mostly illegible from injury. In the abbey library, some very interesting MSS. are preserved, and in the college is a pretty collection of natural history. Other curiosities at St. Maurice are: the Stone Bridge of a single arch, from plans drawn up by a Valasian bishop, who might justly obtain the name of Pontifex; the Town Hall, in a good style; the Hermitage of Nôtre Dame du Sex, cut in the rock at a considerable height, and offering a fine view. Not far from St. Maurice, towards the Lake of Geneva, was Epaunum, a spot celebrated in church history, and destroyed by a land slip.

[Excursions.—On the route from St. Maurice to Martigny, near the village of Miville, are two interesting sights.]

1. The Pissevache or Salanche waterfalls, consisting of several consecutive cascades, terminating in a fine leap from a perpendicular rock, 300 feet high, near the road. It is best seen in the morning, and from the east is the finest point of view.

2. The Bridge of Trient, where this torrent issues in an impetuous stream from a rent cut in the rock by its waters in the course of ages. The rocky channel through which the water has worn away is 1,000 feet high, and yet it is scarcely large enough to admit the passage of the water and spring floods. This sight has been closed to the visitor by an artificial fence, with the view of extorting money. Such impositions are not to be sanctioned.

Monthey.—On the ligne d'Italie railway, between St. Maurice and Boveret the present terminus of the line, on the Lake of Geneva. Only interesting as placed at the entrance of the charming Val d'Illiez, watered by the Viège, and leading up to the immediate foot of the Dent du Midi.

[Prices from Monthey — Guides and porters to Morgin or Champery, 5*fr.*; to Champery, by the Portes du Soleil, 7½*fr.*; Everywhere else, 6*fr.* per day. Horses and mules the same price as guides. For excursions round Champery there are special tariffs.]

Turning to the left from Monthey, you ascend through vineyards to Muren, then passing through fine chesnut woods and lovely country, with charming views, you advance through the rich pasture valley of the Viège, noted for its pastures, its cascades, its numerous châlets, its adventurously placed bridges, and its rare Alpine plants, and numerous erratic blocks. In the summer season, the women put on male attire, which must be a comfort and relief in such a rough country. The Val d'Illiez district is the richest part of the Canton de Valais.

To the left branches off the charming valley of Morgin, at the head of which there is a bathing establishment, and a fine echo, repeating as many as five syllables. The red source, containing calcareous sulphuric acid, is especially recommended for pale complexions. At the bath, is an excellent hotel, where you may obtain good strawberries, fresh butter, capital cream, and for dinner cogs de bruyère (grouse), and marmottes. The service is extremely homely and simple, but good.

Further up the Val d'Illiez, to the right,

on the top of a rock, stands the Church of Trois Torrents, in a picturesque situation. Advancing, you pass the fall of Nant de Fayou, leaping over a rock 130 feet high, but often waterless in summer. The next place is Val d'Illiez parish Church and Cemetery, with a charming view. The hotel and pension of Monrepos are opposite the church. Val d'Illiez is a very picturesque village, and Berlepsch says that its female population are remarkable for handsome features.

11. (3 m.) further up the valley is Champery, a considerable village, now much visited (Hotel de la Dent du Midi; Hotel de la Croix Federale, cheaper) on account of the great number of most interesting excursions that may be made in the neighbouring mountains. We shall proceed to point out the most desirable excursions in the neighbourhood of Champery. 1. To the Calvary, with the view of a cascade; (price of guide, 2fr.) 2. On Mont Crettaz; guide, 2½fr. 3. To Ayerne, with views over the Val and Glacier of Sezanfe. 4. From the Portes du Soleil is a grand view of the Dent du Midi; the ascent takes 3 hours. 5. On the Culet, 2½ l. (7½ m.) is a magnificent view of the chain of Dent du Midi and of the whole valley, 4½fr. 6. Les Esserts, 1½ l. (4½ m.) commands a view of Val d'Illiez and of the Rhone valley. To Mont de Ripaille the distance is 2½ l. (7½ m.), 5fr. To the Dent de Bonnaveau, 4 l. (12 m.), 8fr. To the Alp of Anthemoz the guide costs 5fr. To the Pointe de la Valerette, with a view of Lake Leman, 4 l. (12 m.), the guide costs 6fr. The ascent of Dent du Midi can only be recommended to sturdy travellers free from vertigo, 8 l. (24 m.); guide, 13fr.

From Champery several charming routes lead to the district of Sixt, in Savoy.

1. By the Col de Coux, passes by the Châlets de la Croix, and is a few minutes shorter. 2. By the Châlets de Goleze, where wine, bread, and cheese may be had. These routes are amidst fine timber and magnificent limestone crags. Time, 8 hours. Height: Col de Coux, 6,400 feet; Col de Goleze, 4,600 feet. These are the routes to Samoens Champery communicates direct with Sixt—1st, by

the Col de Sageroux; 2nd, by the Golette d'Oulaz. The first route passes through scenes of the utmost sublimity and beauty, by Châlets de Sesanfe and Bonnaveau. Time, not including halts, 8 hours. The second route, by the Golette d'Oulaz, passes Châlets de Vauzolle and Châlets de Barme, 7 to 8 hours.

1. Fares by the Col de Coux, rather an arduous trip, 5fr. 2. By Col de Coux and Col de Goleze, 12fr. 50c. In taking wine and provisions for these excursions it is important to ascertain before starting that they are of good quality. It is often found that the charges demanded by guides are quite exorbitant, and that the provisions furnished by them are of very inferior nature.

[Three routes conduct from Champery to Chamouni:—
1. By Bonnaveau, Col de Sesanfe (2,420 metres), Luisin, and Salvan (10 hours), from which you can proceed either to Martigny or Chamouni.
2. By Col de Sesanfe, Salanfe (7 hours), Col d'Emaney (3 hours, 2,457 metres), to Trinquent or Finhant (2h. 30m.) From Finhant to Barberine Hotel, 1h. 10m. Barberine Hotel (good), on the Tête Noire Pass to Chamouni, 4 hours.
3. After passing Col d'Emaney, ascends Col de Barberine (2,480 metres), and leads to Châlets de Barberine (4½ hours) from the Hotel de la Barberine. This route passes by beautiful waterfalls in the granitic district of the Aiguilles Rouges. Many paths lead through fine scenery, forming delightful excursions from the Barberine Hotel, especially over the Vernayes Pass to Martigny, much finer than the Forclaz, but bad guides always try to take you by the latter. It leads you by waterfalls and fine views. Chatelard, Cascade des Jeurs. Trinquent, and Salvan; 8 hours from Chamouni to Martigny this way.]

To return and issue from the valley you take the right bank of the Vièze and arrive near St. Maurice. You can also cross the Rhone and follow a footpath to Bex, and those who ascend the Dent du Midi from Val d'Illiez can descend on the other side into the Rhone valley, near the Salanche and Trient chasm.

Möril.—In the Upper Valais, 1¾ l. (5¼ m.) from Lax, 2,520 feet above the sea (Hotel de l'Æggischhorn), is in a charming situation, embowered among fruit trees. On a rocky eminence are the ruins of Mangepan, destroyed by the people in 1262. A little further on, placed on a naked rocky vall. is the solitary Church of Hohfluh. The Rhone is seen dashing and foaming in its rocky bed below. To the right, up the rocks, is a hermitage reached by a narrow path. The Rhone has made a great deposit of sand about here, and is joined by the Massa, a furious torrent, descending from the Aletsch Glacier, and which has bored a deep crevasse through the rock.

Münster.—About 3½ l. above Viesch, in the Upper Valais, 4,168 feet above the sea. (Hotel: Golden Cross, well kept.) A horse with guide to Viesch, Grimsel, and Furcka, returning same day, 10*fr.*; to Brieg, Hospenthal, Andermatt, Airolo, Tosa falls, and Formazza, 12*fr.* The traveller is surprised in this district to see the barns raised on piles to preserve the corn from mice.

Excursions may be made from Münster —1. To the Chapel of St. Anthony, with a fine view into the valley. 2. On the Löffelhorn, for good walkers, free from vertigo. For guide, Peter Bacher, of Münster, is recommended. Take provisions; none to be had on the way. Start 3 a.m. Rise above Geschenen, descend the valley of Trutzi to the Lower Staffel, châlet, 2 l. (6 m.); on to Upper Staffel, 1 l. (3 m.); then steep ascent to Trützi Lake, and by snow fields to summit, which has only room for six to eight persons. Height, 9,512 feet. It affords an extraordinary panoramic view; at your feet all the lower Aar Glacier; just above it the Thierberg and the Scheuchzerhorn, and higher up the formidable peaks of the Schreckhorn; more to the right those of the Wetterhörner; to the left the Oberaarhorn and Finsteraarhorn; and on the side of Valais the Matterhorn and the Mischabelhörner, concealing Monte Rosa.

Light cars from Münster to Viesch, containing three persons, 10*fr.*; to Brieg, 18*fr.*; to Viège, 20*fr.*

' *Obergestelen*, 2 l. (6 m.) from the Grimsel, near the Rhone Glacier, is the centre from which irradiate the three mountain roads: 1, to the *Grimsel*; 2, by *Nufenen* and the Gries Glacier to the Canton of Tessin; 3, by the Rhone Glacier and Furcka to St. Gothard. In February, 1720, Obergestelen was overwhelmed by an avalanche, by which 84 persons lost their lives, as is attested by an inscription on the wall of the church. (Hotel du Cheval Blanc; Alex Berther is a neat house with 12 rooms, and good wine of Bailloz.) Rates from Obergestelen. Horses: 1 horse with guide to Grimsel or Furcka (returning same day) 10*fr.*; to Hospenthal and Andermatt, 20*fr.*; to the Glacier of Gries, 10*fr.*; to the Falls of the Toccia and to Formazza, 20*fr.*; to Premia, 30*fr.*; to Nufenen, 10*fr.*; to Airolo, 20*fr.*

Obergestelen is the starting point for crossing the Gries Glacier to Andermatten Premia and the Val Formazza. The best plan is to sleep at Andermatten, if you have left Grimsel the same morning, but if you sleep at Obergestelen you can get on to Premia 10½ l. (31½ m.) The following is a brief outline of the route:— Crossing the Rhone you arrive at the hamlet of Im Loch, ¾ l. (2¼ m.), where a fine waterfall occurs. You cross the stream, ascend the valley 1½ l. (4½ m.), leaving to the left the Blasihorn and the Galmihörner; there is another water called the Hundsschürpfe, recrossing the stream and passing châlets you arrive at a point where the road forks. The left branch ascends by the Nufenen Joch to Val Bedretto. The direct road leads to the Gries Glacier. From the Altstaffel you ascend over slaty rocks, then fields of snow, till you reach the ice. The glacier is smooth, and having few crevasses, is crossed in 20 minutes, the proper direction being marked by poles; accidents are rare, but in 1843, three travellers (two M. M. Leonard, of Paris, and M. Wolfrat, of Frankfort,) were overtaken by an avalanche and perished about here. The Col, 7,530 feet high, is the boundary line of Switzerland in Italy. It is 3 l. (9 m.) from Obergestelen. The summit is surrounded by sharp bare rocks and snow slopes. In fair weather you have a ver fine view of the Bernese Alps. La Punta di Pasodan is the first station in Tessin. A rapid descent brings you to the Châlets of Bettelmatten, 1 l. (3 m.), then to the Châlets of Morass, 40 minutes, you follow the Griesbach to Kohrbächi, ½ l. (1½ m.), here occurs traces of glacier action in polishing the granite, and now vegetation begins to re-appear. ½ l. (1½ m.) on is Sulla Frutta, with the famous Toccia or Tosa Falls, the finest that occur throughout the Alps. The thunder and roar of its raging waters are heard long before the eye is gladdened and rivetted by the glancing waters and the dancing spray. The Toccia leaps from a rocky precipice of 400 feet, with a breadth of 80 feet, forming three magnificent shoots, which appear to dissolve into air, and fill the nether world with a cloud of vapour. Fruthwald is ½ l. (2½ m.) further on, then Gurflen, ¼ l. (¾ m.), then Zum Steg, ¼ l. (¾ m.), where the municipal council of the valley holds its meetings. It will be perceived from their names, that these villages like those of the Italian valleys S. of Monte Rosa, are occupied by a German population, and recent travellers have ascribed to them the same qualities of honesty, piety, industry, and physical superiority over their Italian neighbours, which form such a striking characteristic of the people of Gressenay, Alagna, and Macugnaga. Mr. King, who visited the district in 1859, is profuse in his praise of the beauty of the scenery throughout the Toccia Valley, and the same sentiments are re-echoed in the *Lady's Tour round Monte Rosa*. Picturesque villages, with glistening campaniles, deep chesnut groves, festoons of vines, emerald meadows, glancing streams, the thunder of waterfalls, and a noble back-ground of snowy Alps complete the picture of this favoured valley.

Pommat (in German), *Formazza* (in Italian), is ¼ l. (¾ m.) from Zumsteg, on the right bank of the river, and has an inn. Andermatten, ¼ l. (¾ m.) further down is 3,823 feet above the sea, and has

the best inn in the valley. From this point the road improves, and follows the right bank. Unterwald is 1¼ l. (3¾ m.) further down. Belepsch affirms that, according to the tradition of these people, they came originally from the Entlibuch in the Canton of Lucerne, and he says that they adhere tenaciously to their old language, and that they are distinguished by their dress. Below this point the road passes through the picturesque defile of Foppiano, containing large garnets in the slate. Issuing from the defile you plunge at once into the sweet south, with its magic tints and lights. The houses are scattered about among the chesnut trees; at Rocco occur the first vines and soon fig trees. At 1¼ l. (3¾ m.) from Unterwald you reach Premia (Hotel del Angelo). This place is a good centre for excursions. To the east, a path by the Scaletti di Forno leads into the Val di Campo (Tessin) and into Val Maggia. To the west is the entrance of the Val Dovera by which you can pass in 12 hours into the Binnenthal in the Valais. Lower down Val Formazza takes the name of Val Antigoria. At every step the beauty of the scenery increases. The road passes Cravegna and Crodo, always following the Toccia, and at Crevola Ossolano joins the Simplon route. From the Grimsel to Domo d'Ossola, this way, the distance is 17 l. (51 m.)

Oberwald is a village in the main Rhone valley, at the head of the Upper Valais, 1¼ l. (3¾ m.) from the Rhone Glacier, and 4,153 feet above the sea. The general character of the Upper Valais is stern and melancholy. Its rocky walls are crowned with dark forests of pine, but the bottom of the valley is generally carpeted with rich meadows, clothed with châlets blackened by age. Almost throughout the Upper Valais you have before you the magnificent pyramid of the Weisshorn, and behind you the imposing mass of the Galenstock.

Nicholas (St.)—See Visp.

Randa.—See Visp.

Riffelberg.—See Visp.

Saas.—See Visp.

Sierre.—Terminus of the Ligne d'Italie Railway. (Hotels: the Sun, clean and moderate. Pension: Baur, out of the town in a delightful position). There are four trains a-day hence to the Lake of Geneva. Those going on to Vevay and Lausanne, by the West Swiss line, must change carriages at St. Maurice. Fare from Sierre to Sion.: 1st class, 1*fr.* 95c.; 2nd class, 1*fr.* 30c.; 3rd class, 95c. From Sierre to Martigny: 1st, 5*fr.* 5c.; 2nd class, 3*fr.* 40c.; 3rd class, 2*fr.* 50c. Post car over the Simplon, twice a-day. The vegetation round Sierre is almost tropical. Accordingly it is surrounded with splendid gardens, and though the climate is none of the most healthy, this district is patronised by the Valaisan nobility. Sierre itself is an uninteresting place, but the country round it is charming. You can obtain excellent Malvoisie wine, but the water is detestable. French and German are both spoken here; the Romance element prevailing hence down the Rhone, and the Teutonic up it. Excursions, immediately round Sierre, may be made to the tower of Goubin, traced up to the time of the Saracens; to the Chartreuse of La Gerondc, on a scarped rock, with a fine view; and a more distant expedition is that of Val d'Anniviers, or Einfisch Thal and up the Bella Tola. Though most of these lateral valleys in this Canton wcre till lately almost unknown and unexplored, few in the whole range of the Alps, so well deserve a visit, and even a stay, and among them few present such striking scenery as the Val d'Anniviers. The passes leading thence to Zermatt are especially sublime and singular. Up to Zinal the traveller can proceed by a good mule track, and there are decent inns at Zinal and at St. Luc. The usual rate of guides in the valley is 5*fr.* per day. To this 1*fr.* is added to maintain the roads.

The *Navisanche river flows* through the *Pontis Gorge into the Rhone,* nearly 1 m. east of Sierre. It is not easy, even in the Alps, to find any gorge exceeding the grandeur of the defile through which the Navisanche has broken its way into the Rhone. In some places it is a mere cleft like the Via Mala. Passing Fang, a hamlet among walnut trees, you arrive at Vissoye, the chief place of the valley. It had no inn in 1863, but a good auberge has been opened at St. Luc, high up on the Eastern slope of the valley. The inhabitants of this district are remarkably industrious, and show much care and forethought in the water channels they have made in different directions. The number of dwellings and mayens or summer habitations of the peasantry give the valley a populous and cheerful appearance. Fires have been frequent and very serious in this valley. At the poor villages of Mission and Ayer, the Val de Torrent joins that of the Navisanche. Above Ayer, you find nothing but mayens. Zinal is on the left bank of the river, six miles fuither on and higher up. It has a decent little mountain inn. Near it a grand view may be obtained by ascending the Arpitetta Alp, commanding the Weisshorn ridge. Mont de la Leè, on the west side of the valley, is also deserving of a visit. At a greater distance, Lo Besso can be ascended, presenting a remarkable obelisk of bare rock on the east side of the Glacier, and rising to 12,057 feet, without offering resting place for snow. The Trift Joch or Col de Zinal from Zermatt is not considered too difficult a pass for male pedestrians, used to mountaineering. The difficulty has been diminished by a fixed ladder and chain, 70 feet long, at the most awkward spot.

Just under Lo Besso, above the ice rapids of the Glacier de Zinal, the traveller reaches the upper level of the glacier, and finds himself amidst some of the grandest scenery in the Alps. The amphitheatre, surrounding the top of the Zinal Glacier, offers 4 summits, exceeding 13,000 feet. These are the Rothhorn (13,855 feet), the Gabelhorn (13,363 feet), the Dent Blanc

(14,318 feet), and the Grand Cornier of 13,022 feet. Such a chain is almost unrivalled. You can reach Zermatt from Zinal in nine hours. The Col is 11,614 feet high, and is a notch in the ridge between the Gabel and the Trifthorn (12,261 feet). It is so narrow that one can sit astride of the ridge. It is possible to go down from it direct to Zermatt by the narrow ravine of the Triftbach.

Another pass from Zinal leads by the Col Durand, or de la Dent Blanche, to Zermatt. This route requires 11 hours without counting halts. This is the south termination of the Zinal Glacier, half-way in the ridge connecting the Dent Blanche with the Gabelhorn. A view may be obtained of it from many points in the Val d'Anniviers, with the summit of Mont Cervin. here known as the Grand Couronne, rising above it.

The summit of this Col is about 11,398 feet, and 6 or 6½ hours from Zermatt. A great Bergschrund, 30 feet wide, across the head of the glacier, is the only difficulty. Persons supposed competent to judge have affirmed that the view from or near the summit is the finest in the whole Pennine Alps. You descend down the slopes of the Ebihorn, but different tracks have been taken at sundry times. Two-and-a-half hours below the summit you obtain a grand view of everything between the Col d'Erin and Alphubel, You can reach Zermatt, if you prefer it, by the slopes north of the Zermatt Glacier, but it is thought more prudent to cross to the right side of the glacier and fall into the usual track to Zermatt.

The western branch of the Val d'Anniviers is the Val de Torrent. The two branches into which the main valley is bisected are connected by four passes. 1. Col de Bréona (9,574 feet). 2. Col du Châtel or Zate (9,433 feet). 3. Col de Torrent (9,593 feet). 4. Pas de Lona (8,928 feet). From Eison, 1½ hour below Evolena, you pass to Cremenz by an easy road in 6 hours. You pass between two

lofty points, the Sasseneire (10,692 feet) and Bec de Bossons (10,368 feet).

The Col de Sorebois offers another good means of communication from Evolena to Zinal without passing by Cremenz or Ayer. The time required is 12 hours, and it affords a good mule track throughout.

From St. Luc, a good centre, with a good inn (Hotel: Bella Tola), a little above Vissoie, several excursions can be made up the ridge separating the Val d'Anniviers from the Turtmanthal. St. Luc can also be reached direct from Lenk in the main Rhone valley by a torrent from the little Illsee, under the Illhorn (8,939 feet). From Lenk to St. Luc by this route requires 5 to 6 hours.

The principal excursion at St. Luc is up the Bella Tola (9,929 feet), which can be ascended by ladies, and affords a very fine panoramic view of the Bernese and Pennine chains. The top can be reached by a mule track from St. Luc in 3 hours.

The most direct way from St. Luc to the Turtmanthal is by a pass south of the Bella Tola, called Pass du Bœuf (9,154 feet), close to the Borterhorn (9,745 feet). You descend into the Turtmanthal by the Borterthal, then to Châlets of Pletschen. Distance, six hours from St. Luc to Zmeiden. Going down to Turtman you pass through one of the finest ancient pine forests in the Alps.

Another interesting route may be followed from St. Luc to Zermatt by the Zmeiden Pass and Jung Joch, 11 hours. This takes you through a scene of great desolation at the head of the Turtmanthal, and with a grand view of the Turtman Glacier. Zmeiden is a group of mayens, five hours from St. Luc, and a little further is another called Gruben, with a small inn, good and clean. Many excursions may be made from this as centre. You can cross from Gruben to Randa by the Turtman and Bies glaciers. The path from Gruben to Zermatt leads to the Chapel and Châlets of Jung, the

Jungthal and the Jung Joch, with a fine view of the Mischabelhörn. A long and rugged descent brings you in six hours from Zmeiden to St. Niklaus.

Sion (Sitten). — The capital of the Canton (the Sedunum of the Romans) stands in the finest part of the Rhone Valley. (Hotels: Golden Lion; Hotel de la Poste; Pension Musson, with a grape wine establishment). Four trains a-day to Geneva. [Fares to Sierre: 1st class, 1*fr.* 95*c.*; 2nd class, 1*fr.* 30*c.*; 3rd, class, 95*c.* To Martigny: 1st class, 3*fr.* 10*c.*; 2nd class, 2*fr.* 10*c.*; 3rd class, 1*fr.* 55*c.* St. Maurice: 1st class, 5*fr.* 5*c.*; 2nd class, 3*fr.* 35*c.*; 3rd class, 2*fr.* 50*c.* Monthey (Val d'Illiez): 1st class, 5*fr.* 75*c.*; 2nd class, 3*fr.* 85*c.*; 3rd class, 2*fr.* 90*c.* Bouverat: 1st class, 7*fr.* 70*c.*; 2nd class, 5*fr.* 10*c.*; 3rd class, 3*fr.* 85*c.* Post cars: Every day from Sion (twice) to Sierre, 3¼ l. (9¾ m.), in 1 hour 35 minutes, 2*fr.* 60*c.*; 2*fr.* 10*c.* To Turtman: 6¼ l. (18¾ m.), in 3¼ hours, 5*fr.*; 4*fr.* 5*c.* To Visp: 9¼ l. (27½ m.), in 5 hours, 7*fr.* 30*c.*; 5*fr.* 90*c.* To Brieg: 11 l. (33 m.), in 6 hours, 8*fr.* 70*c.*; 7 *fr.* 5*c.* Once every day to the Simplon, 19 l. (57 m.), in 14½ hours, 17*fr.* 90*c.*; 15*fr.* 5*c.* To Domo d'Ossola, 25½ l. (76½ m.), in 18½ hours, 24*fr.* 95*c.*; 21 *fr.* 80*c.* To Arona, 37¾ l. (113¼ m.), in 24 hours, 35*fr.* 50*c.*; 29*fr.* 80*c.*]

Population of Sion, 2,926 inhabitants. Height above the sea, 1,625 feet. Stands on the Sionne, near the Rhone, at the foot of two isolated wild looking rocks; one crowned by the old church and Castle of Valeria, still inhabited, though traced up to the Romans; the other, still higher, bearing on its side the castle of Tourbillon, and on its base that of Marjoria, once the episcopal residence. These latter castles are falling into ruins. The position of Sion is gay and pleasing, surrounded by sloping vineyards, cultivated fields, and verdant prairies, and fine fruit trees; it has a highly picturesque appearance, and forms a pretty picture with its background of lofty mountains. The old narrow streets, castellated houses, and arcades, give it a quaint appearance. It is surrounded by ditches and ramparts.

The principal square, called Grand Pont, is surrounded by substantial buildings.

PUBLIC EDIFICES.—The Cathedral, in the Byzantine style, contains several Roman inscriptions, 15 altars, and many fonts. The Church of St. Theodule, built by Cardinal Schinner. The Hotel de Ville is a fine specimen of mediæval architecture; the Chancery; the old Jesuit College, in a fine position; the Arsenal; Les Calendes, a tower dating from Charlemagne, now used as the residence of the Cathedral chapter. It was in this tower that, in 1308, twenty Valaisan patriot citizens, who opposed the subjugation of the Valais, by the Duke of Savoy, were shut up and secretly put to death. The hospital is administered by a prior and eight sisters of la Misericorde, called Sœurs Blanches. Any sick person, either of the town or country, is taken in and well nursed in it. Just outside the town is the Capuchin Convent, inhabited by ten monks, and placed in a charming position.

Sion is the seat of the cantonal government; of the Bishop; it is also the residence of the most distinguished families of the Canton.

[Excursions near the town: the walks and excursions round Sion are delightful. The whole vicinity is like one charming garden. The most interesting are those towards the Rhone, and on the slopes called Mayens de Sion, the other side of the Rhone. The hamlets and country houses on those slopes offer fine air and a pleasant view over the valley. The finest views, however, are from the Châteux of Valeria and Tourbillon, previously noticed. Near Valeria is the Church of St. Catherine, with old frescoes, and said to date from the ninth century. Other excursions may be made to Mont d'Orge, ½ l. (1½ m.) To the Hermitage of Longeborgne,

(3¾ m.) More distant excursions from this centre lead to:

1. Grion, above Bex; Canton de Vaud, below Diablerets, by Pas de Cheville and Enzeindaz. Distance, 12 l. (36 m.)

2. To Gsteig (Châlet) and Saanen (Gessenay) in the Canton of Berne, passing over the Saanetsch Pass. Distance, 11 or 12 l. (34 m.) See Wildstrubel (Canton of Berne.)

3. To Lenk and Zweysimmen (Canton of Berne) over the Rawil Pass. Distance, 12 or 13 m.

4. To Biona in Val Pellina, by the Val d'Herens (Eringerthal) and by St. Barthelemy, 9 l.

The latter valley, Eringerthal or Val d'Herens, opens into the Rhone Valley, nearly opposite Sion, and leads up to grand scenery and a convenient centre— Evolena with a fair hotel. A bridle path leads up to top of the valley; but to pass from the Val d'Herens into those of Anniviers or Heremence, a guide is wanted. Charge, 4½ fr. per day; porters, 5fr.; porters of *chaise* 6fr. Sion to Evolena, 5½ l.

Opening south-east of Sion, the Eringerthal is 12 l. (36 m.) long, and watered by the Borgne. About 3 l. (9 m.) from the entrance, it divides into two branches; the eastern preserving the name of Val d'Herens, while the western is known as the Val d'Heremence. These branches are divided by an icy ridge, including the Pointe de Vouasson (10,766 feet). Near Evolena, the Val d'Herens forks again, the right branch taking the name of Vál d'Arolla. All three branches are noted for fine cascades and glaciers. The people, as in the Val d'Anniviers, are not yet corrupted, and still show patriarchal simplicity in their manners. The language is a French patois. Hotels are not very well arranged, but many will prefer this discomfort to the impositions and worldliness of more frequented centres. First station from Sion is over the Borgne to *Bramois*, crossing a narrow crevasse ⅓ l. (1¼ m.); advancing in ½ l. (1½ m.) you arrive at *Longeborgne*, picturesque hermitage on

the rock inhabited by two hermits, church altar, stairs, cells, all are cut out of the rock. Turning back to Erbio and the head of a gorge you reach Mage, 1½ l. (4½ m.); by the Mayen de Pras, you can here ascend the Mont Noble (8,232 feet), easy to reach, with a splendid view. Next place, Suen, is 1 l. (3 m.), and thence St. Martin, ¼ l. (¾ m.), a large scattered parish. At the place where Val d'Heremence forks, is Enseigne, noted for its natural earth pyramids, called Combes.

From St. Martin, easy wooded slopes, among rocks, bring you to a stream, from which you reascend, catching sight of the rocky peaks of the Grand Dents, Tête Blanche, Dent d'Herens, and Mont Cervin.

Evolena (2½ l., 7½ m. from St. Martin) is a large parish of dispersed houses, with the Hotel of La Dent Blanche. Height above the sea, 4,242 feet. This is an excellent centre for many excursions.

1. To the Glacier of Ferpècle 2 l.(6 m.), 5,546 feet, in the midst of which rises, like an island, Mont Miné, with traces of old mines. The Glacier has encroached on what used to be rich meadows, where, thirty years ago, Roman coins and lances were found. Guide, 3fr. Fine view from here of the Dent Blanche, Dent d'Herens, and Grand Cornier, you can ascend 1½ l. (4½ m.) higher, to the edge of the Glacier.

2. To the Glacier de Vouasson (2 l. on the mountain de l'Etoile). Guide, 3fr.

3. To the Gorges de l'Agueillon. Guide, 4fr.

4. On the Sè Viol, 4fr.

Other more arduous excursions are these:

(a) To the Sasseneire, near the Col du Torrent (10,034 feet), very steep at the upper part. View of the whole valley very striking, including the frightful chaos of rocks and ices, from the Trifthorn to the Gabelhorn. Guide, 6fr.

(b) To the Couronne de Bréona (9,740 feet). Grand scenery; easy ascent. Guide, 5fr.

(c) The Sè Blanc de l'Arzinol. Fine view, 5fr.

(*d*) To the Trois Dents du Visivi and Glacier de Zarmil. Grand view. Guide, 7*fr.*

(*e*) The ascent of the Dent Blanche should only be attempted by sturdy climbers (13,434 feet). Each traveller should have two guides, (50*fr.* each) and a proper staff of porters. Climbed first by Kennedy and Wigram, July 18th, 1862.

The *Col d'Herens*, forms a communication between Evolena and Zermatt by one of the finest of glacier Passes. Road is as follows: Evolena to Châlets of Ferpêcle 2½ l., (7½ m.) to the Alp of Abricolla 1½ l., (4½ m.), where you can pass the night at Hotel de Cretaz. Starting early descend a difficult crevassed glacier and over a ridge or wall of rock, extending from the Tête Blanche to the Dent Blanche. If time allows, ascend the Tête Blanche (11,544 feet), up a steep snow slope, with a view of Monte Rosa, too sublime for language. Down the Glacier de Stock, over the difficult rocks of Stockje you come to the Zermatt Glacier and to Zermatt; 9 hours march over ice and snow.

(*f*) To Col de Torrent, Guide 5*fr.*, if you proceed to Vissoye, 10*fr.*, to the Bella Tola, 18*fr.*, return included.

The Val d'Arolla is a branch of the Val d'Herens from which it forks at Haudieres above Evolena. It leads up to the Mont Blanc de Cheillon and the Pigne d'Arolla. Roads stiff. Guide wanted. Take provisions. Have a good pole and shoes.

[Excursions in Val d'Arolla. 1. To the Glacier d'Arolla. Evolena to Haudieres, 1 l., (3 m.) over the Borgne to Châlets de Praloin and the Chapel of St. Barthelemy ¼ l., (2¼ m.) by marshy meadows to Mayens de Monta 1 l., (3 m.), and 1 l., (3 m.) to the Glacier, Guide 5*fr.* From Monta a difficult excursion. 2. To the Aiguille de la Za, a peak of the Grand Dents; fine view of Mont Collon, the Glacier of Arolla, the Pigne de l'Arolla, the Tête Blanche, and the snows of Col d'Herens, some *frs.* more wanted for this tour. *From Monta you also reach*

3. The Glaciers des Rosettes de Prazgras. Guide from Evolena, 5*fr.* If you wish to see the Mineral de la Casiorte, 2*fr.* more. 4. To the Cascade of Ignos, 500 feet high between the Chapel of St. Barthelemy and the Châlets of Monta. Guide from Evolena, 4*fr.* The following more arduous trips may be recommended to good walkers. 5. Ascent of Mont Collon (11,480 feet). Two guides 30*fr.* each and porters. 6. To the Pignon de l'Arolla (11,700 feet). Two guides, 30*fr.*, and porters. 7. To the Glacier of Arolla and by the Col de Collon to Bionnaz in the Val d'Aosta; two guides, 20*frs.* a hard day of 13 or 14 hours. 8. To the Col of Riedmatten and Glacier of Chailly; over the Glacier of Getroz and the Col of Mont Rouge, to the Glacier of Breney, and into the Val of Chermontane, then up the Glacier, over the Col de Fenêtre, down to Ollomont. This is the high-level Alpine Club route. Two guides, 22*fr.*, only to Chermontane, and Val de Bagne, 18*fr.*

The Val d'Heremence is the other main branch from the Val d'Herens. You reach it from Sion by the same Gorge of the Borgne. At 1¼ l., (4½ m.) you come to Vex, where quarters can be obtained at the Curé's. Behind the village are three roads. You take the upper one, passing through immense fragments of rock, and amidst fine views over the Borgne, 1,000 feet below, you come, 1 l., (3 m.) to Heremence, passing the Hermitage of Longeborgne, and the village of Nax. This is a somewhat wild and primitive district, attested by the heads of lynxes, bears, wolves, and other occupants of the neighbouring forests, formerly very numerous. Opposite Heremence are cascades, in front of you Mage; St. Martin, and the Dent d'Herens close the back ground. This is the proper beginning of the Val d'Heremence, called higher up Val d'Orsera. The river is called the Dixence or Durance. To the left a road leads to singular earth columns, called les Colonnys or les Peramides. A descen brings you to a very picturesque bridge. Beyond is Euseigne. The upper path leads to Marche, 1 l. (3 m.) Lynxes still exist in the forest hereabouts. Above it is the Caverne des Fées, still paved and formerly inhabited. The Mayens de Praz-long, 2 l. (6 m.), are châlets on the banks of a stream. From hence you ascend by a zig-zag path to the Col d'Arzinol, leading in 5 hours to Evolena. Further up the valley you reach the Alpe de Meribé, 1 l. (3 m.), where all progress seems barred by a rock. Ascending to avoid it you reach the Châlets de Teichons, where a rare white variety of the Alpine rose is found growing. Passing by a glacier which often increases largely, you come to the Alpe de la Barma, 1 l. (3 m,), you then proceed from the Châlets de Lautaret to those of Liappey. The Gla-ciers of Cheillon and of Lendarey fill up the head of the valley, thence following a rocky path, the traveller proceeds to the Col de Riedmatten, forming in the rocks a defile only a few feet in width. Look-ing back a sublime view of the Val d'Arolla is presented to the spectator. The descent is convenient to the Alpe de Monta. The principal passes out of the head of the valley are those of the Mont Rouge and the Col de Fenêtre.

For a description of the Pas de Cheville pass from Sion to Bex, see *Bex* under Canton de Vaud.

For the Ravil and Saanetsch Passes, see Canton of Berne, *Wildstrubel* and *Simmenthal.*

Turtman or *Tourtemagne,* (Hotels, Golden Lion or Post; Sun). The situation is un-healthy, owing to neighbouring marshes in the Rhone valley. Distance from Visp, 3 l. (9 m.); from Sierre, 3 l. (9 m.); from Sion, 3¾ l. (11¼m). Behind the town is a fine waterfall ; distance 10 minutes.

This is the centre from which to make excursions into the Turtmanthal, to the Schwarzhorn, by the Pas du Bœuf, and that de la Forcletta into the Valley d'Anni-

The Turtmanthal deserves a visit. It runs throughout magnificent forest,

rock, and pasture scenery. The forests are among the most ancient in the Alps. Nothing but mayens or summer châlets are found in it, so that at other seasons it is perfectly deserted. The entrance of the valley resembles a crevasses. The road behind the inn, ascends very high, through a forest, to Dubenwald, 2¼ l. (6¾ m.) in length. Grand primeval sylvan scenery. Pass to right bank of stream to Vollen-steg, then by the farms of Niggelingen, Tschaffel, and Pietschen, to the hamlet of Zmeiden 8 l. (9 m.); 5,686 feet high. The hotel of the Weisshorn is described as very expensive. Theodule Epinay, of Sierre, is said to be a good guide.

Excursions from Zmeiden. 1. To the Gruben and up the Schwarzhorn (9,870 feet), 3½ l. (10½ m.) Grand view. 2. From Zmeiden to the Great Turtman Glacier (called Weisshorn Glacier, in the valley), 2½ l. (7½ m.) This is a splendid excursion. 3. Up the Zmeidenhorn, com-manding a perfect view of the Weisshorn, Barrhorn, Rothhorn, &c. A lower point, the Kaltenberg, offers a fine view. To the west, the Col de Zmeiden leads to St. Luc (Val d'Anniviers), 5 hours. Another pass from a lower part of the valley at Zerbizren, ¾ l. (2¼ m.) from Zmeiden, leads by the Pass de la Forcletta (9,200 feet), over snow fields to Ayer, in the Val d'Anniviers. Many excursions that may be made in the Turtmanthal are scarcely known as yet. The Jung Pass (9,800 feet), to St. Nicholas, in the Visperthal has been noticed. The Schwarzhorn Pass is another way to the same point, through very fine scenery. From Zmeiden you zig-zag up a forest to a châlet, 1 l. (3 m.) Then on through a solitary district only frequented by marmottes, to the Col, 1½ l. (4½ m.), commanding splendid views of the Balferin, Mischabelhorner, Rothhorn, and Diablons. Descending over small snow fields by piles of stones, raised to point out the way, down to the hamlet of Jungen, with a chapel, 3 l. (9 m.) Zig-zag down through the forest to the Jung-bach. To St. Nicholas, 1 l. (3 m.)

Viège.—The river watering the beautiful Val d'Illiez. (See Monthey.)

Viège.—See Visp.

Viesch.—Charming position in the Rhone Valley, three hours above Brieg, at the foot of the Æggischhorn, now one of the main centres for excursions. (Hotel du Glacier, service objected to, wine good, 3*fr.* the bottle); horse and guide to the Æggischhorn, Brieg, or Münster, 10*fr.*; to Obergestelen, 14*fr.*; to Viège or Oberwald, 15*fr.*; to the Glacier du Rhone, 20*fr.* Viesch is the point from which to reach its highly crevassed glacier, ¾ l. (2¼ m.), near which night quarters may be obtained at Titor, and here the road diverges up the Æggischhorn. Cars with one horse to Brieg, 8 to 10*fr.*, to Viesch 12*fr.* Two ways up from Viesch to Æggischhorn, a stony, devious bridle path, and a pleasanter shorter cut for pedestrians. Arrived at the Viescherstaffel you see the hotel de la Jungfrau, which is reached in three hours from Viesch. At the hotel, which is often crowded, 25 beds, lodging 2*fr.*, dinner 3½*fr.*, supper 3*fr.*, wine not included. Good walkers can sweep round by the glacier to Aletschbord and reach the Æggischhorn, avoid the hotel, and back to Viesch same evening. Guide tariff, April, 1864: from Jungfrau Hotel to Oberaarjoch or Löetschjoch, 30*fr.*; to the Finsteraarhorn or Aletschhorn, 50*fr.*; to the Mönchjoch, 60*fr.*; to the top of the Jungfrau, 70*fr.* Porters to the Oberaarjoch or Löetschjoch, 20*fr.*; to Bell Alp, 8*fr.*; to Viesch, 5*fr.*

The following attractions have made the Jungfrau Hotel, opened by a spirited Valaisan in 1857, one of the most frequented centres in Switzerland. It is just above the Aletsch Glacier, the largest in the Alps. The summit of the Æggischhorn (9,054 feet) is very accessible from the hotel, which is built on its east slope, and commands one of the finest views in the Alps. Lastly, the highest and grandest summits of the Oberland chain are most easily ascended from this point. Another attractive object is the Märjelen Lake (7,230 feet), with floating icebergs on its blue waters, detached from its icy borders. Its waters escape at certain seasons by subterranean channels, partly of artificial construction.

A path, practicable for ladies who walk well, leads down by Riederalp (a little inn here) and the Furkeli on to the Aletsch Glacier and Bell Alp or Aletschbord Hotel. The Märjelen Lake is about 1½ hours from the Jungfrau Hotel. Its depth is various. It forms one of the most striking and polar scenes in the Alps.

The crevasses on the Aletsch Glacier are neither numerous nor difficult. As you go up the glacier you have a view of the ridge south-west of the Jungfrau, separating Löetsch from Lauterbrunnen and the Gasterenthal. These peaks are the Gletscherhorn, Mittaghorn, Grosshorn, ane Breithorn. The height of the Aletsch Glacier, at the point where the lateral valley to Löetsch branches off, is 9,148 feet by the government survey. From this point to the Aletschhorn you have only to rise 4,620 feet higher. This Aletschhorn is much the most striking object among all the surrounding mountains, is 132 feet higher than the Jungfrau, and the third point in elevation of the g oup

Near this part of the Glacier of Aletsch is the Cave of the Faulberg, where people sleep who ascend the Jungfrau or Finsteraarhorn from this side. A beautiful snow-covered mountain, called the Trugberg by Agassiz, is to the right of the Aletsch Glacier near its head. The view of the Oberland from the Col de la Jungfrau is grand. Height, about 11,500 feet, but there is no pass over this way to the Wengerenalp, for the snowy descent brings you to a great precipice of limestone which stops you. The ascent from the Märjelen Lake to the Jungfraujoch is 10 m. The whole excursion is 27½ m. There is no medial moraine cn the Aletsch Glacier.

A considerable glacier, rather steep and crevassed, not marked on any map except the Federal Swiss, descends between

Trugberg and the Grünhorn. In the interstices overhanging the Trugberg Glacier is a considerable accumulation of soil, resulting from the disintegration of the adjoining rock, and producing specimens of thymus serpyllum, with bright red flowers, and still higher the ubiquitous fern *cistoperis fragilis.*

Other interesting excursions from the Æggischhorn for good climbers, are: 1. To the Finsteraarhorn (14,026 feet.) The ascent from the Faulberghorn is 9 or 10 hours. 2. To the Jungfrau (13,671 feet) ascent, and return to the Faulberg, 17½ hours. Has been effected in 10½ hours. 3. The Aletschhorn (13,803 feet.) The summit has been reached from Bell Alp in one long day, starting at 1 a.m. The view extends to Mont Pelvoux, in Dauphiny, 135 miles off.

Nearer objects of interest at the Jungfrau Hotel, are the Viesch Glacier, and to the Gorge of the Massa, where the Aletsch Glacier ends rather suddenly, in a narrow glen, between very steep rocks. The passes of the Oberaarjoch and Studerjoch, from the Grimsel to the Æggischhorn, has been noticed under the head of Grimsel (Canton of Berne).

Two other passes lead from Viesch south, to Italy. 1. By the Binnenthal Albrun Pass, and Pommat to Andermatten, 11½ hours, 30 miles. The Binnenthal is specially interesting to geologists, for its granite metamorphic rocks, saccharoid dolomite, and rare minerals; such as tromelite, corundun, tourmaline, &c. At Binn, the principal village, (4,784 feet), there is a poor inn. There are some fine larches at Imfeld. The Albrun Pass is 8,005 feet. You descend by a granitic scene to Lake Lelenda, and waterfall, to Formazza. Many tracks diverge from this main pass, but it is easy to lose your way here without a guide. 2. From Viesch you can also reach Premia by the Binnenthal. About 12 hours, *walk.* There are two passes from the *Binnenthal to Val Antigeni.* 1. By the *— Pass.* 2. By the Col della Rossa.

In the first pass after reaching the summit of the Albrun Pass (already described), in 6 or 7 hours, you proceed by the Deveroalp pastures to the Devero Châlets, called Al Ponte, (6,273 feet.) You can rough it for a night here. On by German village Ayer, through beautiful Devero Valley to Crode and Premia. 2. Col della Rossa, a direct way from Imfeld in the Binnenthal to Deveroalp. You ascend to a lake, Geissfbad See (7,800 feet), and the Col, only 300 feet above it (8,120 feet.) Way across marked by stone cairns. 3. Kriegalp Pass is the most interesting way from Viesch to Premia. Take S. W. branch of Binnenthal by Heiligenkreuz, 3½ hours from Viesch. Top of pass 7 hours from Viech. 1¼ hour from the top, you descend to Al Ponte.

A further pass leads from Viesch to Isella. It is called the Ritter Pass (8,858 feet) ; a laborious day's walk. Way is up branch of the Binnenthal, called Langthal to hamlet of Heiligenkreuz (4,938 feet). No provisions to be got on the road. On through a further fork of the Langthal, called Jaffischthal to Col south of Tunnetschhorn. You may descend hence to the Simplon Road. By another branch valley, the Mättithal, you approach the Ritter Pass. Highest châlets, Gaumen (6,851 feet), only used a few weeks in summer. At summit of Pass, grand view of Monte Leone and other contiguous peaks (11,698 feet). Down to the Divegliaalp and Val Cherasca (9 hours from Viesch), and hence to Isella (3½ hours). Beautiful views of Val Vedro. Hotel de la Poste, at Isella, comfortable. A chamois hunter, Franz at Frasquera, best guide.

Visp (*Viège*) : 2 l. (6 m.) from Brieg; 3 l. (9 m.) from Turtman ; 6 l. (18 m.) from Sierre; 9¾ l. (29¼ m.) from Sion. (Hotels : Sun, reasonable; Hotel de la Poste). Post car, twice a-day, to Brieg, 1⅞ l (6 m.) in 1 hour, 1*fr.* 40c.; 1*fr.* 15c.; to Sion, 9 l. (27 m.), 5 hours, 7*fr.*. 50c.; 5*fr.* 90c.

Horses and Guides : 1 horse from Visp

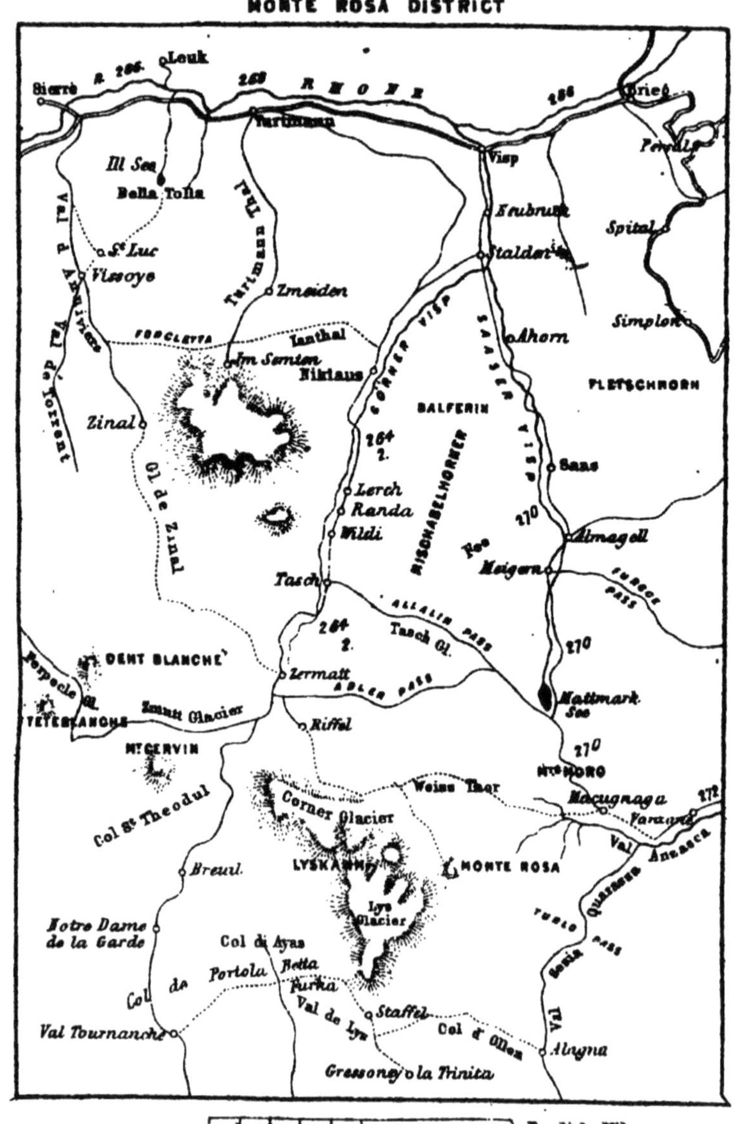
MONTE ROSA DISTRICT
Leuk
Sierre
R. 265.
258
RHONE
266
Brieg
Turtmann
Visp
Ill Sea
Pendle
Bella Tolla
Neubruck
Spital
St Luc
Stalden
Vissoye
Zmeiden
Ahorn
Simplon
FORCLETTA
Ianthal
Im Santen
PLETSCHHORN
Niklaus
BALFERIN
GORNER VISP
SAASER VISP
Zinal
264
2.
Saas
Lerch
Randa
270
Wildi
RISCHABELHORNER
Col de Zinal
Almagell
Fee
FURGGE PASS
Meigern
Tasch
ALLALIN PASS
264
Tasch Gl.
2.
270
DENT BLANCHE
Zermatt
ADLER PASS
Perpecle Gl.
Mattmark
TETEBLANCHE
Zmutt Glacier
See
Riffel
270
Mt CERVIN
Mte MORO
Col St Theodul
Weiss Thor
Macugnaga
272
Gorner Glacier
Varazze
Breuil
Val Anzasca
LYSKAMM
MONTE ROSA
Notre Dame
Lys
de la Garde
Glacier
TURLO PASS
Col di Ayas
QUARAZZA PASS
Col de Portola
Betta
SESIA PASS
Furka
VAL
Val Tournanche
Val de Lys
Staffel
Col d'Ollen
Alagna
Gressoney la Trinita
1 2 3 4 5
10 English Miles.

to Stalden, 5*fr.*; to St. Nicholas, 10*fr.*: if the guide and horse must sleep there, 12*fr.*, and 22*fr.* to Zermatt. Chair porters, 6*fr.* per day; luggage porters, 5*fr.* Distances from Visp to Stalden, 2 L.; to St. Nicholas, 2½ l. (7½ m.); to Randa, 2½ l. (7½ m.); to Tasch, ¾ l. (2¼ m.); to Zermatt, 1½ l. (4½ m.) Total, Visp to Zermatt, 9 l. (27 m.)

Visp does not offer many curiosities except its skull and bone houses, by the church, a custom common to the whole Balferin is obtained from the church-yard. Much harm was done here and in Monte Rosa district. A fine view of the the Vispthal, by the earthquake of July 25, 1855. The Baltschied Valley on the opposite side of the Rhone, is interesting to mineralogists.

The Vispthal forks at Stalden, the right branch to Zermatt being that of Saint Nicholas, and leading to Zermatt and over the Saint Theodule Pass, at the foot of Mont Cervin, to Breuil in the Val Tournanche; the left, or Saasthal, taking you by the Monte Moro Pass to Macugnaga, in the Val Anzasca. The two branches are watered by two Visps, and separated by a magnificent ridge, containing some of the highest mountains in the Alps. This latter range, called the Saas Grat, extending from the Strahl-horn to the Balferin, ranks the next in height after those of Mont Blanc and Monte Rosa, and the four passes leading from Saas to Zermatt are among the most formidable in the Alps, and should not be attacked by any but good mountaineers, well trained to such work. The Dom, one of the Mischabelhörner, in this range, is according to Canon Berchtbold, of Sion, 14,941 English feet above the sea. The height of Mont Blanc is 15,784, and of Monte Rosa, 15,223 feet. The valley of St. Nicholas, at the bridge of Randa, is, according to Schlagintweit, 4,754 feet; and the height of the Dom above the village and bridge, 10,000 feet. Berchtbold has given the Täschhorn 4 metres, or 13 feet over its twin brother, the Dom.

Both are decidedly higher than the northern peak of this ridge, and the general opinion at Zermatt and Saas is in favour of the Dom, an opinion in which Mr. Gottlieb Studer concurs. It is, therefore, still somewhat doubtful which of the two may claim the supremacy among the Alps exclusively Swiss.*

The nature and duration of a tour round Monte Rosa depends on the object and time at the disposal of the visitor. The following are suggestions for excursions of greater or lesser duration:—

Tour of 16 Days and of 10 Days round Monte Rosa.

	DAY.
From Leukerbad, Turtman or Brieg, to Saas...	1
Saas (including a visit to the Fee Valley in the Saas Grat) to Mattmarksee.........	1
Mattmarksee over the Monte Moro to Macugnaga	1
Belvedere and Glacier of Macugnaga Pedriolo, &c.	1
Macugnaga to Ponte Grande (a four hours' walk)............................	1
Ponte Grande, over the Baranca Pass, to Fobello	1
Fobello to Varallo, visit to Monte Sacro and Monte de Tre Croci	2
Varallo to Alagna	1
Excursion from Alagna to the Pile Alpe, Val di Bors and Glacier	1
From Alagna, by the Col d'Ollen to Gressenay	1
Excursion from Gressenay to the Lys Glacier..	1
From Gressenay, by Col di Renzola and Col de Jon, to Chatillon......................	1
Chatillon to Breuil	1
Breuil, over St. Theodule, to Zermatt	1
Up Riffelberg and Görner Grat.............	1
Return from Zermatt to Visp, and thence in a carriage to Brieg or Turtmann	1
	16

Tour of 10 days.

	DAY.
Visit to Fee Valley dispensed with; Mattmarksee, reached the first day...........................	1
Visit Belvedere, and descent to Ponte Grande, not seeing Glacier of Pedriolo.....................	1
Ponte Grande to Varallo	1
Visit Sacro Monte early in the morning, and to Alagna in the evening, ordering a carriage to be ready to take you from Varallo to Piode...	1
Excursion to Pile Alpe, Val di Bors, thence by the Col d'Ollen to Gressenay; may be accomplished in one long day	1

* Monte Rosa is partly Italian.

Excursions from Gressensy to the Lys Glacier may be omitted.

A fortnight would be ample time for making the tour, without making any deviations from the direct route.

In our survey of the Visp district we shall conduct the traveller, first, to Zermatt, now, perhaps, the favourite centre in the Alps, after Chamouni and Interlaken. The road is good from Visp to Stalden. Bed of the river, sandy. Pass some vineyards. View of the Balferin. Start early. The road is hot. Passing Visper Tenninen, in 1½ l. (4½ m.) to the new bridge over to the left bank.

Stalden (½ l., 1½ m.): Rustic inn, cheap. Good wine. A picturesque village, with church on rock. On to Zermatt, by meadows and among fine walnut trees. Vines to the left. Muhlbach ½ l. (1½ m.) Church of Emd, above. Brunegghorn and Weisshorn tower grandly to the right. Shorter cut by foot path. Kalpetran, ½ l. (1½ m.) Kipfen, ¾ l. (2¼ m.) Over Bridge of Seli. Road less good about here. Over the Jungbach to St. Nicholas, ¾ l. (2¼ m.) 3,583 feet. White Cross: indifferent inn, rooms 1½ fr. to 2 fr., tea 1½ fr., moderate beer and wine; bad attendance, 75c. A dirty village, suffered from the earthquake of 1855. From hence, to Zermatt, five hours. To the left, the village of Grächen, is the birth-place of Thomas Platter, who, from being a Goatherd, raised himself, by his love of study and learning, to be one of the best Greek scholars of the day, and, after immense struggles, succeeded in attending the German Universities and in becoming, ultimately, Greek Professor at Bâle.

Excursions from St. Nicholas. The Jungalp, 1½ l. (4½ m.); hence to the Sparrenhorn. Superb view. The Schwarzhorn (9,872) panoramic view. Rothhorn and Barrhorn for sturdy climbers. Pleasant walks to Hoellenen, Grächen, and the Hannigalp. View of Bernese chain, 3½ hours there and back.

Advance up valley from Stalden by good road through pine forest. Grand summit

of Breithorn in front. Over the Biffigbach to the hamlet of Mattsand, by the cascades of Dümmibach, over the Wildibach by a bad road to Herbigen 1 l. (3 m.) a wretched exposed village. Next hamlet of Breitenmatt, then over the bed of Lerchenzug, impassable late in the day from the waters emanating from melting of the snow. *Lerch* hamlet is ¾ l. (2¼ m.) further. To the right you have the Bies or Weisshorn Glacier seeming suspended over the valley. The Weisshorn peak, scaled by Professor Tyndale, 1861, towers a pyramid of pure glistening snow above the glacier.

Valley widens. Over the Lerchen Zug, coming from the Graben Glacier. Next place is Randa, ¾ l. (2¼ m.), 4,448 feet. Hotel du Dome, a fine house, recently opened, twelve beds, clean, but dear. Randa has suffered immensely from avalanches in 1636 and 1819, when the pressure of the air above did great injury. Further on ½ l. (1½ m.), *In der Wildi*, here is a chaos of rocks which buried a whole village and every soul in it. Look back to the Mischabels, the Glacier of Kien, and of Festi, and to the right the Mettelhorn. A-head the Theodulehorn, Glacier of St. Theodule and of Hohelicht. Täsch, 1 l. (3 m.) is a little village on the Täschbach. Here the paths diverge that lead to the Alphubeljoch (11,700 feet), the Täschalp and the gigantic Fee Glacier, to Fee in the Valley of Saas. Also path to Allelin Pass (10,990 feet), and the Mattmarksee.

Valley narrows. Soon the colossal obelisk of the Matterhorn (13,795 feet,) comes in view, looking doubly threatening since the awful accident in July, 1865. Görner Glacier also in view. Zermatt, 1½ l. (4½ m.), called in Italian Praborgne, 5,073 feet above the sea. Hotel du Mont Cervin with sixty beds: fine views from Nos. 40 to 45 (third story); baths; good fare; good attendance. Hotel Monte Rosa, kept by the brothers Seiler, who also own the Riffel hotel. Prices same at both. Rooms, 2 to 3 fr.: table d'hôte, without wine, 3 fr.; breakfast, 1½ fr. Good horses

kept. Tariff of guides* &c.—To the Görner, Findelen, and Zermatt Glaciers, half
a day, 3*fr.*; to the Görner Grat, the Rothhorn, the Hörnli, and the Schwarz See. 6*fr.*;
to the Col de St. Theodule. 8*fr.*; to Cima
de Jazzi, 10*fr.*; to Mon e Rosa, Höchste
Spitze, each guide 50*fr.*; by Col St. Theodule to Val Tournanche, 15*fr.* to Châtillon,
20*fr.*; by the Weissthor to Macugnaga,
25*fr.*; by the Glaciers of Zermatt and Ferpêcle, or to the Col of Evolena, 30*fr.*; by
the Trift Glacier to the Col d'Anniviers, to
Ayer, Val d'Anniviers, 30*fr.* Return fare
included. Grand tour of Monte Rosa. 7*fr.*
per day. By other ways to Saas and Visp
6*fr.* per day. Porters 5*fr.* per day. Horse
and attendant: Zermatt to Riffelberg,
10*fr.*; to Schwarz See, Theodule Joch or
on Rothhorn, 10*fr.*; by Theodule Glacier
to Tournanche, 40*fr.*, return fare included. General excursions 10*fr.* per
day. The Zermatt flora is the finest and
rarest in the Valais.

To appreciate the unrivalled scenery of
this district you must stop at least two
days at Zermatt. The first day you should
visit the Görner Grat (eight hours there
and back). Second day to the Schwarz See
and on the Hörnli. A third day would
be well bestowed in ascending the Col du
Cervin.

Excursions from Zermatt may be classed
as first easy, second harder, third hardest
for practised cragsmen, fourth fool-hardy
for neck-or-nothing men. To the first
class are those to the Findelen, Görner,
and Zermatt Glaciers, to the Schwarz See,
Hörnli and Görner Grat. To the second
belong the ascent of the Mettelhorn,
Theodulejoch, and Cima de Jazzi. To
the third, Monte Rosa, the Weissthor and
Adler Pass to Saas; to Riffelhorn, the Cols
of Evolena, and of Trift. The fourth comprises the ascent of Mont Cervin. From
Zermatt to the Findelen glacier, 1 l. (3 m.),
it is 2½ L. (7½ m.) long and comes from
the Cima de Jazzi; finest point of view
from Fluhalp (7,942 feet) above the
Stelli Lake. Distance to the Görner Glacier
1 l. (3 m.) After the Aletsch, the largest
glacier in Switzerland. Length, 4 L. (12 m.)
Surface, 40 square kilometres. Its needles
cover 10,000 square mètres and are considered among the finest in Switzerland.
Advance, 30 feet a year. Distance to
Glacier of Zermatt 2½ l. (7½ m.) Guide
not wanted. It is near the Riffelberg,
under the Riffelhorn, and Görner Grat.
Cross meadows for one hour. Mont Cervin towers aloft above you in savage,
stern sublimity.

Great point to visit near Zermatt is the
Görner Grat. This is best attained from
the Riffelhaus, an hotel built in 1854,
7,903 feet above the sea, or 2,900 feet
above Zermatt, and 3 l. (9 m.) from it.
To reach it you pass the Triftbach, the
chapel of Winkelmatten, the Findelinbach
the Châlets of Moos, through a forest to
Schwegmatt, half an hour further to the
châlets of Augstkumme, 6,822 feet, and
in three quarters of an hour to the Riffelhaus.

(*a*) The Görner Grat is 9,654 feet high,
and is a rocky ridge, 1½ hour from the hotel,
in the midst of glaciers, and peaks, with
one of the finest panoramic views in the
world. (*b*) The Cima de Jazzi (13,240
feet), is easily reached in five hours from
the Riffelhorn, view almost as fine as from
Monte Rosa, especially into the Vale of
Macugnaga. Veil, a guide, and good
shoes wanted. Start 3 a.m. (*c*) The Mettelhorn (10,794 feet), five hours from
Zermatt. Take a guide. Panorama much
grander than from the Görner Grat, takes
in Monte Rosa, Lyskamm, Breithorn, the
Mischabels, Aletsch, Mont Cervin, and
below villages, streams, and verdant
meadows. (*d*) Monte Rosa, now frequently ascended, even by ladies. Start

---

* Guides of Zermatt not equal to those of Chamouni, or the Oberland. Do well, as cragsmen,
generally, but are afraid of the ice. The following
are spoken well of: Matthew, Joseph, Peter, and
Stephen Zum Taugwald (not to be confounded with
the Taugwalders, who escaped the fatal accident on
Mount Cervin in 1865. Joseph and Ignatius Binner,
Peter Perm, and John Kronig. The Alpine Guide
calls Peter Perm, "first-rate, the best guide at
Zermatt."

2 in the morning from the Riffel. Reach summit at 11 a.m. Return in the evening. It is usual to form a party. In 1864, 400 tourists went up. Monte Rosa has seven summits. 1. Nordende (14,153 feet), Gornerhorn or Pic Dufour (14,284 feet), Zumstein Spitze (14,064 feet), Signal Kuppe (14,044 feet), Parrot Spitze, Ludwig Spitze (13,350 feet), Vincent's Pyramid (13,003.) The ascent of most of these points though arduous is not dangerous. By a Max thermometer left on Monte Rosa, in 1861, it appears that the summer heat varied from 1 to 7 degrees. The group of Monte Rosa consists of gneiss and veined granite.

Mont Cervin rising above the Zermatt Glacier, and Theodulejoch, is a graceful obelisk of calcareous rock, whose precipituous sides scarce admit the lodgment of snow towering aloft in a single shaft of 4,000 feet. After being vainly attacked for several seasons by the Alpine Club, it as at length ascended, and its summit eached, in July, 1865, by the party of Lord F. Douglas, with two Taugwalders, of Zermatt, and Croz, of Chamouni, for guides. On the descent, unfortunately, one of the party slipped, and swept down the rest all of whom went over the precipices and perished, except Mr. Whimpper and the two Taugwalders, the youngest of whom is represented as having behaved in a cowardly and unfeeling manner on the occasion. The body of Lord Francis has not been found.

The Weissthor is a difficult pass from Zermatt to Macugnaga (11,188 feet), only to be attempted by good cragsmen. The Schwarz See and Hörnli are easily reached from Zermatt; also the Col du Cervin or of St. Theodule. Wants a good guide. Highest pass in Europe (10,242 feet.) Road passes over Theodule Glacier, six hours. On the top are châlets, with refreshments. After seven hours' walk you come to Breuil, in Val Tournanche, with hotel, du Mont Cervin. Hence in *6½ l. (19¼ m.), to Châtillon.* Then down the Dora Baltea to Ivrea, and on to Turin by rail. Tournanche is a pretty village 2 l. (6 m.) from Breuil. Hotel, Monte Rosa, new, good, clean. Bed, 1f. 50c.; coffee, 1½f.; supper, 2f. 75c.

Mr. Blatter, who with two other meterologists passed the winter of 1865-66, on a part of the Matterhorn, 10,000 feet high, to make observations, came to Meyringen in May, 1866. Mr. Blatter and his brother enjoyed excellent health all the time, but their companion, an Italian, suffered severely. The extremest cold experienced was 23° Reaumur, or 19½ below zero, Fahrenheit. March 24th, the temperature was 23 9-10ths Reaumur. The average throughout the winter was 16° Reaumur, 4° below zero, Fahrenheit. Their provisions consisted of meat from the Valais, dried in the air, and which had remained almost perfectly sweet. The only living creatures the observers had seen were chouca, a kind of jackdaw, which flew round the hut without the slightest timidity.

Any one feeling strong enough may undertake from Breuil the high Glacier Passes connecting the Italian valleys, S. of Monte Rosa. Those who have leisure and wish to explore all the beauties of these unrivalled valleys, may follow the plan of Mr. King, who with his wife passed several weeks inspecting the choice scenery of this favoured district, combining all that is sublime and beautiful in nature, with what is most interesting in man. The transluceut ultramarine and emerald streams, the ancient forests, with their undergrowth of rare and lovely flowers, the Italian sky. the soft beauties of Lago d'Orta, and the lower valleys, the vigour and classical beauty of the female population, the thrift, piety and honesty of the German settlers in the upper valleys, who form a striking contrast to their Italian neighbours, and adhere to the Teutonic idiom and old Burgundian costume, the stately churches, all the features of these happy valleys combine. to produce an impression of enchantment on those who visit them.

They may be visited as follows: from Breuil from which a guide should be taken to Macugnaga. First day by Cimes Blanches 2½ l., 7½ m.), in the Valley of Challant to St. Jacques d'Ayas 3½ l., (10½ m.) In the afternoon follow the Resy and up the Betta Furka (8,106 feet); descending in 1¾ hours to the Châlets of Betta, with a fine view of Monte Rosa and the Lys Glacier. Thence descend to Gressenay la Trinita with its comfortable substantial houses and lovely pastoral and sylvan scenery. Excellent quarters at the hotel. This is a day's march of 11 or 12 hours. The second day by the Valley of Netsch brings you to the lake and Châlets of Gabiet. Thence by steep snow slopes to the Col d'Ollen (8,956 feet); a wild isolated spot, surrounded by rocks and snows, with a splendid view of Lago Maggiore and Val Sesia. This is a 6 or 7 hours' march. Third day, up to Alagna ¾ l., (2¼ m.), to Ponte ¼ l., (¾ m.), Merletto 1½ l., (4½ m) and the Châlets of Sant Antonio ¾ l., (2¼ m.) commanding a view of Monte Rosa. Then on by a tedious stony Pass, over rocks and grass slopes called the Turlo (8,526 feet), with a cross on the summit. Difficult descent over snow fields to the Châlets of Plana 2 l., (6 m.), after this a charming country, with beautiful cascades, to Isella 1½ l., (4½ m.) and Macugnaga 1½ l., (1½ m.). The Turlo may be avoided by taking some higher glacier passes, or by going down Val Sesia and crossing over to Val Anzasca, by the Mastalon and beautiful paradisaical scenery. From Macugnaga you reach Saas and Visp by Monte Moro Pass, as will be seen presently. But adventurous spirits sometimes attempt the Weissthor to Zermatt, while others cross the Lyskamm and Joch close to Monte Rosa over to the Riffel.

The other branch of the Visperthal, called the Saasthal, forks at Stalden.

As far as Stalden the road is the same as that to Zermatt. Distances from Visp to Macugnaga by the Monte Moro Pass are as follow :—

To	Hours walk.		English miles.
Stalden	1½		5
Saas	3¾		10
Mattmarksee	3		8¼
Monte Moro	2		5
Macugnaga	4		8
	14		36¼

The path through the Saasthal is fit for mules almost to top of Monte Moro Pass. Charge of 20*fr.* for a mule from Visp to Saas, is considered too high. From Saas to Monte Moro the charge is 10*fr.* Above Stalden a path strikes off to the left, over the Kinnebruck, a single arch of 150 feet, thrown across the Görner Visp, and follows ascending the east branch valley, watered by the Saaser Visp. The vale soon narrows and higher summits are shut out. No houses appear till you come to the village of Balen at the base of the Balferin, then the vale widens a little, and some of the peaks above it become visible. The walk from Stalden to Saas takes 3¾ hours. The two inns at Saas have undergone many changes. The hotel of Monte Rosa, conducted by Fr. Andermatten, is said not to be so good as in 1862. Hotel Monte Moro was fair and cheap in 1862. The inn at Mattmarksee is better situated, and has been improved. Saas is 5,267 feet above the sea. There are not many fine views from the village, but close to it are some of the the finest in the Alps, including the Fee and Gletscher Alps, which are close at hand, and can be visited by most persons. The Fee Glacier is in a recess of Saas Grat, surrounded by an amphitheatre of fine peaks. The Gletscher Alp rock bisects the Fee Glacier. To enjoy the scenery fully you should go to the top of the Gletscher Alp, where are seen the three horns of the Mischabelhörner, all above 14,000 feet, forming the right side of the amphitheatre. Next to them is the Alphubel (13,803 feet). A spur of the Alleleinhorn (13,235 feet) shuts in the Fee Valley and completes the circular view which has in its centre the Alphubel Pass. Another excursion may be made from Saas to the Triftalp, 2½ hours, above a village on the east side of the valley of Saas. The road from Visp to Monte Moro follows the course of the Saaser Visp. The scenery is savage and desolate, but fine peaks shew themselves now and then. You pass the village of Almagell, near the highest limit of trees, at the junction of the Lehmbach with the Visp. A fine cascade occurs at this point. Pass on to Zwichenbergen, then over a torrent from the Furgethal, beyond which the scenery increases in wildness and the road mounts. Three hours from Saas brings you to a point where the road looks down on the Mattmarksee, a lake formed by the waters of the Visp, dammed up by the Allelein Glacier. A small inn has been opened south of the lake, around which botanists may revel in a rare Alpine flora, including *pleurogyne carinthiaca*. From this point the ascent is steep, and by an ancient paved road, you proceed over moderately steep snow slopes, and reach the top of the Pass, when the eye catches the east face of Monte Rosa to the Weissthor, while, on the opposite side of the deep basis of Macugnaga, rises the Pizzo Bianco. The view is very grand. Height of Pass, 9,390 feet.

A point, east of the Pass, called the Joderhorn is deserving of a visit, on account of its view over Italy and the southern ranges of the Alps. The descent from the Moro to Macugnaga is long and steep, requiring 3½ hours. The name, Monte Moro, and others about here, such as Mischabel and Allelein, seem to show that this route was occupied at an early period by the Saracens. Careful observations on the natural history and physique of the Alps were made by the brothers Schlagintweit, in 185–, who resided for some time in a hut built for them on the south side of Monte Rosa. They found phanerogamous plants at a great elevation, one the cherleria sedoides, occurring *at 11,770 feet.* The snow limit was 9,200

feet; Rhododendra occurred at 9,350 feet; the highest grass and bushes at 7,000 to 7,500 feet; the pinus cembra at 6,600 feet, and the pinus larix or larch at 6,600 also.

Macugnaga is probably placed in the most enchanting position on our earth. Hence, those who can should try to stay a few days there. But I beg them not to corrupt or disgust the honest, pious German natives, by reckless extravagance or ridiculous hauteur. Hotel, du Monte Rosa. The host, Fr. Lockmatter, is a good guide. Complaints are made of want of order in his establishment. 20 rooms at 2*fr.*; coffee, 1½*fr.* Hotel du Monte Moro is said to be better. The view from Macugnaga is unrivalled. The parish includes six villages in a half circle of meadows, crowned by the snows of Monte Rosa. The Glacier of Macugnaga appears suspended at a vast height, and can be best seen from the Belvedere. Gold mines have been worked in the Val Anzasca since Roman times; the most important is at Pestarena on the road to Vogogna.

Excursions from Macugnaga to the Belvedere, 1½ l. (3½ m.) from the village. Guide useless. From the Belvedere on to the glacier and to the Jazzialp, ¼ hour; then to the top, ¼ hour, to the Alpe Fillar, among the moraines of the Fillar Glacier coming from the Old Weissthor Pass, no longer used. Then to the Macugnaga Glacier, to the Châlets of l'Alpe Pedriolo (6,522 feet), where milk may be had; hence to the Alpe de la Croza, descending to Onigo and back to Macugnaga. More than ha'f-a-day wanted. From Macugnaga, walks can be taken, ½ l. (1½ m.) to Borgo; ½ l. (1½ m.) to Pestarena; 1 l. (3 m.) to Prequartero; ½ l. (1½ m.) to Ceppo Morelli; 1¼ (3¾ m.) to Borgone. ¾ l. (2¼ m.) to San Carlo; 1 l. (3 m.) to Ponte Grande, with a very fine view; ½ l. (1½ m.) to Pic di Mulcra; 1 l. (3 m.) to Vogogna. Several beautiful lateral passes connect Val Anzasca with Vals Strona and Mastalone. The whole country is perfectly enjoyable and full of interest to geologist, botanist, and sportsman, for it has fine trout streams.*

[Supplementary information on, and mileage of, the High Level Passes in the Valais and Italian valleys south of Monte Rosa.]

ROUTE *(Aleph)*—From Aosta to Zermatt, up the Val Pellina and the Col of Val Pellina.—19 to 20 hours.
Val Pellina, 3 hours; Prarayen, 6 hours 40 min.; Last Châlet, 45 min.; Great Glacier of Zardezan, 30 min.; Leave Glacier, 3 hours 15 min.; Couloir, 1 hour; Col Val Pellina, 1 hour 15 min. (3,562 metres); by rocks of Stockje and Glacier of Zmutt to Zermatt 10 hours 30 min.

ROUTE *(Beth)*—From Prarayen to Val Tournanche and Breuil, by the Col de Vacornere or Cornguier (3,150 metres), 5 or 6 hours; ascent of the Château des Pames (3,657 metres); paths fork at the Châlets de Chignane.
First, to Val Tournanche, 7 hours.
Second, by Col de Dza to Breuil, 7 hours. Pass good inn at Glomen.

ROUTE *(Gimel)*—Zinal to Zermatt.
a By Col Durand, 13 to 14 hours (3,474 metres).
b By Trift Joch, 11 hours, dangerous (3,450 metres).
c Zinal to Zermatt, by Col Morning, 12 hours, (3,877 metres).
d Zinal to Zermatt, by Col de Schallens, 14 hours, from Zinal to Randa.

ROUTE *(Daleth)*—Zmeiden to Randa.
a By Col de Bies, 16 hours (3,700 metres). Dangerous, by Turtman Glacier.
b By Col de Diallons or Traucit, 8 or 9 hours. Glacier Pass (3,252 metres).

ROUTE *(Heth.)* — Zermatt to Verrex, by the Schwarzthor. A long day from the Riffel Hotel, to San Giacomo and Ayas (little hotel with four beds), 3,849 metres; Verrex, 6 hours from San Giacomo.

ROUTE *(Yod.)*—
a By the Col de Lys or Silber Pass from Zermatt to Pont Saint Martin. 19 hours from Riffel to Gressenay. Highest pass in the Alps. In fine weather not very difficult (4,344 metres), 294 metres lower than Monte Rosa. Pass is between two peaks of Monte Rosa. Parrot Spitze to the E. and Ludwigshohe to the W. Pont St. Martin is 26 kilometres from Gressenay.
b By the Col des Jumeaux (3,962 feet) 20 hours; 10 hours to the Châlet de Lys.

ROUTE *(Koph)*—Alagna to Zermatt, by the Col Sesia (doubtful and dangerous), 18 hours, 4,400 metres, near the Parrot Spitze of Monte Rosa.

* For information respecting the lower part of the valleys south of Monte Rosa, and the Italian Lakes; see *Canton of Tessin.*

ROUTE *(Llamed)*—Zermatt to Macugnaga.
a By the Alt Weissthor, 14 hours (3,612 metres), near Cima de Jazzi.
b Neu Weissthor, 11 to 12 hours (3,612 metres). From Riffel to Macugnaga, 9 to 10 hours by this route. By Findelen Glacier.

Tour of Monte Rosa.

ROUTE *(Mem)*—High Glacier Passes.
a Zermatt to Breuil, by St. Theodule Col.
b Breuil to Gressenay St. Jean, by le Col des Cimes Blanches and the Betta Furka, 9 to 10 hours; Cimes Blanches (3,041 metres), Betta Furka (2,633 metres).
c From Cour de Lys, by Col della Piscie to Pile Alpe (3,162 metres).
d From Pi'e Alpe to Macugnaga, by Col delle Loccie, 14 to 15 hours (3,647 metres).

ROUTE *(Nun)*—Intermediate Passes (between Val Tournanche and Val Anzasca).
a Val Tournanche to Ayas by Col de Portola. First day (2,436 metres). Brussone or Champolien better night quarters than Ayas.
b Champolien to Gressenay St Jean by the Col de Pinta, 6 hours. Easy Pass (2,499 metres). Fine waterfall.
c From Gressenay St. Jean to Alagna by Col d'Ollen, 8 hours. Mule path Col (2,909 metres).
d Alagna to Macugnaga and Pestarena by the Turlo Pass (2,770 metres) 10 hours.

ROUTE *(Shin.)*—Lower Passes (of Italian valleys).
a Chatillon to Brussone by Col de Joux, 4 hours 30 min. Mule path.
b Brussone to Gressenay St. Jean by the Col de Ranzola, 4 hours 30 min. Mule path (Hotel Delapierre at Gressenay).
c Gressenay to Riva by Col de Valdobbia, 6 to 7 hours. Col (2,548 metres). Little hospice at top. At Riva (bad inn). Sleep at Alagna or Mollia. Fine church with frescoes.
d Riva to Rimasco by Col de Moud, 7 hours. Mule path. At Châlets de Moud, good milk.
e Riva to Rimasco by the Sesia and Sermenta valleys. Carriage road, 8 hours. Inn at Rimasco, dirty. Mine host civil.
f Rimasco to Ponte Grande, 8 hours, by Col d'Egua (2,153 metres), and Col de Baranca. Delightful excursion through Val Mastalone, Val Fobello or direct by Val Olloccia, through primeval forests by ultramarine streams, and among a rare Alpine flora.

ROUTES *(Teth.)* south from Macugnaga and to Vogogna, 9 hours, by Ceppo Morelli and Val Anzasca, one of the finest in the Alps. At Pestarena (Albergo de Minieri Good), 1½ hours, Ceppo Morelli (small inn) splendid view, 4½

Vanzone (Hotel des Chasseurs, Sole Moro) Italian town. Pretty churches, 3½ hours from Macugnaga; Ponte Grande (large Hotel di Ponte Grande (inn), 45 min.; Castiglione, 1½ hours; Vogogna (Simplon Road), 1 hour; Ponte Grande to Orta, by Val Mastalone, delicious (55 to 66 kilometres, too much for one day); Col de Barranca (1,752 metres); Agazzo in Val Fobello; Fobello (inn); Ferrara; Ponte della Gula.

By Val Strona. Ponte Grande to Campello foot path. Campello to Omegna (Mule path), 5 hours; Omegna to Orta, road or sail on lake, 2 hours.

Delightful expedition through a paradise of beauty, glancing streams, tropical vegetation, view of icy peaks and a classical population with picturesque costumes.

Varallo to Alagna (42 kilometres), 7 to 8 hours by Sermenta and Val Sessia. Good dear inn at Varalla, Albergo d'Italie. See Canton of Tessin, Baveno. Excursions. Vocca 1½ hour; Scopa, good inn, 2 hours 50 min.; Scopello, 3½ hours (dear inn); Pila, 3 hours 40 min.; Piodre, 4½ hours; Mollia, good inn, 5½ hours; Riva, 38 kilometres, 7 hours, middling inn; Alagna, 8 hours.

ROUTES FROM SION

To Aarau, by Aarberg (Nos. 262 and 216), and Solothurn (No. 16), or by Berne (Nos. 73 or 74 and 6).

ROUTE 262.

AARBERG. (Rail through Aigle, Vevay, Lausanne, and Berne), or road, 30¾ l., (92¼ m.)

	Leagues.	Miles.
Bex (No. 74)	8¾	26¼
Aigle (No. 58)	1½	4½
Vevay 14 l. (42 m.), (No. 54.)	3¾	11¼
Chexbres	1	3
Essertes	2	6
Mezieres	½	1½
Carrouge	½	1½
Moudon 19½ l. (58½ m.)	1½	4½
Lucens	1	3
Hennez	1	3
Marnand	½	1½
Payerne 23 l. (70½ m.)	1½	4½
Corcelles	½	1½
Dompierre	½	1½
Domdidier	½	1½
Avenches	½	1½
Faoug	½	2¼
Morat 27 l. (81 m.)	½	2¼
Kczerz (Chiètre)	1¾	5¼
Fräschels	½	1½
Kalnach	½	1½
Bargen	½	1½
Aarberg	½	1½
	30¾	92¼

Aigle, Rail or (Nos. 74 and 58), Altdorf (No. 261), or by Berne (Nos. 74 and 66, 67, or 68), and Lucerne (No. 147), Altstaetten, by Aarberg (Nos. 262 and 216), Solothurn (No. 16), Aarau (No. 16), Zurich (No. 196), and St. Gallen (No. 180).

ROUTE 263.

AOSTA (20¾ l., 62¼ m.)

	Leagues.	Miles.
Vetro	1½	4½
Ardon	½	1½
St. Pierre	½	1½
Riddes	½	1½
Saxon	¾	2¼
Chataz	1¼	3¾
Martigny (6 l. 18 m.)	1	3
La Bourg	¼	¾
Bovernier	1	3
St. Branchier	¾	2¼
Orsières	1¼	3¼
Liddes	¾	2¼
Alève	½	1½
St. Pierre	½	1¼
Hospice of St. Bernard	3	9
St. Remy	2	6
St. Oyen	1	3
Etroubles	½	1¼
Ginod	2	6
Aosta	1¼	3¾
	20¾	62¼

Appenzell, by Aarberg (Nos. 262 and 216), Solothurn (No. 16), Aarau (No. 18), and Zurich (No. 28), or by Berne (Nos. 73, or 74, and 79), and Zurich (No. 28), or Thun (No. 73 or 65), Lucerne (No. 253), and Rail to Zurich.

Art, by Berne (Nos. 73, 74, and 78), or Thun (Nos. 73 and 65), Lucerne (No. 253), and Zug (No. 281).

Baden, by Aarberg (Nos. 262 and 216), Solothurn (No. 16), and Aarau (No. 2), or by Bex (No. 74), Aigle (No. 58), and Berne (No. 54 and 56), or by the Simmenthal and Saanetsch (No. 72).

Bâle by Berne (Rail), and by Solothurn (Nos. 16 and 43), or by Bienne and the Münsterthal (Nos. 264 and 29).

Bellinzona (No. 236), Berne (Nos. 72, 73, 74), Bex, Rail or (No. 74).

ROUTE 264.

BIENNE, 32¾ l (98¼ m.)

	Leagues.	Miles.
Aarberg (No. 262)	30¾	92¼
Bienne (No. 59)	2	6
	32¾	98¼

ROUTE 264 (1.)

BIONA (Val Pellina), and Aosta.

	Leagues.	Miles.
Martigny	6	18
Bovernier	1¼	3¾
St. Branchier (or Chables)	1¼	3¾
Champsec	2	6
Loutier	½	1½
Pont du Mont Voisin	2½	7½
Châlets de Torenbec	1½	4½
Col de Fenêtre	4	12
Biona	1¼	3¾
Valpellina, from the Col	2¾	8¼
4 l., (12 m.)		
By Roysan to Aosta	3	9
(31 from Valpellina to Aosta)	26	78
To Biona	19	57

ROUTE 264 (2.)

BREUIL AND VAL TOURNANCHE TO IVREA.

	Leagues.	Miles.
Visp	6½	19½
Zermatt	9	27
Col de St. Theodule	3	9
Breuil	2	6
Val Tournanche	2	6
Chatillon	3¼	9¾
Donnaz	5	15
Ivrea	4	12
	34¾	104¼

To Breuil, 20½ l. (61½ m.), Brougg, by Aarberg (Nos. 262 and 216), Solothurn (No. 16), and Aarau (No. 7), or by Berne (No. 73, 74, and 197), Bulle (Nos. 74, 58, and 54), Burgdorf, by Berne (Nos. 73, or 74, and 60).

ROUTE 265.

CHAMOUNI, 15¼ l. (45¾ m.

	Leagues.	Miles.
Martigny (No. 263)	6	18
The Forclaz	2	6
Trie[nt]	½	1½
Frontier of the Valais	2	6
Châlet de Charmillan	1	3
La Tour	¾	2¼
Argentiere	1	3
Chamouni	2	6
	15¾	45¾

Chaux de Fonds, by Lausanne (Nos. 267 and 173 or 174), and Neuchâtel (No. 169), Chiavenna, by Bellinzona (Nos. 236 and 230), Chur (No. 235).

ROUTE 266.

DOMO D'OSSOLA 22½ l. (67½ m.)

	Leagues.	Miles.
St. Leonard	1	3
Sierre	2	6
Loesch	1¼	3¾
Turtman	½	1½
Brunk	¾	2¼
Visp	1	3
Gambsen	¾	2¼
Glys	¾	2¼
Brieg	¼	¾
Ried	1¼	3¾
Persal	2	6
Simplon Hospice	2¼	6¾
Simplon (Village)	1½	4½
Ruden	2	6
Divedro	2¼	6¾
Crevola	2	6
Domo d'Ossola	1	3
	22½	67½

Einsiedeln and Engelberg, by Berne (Nos. 73 or 74. and 66, 67, or 68), and Lucerne, (Nos. 152 ard 153).

Frauenfeld, by Aarberg (Nos. 262 and 216), Solothurn (No. 16), Aarau (No. 18), and Zurich (No. 245 ; or by Berne (Nos. 73 or 74 and 79) and Zurich (No. 245).

Fribourg (Nos. 74, 58, and 54).

Gais, by Aarberg (Nos. 262 and 216), Solothurn (No. 16), Aarau (No. 18), Zurich (No. 196), and St. Gallen (No. 186); or by Berne and Zurich.—Routes as before.

Geneva (No. 98), or by south side of lake, through St. Gingoulph and Thonon.

Glarus, by Altdorf (Nos. 261 and 103); or by Aarberg, Solothurn, and Zurich.—See routes above.

Herisau, by Aarberg (Nos. 262 and 216), Solothurn (No. 16), Aarau (No. 18) and Zurich (No. 301), or by Berne (Nos. 73 or 74 and 79) and Zurich (No. 301).

Hofwyl, by Berne (Nos. 73, 74, and 62).

Lauffenbourg, by Aarberg (Nos. 262 and 216), Solothurn (No. 16), and Aarau (No. 10) ; or by Berne (Nos. 73 or 74 and 6) and Aarau (No. 10).

ROUTE 267.

LAUSANNE, 18 L (54 m.)

	Leagues.	Miles.
Vevay (No. 262)	14	42
St. Saphorin	¾	2¼
Cully	1½	3¼
Lutry	¾	2¼
Lausanne	1¼	3¼
	18	54

ROUTE 268.

LOESCH (BATHS), 7 L (21 m.)

	Leagues.		Miles.
St. Leonard	1	......	3
Sierre	2	......	6
Loesch (4¼ l.)	1¼	......	3¾
Varen	1¼	......	3¾
Loesch (Baths)	1½	......	4½
	7		21

ROUTE 269.

LOCARNO 32¼ L. (97¼ m.)

	Leagues.		Miles.
Domo d Ossola (No. 266)	22¼	......	67¼
Malesco	2	......	6
Masera	1	......	3
Olgia	1	......	3
Borgnone	1	......	3
Verdasia	¾	......	2¼
Rosa	¾	......	2¼
Losona	1	......	3
Locarno	2½	......	7½
	32¼		97¼

Locle, by Lausanne (Nos. 267 and 173 or 174) and Neuchâtel (No. 175), Lucerne, by Berne (Nos. 73 or 74 and 66, 67, or 68, or 55 and 76).

ROUTE 270.

LUGANO 38¾ l. (116¼ m.)

	Leagues.		Miles.
Locarno (No. 269)	32¼	......	97¼
Over the lake, to Magadino	1¼	......	3¾
Cadenazzo	1	......	3
Bironico	1½	......	4½
Taverne	1	......	3
Cadempino	1	......	3
Vesia	¼	......	¾
Lugano	¼	......	¾
	38¾		116¼

LYS (VAL DE) GRESSENAY LA TRINITA AND GRESSENAY ST. JEAN.

	Leagues.		Miles.
Visp	6¼	......	19¼
Stalden	2	......	6
Balen	2	......	6
Chapel of St. Anthony	¾	......	2¼
Saas-im Grund	¼	......	¾
Mattmark Hotel	3	......	9
Distelalp	¼	......	¾
Telliboden	½	......	1½
Col de St Pierre Bodmen-alp	2	......	6
Macugnaga	1	......	3

ROUTE 270—(Continued.)

			Miles.
Macugnaga to Gressenay by the Turlo Pass to Alagna	7¼	......	21¾
Thence by Col d'Ollen to Gressoney la Trinita	7¼	......	23¼
	33¼		99¾

MACUGNAGA (and thence to VOGOGNA).

	Leagues.		Miles.
Sion to Macugnaga (see last Route)	17¾	......	53¼
Macugnaga to Borgo	⅓	......	1¼
Pestarena	⅓	......	1¼
Ceppo Morelli	1¼	......	3¾
Borgone	⅔	......	2¼
Ponte Grande	1	......	3
Pic de Mulera	½	......	1¾
Vogogna	1	......	3
	23¼		69¾

ROUTE 271.

MENDRISSIO (42¼ l., 126⅜ m.)

	Leagues.		Miles.
Lugano (No. 270)	38¾	......	116¼
Mendrissio (No. 235)	3½	......	10¼
	42¼		126⅜

ROUTE 272.

MILAN (53¼ l., 160½ m.)

	Leagues.		Miles.
Domo d'Ossola (No. 266)	22¼	......	67¼
Marguzzo	6	......	18
Sesto	7	......	21
Casina del bon Jesu	8	......	24
Rho	6	......	18
Milan	4	......	12
	53¼		160½

Morat (No. 252).

ROUTE 273.

MORGES (20 l., 60 m.)

	Leagues.		Miles.
Lausanne (No. 267)	18	......	54
Morges	2	......	6
	20		60

Moudon (No. 262).
Neuchâtel, by Lausanne (Nos. 267 and 173 or 174).
Orbe, by Lausanne (Nos. 267 and 174).
Payerne (No. 252).
Pfeffers (Baths), by Chur (Nos. 135 and 131).
Righi (The), by Berne (Nos. 73 or 74 and 66, 67 or 68). and Lucerne (Nos. 158 or 159).
Saint Gallen, by Aarberg (Nos. 262 and 216), Solothurn (No. 16), and Aarau (No. 19), and Zurich (No. 196); or by Berne (No. 73), or Thun (No. 65), Lucerne and Zurich.

Schaffhausen, by Aarberg (Nos. 262 and 216) Solothurn No. 16) and Aarau (No. 18), and Zurich (No. 193); or by Berne, Lucerne, and Zurich as before.

Schwyz, by Altdorf (Nos. 261 and 207).

Solothurn (No. 227).

Staus, see Unterwalden.

ROUTE 274.

THUN (18½ L., 55½ m.)

	Leagues.		Miles
Zwelsimmen (No. 73) ...	10¼	......	32¼
Thun (No. 72)	7¾	....	23¼
	18½		55½

Trogen, by Aarberg (No. 262 and 216), Solothurn (No. 16), Aarau (No. 18), Zurich (No. 196). and St. Gallen (No. 193), or by Berne and Zurich, as before.

ROUTE 275.

TURIN, 55¾ L, (167¼ m.)

	Leagues.		Miles.
Aosta (No. 263)................	20¼	....	62¼
Chatillon	6	....	18
Verns	6	....	18
Vittone...............................	5	....	15
Ivrea..................................	6	....	18
Fogliazzo	6	....	18
Turin	6	....	18
	55¾		167¼

b Or by Valpellina (No. 264).

	Leagues.		Miles.
Aosta (No. 263)	26	....	78
Aosta to Turin (No. 275)	35	....	105
	61		183

c Or by Breuil and Val Tournanche.

	Leagues.		Miles.
Tournanche (No. 264, 2)...	34¾	....	104¾
Ivrea to Turin....................	18	....	54
	52¾		158½

Unterwalden, by Altdorf (Nos. 261 and 251), Vevay (No. 262), Winterthur, by Aarberg (Nos. 262 and 216), Solothurn (No. 16), Aarau (No. 18), and Zurich (No. 301), or by Thun (274), Lucerne (Nos. 253 and 255), and Zurich (No. 301), or Rail from Lucerne to Zurich, and on to Winterthur. Yverdun, by Lausanne (Nos. 267, 173, or '74.) Zug, by Aarberg (Nos. 262 and 216), Solothurn (No. 16), and Aarau (No. 17), or by Berne (Nos. 73, or 74, and 78), or Thun No. (274), Lucerne (Nos. 253 and 255), and rail or boat to Zug.

Zurich, by Aarberg (Nos. 262 and 216), Solothurn (No. 16) and Aarau (No. 18), or by Berne (No. 73 or 74 and 79), or by Thun and Lucerne as in the last number.

N

Zurzach, by Aarberg (Nos. 262 and 216), Solothurn (No. 16). and Aarau (No. 14), or by Berne (Nos. 73 or 64, and 197).

Strasburg, Frankfort, and the Rhine, by Lausanne, Berne, Olten, and Bâle; (rail.)

Bavaria, Austria, and East Germany, by Berne or Thun. Lucerne, Schaffhausen, and Ravenshorn, to Friedrichshafen. (Rail from Lucerne, and over lake of Constance.)

Paris, Lyons, and France, by Geneva, or Paris direct, by Neuchâtel and Pontarlier.

ROUTE D.

Route D brings us direct from Paris through Macon to Geneva, whence you can proceed direct by rail or lake to the Canton de Valais, and the Rosa district, or diverge by Chamouni or Sixt, and eventually reach the Valais by the Col de Balme or Tête Noire, after exploring the wonders and beauties of the Mont Blanc district.

Fares from Paris to Geneva, 1st class, 70f.; 2nd, 52f. 50c.; 3rd, 38f. 50c. Express leaves Paris 8 40 p.m., reaches Geneva 10 40 a.m.

A direct 1st, 2nd, and 3rd class day Train leaves Paris at 6 40 a.m., and reaches Geneva at 11 5 p.m.

Some writers give this Canton 93 English square miles, others make it 100.

Our 4th main approach is by the

CANTON OF GENEVA

from Paris, Route D.

LIMITS.—This Canton only touches the rest of Switzerland on one side, when it meets the Canton de Vaud; on all other sides being surrounded by France, and its newly annexed territory of Savoy.

AREA, SOIL AND CLIMATE.—The area of the Canton of Geneva* is smaller than that of any other Canton, for it has only 11 square leagues (283 square kilometres). It is situated at the western extremity of Switzerland, between the Alps and the Jura; a position which may perhaps help

*J. F. Cooper says, "In extent it is the smallest state but one of the Confederation, Zug being the most minute of the sisterhood. The Canton is irregular in shape, extending on both sides of the lake; but its greatest length is less than 14 miles, and its greatest breadth less than 7." (Page 219, v. 2. Excursions in Switzerland, 1836.)

Vanzone (Hotel des Chasseurs, Sole Moro) Italian town. Pretty churches, 3½ hours from Macugnaga; Ponte Grande (large Hotel di Ponte Grande (inn), 45 min.; Castiglione, 1½ hours; Vogogna (Simplon Road), 1 hour; Ponte Grande to Orta, by Val Mastalone, delicious (55 to 66 kilometres, too much for one day); Col de Barranca (1,752 metres); Agazzo in Val Fobello; Fobello (inn); Ferrara; Ponte della Gula.

By Val Strona. Ponte Grande to Campello foot path. Campello to Omegna (Mule path), 5 hours; Omegna to Orta, road or sail on lake, 2 hours.

Delightful expedition through a paradise of beauty, glancing streams, tropical vegetation, view of icy peaks and a classical population with picturesque costumes.

Varallo to Alagna (42 kilometres), 7 to 8 hours by Sermenta and Val Sessia. Good dear inn at Varalla, Albergo d'Italie. See Canton of Tessin. Baveno. Excursions. Vocca 1½ hour; Scopa, good inn, 2 hours 50 min.; Scopello, 3½ hours (dear inn); Pila, 3 hours 40 min.; Piodre, 4½ hours; Mollia, good inn, 5½ hours; Riva, 38 kilometres, 7 hours, middling inn; Alagna, 8 hours.

ROUTES FROM SION

To Aarau, by Aarberg (Nos. 262 and 216), and Solothurn (No. 16), or by Berne (Nos. 73 or 74 and 6).

ROUTE 262.

AARBERG. (Rail through Aigle, Vevay, Lausanne, and Berne), or road, 30¾ L, (92¼ m.)

	Leagues.	Miles.
Bex (No. 74)	8¾	26¼
Aigle (No. 58)	1½	4½
Vevay 14 L.(42 m.), (No. 54.)	3⅝	11⅓
Chexbres	1	3
Essertes	2	6
Mezieres	½	1¼
Carrouge	½	1½
Moudon 19½ L. (58½ m.)	1½	4½
Lucens	1	3
Hennez	1	3
Marnand	½	1½
Payerne 23 L. (70½ m.)	1½	4½
Corcelles		1¼
Dompierre		1½
Domdidier		1½
Avenches		1½
Faong		2¼
Morat 27 L. (81 m.)		2¼
Kezerz (Chiètre)	1½	5¼
Fräschels		1½
Kalnach		1½
Bargen		1½
Aarberg	½	1½
	30¾	92¼

Aigle, Rail or (Nos. 74 and 58), Altdorf (No. 261), or by Berne (Nos. 74 and 66, 67, or 68), and Lucerne (No. 147), Altstaetten, by Aarberg (Nos. 262 and 216), Solothurn (No. 16), Aarau (No. 18), Zurich (No. 196), and St. Gallen (No. 180).

ROUTE 263.

AOSTA (20¾ L, 62¼ m.)

	Leagues.	Miles.
Vetro	1½	4½
Ardon	½	1½
St. Pierre	½	1½
Riddes	½	1½
Saxon	¾	2¼
Chataz	1¼	3¾
Martigny (6 L. 18 m.)	1	3
La Bourg	¼	¾
Bovernier	1	3
St. Branchier	¾	2¼
Orsières	1¼	3¼
Liddes	¾	2¼
Alève	½	1½
St. Pierre	½	1½
Hospice of St. Bernard	3	9
St. Remy	2	6
St. Oyen	1	3
Etroubles	½	1¼
Ginod	2	6
Aosta	1¼	3¾
	20¾	62¼

Appenzell, by Aarberg (Nos. 262 and 216), Solothurn (No. 16), Aarau (No. 18), and Zurich (No. 28), or by Berne (Nos. 73, or 74, and 79), and Zurich (No. 28), or Thun (No. 73 or 65), Lucerne (No. 253), and Rail to Zurich.

Art, by Berne (Nos. 73, 74, and 78), or Thun (Nos. 73 and 65), Lucerne (No. 253), and Zug (No. 281).

Baden, by Aarberg (Nos. 262 and 216), Solothurn (No. 16), and Aarau (No. 2), or by Bex (No. 74), Aigle (No. 58), and Berne (No. 54 and 56), or by the Simmenthal and Saanetsch (No. 72).

Bâle by Berne (Rail), and by Solothurn (Nos. 16 and 43), or by Bienne and the Münsterthal (Nos. 264 and 29).

Bellinzona (No. 236), Berne (Nos. 72, 73, 74), Bex, Rail or (No. 74).

ROUTE 264.

BIENNE, 32¾ L (98¼ m.)

	Leagues.	Miles.
Aarberg (No. 262)	30¾	92¼
Bienne (No. 59)	2	6
	32¾	98¼

ROUTE 264 (1.)

BIONA (Val Pellina), and Aosta.

	Leagues.		Miles.
Martigny	6	......	18
Boveruier	1½	......	3¾
St. Branchier (or Chables)	1¼	......	3¾
Champsec	2	......	6
Loutier	½	......	1½
Pont du Mont Voisin	2½	......	7½
Châlets de Torenbec	1½	......	4½
Col de Fenêtre	4	......	12
Biona	1¼	......	3¾
Valpellina, from the Col	2¾	......	8¼
4 L, (12 m.)			
By Roysan to Aosta	3	......	9
(31 from Valpellina to Aosta)	26	......	78
To Biona	19	......	57

ROUTE 264 (2.)

BREUIL AND VAL TOURNANCHE TO IVREA.

	Leagues.		Miles.
Visp	6½	......	19½
Zermatt	9	......	27
Col de St. Theodule	3	......	9
Breuil	2	......	6
Val Tournanche	2	......	6
Chatillon	3¼	......	9¾
Donnaz	5	......	15
Ivrea	4	......	12
	34¾		104¼

To Breuil, 20½ l. (61½ m.), Brougg, by Aarberg (Nos. 262 and 216), Solothurn (No. 16), and Aarau (No. 7), or by Berne (No. 73, 74, and 197), Bulle (Nos. 74, 58. and 54), Burgdorf, by Berne (Nos. 73, or 74, and 60).

ROUTE 265.

CHAMOUNI, 15¼ l. (45¾ m.

	Leagues.		Miles.
Martigny (No. 263)	6	......	18
The Forclaz	2	......	6
Trient	½	......	1½
Frontier of the Valais	2	......	6
Châlet de Charmillan	1	......	3
La Tour	¾	......	2¼
Argentiere	1	......	3
Chamouni	2	......	6
	15¼		45¾

Chaux de Fonds, by Lausanne (Nos. 267 and 173 or 174), and Neuchâtel (No. 169), Chiavenna, by Bellinzona (Nos. 236 and 230), Chur (No. 135).

ROUTE 266.

DOMO D'OSSOLA 22½ l. (67½ m.)

	Leagues.		Miles.
St. Leonard	1	......	3
Sierre	2	......	6
Loesch	1¼	......	3¾
Turtman	½	......	1½
Brunk	¾	......	2¼
Visp	1	......	3
Gambsen	¾	......	2¼
Glys	¾	......	2¼
Brieg	¼	......	¾
Ried	1¼	......	3¾
Persal	2	......	6
Simplon Hospice	2¼	......	6¾
Simplon (Village)	1½	......	4½
Ruden	2	......	6
Divedro	2¼	......	6¾
Crevola	2	......	6
Domo d'Ossola	1	......	3
	22½		67½

Einsiedeln and Engelberg, by Berne (Nos. 73 or 74. and 66, 67, or 68), and Lucerne, (Nos. 152 ard 153).

Frauenfeld, by Aarberg (Nos. 262 and 216), Solothurn (No. 16), Aarau (No. 18), and Zurich (No. 245 ; or by Berne (Nos. 73 or 74 and 79) and Zurich (No. 245).

Fribourg (Nos. 74, 58, and 54).

Gais, by Aarberg (Nos. 262 and 216), Solothurn (No. 16), Aarau (No. 18), Zurich (No. 196), and St. Gallen (No. 186); or by Berne and Zurich.—Routes as before.

Geneva (No. 98), or by south side of lake, through St. Gingoulph and Thonon.

Glarus, by Altdorf (Nos. 261 and 103); or by Aarberg, Solothurn, and Zurich.—See routes above.

Herisau, by Aarberg (Nos. 262 and 216), Solothurn (No. 16), Aarau (No. 18) and Zurich (No. 301), or by Berne (Nos. 73 or 74 and 79) and Zurich (No. 301).

Hofwyl, by Berne (Nos. 73, 74, and 62).

Lauffenbourg, by Aarberg (Nos. 262 and 216), Solothurn (No. 16), and Aarau (No. 10) ; or by Berne (Nos. 73 or 74 and 6) and Aarau (No. 10).

ROUTE 267.

LAUSANNE, 18 l. (54 m.)

	Leagues.		Miles.
Vevay (No. 262)	14	......	42
St. Saphorin	½	......	2¼
Cully	1¼	......	3¾
Lutry	½	......	2¼
Lausanne	1¼	......	3¾
	18		54

Vanzone (Hotel des Chasseurs, Sole Moro) Italian town. Pretty churches, 3½ hours from Macugnaga; Ponte Grande (large Hotel di Ponte Grande (inn), 45 min.; Castiglione, 1½ hours; Vogogna (Simplon Road), 1 hour; Ponte Grande to Orta, by Val Mastalone, delicious (55 to 66 kilometres, too much for one day); Col de Barranca (1,752 metres); Agazzo in Val Fobello; Fobello (inn); Ferrara; Ponte della Gula.

By Val Strona. Ponte Grande to Campello foot path. Campello to Omegna (Mule path), 5 hours; Omegna to Orta, road or sail on lake, 2 hours.

Delightful expedition through a paradise of beauty, glancing streams, tropical vegetation, view of icy peaks and a classical population with picturesque costumes.

Varallo to Alagna (42 kilometres), 7 to 8 hours by Sermenta and Val Sessia. Good dear inn at Varalla, Albergo d'Italie. See Canton of Tessin, Baveno. Excursions. Vocca 1½ hour; Scopa, good inn, 2 hours 50 min.; Scopello, 3½ hours (dear inn); Pila, 3 hours 40 min.; Piodre, 4¾ hours; Mollia, good inn, 5¼ hours; Riva, 38 kilometres, 7 hours, middling inn; Alagna, 8 hours.

ROUTES FROM SION

To Aarau, by Aarberg (Nos. 262 and 216), and Solothurn (No. 16), or by Berne (Nos. 73 or 74 and 6).

ROUTE 262.

AARBERG. (Rail through Aigle, Vevay, Lausanne, and Berne), or road, 30¾ L., (92¼ m.)

	Leagues.	Miles.
Bex (No. 74)	8¾	26¼
Aigle (No. 58)	1½	4¼
Vevay 14 L. (42 m.), (No. 54.)	3¾	11¼
Chexbres	1	3
Essertes	2	6
Mezieres	¼	1¼
Carrouge	½	1½
Moudon 19½ L. (58½ m.)	1½	4½
Lucens	1	3
Hennez	1	3
Marnand	½	1½
Payerne 23 L. (70½ m.)	1½	4½
Corcelles	½	1½
Dompierre	½	1½
Domdidier	½	1½
Avenches	½	1½
Faoug	¾	2¼
Morat 27 L. (81 m.)	¾	2¼
Kezerz (Chiètre)	1½	5¼
Fräschels	½	1½
Kalnach	½	1½
Bargen	½	1½
Aarberg	½	1½
	30¾	92¼

Aigle, Rail or (Nos. 74 and 58), Altdorf (No. 261), or by Berne (Nos. 74 and 66, 67, or 68), and Lucerne (No. 147), Altstaetten, by Aarberg (Nos. 262 and 216), Solothurn (No. 16), Aarau (No. 18), Zurich (No. 196), and St. Gallen (No. 180).

ROUTE 263.

AOSTA (20¾ L, 62¼ m.)

	Leagues.	Miles.
Vetro	1½	4¼
Ardon	¼	1¼
St. Pierre	¼	1¼
Riddes	¼	1¼
Saxon	¾	2¼
Chataz	1¼	3¾
Martigny (6 L. 18 m.)	1	3
La Bourg	¼	¾
Bovernier	1	3
St. Branchier	¾	2¼
Orsières	1¼	3¼
Liddes	¾	2¼
Alève	½	1½
St. Pierre	½	1½
Hospice of St. Bernard	3	9
St. Remy	2	6
St. Oyen	1	3
Etroubles	½	1¼
Ginod	2	6
Aosta	1¼	3¼
	20¾	62¼

Appenzell, by Aarberg (Nos. 262 and 216), Solothurn (No. 16), Aarau (No. 18), and Zurich (No. 28), or by Berne (Nos. 73, or 74, and 79), and Zurich (No. 28), or Thun (No. 73 or 65), Lucerne (No. 253), and Rail to Zurich.

Art, by Berne (Nos. 73, 74, and 78), or Thun (Nos 73 and 65), Lucerne (No. 253), and Zug (No. 281).

Baden, by Aarberg (Nos. 262 and 216), Solothurn (No. 16), and Aarau (No. 2), or by Bex (No. 74), Aigle (No. 58), and Berne (No. 54 and 56), or by the Simmenthal and Saanetsch (No. 72).

Bâle by Berne (Rail), and by Solothurn (Nos. 16 and 43), or by Bienne and the Münsterthal (Nos. 264 and 29).

Bellinzona (No. 236), Berne (Nos. 72, 73, 74), Bex, Rail or (No. 74).

ROUTE 264.

BIENNE, 32¼ L. (98¼ m.)

	Leagues.	Miles.
Aarberg (No. 262)	30¾	92¼
Bienne (No. 59)	2	6
	32¼	98¼

ROUTE 264 (1.)

BIONA (Val Pellina), and Aosta.

	Leagues.	Miles.
Martigny	6	18
Bovernier	1¼	3¾
St. Branchier (or Chables)	1¼	3¾
Champsec	2	6
Loutier	¼	1½
Pont du Mont Voisin	2¼	7½
Châlets de Torenbec	1½	4½
Col de Fenêtre	4	12
Biona	1¼	3¾
Valpellina, from the Col 4 l, (12 m.)	2¾	8¼
By Roysan to Aosta	3	9
(31 · from Valpellina to Aosta)	26	78
To Biona	19	57

ROUTE 264 (2.)

BREUIL AND VAL TOURNANCHE TO IVREA.

	Leagues.	Miles.
Visp	6½	19½
Zermatt	9	27
Col de St. Theodule	3	9
Breuil	2	6
Val Tournanche	2	6
Chatillon	3¼	9¾
Donnaz	5	15
Ivrea	4	12
	34½	104¼

To Breuil, 20½ l. (61½ m.), Brougg, by Aarberg (Nos. 262 and 216), Solothurn (No. 16), and Aarau (No. 7), or by Berne (No. 73, 74, and 197), Bulle (Nos. 74, 58, and 54), Burgdorf, by Berne (Nos. 73, or 74, and 60).

ROUTE 265.

CHAMOUNI, 15¼ l. (45¾ m.

	Leagues.	Miles.
Martigny (No. 263)	6	18
The Forclaz	2	6
Trient	¼	1½
Frontier of the Valais	2	6
Châlet de Charmillan	1	3
La Tour	¾	2¼
Argentiere	1	3
Chamouni	2	6
	15¼	45¾

Chaux de Fonds, by Lausanne (Nos. 267 and 173 or 174), and Neuchâtel (No. 169), Chiavenna, by Bellinzona (Nos. 236 and 230), Chur (No. 135).

ROUTE 236.

DOMO D'OSSOLA 22½ l. (67½ m.)

	Leagues.	Miles.
St. Leonard	1	3
Sierre	2	6
Loesch	1¼	3¾
Turtman	½	1½
Brunk	¾	2¼
Visp	1	3
Gambsen	¾	2¼
Glys	¾	2¼
Brieg	¼	¾
Ried	1¼	3¾
Persal	2	6
Simplon Hospice	2¼	6¾
Simplon (Village)	1½	4½
Ruden	2	6
Divedro	2¼	6¾
Crevola	2	6
Domo d'Ossola	1	3
	22½	67½

Einsiedeln and Engelberg, by Berne (Nos. 73 or 74 and 66, 67, or 68), and Lucerne, (Nos. 152 ard 153).

Frauenfeld, by Aarberg (Nos. 262 and 216), Solothurn (No. 16), Aarau (No. 18), and Zurich (No. 245 ; or by Berne (Nos. 73 or 74 and 79) and Zurich (No. 245).

Fribourg (Nos. 74, 58, and 54).

Gais, by Aarberg (Nos. 262 and 216), Solothurn (No. 16), Aarau (No. 18), Zurich (No. 196), and St. Gallen (No. 186); or by Berne and Zurich.—Routes as before.

Geneva—No. 98), or by south side of lake, through St. Gingoulph and Thonon.

Glarus, by Altdorf (Nos. 261 and 103); or by Aarberg, Solothurn, and Zurich.—See routes above.

Herisau, by Aarberg (Nos. 262 and 216), Solothurn (No. 16), Aarau (No. 18) and Zurich (No. 301), or by Berne (Nos. 73 or 74 and 79) and Zurich (No. 301).

Hofwyl, by Berne (Nos. 73, 74, and 62).

Lauffenbourg, by Aarberg (Nos. 262 and 216), Solothurn (No. 16), and Aarau (No. 10) ; or by Berne (Nos. 73 or 74 and 6) and Aarau (No. 10).

ROUTE 267.

LAUSANNE, 18 L (54 m.)

	Leagues.	Miles.
Vevay (No. 262)	14	42
St. Saphorin	¾	2¼
Cully	1¼	3¾
Lutry	¾	2¼
Lausanne	1¼	3¾
	18	54

unally, that the town contains 50 watch-makers' and 70 jewellers' shops, and that 75,000 ounces of gold are used in them annually. A good watch costs about 450 francs.

Other manufactures are schalls, especially those of M. Prevost-Picter, which are considered almost equal to the native Indian schalls; also hats, leather, cotton, and other branches of industry, give occupation to the sturdy democrats of Geneva.

For the information of visitors it may be useful to add that Geneva has good native physicians, allopathic and homeopathic, besides a well-known countryman of our own, Dr. Metcalfe. It has also a British consul, an English club, an electric telegraph, a Genevese club or cercle, two railway routes to Paris, other lines to Lausanne, Neuchâtel, Berne, and Sion, besides daily steamboats, which run to the end of the lake in five hours.

WALKS, &c., NEAR GENEVA.—In Geneva the best walks, commanding the finest views, are—1st, the Bastion Bourgeois. 2nd, the Bastion d'Hollande, planted with trees, and offering fine views of the lake. 3rd. The petit Languedoc, a sheltered winter walk. 4. La Treille, a terrace with trees and seats, commanding a very fine view. 5. The Observatory, immediately above the town, commands a fine view. 6. The Russian church. 7. The Cemetery, with the tombs of Sir Humphry Davy and De Candolle. 8. Campagne Rothschild, pretty grounds, open Tuesday and Friday. Villa Peel, Villa Beaulieu, with two noted cedars; Bois de la Batie (20 minutes), &c., &c.

Carouge.—This is a large borough almost contiguous to Geneva, on the old Chambory road. Its inhabitants, mostly Catholics, are actively engaged in manufacturing industry.

Fernex or *Fernay* is celebrated as the residence of Voltaire, and for a splendid *view of Mont Blanc.* Fernay, though only five miles from Geneva, is within the frontiers of France, on the road to Paris by Gex. The great French satirist lived here from 1759 to 1777. His château is prettily situated, but has been much altered by recent proprietors. The furniture used to be in great request with visitors, who tore Voltaire's bed curtains into rags to keep as relics. The church built by Voltaire is used as a hayloft. The gardens surrounding the château are pretty, and command striking views.

Chambesy, Genthod, Pregni, and Varambé are villages charmingly situated near Geneva, and offering delightful views.

Sacconex (Petit and Grand), Saint Gervais, and Saint Jean are eminences near Geneva, offering fine views of the Lake, the Alps, and the Jura.

WATER EXCURSIONS.—Trips on the lake will be found perfectly delightful. The lake itself is an object of constant interest and beauty; the fishing is excellent, and the back-ground presented by the Alps, especially about sun-set in summer, requires the pen of Byron to do it justice.

EXCURSIONS ON LAND.

Boisy.

Chamouni. (See further on.)

Dole (The). See Vaud (Canton of).

L'Ecluse. (Fort de) On a rock, forming the line of demarcation between France and Savoy till 1792. This little fortress, blocking a very narrow defile, has a very striking appearance.

Mole (The).—A fine pyramidal mountain, with a good view, above Contamines, 2¾ l. (8¼ m.) from Geneva.

Rhone (The Perte du) is two leagues (6 miles) from Geneva, close to the road to Lyons, and presents a singular phenomenon, consisting of the sudden disappearance of a river 50 or 60 feet deep, and only 15 or 20 in width, under great masses of rock, and its silent reappearance, issuing from its subterranean course 60 paces further on; when, however, heavy rains have prevailed for some time, all the water of the river is not entirely received underground, but some escapes by over-flowing above.

Salevè (Mont).—Reached through Carouge and Veiri is two leagues (six miles) from Geneva, and just beyond the limits of the Canton, in Savoy. It consists of the great and little Salevè, separated by a valley, enclosing the village of Moneti or Monetier, which may be reached by char-a-banc by going round the Petit Salevè, involving a detour of three miles. From Monetier, the distance to the Grand Salevè is one league (3 m.), and half a league (1½ m.) to the Petit Salevè. Both summits command delightful views, and the Petit Salevè is noted for certain plants, the Balme de l'Hermitage being found lower down, and higher up the Balme du Demon, but the ascent used to be considered dangerous.

Voirons (The). This mountain is situated in the Chablais (now France). It has two hotels since 1859, Hotel Châlet, and Hotel Pension, directed by M. Gaillard. Pension, 5½ *fr.*, all included. Whey, goats' milk, and asses' milk. A doctor attached. Mineral spring (ferruginous, with carbonic acid gas).

The principal excursion from Geneva is Chamouni, which, though before 1859 a part of Savoy, and since that date of France, is so closely connected with Switzerland, that it cannot be omitted in a Swiss Guide. The following is a brief notice of the route from Geneva to Chamouni: First to Bonneville, 5¼ l. (15¾ m); thence to Vougy, 1½ l. (4½ m.); on to Sinongy, 1 l. (3 m.); to Cluse, 1 l. (3 m.); to the Pont de l'Arve, from which a grand view is obtained. From Cluse to Maglan, 1½ l. (4½ m.); and thence by the Valley of St. Martin, 2½ l. (7¼ m.) Near Maglan you pass the Nant d'Orli (Nant, Gaelic for stream), a fine waterfall, and further up Nant d'Arpena, 800 feet high, the Staubbach of this district. Near the inn at St. Martin is a splendid view of Mont Blanc, by some thought finer than any view of the monarch near Chamouni. From this to Chêde, 2 L (6 m.), and near

that the beautiful cascade of Chêde; not far on, at Servoz, the fragments of Anterne, which in 1751 rolled down from the mountain of Varens. From Servoz a path leads by Boujet in three hours to the Col d'Anterne (6071), with grand views, by the lake d'Anterne to the Collet d'Anterne, 2 l. (6 m.), through some poor Savoyard villages. Pelly de Salles, 1½ L (4½ m.), Lignon and Fardalet ¼ l. (2¼ m.), and by a steep descent to Salvagny, 1 l. (3 m.), in the Vale of Sixt, and to Sixt itself. (See further on.) From Chêde to Servoz, distance 1½ l. (4½ m.), and thence to the Priory, by a wild gorge, 2½ l. (7½ m.); in all 18½ l. (55½ m.) from Geneva. The road is throughout fit for carriages; above St. Martin, for small cars. As regards hotels, at Bonneville are the Couronne, Balance; at Cluses, the Ecu de France and Union; at St. Martin, Hotel du Mont Blanc, first class; at Servoz, the Universe and Balance. Fares from Geneva, diligences to Sallenches, 11 L (33 m.), in six hours, 10 *fr.*; hence to Chamouni in chars-a-banc, &c.; which route takes 10 hours, 15 *fr.* Good walkers take post car to St. Martin, and thence on foot to Chamouni. Carriages from Geneva, one-horse, to Sallenches or St. Martin, 30 *fr.*, to Chamouni 45 *fr.*, from St. Martin to Chamouni 15 or 20 *fr.*

The Valley of Chamouni is 2,040 feet above the Lake of Geneva. In 1099 a certain Count of Geneva founded there a Benedictine Priory, round which the village of Chamouni gradually sprang up, and ultimately gave its name to the valley. It is said afterwards to have been so overlooked that the population relapsed into barbarism, till in 1741 Pococke and Windham, with an armed band, discovered the valley. This is probably a myth, though they were perhaps the first tourists who made known the charms of the valley. Since that date it has increased every year in popularity, and is now probably the most frequented spot among the High Alps.

Hotels; Hotel Royal de Londres

Hotel de Londres et d'Angleterre; Hotel de Saussure. The first hotels are so crowded in August that it is difficult to get room. Prices in the first hotels: rooms 3 to 4*fr.* a day; breakfast 1½ to 2*fr.* Crown, Mont Blanc, Nord, Balance, are other hotels. ' Pension des Alpes.

Guides: The best Chamouni guides are J. Baptist Croz (his brother, M. Croz, was killed at Mont Cervin in 1865 accompanying Lord Douglas; J. M. Claret, Joseph Tairraz, Michel Payot, first-rate; Victor Tairraz, first-rate, is a little passé in age; Zachary Cachat, good but eccentric; Jean Pierre Cachat, good. To Mont Anvert, La Flegere, &c., a guide not wanted. To the Glacier of Bossons, the Chapeau, &c., a boy can be taken. For more arduous expeditions a guide. Prices by tariff, 6*fr.* per day to ordinary excursions; to the Jardin, 10*fr.*; Buet, 15*fr.*; Grands Mulets, 40*fr.*; Col du Géant, 50*fr.*; on Mont Blanc, 100*fr.*, with 10 to 15*fr.* pour boire. Martigny guides cannot be employed at Chamouni, but Chamouni guides are allowed in Switzerland. Horse and servant 12*fr.* per day. To Martigny by Col de Balme or Tête Noire, 12*fr.*; the same for a horse. Two days at least required to see the favourite points visited at Chamouni.

The valley is 5 l. (15 m.) long and 20 minutes broad. It produces nothing but pastures and alpine p'ants, from the latter of which the bees extract the sweets that make the celebrated Chamouni honey. The Aiguilles, that form a characteristic feature of the scenery, are supposed to result from the disintegration of protogyne rocks, which were here raised up by radiation, and it is thought that the quicker or slower decomposition of this rock, under atmospheric and other influences, has occasioned the phenomenon. Mont Blanc, the highest mountain in Europe (14,793 French feet, 15,784 English, above the sea) is of the rock called by Saussure protogyne *granite*. Ascended for the first time in *1786 by Dr. Paccard and Jaques Balmat, and next year by Saussure*; it has now

become a familiar and popular excursion even for ladies, attended with little danger, but some fatigue. You are obliged to take four guides, 700*fr.* the usual cost; provisions wanted, three days are sometimes consumed. Usual route by the Grande Mulets, where is a hut to sleep in. The top is called the Bosse or Hump of the Dromedary. The point seen from Chamouni, and taken for the summit, is the Dome de Gouté. There is said to be an easier way to the top from the Pavillon de Bellevue, and it is reported that you can easily reach the summit and back from that point in one day.

Without going so high you have a grand view of Mont Blanc and the valley from the Brevent opposite (8,380 feet). Ascent rather steep at the Cheminée, but ladies have mounted it easily with the writer. A few snow fields (with red snow) at the top. The view one of the finest in Europe, five hours from Chamouni, three to Planpraz, where you can sleep, can be ridden on mules.

Other ordinary excursions about the valley, now as well known as the Bois de Boulogne, are to the (2¼ hrs.) Mont Anvert, with a pavilion and night quarters. Hence descend on the Mer de Glacé. Mont Anvert is covered with rhododendra in the season, and is a delightful spot to roam about freely without guides. From the Aiguille du Dru, opposite, looking like a cathedral spire, you frequently see avalanches. The principal peaks near are the Dru (11,489 feet), the Aiguille Verte (12,603 feet), Great and Little Jorasse (11,490 and 12,663 feet), the Aiguille du Tacul (10,323 feet), and the Géant (12,290 feet). Height of Mont Anvert 5,911 feet, distance from Chamouni 2¼ hours.

The *Chapeau* is opposite Mont Anvert. There is now an inn here. The view is very fine. Glacier movements sometimes heard from here like a cannonade.

The *Jardin* or *Courtil* is a rock amidst the ice, covered with Alpine flowers in summer, and reached from Mont Anvert and back, over the ice, in ten hours.

Heat great in summer. Ladies often go. View sublime towards the Géant.

Opposite Mont Anvert is La Flegerè (5,806 feet), a terrace of the Aiguilles Rouges, attainable on horseback (2½ hours) from Chamouni. Fine view of Mont Blanc and the valley. Small Auberge at the top. Other favourite points to visit are the Col de Balme (7,086 feet), five hours from Chamouni, and two from Trient in the Valais, by which you reach Martigny, passing the Forclaz, in 9 or 10 hours. The Col de Balme closes the valley to the east, and furnishes the first water to the Arve. The sun-rise view of Mont Blanc from the Col is celebrated and justly.

The glaciers most usually visited are the Bossons and Bois, though that of Argontiere and La Tour are well worth a visit. The Bossons descends from the Dome du Gouté nearly to Moncouard, a hamlet of Chamouni. It is remarkable for the beauty of its ice pyramids. The Bois Glacier is the continuation of the Mer de Glacé, and the source of the Arveyron, which issues from a superb icy grotto, which, however, it is unsafe to enter.

The Cascade des Pelerins, once noted, is now nearly destroyed by a fall of rock.

More distant and hazardous excursions embrace a visit to the foot of the Aiguille de Charmoz, and the other Aiguilles immediately above Chamouni, and especially the passage of the Col du Géant to Cormayeur, in Piedmont. To effect this passage you must take experienced guides, ropes, veil, &c., and start at midnight, walking eighteen hours over the snow, and over certain highly crevassed and intricate parts of the glaciers. The Col is 10,458 feet high, and the descent on the Italian side requires care on account of slippery precipices and couloirs. Some English travellers and their guide perished on this descent, from want of care, a few years ago.

The most interesting excursion is the tour of Mont Blanc, either crossing the Géant or going round by the Col de Balme and Martigny to the Val de Ferret, or cutting off this distance by crossing directly up the Glacier of La Tour. In either way you come round to Cormayeur, the Chamouni of Piedmont, in the upper part of the Dora Baltea course. Hence you continue at the foot of the Brenva and Allèe Blanche Glaciers to the Col de Bonhomme, and return to Chamouni, striking into the Geneva road between Servoz and Chamouni. It is estimated that this tour, if taken to Martigny, requires five days, walking seven or nine hours a day. A guide, at 6fr., is wanted for each traveller. The route may be reversed by beginning with the Col de Voza to Contamines, 7 l., first day; second, by the Col de Bonhomme to Chapiu, 8 l. (24 m.); third, by the Col de la Seigne to Courmayeur, 9½ l. (28½ m.); fourth, by the Col de Ferrex to the Châlets of Ferrex, 8 l. (24 m.); fifth, by the valley of Ferrex to Martigny.

Height of the Col de Voza 5,571 feet. Fine view of Mont Blanc and its chain. Descent to Bionnay: four large glaciers d scend into this valley—Miage, Bionassey, Armancette, and Tré la Tête. Road forks here—right to Baths of St. Gervais, left to Contamines, a large Alpine village, 4 l. (12 m.) from Chamouni. You must sleep there; no night quarters for 8 l. (24 m.) further.

Next day, 2 l. (6 m.), to Châlets of Nant Bourant and Mont Joli, under Aiguille de Tré la Tête, to Mont Joie (Mons Jovis): magnificent view. On to Col du Bonhomme, by Place des Dames, where two English ladies, with guides, were buried by an avalanche. Wild district. Bad road; somet mes snow. Croix du Bonhomme (7,520 feet). Fine view of Bonneval Vale, towards the Isere, Mont Cenis, and the Aiguille de Vanoise. Fr m Nant Bourant to Col 3½ l. (10½ m.) A descent of two hours to Chapiu, a poor village. Hotels du Soleil and Pavillon. Dear, and rather meagre fare. You can diverge from here by the Val de Bonneval to Bourg St. Maurice, 3 l. (9 m.), or to the Little St.

Bernard, and thence by Pré St. Didier to Courmayeur.

Third day, from Chapiu by Motet, 1 l. (3 m.), wretched châlets, with l'Ancien Hotel and the Repos, bad service, extravagant prices, you rise to Col de la Seigne (7,800 feet); striking view—Val Ferrex 12 l. (36 m.) seen in all its length; upper part of it called the Alleè Blanche. Mont Blanc looks quite different this side—an enormous precipice of 9,000 feet above the Glacier of Miage. The Alleè Blanche takes its name from the numerous glaciers that descend from this precipice into it. These glaciers are those of Broglia, Fressenay, Brenva, Mont Frety, Entreves, Rochefort, Planpansiere, &c. 2 l. (6 m.) hence to Courmayeur. You cross the Dora several times. Brenva Glacier completely occupying the valley, the river has been forced to tunnel a way under it. Opposite the glacier the Chapel of Nôtre Dame de Guérison.

Courmayeur. — Hotels : Royal, Ange, Mont Blanc, Union. Post car to Aosta, 7*fr.*, five hours; carriages with one horse to Aosta, 15 to 18*fr.*; with two horses, the double. Courmayeur is much crowded with visitors, especially Italians, in summer. It is an excellent centre for many beautiful excursions, especially to the Grammont, with Mont Blanc opposite. Road easy, 1½ hours. Another easy excursion to Montagne de Saxe; fine view of the valley. Several fine views from Courmayeur to Aosta; only drawbacks, crétins. A short cut by Col Ferret to Martigny direct, or by St. Bernard, without going to Aosta.

The baths of St. Gervais are another point of attraction near Chamouni. They are a little off the road to Geneva, near Sallenches, in the Val Mont Joie. Hotels du Mont Joli and de Genève Carriage, with one horse, from Sallenches, 6*fr.* These baths, with sulphur springs, are much visited. Heat of spring 40° centigrade. Bathing establishment has 100 beds. Price moderate. *Near the fine fall of the Bonnant. Pretty walks round the bath.*

Another favourite excursion is that to Sixt, a charming spot, from which Champery, in the Val d'Illiez, may be reached. From Chamouni you can pass to Sixt, either by the Col d'Anterne, already noticed, to which you diverge at Servos or by the Aiguilles Rouges, diverging from the Tête Noire on the way to Martigny.

The latter route (by the Aiguilles Rouges to Sixt) is nearly the same as that followed to ascend the Buet. In fact, you take the summit of the Buet from Chamouni this way, or reverse the expedition, which involves 14 hours, or only 12 by passing the night at the Châlets de Fonds, above Sixt. Leaving Sixt you advance up the valley of Fonds, which is considered the most beautiful of all those surrounding Sixt, itself a centre of beauty. From the Châlets de Fonds there are two ways to the top of the Buet; the direct route is by Beaux Prés, by a limestone ridge and a rather steep glacier (4½ hours) from the châlets. The longer way, more frequented, takes by an easy path, in 3½ hours to the Col de l'Echaud (8,058 feet), connecting the Vallée des Fonds with that of the Dioza; and thence to the top by slate rocks (2½ hours),

Height of Buet 10,207 feet. View from it almost indescribable in grandeur. Descending by a curious limestone rock, Table au Chantre, and two hours from summit, to Pierre a Berard (7,498 feet), a huge rock, where visitors used at one time to bivouac, and a rather dear châlet inn has been opened, you come to a mule path through larches, and gain the Eau Noire Valley, or Col de Berard, near the Cascade de Poyaz, by the beaten track of the Tête Noire, to Chamouni. This is the district of the Aiguilles Rouges, a granitic groupe. Valorsine, on the Tête Noire pass, 4½ hours from Buet (6½ ascending). Fair quarters at inn by Cascade de la Barberine. Argentiere 1½ hour. Chamouni 3 from here. There are other diverging routes from Buet, through Aiguilles Rouges, by Col de Berard to Trient. You can also pass from Valorsine to Servoz in 8½ hours, by Col de Salenton (8,160 feet) and the Châlets de Villy.

Sixt has been known for some years as one of the choicest centres in the Alps. (Hotel du Fer a Cheval).

The best local guide is Mr. Alfred Will's, "Eagle's Nest." The entire district is the perfection of the picturesque, and, in part, sublime. Rocks, waterfalls, pine forests, nothing is wanting to complete the picture. On the road to Samoens, excursions should be made to the Gouffres des Tines, and the Fall of the Nant Dant, falling 650 feet from Mont Aubenè. Samoens, 1½ l. (4½ m.) from Sixt, (Hotel de la Croix d'Or) is on the road down the valley to Geneva. From Samoens you can pass by the Col du Mont Jouplane and the valley of the Dranse to Thonon, on the Lake of Geneva, 10 l. (30 m.)

Three paths lead from Sixt, through beautiful scenery, to Champery, in the Val d'Illiez (see Canton of Valais, Champery), many other excursions full of interest and beauty can be made from this centre.

Two main thoroughfares and beaten tracks lead from Chamouni to Martigny, in the Valais:—1. The Col de Balme; 2. The Tête Noire. By the Col de Balme, distance 10 l. (30 m.); Guides useless; a horse or mule 12fr. Ascending from Martigny, you reach the Col de Forclaz, 4,687 feet, with a fine view of the Valais, in 2¾ hours. There is an auberge on the Col. Descent through a fine aged fir forest, with plenty of whortleberries under foot, 20 minutes. In Trient Valley, roads fork; that to the right leads to the Tête Noire. Pass village of Trient, over the Nant Noire, through forest of Magnin, laid waste by avalanches, and a steep path to top, 3 l. (9 m.), passing Châlets of Herbagères, with ridiculously dear châlet inn. Col de Balme, 6,783 French feet, is the limit of France, since 1859. Dear hotel, Pavillon du Col de Balme, also a Swiss auberge near it. Few views finer. Descent

to Arve ¾ l. (2¼ m.). To the hamlet of Tours, ¼ l. (1½ m.) to Argentières where you rejoin path over Tête Noire, ½ l. (1½ m.) to Levancher, 15 minutes; Les Tines, 30 minutes; Le Praz, and Chamouni, ½ l. (1½ m.)

Leaving Trient, the Tête Noire route passes through gorges in the Aiguilles Rouges district. Distance 9 l. (27 m.) to Argentières, 7 l. (21 m.) The Trouperdu is the wildest gorge on the way. 1 l. (3 m.) from Trient is the Hotel de la Tête Noire, 3,676 feet. Fine narrow glen, with wild scenery, thence to the Hotel de la Cascade, half way; ½ l. (1½ m.) on is the Cascade de la Barberine. ½ l. (1½ m.) further, Valorcine, among precipices, and subject to avalanches. Then, on to village of Nant, under the Aiguilles Rouges. ½ l. (1½ m.) from the road is the Cascade de Poyaz, you reach it by a path through tunnels and among pines and rhododendrons. Water falls into a terrible abyss with the noise of thunder. In the morning an iris spans the fall. Thence to Argentières, where you join the Col de Balme route.

ROUTES FROM CHAMOUNI.

To Blanc (Mont) 17 hours ascent, 8 hours descent; tariff of guides, 100fr. to top. To Grands Mulets, 40fr. Dome du Gouté, 60fr. The Corridor, 80fr. The trip to the Grands Mulets, only 20fr.; in two days, 30fr. Aiguille du Gouté, by the Pavillon de Bellevue, 30fr. Porters, to summit, 40fr., not to carry more than ten kilogrammes from the Grand Plateau to the summit.

a Usual route by hamlet of Pelerins, Glacier of Bossons, to Grand Mulet (3,050 metres); thence by Petit Plateau and Grand Plateau, to Rochers Rouges (4,492 metres). On by Corridor, where Dr. Hamel was lost, in 1820; up Mur de la Côte. Then by the Petits Mulets to the summit.

b By St. Gervais and the Dôme du Gouté.

Mont Blanc has been ascended on this side in 1855. Very difficult couloir, at an angle of 43°. The best way on this side is by the Cabane Guichard and Col de Voza.

c Chamouni to Cormayeur, by the Col du Géant, in 16 hours 30 min. (3,370 metres). Ascent from Cormayeur, 6 hours.

d Ditto by Col de Triolet, 3,700 feet. To Châlets of Pré de Bar 8 hours 35 min., from foot of Glacier de Talefré, where you sleep.

e Chamouni to Orsieres, by the Col d'Argentière, 20 hours; difficult. Sleep first night at Châlets de Lognant. Route passes over the Glacier d'Argentière.

f By the Col de la Tour Noire; extremely difficult; discovered, 1863.

g By Col du Tour, 1½ day; guide, 40*fr.* You sleep at Col de Balme, and ascend the Glacier la Tour.

h By the Cols du Chardonnet and the Fenétre de Salenaz. Start from Châlets of Lognant; takes 12 hours.

i By the Col de Forclaz and lake Champery, 10 hours 30 min. By Signal de Bovine, Châlets and Croix de Bovine.

k Chamouni to Sixt, by the Col de Genevrier, 12 hours.

l Chamouni to Sixt, by the Col de Tenneverges and the valley of Barberine, 14 hours (see above).

m Ditto by the Grenairon, 11 hours, 18*fr.*

n By the Buet and Brevent, the Col de Lechaud and the Châlets of Villy.

ROUTES FROM AND TO SIXT.

Two principal routes lead from Geneva to Sixt, both practicable for carriages, three minor routes and footpaths lead over the hills, by deviations.

1. The first main route from Geneva to Sixt by St. Jeoire presents the following itinerary, with hotels:—

	Kilometres.	Miles (Eng.)
Geneva to Nangy	15	9¼
St. Jeoire (Hotel la Couronne)	13	8
Tanninges (Hotel les Balances le Lion d'Or)	14	8¾
Samoens (Hotel Croiz d'Or)	14	8¾
[Guides Gurnie de Vallon Clement Gallet.]		
Sixt (Hotel et Pension des Cascades	8	5
	64	40

Conveyances, as far as Tanninges carriages, thence to Sixt in chars.

2. Geneva to Sixt through Chatillon. Itinerary from Geneva.

	Kilometres.	Miles (Eng.)
Bonneville	28	17½
Chatillon	—	8
Tanninges	—	—
Sixt	36	23½
	49	49

From Cluses and St. Martin on the direct road from Geneva to Chamouni, you can reach Sixt in three ways.

(*a*) By the Col d'Alberon—footpath. Turn off from high road to Sallenches at Magland and ascend to Col by village of Colonnaz, through pine woods. The Col is 4,487 feet high near little Lake of Flaine. Time from Cluses to Sixt, 8 to 9 hours. Direct Route from Cluses to Sixt by lake of Gers, through fine scenery, 7½ hours.

(*b*) By *St. Martin.*—This route takes you by the fine tall of Nant d'Arpenaz and near the Lac de Flaine, over the Desert de Platey and close to Croix de Fer (2.317) to Sixt; to Nant 1 hour; Châlets of Vange. 1 hour 10 min.; Haon, 40 min. (Eocene limestone, with fossils, abundant at Croix de Fer); Desert of Platey, 2 hours; Two paths down hence to Sixt, one by Lac de Flaine, the other by valley of Salles, 2½ hours.

(*c*) By *Passy* and *La Portette.*—Passy is almost equidistant from Sallenches, St. Gervais, and Servoz. A route from Passy to Sixt, little frequented is said to ue as fine as the Gemmi; time 7 or 8 hours.

Steep ascent up almost inaccessible precipices; Escaliers or Degres de Platey, 3 hours up, 2 down, Châlets de Platey.

	Hours.	Minutes.
Portette (fine view)	0	25
Châlets de Salles	1	30
Châlets de Lignon (cascade)	0	45
By two waterfalls Du Rouge to Salvagny	0	30
By Cascades des Deschargeux	0	30

From Sixt to Champery (see Monthey), under Canton of Valais.

Sixt to Thonon on the Savoy side of the lake of Geneva, opposite Rolle.

From Thonon to Samoens the itinerary is as follows :—

	Hours walk.	Miles.
La Vernaz	3	9
Biot	1¾	5¼
Montrioud	1¾	5¼
Samoens	4	12
	10½	31½

This route passes by ruins of Abbey of St. Jean d'Aulph (Inn chez Doller and Le Cheval). From Foron a path leads to Tanninges, 5¼ hours from Biot, 10 from Thonon. From head of stream above Morzine, two paths lead to Samoens, one by Col de Goleze, two by Col de Coux.

From Bonneville to Thonon you can take three routes.

1. By Bonne and Machilly, post road, 26½ m.

2. By Boege, char road, about 34 m.

3. By St. Jeoire and Megevette about 30 m.

From Thonon several routes may be taken to the Val d'Illiez (see Monthey, Canton of Valais); but the principal are

(1.) The Col d'Abondance, 13 hours.

(2.) The Col de Chesery, 12 hours.

(3.) The Col de Coux.

1. Follows the Dranse d'Abondance. Best inns *en route* at La Vacheresse (Croix d'Or).

This is the place from which to ascend the Dent d'Oche with grand view of Lake of Geneva; Nôtre Dame d'Abondance (Inn chez Cretin La Croix), and La Chapelle (Inn La Croix).

The Col d'Abondance is the Swiss frontier (4,629 feet).

2. The Col de Chesery has been little explored—it is near S. side of Point de Mossetta (7,536 feet).

3. Col de Coux.—This route follows Middle Dranse to its source about Morzine and then over the Col to Champery.

For routes from Champery to Sixt (see Champery under Monthey, Canton of Valais).

Sixt to Martigny, 4 routes. There are conflicting accounts of this district, which has not been minutely or carefully inspected. Easiest way from Sixt to Martigny is

a. By a summit called Tête Noire, forming the centre of the Fer a Cheval.

Thence to Châlets des Vieux Emoussons 7½ hours ; Jeunes Emoussons, 1 hour; Cascade de la Barberine to junction with Eau Noire at the inn. Thence to Martigny, 3 hours. (Mr. Ball would give this nameless pass the appellation of Col de Grenairon, 8,500 feet.)

b. Route to Martigny by Col de Tennevergues is more difficult ; not well known to guides. Passing under S. side of Pic de Tennevergues, it joins the former path (*a*) at Châlets d'Emoussons.

These two routes when joined at Eau Noire, the true source of the Trient below Valoisin, pass thence to Martigny, by the known old Tête Noire route.

c. Another route takes you from Sixt, by Salenche or Salenfe torrent into Rhone Valley, at Varreayas, and thence to Martigny.

d. A fourth brings you by Châlets d Emaney to the Trient at Trinquet

This district, consisting of Jurassic limestone is full of beautiful scenery, fine waterfalls, and ancient forests, the paths leading over the great range parallel to the two chief valleys that enclose it on either side Vals d'Illiez and of Trient.

ITINERARY FROM GENEVA.

Geneva to Aarau, by Lausanne (Nos. 96 and 63), and Berne (No. 6), or by Lausanne (Nos. 96 and 223), and Solothurn (No. 16).

Aarberg, by Lausanne (Nos. 96 and 276).

Aarbourg, by Lausanne (Nos. 96 and 63), and Berne (No. 6).

Aigle, by Bex (Nos. 94 and 58).

Altdorf, by Lausanne (Nos. 96 and 63); Berne (Nos. 66, 67, and 68) and Lucerne (No. 147).

Altstaetten, by Lausanne (Nos. 96 and 63); Berne (No. 79); Zurich (No. 196), and St. Gallen (No. 180).

Appenzell, by Lausanne (Nos. 96 and 63); Berne (No. 79), and Zurich (No. 28).

Art, by Lausanne (Nos. 96 and 63); Berne No. 78), and Zug (No. 281)

Baden, by Lausanne (Nos. 96 and 63), and Berne (No. 56), or by Lausanne (Nos. 96 and 223); Solothurn (No. 16), and Aarau (No. 2).

Bâle, by Neuchâtel (Nos. 97 and 40), and Aarberg (No. 29), or by Lausanne (Nos. 96 and 63), and Berne (No. 32).

Bellinzona, by Sion (Nos. 98 and 236).

Berne, by Lausanne, (Nos. 96 and 63), or by Lausanne (Nos. 96 and 279), and Fribourg (No. 54).

ROUTE 94.

BEX, 16½L (49½ m.)

	Leagues.	Miles.
Coligny	¼	1¼
Corsy	1¼	3¼
Dovain	1	3
Massongy	¾	2¼
Condre	½	1½
Anty	¾	2¼
Thonon	½	1½
Evian	2	6
Maxelly	½	1½
La Tour Ronde	½	1½
Meillerie	1	3
St. Gingoulph	1½	4½
Boveret	¾	2¼
Vauvrier	1¼	3¼
Vionnaz	½	1½
Murat	½	1½
Monthey	1	3
St. Maurice	1	3
Bex	½	1½
	16½	49½

Bienne, by Lausanne, (Nos. 96 and 276), and Aarburg (No. 59).

Breuil—See Canton of Valais, Zermatt; Italian Valleys, Ayas (Val. d') and St. Theodule (col. de), (No. 264). and Route Mem. a.

Brougg, by Berne, (Nos. 96 and 97), or by Lausanne (Nos. 96 and 223); Solothurn (No. 16), and Aarau (No. 7).

Bulle, by Lausanne (Nos. 96 and 278).

Burgdorf, by Lausanne (Nos. 96 and 63), and Berne (No. 60).

ROUTE 95.

CHAMOUNI, 18½L (55½ m.)

MURRAY makes it 53½ English miles; 86 kilom.

	Leagues.	Miles.
Chesne	¼	1¼
Vetro	1¼	3¼
Nangy	¾	2¼
Contamine	¾	2¼
Bonneville	2	6
Vangy	1½	4½
Siongy	1	3
La Cluse	1	3
Maglan	1½	4½
St. Martin	2½	7½
Salenche	¼	¾
Chêde	1¾	5¼
Servoz	1½	4½
Ouches at the entrance of the valley	1	3
Moncouart	½	1½
The Priory or Village of Chamouni	¾	2¼
	18½	55½

ROUTE 95 (2).

Chatillon, Geneva to Aosta, by Great St. Bernard. See (No. 263).

	Leagues.	Miles.
Quart	1½	3½
Nuz	1¼	3¼
Chatillon	2½	7½
Kilometres 24.	5	15

Chaux de Fond, by Neuchâtel (Nos. 97 and 169).

Chiavenna, by Sion (No. 98 and 236), and Bellinzona (No. 230).

Coire, by Lausanne (No. 96 and 63); Berne (No. 79), and Zurich (No. 142).

Courmayeur, by the Col de Bonhomme, or the Col du Géant. See Chamouni, (Routes c. d. e. f. g. h. i.). By Orsieres and the Col de Ferret. See Valais (Canton of), and do.

Einsiedeln, by Lucerne (Nos. 96 and 63); Berne (Nos. 66, 67, or 68), and Lucerne (No. 152).

Engelberg, by Lausanne (Nos. 96 and 63); Berne (Nos. 66, 67, or 68), and Lucerne (No. 153).

Frauenfeld, by Lausanne (Nos. 96 and 63); Berne (No. 79), and Zurich (No. 245), or by Lausanne (Nos. 96 and 223).

Solothurn (No. 16); Aarau (No. 18), and Zurich (No. 245).

Fribourg, by Lausanne (Nos. 96 and 83, or 279).

Gais, by Lausanne (Nos. 96 and 63); Berne (No. 79); Zurich (No. 296), and St. Gallen (No. 186), or by Lausanne (Nos. 96 and 223).

Solothurn (No. 16), Aarau (No. 18), Zurich (No. 196), and St. Gallen (No. 186).

Glarus, by Lausanne (Nos. 96 and 63), Berne (No. 79), and Zurich (No. 116).

Gressenay, St. Jean, in the Val d'Ayas.

Geneva to Visp, (Nos. 96, 267, 266).

Visp to Zermatt, (No. 264).

Zermatt to Gressenay, by Col St. Theodule, Breuil, and St. Giacomo, or by the higher passes, including the Schwarz-Thor, the Col de Lys, the Col des Jumeaux, &c. See under Canton of Valais, 270—2, Zermatt and Riffel, and under the Italian Valleys, Ayas (Val de) Gressenay Lys (Val de,) and Tournanche (Val). See Canton of Valais. Routes, Koph, Yod, Llamed.

Herisau, by Lausanne (Nos. 96 and 63), Berne (No. 79), and Zurich (No. 301), or by Lausanne (Nos. 96 and 223), Solothurn, (No. 16), Aarau (No. 18), and Zurich (No. 301).

Hofwyl, by Lausanne (Nos. 96 and 63), and Berne (No. 62).

Lauffenbourg, by Lausanne (Nos. 96 and 63), Berne (No. 6), and Aarau (No. 10), or by Lausanne (Nos. 96 and 223), Solothurn (No. 16), and Aarau (No. 10).

ROUTE 96.

LAUSANNE, 10¼ L (32¼ m.) by land.

	Leagues.	Miles.
Versoix	1¼	5¼
Coppet	¼	2¼
Cran	¼	2¼
Nyon	¾	2¼
La Ligniere	1	3
Rolle (6 L)	1	3
Allaman	1	3
Morges	1¼	5¼
Lausanne	2	6
	10¼	32¼

By Steamboat in 3 hours.

Locarno, by Sion (Nos. 98 and 236), and Bellinzona No. 222).

Locle by Neuchâtel (Nos. 97 and 175).

Loesch (Baths), by Sion (Nos. 98 and 265).

Lucerne, by Lausanne (Nos. 96 and 63), and Berne (Nos. 66, 67, and 68).

Lugano, by Sion (Nos. 98 and 236), and Bellinzona (No. 233).

Macugnaga.—See Canton of Valais, Zermatt, Monte Moro, and Weiss Thor; also Italian Valleys— (Nos. 270—3 and 270—4).

Mastalone.—See ditto Route B.

Mendrisio, by Sion (Nos. 98 and 236), and Bellinzona (No. 235).

Morat, by Lausanne (Nos. 96 and 276).

Morges (No. 96).

Moudon, by Lausanne (Nos. 96 and 276)

ROUTE 97.

NEUCHÂTEL, 22¼ L (66¾ m.)

	Leagues.	Miles.
Morges (No. 96)	8¼	26¼
Cossonay	2	6
Lasarraz	1	3
Orbe (133) 4 L	2	6
Mathoud		2¼
Succevaz		
Treycovagnes		1¼
Yverdun (15¾ L)		1¼
Grandson		2¼
Ouens		2¼
Concise		
Vaumarcus	1¼	5
St. Aubin		1¼
Bevais		2¼
Boudry		
Colombier		
Auvernier		
Serriere		1¼
Neuchâtel		1¼
	22¼	66¾

Omegna.—See Canton of Valais, Italian Valleys.

Saas. Anzasca (Val)., Mastalone (Val). (No. 270, 2 Band S.)

Orbe (No. 97).

Orta.—See Canton of Valais, Italian Valleys

Payerne, by Lausanne (Nos. 96 and 276).

Pfeffers (baths), by Lausanne (Nos. 96 and 63), Berne (No. 79), and Zurich (No. 304), or by Lausanne (Nos. 96 and 223), Soleure (No. 16), Aarau (No. 18), and Zurich (No. 304).

Riffelberg (see Canton of Valais). Route Yod, A. and B.

Righi (The), by Lausanne (Nos. 96 and 63), Berne (Nos. 66, 67, or 68), and Lucerne (Nos. 158 or 159).

Saas, by lake and rail to Sion (Nos. 96, 267, and 270—2), thence to Visp and up the valley (See Canton of Valais, Saas).

Saint Gallen, by Lausanne (Nos. 96 and 63), Berne (No 79), and Zurich (No 196), or by Lausanne (Nos. 96 and 223), Solothurn (No. 16), Aarau (No. 18), and Zurich (No. 196).

Schaffhausen, by Lausanne (Nos. 96 and 63), and Berne (No. 197), or by Lausanne (Nos. 96 and 223).

Solothurn (No. 16), and Aarau (No. 14).

Schwyz, by Lausanne (Nos. 96 and 63), Berne (Nos. 66, 67, or 68), and Lucerne (No. 161).

Simplon, rail to Sion, or by lake to Boveret, rail to Sion (see Sion, Canton of Valais), thence through Brieg to the Hospice. top of Simplon Pass, Domo D'Ossola and Baveno. See Canton of Valais (No. 266).

ROUTE 98.

Sion, rail throughout or by lake to Boveret, thence by rail (see Sion, Canton of Valais), 24½ l. (72¾ m.)

	Leagues.	Miles.
To St. Maurice (No. 94),	16	48
Thence to Sion (No. 74),	8½	24¾
	24½	72¾

Solothurn, by Lausanne (Nos. 96 and 223), or by Lausanne (Nos. 96 and 63), and Berne (No. 75).

Stans (see Canton of Unterwalden).

Thun, by Lausanne (Nos. 96 and 63), and Berne (No. 55).

Trogen, by Lausanne (Nos 96 and 63), Berne (No. 79), Zurich (No. 196). and Saint Gallen (No. 193), or by Lausanne (Nos. 96 and 223), Solothurn (No. 16) Aarau (No. 19), Zurich (No. 196), and Saint Gallen (No. 193).

Unterwalden, by Lausanne (Nos. 96 and 73), Berne (Nos. 66, 67, or 68), and Lucerne (No. 153).

Varallo (see Canton of Valais), Sass, Weiss Thor, and Italian Valleys, Val Sesia, Val Mastalone, and Val Anzasca (270-2, B. and S.)

ROUTE 99.

VEVAY, 15½ L (46½ m.)

	Leagues.	Miles.
Lausanne (No. 96)	10¾	32¼
Lutry	1	3
Cully	1¼	3¾
St. Suphorin	1½	5¼
Vevay	¾	2¼
	15½	46½

ROUTE 97 (2).

Finest panoramic view in Switzerland after the Righi.

	Leagues.	Miles.
Weissenstein (The), by Solothurn (Nos. 16 and 18)	23	69
Solothurn to Weissenstein	3	9
	26	78

Winterthur, by Lausanne (No. 96 and 63), Berne (No. 79), and Zurich (No. 301), or by Lausanne (Nos. 96 and 223), Solothurn (No. 16), Aarau (No. 18), and Zurich (No. 301).

Yverdun (see No. 97).

Zug, by Lausanne (Nos. 96 and 63), and Berne (No. 78).

Zurich, by Lausanne (Nos. 96 and 63), and Berne (No 79). or by Lausanne (Nos. 96 and 223), Solothurn (No. 16), and Aarau (No. 18).

Zurzach, by Lausanne (Nos. 96 and 63), and Berne (No. 167), or by Lausanne (Nos. 96 and 223), Solothurn (No. 16), and Aarau (No. 18).

Routes from Geneva to France, Germany, and Italy.

GERMANY.—From Geneva to—

Baden (Duchy of)
Darmstadt,
Frankfort and the Rhine (by Lausanne).
Berne and Bâle. or by Neuchâtel and Bâle.
To Austria, Bavaria, Suabia, Wurtemberg, by Lausanne, Berne, Olten, Zurich, Romanshorn, the Lake of Constance, and Friedrichshafen; rail, through Berne, Winterthur, or St. Gallen, or Schaffhausen (No. 200).

FRANCE.—To Lyons, by rail, or road, 42 l. (126 m).

To Paris, by rail. through Lyons, Macon, or Pontarlier, or by road.

ITALY.—From Geneva to Turin by rail.

Another Route by the St. Bernard Pass to Aosta (No. 263). and Chatillon, thence to Turin, taking rail at Ivrea.

Distance from Geneva to Chatillon, 40 l. (120 m.)

	Leagues.	Miles.
Chatillon to Donas	4	12
Donas to Ivrea	7	21
Ivrea, by rail, to Turin	11¼	33¾
	32¼	66¾
To Chambery & St. Michel	6¾	20¼
Thence by road to Suza over Mont Cenis, St. André	4	12
Villars Oudin	3	9
Bramant	2	6
Lans-le-bourg	4	12
Aux Tavernettes	3	9
Over Mont Cenis to Novalaise	4	12
Susa	2	6
Rail to Turin	11	33
	39¾	119¼

To Milan, Central and Eastern Italy, by Sion and the Simplon, Canton de Valais, Simplon, Domo d'Ossola, Baveno, Lago Maggiore and Milan (No. 266).

Our fifth main approach (Route E) to Switzerland brings us to Friedrichshafen on the Lake of Constance. This route is the best access for all coming from Central and Southern Germany, and even from the Rhine, if the visitors object be the Grisons and East Switzerland. Friedrichshafen is in Wurtemberg, on the N. of the lake of Constance. 2,000 inhabitants. Hotels: Maison Allemande, splendid view. Hotel Nestle; Crown; King of Bavaria.

Railway: Fares in Florins and Kreutzers.

(1 florin=2 francs 10 cents.)

	1s cl.		2nd cl.		3rd cl.	
	fl.	k.	fl.	k.	fl.	k.
Ulm	4	15 ...	2	51 ...	1	57
Augsburg	7	42 ...	5	9 ...	3	30
Munich	10	12 ...	6	48 ...	4	36
Stuttgardt	8	0 ...	5	15 ...	3	33
Heidelberg	12	27 ...	8	9 ...	5	30
Frankfort	16	0 ...	10	30 ...	7	3

Steam boats: Fares in Florins and Kreutzers.

	1st cl.		2nd cl.	
	fl.	k.	fl.	k.
Every day—Twice to Bregenz ...	1	15 ...	0	51
Do. Four times to Constance...	1	6 ...	0	42
Do. Twice to Lindau	0	57 ...	0	39
Do. Once to Ludwigshafen	1	4 ...	1	12
Do. Twice to Meersburg..........	0	48 ...	0	30
Do. Four times to Romanshorn.	0	33 ...	0	21
Do. Four times to Rorschach...	0	54 ...	0	36

Friederichshafen has developed immensely of late years. Its old name was Buchhorn. Its is now the summer residence of the Royal family of Wurtemberg, who inhabit an old convent, Hofen, founded in 1050 by St. Conrad, Bishop of Constance. Finest view of the Alps from the N. bank of lake is here. It takes in Appenzell, Glarnish, Rhaetikon, Scesaplana, and Vorarlberg. Good pictures of Hess and others in the Castle.

LAKE OF CONSTANCE.

Lacus Brigantinus of the Romans. In the ninth century, Lacus Bodamicus, in German, Boden See. It is easily reached by the Bavarian Railway lines, at Lindan, of Wurtemberg, at Friedrichshafen, and by the Swiss Lines, Zurich-Romanshorn, Zurich, Rorschach, Chur-Rorschach, and Bâle Shaffhausen at Romanshorn, Rorschach, &c. (see *Bradshaw's Continental Railway Guide*). The opening of these lines has led to much activity in the navigation of the lake.

The circuit of the lake is 53 leagues. Its banks are rather flat, but its vast sheet of water, 500 square kilometres, and the Alps seen in the distance give it a grand character. It is 14 l. (Swiss) in length, 3 l. (9 m.) wide between Friedrichshafen and Romanshorn, and is 8 l. sq. less surface than the Lake of Geneva. Height 1,225 feet above the sea. Climate mild. In the last four centuries is has been only five times completely frozen over. Greatest depth between Arbon and Friedrichshafen, 964 ft. Twenty-two steamboats traverse it in all directions, it has also many sailing vessels which carry about 1,500 quintals. The amount of grain and bread entering this way into Switzerland from Germany, may be estimated at 1½ million quintals. Navigation is safe. It is only the Föhn or S.W. wind that blows heavily. Lake well stocked with fish. It has 25 kinds; silures of almost 100lbs., blue salmon, of which 3,000 are taken per day in summer, trout of 40 to 50lb., &c. Salted salmon is a great article of trade. On the Swiss side angling is free, except on Sundays and fête days during Divine Service.

Its waters wash the shore of three Swiss Cantons; 1, Thurgau; 2, Saint Gallen; and 3, Grisons. As Romanshorn, the nearest Swiss terminus opposite Friedrichshafen, is in the Canton of Thurgau, we shall give it a brief notice first, passing thence to Saint Gallen and the Grisons, by Appenzell.

CANTON OF THURGAU.

LIMITS.—To the east, the Lake of Constance; north, the same lake and the Rhine; to the west, the Canton of Zurich; south, Canton of St. Gallen.

AREA, SOIL, CLIMATE.—The area is 41½ square Swiss leagues (370 English square miles). Save in low marshy corners near the lake, its surface consists generally of

78

hills and fertile valleys. It is thickly peopled and very productive; but as the scenery is tame tourists only pass through it. Climate mild, suited to all kinds of crops.

MOUNTAINS.—The mountain ridge of Allmanns, belonging properly to the Canton of Zurich, shades away gradually, into that of Thurgau. No remarkable eminence occurs in the interior.

LAKES, RIVERS, &c.—The Lake of Constance, separates Thurgau from Wurtemberg, Bavaria, and from Baden to the E. and N. There are three other lakes (all small), those of Bichel, Huttwyl, and Huttlingen, only remarkable for being very well stocked with fish.

RIVERS.—1. The Thur gives its name to the Canton and is its principal river, though it does not rise in it, only reaching it at the hamlet of Heidelberg, and passing through it from E. to W., when it issues, from it into that of Zurich. Though swollen with some considerable streams, the Thur is not properly navigable in this Canton.

2. The Murg is formed by the confluence of several streams, of which the most important issues from the Schnabelhorn, it enters the Canton near Anderwyl, the last village on its southern frontier, it is increased by the accession of several streams, and falls into the Thur below Frauenfeld.

3. The Sitter comes from the Cantons of Appenzell and Saint Gallen, enters that of Thurgau near the village of Gotthaus, and joins the Thur near Bischoffzell.

4. The Rhine borders the Canton for some distance on the side of Schaffhausen.

RIVULETS.—Several, but inconsiderable.

AGRICULTURAL AND INDUSTRIAL PRODUCTIONS.—Thurgau has much cattle, and many pigs. Game is plentiful, including hares, foxes (?), badgers, gelinottes, partridges, &c.; fish is caught in abundance. Large crops of cereals are raised, and the vine grown exceeds the consumption. Fruit (especially apples), is so abundant that they make a good deal of cider. Thurgau yields hemp, flax, &c.; it has fine forests, and a little coal. The industrial branches consist in cotton, prints, muslins, silk stuffs.

POPULATION AND RELIGION.—There are 90,000 inhabitants, of whom 68,000 are Protestants, and 20,000 Catholics.

ABBEYS AND CONVENTS.—Some of these are secularised, such as the Capuchin Convent at Frauenfeld. There are chapters of canons of St. Pelagius, at Bischoffzell; an abbey of St. Benedict, at Fischingen; another of Augustinians at Kreutzlingen, and a Chartreuse or Carthusian monastery, at Ittingen. There are five convents at Dänicken, Kalchern, Feldbach, Munsterlingen, and St. Catharinenthal. The three former are, or were, of the Cistercian, the fourth of the Benedictine, and the fifth of Dominicanesses.

EDUCATION AND CHARITIES.—Education is now carefully attended to. There are Latin grammar schools at Frauenfeld, and some other places, but there is no college. There is no general charitable institution: each parish is obliged to support its own poor.

FRAUENFELD.—Pop. 3,900. Hotels: Crown, Falcon, Ox. Post car to Constance every day, in 3½ hours, 3fr. 30c.; to Stein in 2½ hours, 2fr. 75c.; and to Wyl in 2 hours, 2fr. 30c. The town is built on an eminence above the Murg, and was burnt in 1788, being reconstructed on a more regular plan, with broader streets. It has some cotton and silk mills, but the people are principally devoted to agriculture The public buildings are the Hotel d Ville, in which, before 1798, the Diet the Confederation used to meet; the o castle with a tower, built 1,000 years ag the cathedral, &c. Neighbourhood agr able. Many pretty walks, and pleas views of the Alps from the hills, near town. It is now a station on the Zu

Romanshorn railway. You do not change carriages between these two places. Five trains a-day each way.

ROMANSHORN.—Terminus of the Zurich railway. Port on the lake of Constance, landing place for steamers. (Cornu Romanorum.) Hotels: Bodan, Römerhorn, Schwezierhaus, The rails have made the place. Its port is the best on the lake. Steamers three times a day to Bregenz, 2*fr.* 20*c.*; 1*fr.* 95*c.* To Constance, ditto, 1*fr.* 95*c.*; 1*fr.* 30*c.* To Friederichshafen four times a-day, 1*fr.* 20*c.* and 75*c.* To Lindau, three times, 2*fr.* 5*c.*; 1*fr.* 50*c.* To Rorschach, three times, 1*fr.* 50*c.*, and 85*c.* A telegraphic wire passes under the lake to Friedrichshafen.

RAILROADS. — Fares, in Francs and Cents.

From Romanshorn to	1st class.		2nd class.		3rd class.	
	fr.	*c.*	*fr.*	*c.*	*fr.*	*c.*
Bâle	15	50	10	85	7	75
Berne	22	50	15	75	11	25
Fribourg (Swiss)	26	0	18	20	13	0
Geneva	38	10	26	90	19	30
Glarus	15	55	10	90	7	80
Lausanne	32	75	22	95	16	40
Lucerne	15	25	10	65	7	60
Neuchâtel	25	40	17	90	12	85
Schaffhausen	6	45	4	95	3	25
Thun	25	65	17	95	12	85
Vevay	35	0	24	70	17	75
Winterthur	6	0	4	20	3	0
Zug (by Righi)	13	0	9	10	6	50
Zurich	8	75	6	10	4	35

Weinfelden on the Zurich Romanshorn Railway, is the richest place in Thurgau. Hotels: Traube, Krone. Post cars every day to Constance, 1¾ hours, 1*fr.* 60*c.*, and to Wyl, two hours, 1*fr.* 70*c.* The town stands at the foot of the Ottenberg, and is noted for its wines. It has an old castle.

Taking another steamer from Friedrichshafen you reach Rorschach, a port on the Lake of Constance, in the Canton of Saint Gallen, and the nearest way from Germany to the Grisons. Or if coming from East Germany (Vienna, Munich, &c.) the best way is to cross by steamer from Lindau, in Bavaria.

Lindau (3,700 inhabitants) is on the north-east side of the lake, and built on an island, united to the mainland, by a railway bridge and by a wooden bridge, 1,000 feet long. In the middle ages it was a free town, with much trade. Its curiosities are the New Port, Maison de Ville, built 1422; monument of King Maximilian II., by Halbig, prepared at Munich by Miller; Roman walls, &c. Hotels: Bayern, Krone, Gans, Germanischer Hof, Helvetia.

Railways: Fares in Florins and Kreutzers.

	1st cl.		2nd cl.		3rd cl.	
	fl.	*k.*	*fl.*	*k.*	*fl.*	*k.*
Kempten	3	36	2	24	1	36
Augsburg	7	48	5	12	3	30
Munich	10	18	6	51	4	36
Nuremberg	14	42	9	18	6	36
Bamberg	17	6	11	24	7	39
Wurzburg	21	9	14	6	9	27
Leipzig	28	51	20	4	13	51
Dresden	34	6	24	2	16	30
Madgeburg	34	27	23	48	16	10
Berlin	39	56	27	40	19	4

Steamboats: Fares in Florins and Kreutzers.

	1st cl.		2nd cl.	
	fl.	*k.*	*fl.*	*k.*
Every day—Four times for Bregenz	0	21	0	15
Do. Three times for Constance	1	57	1	18
Do. Three times for Friedrichshafen	0	57	0	37
Do. Once for Ludwigshafen	2	39	1	45
Do. Three times for Meersburg	1	42	1	6
Do. Four times for Romanshorn	1	6	0	42
Do. Four times for Rorschach	0	45	0	36

Around Lindau are a multitude of places and walks: to Hoyersberg, ½l. (1½ m.); to Villa Gruber, open Tuesday and Friday; to Villa Am See; to Villa Lenchtenberg; to the Schachenbad, with sulphur springs; to Wasserburg (2,500 inhabitants), with tomb of the composer, Lindpaintner, (+ 1856); to the Steig, Egghalden, Aeschach, &c., &c.

ROUTES FROM FRAUENFELD.

To Aarau, by Zurich (Nos. 245 and 18).

Aarberg, by Zurich (Nos. 245 and 79), and Berne (No. 53), or by Zurich (Nos. 245 and 18), Aarau (No. 16), and Solothurn (No. 216).

Aarburg, by Zurich (Nos. 245 and 18), and Aarau (No. 1).

Aigle, by Zurich (Nos. 245 and 79), and Berne (No. 54), or Thun (No. 255), and the ——— (No. 54).

Altdorf, by Zurich (Nos. 245 and 215), and Schwyz (No 207).

Altstactten, by Saint Gallen (Nos. 185 and 180).

Appenzell (No. 22).

Art, by Zurch (Nos. 245 and 295, or 296), and Zug (No. 281).

Baden, by Zurich (Nos. 245 and 18).

Bâle, by Zurich (No. 245 and 44), or by Schaffhausen (Nos. 190 and 41).

Bellinzona, by Chur (Nos. 127 and 119, or 120), or by Zurich (Nos. 245 and 215), Schwyz (No. 207), and Altdorf (No. 229).

Berne, by Zurich (Nos. 245 and 79).

Bex, by Zurich (Nos. 245 and 79), and Berne (No. 58).

Bienne, by Zurich (Nos. 245 and 79), and Berne No. 59), or by Zurich (Nos. 245 and 18), Aarau (No. 16), and Solothurn (No. 218).

Brougg, by Zurich (Nos. 245 and 298).

Bulle, by Zurich (Nos. 245 and 79), and Berne (No. 54).

Burgdorf, by Zurich (Nos. 245 and 18), and Aarau (No. 18); or, after Zurich, by the Route (No. 302) to Morgenthal, and (No. 6) to Kirchberg, and thence to Burgdorf.

Chamouni, by Zurich (Nos. 245 and 79), Berne (No. 63), Lausanne (No. 96), and Geneva (No. 95), or by Zurich (Nos. 245 and 18), Aarau (No. 16), Solothurn (No. 223), Lausanne (No. 96), and Geneva (No. 95).

Chaux de Fonda, by Zurich, Aarau, and Solothurn (same routes as above, and 220).

Chiavenna, by Chur (Nos. 127, 121, 122, or 123).

Chur (No. 127).

ROUTE 240.

CONSTANCE, 5 l. (15 m.)

	Leagues.		Miles.
Fäwen	¾		2¼
Pfyn	½		1½
Mühlheim	¾		2¼
Heffenhausen	1		3
Waldi	¾		2½
Constance	1¼		3¾
	5		15

Einsiedeln, by Zurich (Nos. 245 and 299, or 300).

Engelberg, by Zurich (Nos. 245 and 160), and Lucerne (No. 153).

Fribourg, by Zurich (Nos. 245 and 79), and Berne (No. 54), or by Zurich (Nos. 245 and 18), Aarau (No. 16), and Solothurn (No. 221).

Gais, by St. Gallen (Nos 185 and 186).

Geneva, by Zurich (Nos. 245 and 79), Berne (No. 63), and Lausanne (No. 96), or by Zurich, Aarau, Solothurn, and Lausanne (see Chamouni, further back. Glarus (No. 109).

ROUTE 241.

HERISAU, 7 l. (21 m.)

	Leagues.		Miles.
Mazingen	1		3
Schönenberg	½		1½
Munchwyl	½		1½
Wyl 2¼ l. (8¼ m.)	¾		2¼
Burenbrucke	1¼		4
Niederwyl	¾		2¼
Gossau	¾		2¼
Herisau	1¼		3¾
	7		21

Hofwyl, by Zurich (Nos. 245 and 302).

Lauffenbourg, by Zurich (Nos. 245 and 303).

Lausanne by Zurich (Nos. 245 and 79), and Berne (No. 63), or by Zurich (Nos. 245 and 18), Aarau (No. 16), and Solothurn (No. 223).

Locarno, by Chur (Nos. 127 and 119, or 120), and Bellinzona (No. 232), or by Zurich, Schwyz, and Altdorf.

Locle, by Zurich (Nos. 245 and 18), Aarau (No. 16), and Solothurn (No. 221).

Loesch (Baths), by Zurich (Nos. 245 and 79), and Berne (No. 65), or from Berne to Sion (No. 74), and thence to Loesch (No. 26-), or by Thun (No 253), and the Simmenthal (No. 55).

Lucerne, by Zurich (Nos. 245 and 160).

Lugano, by Chur (No 127 and 119, or 120), and Bellinzona (No. 233), or by Zurich, Schwyz, and Altdorf.

ROUTE 242.

LEICHTENSTEIG, 6¾ l. (20¼ m.)

	Leagues.		Miles.
Wyl (No. 241)	2¾		8¼
Rikenbach	½		1½
Gonzenbach	1¾		5¼
Butschwyl	1		3
Diefurt	½		1¾
Liechtensteig	½		1¼
	6¾		20¼

Mendrisio, by Chur (Nos. 127 and 119, or 120), and Bellinzona (No. 235), or by Zurich, Schwyz, and Altdorf.

Morat, Morges, and Moudon, by Zurich and Berne, or by Zurich, Aarau, and Solothurn. (See those different routes).

Neuchâtel, by Zurich (Nos. 245 and 18), Aarau (No. 16), and Solothurn (No. 178), or by Zurich (Nos. 245 and 79), and Berne (No. 79).

Orbe, by Zurich (Nos. 245 and 18), Aarau (No. 16), Solothurn (No. 178), and Neuchâtel (No. 97), or by Zurich and Berne.

Payerne, by Zurich (Nos. 245 and 79), and Berne (No. 77), or by Zurich, Aarau, Solothurn, and Morat.

Piexers (Baths), by St. Gallen (Nos. 185 and 188).
Righi (Mount), by Zurich (Nos. 245 and 215), and
   Schwyz (No. 212).
Saint Gallen (No. 185).

ROUTE 243.

SCHAFFHAUSEN, 5½ L. (16½ m).

	Leagues.	Miles.
Horgenbach	1	3
Usslingen	½	¾
Dietingen	½	1½
Neuforn	½	2½
Schlatt	1½	4½
Schaffhausen	1½	4½
	5½	16½

Schwyz, by Zurich (Nos. 245 and 225).
Sion, by Zurich (Nos. 245 and 79) and Berne (Nos.
   73 and 74), or by Zurich (Nos. 245 and 18),
   Aarau (No. 16), and Solothurn (No. 227), or
   Lucerne (No 160). Thun (No. 255), and the
   Simmenthal (No 65).
Thun, by Zurich (Nos. 245 and 79), and Berne,
   (No. 55).
Trogen, by St. Gallen (Nos. 185 and 183).
Unterwalden, by Zurich (Nos. 245 and 160), and
   Lucerne (No. 153).
Vevay, by Zurich (No. 245 and 79), and Berne (No
54), or by Lucerne (No. 160), Thun (No. 255), and
the Simmenthal (No. 55).

ROUTE 244.

WINTERTHUR, 2¾ L (8¼ m.)

	Leagues.	Miles.
Islikon	1	3
Ober-Winterthur	1½	3¾
Winterthur	¼	1½
	2¾	8¼

Yverdun, by Zurich (Nos. 245 and 79), and Berne
   (No. 77), or by Zurich (No. 245 and 18), Aarau
   (No. 16), and Solothurn (No 228).
Zug, by Zurich (Nos. 245 and 295, or 296.)

ROUTE 245.

ZURICH, 6¾ L. (20¼ m.)

	Leagues.	Miles.
Winterthur (No. 244)	2¾	8¼
Zurich (No. 196)	4	12
(or by rail).		
	6¾	20¼

ROUTE 246.

ZURZACH, 12½ L. (37½ m.)

	Leagues.	Miles.
Schaffhausen (No. 243)	5½	16½
Zurzach (No. 14)	7	21
	12½	37½

Or by Zurich (Nos. 245 and 305, or 306,)

To Germany. Augsburg, Munich, and Ulm, through
Romanshorn. The Rhine, Stuttgardt, and
Frankfort, do. The Rhine, Strasburg, and
Paris, through Schaffhausen, and Bâle. Lyons,
Piedmont, and Geneva, through Zurich, Berne,
and Geneva. Milan and Italy, by Chur, or by
Schwyz, Altdorf, and Bellinzona.

The traveller bound from Bavaria and
Central Germany to the Grisons, takes the
steamer from Lindau to Rorschach, which
brings him first to the

CANTON OF ST. GALLEN,

Northern limits, Thurgau and the Lake
of Constance. Western, the Lakes of
Zurich, Schwyz, and Glarus; south, the
Grisons; east, the same; and the Vorarlberg (in Austria).

AREA, SOIL, AND CLIMATE.—The surface of this Canton is 104½ square Swiss
leagues, and consists generally of fertile
plains and cultivated hills. Nevertheless
it has several high mountains, especially
in its southern and south-western parts,
where they rise to the High Alps. These
higher ridges are, in fact, nothing more
or less than the continuation of the Alps
of the Grisons and Appenzell, and are for
the most part covered with glaciers. Their
highest points are the Hohenkasten, the
Hohenmessmer, the Sentis, the Kuhfirsten,
the Speer, &c. In these uplands the
climate is severe most of the year, but in
the north and east of the Canton, it is temperate and favourable not only to the
cultivation of cereals and fruits, but even
to vine culture.

MOUNTAINS.—These have been named
in the last section.

LAKES, RIVERS, AND RIVULETS.—
1. The Lake of Constance which does
not properly belong to the Canton of St.
Gallen, but bathes a strip of it from Alt-
Rhein to Steinach.

2. The Lake of Zurich. Only a portion
of the S. W. extremity of this lake
enters a little way into the territory of
St. Gallen.

3. The Lake of Wallenstadt, extends E. and W. to a length of 4 l. (12 m.,) from Wallenstadt to Wesen. Its greatest width does not exceed 1 l. (3 m.,) but its depth is very considerable, (600 feet). The north side of the lake consists almost entirely of a precipitous wall of lofty rocks, furrowed with watercourses, sparkling with waterfalls, and descending sheer into the lake, giving no landing place, and rendering the navigation at certain times dangerous. It was thus that in December 1850, a steamer overtaken by a squall, sunk with 15 passengers under the rock of Batlis, near the N. E. end of the lake. The only landing places on the north side are Quinten and Mühlehorn. Accordingly it is on the south side that the railway from Zurich to Chur by Wesen and Ragatz has been carried. In summer, the winds on the lake are tolerably regular; but since the finishing of the Railway there are no steamers on this lake, which is one of the wildest and sternest of these among the Alps.

The three lakes of Murg· are situated at top of the Murg Alp, 4 l. (12 m.) South of the Lake of Wallenstadt. Many trout are caught in them, but they are generally covered with ice till far in the summer.

RIVERS.—1. The Rhine borders this Canton throughout its Eastern frontier. 2. The Tamin or Tamina issuing from the Kalfeuserthal, passes by Pfeffers Baths and falls into the Rhine, near Ragatz. 3. The Thur issues from several sources near Wildhaus, in the district of Toggenburg, through which it flows, entering the Canton of Thurgau, near Bischoffzell. 4. The Sitter descends from the Hohen Säntis, flows through the Ausser Rhoden, in the Canton of Appenzell, and unites with the Thur near Bischoffzell. 5. The Necker or Neckar, also issuing from the Hohen Säntis, also joins the Thur near Lutisburg. 6. The Glatt, rises similarly in the Canton of Appenzell and in Toggenburg; it also joins the Thur *near Ober-Buren.* 7. The Sees issues

from the Kalfeuserthal, and falls into the lake of Wallenstadt. 8 and 9. The Godach and the Steinach both rise in the Canton of Appenzell; the former rises near Trogau, and falls into the Lake of Constance, near Horn, the latter, coming from the Vögelisegg, falls into the same lake, near Steinach. 10. The Lint comes from the Canton of Glarus, and forms the frontier of St. Gallen, Glarus and Schwyz, from Ziegelbrucke to the Lake of Zurich into which it falls.

RIVULETS.—The Saar, the Schilzbach, the Steinibach, are a few out of many others.

AGRICULTURAL PRODUCTIONS, MANUFACTURES.—This Canton breeds a great many cattle, horses, sheep, goats, and pigs; it has also many bees. Fish are caught in abundance, and the sportsman may find a good deal of game here, hare white partridges, gelinottes, and even chamois, but the rocky parts of the mountains are the resort of vultures, and other birds of prey. The soil is generally fertile in St. Gallen, yielding cereals of all kinds, fruit, vegetables, and wine. It has fine meadows and vast forests. Among its mineral productions, may be remarked calcareous schist, coal, crystal saltpetre, and mineral springs. The people prepare great quantities of cheese and dairy produce; and they manufacture linen, embroidered muslins, &c., having many power looms, bleaching grounds and glass works, at Mels.

HOT SPRINGS, &c.—The Baths of Pfeffers are widely known, both on account of their efficacy and their wild and singular situation. The waters have their source, a temperature of 30° Reaumur. Other baths occurring in this Canton, are those of St. Margaret, Balgach, Humelwald, Kobelwies, Ennetbuhl, &c. They are in less repute.

POPULATION AND RELIGION.—The present population of this Canton is 180,000. 5-9ths of the population are Catholic, 4-9ths are Protestants, the former most

conservative, the latter radicals. Hence, as the two parties are numerically nearly even, there are warmer discussions here than in most parts of Switzerland.

ABBEYS AND CONVENTS.—Four of men, 11 of women. The Abbey of St. Gallen, and a convent at Schännis have been suppressed.

EDUCATIONAL AND CHARITABLE INSTITUTIONS.—Most of the villages have fair schools; in the towns they are good, and especially that of Altstaetten. Those who aspire to higher studies, attend the College of St. Gallen. Literary and scientific associations are rather numerous in this Canton. Each parish is bound to support its poor, and vary according to the local means. Savings' banks and benefit societies exist, but no great charities, the good people appearing to prefer to dispute in cafés about the *summum bonum*, rather than adopt practical measures of immediate utility and indisputable charity.

SURVEY OF THE CANTON.

Calfeuser or *Kalfeuserthal*. See *Pfëffers*.

Pfëffers (Bad).—The position of this place in a mere rent in the lofty perpendicular rocks is striking and rather awful. Great improvements have been made in the Bathing establishments since the days when patients were let down by ropes to be drenched and ducked, and exposed to a kind of kill-or-cure treatment, which if they survived, they were dragged up again to life and liberty. The present buildings are enlarged, but the place is gloomy enough to bore you to death, and most prefer to take the waters at Ragatz, whither they are now conducted by pipes. Nevertheless, the place is well worth a visit, though every door you pass through (of which many seem useless, except for extortion), costs a douceur, and something more.

The bath house is situated at the bottom of a deep ravine, shut in by lofty, wall-like rocks, through which the impetuous Tamina has cut its way, and rushes along in its headlong course. It

is only in the heart of the summer that the sun penetrates into this desolate spot, and then only from 11 a.m. to 3 p.m. But though these baths present few attractions to the gay, and are rather repulsive in position and character, they are frequented by crowds on account of their efficacy, and probably, al-o, of the beauty and sublimity of the neighbouring scenery. The hot spring is 700 feet from the bath establishment, in a sort of cavern. Charge for entrance, 1*fr.* (Height of Pfëffers Baths above the sea, 2,110 feet; above Ragatz, 510 feet. The bath house was built in 1701, has 140 rooms, can hold 300 patients, has 23 baths of which 4 are common). In summer the springs furnish 1,500 pots a-day. In winter very little. The water is tasteless, colourless, and clear as crystal. Good in scrofula, rheumatism, stomach and nerve complaints, old wounds, &c. It was discovered by hunters in 1038, and the first bath was built by Abbot Hugh II. In some places the two walls of rock enclosing the ravine, approach so near, at a height of 80 or 100 feet, that you can step over. A new valuable spring was discovered, October 2nd, 1860. You can go back to Ragatz, by a path leading to the top of the rocks, ¾ l. (2¼ m.), or immediately behind the baths, by the Beschluss, to the village of Pfëffers, the Kalfeuserthal and the Col of Gungel. Distance from Ragatz, directly up the Tamina Gorge, to the baths, 1 l. (3 m.)

The Calfeuserthal, near Pfëffers is described by Alpine Clubmen, as one of the finest in the Alps, fit to compete with Val Anzasca. The best way to reach it is from the hotel of Ragatz to the village of Pfëffers, thence on, above the Tamina, to Tschenner, Teuf, and Väson, 2½ l. (7½ m.) by the left side of the gorge, or by the right to Vadura, 2 l. (6 m.) and near Monte Luna, 4,737 feet. Vättis is 3½ l. (10½ m.) from Ragatz, at the foot of the Drachenberg. Hence to the right you can reach Reichenau, by Gungel, 6½ l. (19½ m.), or by the right to Martinsfal you can pass

3. The Lake of Wallenstadt, extends E. and W. to a length of 4 l. (12 m.,) from Wallenstadt to Wesen. Its greatest width does not exceed 1 l. (3 m.,) but its depth is very considerable, (600 feet). The north side of the lake consists almost entirely of a precipitous wall of lofty rocks, furrowed with watercourses, sparkling with waterfalls, and descending sheer into the lake, giving no landing place, and rendering the navigation at certain times dangerous. It was thus that in December 1830, a steamer overtaken by a squall, sunk with 15 passengers under the rock of Batlis, near the N. E. end of the lake. The only landing places on the north side are Quinten and Mühlehorn. Accordingly it is on the south side that the railway from Zurich to Chur by Wesen and Ragatz has been carried. In summer, the winds on the lake are tolerably regular; but since the finishing of the Railway there are no steamers on this lake, which is one of the wildest and sternest of these among the Alps.

The three lakes of Murg· are situated at top of the Murg Alp, 4 l. (12 m.) South of the Lake of Wallenstadt. Many trout are caught in them, but they are generally covered with ice till far in the summer.

RIVERS.—1. The Rhine borders this Canton throughout its Eastern frontier. 2. The Tamin or Tamina issuing from the Kalfeuserthal, passes by Pfeffers Baths and falls into the Rhine, near Ragatz. 3. The Thur issues from several sources near Wildhaus, in the district of Toggenburg, through which it flows, entering the Canton of Thurgau, near Bischoffzell. 4. The Sitter descends from the Hohen Säntis, flows through the Ausser Rhoden, in the Canton of Appenzell, and unites with the Thur near Bischoffzell. 5. The Necker or Neckar, also issuing from the Hohen Säntis, also joins the Thur near Lutisburg. 6. The Glatt, rises similarly in the Canton of Appenzell and in Toggenburg; it also joins the Thur near Ober-Buren. 7. The Seez issues from the Kalfeuserthal, and falls into the lake of Wallenstadt. 8 and 9. The Goldach and the Steinach both rise in the Canton of Appenzell; the former rises near Trogau, and falls into the Lake of Constance, near Horn, the latter, coming from the Vögelisegg, falls into the same lake, near Steinach. 10. The Linth comes from the Canton of Glarus, and forms the frontier of St. Gallen, Glarus, and Schwyz, from Ziegelbrucke to the Lake of Zurich into which it falls.

RIVULETS.—The Saar, the Schilzbach, the Steinibach, are a few out of many others.

AGRICULTURAL PRODUCTIONS, MANUFACTURES.—This Canton breeds a great many cattle, horses, sheep, goats, and pigs; it has also many bees. Fish are caught in abundance, and the sportsman may find a good deal of game here, hares, white partridges, gelinottes, and even chamois, but the rocky parts of the mountains are the resort of vultures, and other birds of prey. The soil is generally fertile in St. Gallen, yielding cereals of all kinds, fruit, vegetables, and wine. It has fine meadows and vast forests. Among its mineral productions, may be remarked calcareous schist, coal, crystals, saltpetre, and mineral springs. The people prepare great quant.ties of cheese and dairy produce; and they manufacture linen, embroidered muslins, &c., having many power looms, bleaching grounds, and glass works, at Mels.

HOT SPRINGS, &c.—The Baths of Pfeffers are widely known, both on account of their efficacy and their wild and singular situation. The waters have at their source, a temperature of 30° Reaumur. Other baths occurring in this Canton, are those of St. Margaret, Balgach, Hummelwald, Kobelwies, Ennetbuhl, &c. They are in less repute.

POPULATION AND RELIGION.—The present population of this Canton is 180,000, 5-9ths of the population are Catholics, 4-9ths are Protestants, the former mostly

conservative, the latter radicals. Hence, as the two parties are numerically nearly even, there are warmer discussions here than in most parts of Switzerland.

ABBEYS AND CONVENTS.—Four of men, 11 of women. The Abbey of St. Gallen, and a convent at Schännis have been suppressed.

EDUCATIONAL AND CHARITABLE INSTITUTIONS.—Most of the villages have fair schools; in the towns they are good, and especially that of Altstaetten. Those who aspire to higher studies, attend the College of St. Gallen. Literary and scientific associations are rather numerous in this Canton. Each parish is bound to support its poor, and vary according to the local means. Savings' banks and benefit societies exist, but no great charities, the good people appearing to prefer to dispute in cafés about the *summum bonum*, rather than adopt practical measures of immediate utility and indisputable charity.

SURVEY OF THE CANTON.

Calfeuser or *Kalfeuserthal.* See *Pfëffers.*

Pfëffers (Bad).—The position of this place in a mere rent in the lofty perpendicular rocks is striking and rather awful. Great improvements have been made in the Bathing establishments since the days when patients were let down by ropes to be drenched and ducked, and exposed to a kind of kill-or-cure treatment, which if they survived, they were dragged up again to life and liberty. The present buildings are enlarged, but the place is gloomy enough to bore you to death, and most prefer to take the waters at Ragatz, whither they are now conducted by pipes. Nevertheless, the place is well worth a visit, though every door you pass through (of which many seem useless, except for extortion), costs a douceur, and something more.

The bath house is situated at the bottom of a deep ravine, shut in by lofty, wall-like rocks, through which the impetuous Tamina has cut its way, and rushes along in its headlong course. It

is only in the heart of the summer that the sun penetrates into this desolate spot, and then only from 11 a.m. to 3 p.m. But though these baths present few attractions to the gay, and are rather repulsive in position and character, they are frequented by crowds on account of their efficacy, and probably, also, of the beauty and sublimity of the neighbouring scenery. The hot spring is 700 feet from the bath establishment, in a sort of cavern. Charge for entrance, 1*fr.* (Height of Pfëffers Baths above the sea, 2,110 feet; above Ragatz, 510 feet. The bath house was built in 1701, has 140 rooms, can hold 300 patients, has 23 baths of which 4 are common). In summer the springs furnish 1,500 pots a-day. In winter very little. The water is tasteless, colourless, and clear as crystal. Good in scrofula, rheumatism, stomach and nerve complaints, old wounds, &c. It was discovered by hunters in 1038, and the first bath was built by Abbot Hugh II. In some places the two walls of rock enclosing the ravine, approach so near, at a height of 80 or 100 feet, that you can step over. A new valuable spring was discovered, October 2nd, 1860. You can go back to Ragatz, by a path leading to the top of the rocks, ¾ l. (2¼ m.), or immediately behind the baths, by the Beschluss, to the village of Pfëffers, the Kalfeuserthal and the Col of Gungel. Distance from Ragatz, directly up the Tamina Gorge, to the baths, 1 l. (3 m.)

The Calfeuserthal, near Pfëffers is described by Alpine Clubmen, as one of the finest in the Alps, fit to compete with Val Anzasca. The best way to reach it is from the hotel of Ragatz to the village of Pfëffers, thence on, above the Tamina, to Tschenner, Teuf, and Väson, 2½ l. (7½ m.) by the left side of the gorge, or by the right to Vadura, 2 l. (6 m.) and near Monte Luna, 4.737 feet. Vättis is 3½ l. (10½ m.) from Ragatz, at the foot of the Drachenberg. Hence to the right you can reach Reichenau, by Gungel, 6½ l. (19¼ m.), or by the right to Martinsfal you can

3. The Lake of Wallenstadt, extends E. and W. to a length of 4 l. (12 m.,) from Wallenstadt to Wesen. Its greatest width does not exceed 1 l. (3 m.,) but its depth is very considerable, (600 feet). The north side of the lake consists almost entirely of a precipitous wall of lofty rocks, furrowed with watercourses, sparkling with waterfalls, and descending sheer into the lake. giving no landing place, and rendering the navigation at certain times dangerous. It was thus that in December 1850, a steamer overtaken by a squall, sunk with 15 passengers under the rock of Batlis, near the N. E. end of the lake. The only landing places on the north side are Quinten and Mühlehorn. Accordingly it is on the south side that the railway from Zurich to Chur by Wesen and Ragatz has been carried. In summer, the winds on the lake are tolerably regular; but since the finishing of the Railway there are no steamers on this lake, which is one of the wildest and sternest of these among the Alps.

The three lakes of Murg· are situated at top of the Murg Alp, 4 l. (12 m.) South of the Lake of Wallenstadt. Many trout are caught in them, but they are generally covered with ice till far in the summer.

RIVERS.—1. The Rhine borders this Canton throughout its Eastern frontier. 2. The Tamin or Tamina issuing from the Kalfeuserthal, passes by Pfeffers Baths and falls into the Rhine, near Ragatz. 3. The Thur issues from several sources near Wildhaus, in the district of Toggenburg, through which it flows, entering the Canton of Thurgau, near Bischoffzell. 4. The Sitter descends from the Hohen Säntis, flows through the Ausser Rhoden, in the Canton of Appenzell, and unites with the Thur near Bischoffzell. 5. The Necker or Neckar, also issuing from the Hohen Säntis, also joins the Thur near Lutisburg. 6. The Glatt. rises similarly in the Canton of Appenzell and in Toggenburg; it also joins the Thur near Ober-Buren. 7. The Sees issues

from the Kalfeuserthal, and falls into the lake of Wallenstadt. 8 and 9. The Goldach and the Steinach both rise in the Canton of Appenzell; the former rises near Trogau, and falls into the Lake of Constance, near Horn, the latter, coming from the Vögelisegg, falls into the same lake, near Steinach. 10. The Linth comes from the Canton of Glarus, and forms the frontier of St. Gallen, Glarus, and Schwyz, from Ziegelbrucke to the Lake of Zurich into which it falls.

RIVULETS.—The Saar, the Schilzbach, the Steinibach, are a few out of many others.

AGRICULTURAL PRODUCTIONS, MANUFACTURES.—This Canton breeds a great many cattle, horses, sheep, goats, and pigs; it has also many bees. Fish are caught in abundance, and the sportsman may find a good deal of game here, hares, white partridges, gelinottes, and even chamois, but the rocky parts of the mountains are the resort of vultures, and other birds of prey. The soil is generally fertile in St. Gallen, yielding cereals of all kinds, fruit, vegetables, and wine. It has fine meadows and vast forests. Among its mineral productions, may be remarked calcareous schist, coal, crystals, saltpetre, and mineral springs. The people prepare great quant.ties of cheese and dairy produce; and they manufacture linen, embroidered muslins, &c., having many power looms, bleaching grounds, and glass works, at Mels.

HOT SPRINGS, &c.—The Baths of Pfeffers are widely known, both on account of their efficacy and their wild and singular situation. The waters have at their source, a temperature of 30° Reaumur. Other baths occurring in this Canton, are those of St. Margaret, Balgach, Hummelwald, Kobelwies, Ennetbuhl, &c. They are in less repute.

POPULATION AND RELIGION.—The present population of this Canton is 180,000, 5-9ths of the population are Catholics, 4-9ths are Protestants, the former mostly

conservative, the latter radicals. Hence, as the two parties are numerically nearly even, there are warmer discussions here than in most parts of Switzerland.

ABBEYS AND CONVENTS.—Four of men, 11 of women. The Abbey of St. Gallen, and a convent at Schännis have been suppressed.

EDUCATIONAL AND CHARITABLE INSTITUTIONS.—Most of the villages have fair schools; in the towns they are good, and especially that of Altstaetten. Those who aspire to higher studies, attend the College of St. Gallen. Literary and scientific associations are rather numerous in this Canton. Each parish is bound to support its poor, and vary according to the local means. Savings' banks and benefit societies exist, but no great charities, the good people appearing to prefer to dispute in cafés about the *summum bonum*, rather than adopt practical measures of immediate utility and indisputable charity.

SURVEY OF THE CANTON.

Calfeuser or *Kalfeuserthal.* See *Pfëffers.*

Pfëffers (Bad).—The position of this place in a mere rent in the lofty perpendicular rocks is striking and rather awful. Great improvements have been made in the Bathing establishments since the days when patients were let down by ropes to be drenched and ducked, and exposed to a kind of kill-or-cure treatment, which if they survived, they were dragged up again to life and liberty. The present buildings are enlarged, but the place is gloomy enough to bore you to death, and most prefer to take the waters at Ragatz, whither they are now conducted by pipes. Nevertheless, the place is well worth a visit, though every door you pass through (of which many seem useless, except for extortion), costs a douceur, and something more.

The bath house is situated at the bottom of a deep ravine, shut in by lofty, wall-like rocks, through which the impetuous Tamina has cut its way, and rushes along in its headlong course. It is only in the heart of the summer that the sun penetrates into this desolate spot, and then only from 11 a.m. to 3 p.m. But though these baths present few attractions to the gay, and are rather repulsive in position and character, they are frequented by crowds on account of their efficacy, and probably, also, of the beauty and sublimity of the neighbouring scenery. The hot spring is 700 feet from the bath establishment, in a sort of cavern. Charge for entrance, 1fr. (Height of Pfëffers Baths above the sea, 2,110 feet; above Ragatz, 510 feet. The bath house was built in 1701, has 140 rooms, can hold 300 patients, has 23 baths of which 4 are common). In summer the springs furnish 1,500 pots a-day. In winter very little. The water is tasteless, colourless, and clear as crystal. Good in scrofula, rheumatism, stomach and nerve complaints, old wounds, &c. It was discovered by hunters in 1038, and the first bath was built by Abbot Hugh II. In some places the two walls of rock enclosing the ravine, approach so near, at a height of 80 or 100 feet, that you can step over. A new valuable spring was discovered, October 2nd, 1860. You can go back to Ragatz, by a path leading to the top of the rocks, ¾ l. (2¼ m.), or immediately behind the baths, by the Beschluss, to the village of Pfëffers, the Kalfeuserthal and the Col of Gungel. Distance from Ragatz, directly up the Tamina Gorge, to the baths, 1 l. (3 m.)

The Calfeuserthal, near Pfëffers is described by Alpine Clubmen, as one of the finest in the Alps, fit to compete with Val Anzasca. The best way to reach it is from the hotel of Ragatz to the village of Pfëffers, thence on, above the Tamina, to Tschenner, Teuf, and Väson, 2½ l. (7½ m.) by the left side of the gorge, or by the right to Vadura, 2 l. (6 m.) and near Monte Luna, 4,737 feet. Vättis is 3¼ l. (10½ m.) from Ragatz, at the foot of the Drachenberg. Hence to the right you can reach Reichenau, by Gungel, 6¼ l. (19¼ m.), or by the right to Martinsfal you can go

3. The Lake of Wallenstadt, extends E. and W. to a length of 4 l. (12 m.,) from Wallenstadt to Wesen. Its greatest width does not exceed 1 l. (3 m.,) but its depth is very considerable, (600 feet). The north side of the lake consists almost entirely of a precipitous wall of lofty rocks, furrowed with watercourses, sparkling with waterfalls, and descending sheer into the lake. giving no landing place, and rendering the navigation at certain times dangerous. It was thus that in December 1830, a steamer overtaken by a squall, sunk with 15 passengers under the rock of Batlis, near the N. E. end of the lake. The only landing places on the north side are Quinten and Mühlehorn. Accordingly it is on the south side that the railway from Zurich to Chur by Wesen and Ragatz has been carried. In summer, the winds on the lake are tolerably regular; but since the finishing of the Railway there are no steamers on this lake, which is one of the wildest and sternest of these among the Alps.

The three lakes of Murg· are situated at top of the Murg Alp, 4 l. (12 m.) South of the Lake of Wallenstadt. Many trout are caught in them, but they are generally covered with ice till far in the summer.

RIVERS.—1. The Rhine borders this Canton throughout its Eastern frontier. 2. The Tamin or Tamina issuing from the Kalfeuserthal, passes by Pfeffers Baths and falls into the Rhine, near Ragatz. 3. The Thur issues from several sources near Wildhaus, in the district of Toggenburg, through which it flows, entering the Canton of Thurgau, near Bischoffzell. 4. The Sitter descends from the Hohen Säntis, flows through the Ausser Rhoden, in the Canton of Appenzell, and unites with the Thur near Bischoffzell. 5. The Necker or Neckar, also issuing from the Hohen Säntis, also joins the Thur near Lutisburg. 6. The Glatt, rises similarly in the Canton of Appenzell and in Toggenburg; it also joins the Thur near Ober-Buren. 7. The Sees issues from the Kalfeuserthal, and falls into the lake of Wallenstadt. 8 and 9. The Goldach and the Steinach both rise in the Canton of Appenzell; the former rises near Trogau, and falls into the Lake of Constance, near Horn, the latter, coming from the Vögelisegg, falls into the same lake, near Steinach. 10. The Linth comes from the Canton of Glarus, and forms the frontier of St. Gallen, Glarus, and Schwyz, from Ziegelbrucke to the Lake of Zurich into which it falls.

RIVULETS.—The Saar, the Schilzbach, the Steinibach, are a few out of many others.

AGRICULTURAL PRODUCTIONS, MANUFACTURES.—This Canton breeds a great many cattle, horses, sheep, goats, and pigs; it has also many bees. Fish are caught in abundance, and the sportsman may find a good deal of game here, hares, white partridges, gelinottes, and even chamois, but the rocky parts of the mountains are the resort of vultures, and other birds of prey. The soil is generally fertile in St. Gallen, yielding cereals of all kinds, fruit, vegetables, and wine. It has fine meadows and vast forests. Among its mineral productions, may be remarked calcareous schist, coal, crystals, saltpetre, and mineral springs. The people prepare great quant.ties of cheese and dairy produce; and they manufacture linen, embroidered muslins, &c., having many power looms, bleaching grounds, and glass works, at Mels.

HOT SPRINGS, &c.—The Baths of Pfeffers are widely known, both on account of their efficacy and their wild and singular situation. The waters have at their source, a temperature of 30° Reaumur. Other baths occurring in this Canton, are those of St. Margaret, Balgach, Hummelwald, Kobelwies, Ennetbuhl, &c. They are in less repute.

POPULATION AND RELIGION.—The present population of this Canton is 180,000, 5-9ths of the population are Catholics, 4-9ths are Protestants, the former mostly

conservative, the latter radicals. Hence, as the two parties are numerically nearly even, there are warmer discussions here than in most parts of Switzerland.

ABBEYS AND CONVENTS.—Four of men, 11 of women. The Abbey of St. Gallen, and a convent at Schännis have been suppressed.

EDUCATIONAL AND CHARITABLE INSTITUTIONS.—Most of the villages have fair schools; in the towns they are good, and especially that of Altstaetten. Those who aspire to higher studies, attend the College of St. Gallen. Literary and scientific associations are rather numerous in this Canton. Each parish is bound to support its poor, and vary according to the local means. Savings' banks and benefit societies exist, but no great charities, the good people appearing to prefer to dispute in cafés about the *summum bonum*, rather than adopt practical measures of immediate utility and indisputable charity.

SURVEY OF THE CANTON.

Calfeuser or *Kalfeuserthal.* See *Pfëffers.*

Pfëffers (Bad).—The position of this place in a mere rent in the lofty perpendicular rocks is striking and rather awful. Great improvements have been made in the Bathing establishments since the days when patients were let down by ropes to be drenched and ducked, and exposed to a kind of kill-or-cure treatment, which if they survived, they were dragged up again to life and liberty. The present buildings are enlarged, but the place is gloomy enough to bore you to death, and most prefer to take the waters at Ragatz, whither they are now conducted by pipes. Nevertheless, the place is well worth a visit, though every door you pass through (of which many seem useless, except for extortion), costs a douceur, and something more.

The bath house is situated at the bottom of a deep ravine, shut in by lofty, wall-like rocks, through which the impetuous Tamina has cut its way, and rushes along in its headlong course. It is only in the heart of the summer that the sun penetrates into this desolate spot, and then only from 11 a.m. to 3 p.m. But though these baths present few attractions to the gay, and are rather repulsive in position and character, they are frequented by crowds on account of their efficacy, and probably, also, of the beauty and sublimity of the neighbouring scenery. The hot spring is 700 feet from the bath establishment, in a sort of cavern. Charge for entrance, 1*fr.* (Height of Pfëffers Baths above the sea, 2,110 feet; above Ragatz, 510 feet. The bath house was built in 1701, has 140 rooms, can hold 300 patients, has 23 baths of which 4 are common). In summer the springs furnish 1,500 pots a-day. In winter very little. The water is tasteless, colourless, and clear as crystal. Good in scrofula, rheumatism, stomach and nerve complaints, old wounds, &c. It was discovered by hunters in 1038, and the first bath was built by Abbot Hugh II. In some places the two walls of rock enclosing the ravine, approach so near, at a height of 80 or 100 feet, that you can step over. A new valuable spring was discovered, October 2nd, 1860. You can go back to Ragatz, by a path leading to the top of the rocks, ¾ l. (2¼ m.), or immediately behind the baths, by the Beschluss, to the village of Pfëffers, the Kalfeuserthal and the Col of Gungel. Distance from Ragatz, directly up the Tamina Gorge, to the baths, 1 l. (3 m.)

The Calfeuserthal, near Pfëffers is described by Alpine Clubmen, as one of the finest in the Alps, fit to compete with Val Anzasca. The best way to reach it is from the hotel of Ragatz to the village of Pfëffers, thence on, above the Tamina, to Tschenner, Teuf, and Väson, 2½ l. (7½ m.) by the left side of the gorge, or by the right to Vadura, 2 l. (6 m.) and near Monte Luna, 4,737 feet. Vättis is 3½ l. (10½ m.) from Ragatz, at the foot of the Drachenberg. Hence to the right you can reach Reichenau, by Gungel, 6½ l. (19½ m.), or by the right to Martinsfal you can pass

Morges and Moudon, by Zurich (Nos. 196 and 79), and Berne (No. 63). You can also follow the Routes of Zurich (Nos. 196 and 18), Aarau (No. 16), and Solothurn (No. 228).

Neuchâtel, by Zurich (Nos. 196 and 79), and Berne (No. 79), or by Zurich (Nos. 196 and 18), Aarau (No. 16), and Solothurn (No. 178).

Orbe, by Zurich (Nos. 196 and 79), and Berne (No. 71), or by Zurich (Nos. 196 and 18), Aarau (No. 16), Solothurn (No. 178), and Neuchâtel (No. 97).

Payerne, by Zurich (Nos. 196 and 79), and Berne (No. 77), or by Zurich (Nos. 196 and 18), Aarau (No. 16), and Solothurn (No. 228).

ROUTE 188.

PFÄFFERS (Baths), 19½ l. (58½ m.)

	Leagues.		Miles
Ragatz (No. 181)	17½	......	52½
Valens	1½	......	4½
Pfäffers	½	......	1½
	19½		58½

ROUTE 189.

RAPPERSCHWYL, 15¼ l. (45¾ m.)

	Leagues.		Miles.
Usnach (No. 183)	11½	......	34½
Schmerikon	1¼	......	3¾
Wurmspach	1½	......	4½
Rapperschwyl	1	......	3
	15¼		45¾

Righi (The), by Schwyz (Nos. 191 and 212).

ROUTE 190.

SCHAFFHAUSEN (by rail), see St. Gallen (town), and Schaffhausen (town), or post road, 13½ l. (40½ m.)

	Leagues.		Miles.
Frauenfeld (No. 185)	8	......	24
Horgenbach	1	......	3
Usslingen	¼	......	¾
Dietigen	½	......	1½
Neuforn	¾	......	2¼
Schlatt	1½	......	4½
Schaffhausen	1½	......	4½
	13½		40½

ROUTE 191.

SCHWYZ, 23½ l. (70½ m.)

	Leagues.		Miles.
Altendorf (No. 183)	14¾	......	44¼
Pfäffikon	1¼	......	3¾
Richtenschwyl	1½	......	4½
Schindellegi	1	......	3
Rothen-Thurm	2½	......	7½
Sattel	½	......	1½
Steinen	1	......	3
Seewen	½	......	1½
Schwyz	½	......	1½
	23½		70½

Sion, by Zurich (Nos. 196 and 79), and Berne (Nos. 73 or 74), or by Chur (Nos. 181 and 185).

Solothurn, by Zurich (Nos. 196 and 18), and Aarau (No. 16).

Stanz, see Unterwalden.

ROUTE 192.

STEIN (am Rhein), 11 l. (33 m.)

	Leagues.		Miles.
Frauenfeld (No. 185)	8	......	24
Wart	1	......	3
Huttwyler	1	......	3
Stein	1	......	3
	11		33

Thun, by Zurich (Nos. 196 and 79), and Berne (No. 55), or Lucerne (No. 160), and Meyringen (No. 255).

ROUTE 193.

TROGEN, 2 l. (6 m.)

	Leagues,		Miles.
Speicher	1	......	3
Trogen	1	......	3
	2		6

Unterwalden, by Schwyz (Nos. 191 and 213).

Vevay, by Zurich (Nos. 196 and 79), and Berne (No. 54); or by Zurich (No. 196), Lucerne (No. 160), Thun (No. 255), and the Simmenthal (No. 55).

ROUTE 194.

WALLENSTADT, 19½ l. (58½ m.)

	Leagues.		Miles.
Sargans (No. 181)	16½	......	49½
Halbmeil	1½	......	4½
Berchis	¾	......	2¼
Wallenstadt	¾	......	2¼
	19½		58½

Winterthur, by rail or post road (Nos. 160 or 196).

Yverdun, by Zurich (Nos. 196 and 79), and Berne (No. 77); or by Zurich (Nos. 196 and 18), Aarau (No. 16), and Solothurn (No. 228).

ROUTE 195.

ZUG, 22½ l (67½ m.)

	Leagues.		Miles.
Richtenschwyl (No. 191)	17½	......	52½
Wädenschwyl	¾	......	2¼
Horgen	1	......	3
Sihlbrucke	1¾	......	5¼
Baar	¾	......	2¼
Zug	¾	......	2¼
	22½		67½

ROUTE 196.

Zurich, by rail see Zurich, (town) and St. Gallen (town), or by post road, 14 L. (42 m.)

	Leagues.	Miles.
Munchwyl (No. 185)	6	18
Dutwyl	1	8
Aadorf	¼	1½
Elg	¼	1½
Räterschen	1¼	3½
Winterthur	¼	2¼
Tös	¼	¼
Breite	¼	2¼
Bassersdorf	¼	2¼
Rieden	¼	2¼
Wallisellen	¼	¼
Schwammendingen..............	¼	¼
Zurich	1	3
	14	42

Zurzach, by Zurich (Nos. 196 and 305, or 306)

Milan and Italy, by Chur.

Wurtemberg and North Germany, by Rorschach and Lindau, or Friedrichshafen.

The Rhine, Strasburg, and Paris, by Zurich and Bâle, or Rorschach and Friedrichshafen.

Lyons and South France, by Zurich, Berne, and Geneva.

Closely connected with St. Gallen is the

CANTON OF APPENZELL.

LIMITS.—This Canton, being enclosed on all sides by that of Saint Gallen, has no other frontier, and though seldom visited is a charming pastoral Alpine land, full of various attractions.

AREA, SOIL, AND CLIMATE.—The area of the Canton of Appenzell is 19½ Swiss square leagues (420 square kilometres). The surface is very various, as it is almost throughout intersected by mountains of different elevations, and by valleys, generally narrow, and in certain places very deep. In the southern part of the Canton appear a few summits that may be classed with the high Alps, culminating in the Geyrenspitz (part of Mount Sentis), and the Hohenkasten (the summit of Mount Kamor). In these higher regions the climate is naturally very severe, while in the lower districts it is milder, though they are generally exposed to the north, for which, and other reasons, they are but little adapted to agriculture.

MOUNTAINS.—The Alps of Appenzell consist principally of three chains of mountains running from east to west, and surrounding the Canton almost entirely on three sides. The slope of Mount Sentis is covered with a glacier, its highest point, the Geyrenspitz or Gyrspitz, is 7,670 feet above the sea, and the Hohenkasten, the summit of Mount Kamor, is 5,418 feet above the Mediterranean. The view from the summit of both is delightful, but the ascent is in both cases rather difficult, and used to be considered even dangerous.

LAKES, RIVERS, AND RIVULETS.—The largest lake in the Canton is called See-Alp, it has a length of one league (three miles), and a width of a quarter of a league (three-quarters of a mile). It is very deep, and well stocked with excellent trout. The small tarns, such as the Fahler and Sätmis Lakes, hardly deserve to be noticed.

RIVERS.—The Sitter is a tributary of the Thur, and flows through the Cantons of Appenzell, St. Gallen, and Thurgau or Sentis. It rises in the chain of the high Säntis, the highest mountain chain of north-eastern Switzerland. Its sources converge from all the lateral glens, and constitute the main stream in the depth of the valley.

The division of the Canton, ca...ed the Inner Rhode, is only the upper basin of the Sitter, in which the stream originates in a variety of rivulets. This basin is about three German square miles in area, walled round on all sides by mountains covered with pastures to their summits. The dwellings of the men of Appenzell are dispersed all over this basin; villages only occur here and there. There are said to be only six in the whole state. In the middle of the basin stands the main village—Appenzell.

The Sitter takes that name at the confluence of three rivulets, which form it near Weissbad. It falls into the Thur near Bischoffszell. The Urnäsch rises on the Schwäg Alp, and falls into the Sitter near the frontier of the Canton. The Goldbach issues from several sources at Trogen, Speicher, and Rohrtobel, and falls into the Lake of Constance, between Rorschach and Horn.

RIVULETS.—The Bärbach, the Schwindibach, the Weisswasser, are the three streams which. uniting at Weissbad, form the Sitter. The Rothbach falls into the same river near the Convent of Wonnenstein.

AGRICULTURE AND INDUSTRY.—Appenzell breeds much cattle of a fine race; the horses are few in number, nor are there many sheep or pigs, but goats are very numerous. The Canton has very little game or poultry, but a fair supply of fish and many bees. Its pastures and meadow land are excellent. The crops of cereals are scanty, and vegetables, as well as fruit, are not very plentiful. This Canton has large forests of fine timber trees; and among its mineral productions we may enumerate sandstone of very fine quality, crystals and mineral springs. A great quantity of cotton goods, cambric muslins, and other very fine muslins, elegantly embroidered, represent the manufacturing produce of the canton.

MINERAL SPRINGS AND COLD BATHS.—There are three springs and baths of mineral waters in the Canton of Appenzell. 1st. Those of Gonten, situated between the village of that name and the town of Appenzell; its waters are sulphureous, vitriolic, and aluminous. 2nd. Another spring is at Weissbad, 1 l. (3 m.) from Appenzell; its waters contain principally carbonate of lime. 3rd. The baths of Waldstadt are 1 l. (3 m.) from Herisau; its waters contain carbonate of lime, iron, and a very little selenite. The village of Gais is more noted than either of the foregoing baths. It is frequented every year by a great number of strangers, as well as natives, who take up their abode there in order to undergo a treatment, consisting of goat's whey diet. *Gais stands* very high, and is 3 l. (9 m.) *from St. Gallen,* 1½ l. (4½ m.) from Alt-

stätten, 2 l. (6 m.) from Trogen and Speicher, 4 l. (12 m.) from Herisau, and 1½ l. (4½ m.) from Weissbad. The principal inn (the Ox) is often unable to accommodate the great influx of visitors, but the inhabitants generally show great willingness to let furnished apartments. In the vicinity of Gais, and within a radius of 1 l. (3 m.), are many charming views, especially the Stoss, ¾ l. (2¼ m.) a spot noted for the defeat of the Austrians, by the men of Appenzell, in June, 1406. Other pleasing walks may be made to the Gabris 1 l. (3 m.); to the Golderstock, 1 l. (3 m.); to the Sommersberg, ¾ l. (2¼ m.)

POPULATION AND RELIGION. — The Canton of Appenzell has now 56,000 inhabitants; its increase during the last thirty years having been only 1,000. Since 1597, the Canton has been divided, politically, into two Rhodes (Rotten or Cohorts), Inner Rhoden and Outer Rhoden.

The Outer Rhode (see next page) of Appenzell is very industrious, giving occupation even to many in the Inner Rhode, and in the Vorarlberg, in Austria. Muslin is the staple of their manufactures. All kinds of handsome and variegated emb .. .ery are prepaired by the women in their ,..cturesque Alpine cottages. Altar cloths, sace. dotal vestments, and corporals are much worked, besides surplices, counterpanes, veils, shawls, turbans, carpets, &c.

The master manufacturers belong many of them to old Swiss familes, and are described as men of enlightened. patriotic, and liberal mind. and of even literary taste and attainment. — (See *Kohl's Alpen Reisen.*)

The people of the Inner Rhode are Catholics, those of the Outer Rhode, Protestants. The former only form four parishes, while thirty fall to the share of the latter.

ABBEYS AND CONVENTS.—Near Appenzell, there is a Monastery of Capuchin friars and a convent of nuns. At Wonnenstein, near Teufen, there is another convent of nuns.

EDUCATIONAL, SCIENTIFIC, AND CHARITABLE INSTITUTIONS.—Until lately education was rather neglected in the Inner Rhode. In the Outer Rhode, free schools

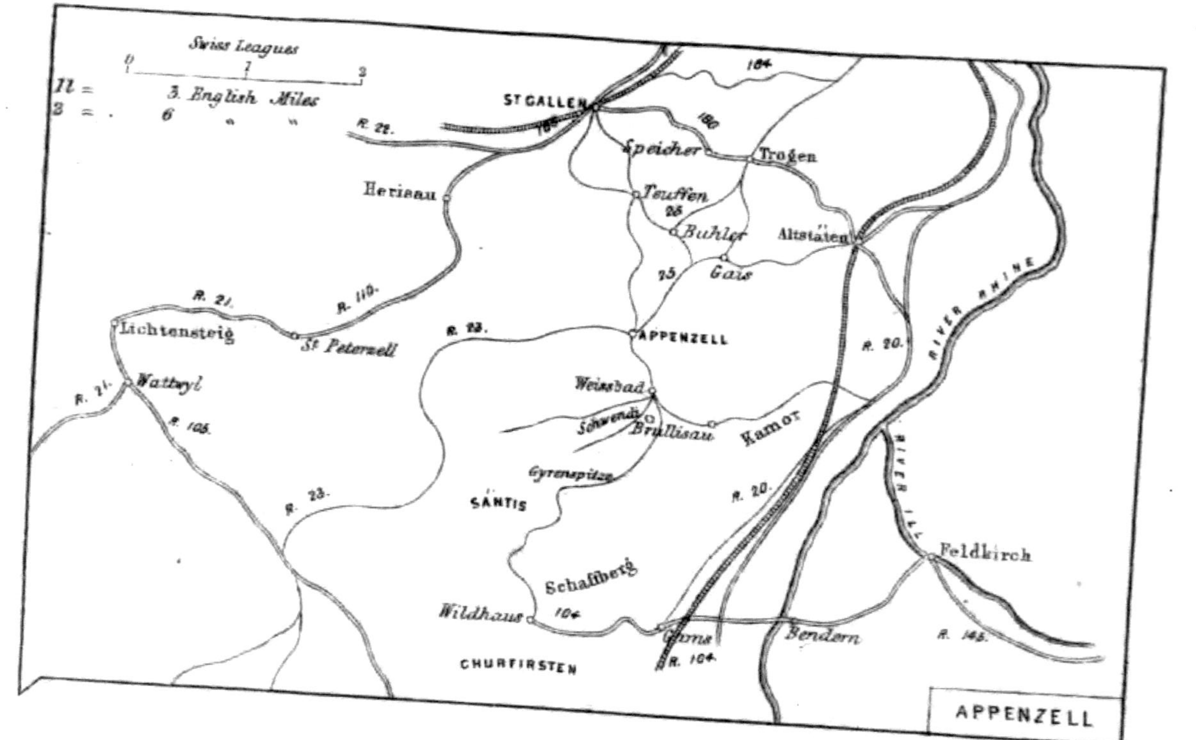

Swiss Leagues
0   1   3
R = 3. English Miles
3 = 6   "   "
R. 22.
ST GALLEN
104
180
Speicher
Trogen
Herisau
Teuffen
26
Buhler
Altstaten
25
Gais
R. 21.
R. 110.
Lichtensteig
St Peterzell
R. 23.
APPENZELL
R. 20.
RIVER RHINE
R. 21.
Wattwyl
Weissbad
R. 105.
Schwendi
Brullisau
Kamor
Gyrenspitze
R. 20.
R. 23.
SÄNTIS
RIVER ILL
Schaffberg
Feldkirch
Wildhaus
104
Gams
Bendern
R. 145.
CHURFIRSTEN
R. 104.
APPENZELL

have been established in almost every parish, where the children are suitably instructed, and Herisau has for many years contained a very fair library. No general charitable institution exists in the Canton. Each parish is bound to take care of its poor; some of them, especially Trogen, have excellent poor-houses, where the paupers of the parish receive suitable support.

POLITICAL DIVISIONS OF THE CANTON. We have seen that this Canton is divided into interior and exterior Rhodes, and the latter is, moreover, subdivided into parishes *this side* and *beyond* the Sitter. Both Rhodes are, absolutely, independent of each other, though they have only one vote in the Diet of the Confederation, and they are both equally democratic in spirit and character.

Ausser, or Outer Rhoden, extends almost to the Rhine and Lake of Constance, and consists of a group of mountains, of 3,000 or 4,000 feet, lying scattered, but nowhere constituting a chain. Their dome-like summits are separated by basins and valleys, whilst the principal towns and villages stand mostly on lower ridges and eminences. There are no long valleys, nor are there any large places. Most of the villages, consisting of handsomly built houses, are inhabited mostly by rich manufacturers. Yet these dwellings combine the advantages and appearance of substantial farms, with city arrangements; hence, these villages, for there are no towns, properly speaking, bear the appearance of towns. The name, Appenzell, is said to be derived from the cell of an Abbot of St. Gallen. The history of the division of the Canton into two Rhodes is curious and interesting; as throughout Switzerland, the Conservative, old Swiss, and Radical new Swiss, elements were nearly balanced, and as they could not well agree, they agreed to differ, and virtually split the Canton into two sub-cantons.—*Alpenreisen, Kohl*, Vol. 2, p. 28.

Of these Rhodes, Fennimore Cooper remarks that : the first (the Exterior Rhode) is the wealthiest, the most industrious, and the most populous; the latter (the Inner Rhode) being purely, I may say eminently, pastoral. Both polities are purely democracies, the people enacting the laws in their original assemblies. This system, however, has some check, but no balance, namely, in the councils, which exercise a species of veto. In the Protestant Rhode, all males of sixteen have a voice, and in the Catholic, all males of eighteen.*

The parishes on both banks of the Sitter, in the Outer Rhode, have an equal vote in the nomination of their magistrates. From this division, it results that there are three capitals to the Canton.

As regards Divine worship and sectarian difference, it is delightfully refreshing, amidst the bigotry and strife of parties, to read that the Catholics and Protestants of Lichtensteig use the same building, resorting to it at different hours.

SURVEY OF THE CANTON.

INNER RHODE.

[The Inner Rhode contains 2½ German square miles, and 12,000 inhabitants. All the little Swiss capitals contain interesting remains of antiquity, and illustrations of national history. Even Appenzell has preserved many German, Austrian, and Italian flags, the trophies of its valiant sons.]

Appenzell.—The two principal inns, are the Lion, the Eagle and the Pike.

[About 2½ miles south-east of Appenzell, is a decent, but unpretending, pension and bathing establishment, call'd Weissbad. The grounds and walks in the vicinity, are charming. The Rössli, is another inn, and if full, there is a third at Schwendi, at an old woman's called Catharine. The Lauenbach Waterfall, 1 l. from Weissbad.]

This little town is neatly built on the Sitte, which is crossed by two covered bridges. It has 3,000 inhabitants, and some trade. Its principal buildings are: the parish Church, which dates back before 1069 and contains some flags taken from the enemy in very ancient battles.

The Hotel de Ville, decorated with the portraits of several of their Landammans, the Arsenal containing a picture of the battle of Stoss. Every year, on the 7th and 8th of May, the legislative assembly of the Catholic population (Landsgemeinde) is held in this borough.

Post car, twice a-day, to St. Gallen, 2½ hours. Fares, 1*fr*. 90*c*.; two-horse carriage, to Weissbad, 18*fr*.

*Excursions in Switzerland, by T. R. Gasparin, vol. I., p. 192.

Excursions near Appenzell.

Kamor (The). To reach this mountain you must pass by Weissbad, and thence proceed by a path called the goat path (Geissweg), to reach the top which bears the name of Hohenkasten, and is 3 l. (9 m.) from Appenzell, commanding a magnificent view. Several paths lead from this mountain to the valley of the Rhine (the Rheinthal).

The name Camor is said to be of Rhaetian derivation. Its elevation is like that of the Righi, adapted to secure both an extensive and a minutely interesting view which is especially directed to the north, embracing the glorious champagne country of St. Gallen, Thurgau, and the Outer Rhode, including the whole area of the Lake of Constance, with the German shores of Wurtemberg and Bavaria. To the east the eye takes in Austrian Tyrol, the whole Valley of the Boden See, the Rhine Valley forming a great curve from the Grisons to the Lake of Constance, while close in front is the little principality of Lichtenstein and the Republic of the Inner Rhode. Behind is the high Santis close at hand with its mighty rocks and masses of ice, and its sides broken into two dark ravines, clothed with fir forests and containing two calm, dark-looking lakes, the Santis See and the See Alp See. The summit of the Kamor is a kind of grassy dome, clothed in summer with gay flowers. The descent to the Rhine Valley is of 4,000 feet, and takes three hours over a very steep and rocky path.*

Sentis (The). This, the highest mountain in the Canton is 8 or 9 l. (24 to 27 m.) from Appenzell, and is reached also through Weissbad, from which three different paths lead to the top of the mountain. These paths are said by some writers to be attended with danger to persons subject to vertigo, but late experience has proved that the difficulties attending Alpine climbing, were rather exaggerated a few years ago. The traveller who does not dread a little fatigue and has a steady head will find ample compensation for all trouble and hardships in the enchanting view he will obtain from the summit.

Wildkirchlein (To). 2½ l. (7½ m.) from Appenzell. The road leads again through Weissbad, and thence by a continual

*The Säntis is 8,280 feet above the sea, and can be ascended in five hours from Weissbad.

ascent by the Bodmenalp to a rough wooden bridge, which crosses a frightful abyss at a height of 250 feet above it. It requires some courage to venture across this bridge, which must be passed to reach Wildkirchlein, which is close at hand. This place is formed by two caverns, one of which encloses a chapel, while the other was lately occupied by a hermit. The view from this place is also very delightful. There is a clean little inn close to the rocks of the Wildkirchlein.

THE OUTER RHODE.—*Beyond the Sitter.*

The Outer Rhode has five square miles. Consists mostly of Alp pasture land, with a population of 44,000 souls. The population is employed in the care of cattle, and also in manufacturing industry.

Herisau.-Hotels: Löwe, Cigogne, Pike. Post twice a-day from St. Gallen to Herisau 1*fr.*; 2 l. (6 m.) Is the handsomest and largest town in the Canton; it contains an orphanage, other good charitable institutions for the poor beyond the Sitter; an arsenal, and a powder mill. Its principal inns are the Pike and the Lion. A considerable trade is carried on at Herisau which has a good many well-built houses and some rather extensive manufactures of cotton. Its most remarkable buildings are the Church with its ancient tower, the orphanage, and the town-house. Fennimore Cooper describes Herisau as a neat and striking little town, in which there is a mixture of the ancient and of the modern Swiss architecture. Manufactures, aided by a fire, have been the parents to the latter. The public square of Herisau, like that of Gais is exceedingly neat and pleasing.

Hohe-Fall, is a pretty cascade 1½ l. (4½ m.) from Appenzell, near the Convent of Wannenstein.

Hundwyl.—Inns: Krone; Ochs; Bär, simple and rustic but good. Is a fine village, the centre of a parish of 1,600 inhabitants, but offering nothing very remarkable except the fact that the council called Landsgemeinde assembles there every two years, the alternate meetings being held at Trogen.

Rosenberg and *Schwänberg* are the ruins of two forts destroyed by the men of Appenzell, standing on a height near the town and offering a very fine view.

This Side the Sitter.

Trogen.—[HOTELS: Schäfli, Krone, Löwe]. Is a pretty town with a greater deal of trade, built at the foot of Mount Gäbris, and containing 3,000 inhabitants. The parish church stands in a handsome platz surrounded by good buildings. The legislative assembly of the Protestant population of the Canton (Landsgemeinde) is held at Trogen and Hundwyl, in alternation, but the criminal trials (Assizes) are held exclusively at the town-house of Trogen. This parish possesses fine charitable institutions.

EXCURSIONS NEAR TROGEN.

Gais lies in one of the little dales into which the country is broken. It presents a very lively "bit of life," and consists of about 100 houses scattered over the lawn-like meadows, with no attention to regularity. They are of various colours, and the church is spacious and white. Naked earth is nowhere visible.

Gais is noted for its whey-cure treatment, in German, Molken Kur; in French, cures de lait or petit lait. The best inn is the Krone, excellently managed, with very good wine de la chartreuse. The Ochs is a good inn. The Rothbach, simpler. Drei Könige, one room per week, 8*fr.* to 10*fr.* Table d'hote, 2 to 2½*fr.* Post car twice a-day from Saint Gallen, 1*fr.* 60*c.* To Appenzell, post starts at noon. Coupé, 90*c.* Interior, 75*c.* From the Alstäetten station, post starts for Gais every evening. Fare, 1*f.* 65*c.* Time, 1h. 25m.

Neither cattle, trees, nor grain, scarcely shrubs are to be seen for miles, the eye rests on nothing but meadows, as closely cut as velvet, houses looking like large boxes laid carelessly on enormous grass carpets, and a road just wide enough, and quite good enough for a park. Gais is 2 l. (6 m.) from Trogen.

o

Gäbris (Mount), is 1 l. (3 m.). from Trogen. Several large châlets are met on the slope of this mountain, which commands admirable views in all directions.

Speicher is rather a well-built village, with a fine new octagonal Church, ½ l. (1½ m.), from Trogen. It was here that the men of Appenzell gained their first victory over the Abbot of Saint Gallen, in 1403. At Vögeliseck, (¼ l.), the Pigeon, Pension, and Kur, with charming views.

Stoss (Am.)—The way up from Alstaetten is very steep for a carriage road. It takes two hours to walk to the summit The views during the ascent are very fine commanding the Rhine valley, a part of Austria, with villages, churches, and châteaux, the Vorarlberg presenting a sublime grouping of dark mountains, with retiring valleys, and in the foreground, neat, verdant fields, dotted with cottages. Am Stoss, is ¾ l. (2¼ m.) from Appenzell. It was here the Appenzellers defeated the Austrians in 1405.

Teuffen is a village 1½ l. (4½ m.), from Trogen, within ¼ l. (¾ m.), of the fine fall of Hohefall, formed by the Rothbach, near the Convent of Wonnenstein, to which we have already alluded.

Hotel et pension des Alpes (propietor, Zürcher), is a milk and whey kur, capitally managed, with a very fine view. Another pension and kur is at the Poste, chez Madame Muller. Besides these, in the town or village, is the Pike Inn, and out of the village, Hotel du Tilleul or the Linde Hotel. Distance from Appenzell village, 1½ l. (4½ m.), from Gais the same. Post car twice a-day from Saint Gallen, 75*c.*

The kur, by goat's whey, is a special feature of the Canton. It is drunk warm. Charge, 6*c.* or 8*c.* a-day. A walk is taken after the draught. It is used for inflammations. Gais, Helden Gonten, and Heinrichsbad, are the most noted places of kur.

ROUTES FROM APPENZELL.

Appenzell to Aarau, by Zurich (Nos. 28 and 18).

Aarburg, by Zurich (Nos. 28 and 18).

Aarau (No. 16), and Solothurn (No. 216), or by Zurich (Nos. 28 and 79), and Berne (No. 89)

Aarburg, by Zurich (Nos. 20 and 18), and Aarau (No. 1).

Aigle, by Zurich (Nos. 28 and 79), and Berne (No. 54).

Altdorf, by Glarus (Nos. 23 and 103).

ROUTE 19.

ALTSTAETTEN, 3 l. (9 m.

	Miles.
Gais	3
Am Stoss	2½
Altstaetten	3¼
	9

Art, by Schwyz (Nos. 26 and 208).

Baden. by Zurich (Nos. 28 and 18).

Bâle, by Zurich (Nos. 28 and 44.)

Bellinzona, by Schwyz (Nos. 26 and 207), and Altdorf (No. 22).

Berne, by Zurich (Nos. 28 and 79).

Bex, by Zurich (Nos. 28 and 79), and Berne (No. 58).

Brougg, by Zurich (Nos. 28 and 278).

Bulle, by Zurich (Nos. 28 and 79), and Berne (No· 54).

Burgdorf by Zurich (Nos. 28 and 18), and Aarau (No. 8): or from Zurich, by the Route (No. 302), to Morgenthal, thence by the Route (No. 6), to Kerchberg, and thence to Burgdorf.

Chamouni, by Zurich (Nos. 28 and 79), Berne (No· 63), Lausanne (No. 96). and Geneva (No. 95) or by Zurich (Nos. 28 and 18), Aarau (No. 16) Solothurn (No. 223), Lausanne (No. 96), and Geneva (No. 95).

Chaux de Fonds, by Zurich (Nos. 28 and 18), Aarau (No. 16), and Solothurn (No. 220), or by Zurich Nos. 28 and 79), Berne (No. 70), and Neuchâtel (No. 169).

Chiavenna by Coire (Nos. 20, and 121, 122, or 123).

ROUTE 20.

COIRE or CHUR, 18¼ L. (55¼).

	Miles.
Alstaetten (No. 19)	9
Sennwald	9
Salez	3
Haag	3
Werdenberg	3
Trubbach	9
Ragatz (14 leagues)	42
Oberzollbrucke	4½
Zizers	1¼
Masans	6
Coire or Chur	¾
	Leagues, 18¼ miles, 55¼

ROUTE 21.

EINSIEDELN, 16¼ L. (48¾ m.)

	Leagues.		Miles.
Hundwyl	1	……	3
Wallstadt	½	……	1½
Schönengrund	½	……	1½
Merschwändl	¾	……	2¼
Peterszell	½	……	1½
Brunnadern	¾	……	2¼
Lichtensteig 5½ L. (16½ m)	1¼	……	4
Wattwyl	½	……	1½
Hummelwald	1	……	3
Bildhaus	½	……	1½
Uznach 9¼ l. (28¼ m.)	2	……	6
Grinau	¼	……	¾
Tuggen	¾	……	2¼
Wangen	1	……	3
Lachen	1	……	3
Altendorf	¾	……	¾
Ezel-Höhe	2¼	……	6¾
Einsiedeln	1¼	……	3¾
	16¼		48¾

Engelberg. by Schwyz (Nos. 26 and 213), and Stans (No. 252).

ROUTE 22.

FRAUENFELD, 9 l. (27 m.)

	Leagues.		Miles.
Hundwyl	1	……	3
Herisau	1	……	3
Gossau	1¼	……	3¾
Niederwyl	¾	……	2¼
Buren	¾	……	2¼
Wyl	1¼	……	4¼
Munchwyl 7 l. (.1 m.)	¾	……	2¼
Mazingen	1	……	3
Frauenfeld	1	……	3
	9		27

Fribourg, by Zurich (Nos. 28 and 79), and Berne (No. 54).

Geneva, by Zurich (Nos. 28 and 79), Berne (No. 63), and Lausanne (No. 96), or by Zurich (Nos. 28 and 18), Aarau (No. 16), Solothurn (No. 223), and Lausanne (No. 96).

ROUTE 23.

GLARUS, 14¾ l.) 44¼ m.)

	Leagues.		Miles.
Uznach (No. 21)	9¼	……	28¼
Kaltbrunn	¾	……	2¼
Schännis	¾	……	2¼
Ziegelbrücke	1½	……	4½
Uznach	½	……	1½
Näfels	½	……	1½
Netstall	½	……	1½
Glarus	¾	……	2¼
	14¾		44¼

Herisau (No. 22).

Hofwyl, by Zurich (Nos. 28 and 30).

Lauffenburg, by Zurich (Nos. 28 and 303).

Lausanne, by Zurich (Nos. 28 and 29), and Berne (No. 63), or by Zurich (Nos. 28 and 18), Aarau (No. 16), and Solothurn (No. 223).

Locarno, by Coire (Nos. 20 and 119, or 120), and Bellinzona (No. 232).

Locle (Au), by Zurich, (Nos. 28 and 218), and Solothurn (No. 224), or by Zurich (Nos. 28 and 79), Berne (No. 70), and Neuchâtel (No. 175).

Loesch (Baths), by Zurich (Nos. 28 and 79), and Berne (No. 65), or by Zurich (Nos. 28 and 18), Aarau (No. 16), Solothurn (No. 227), and Sion (No. 268).

Lucerne, by Schwyz (Nos. 26 and 161).

Lugano, by Coire (Nos. 20 and 119, or 120), and Bellinzona (No. 233).

Mendrisio, by Coire (Nos. 29 and 119, or 120), and Bellinzona (No. 235).

Morat, Morges, and Moudon, by Zurich (Nos. 28 and 79), and Berne (No. 63), or by Zurich (Nos. 28 and 18), Aarau (No. 16), and Solothurn (No. 225).

Neuchâtel, by Zurich (Nos. 28 and 18), Aarau (No. 16), and Solothurn (No. 178), or by Zurich (Nos. 28 and 79), and Berne (No. 76).

Orbe, by Zurich (Nos. 28 and 79), and Berne (No. 71), or by Zurich (Nos. 28 and 18), Aarau (No. 16), Solothurn (No. 178), and Neuchâtel (No. 9).

Payerne, by Zurich (Nos. 28 and 79), and Berne (No. 77), or by Zurich (Nos. 28 and 18), Aarau (No. 6), and Solothurn (No. 223).

ROUTE 24.

PFEFFERS (Baths), 16 l. (48 m.)

	Leagues.	Miles.
Ragatz	14	42
Valens	1½	4½
Pfeffers	½	1½
	16	48

Righi (Monte), by Schwyz (Nos. 26 and 212).

ROUTE 25.

ST. GALLEN, 4 l. (12 m.)

	Leagues.	Miles.
Gais	1	3
Bueler	½	1½
Teufen	1	3
St. Gallen	1½	4½
	4	12

Schaffhausen, by Frauenfeld (Nos. 22 and 190).

ROUTE 26.

SCHWYZ, 20¼ l. (60¾ m.)

	Leagues.	Miles.
Einsiedeln (No. 21)	16½	48¾
Rothen-Thurm	1¼	4
Sattel	¾	1½
Steinen	1	3
Seewen	¼	1¼
Schwyz	¼	1¼
	20¼	60¾

Sion, by Zurich (Nos. 28 and 79), and Berne (Nos. 73 or 74), or by Zurich (Nos. 28 and 18), Aarau (No. 16), and Solothurn (No. 227).

Stanz. See Unterwalden.

Thun, by Zurich (Nos. 28 and 79), and Berne (No. 56).

Trogen, by St. Gallen (Nos. 25 and 193).

Unterwalden, by Schwyz (Nos. 26 and 213).

Vevay, by Zurich (Nos. 28 and 79), and Berne (No. 54), or by Zurich (Nos. 28 and 18), Aarau (No. 16), and Solothurn (No. 227).

ROUTE 27.

WINTERTHUR, 11 l. (33 m.)

	Leagues.	Miles.
Munchwyl (No. 22)	7	21
Dutwyl	1	3
Aadorf	½	1½
Elg	½	1½
Rätschen	1¼	3¾
Winterthur	¾	2¼
	11	33

Yverdun, by Zurich (Nos. 28 and 18), and Berne (No. 77), or by Zurich (Nos. 28 and 18), Aarau (No. 16), Solothurn (No. 179), and Neuchâtel (No. 97).

Zug, by Zurich (Nos. 28 and 295, or 296).

ROUTE 28.

ZURICH, 15 l. (45 m.)

	Leagues.	Miles.
Winterthur (No. 27)	11	33
Törs	¾	¾
Breite	¾	2¼
Bassentorf	¾	2¼
Rieden	¾	2¼
Wallisellen	¾	¾
Schwammedingen	½	¾
Zurich	1	3
	15	45

The principal object in reaching Switzerland by Route E, and in visiting the shores of the Lake of Constance and

Gallen, will be to proceed on to the Grisons and penetrate into the recesses and examine the sublimities and beauties of this great Canton which, though less visited, is scarcely less interesting and far more bracing than the favoured districts of Interlaken, Chamouni, and even Zermatt.

Route E, from Rorschach and St. Gallen brings us direct by rail or road into this Canton, leaving that of Glarus (to be noticed presently) to the W

CANTON OF GRISONS.

(German Graubundten).

LIMITS.—To the E. the Tyrol, to the W. also the Tyrol, the Vorarlberg, and the Cantons of St. Gallen, Glarus, and Uri. to the W. Uri again and Tessin, to the S. Italy.

SURFACE, SOIL, AND CLIMATE —The surface of this Canton comprises 318½ square Swiss leagues (3,080 English square miles). It is almost entirely encompassed and intersected throughout by glaciers and high mountains, forming about sixty valleys of various dimensions. The climate varies according to the position of the valleys (some of which contain the highest villages in Europe) being tolerably mild in those that open to the N.E., whilst it increases in severity as you advance into the S.W. districts.

MOUNTAINS.—The main chains of the highest Alps running through the Grisons follow almost invariably a N.E. and S.W. direction. The first chain you encounter entering the Canton from the N., is the border chain separating the Grisons from St. Gallen, from Glarus, and Uri, and extending from the Calanda to the Crispalt and the St. Gothard. In the southern part of this Canton, there is another chain following almost exactly the same direction and reaching from the Luckmanier, *a mountain* on the S.W. frontier of the *Canton to the Fermunt*, situated on the *borders of the Tyrol.* The latter chain

forms remarkable bends almost throughout its length, and contains among other remarkable peaks and passes, the Luckmanier (5,740 feet on the top of the pass), the Vogelberg. the Bernardin, the Splugen (6,170 feet), the Septimer, the Julier (6,830 feet), the Albula, the Scaletta, the Fluela, and the Piz Linard. To the S. of the Septimer rises the Maloja (5,850 feet), separating the valley of Bergaglia or Bergell, from the Upper Engadin, which is also separated from the Val Poschiavo, by the Bernina, and f.om the district of Bormio, by the Casanna. The latter district is also cut off from the valley of Münster by the Umbrail and the Wörmser Joch. Almost all these colossal mountains are covered with everlasting snow and ice of prodigious thickness. The Bernina in particular is one of the largest and most remarkable glaciers in the Alps, and has latterly attracted considerable attention among foreign scientific travellers, and members of the Alpine Club.

LAKES, RIVERS, AND RIVULETS.—The lakes are numerous, but mostly only mountain tarns in this Canton. The largest is that of Sils, which has a length of 2 l. (6 m.) and a breadth of 1 l. (3 m.); its waters are discharged into the Lake of Silva-plana, which is at a short distance; and the latter communicates with the Lake of St. Moritz. The two latter are smaller than the Lake of Sils. On the Bernina there are three little lakes that discharge their waters into the Poschiavo Lake, which has a length of ¾ l. (2¼ m.) and a breadth of ¼ l. (¾ m.) Another lake near Davos, called the Great Lake, is not larger than the Poschiavo, and the Schwarz See or Black Lake, close at hand, is still smaller. On the Hinzenberg, four little tarns are encountered, called respectively the Luscher, the Comina. the Bischol, and the Alpotta. The first of these has apparently no tributary and no outlet, and may interest adventurous travellers in search of paradoxes. Most of these mountain tarns are well stocked with fish.

RIVERS.—The Rhine rises in this Canton and is composed of the junction of three main branches, fed by the highest glaciers on the frontier of the Grisons. The Hinter-Rhein issues from the Glacier of Baduz, forming a part of the Crispalt, and situated in the highest and remotest part of the valley of Tavätsch, and from a little lake near the St. Gothard. Subsequently it flows through this valley and unites near Dissentis with the Middle Rhine, which proceeds from a little lake situated on the Luckmanier at the bottom of the valley of Madels. After the confluence of these two rivers, the Rhine receives further accessions, at Ilanz of the Glenner, issuing from the glaciers of the valley of St. Pierre, and lastly at Reichenau, the Vorder-Rhein. The latter branch is formed by the union of 12 torrents issuing from the immense glacier, situated at the extremity of the Valley of Rheinwald. This raging torrent cuts its way with perpetual roar of its foaming waters through the deep and dismal chasm of the Viâ Mala, near the Splugen, where it forms a beautiful waterfall, receives near Thusis, the Black Nolla, and is joined a little further on by the Albula. Below Reichenau the Rhine becomes navigable for rafts. At Chur (Coire) it is further augmented by the Plessour and near Mallans by the Landquart, and it ultimately leaves the Canton near Luciensteig.

The Inn issues from the Glacier of the Maloja, in the Upper Engadin, where it is called the Oen. It supplies the Lakes of Sils, Schwarz See, and St. Moritz, receives a number of tributary rivulets in the Upper and Lower Engadin, and enters the Tyrol near Finstermünz. Length of Engadins, 19 l. (57 m.)

The Glenner is formed by the junction of waters flowing from the glaciers of the valley of St. Pierre, and joins the Rhine near Ilanz.

The Albula proceeds from a small and very deep lake, situated above Dörfli, in the Valley of Davos. This river describes a semicircle in its course, and drains the waters of the above valley (Davos), and of Ober-Halbstein: it ultimately falls into the Rhine, near Sils and Thusis.

The Muesa descends from the Bernardin, runs through the valley of Misocco, which it leaves near Roveredo, where it joins the Calancasca, which issues from the Valley of Calanca; beyond Monticello the united waters of these two streams enter the Canton of Tessin.

The Maira takes its source at the Septimer and on the Maloja, runs through the valley of Bergell, and leaves the Canton, near Castasegna.

The Landquart comes from the highest part of the Valley of Prättigau, which it waters throughout its length, and falls into the Rhine, near the bridge of Tardis, not far from Mallans.

RIVULETS.—Among the multitude of torrents and streams that intersect the valleys of this Canton, it will suffice to name the Black Nolla (Schwarz Nolla), separating the valley of Schanns from that of Domleschg; the Savienbach; the Plessour; and the Rabius.

CROPS, INDUSTRY, &c.—The Canton of Grisons has large herds of horned cattle, amounting to above 90,000 head. Sheep, are also abundant, as well as goats and pigs. Fish, game, and poultry are very plentiful. The mountains are not only frequented by rabbits, foxes, chamois, grey and white hares, marmottes, &c.; but even wolves, bears, eagles, vultures, &c., are occasionally met with, especially the latter. The crops consist of wheat, maize, vegetables, potatoes, flax, hemp, &c.; a little wine is obtained and some fruit. Many parts of the Canton are still clothed with magnificent forests, though the axe of the woodman has latterly made sad ravages amongst them. The minerals consist of marble, alabaster, porphyry, serpentine, marl, and clay. Some of the mountains have veins of iron, lead, copper, silver, and gold ore. Nor is the Canton without springs of saline and mineral waters.

As regards industry the manufactures consist of woollen stuffs, cotton and Irish linen; but the principal industrial productions are brandy and cheese. There is also a considerable transport trade through the Grisons from Germany and Switzerland to Italy. Another commercial feature of the country consists in the tendency of the people to emigrate and set up as confectioners in the principal capitals of Europe. This business is often found to be successful, and the exiles ultimately return to their homes with a fair little property.

THERMAL WATERS, BATHS, &c. — No canton of Switzerland contains so many mineral waters as the Grisons, but hitherto they have not been much frequented, at least by the English, because they were deficient in comfortable bathing establishments. The most frequented and valued baths are at St. Moritz, in the Upper Engadin; at Schuls and Zermetz, in the Lower Engadin; at Fideris in the Prattigau; at Alveneu and Malix, in the jurisdiction of Belfort, and at Lurli, near Massans. On the Rabius there is a mineral spring said to be very efficacious in cases of goitres. *

POPULATION AND RELIGION.—The Grisons have a population of 89,840 inhabitants, of whom 51,855 are Protestants, and 38,039 Catholics. In some respects the population of this Canton is the most interesting in Switzerland; as reasons exist that make it probable that they as well as the neighbouring Tyrolese derive their origin at least in part, from the primitive inhabitants of Italy, especially the Etruscans. Some of the first scholars of Germany and of Europe, including Niebuhr, have argued with much ability in favour of this view and the names of a vast number of places, both in the Grisons and the Tyrol seem to point clearly to a

close connection between the early population inhabiting this part of the Alps and the ancient Etruscans. The name given by the German scholars to this early colony of Etruscans in the Alps is that of Rasseni. One German author, Ludwig Steub, traces names of Etruscan derivation in many cantons in the East of Switzerland and does not hesitate to infer that a large part of that country was subject to Etruria. He makes the east of Valais and of the Bernese Oberland and Unterwalden, the west end of this Etruscan territory, which in his opinion extended to the Kamor and Santis in Appenzell. He follows them to the Inn and throughout Tyrol in the east, and takes in the Grisons, Saint Gallen, and Glarus in the centre. In a large part of this territory the language now spoken is Rhoeto-Romance, a corruption of the Latin comparable to the Provençal. This tongue was evidently imposed on the people by the Romans, but the primitive names of rivers, mountains, &c., throughout the district are of different origin, and are thought to be Etruscan. The strange intermixture of German, Rhoeto-Romance, and Italian in many of the valleys of the Grisons, dwelt on by Kohl, is the result of the conflict of races in these Alpine territories in the dark and middle ages. Instances of these names of Etruscan derivation occasionally adopted and transformed by Roman influence in the Rhoeto-Romance, are presented in the Rhine, said to be derived from Etruscan names, Reunus and Rionchus. Again a multitude of places beginning with Ver, are referred to this origin. Thus Vern is a glacier in the Tyrolese German. This gave rise to Verona, to Verniol near Mels in St. Gallen, and Vermuna in the Vorarlberg.

Vet, is found in Vetisa near Pfäffers Baths; Vetan or Vetana, in the Engadin, and Vazerol or Vatural near Brienz in Grisons.

Tut, Tat, Tet, and *Tit*, are found in Dödi in Glaris, Titlis in Unterwalden, and Zuz or Tutisa in Engadin.

* St. Moritz is a recently established bathing place near the Lake of Silva-plana in the Julier Pass. *See Julier* under "Peaks and Passes of the Rhoetian Alps."

Tum, gives the Tamina river in St. Gallen, Tumunisa or Tamins on the Vorder-Rhein and Tomils in Domleschg.

Thu, is seen in Thusis and Dissentis.

Thal Thalna, was an Etruscan Goddess, and we find her name in Thalas near Tussis.

The root Tar occurring in Tarquiniæ the capital of Etruria is found in Tarsol on the Tamina in St. Gallen and Tertschein in the Upper Inn Thal.

Suth is found at Suss in the Engadin, and even in the eminent family of Salis of military repute. Sadurna also occurs on the Vorder-Rhein.

Pur gives Poschiavo, the Brenta, Pardisla near Maienfeld, Brienz-Purnisalisa, the valley of Prättigau, &c.

The root Ar is found in Arusa-Arosa near Davos. Arduna now Dardin occurs near Dissentis, and Ardez in Engadin. In the latter name we find again the Etruscan Au as it was originally. Augadin and the river Inn was known to the Romans as the Ænns. Lastly all names connected with Alp, such as the Albula are referred to an Etruscan root.

It will be seen from these specimens which may be greatly multiplied that there is some ground for the belief that there was a connection between the Grisons and Etruria. But the evidence of the influence of Roman sway as detected in the existing Rhoeto-Romance language is much stronger. The noted traveller Kohl,* has examined this matter closely, and shewn the near affinity of the Rhoeto-Romance to the Latin. (Also Professor Diez of Bonn.)

ABBEYS AND CONVENTS.—These consist chiefly of the chapter of canons at Coire, and of that at Poschiavo or Puschlaf, where there is also a convent of nuns; another convent occurs at Münster. A Monastery of Benedictines is established at Dissentis, and one of Dominicans at Katsis.

* Alpen Reisen, ubi supra,

EDUCATIONAL, SCIENTIFIC AND CHARITABLE INSTITUTIONS.—Education has not been very zealously promoted in this Canton, and is confined in the villages to elementary schools which are only attended in the winter. In the towns the educational establishments are more regularly organised, and Coire possesses, besides a primary school, a very good Lyceum (the Cantonal School of the Protestants), and a Latin School for the Catholics.

LIBRARIES.—These are the Town Library at Coire; that of the Lyceum; private collections, and the Literary Society.

CHARITY.—Every parish is obliged to provide for the wants of its sick and poor. Chur has some well-regulated charitable institutions. It also possesses an Economical Society, deserving especial notice, founded in 1778, extinct for a time, and revived in 1804, when its organisation was remodelled.

POLITICAL DIVISIONS OF THE GRISONS. Politically the Grisons used to form almost as many republics as villages and valleys. They were called Hochgerichte, but the smaller ones have been suppressed since 1848. In fact, the Grisons present a miniature picture of the whole Switzerland. The Canton is divided into 150 valleys, and in the struggle of the people against the barons, who once possessed 186 castles, of which the ruins remain, they formed Bunds or Confederations. The chief of these Bunde are three in number. 1st. The Bund des Gotteshauses. 2nd. Ober, or Graue Bund, so called from the grey cloth prepared in that district. 3rd. The Bund of the Zehn Gerichte, or Ten Jurisdictions. The first was founded A.D. 1396; the Graue Bund, A.D. 1424; the third, 1428 to 1436. In 1748 the three Bunde agreed to form a common Confederacy. Analysing the Canton according to these three Bunde, we find—

I. That the Gotteshaus Bund has eleven Superior jurisdictions (Hochgerichte), forming the east part of the Canton, peopled mostly by a Romantsch race, and containing Chur or Coire, the capital, Reichenau, Poschiavo, Sta. Maria in the Münsterthal, and Soglio. This Bund comprises the two Engadins. In the Upper Engadin, occur Bevers, Samaden, Silva-plana, and St. Moritz. In the Unter Engadin, are Lavin, Martinsbrucke, Schmols, Siss, and Tarasp (once the residence of the Dietrichstein family).

II. The Graue Bund has eight superior jurisdictions, and mostly a Romantsch population. Its principal boroughs are Dissentis, Ilanz, and Thusis.

III. The Zehngerichte Bund, with seven superior jurisdictions. This forms the north centre of the Canton, and is mostly peopled by Germans. It contains Davos, Fideris, Mayenfeld and Seewis, the birthplace of Salis, the historian (+ Dec. 26, 1762), Klosters, and other places.

SURVEY OF THE CANTON OF GRISONS.

Adula (Group). See Peaks and Passes of the Rhoetian Alps.

Alveneu (Romantsch Alvanova), situated on a steep slope, on the route from Chur to Pontè, in the Engadin by Tiefenkasten, 15 l. (45 m.) It is reached from Lenz by a path along the Albula, passing the ruins of Belfort (destroyed in 1499, belonging to the Barons of Vatz) and through the hamlet of Surava, under the Piz St. Michel, Piz d'Aela, Piz d'Err, Cima da Flix, and Piz d'Uertsch. Alveneu has a handsome Church, with the remains of an ancient altar, in sculptured wood. A very fine view is obtained from the Chapel of St. Anthony.

Alveneu (Baths), ½ l. (1½ m.) from Alveneu village (Romantsch. Igl Boign), has been known for four centuries on account of its cold sulphur springs (6° Reaumur). It is a rustic establishment, with 45 rooms. Ask for vin du pays, and inquire after the price of everything. *A little church near* commemorates the plague of 1629. The vegetation around is very rich. Distance from Chur, 5 hours 45 minutes.

Arosa, a pastoral idyllic district, consisting of a plateau, near the Schanfig Valley and Sattel Alp, reached from Chur by the Plessur. Arosa is 6,208 feet high, and the highest spot, except the Engadins, where potatoes are grown. It is on the west side of the Welsch Tobel. Fair quarters to be had at the house of Obman Told. Several interesting excursions may be made from Arosa, attractive to geologsts and botanists. You can pass h-nce by the Alveneuer Alp (a difficult path) to Alveneu, 7 l. (21 m.) Passes by the Welsch Tobel.

Other routes from Alveneu:—

(a) West, by Lake of Schwelli, Aaroser Schaf Aélpli Belle Bleise (8,200 feet), and the Parpan Rothhorn (8,930 feet), to Parpan, 7 l. (21 m.) Hard day.

(b) By Alp of Brienz and Sandhubel, fine view (8,515 feet), volcanic aspect, through Altein Pass to Wissen, 6 l. (18 m.)

(c) By Aélpli, of Maienfeld and Fürkli, two hours, to Kummerhubel, porphyry country, Frauenkirch and the Davos Thal, four hours.

Bergel (The) or Bregaglia, is a narrow valley rising in terraces, watered by the Maira, or Mera, and forming the south-west approach to the Maloja Pass into Italy, of which it in some degree enjoys the climate. Its population is distinctly Italian. Length of valley from Maloggia to Chiavenna 8 l. (24 m.), six of which leagues belong to Switzerland, and two to Italy. Distance from Samaden to Chiavenna, by Bergel, 11¼ l. (33¾ m.) Post car every morning, 9fr. 5c. Road passes Silva-plana, Sils (5,531 feet), Maloggia, Casaccia (Mr. Maier, schoolmaster, keeps the inn), Vicosoprano (inn, Crown), Stampa (Post Inn), Promontogno (Hotel Galleria, Ganzoni's, well kept), Castasegna (2,216 feet, inns—Poste and Alla Liberia), Swiss frontiers, Plurs, the Aqua Fraggia Cascade, and Chiavenna. From Val

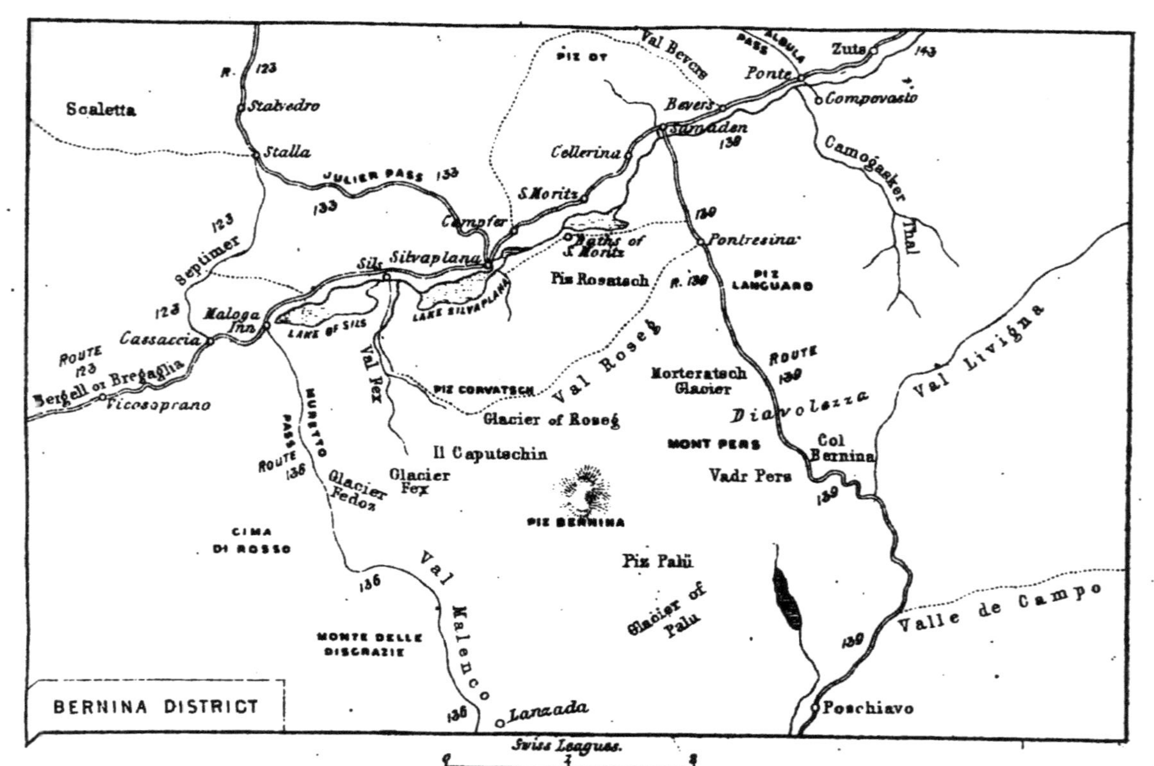

BERNINA DISTRICT
Scaletta
R. 123
Stalvedro
Stalla
Septimer
123
JULIER PASS 133
133
Campfer
Sils Silvaplana
PIZ OT
Val Bevers
ALBULA PASS
Zuts
143
Ponte
Compovasio
Bevers
Samaden
138
Camogasker Thal
Cellerina
S. Moritz
Baths of S. Moritz
Pontresina
130
Piz Rosatsch
R. 130
PIZ LANGUARD
LAKE SILVAPLANA
Maloga Inn
Cassaccia
LAKE OF SILS
Val Fex
Val Roseg
Morteratsch Glacier
ROUTE 130
Val Livigna
ROUTE 123
Bergell or Bregaglia
Vicosoprano
123
MURETTO PASS
PIZ CORVATSCH
Glacier of Roseg
Diavolezza
ROUTE 136
Glacier Fedoz
Il Caputschin
Glacier Fex
MONT PERS
Col Bernina
Vadr Pers
139
CIMA DI ROSSO
PIZ BERNINA
Piz Palü
136
Val Malenco
Glacier of Palu
Valle de Campo
MONTE DELLE DISGRAZIE
139
136
Lanzada
Poschiavo
Swiss Leagues.
0   1   2

gel, fine views to be
alachina, one point
the other 7,976 feet

h inn, at Landame-
e.ta), 408 Protestant
ts on the Albula
Ponte, 1.389 metres
ands at the entrance
, with Romantsch
metres), by which
esch (3,417 metres),
metres), and descend
the Engadin (three
ergüu to Filisur and
., through Bergüner-
ke Viâ Mala. Road
rock, on right bank
t above it, 1¾ hours
ur. Carriage road
ar road.
leagues from Sama-
sina (6,308 feet), on
od wine, decent ac-
good centre for Val
sch Glacier. &c. See
the Rhœtian Alps."
4 feet, highest peak
a great group, south
ey. First ascended
urs; descent, 8.
, ¾ l. (2¼ m.) from
d of the Engadin, is
base of a precipice
The schoolmaster,
ollections of plants
nt excursions to Val
le Suvretta, by the

—Chez Lanz), 1,776
f routes over Septi-
es. Routes hence,
urs, mule path; and
3 hours, mule path.
y Col de la Vailetta
netres), or by Furkel
d Val Avers, through
e highest hamlet in
very modest inn, kept
l (*Germ. Hundeloch*;

inn—Chez Salis), fine waterfal's, Aversbach, by Val Ferrara or Avers, to Hinter-
Rhein at Andeer.

Second route, by Col de la Furkel, descent in 1 hour to old deserted inn of
Septimer (2,300 metres), and in 2 hours
to Casaccia.

Bonaduz, a covered bridge behind Reichenau, leads to this place, called Beneduces, in the middle ages, and standing
at the entrance of the delightful valley of
Domleschg. Hotels: De Giacomi, Crown.
The population of Bonaduz is Catholic.

Bormio, or Worms (Baths of), in a
delightful neighbourhood in the Valtelline, between the Stilfzer Joch and the
Lake of Como. The new baths are a magnificent establishment, with room for 100
bathers. For prices, climate, &c., see
" Peaks and Passes of the Rhoetian Alps."
Elevation, 4,460 feet ancient bath, and
4,125 modern. Distance from Col de
Bormio, 4 l.; Bormio to Sondrio, 12½ l.
Diligence every day at 11 a.m. Sondrio
to Colico, on Lake of Como, 7½ l., twice
a-day, in 4½ hours, 5½ fr., all included.

Bormio (Town), ¾ l. (2¼ m.), from the
baths. Dismal, quaint, old fashioned
Italian town. Burnt, 1855. Fine fresco
in church of the Crucifix, Strada Combo.
See " Peaks and Passes of the Rhoetian
Alps."

Bormio (Col of), or Wörmser Joch.
Highest good turnpike road in Europe,
between Engadin at Schuls and Valtellina,
leading to Chiavenna and the Lake o
Como. Elevation, 8,242 feet The Bormio is the ancient pass. The more modern
pass of Stelvio, or Stilfzer Joch, is 9,177
feet high. It was constructed by Donegani, in 1825, by order of the Austrian
government, and is called a " marvellous
road." Route.

English Miles from Bormio.

	Miles.
Santa Maria ...	10¼
Trafoi	9
Prad	8
Mals	8¼
	38

d'Ordlegna, near Bergel, fine views to be had by ascending Salachina, one point 7,671 feet (1½ hour), the other 7,976 feet in 3 hours.

Bergün (Romantsch inn, at Landamman's, or Mayor's Cloeta), 408 Protestant Romantsch inhabitants on the Albula Pass from Chur to Ponte, 1,389 metres above the sea. It stands at the entrance of the Val Tuors, with Romantsch village Latsch (1,600 metres), by which you can ascend Piz Kesch (3,417 metres), and Piz Uertsch (3,273 metres), and descend thence to Ponte in the Engadin (three hours). Road from Bergün to Filisur and Chur leads by Albula, through Bergünerstein, a wild gorge like Viâ Mala. Road made in 1696, cut in rock, on right bank of the Albula, 600 feet above it, 1¼ hours from Filisur, 9 to Chur. Carriage road to Chur; to Ponte, car road.

Bernina (Inn), three leagues from Samaden, two from Pontresina (6,308 feet), on the Bernina Pass, good wine, decent accommodation; very good centre for Val Diavolezza, Morteratsch Glacier, &c. See " Peaks and Passes of the Rhoetian Alps."

Bernina (Piz) 13.294 feet, highest peak of Grisons, centre of a great group, south of the Engadin Valley. First ascended 1851. Ascent, 12 hours; descent, 8.

Bevers (5,264 feet), ¾ l. (2¼ m.) from Samaden, at the head of the Engadin, is a rich village, at the base of a precipice called Cresta Mora. The schoolmaster, Krättli, sells good collections of plants and minerals. Pleasant excursions to Val de Bevers and Val de Suvretta, by the Giop Alp, to Moritz.

Bivio, or Stalla (inn—Chez Lanz), 1,776 metres, at junction of routes over Septimer and Julier Passes. Routes hence, first, to Andeer, 11 hours, mule path; and second, to Casaccia, 13 hours, mule path.

Route first passes by Col de la Vailletta or Stallerberg (2,581 metres), or by Furkel Col (2,675 metres), and Val Avers, through Juf (2,040 metres), the highest hamlet in Switzerland, Cresta (very modest inn, kept by Shepherd), Canicul (Germ. Hundeloch;

inn—Chez Salis), fine waterfals, Aversbach, by Val Ferrara or Avers, to Hinter-Rhein at Andeer.

Second route, by Col de la Furkel, descent in 1 hour to old deserted inn of Septimer (2,300 metres), and in 2 hours to Casaccia.

Bonaduz, a covered bridge behind Reichenau, leads to this place, called Beneduces, in the middle ages, and standing at the entrance of the delightful valley of Domleschg. Hotels: De Giacomi, Crown. The population of Bonaduz is Catholic.

Bormio, or Worms (Baths of), in a delightful neighbourhood in the Valtelline, between the Stilfzer Joch and the Lake of Como. The new baths are a magnificent establishment, with room for 100 bathers. For prices, climate, &c., see " Peaks and Passes of the Rhoetian Alps." Elevation, 4,460 feet ancient bath, and 4,125 modern. Distance from Col de Bormio, 4 l.; Bormio to Sondrio, 12½ l. Diligence every day at 11 a.m. Sondrio to Colico, on Lake of Como, 7½ l., twice a-day, in 4½ hours, 5½ fr., all included.

Bormio (Town), ¾ l. (2¼ m.), from the baths. Dismal, quaint, old fashioned Italian town. Burnt, 1855. Fine fresco in church of the Crucifix, Strada Combo. See " Peaks and Passes of the Rhoetian Alps."

Bormio (Col of), or Wörmser Joch. Highest good turnpike road in Europe, between Engadin at Schuls and Valtellina, leading to Chiavenna and the Lake o Como. Elevation, 8,242 feet. The Bormio is the ancient pass. The more modern pass of Stelvio, or Stilfzer Joch, is 9,177 feet high. It was constructed by Donegani, in 1825, by order of the Austrian government, and is called a " marvellous road." Route.

English Miles from Bormio.

	Miles.
Santa Maria	10½
Trafoi	9
Prad	8
Mals	6½

See "Peaks and Passes of the Rhoetian Alps."

Bregenz.—Capital of Austrian Vorarlberg, on the Lake of Constance (Brigantium of Strabo and Ptolemy), 3,200 inhabitants. Hotels: Oestreichischer Hof, on the lake; Schwarzer Adler, cheaper; Goldener Adler.

Fine views near the town. Riedernburg is a ladies' school of the Sacré Cœur. Gebhardsberg ¾ hours, a hermitage. Higher up, a rustic inn. The Pfändler, 2,135 feet above the Lake of Constance, has a complete view of the lake and mountain. No Inn. 2½ hours. Two routes from Chur to Bregenz.

1. By Rheineck, 95 kilometres. Rail or post road. Four trains a-day in 3 hours. 1st class, 8*fr.* 90*c.*; 2nd, 6*fr.* 25*c.*; 3rd, 4*fr.* 45*c.* 2. By Feldkirch. Rail to Mayenfeld. Post road from Mayenfeld to Feldkirch (by Luziensteg, defile.) Mail post once a-day; time 2¼ hours 45 min. Fare, 2*fl.* 66*k.* Omnibus twice a-day. Fare, 1*fl.* 5*k.* from Feldkirch to Bregenz (2 hours).

Brienz, a village on the Albula Pass from Chur to Ponté in the Engadin, ¾ l. (2¼ m.), from Lenz, by a path, leading under rocks, and above the Albula to Alvenen. (See that place).

Buffalora.—One of the finest waterfalls in the Alps, on the Bernardin Pass, near Misocco, 1½ l. (4½ m.), Albergo Toscani, the road descends the valley amidst a rich southern vegetation, flanked on either side by rocks furrowed by waterfalls, and near the Château of Misocco, belonging to the Signeur of Sax. It was ruined 1527. The Buffalora Fall, near Soazza, to the right, descends 200 feet, presenting the appearance of a crystal column. The Fall of Cabbiolo is ¾ l. lower down. (See Bernardin, under "Peaks and Passes of the Rhoetian Alps."

Calanca (Val), opens between Grono and Roveredo, in Val Misocco, extending 4 l. (15 m.), to Pizzo di Muccia (2,963 metres), and the Adula Group. It is reached from Chur by the Bernardin Pass, and is ascended by a good carriage road. Ruins of Château of Calanca, near Santa Maria, 4 l. (12 m.), from Roveredo, at Augio, two different paths branch off, leading to Misocco (3 hours), or to Soazza, by the Buffalora Fall (3½ hours). From Valbella (1,336 metres), the last hamlet in Val Calanca, you can reach Misocco (in 3 hours), by the Col di Trasculmene (2,153 metres), and from the Châlets of Alogna (1,419 metres), you can follow a road that takes you (3 hours) to San Bernardino, by the Col di Passeti (2,075 metres).

Calanda (The) or Galanda, 6 l. (or 18 m.) from Chur, presents one of the finest views in the Grisons. The summit is 8,650 feet high. View embraces Grisons, Appenzell, and Glarus Alps, and to the N.W., the whole country, to Lake of Constance. The easiest ascent to this mountain, is from Chur (6 or 7 hours), and you can descend from the top to Pfëffers Baths in 6 hours.

Campfer is a pretty hamlet (in the Upper Engadin,) ½ hour below Silva-plana, where the aspect of the valley improves, and becomes quite charming. It gives its name to one of the lakes of Silva-plana, and is chiefly noticeable as the residence of a chamois hunter, Adam Engler, a clever, prudent, and obliging guide.

Casaccia.—On Maloja Pass, from St. Moritz to Chiavenna. Romantsch Casetsch, German Casatch. Hotels: Chez Bart, Giønannini, Poste, Chez Michael (1,406 met.), at junction of Maloggia to Septimer roads. Near it superb Fall of Ordlegna. A path hence to Sondrio (in 10 hours), by Val Ordlegna, Col de Muretto (2,557 metres), and Val Malenco.

Casaccia (Hospice of), above Val Jura, in Tessin.

Casanna, on the Lukmanier, 1 l. from Olivone.

Casanna (Valley of), leading out of the Engadin, near Scanfs.

Casanna (2,562 metres), a mountain near Klosters am Platz (Prättigau). Hotel Hirsch. Can be ascended.

Canicul, or Inner Ferrera, near the Val d'Averse, between Splugen and Engadin. Situated under Piz Starlera. To the right is the Val d'Emet. Lodgings at the cure's. Falls near it. Close by to right, Val di Lei, with snowy peaks of Pizzo Stella (10,485 feet). A difficult pass from Val di Lei (8,240 feet) leads by the Lago Ghiacciato, and Lago di Aqua Fraggia to Chiavenna.

Capütschin Piz (10,446 ft.), in the Bernina district, above Val Rosegg. See "Peaks and Passes of the Rhœtian Alps."

Castasegna.—On route from Samaden to Chiavenna, by Val Bergel, (2,216 feet). Post inn chez meng; Alla Liberia. 2 l. to Chiavenna. Many silk worms. Fine chesnut woods. Road passes to Chiavenna through Plurs, where in 1618 (Sept. 4th), 2,430 people lost their lives, by a landslip of Mont Conto. Sixty feet of rock cover the buried village.

Chur, (Quera, Coira, Curia, Rhaetorum), is the capital of the Canton of Grisons, the seat of the government, a bishop's see, and the centre for the posts, telegraphs, and customs of E. Switzerland. It stands opposite the Calanda, on the river Plessur, and between the Piz-Okel and the Mittenburg, and exhibits in its precincts the traces of old fortifications. It is divided into the high town or bishop's court, and the modern town. Chur is supposed to have been built at the time of Constantine.

RAILWAYS.—4 trains per day. Luggage in hand not charged. Tickets direct to following places. Fares in francs and cents

	1st cl.	2nd cl.	3rd cl.
	fr. c.	fr. c.	fr. c.
Aix-la-Chapelle	34 80	70 10	...
Augsburg (express)	31 75	22 0	...
Bâle	24 45	17 5	12 20
Berné	27 45	19 15	13 70
Cologne	85 20	63 0	...
Geneva	44 30	30 90	22 15
Glarus	7 40	5 20	3 70
Leipzig	93 30	67 75	...
Lucerne	20 20	14 10	10 19
Mayence	66 30	48 75	...
Munich	38 25	26 40	...
Paris	86 70	64 60	...
Ragatz	2 30	1 60	1 15

RAILWAYS—*(Continued).*

	1st cl.	2nd cl.	3rd cl.
	fr. c.	fr. c.	fr. c.
Rapperschwyl	9 0	6 30	4 50
Rorschach	9 80	6 85	4 90
St. Gallen	11 10	8 5	5 75
Schaffhausen	17 70	12 35	8 25
Solothurn	24 75	17 25	12 85
Strasburg	40 45	29 5	...
Stuttgardt	28 90	20 5	...
Thun	30 60	21 35	15 30
Vienna	105 25	76 65	...
Winterthur (by lake of Wallenstadt)	14 70	10 25	7 35
Wesen	6 20	4 80	3 10
Zurich (by Lake of Wallenstadt)	13 70	8 80	6 0

On Sundays, tickets at reduced prices for 2 days. Five days return tickets de circulation (on the Swiss Union Railway). Chur, Wallenstadt, Glarus, Zurich, Schaffhausen, Constance, and Rorschach. Post cars, every half-hour after the arrival of the trains. Two post cars by Splugen and Bernardin ; three times a day to Thusis, Viâ Mala and the village of Splugen; twice to Oberhalbstein, and the Engadin, St. Moritz, and Tarasp ; and once to the Vorder-Rhein district. Summer fares, from Chur to Bellinzona, 26 l. (78 m.), in 16 hrs., 28*fr.*; 24*fr.* 10c. Chiavenna, 19 l. (57 m.), in 13 hrs., 21*fr.*; 18*fr.* 20c. Disentis, 13 l. (39 m.), in 9 hrs., 10*fr.* 40c.; 8 *fr.* 45c. Genoa by Bellinzona, 77½ l. (232½ m.), in 38 hrs. 47*fr.*; 42*fr.* 70c. Ilanz, 6¾ l. (20¼ m.), in 4½ hrs., 4*fr.* 40c. Lugano, 32 l. (96 m.), in 19 hrs., 33*fr.* 20c.; 28*fr.* 30c. Magadino, 28¾ l. (86¼ m.), in 18¼ hrs., 30*fr.* 50c.; 26*fr.* 10c. Milan by Chiavenna, 44 l. (132 m.), in 29 hrs., 38*fr.* 65c., or 33*fr.* 50c. by taking second class on the Lake of Como steamer, and third class on the rail, (3*fr.* 20c. less). Milan by Bellinzona, 36*fr.* 60c. Poschiavo, 25 l. (75 m.), in 33 hrs., 19*fr.* 90c. Samaden, 17 l. (51 m.), in 13 hrs., 17*fr.* 25c.; 14*fr.* 70c. St. Moritz, 16½ l. (49½ m.), in 12½ hrs., 16*fr.*; 13*fr.* 60c. Schuls-Tarasp, 28½ l. (85¼ m.), in 29 hrs., 26*fr.* 55c.; 22*fr.* 5c. Splügen, 10¾ l. (32¼ m.), in 7¼ hrs., 11*fr.* 35c.; 9*fr.* 80c. Thusis, 5¼ l. (15¾ m.), in 3 hrs., 5*fr.* 35c.; 4*fr.* 55c. Truns, 10½ l. (31¼ m.), in 7¼ hrs., 6*fr.*; 80c. Turin by Bellinzona in 36 hrs., 41*fr.* 85c.; 40*fr.* By Milan, 47*fr.* 60c.; 43*fr.* 90c. The first prices mentioned are for the coupé, the others for the inside.

CARRIAGES.—To Reichenau, 1 horse, 6*fr.*; 2 horses, 10 to 12*fr.* Ilanz, 1 horse, 18*fr.*; 2 horses, 30 to 35*fr.* Truns, 40 to 45*fr.* Dissentis, 60 to 70*fr.* Thusis, 1 horse, 12*fr.*; 2 horses, 20 to 24*fr.* St. Andeer, 45 to 50*fr.* Splügen, 60 to 70*fr.* Chiavenna, 120 to 140*fr.* Colico, 140 to 150*fr.* Bellinzona, 160 to 170*fr.* St. Moritz, in the Engadin, 80 to 90*fr.* Pour-boire, not included.

It is recommended to distrust the Italian *cochers*, who almost always deceive. It is best to make all arrangement with the hotel-keeper, with whom you lodge at Chur.

HOTELS.—The Luckmanier, at the entrance of the town, near the station—clean. Steinbock, very good.

Freleck. Weisserkreuz, Stern, and Rother-Löwe. The Cafés are the Luckmanier aud the Löwe.

The Protestants at Chur number three-fourths, and the Catholics about one-fourth of the population. represented by Berlepsch as 7,400. and by Joanne as 6,978 inhabitants. Its elevation is 673 metres. The town is built at the foot of the Mittenberg, and of the Spontiskopf, and about 30 minutes' walk from the confluence of the Rhine and Plessur.

The place, or square, has been adorned by a public fountain, erected 1860, and the upper town, or Bishop's Hof, contains the episcopal palace, and the Cathedral (in the Roman style), built on the site of a Roman temple destroyed in the third century; the Cathedral was built in the twelfth or thirteenth centuries, and is of a very irregular form. A Roman Mosaic may be seen in the crypt. Many of the ornaments, sculptures, and pillars, are rough, and even grotesque. To the right, on entering, is the sarcophagus, in red marble, of the Bishop Ortlieb von Brandis. A very curious Roman altar is shown under the existing altar in the Chapel of Canons. The first side chapel contains an altarpiece, by Stumm, a pupil of Rubens; the altarpiece in the chapel of St. Lawrence, to the right at the end, is attributed to Holbein, the younger; surrounding it, are smaller paintings by Keller. There are paintings of Albert Durer, on the second altar, on the left aisle. The Cathedral has a vast crypt, called *Eglise des Capucins*. In the choir or Eglise des Chanoines (Domherren Kirche) are some fine wood carvings on the main altar (of the fifteenth century); also paintings of Holbein the younger; and the sacristy contains an ostensorium and busts of the age of the Crusades; embroidered stuffs of the times of the Saracens; (among others an unique specimen of silk embroidery of the age of Justinian), a chasuble with an Arabic inscription, &c. The high tower "Marsoel" is of the time of the Romans, which contains the episcopal chapel and archives. A cabinet of natural history under the direction of Professor Theobald deserves *a visit. It contains* the oryktognostic *collection of the monk Placidus*, a speaker

of the Dissentis Monastery, and specimens of the Swiss flora by Moritzi. Fine specimens of bears. In the same building is the Cantonal Library, with MSS. of Galer de Wyneck, Ardüser and Rosius Porta, Grisons historians. Many other MSS. bearing on local history and portrait of a Grisons hero, Benedikt Fontana, as well as bust of Gaudenz de Salis, a Swiss poet. In the ancient cantonal school are chemical and physical laboratories, and episcopal archives of the time of Charlemagne. M. de Moor has a collection of 10,000 documents. Stained glass with a visa in the Salle du Conseil.

WALKS NEAR CHUR.—To the summer châlet Rosenberg 10 m. To the Felsenkeller with an equally fine view. The Lurlibad, Chapel of St. Lucius and Piz Okel are other pleasant walks.

EXCURSIONS. — Scalära Tobel a wild gorge, said to be the scene of the revels of evil spirits, 1 l. (3 m.). Rich flora with orchises and cyclamens by the way.

A very fine view is obtained from the Stätzerhorn (5¼ l.), post road by Malix and Parpan, 2¼ l.

Davos —(Romantsch, Dafas, meaning behind). This valley is on the direct road from Klosters to Thusis, and consists of one principal valley 4 to 5 l. long, and of the lateral valleys of Fluella, Dischma, Sertig, and Monstein, leading towards the Engadin. It is watered by the Landwasser, which flows into the Albula, below Alveneu Baths, and it communicates North by the Stutz Pass with the Prättigau, and south-west with Chur by the Strela; with the Engadin by the Cols of Sertig, Scaletta, and Fluella. Distance:—From

* The ascent is by bridle and foot path to the Observatzer Maiensass Sporz. ascent 2¼ l. (7,930ft.) View of Grisons mountains very complete, including Ringelspitz. 10,000 ft.; Piz Urlaun, 10,380 ft.; Piz Tumbif, 9.900 ft.; Piz Rhein, Rheinwaldhorn, Tambohorn, the chaos of peaks about Oberhalbstein, Davos, Bergun, and the Prättigau, the Piz Linard, even the Bernina is clearly seen, distant 8 or 9 l. (27 m.), besides the whole district of Domleschg and 60 villages.

Davos to Chur, by the Strela, 9h. 30m. From Davos to Engadin, by the Scaletta, 9 hours. From Klosters to Thusis by Davos, 13 hours. Car route: Carriages to Davos, 4fr. By Col de Fluela to Engadin, 7 hours.

Davos am Platz or Am Platz (Hotel Rathaus zum Strela by Erhard Michel, pension, 4fr., excellent wine of Valtelline) (4,800 feet), chief place in the valley, is a scattered village, among meadows. Wolves and bears' heads are nailed up to the communal house. The Salle of this house has some good stained-glass paintings, representing the armorial bearings of families who have deserved well of their country.

The valley of Davos was formerly covered with forests, and was cleared by the Baron of Vatz, who, in the 13th century, caused his huntsmen to explore it, and gave them land in it with great privileges, which led to their being called the freemen of Davos.

Dissentis.—(3,540 ft.) 13 to 14 hours from Chur. Disertinum, the Desert, in Romantsch, Muster or Monastery. (Hotels: Condrau, Krone, Rathaus, and Poste). Near the junction of the Vorder-Rhein and Medels-Rhein, on the rivulet Magriel. It contained a Benedictine Abbey founded in the 7th century by the Scotch monk, Siegbert, a companion of St. Gallen, and burnt by the civilising French, in 1799, with its valuable library, containing a rare mineralogical collection of Father Placidus a Spescha, a man of much science, born at Trons, in 1732. The Abbey, rebuilt, was burnt again in 1846, and has been built again for the third time. In its vast church of the date of 1712, are tombs of St. Placidus and St. Columban. At 30 m. distance in the chapel of Acletta is a much admired Madonna. For ascensions from Davos, see "Peaks and Passes of the Rhoetian Alps," at the end.

EXCURSIONS FROM DISSENTIS.—To Piz Pazola on horseback. Fine view of Medels Glacier. To the Alpe de Lumpegnia, 1 hour on horseback, 1¼ hour on foot.

Piz Murainn (8,924 ft.), 4 hours on horseback, to within ½ l. of summit. Coming down pass by hamlet of Soliva to Medels Glacier (3 l.). Passes from Dissentis:— 1. To Amsteg by Oberalp, 8 l. (24 m.)—(Route 117). 2. To Maderanerthal by the Glacier of Bruni, and on to Amsteg, 12 l. (36 m.) 3. To Amsteg by the Kreuzli 11 l. (33 m.) 4. To Airolo by the Pass dell' Uomo (10½ l.) To Olivone in the Val Blegno by the Luckmanier (9½ l.) The best chamois hunter about Dissentis is a certain Tennez.

Behind Dissentis is the Tavetsch district, amidst high Alps and Glaciers, forming the source of the Vorder-Rhein. This was the scene of much fighting in 1799.

Domleschg.—(Valley). Val Tomiliasca, or Vallis Domestica, 2½ l. long (7½ m.) in some places, ¼ l. (2¼ m.) wide, has 22 villages, 6,000 inhabitants, and 20 ruined castles. Shut in to W. by Heinzenberg, with many villages, to the E. by the Malix and Stätzerhorn. Climate mild. Peaches ripen out of doors. But for inundations would be the richest valley in Switzerland. Great variety of religion and languages in the population. Bonaduz and Rhaezuns are Romantsch Catholic. Rothenbrunnen is German and Protestant. Scheid is Romantsch Protestant. Tomils, Paspels, and Rothels, are Romantsch and Catholic. Almens is German and Protestant. Katzis, Romantsch and Catholic. Musein, German and Protestant. Scharans, Romantsch and Protestant. Thusis, Romantsch and Protestant, &c.

The valley of Domleschg opens into the Hinter-Rheinthal at Reichenau and Bonadu.

Engadin.—Upper and Lower, extends from the Maloggia pass to Martinsbrücke 18 l. (54 m.), between two main Alpine chains, and is watered throughout by the Inn which at its upper extremity forms the two lakes of Sils and Silva-plana. It is one of the highest inhabited valleys in Europe. The population 10,149, are of

Romantsch or Italian origin, and Protestants. They supply Europe with waiters and confectioners, who returning to the Engadin, erect substantial stone houses and live very comfortably. Upper Engadin is 7 l. (21 m.) long, and 30 m. broad, and an elevation of 1,862 to 2,650 metres. Lower Engadin is 11 l. long (33 m.), from Brail to Martinsbrucke.

See "Peaks and Passes of the Rhoetian Alps."

Feldkirch. See Montafun.

Felsberg (New), a village, 1 l. from Chur, built by removing from Old Felsberg, threatened with a landslip by the mountain impending over it.

Fideriser Au.—Hotel Chez Nigli, telegraph office. Carriages on hire. A village in the Prättigau. Route from Chur to Klosters.

Fideris (Village). Hotel: Star, good Malans wine; cheap pension, chez Clas Bohner. Mine host is a mighty hunter and knows the mountains well. Lion, whey-cure. Between village and baths is the new Hotel of Quadera.

Fideris (baths), ¼ l. from the village (3,251 feet), in a desert gorge, only accessible for very light carriages. Alkaline-ferruginous springs, good for stomach complaints, scrofula, &c. Bath house, simple, but full in summer. Good cellar and good kitchen. 5 *fr.* for use of the waters during the process of cure.

Excursion to the Gyrenspitz (6,742 feet), 1½ l. (4½ m.) To the Kistenstein (7,633 feet) same route ¾ l. (2¼ m.) further.

Near Fiderisau 1h. 30m., an excursion to the Druserthal, watered by the Schranbach. Three paths that separate at Schniders lead into the valley of Montafun. 1. By Drusenalp (1,633 metres), and Drusenthor (2,384 metres) 8 hours. 2nd. By the Schweizerthor (2,170 metres) 8 hours; 3rd, by Caveli Col (2,303 metres); 40 min from *Fideris* is the picturesque valley of Rats-*ahits leading to baths* from which a path *Langwies (3 hours) leads to the Schan-*

figgthal, and another path descends direct to Kublis in 1 hour.

Filisur, near Alveneu on the Albula pass. Inn: Chez Schmit. A pretty village built of stone. Height (3,260 feet). Close at hand precipices of the Crochetta, and ruins of Greifenstein. Much copper and iron ore, also silver and lead.

EXCURSION. — To Stulsergrat (7,950 feet). Very fine view of Albula and Davos valleys.

Hinter-Rhein.—The highest village in the Rheinwald (5,000 feet) near the sources of the Rhine, 3½ l. (10½ m.) from the village of Splugen.

Excursion to sources 7 or 8 hours. Guide wanted. Hinter-Rhein issues from a large crevasse (2,216 metres) at the base of the vast Glacier of Zapport, under the Adula Groupe (Guferhorn 3,393 metres) Pic. (Val Rhein 3,398 metres, &c.) 1 hour from Hinter-Rhein you ascend and pass through a savage glen (Hoelle), opposite pastures called Paradies (2 hours) to the ice grotto, often a splendid sight, from which the Rhine issues.

Ilanz.—6h. 30m. from Chur on the road to Dissentis and Andermatt (Route 117), in Romantsch, Glion or Ilon. Hotels: Lukmanier and Oberalp, near the covered bridge; Löwe Schweizerkreuz (658 metres) mixed Romantsch and Germans, 718 metres high near the confluence of the Vorder-Rhein and the Glenner descending from the Valley of Lungnetty. Ilanz contains some very old houses, a hotel de ville, and a wooden bridge over the Rhine, built 1851. Near it are the ruins of many castles. Piz Mundaun can be ascended hence in 3 hours. Ilanz is a good centre for excursions.

Julier.—See "Peaks and Passes of the Rhoetian Alps."

Klosters am Platz—Reached from Chur by the Prättigau. To Landquart 15 kilometres. Rail. From thence to Klosters, 7h. 30m. Hotel: Hirsch. 1,044 inhabitants, consists of 5 hamlets, Ueber'm-bach, Doerfli, Aeuje, Am Platz, and Beider Brucke (3,700 feet high). Another hamlet, once belonged to Klosters, and was destroyed by a landslip, in 1768. The valley is closed by the Silvretta Glacier.

Excursion with guide to Col of Vereina (2,479 m.) By Châlets of Nowai to the Stutzalp, where the ghost of a shepherd is supposed to wander at night. Pass on opposite Hafenhorn (9,183 feet) over blocks of gneiss to cavern of Baretto Balma, once said to have been inhabited by wild men. Hence turn down Susserthal, under Piz Linard (10,516 feet) to Col (7,630 feet) among many little tarns; descend by Val Fles and Susasca to Sus and the Engadin, 8 or 9 hours. Another excursion by Col of Lavine takes you to Lavine in the Engadin in 10 to 12 hours. It strikes out from the last road of Col Vereina, at Cavern of Baretto Balma, takes you to Glacier of Piller, where you behold a wilderness of snow broken by the black rocks of the Silvretta. It is one of the grandest and most awful chaotic views in Switzerland. You descend by Val Lavinuoz over ice and rocks to Alpe de Merangun and thence to Lavine. Sure head and feet required. Another path by Roggengrat to Val Sardasca has even greater attractions. It is a hard day's work.

Kublis (Crown Inn), in the Prättigau, 1¾ l. (5¼ m.) from Klosters near the Serneus Baths (see that place), ⅔ l. (2¼ m.); from Kublis, towards Fideris at Delfazza is the retired Valley of St. Anthony, inhabited by shepherds in scattered châlets, constantly threatened by avalanches. Many lakes at the head of the valley; the largest is the Putznauer, ⅔ l. (2¼ m.) round. The Sulzfluh rising above it has an unrivalled echo.

Langwies, 5 hours from Chur in the Schalfick or Schanfiggthal (inn), 341 inhabitants, (1,377 feet) at the foot of the Strela. The Church is at the entrance of the Valley of Fundey leading to Fideris or to Conters (3h. 30m.) in the Prättigau. By village and torrent of Arrosewasser a branch of the Plessur or path to Wiesen in Valley of Davos. (Inn at Wiesen, Chez Palmi.)

Two other routes from Chur to Langwies, besides Schalfickthal. 1. Difficult up course of Plessur. 2. By Bruck, Prada (1,160 metres), and Tchiertscheon (1,351 metres).

Lavin, or Luvin, in Lower Engadin (bad inn), 317 inhabitants, (1,430 metres high), on the Lavinuoz. Fine waterfall. Ascension of Piz Linard, fatiguing, best made hence (3,416 metres.) Highest point of Selvretta group (5 hours) Panoramic view one of the finest in the Alps. Inn at Lavin, Chez Jacob Juon, not dear, fair. Bad coffee at Poste.

Walks from Lavin, to Val Lavinuoz, to the Glacier of Tiascha (1½ hour). Ascension of Piz Mezzdi (9,000 feet), fine view from Mount Mortera.

Lukmanier.—See "Peaks and Passes of Rhoetian Alps".

Maloggia (Col de), or Maloya (1,811 metres.) Inn. Connecting Upper Engadin with Val Bergel. 1h. 15m. from Col. is Sils. 1 hour further, Silva-plana, and 1h. 30m. Saint Moritz.

Mayenfeld, on the Rhine, crossed by a wooden bridge. Capital of the Zehntgerichtsbund. Contains 1,200 inhabitants. Wine grown about here. Close at hand, is the Luziensteig Federal Fortress. Old tower at Mayenfeld, dates from 367 Very good wine called Completer, to be had at the Kaufhaus. Luziensteig has fortified after plans designed by General Dufour. Numerous blockhouses defend its approach. Artillery practice in summer. Principal strength of the place is a defile, 350 paces wide, leading through the works. On W. side Flaescherberg (1,444 metres), and E., Guscheralp. Douane and Church of St. Lucius, oldest in Grisons. (Inn).

Mayenfeld is a station on the Bregenz rail, 19 kilometres from Chur. Trains four times a-day.

Misocco (Thal or Misorex), also called Cremeo, the S. descent from the Bernardine Pass. At the village of Misocco, is an Auberge, Tossani. The valley shows a luxurious southern vegetation, has a fa castle of the Counts of Sax, and some fine waterfalls. This valley contains th.. Falls of Buffalora, already noticed. At Cana, you find the first fig trees, and the vine grows in festoons. To the left, is a difficult path by the Val Cana and Forcola to Gravedona, on the Lake of Como. At Grono, is a Chapel, near the Château of Fiorentino, containing some very ancient frescoes. To the right, opens Val Calanca, with 2,2 0 inhabitants, who (the men), every year go abroad, as chimney sweeps, glaziers. &c. Chief place of Lower Misocco is Roveredo, with many fine houses, but much injured by a hurricane in 1834. Fine Church of the Madonna. Ruins of the Palace of the Trivulzi. (Croce Bianca, and Canone d'Oro. Inns fair. Population, 1,000.)

Route hence to Bellinzona (No. 120).

Morteratsch (Glacier). (1h. 30m.), from Pontresina, 4fr. (See "Peaks and Passes," &c.)

Morteratsch (Piz), (3,754 metres.) Guide wanted for ascension, 25fr. Ascent 3 or 5 hours. (See "Peaks and Passes," &c.)

Molins or Mühlen, 9¾ l. (29¼ m.) from Chur on road to Julier Pass. Post inn. Dinner dear. Romantic position in deep glen. Fine view of cascade from bridge on Rhine. Near it, ruins of Marmels, an ancient den of robber knights, in an almost inaccessible position.

Montafun, is a valley 10½ l. (31½ m.), through bright, cheerful scenery, but with indifferent accommodation. Afun appears to be the old Celtic Avon—river. The people, as in the Engadin, are migratory. The men go forth in the spring, as masons, confectioners, and scythe dealers. The women's costume is very original: red robes and stockings, felt hats and long tresses.

Bludenz, is a little town in this valley. (Hotel de la Poste), with a fine view from the Church and Castle of Steinbach.

Excursion to the Scesaplana (7 hours). From the Wallgau and Montafun an almost *infinite* number of paths lead over the *Rhätikon* ridge, to the Prättigau. Most

of these passes lead over glaciers, and are named thors, thus: Schweizerthor, Drusenthor, &c. Thor—Gate. The Wallgau behind Bludenz, 5 l., separates into two valleys, one (the southern), running along the Rhätik.n, is the Montafun (Mont d'Avon, in opposition to Mont d'Avos, according to Berlepsch), the other is the Klosterthal, watered by the Alfensbach. This is the post road into Vorarlberg and Tyrol. Vorarlberg is an Austrian province, with 107,000 Catholic inhabitants, divided into the three districts of Bregenz, Feldkirch, and Bludenz. From the railway station, Haag. Post every day for 1fr. 45c. to Feldkirch. (Inns, the Angel and the Post).

Münster (1.248 metres), 473 Catholic inhabitants. Very old Benedictine Abbey. Road from Grisons to Tyrol. Münsterthal, elevated valley, watered by the Rambach, and up it runs the road that passes by Würmser Joch, into the Valtelline. It has many lateral valleys, occupied by a Romantsch or Ladin population.

The valley contains Cierfs, the hamlet of Lü (5,900 feet); ¾. thence, Valcava, an Alpine village, to the right, in Val Fraele, and Piz Lat (8,876 feet), and Piz Umbrail (9,340 feet). Santa Maria, is a comfortable village. Hence to Stelvio Pass (3½ hours). The Malserhaide is noted for the spot where Benedict Fontana met a hero's death, saving his honour, his country, and liberty, 1499. Many bears in this district.

Malins, in Hinter-Rhein valley, romantically situated, near waterfalls, and in meadows, surrounded by precipices of Flimserstein. To the left, was the Flimser forest, and 1 l. hence, Flims (3,329 feet). Hotel Poste, so called from its numerous springs. Flirum, is Romantsch—flowing water.

Nauders. (See "Peaks and Passes.")

Oberhalbstein, a valley affording good pasturage, and watered by the Oberhalbsteiner Rhine, with a Romantsch population.

Piz, Palu. (See "Peaks and Passes.")

Panixer Pass, between Elm and Ilanz. (See Canton of Glarus.

Parpan, a village on the Julier Pass. Inn, Löwe. Elevation, 1,505 metres. To the E., the Rothhorn of Parpan (2,904 metres).

Piz Ault,	Piz Linard,
Piz Bernina,	Piz Morteratsch,
Piz Beverin,	Piz Mundain,
Piz d'Err,	Piz Rosegg,
Piz Landquart,	Piz Valrhein.

(See "Peaks and Passes of the Rhoetian Alps.")

Platz. (See Davos.)
Ponte. ⎱ (See "Peaks and Passes
Pontresina. ⎰ of the Rhoetian Alps.")

Poschiavo, or Pushlav, is an elevated valley, extending from the Bernina, to the borders of the Valtellina, and watered by the Poschiavino, which flows through it to join the Adda. In its northern part occurs savage Alpine scenery and beautiful pastures, while in its southern reaches, you encounter an Italian climate, crops, orchards, and chesnut groves. The population (2-3rds catholics), though the valley is Swiss.

Poschiavo, is a small market borough. Albergo Albrici, with a civil landlord; and Albergo Bernina, smaller; a third, is Albérgo Sanadeni; and a fourth, Croce Bianca, chez Dorizzo. Elevation, 3,112 feet. Looks like a town, having many good looking houses and villas near it. Much trade in Valtelline wine. Cigar manufactory. An Italian patois is spoken in the valley, but German is taught in the schools. Communal town house with a "Witch's Tower," a relic of the superstitions of the 16th and 17th centuries, in which canny Scotland put to death many thousand grannies in a few years, and Lord Bacon expressed a strong dread of sorcery. Country round Poschiavo charming.

Pleasantest excursions, a good climb to the Pizzo Sassalbo (2,858 metres or 9,798 feet), 5 hours from Poschiavo, com-

manding a magnificent panoramic view. Nearer Poschiavo are a pretty garden and grotto, ortini, and an old ruin castello of the 14th century.

Prese (La).—Baths at point where the Poschiavim enters the lake of La Prese or Presse. This lake is two kilometres long, 1,000 yards broad, 68 or 70 deep. Its height is 2,880 feet above the sea (Ball says 3,215 feet.) Mean temperature in summer, 68° or 70°. Fahrenheit. It is a delightful sheet of water, noted for its trout. The baths are much frequented, and are in a handsome structure. The best hotel in Poschiavo on the N. side of the lake. The waters are sulphurous. Living, 6*fr.* a-day. Rooms, 1½*fr.* to 4*fr.* Dinner, 3*fr.* without wine. Breakfast, 1*fr.* A bath, 1*fr.* 30c. A carriage, with one horse, to Selva, 15*fr.*; two horses, 25*fr.* to 30*fr.* To Pontresina, carriage, with one horse, 30*fr.*; with two horses, 45*fr.* to 50*fr.* To Tirano, carriage, with one horse, 8*fr.*; with two horses, 14*fr.* To Selva, a donkey, 8*fr.* Trout in lake weigh sometimes 15lb.

Prättigau.—Distances: Chur to Landquart (15 kilometres.) Ragatz to Mayenfeld (4 kilometres.) Rail: Landquart to Klosters, 7h. 30m. Carriage road: Diligence once a-day, from Landquart to Kublis, 4 l. 2-8th. (13½ miles), in 2h. 45m., for 2*fr.* 25c., and to Davos, in 7h. 45m.; for 4*fr.* 80c. from Chur.

The Prättigau is a valley 11 l. (33 miles) long, rich in hay and fruit, lying between the ridges of the Rhätikon to the N.E., the Engadin Alps to the S., to the W., by the Hochwang chain, and the Mountains of Davos. The Landquart torrent issues from it. It takes its name from the Mediæval Latin name, *Prati govia* (Canton of Meadows.) Population, 11,000 Protestants, laborious, vigorous, proud of their nationality to a fault, living by the produce of their flocks and herds. The Prättigau cattle are the best in the Grisons. Romantsch was formerly the local idiom, and many spots retain a

P

mantsch names. In the 17th century, the Prättigau obtained an illustrious name from the bravery with which it gallantly repelled the bands of the Austrian, Baldi-ron. In 1649, the district purchased its freedom from Austria. The Prättigau forms the Route from Ragatz to Klosters.

Principal places in the valley. Land-quart, Hotel Zollbrücke; Seewis, whey cure establishment of Schlössli, chez Andrew Walser; Jenatz (Inns, Crown and Post), good, and not dear. Omnibuses. Kublis (Crown Inn).

Fideris and Klosters.—(See the two latter places.

Reichenau, 3 hours from Chur, 45 miles from Thusis, at the confluence of the Vorder and Hinter-Rhein. (In Romantsch, Lo Pon, or Pon Sol), 586 metres above the sea. Contains a château, in which was a school where it is said Louis Phillipe, in exile, acted as mathematical master, in 1793, under the name of Chabot. Hotel de l'Aigle, good. The château belongs to M. Planta. Berlepsch says, "there are only three houses in the village."

Rheinwald (Valley), is a mild district watered by the Hinter-Rhein, and containing only a German population.

Rhaetian Alps.—(Peaks and Passes of the.)

The Rhoetian Alps fall into the following principal groups :—

1. The Lukmanier and the Adula Groupe from St. Gothard to the Splugen.

2. The chain extending from the Splugen N.E. on the left bank of the Inn, and containing the Albula and Selvretta Alps.

3. The S.E. branch on the right bank of the Inn, containing the Bernina Groupe and passing around converging with the former into the Tyrol.

To the east of the St. Gothard stands the Lukmanier (locus magnus?) over which a mule path leads from Medels in the Rheinthal to the Tessin. This is the lowest of all the Alpine passes in Switzer-

land, being 5,948 feet above the s late plans in favour of a railro Switzerland through the Alps, to this point. As regards the gr the ascent on the side of the Rhin this would be feasible. From the this valley it has been proposed t tunnel three miles in length, thr Lukmanier Kopf and the Platifer were accomplished, the locomotiv everlasting snow and ice, would l light of day and reach it agai chestnut and mulberry trees, ab way between Airolo and Bellinzo

After passing to the East of manier you reach immediately the Adula * Groupe, covering a squar of 24 German miles (380 square, This central knot of mountains in other chains mostly to the N remarkable for savage scenery, and the mass of its glaciers and sno intersected by valleys inhabited l lations of German, Italian, and Rc origin, and it hence follows that valley you find a different nam same peak. The N.W. column central knot is formed by the Rh horn 10,454 feet high; further Zaporthorn, 10,439 feet. The bac of the semicircle to the S. of th waldhorn is formed and filled by rugged ridge called sometimes the or Vogelberg, and sometimes th in the narrower sense of that te the S.E. side of this ridge rise mits of the Moschelhorn, 9,611 surrounded by the icy envelope Vorder, Hinter, and Ober Mosc ciers, sending their tribute to th in the shape of seven silver w threading the precipices at the From the Moschelhorn a broad n

* Berlepsch asserts that according to into the etymology of the Celtic languag means the same thing, as "Father Sun"; the term would here signify the mighty A Sun, formed by the great ice dome sparkl radiance. Others trace the term to Ad, dula, point –Vogelspitz.

ridge runs Eastward, from which springs the Ramithorn, 8,770 feet high, and then gradually sinks to the Bernhardin pass, which unites the Adula with the Suretta Groupe. The Bernhardin is a very ancient pass, deriving its name from a small chapel, dedicated to St. Bernardin of Sienna (on the southern slope, by the village of the same name), who travelled along the southern slope of the Alps in the years 1432—1436, preaching and evangelising the people. From the village of Splügen, 4,448 feet high, a road leads S.W. through Medels, Nüfenen, Hinter-Rhein, 4,987 feet, which is situated 3 l.(9 m.) from the leap or source of the Hinter-Rhein, * to the steep summit of the Splugen pass, 6,584 feet above the sea. This ascent is in the form of a zig-zag, describing 16 windings. The Moesa issues near this spot from a small lake on the summit, where the traveller now finds a refuge and an inn, from which the road descends rapidly, and by many windings on the Italian side. In the Misoxerthal or Val Mesocco, which extends 9 l. (27 m.) San Bernandino is the first and highest village encountered by the traveller; and after passing this point all the scenery becomes distinctly Italian. The ruin of the castle of Misoc. and the town of the same name stand in a charming situation. at an elevation of 2,390 feet. The valley descends west, thence by many windings to Roveredo and Bellinzona. The present road

over the Splugen was completed in 1821, is 16 feet wide, and provided with the usual securities of refuges and a hospice. But this pass which was much frequented even in the middle ages was only traversed by mule paths till 1818. Two paths led over the mountain, one following the course of the Rhine, and called the Schlecten Weg, through the Verlorene Loch; the other, the Guten Weg over the precipices above the torrent. The Rhine has cut such a deep chasm through the rocks at the Viâ Mala (300 to 400 feet below) that the road has been carried up the side of the precipices by parapets and adventurous bridges. In many cases on looking down the giddy depths below, you see nothing of the river and only know of its existence by the roar or the ascending spray.

Such is the Viâ Mala, 2 l. (6 m.) in length, after which the pass expands into the smiling Schamserthal, 2,663 feet high, from which you pass into the Rhinewald-thal, by another savage pass the Rofla, 1 l. (3 m.) in length. The river cuts its way through this ridge in cascades and chasms, and the traveller after passing it reaches the old valley of "Frezen am Rhein," through a sort of rocky gate called the Sasaplana. This district is inhabited by a German population as far as the Hinter-Rhein Glacier. Their principal village is that of Splugen. This German colony is said to have been brought here for the protection of the pass by Frederic Barbarossa, Emperor of Germany. They form a little German state, consisting of the following villages, Suvers, Splugen, Medels, Hinter-Rhein, &c. At Splugen, which is said to take its name from the Latin, Specula (a prospect or beacon), the two roads over the Bernhardin and Splugen passes fork. The slope on the Italian side of the Splugen is even greater—and therefore the scenery is even wilder and the road a work of greater difficulty in its construction. But on this side instead of descending as low in the ravine as in the case of the Viâ

---

* To the source of the Rhine a guide is required, and provisions. Some spots are dangerous from avalanches. Distance, 3 l. (9 m.) Pass by the Alpe of Zapport, over tracts covered with rhododendrons and polypodium rhaetium. The valley narrows, and is often blocked up by avalanches forming snow bridges over the Rhine. Caution required. Reach the last châlets and end of road over an abyss into which the Rhine leaps, called l'enfer, by the people, opposite a verdant spot called "paradise," in the midst of the glaciers. Head of valley blocked up by large Zapport Glacier, from whose cavern issues a large jet of water. It is the source of the Rhine. Above tower aloft the Kanalhorn, Guferhorn, and the Rheinwaldhorn. This spot was sacred in the time of the ancients; and the Romans had built here a temple, dedicated to the Nymphs. The scene is majestic, solemn, and savage in the extreme.

Mala, it has been carried higher up the precipices, by means of countless galleries, buttresses, bridges, and breastworks. In one place the Madesimo plunges headlong into the abyss, and at every turn of the road the traveller expects that it will terminate at the edge of some awful precipice. In fact, it is a triumph of skill.

At Campo Dolcino softer scenery commences and henceforth all is Italian. Men, houses, vegetation, all present a new aspect. Your carriage rolls along amid chestnut woods, the valley widens, and you at length reach the first Italian town, Chiavenna, at the point, where the stream from the Jacobsthal meets the Maira descending from that of Bergell.

From the ridge of the Splugen to that of the Brenner the Rhoetian Alps extend east under different names, but chiefly known as the Grisons and Tyrolese Alps. Their general elevation has taken place more in masses than has been the case in the western alps. To the west a disposition to develop peaks predominated, hence it has the most remarkable summits and the deepest valleys. On the other hand, to the east of the St. Gothard group, the whole crust of the earth, including both mountains and valleys, has been extraordinarily raised. This is most evident in the small comparative elevation of the peaks above the adjacent valleys, though both have received a very considerable elevation. It was this elevating law in the eastern Swiss alps which created such a number of very high valleys, affording cultivation and produce quite close under the highest summits, as in the Upper Engadin, Avers (the highest valley in Europe, occupied by villages), Rheinwald, Tavetsch, &c., places which not only equal but even considerably exceed the bald summits of the Riesengebirge and Harz mountains in Germany. Nevertheless, the Rhaetian Alps are not a mere high plateau, but a highland district opened up by many fine valleys, and *offering much diversified scenery.* Many *of the peaks* are also very high, and

sharply defined. But these lie mostly in the midst of vast glaciers, and at the head of uninhabited valleys, remote from all means of accommodation and appliances of civilized life. Hence many of these mighty peaks have not even received a name, as is the case with those above 10,000 feet high near the source of the Hinter or Posterior Rhine. The Bernina groupe may compete with that of the Jungfrau and Finsteraarhorn.

Eastward from the Splugen you come to the Septimer (called anciently Setmer) and a little to the south-east, the Maloja, where the Inn rises, a ridge above 6,000 feet, holding together the two parallel branch chains of the Rhaetian Alps. On the Col between the two (the Septimer and the Maloja) is the Longhino Lake, which is said to feed the Inn, the Rhine, and the Maira. The Septimer Pass, now almost deserted, was a great thoroughfare between Swabia and Italy in the Middle Ages. A hospice was built on it by Bishop Guido, of Chur, in 1120, in honour of St. Peter. A road still leads over the Maloja.

Beyond the Septimer the Middle Zone begins to fork, and embraces in two mighty branches the Upper Innthal or Engadin, and lower down, the Tyrolese Innthal, is Landeck. In certain points the Innthal resembles the Valais. Both are extensive latitudinal valleys, both are shut in at the end by a gorge; whereof, however, that of the Inn at Finstermunz is much more wild than the Narrows of St. Maurice. Another point of resemblance is this, that the southern chain enclosing it is the highest. This is in the Valais, Monte Rosa, in the Engadin, the Bernina Chain; and as the Finsteraarhorn group closes in the Valais to the north, so in the Engadin the Selvretta chain stretches away to the Vorarlberg. But there is one essential difference between the two valleys; the Valais is deeply depressed from beginning to end, hence the oppressive heat in summer, and the cretins and goitres at Martigny, whereas the Engadin rises up to the very shoulders of the mountains by gradual incline for nine or ten leagues (thirty miles), bringing you to the healthy bracing district of St. Moritz and Silvaplana.

(A) The north-eastern chain, drawing along the left bank of the Inn, is deeply intersected at its west end by the lateral valleys of the tributaries of the Rhine, and presents the aspect of numerous high Alpine peaks (on the average 8,000 feet high), and stretching out their snow-covered branches north-west, towards the Rhine. It is only from the sources of the Inn, where the ridge sinks deeply at the Julier Pass, that an unbroken connection of the chain can be traced. A paved carriage road leads over the Julier Pass from the Oberhalbstein Valley (the Hinter-Rhein) into the Inn Valley. Two mysterious granitic pillars ($4\frac{1}{2}$ metres high), are supposed to be Roman milliaria (mile stones), especially as Roman coins have been found along this road. Some, however, imagine that they are the remains of a Celtic Temple of the Sun, dedicated to Jul. It was over this pass that young Friedrich Hohnstaufen passed to his German inheritance in 1215. Having ascended the pass from the north, and reached the summit, where a small lake supplies the Inn with a sparkling foaming tributary torrent, you discover to your right the Septimer and the Maloja, and directly in front the Bernina, forming the southern wall of the valley; and if you follow down the road by the side of the brawling torrent (before mentioned) your eye is suddenly suprised and delighted with the view of the shining bright green mirror of the lake of Silva-plana at your feet.

To the north of the Julier Pass, lie the Albula Alps, with ten summits, above 9,000 and 10,000 feet; to the N. E. runs the Albula Pass (much frequented, 7,200 feet), from Ponte in the Engadin to Bergün, in the Albulathal, passing over a wild mountain basin, made desolate by frequent avalanches and landslips, and hut in by two snowy peaks of almost equal height (7,000 feet), and called

Crap Alv. To the N. of the Albula Pass, rises a still more imposing mountain mass, the Piz Uertsch, (10,076 feet). Its neighbour is a great icy ridge, called Piz Kesch (10,519 feet), forming the largest connected glacier mass in the Grisons Alps. Proceeding still further N. E. you come to the Scaletta group, reaching 9,956 feet in the Piz Vadret da Brail.

The Selvretta Alps, surrounded by five glaciers, and also called the Fermunt group, form the centre of elevation of the whole mass. Piz Linard approaches Piz Kesch in elevation (10,519 feet) and can be seen throughout Suabia. As far as is known, it was first ascended by a Pfarrer (curate) Zodrell at the beginning of the present century, but he found a pair of horse shoes on the top. In the summer of 1835, it was ascended by the naturalist, Oswald Heer, accompanied by the Glarus guide, Maduts von Matt. Weilermann ascended it in 1858. They passed the night at the foot of the actual pyramid in a charcoal burner's hut; from this point, the ascent, described as fatiguing and dangerous, lasted six hours. The summit consists of a narrow ridge, covered with blocks of rock, and presenting from its central position a magnificent panorama.

At the source of the Illiez, another group, that of the Jamthaler Ferner is linked on to this Selvretta chain. We have no exact measurements of the Jamthaler Alps, in whose centre, are vast icy masses, irradiating along the various branch ridges, and descending as seven distinct glaciers, into the neighbouring valleys.

The main ridge passes on from the Jamthaler Ferner to Landeck, while a lateral chain, called the Rhätikon, runs N.W. between the valleys of Montafun and Prättigau, on the Ill and Landquart, right bank tributaries of the Rhine. Two peaks deserve notice in this Rhätikon ridge; the Scesaplana (9,136 feet), with a splendid view, and the Falkniss (8,010 feet) half a league from the Rhine. The Rhätikon is remarkable for its quaint and grotesquely-shaped peaks. At its end this chain splits into two; one runs straight along the Rhine to Feldkirch, the other runs South, up the Rhine to Mayenfeld, when it ends at the Fläscherberge, (3,512 feet) opposite the S.E. end of the Thur Alps. Between this mountain (the Fläscherberge) and the Falkniss, is a narrow fortified pass, the Luziensteig, (named after St. Lucius, Apostle of Rhoetia), leading from Mayenfeld to Feldkirch. Numerous combats took place here, between the French and Austrians, in 1799 and 1800.

(B) Leaving the Septimer and following the right bank of the Inn, the centre of this southern chain and of all attraction in the Grisons, is the grand Bernina group. In magnificence of peaks and glaciers, it scarcely yields the palm to Monte Rosa district; and the spring green colour of its numerous beautiful lakes adds a special charm to it. The highest point is the Piz Bernina, (12,564 or 13,506 Eng. feet) first ascended by Coaz, Sept. 13, 1850; secondly, Oct. 3, 1858, by Sarras, Jenni, and Ruodi, and afterwards by the Alpine Clnb. A road practicable for light carriages, leads from the Upper Engadin over the top of the Bernina Pass, 6,260 feet high, to Puschlav, Poschiavo, in Valtelline, (Italy). You proceed for 8 hours from Pontresina at the northern foot to Poschiavo, at the southern side of the pass, having throughout that distance and close at hand the splendid Bernina Glaciers. The north ascent is gentle and easy, the southern steep and sudden. The road passes up along a large green lake, and leads by some newly-made walks and plantations, to the sulphur springs of La Prese, descending by easy zig-zags to it. Behind Poschiavo, now a popular resort on account of its sulphur springs and scenery, you proceed again for a league (3 m.) along the banks of the beautiful green lake, and thence by the stream it feeds the Poschiavino, through *a narrow,* deep, and verdant valley, down *to the Adda,* reached at a still lower *level, pouring its impetuous current by*

the village of Tirano. In the west part of the Bernina group, occur the following important peaks and glaciers: the great glacier mass of Monte Rosso di Scersen, from which the Rosetsch Glacier flows down north, the Piz Cambrena (11,110 feet), the Piz di Palu, (12,049 feet), the Piz di Verona, (10,663 feet), the Monte Pers, (9,887 feet.) The N. E. corner of the group is formed by the Piz Bernina itself, Monte Fossagno (9,463 feet); the E. corner of the Tirano, by the Monte Masuccio (8,576 feet), and the Monte Cambolo (8,933 feet), the S.W. corner by Morbegno, by the Monte Spluga (8,750 feet) To the north of the Bernina pass, rises Piz Languard, since 1856 frequently ascended, on account of its surprising and most extensive view, extending from Monte Rosa, to the Gross Glockner, in the Tyrol, and embracing above 1,700 peaks (See below.)

The Bernina district being the Chamouni of the Grisons, we must enter a little more minutely into its accommodations, excursions, and routes. The best centres are Samaden and Pontresina. Samaden is 5,362 feet above the sea; 1 l. (3 m.) from Pontresina and 1 l. from St. Moritz. Hotels—Bernina ; Piz Ott, good cookery—kept by a chemist learned in the mysteries of distilling fire-water from Alpine plants, cheap; Crown chez Gensler. Every day post car by the Julier to Chur and Lake of Constance, by the Maloggia to Chiavenna and the Lake of Como, by Lower Engadin to Tyrol, and by the Bernina Pass to the Valtelline. From Samaden to Zérnetz, 5⅜ l. (16 m.) in 2½ hours. Fares, 4fr. 60c. To Schul Tarasp, 11 l. (33 m.) in 5hrs. (9fr. 30c. 7fr. 35c.). To Nauders, 16⅛ l. (48 m.) 10¼hrs. (10fr. 75c.). To Poschiavo, 8 l. (24 m.) in 7½hrs. (5fr. 20c.) La Prese 9 l. (27 m.) in 8¼hrs. (5fr. 80c.) To Tirano, 11¼ l. (33½ m.), 9½hrs. (7fr. 40c. To St. Moritz, 1¼ l. (3¾ m.), in 1hr. (1fr. 25c., 1fr 10c.) To Col di Maloggia 4¾ l. (14¼ m.), 2¼h (4fr. 85c., 4fr. 15c. To Casaccia, 5½ l. (17¼ m.) in 3¼ h

(5fr. 85c., 5fr). To Vicosoprano, 7¼ l. (21¾ m.) in 4h. (7fr. 35c., 60fr. 30c.) To Chiavenna, 11¼ l. (33¾ m.), 6¼h. (11fc. 25c., 9fr. 60c.) To Tiefenkasten, 11¼ l (33¾ m.), 7¼h. (11fr. 35c., 9fr. 70c.) To Chur, 17¼ l. (51¾ m.), 11¼h. (17fr. 25c., 14fr. 70c.)

The Romance name of Samaden is *Samada* (frozen snow). It is the capital of Upper Engadin, with 517 Protestant well-to-do inhabitants. At the foot of Piz Padella (8,875 feet); built of handsome stone houses. Oldest family, that of the Planta, whose armorial bearings (a bear's paw) are frequently seen in the Engadin. From the church of St. Peter, oldest in the country, a very fine view. Principal excursion from Samaden Piz Ott.

Piz Ott (10,002 feet), 4,650 feet above valley. Guide, 6 to 7fr. Way safe, easy. Ascent, 3 to 3½ h., descent 2½ to 3h. Go up by Piazza de la Polenta, the ridge of the "Three Sisters" (rocks looking like human figures), also called Fra Scala, and Donna Lucrezia—fantastic rocks. To the right Cima di Spinas. Over great blocks of granite. Chamois often seen here. View from summit takes in all Grisons peaks—Tyrol, Piedmont, Savoy, and Valais. Bernina looks grand; stone pyramid on top. Way up made for 1,600 feet by people of Samaden and frequenters of Baths of St. Moritz.

St. Moritz is 1¼ l. (3¾ m.) from Samaden and 5,714 feet above the sea. Hotels —du Culm, by Badrutt of Samaden, 40 rooms; board, 15fr. per day; rooms, 2 to 3fr., in the house; ¼ to ½ less out of the house. Pension Bavier; the Cross; Wettstein; rooms, 1½fr. to 2fr.; Pension, 4fr. per day; Pension Gartmann; Aquila Nera; good lodgings to be had; post cars every day from St. Moritz to Maloggia, 3½ l. (10½ m.), 3fr. 60c., 3fr. 5c. To Casaccia, 4½ l. (13½ m.), 4fr. 60c., 3fr. 90c. To Chiavenna 10 l. (30 m.), 8fr. 50c. To Zernetz, 6¾ l. (19½ m.), 5fr. 75c., 4 fr. 75c. To Shuls 12½ l. (37½ m.), 10fr. 55c., 8fr. 45c. To Chur, 16½ l. (48½ m.), 16fr., 13fr. 60c.

Private Carriages.—A whole day, 1 horse, 15fr., 2 horse, 30fr.; for afternoon, to Pontresina, 5fr.; Maria-Sils, 8fr.; Maloggia, the Morteratsch Glacier, Ponte and Val Bevers, 10fr. each excursion. To Zutz, 10 to 12fr.; into the valley of Rosegg, by small mountin car, without springs, 15fr. per day. Guides—Adam Engler, at Campfer, clever, prudent, and willing.

St. Moritz, in Romantsch San Murezza, is the highest village in the Engadin, being 5,700 feet above the sea. The situation is most charming, on the lake of St. Moritz, and it is now much in request on account of its waters and baths. The iron springs and bath-house are ¼ l. (¼ m.) from the village, on the other side of the lake. Temperature of water, 4½° Reaumur. They have more sulphuric acid than the Schwalbach and Pyrmont springs. A company of shareholders has built, since 1856, a new comfortable bath-house, with 90 rooms, always full in summer (1st July to end of September). The carbonic acid of the springs is collected and used for diseases of the eye. Scenery around peaceful and pastoral, backed by sublime snowy peaks.

EXCURSIONS. — Numberless. To the Acla by Lake of Stats, to Pontresina, 1½ l. (4½ m.) To Johannisberg, ½ l. to ¾ l. from Bath House. Fine lake view. To the Alp of Giop, ¾ l. (2¼ m.), 1,100 feet above the St. Moritz; fine view of Bernina, Rosatch, and the lakes. To the Alp of St. Moritz and the Alp of Margums, 1 l. (3 m.), easy, 1,600 feet above valley, fine view of Engadin. To the Druid's Altar an erratic block, near it Falls of the Inn, issuing from St. Moritz Lake.

Piz Nair (9,262 feet), is an interesting excursion. 8 hours' ascent. Panoramic view of Bernina Chain. You can reach Samaden from St. Moritz, by Val de Bevers, rich in chamois, interesting from structure of mountains, and unique in certain respects. It forms a vast crescent from Piz Ott, without lateral valleys. Its flora is the richest in the Engadin. The

Rosetsch, 4 hours' ascent. The Crapnair, 2 hours. Fuorcla by the Alp of Silvaplana (3 h.), view of Rosegg, Bernina, Morteratsch, and Julier. Way, through forests. On road back visit Rosegg Glacier.

Pontresina is 5,566 feet high, the best centre for High Alp excursions, in the Grisons. On the Bernina Pass (south side), 2½ l. (7½ m.) from Samaden. (See Routes at end of Canton). Hotels: White Cross, by Enderlin; Crown, L. Gredig. In Upper Pontresina, Hotel du Glacier, a little inn, 5 rooms, 1*fr*. each. Good guide, John Colani, son of the Chamois King, a wild character, much known in this country. Colani knows the Bernina district well, has some knowledge of geology and botany, and speaks French, German, and Italian. There is a tariff for guides here.* Pontresina is the best point from which to visit the Bernina. Prices are rising with the influx of English and other gold, to fever heat and famine prices, as in the Bernese Oberland. Settle all fares beforehand. M. Jean Sarraz has a fine ornithological collection, and specimens of Engadin butterflies, &c. He is perfectly acquainted with the whole district, and instructs the guides in their trade.

EXCURSIONS.—To the Muottes, 2½ l. (7½ m.) Muot means height in Romanstch. There is a road to Punt Muraigl; thence on by forest to the Alp of Muraigl and the top. Fine view of Rosegg, of Morteratsch, Upper Engadin, Piz Tschierva, &c.

The Glacier of Rosegg is 3 l. (9 m.) from Pontresina. To be reached in light carriages. Guide, needless. The red granite peak of Piz Rosatsch rises to the right. Can be ascended in 4 hours. A châlet of old Colani is in the valley of Rosegg. The glacier is on a gentle incline, and can be easily ascended. In the middle of it is a rock, covered with verdure, and named Agagliouls (middle point), situated like the Jardin of Chamouni,

amidst the highest peaks, such as Piz Tschierva (10,990 feet), Piz Morteratsch (11,556 feet), the Bernina (12,574 feet), Piz Rosegg (12,140 feet), the Seller (11,042 feet), the Canütschin (10,446 feet), and Piz Corvatsch (10,645 feet).

The Cima da Fex is a fatiguing excursion, but repays your trouble, 7 l. (21 m.), ½ l. (1½ m.) over the snow, which must be reached before 10 a.m., as it is almost impassable when thawed. The panoramic view is splendid. Descent to valley of Fex, steep, but safe. A good guide is requisite. Takes in all 12 hours. The glacier of Morteratsch is 1 l. (3 m.) from Pontresina. Road takes you to bridge of Flatzbach, thence 5 minutes to end of glacier. Guide, needless. At hand Fall of the Flatzbach, beautiful green stream, to be compared to those in the Oberland of Berne. Climb up both sides of stream to see Upper Falls, but be careful of slippery rocks of the moraines. Grand group of peaks seen rising round the glacier: Piz Zuppo (hidden horn), the Bernina's second peak was ascended from Pontresina by Messrs. Jäger and Enderlin. You can ascend the glacier. M. Coaz, forest inspector of the Grisons, went all the way up the glacier, 3 l. (9 m.), to the top of the Bernina (12,474 feet), September 13th, 1850. It has been since then scaled three times, the last time by Messrs. Kennedy and Hardy, in 1861.

An excursion may be made from Pontresina to the Val Diavolezza, near the Inn on the Bernina Pass (6,308 feet). It needs a good guide and good legs. It takes you into a savage mountain basin, 1¼ l. (3¾ m.) from the Inn, surrounded by grand peaks—Cambrena, Palü, Bernina, and Morteratsch. Another excursion from the Inn on the Bernina is to the Black and White Lakes, the former sending its waters by the Inn, into the Black Sea; the latter by the Adda, into the Adriatic. Frozen from October to June. Excellent trout. Distance, ¼ l. (1¼ m.) From the lakes ascend in two hours Piz Lagalp (9,118 feet), fine view.

---

* The best guide is said to be Jenni, but he is a little rough.

In the Lower Engadin Tarasp will be found the best centre for excursions. It is 4,608 feet high, and only 3½ l. (10½ m.) from Schuls, with its mineral springs and comfortable hotels.

Its environs are rich in spar, serpentine, aragonite, &c. Dr. Moos is a good scientific guide. At the Capuchin Convent (Tarasp is the only Catholic place in the valley) good Tyrolese wine may be had. Excursions from Tarasp or Schuls may be made to the Kreuzberg, with views of Piz Pisoc (9,783 feet), Piz Zuort (9,611 feet), and Piz Plafna dam daint (9,771 feet).

From Schuls you can ascend the Piz Chimpatsch (8,989 feet), with the finest view in Lower Engadin. A pleasant expedition of two days may be made from Schuls to the Mingerthal, the Münsterthal, and Val Muranza, on to the Umbrailer Joch, the Stilfzer Joch, and to the Baths of Bormio in Valtellina.

First day by Val Scharl to Val Minger. On to Schmelzboden, a district prolific in bears, to the village of Scarl (5,581 feet), with a simple inn, chez Gaspard Arquint. Nic. Fill, a chamois hunter, is a good guide here. Women's costume hereabouts like that of nuns. Roads fork; ¼ l. on to the right you reach Austria, by Cruschetta and Val Plazer. Proceeding to Val d'Astres, and passing the châlets of Pradatschol, Tamangur da dora, and Pra da Seccia, at the foot of Piz d'Astas (9,180 feet), you come to the largest alp pastures in Switzerland. On by châlet Astra da dora, and da daint to Col Costainas and Val Champatsch. Then by Champatsch forest to Lü da daint, a village, (5,904 feet), one of the highest. At Lü da dora, superb view into Val Münster, and at Santa Maria, decent plain inn, Croix Blanche. Second day from St. Maria to the Wörmser or Stilfser Joch, (3½ l. 10½ m.) Up by an aged larch forest, among quartz blocks, to the Gorge of Scais; to Taufers, Val Muranza, Puntins da daint, with view of the Ortlerspitz in Tyrol. 1¼ l. (3¾ m.) from Muranza,

Châlets, you come to the Umbrail Joch (7,732 feet, and on to the Wörmser Joch. A horse to Bormio Baths, 4 l. (12 m.), 9fr.; 2 horses, 15fr.

The Stilfser Joch is (8,610 feet) on the frontiers of Italy and Austria. It is the finest high pass route in Europe, but the result of the unfortunate dispute of recent years has been that it has been almost ruined as a means of precaution on the part of the Austrian Government. Descending 1¼ h. you arrive at a Refuge, and on to the Post Station, Franzenshöhe, (6,380 feet), good walkers can descend 1½ l. (4½ m.) lower down to see the magnificent Glaciers of the Ortler. Distances from the Joch to Franzenshöhe 1½ k (4½ m.); to Trafoi, 1½ l. (4½ m.); to Gamagayr, a fortress and custom house, 1½ l. (4½ m.); to Pradt, 1½ l. (4½ m.); to Schluderns, 1 l. (3 m.); to Mals.

The road over the Stilfser or Wörmser Joch was made for the Austrian Government in 1820 to 1825 by the engineer Donegani. The descent is by numerous zig-zags, to the Church of St. Rainieri, to the pian di Braulio (7,325 feet), with a surprising view of Monte Cristallo 12,110 feet, pass a fine fall of the Adda under glaciers that seem almost suspended above your head. On by the Casino del Rotteri di Spondalunga to Ponté di Vitelli, destroyed by the Austrians 1859. Through a gallery 13½ feet high, to a second gallery, in 5 minutes 3 others, and then a 6th. This district is exposed in winter to frightful snow whirlwinds. Fine fall near Platta Martina. On through Val de Frael to last gallery, when a road strikes off to Baths of Bormio, in Valtellina, known even in Roman times (to Pliny), called in the middle ages Il Paradiso delle Donne. Temperature of water, 89° cent., 1 more than Pfäffer's, but less than Loesch. Water so plentiful that it gives 760 litres a minute, or 165 baths an hour. It contains Glauber's salt, magnesia, lime, oxide of iron, but less chlorium than Loesch and, Pfäffers. Strongest spring called Pliniana. The old baths were on a high rock.

Modern baths, 335 feet lower, have a fine building, room for 100 persons, 40 baths, part in marble, and all well arranged. Prices at the new baths: breakfast, 1*fr.* 50*c.*; dinner, table d'hôte, at 1 p.m., 3*fr.*, at 4 p.m., 4*fr.*; rooms 1 to 3*fr.*; carriage, with 2 horses to the Joch, 20*fr.*, with 1 horse, 10*fr.*; 2 horses to Tirano, 20*fr.*, 1 horse, 12*fr.*; a mule, 10*fr.*, per day; omnibus to Bormio, 1*fr.*, luggage, 50*c.* The climate of Bormio (4,460 feet) is remarkable. You have cool Alpine breezes and a torrid heat of sun, with tropical plants. The excursions near it defy competition. The special charm of the views near it seems to be the union of Alpine verdure and sublimity with Italian softness and magical lights in the Adda Valley. The favourite excursions are to Val Furva, 3l. (9m.), to Scala di Fraele, (6.115 feet), to the lake of Fraele, solitary, poetical, and with good sport for the line, ¼ a day. To the Val di Dentro, &c. Bormio itself is a little dismal, ruinous town, almost burnt down 1855, but an important trading place in the 15th century. Fine fresco of Camelino in the Church of the Crucifix, Strada Combo. Italian bersaglieri, looking like heroes of penny theatres, begin to shew here.

ASCENSIONS IN THE GRISONS.—Several of these have been already noticed but some further observations on this point are expedient.

1. On the route from Chur to Andermatt (Uri), [Route 117], the following ascensions may be made. Near Ilanz, Piz Mundaun (2,065 metres), splendid view, 1 hour from top an inn, where you can sleep Ascent 3 honrs may be made on horseback.

Near Dissentis. Piz Muraun (2,899 met.) fine view 4 hours. Crap Alv (2,982 met.) one of the summits of the Piz Aul 4 hours. Piz Aul (3,033 met.) very extensive view. You see Mont Blanc. Piz Tgietschen, highest point of Oberalpstock (3,330 met.) between the Vorder-Rhein and the Reuss.

In the Russeinthal near Dissentis, *ascensions of the* Stockgron or Piz Rus-sein (3,478 met.) and the Piz Urlaun (3,372 met.)

Near Thusis and Andeer Piz Beverin, ascent easy (3.000 met.) Guide, 5*fr.*, Mule and driver, 9*fr.* Near Splugen (Hotels: Bodenhaus, and Hosig, good;) ascent of Tambohorn (3,276 met.), 4 hours.

Piz Regina (2,508 met.) fine view, and Piz Aul (3,124 met.) with an immense panorama, are on the road from Ilanz to Hinter-Rhein, by the Diesrut and Greina. Further on Piz Scherboden or Terri de Derlun (3,124 met.) accessible on the side of the Alp Scherboda. Piz Valrhein or Rheinwaldhorn can be visited from Hinter-Rhein (Bernardin Pass), 5 posts ⅔ from Chur, 8 hours ascent. Difficult, rather dangerous. Sleep at Châlet of Lenta. Piz Valrhein (3,398 met.) watershed for rivers to North Sea and Adriatic. View embraces whole of Central Alps. At Hinter-Rhein, hotel, La Poste.

In Prättigau: Ascent of Scesa Plana (2,968 met.), from Seewis (Pension, Scesa Plana, 4*fr.* per day), difficult, 7 hours, guide wanted. Near Klosters, ascension of the Casanna (2,562 met.), Schwarzhorn (2,678 met.), and Weissfluh (2,823 met.)

In Oberhalbstein, a nameless peak of the Piz d'Err ridge, between the Albula, the Julier and the Inn, has an immense panoramic view (3,287 met.) This ridge or massif comprises the Piz Err (3,393 met.) the Piz Aela (3,320 met.), the Cima di Flix (3,356 met.), the Piz Salteras (3,078 met.), and the Piz Curver (2,720 met.) and is said to have a fine fiora.

Ascents in the Bernina district and the Engadin, will be found under the more particular description of this sublime part of the Grisons, given further back.

Rosein (Val), between the Stachelberg, Linththal Glarus, and Dissentis is a beautiful glen, having at the top two or three châlets, called Dissentis Alp, 3 hours from the road between Ilanz and Dissentis. Val Rosein is the way up to the San Grat. It is usually called Russein. Time from Dissentis to Stachelberg, 12 hours.

Height of Upper Sandalp (1,938 met.) Route passes Pantenbrücke.

Rosegg, or Rosana (Val), leading up to Rosegg Glacier and Pizz Rosegg. (See "Peaks and Passes,"&c.), 3 hours from Pontresina. Trientalis Europea (very rare), has been found here. Rosegg (Piz) 12,936 feet, ascended by Mr. Bircham, in Sept., 1863, with P. Jenni and Fleuri, as guides; difficult.

Roveredo. See Misocco.

Saint Moritz—"See Peaks and Passes of the Rhoetian Alps."

Sand Alp.—See Canton of Glarus, and Rosein (Val.)

Santa Maria.—See Munsterthal.

Scaletta.—Pass from Scaufs to Davos (2,619 met.), 8½ hours, passes by Schwarzhorn (3,151 met.), with even a finer panoramic view than that from Piz Languard.

Scesa Plana.—(2,968 met., 9,500 ft.) in the Prättigau, can be ascended from Bludenz (Hotel, de la Poste), in the Montafun valley, in 7 hours, or from Seewis (pension, Scesa Plana, 4 *fr.* per day), in 6 or 7 hours. Good guide wanted. This expedition is wild and romantic. The Alvier makes some fine falls, and you pass a beautiful wildly situated tarn ; the Lüner Lake (4,680 ft.) Last part of the way over blocks of rock and snow. View, embraces Tyrol, Grisons, Uri, Glarus, St. Gallen, Appenzell, and the lakes of Wallenstadt and Constance.

Seewis, village in the Prättigau under the Scesa Plana, burnt, 1863. Pension, see Scesa Plana.

Schams, or Schons, Valley of (Vallis Sexamnes), 930 to 980 met. high, 2 hours long, and 1 hour wide; has a population of 1,700 Romantsch Protestants. It is the elliptical basin of an ancient lake. The slopes of the mountains are sometimes covered with coniferæ, at others with green Alps covered with châlets. It presents a sweet contrast to the savage Via Mala.

Scanfs (Hotel du Raisin). Rich village; many confectioners ; collection of medals, shells, MSS. in the Maison Caratsch.

Entrance of Casanna Valley. See "Peaks and Passes of the Rhoetian Alps" and Casanna.

Schanfigg, or Schalfick (Valley), Scane Vikkum, opens to the E. of Chur, length, 7 or 8 l. (24 m.), to Mont Strela, and watered by the impetuous Plessour. It affords special interest to the pedestrian tourist in the Grisons. It is a series of ravines. Right side is inhabited. Left, wild and rugged. Tours may be made up it—1st, by the Ochsenalp, Weisshorn (8,300 feet), dolomite rock contrasting with the serpentine of the Bruggerhorn, on by Sattelalp to Arosa (see Arosa). Eve Inn, A short day. 2nd, By the Strehla Pass to Langwies, 4 hours (inn), and on by Sertig, fine views of the Selvretta groupe to Davos. No paths on the descent.

Schyn (Defile of) in Romantsch Müras, on the road from Klosters to Thusis, by Davos. Near it is a bridge, at Solis, 56 metres, or 170 feet above the torrent.

Serneus (Baths of), near Klosters and Platz, in the Prättigau (985 metres). Sulphur springs. The baths are half a league (1½ miles) from the village. Temperature of springs 70° Reaumur. Good and cheap inn.

Sils (Lake of), Silser See, largest in the alps at so great a height (5,887 feet); three m. long, one broad; once joined Silvaplana, forming a single sheet of water to Campfer, nine miles. (See "Peaks and Passes," &c.)

Sils (village); this, and Santa Maria near it, are the highest villages in Upper Engadin; neat and comfortable. Pension Gartmann at Maria; fine mountain air. Wilder Mann Inn ; the host a good guide to adjoining Val de Fex, full of attractions to the naturalist.

Silva-plana (Lake), German, Waldebene, divided into Upper and Lower, or Campfer Lake. Height 1,794 metres: length of both lakes, 4,500 metres ; breadth, 1,300 metres; depth, 74 metres. The two lakes communicate by the Stretta del Piz Canal, 13 yards deep, which never freezes lakes are at the head waters of the Inn, in Upper Engadin.

Silva-plana (village), Hotel Kreuz, 204 inhabitants, Protestant and Romantsch, 1,816 metres high, on the level between the lakes.

(See "Peaks and Passes of the Rhoetian Alps.")

Somvixer (Thal), pass from Truns to Olivone, 11 l. (33 m.); watered by Rhine; wild district; lynxes in the woods.

Somvix (village); fine view. New road from Dissentis, finished 1858; fine piece of engineering.

· *Splugen* (See "Peaks and Passes of the Rhoetian Alps.")

· *Stätzer Horn;* mountain, with fine view, near Chur. See Chur.

Süss, on the Inn, near Zernetz, Lower Engadin (Hotels: Krone, Post), at the confluence of the Inn and Susasca; 339 inhabitants. You can reach Davos from here by the Süsser Thal, and Klosters by the Col of Lavin.

Tarasp (Inn, chez Perl), 1,401 metres high, 395 inhabitants, in Lower Engadin. Capuchin Church and a castle by a lake.

Tarasp (Baths), two cold springs, 8° 75. Reaumur. Many excursions. See "Peaks and Passes," &c.

Thusis or *Tusis* (Rom. Tusaun), two posts, 5 hours 30 minutes, from Chur, (Inns: Via Mala, good; Adler and Post; good telegraph office); has 739 German Protestant inhabitants; elevation, 746 metres, under the Heinzenberg, and at the confluence of the Rhine and Nolla; good trout; excellent wines—the Saessello, the Inferno, and the Montagner, 4*fr.* per bottle, Asti, Marsala, &c.; good beds. Horses and donkeys supplied; carriages, one horse, to Via Mala, 5*fr.*; two horses, 10*fr.* To Zillis, one-horse carriage 6*fr.*; two horses, 12*fr.* To Andeer, one-horse carriage 8½*fr.*; two horses, 15*fr.* Mountain horses, by Tschappina and Glas to Savien, 15*fr.* per day. Donkeys 15*fr.* per day. Walks: *1. To Nieder* Tagstein, ½ l. (1½ m.), takes you near Statzerhorn, Balderstein Castle, Sils, the ruins of Ehrenfels, the Crapteig

fir forests, the Jomsergrat, to a place where a great popular gathering takes place in May, with bands and flags. Pleasing excursion to Tagstein Castle, in a kind of natural park. 2. To the ruins of Campi, by Sils, through a wood of fine walnut trees, near Baldenstein. Ascent to Hohen Rätien (one hour), whence a fine view over the whole Domleschg Valley. Tagstein Castle, very old, said to have been built 587 B.C. 3. To the Nolla Gorge. The Nolla is a terrible torrent, working great devastation: cuts its way through masses of slate rock. A quarter of a league above Thusis you have a fine view of the savage gorge, overhung by dark fir forests. Looks well after a storm.

Mountain. Expeditions. 1. To Piz Beverin (3,000 metres), generally ascended from Andeer. Start at one o'clock a.m. from Thusis, or two a.m. from Andeer. From Zillis, a path leads by Donath, the Alps of Anna Rosa, in Nursin, to the top in 5½ hours. Many crystals near the summit. Guide from Andeer, 5*fr.*; horse and man, 9*fr.* 2. To Savien-Platz, in the Savienthal (4 hours), where the shepherds are still honest and true, notwithstanding the new law of nations and principle of annexation going on around them. 3. To Prätzer-horn, 4 hours from Thusis, by Purtein, home of a Grison poetess, Nina Came-nisch; and by Sarn to the Alp of Pratz, a fine district for botanists in July. 4. You can also ascend the Statzerhorn, by the Schaller Alp, in 3½ hours.

Tiefenkasten (Romantsch, chaste). Hotels: Albula, Post, Kreuz. 160 Rom-antsch inhabitants, 889 metres high, at the entrance of the Oberhalbstein Valley (Romantsch Sur Seissa), 8 l. (24 m.) lead-ing to the Septimer and Julier Passes. Even in Roman times, there was a fortified post here to defend the Julier Pass. To the west, above the Albula Valley, is the Schyn Pass, leading to Thusis, in the Domleschg. A road, made from 1837 to 1840, leads by a steep ascent to a place called Am Stein (½ hour), shut in by precipices, and giving the name of Ober halb des Steines to the valley called in Romantsch Seissa. The Rhine foams and frets below in a deep channel.

Tirano, in Valtellina, reached from Saint Moritz, by the Bernina and Piscia-della, 14 to 15 hours. Diligence every day from Samaden to Poschiavo, and from Poschiavo to Tirano (7h. 20m.); total fare, 7fr. 20c., 11⅝ l. (34 m.) Or by Cavaglia, 13h. 30m.; carriage route from Saint Moritz to Lake Piccolo, and from San Carlo to Tirano. Path from Piccolo to San Carlo. Hotel due Torri, Angelo. No curiosities, but cretins. Half a league (1½ mile), at Madonna di Tirano, is a beautiful Church, all of marble, with a bronze statue of St. Michael, to which a miraculous legend is attached. Fine carvings in choir. Albergo chez Molinari.

Trins, 1 l. (3 m.) from Reichenau. Post Inn. Ruins of a castle, built by Pepin le Bref. The village is surrounded by walnuts and cherry orchards.

Truns, or Trons (Hotel Krone), 893 Catholic inhabitants, 860 metres, at the junction of the Ferrera with the Rhine. Fine view from chapel. Armorial paintings of 1425 in the Assembly House of the Deputies of the Grauenbund. Excursions to Val Ferrera, Piz Ner (3,070 met.), and Glacier of Puntaiglas, under Piz Urlaun (3,372 met.), and Frisal (3,295 met.) Passes lead hence—

1. To Stachelberg, in the Linththal, Glarus, by the Sandgrat, 14 hours. Difficult route; good guide wanted.

2. To Stachelberg, by the Kistengrat. Fatiguing; 11½ hours.

3. To Schwanden, by the Panixer Pass.

4. To Olivone, by the Greina, 11 l. (33 m.)

A path may be followed from Obersaxen, near Ilanz, to Truns, more interesting than the post road. Ilanz to Flond, ⅜ l. (2¼ m.), Valata, 1 l. (8 m.), to Meyerhof; fine view; good inn. In ⅜ l. (1½ m.), Gorge of Val Gronda, a deep crevasse with waterfalls and fine views; easy ascent. Hence to Piz Miezdi; superb view. Descent to Rhine Valley at Tavanasa, opposite the heights of Bregels, where lives the best chasseur of the Grisons—Benedetg, Cathomén.

Vals, or St. Peter am Platz, chief village of the Valley of Vals (3,842 feet high); 2¼ l. (8¼ m.) from Ilanz. To the left you pass by the Flinser Alp to Safienplatz. The valley is divided into Val Zafreila, leading to the Glacier of the Adula, to the left, into the Val Peil, leading in 3 hours to the Col of Valserberg, and in 1½ hour to Hinter-Rhein, and by the Lenta Pass, in 7¼ hours, to Olivone.

Val Blegno.—Southern descent of the Lukmanier Pass, from Dissentis to Olivone. Chief place of the district. Inn, Stefano Bello's. Every day there is a fast car in 3 hours to Biasca, in Val Lavigno, 2fr. 85c. (See Canton of Tessin).

Valtellina.—Valley of the Adda, belongs to Italy, since 1857. (See Bormio.) Sondrio is the chef lieu of Upper Valtellina. It stands high, contains large convents, and exhibits the Italian style of architecture. Grosio is a large, well peopled village, with fine church of St. Joseph. Grosetto is a village with a taper spire, where the Virgin is said to have appeared, and driven back a tribe of barbarians, on the point of plundering it. On Sundays, the women go to church with embroidered handkerchiefs on their heads and a fan in their hands. The neighbouring country is extremely beautiful, the mountains assume a softer outline, and are covered with forests or vineyards. Tirano is in Lower Valtellina (see Tirano), which has little to interest. The roads are wearisome and dusty, to the lake of Como. Valley of Veltlin very hot in Summer, but only unhealthy place is Colico. The great military road of the Stilfzer Joch, runs up it. It produces much silk, and excellent wines. Its proper termination is Monrignone, where the Adda is formed by the confluence of two streams, flowing in opposite directions, and meeting near Bormio. The other places in the Valley are Morbegno (Inn, Regina d'Inghilterra. good, 653 feet above the sea. Sondrio (Inns, Albergo Della Maddalena. Im-

Corona, Post, Angelo, small and cheap.)
Good houses and educated inhabitants.
The mineralogist can probably obtain leave
to see the collection of Signor Giuseppe
Sertoli. The botanist will also probably
be able to view the herbarium of Signor
Ferrari (1,198 feet above the sea).

Cretinism and goitre exist in several
parts of the valley, between Sondrio and
Tirano.

The itinerary of the valley from Bormio
is as follows :—

Bormio to	Miles.
Bolladore	14
Tirano	14
Sondrio	18½
Morbegno	16
Colico	11½
	74

Vrin, a scattered village with several
churches. On the pass from Ilanz to the
Somvixthal, by the Disrut Col. Surrounding it are a number of lofty peaks,
such as Piz Aul, the Frunthorn (9,340 feet),
the Terri de Derlun (9,617 feet), and the
Piz Terri de Canal (9,700 feet). One
league from Vrin is Butzatsch, when you
proceed by the Disrutalp, in 1¼ hour, to
the Disrut Col (7,462 feet). Then the road
forks; to the right, leading to the Somvixthal; to the left, by the Greina to Val
Camadra and Olivone in the Tessin.

One league (3 m.) from Vrin, is the
large village of Lumbrein (4,341 feet above
the sea), near which some pleasant excursions may be made. To Piz Cavel
and to Piz Camona (9,060 feet), easy ascent
in 3½ hours, by Val Cava. Fine view.
To Piz Regina, 2 hours, Piz Aul requires
sturdy hands and feet.

A post car proceeds four times a week
from Ilanz to Peiden, by Lungnatz, 2¼
hours. Vrin is 4 hours from Peiden, which
has a source of mineral waters at the
entrance of the Duvin Gorge.

Zernetz.—Hotel, Lion, chez Fili; Crown,
where there is a tame chamois (roast
chamois and marmottes, to be had at the
end of the summer); in Lower Engadin,

3 l. (9 m.) from Scanfs, 9¼ miles from
Zutz.

Many excursions may be made hence.
1. Val Cluozza, leading to the Teufelsthal
and Falsenthal, a frightful solitude, the
select abode of bears. 2. To Mont Bes-
seglia, with view into Val Macun. An
old tradition says that dragons inhabit its
lakes. Every day a post car to Tarasp,
in 6 hours, and to Zutz, in 2½ hours.

Zillis.—(3,061 feet high) very old village.
Church dates from A.D. 940, 1½ m. above
the entrance into the Schamserthal.
(Romantsch name, Ciraun.) An old
fresco on the last house of the village,
date 1590, and a pious inscription in old
German. Piz Beverin can be hence ascended, passing by Andeer (2 m.), with
good inn. Hotel, Frau, reasonable, and
a good centre. Ascent takes 6 hours.
Guide, 5*fr.* Bears occasional visitors at
Andeer.

Zutz.—(See Süss).

ROUTES OF THE GRISONS.

From Chur to

Aarau, by Zurich (Nos. 142 and 18).

Aarberg, by Zurich (Nos. 142 and 79), and Berne
(Nos. 53), or by Zurich (Nos. 142 and 18), and
Solothurn (Nos. 16 and 216).

Aarberg, by Zurich (Nos. 142 and 18), and Aarau
(No. 1).

Aigle, by Zurich (Nos. 142 and 79), and Berne (No.
54), or by Thun and the Simmenthal (No. 55).

ROUTE 117.

ALTDORF, by SCHWYZ (Nos. 134 and 207), or by the
DEVIL'S BRIDGE, 27¾ l. (83¼ m.)

	Leagues.	Miles.
Ems	1¼	3¾
Reichenau	¼	1¼
Tamins	¼	¾
Trins	¼	2¼
Trinser-Mühle	¼	1¼
The Waldhäuser, near Flims	1	3
Laag	1	3
Sagens	½	1½
Schlewis or Lauenberg	¼	1½
Ilanz	¼	1¼
Strada	¼	1½
Schnans	¼	¾
Ruvis	¼	¾
Carried forward	8	24

ROUTE 117—*(Continued)*

	Leagues.	Miles.
Brought forward	8	24
Tavarasca	1½	4¼
Truns	1	3
Somvix	¾	2¼
Dissentis	2	6
Monpertavetsch	1	3
Rugnei	¾	2¼
Sadrun	¼	¾
Camischolas	¼	¾
Sarkuns	¼	¾
Rueras	¼	¾
Sellva	1	3
Ciamut	½	1½
Oberalpsee	1¼	3¾
Andermatt, 20¼ l. (6¼ m.)	2	6
Teufelsbrücke (Devil's Bdg.)	¼	¾
Göschenen	¾	2¼
St. Joseph	¾	2¼
Wasen, 22¼ l. (68¼ m.)	¼	¾
Altdorf	5	15
	27¼	83¼

ROUTE 118.

ALTSTAETTEN, 15 l. (45 m.)

	Leagues.	Miles.
Zizers	1¾	5¼
Ragaz	2¼	6¾
Sargans	1	3
Trubbach	1	3
Werdenberg	3	9
Haag	1	3
Salez	1	3
Sennwald, 12 l. (36 m.)	1	3
Altstaetten	3	9
	15	45

Appenzell (No. 20).

Art, by Schwyz (No. 134 and 208).

Baden, by Zurich (No. 142 and 44).

ROUTE 119.

BELLINZONA, 32 l. (96 m.)

	Leagues.	Miles.
Dissentis (No. 117)	13¼	39¾
Montpermedels	1	3
Platta	1	3
St. Rocco	½	1½
San Giacomo	1½	4½
Hospital San Maria	1	3
Hospital Casaccia	1¼	3¾
Hospital Campier	1	3
Olivone	1¾	5¼
Blasca	4¾	14¼
Osogna	1½	4½
Terracia	1¾	5¼
Bellinzona	1¾	5¼
	32	96

ROUTE 120.

BELLINZONA, by the Splugen, 25½ l. (76½ m.)

	Leagues.	Miles.
Bonaduz	2	6
Rhäzuns	¼	¾
Kazis	2	6
Thusis	½	1½
Viâ Mala to last bridge	1	3
Zillis	¼	¾
The Pigeuner Baths	¼	1¼
Andeer	¼	¾
By the Rofla to the first bridge	½	1½
To the end of the Rofla	1	3
The Splugen, 9¾ l. (29¼ m.)	1½	4½
Medels	½	1½
Ebl	½	¾
Rufenen	½	1½
Hinter-Rhein	1	3
Mount St. Bernardin	3	9
The Piano of San Giacomo	1½	4½
Misox	1	3
Soazza, 18 l. (54 m.)	½	1½
Gabiolo	1	3
Lostallo	¾	2¼
Cama	1¼	3¾
Leggia	¼	¾
Grono	¾	2¼
Roveredo	½	1¼
San Vittore	½	1¼
Monticello	½	1½
Lumino	½	1¼
Caslione	¼	¾
Molinazzi	¾	2¼
Bellinzona	½	1½
	25½	76½

Berne, by Zurich (Nos. 142 and 79).

Bex, by Zurich (Nos. 142 and 79), and Berne (No. 58), or by Thun and the Simmenthal (No. 55).

Bienne, by Zurich (Nos. 142 and 79), and Berne (No. 59), or by Zurich (Nos. 142 and 18), Aarau (No. 16), and Solothurn (No. 218).

Brougg, by Zurich (Nos. 142 and 79), and Berne (No. 54).

Burgdorf, by Zurich (Nos. 142 and 302, as far as Morgenthal), thence by Route No. 6 to Kirchberg, and thence to Burgdorf.

Chamouni, by Zurich (Nos. 142 and 79), Berne (No. 63), Lausanne (No. 96) and Geneva (No. 95), or by Zurich (Nos. 142 and 18), Aarau (No. 16), Solothurn (No. 223), Lausanne (No. 96) and Geneva (No. 95), or by Thun and the Simmenthal to Vevay (No. 55).

Chaux de Fonds, by Zurich (Nos. 142 and 18), Aarau (No. 16) and Solothurn (No. 220), or by Zurich (Nos. 142 and 79), Berne (No. 70) and Neuchâtel (No. 169).

ROUTE 121.

CHIAVENNA, by the Splugen, 16 l. (49 m.)

	Leagues.	Miles.
To Splugen, see No. 120 ...	9¾	29¼
Inn at the top of Pass	2	6
By Tecino to Isola	2	6
Campod Icln	1	3
Preston	¼	¾
S. Maria di Gallipocio	½	1½
Bett	¼	¾
Chiavenna	¼	¾
	16	49

ROUTE 122.

By the S. Bernardin and valley of Misocco, 25¼ l. (75¾ m.)

	Leagues.	Miles.
Soazza. (No. 120)	18	54
To the summit of Mount Furcola	3½	10½
Santa Maria (valley of San Giacomo)	2	6
Chiavenna	1¾	5¼
	25¼	75¾

ROUTE 123.

By the Septimer, 21¼ l. (63¾ m.)

	Leagues.	Miles.
Malix	1½	3¾
Churwalden	¾	2¼
Parpan	¾	2¼
By la Bruyere to Lenz, 4¼ l. (14¼ m.)	2	6
Vazerol	¼	
Tiefenkasten	½	2¼
Conters	1½	4½
Savognin or Schweiningen	½	
Tinzen	½	1½
Rofna	¾	2¼
Mühlen	1	3
Marmels (Marmorera)	1	3
Stallvedro	½	1½
Stalla, 11¾ l. (35¼ m.)	½	1½
Inn on Septimer	2	6
Casaccia, 15¼ l. (45¾ m.)	1½	4½
Vicosroprano	1½	4½
Borgonovo		1½
Stampa		1
La Porta		
Promontogno		
Castasegna	1	3
Villa or Fontella	½	2¼
Sta. Croce		1½
Prosto		1½
Chiavenna	¼	¾
	21¼	63¾

ROUTES 124—125.

Constance.—Rail to Rorschach, and on by steamer; Rail direct.

ROUTE 126.

EINSIEDELN, 19 l. (57 m.)

	Leagues.	Miles.
Wesen, (No. 107 A)	12	36
Urnen	½	1½
Einsiedeln (No. 108)	6½	19½
	19	57

Engelberg, by Altdorf (Nos. 117 and 257, 258, or 259), or by Schwyz (Nos. 134 and 207), and Altdorf (No. 117).

ROUTE 127.

FRAUENFELD, 26¼ l. (78¾ m.)

	Leagues.	Miles.
Wesen (No. 107 A)	12	36
Ziegelbrücke	½	1½
Schännis	1	4½
Kaltbrunn		2¼
Uznach		2¼
Liechtensteig (No. 21)	4	12
Frauenfeld (No. 109)	6½	19½
	26¼	78¾

Fribourg, by Zurich (Nos. 142 and 79) and Berne (No. 54).

ROUTE 128.

GAIS, 17 l. (51 m.)

	Leagues.	Miles.
Altstaetten (No. 118)	15	45
Am Stoss	1½	3¾
Gais	¼	2¼
	17	51

Geneva, by Zurich (Nos. 142 and 79), Berne (No. 54) and Lausanne (No. 96); or by Zurich, Aarau, Solothurn, and Lausanne (See Chamouni).

Glarus (No. 107).

Herisau, by Appenzell (Nos. 20 and 22).

Hofwyl, by Zurich (Nos. 142 and 302).

Lauffenberg, by Zurich (Nos. 142 and 303).

Lausanne, by Zurich (Nos. 142 and 79) and Berne (No. 6?); or by Zurich (Nos. 142 and 16), Aarau (No. 16), and Solothurn (No. 210).

Lindau, rail to Rorschach, and boat over Lake of Constance.

ROUTE 130.

London (Baths), by Zurich (Nos. 142 and 79) and Berne (No. 65); or by Zurich (Nos. 142 and 18), Aarau (No. 16), Solothurn (No. 227), and Sion (No. 268); or by the Saint Gothard, 46½ L. (149¼ m.)

	Leagues.	Miles.
Andermatt (No. 117)	20½	62½
Hospital		2½
Zum Dorf	1½	4½
Reulp	1	3
On the Furka	3	9
Oberwald (in the Valais)	3	9
Obergestelen		1½
Göschenen		2½
Munster		2½
Recklingen		1½
Niederwald	1½	4½
Belwald		2½
Viesch		1½
Lax		1½
Deisch		1½
Mörtl	1½	4½
Naters	2	6
By Brieg to Glys		1½
Gambsen		2½
Visp or Viege		2½
Brunk	1	3
Turtmann		2½
Loesch, town 44 l. (132 m.)		1½
Waren	1	3
Loesch (baths)	1½	4½
	46½	139½

Locarno and Lugano, by Bellinzona (Nos. 119 or 120, and 282 and 283).

Locle, by Zurich (Nos. 142 and 18), Aarau (No. 16), and Solothurn (No. 224); or by Zurich (Nos. 142 and 79), Berne (No. 70), and Neuchâtel (No. 175).

Lucerne, by Schwyz (Nos. 134 and 161).

Mendrisio, by Bellinzona (Nos. 119 or 120), and further on (No. 235).

Morat, by Zurich (Nos. 142 and 79) and Berne (No. 77); or by Zurich (Nos. 142 and 18), Aarau (No. 16), and Solothurn (No. 221).

Morges, by Zurich (Nos. 142 and 79), Berne (No. 63), and Lausanne (No. 96); or by Zurich (Nos. 142 and 18), Aarau (No. 16), Solothurn (No. 223), and Lausanne (No. 96).

Moudon (same routes as the last except Lausanne).

Neuchâtel, by Zurich (Nos. 142 and 79) and Berne (No. 70); or by Zurich (Nos. 142 and 18), Aarau (No. 16), and Solothurn (No. 178).

Orbe, by Zurich (Nos. 142 and 79), Berne (No. 71), or by Zurich (Nos. 142 and 18), Aarau (No. 16), Solothurn (No. 178), and Neuchâtel (No. 97).

Payerne, by Zurich (Nos. 142 and 79), and Berne (No. 77), or by Zurich (Nos. 142 and 18), Aarau (No. 16), and Solothurn No. 223).

Q

ROUTE 131.

Pfeffers (Baths), 4½ L. (14½ m.)

	Leagues.	Miles.
Zizers	1½	5½
Unter-Zollbrücke	1	3
The Abbey of Pfeffers	1½	4½
Pfeffers Baths	½	1½
	4½	14½

Righi (The), by Schwyz (Nos. 134 and 212)

ROUTE 132.

Saint Gallen, 21½ L. (64½ m.

	Leagues.	Miles.
Rorschach	19½	57½
St. Gallen	2½	6½
	21½	64½

Or by Rail (see St. Gallen and Chur).

ROUTE 133.

Saint Moritz, in the Engadin, (16½ L. (50½ m.)

	Leagues.	Miles.
Steila (No. 123)	11½	35½
Silva-plana	4	12
Saint Moritz (Baths of)	1	3
	16½	50½

Schaffhausen, by Rail, through Zurich.

ROUTE 134.

Schwyz, 24½ L. (72½ m.)

	Leagues.	Miles.
Urnen (No. 126)	12½	37½
Bilten	½	1½
Richenburg	½	½
Schubelbach	1	3
Galgenen	½	1½
Lachen	½	1
Altendorf	½	[illegible]
Pfäffikon	1½	3
Richtenschwyl, 18½ l. (54½ m)	1½	4½
Schindellegi	1	3
Rothen—Thurm	2½	7½
Sattel	½	1½
Steinen	1	3
Seewen	½	1½
Schwyz	½	1½
	24½	72½

ROUTE 135.

Sion, 46½ L. (144½ m.)

	Leagues.	Miles.
Loesch (No. 130)	44	132
Siders or Sierre	1½	3½
St. Leonard	2	6
Sion or Sitten	1	3
	46½	144½

Solothurn, by Zurich (Nos. 142 and 18), and Aarau (No. 18), or by Schwyz (Nos. 134 and 161), and Lucerne (No. 162).

ROUTE 136.

Sondrio, 25¼ L. (75¾ m.)

	Leagues.	Miles.
Casaccia (No. 123)	15¼	45¼
Malaja	1	3
Bosso	3	9
Sondrio	6	18
	25¼	75¾

Stanz. See Unterwalden.

ROUTE 137.

Thun, by Zurich (Nos. 142 and 79), and Berne (No. 55), or by the Devil's Bridge, 46 L. (138 m.)

	Leagues.	Miles.
Wesen (No. 117)	22¼	68¼
Thun (No. 55)	23¾	69¾
	46	138

ROUTE 138.

Trogen, 17¼ L (52¼ m)

	Leagues.	Miles.
Altstatten (No. 118)	15	45
Trogen	2¼	7¼
	17¼	52¼

ROUTE 139.

Tirano, 27 L. (81 m.)

	Leagues.	Miles.
Lenz (No. 123)	4¾	14¼
Brienz	1	3
Alveneuer (baths)	1	3
Filisur	1	3
Bergun	1	3
The Weissenstein Inn	2	6
Pont., 14¼ L. (42¾ m.)	3	9
Bevers	1	3
Samaden	½	1½
Pontresina	1	3
The Mountain Inns (Bernina Pass)	1½	4½
La Rosa	2½	7½
Pisciadella	1	3
Poschiavo or Puschlav	1½	4½
Prada	¼	¾
San Antonio	¼	¾
Meschin	1	3
Brus	1	3
Madonna	1	3
Tirano	¼	¾
	26½	80½

Unterwalden, by Schwyz (Nos. 134 and 273).

Vevay, by Zurich (Nos. 142 and 79); and Berne (No. 54).

Winterthur, by Saint Gallen, Rail, (see Chur and Saint Gallen.)

ROUTE 140 (a).

Worms or Bormio, 31¾ L. (95¼ m.)

	Leagues.	Miles.
Zernez (No. 143)	18¾	56¼
Livin	7	21
Worms or Bormio	6	18
	31¾	95¼

ROUTE 140 (b).

By Val Fidriga, 26½ L. (79½ m.)

	Leagues.	Miles.
Scanfs (No. 143)	15½	46½
Casana Alp	2¼	6¾
Casana Pass	1½	3½
Val Fidriga to Luvin	1½	4½
Trepall	½	1½
San Carlo	2	6
Isolaccia	1	3
Bremaglio or Bramei	2	6
Worms	½	1½
	26½	79½

Yverdun, by Zurich (Nos. 142 and 79), and Berne (No. 77), or by Zurich (Nos. 142 and 18) Aarau (No. 16), and Solothurn (No. 228).

ROUTE 141.

Zug, 23¼ L. (69¾ m.)

	Leagues.	Miles.
Horgen (No. 142)	20	60
Zug (No. 115)	3¼	9¾
	23¼	69¾

Zurich, by Rail: see Chur and Zurich.

ROUTE 142 (a).

Zurich, by Horgen, 23¼ L. (69¾ m.)

	Leagues.	Miles.
Richtenschwyl (No. 134)	18¼	54¾
Wadenschwyl	¾	2¼
Horgen, 20 L. (60 m.)	1	3
Oberrieden	⅓	1
Thalwyl	[illegible]	[illegible]
Ruschlikon	[illegible]	1½
Kilchberg	[illegible]	[illegible]
Wollishofen	[illegible]	2¼
Zurich	1	3
	23¼	69¾

ROUTE 142 (b):

By Uznach 24¼ l. (74¼ m.)

	Leagues.	Miles.
Wesen (No. 107 a)	12	36
Schännis	1½	4½
Zurich (No. 116 b)	11¼	33¼
	24¼	74¼

To the Tyrol by the Engadin.

ROUTE 143.

Bolzen (Bozen) 46 l. (138 m.)

	Leagues.	Miles.
Pont (No. 139)	14¼	42¾
Zuz	1	3
Scanf	¼	¾
Capella	⅓	1¼
Cinuscel	⅓	1¼
Pontalto	¼	¾
Zernez, 18¾ l. (56¼ m.)	2	6
Inn on the Ofen	3	9
Cierf	2	6
S. Maria	1	3
Münster	¾	2¼
Taufer	½	1½
Glurns	2	6
Schlanders	5	15
Meran	7	21
Bolzen (Bozen)	6	18
	46	138

ROUTE 144.

Inspruck, 57 l. (171 m.)

	Leagues.	Miles.
Zernez (No. 143)	18¾	56¼
Sus	1½	4½
Lavin	¾	2¼
Guarda	1	3
Fattan	2	6
Schuls	1	3
Remuss	2	6
Strada	1¼	3¾
Martinsbruck	¾	2¼
Nauders	1	3
Pfunds	2	6
Pruz	3	9
Landeck	3	9
Imst	4	12
Heimingen	4	12
Sils	1	3
Sam	1	3
Rieds	1	3
Telfs	1	3
Patnau	2	6
Zierl	2	6
Inspruck	3	9
	57	171

Into the Tyrol by the Adlerberg.

ROUTE 145.

Bolzen (Bozen), 58¼ l. (176¼ m.)

	Leagues.	Miles.
Feldkirch (No. 129)	9¼	28¼
Frastanz	½	1½
Neunzig	1	3
Pludenz	2	6
Praz	2	6
Dalas	1	3
To the Convent	2	6
Zur Stuben	1	3
Adlerberg	1½	4½
St. Anthony	1½	4½
St. Jakob	1	3
Patnai	1	3
Fliersch	1	3
Zum Strengen	1	3
Bianz	1	3
Landeck	1	3
Prunz	3	9
Pfunds	3	9
Nauders	2	6
Mals	4½	13½
Glurns	¼	¾
Schlanders	5	15
Meran	7	21
Bolzen (Bozen)	6	18
	58¼	176¼

ROUTE 146.

Inspruck, 47 l. (141 m.)

	Leagues.	Miles.
By Feldkirch to Landeck, (No. 145)	28	84
From Landeck to Inspruck, (No. 144)	19	57
	47	141

To Bavaria, Austria, and North Germany, as well as Suabia, Franconia, Saxony, and the Rhine, the best route is by Ragatz, Lindau, and Friedrichshafen.—See *Bradshaw's Continental Railway Guide.*

To Paris, Strasbourg by St. Gallen, Zurich, and Bâle. To South France by Zurich, Berne, and Geneva.

To Milan and Italy by Chiavenna.

We have seen that the Grisons are connected by several important passes with the Canton of Glarus, which may also be approached from Zurich, by rail; and from Schwyz, by the Pragel Pass.

We must therefore proceed to examine this in many respects highly interesting Canton

The traveller, if arriving from Zurich, can reach Glarus direct by rail; if from the Grisons, several interesting Passes connect the two Cantons, *i.e.* the Scrnf the Weisstannen, and the Panixer Pass. [For the trains and fares per rail, see Zurich; for the pedestrian Passes to Grisons, see Routes at the end of this Canton.]

CANTON OF GLARUS.

Is bordered to the E. and N. by that of St. Gallen, to the S. by the Cantons of Grisons and Uri, and to the W. by that of Schwyz.

SOIL AND CLIMATE.—The area of the Canton of Glarus is $31\frac{1}{2}$ Swiss sq. leagues* (691 square kilometres), and consists essentially of mountains and valleys. Among the latter only two are habitable, *i.e.*, the Great and the Little Valley. The former, called also the Valley of the Linth, is watered by that river, and extends from the Lake of Wallenstadt, 8 l. (24 m.), N. and S., up to the highest mountains in the Canton, which form its frontier on the side of the Grisons and Uri. The Little Valley, also named Valley of Seinft (Sernft-thal), is to the E. of the former, and begins amongst the Alps of Frugmatt. Descending thence it forms a semicircle as far as Schwanden, where it joins the principal valley. A third little valley, the Klönthal, opens to the N.E., and runs from the frontiers of Schwyz to the little hamlet of Riedern, which is the only inhabited place contained in it. In the northern part of the Canton, some marshes formed by the Linth, used to taint the air and occasion marsh fevers, but this evil has been remedied by canals and drainage, chiefly planned by the genius of an eminent Swiss savant, who thence derived the honourable title conferred upon him by the Government of, Escher von der Linth.

This drainage was carried out by a company of shareholders, and known by the name of the Linth works; with the exception every part of the Canton enjoys a healthy climate, which though cold and severe in the mountains is mild and genial in the valleys.

MOUNTAINS.—Towering mountains and formidable glaciers surround the Canton of Glarus almost on every side, but especially to the south and west; their ramification and buttresses which extend and cross each other in all directions in the interior of the Canton, conspire in forming the three principal valleys mentioned above, all pouring their waters into the Linth. The principal mountains and glaciers in the western part of the Canton are—the Hirzli, the Kupfenstock, the Bocksberg, the Hofläscher, the Wigg whose summit is called Schien; the Deyenstock, the Pfannenstock, the Reiseltstock, the Kammerstock, the Claridenhörner, and the Sheerhorn. To the south occur the following summits—the Gersistock, the Tödi, or Dödi (10,887 Swiss feet, 3,662 metres, 11,883 English feet above the sea), the Kisten, the Selbsanft, the Haustock (10,363 feet above the sea), the Cascharauls is a remarkable peak, 9,340 feet high, near the Sand Glacier. From the south-west to the north-east you come to the Wichlestock, the Vorab, the Ofen, the Falhuber, the Tschingelspitz, and to the east are situated the Spitzmeilen, the Foessi the Schilt, and the Murtschenstock. In the centre of the Canton occur others such as the Wallenberg, the Kirenzer the Mulliberg, and the Frohnalpstock These mountains are on the eastern bank of the Linth, while on its western bank we find the three Glarnisches (anterior middle, and posterior), the Guben, the Bächistock, and the Braunwaldberg Lastly, in the valley of Sernft we have the Gaisstock, the Rothberg, the Karpfstock,* &c., &c.

* 484 English square miles.

* The Karpfstock. 9,180 feet above the sea. The Freiberge extend from the Karpfstock nearly to Schwanden, and include most of the highland that is encircled by the valleys of the Sernft, the

LAKES, RIVERS, AND RIVULETS. — 1. The lake of Wallenstadt (see its description in the Canton of St. Gallen). The lake of Klön and some small mountain tarns also occur in different parts of the Canton.

RIVERS.—2. The Linth, formed by two streams, the Staffel and the Limmeren, flows through the principal valley of the Canton receiving accessions from a multitude of torrents and streams, and ultimately falls into the Lake of Wallenstadt. 2. The Sernft rises in the Frugmatt, at the foot of the Hausstock, has a semicircular course through the valley of the same name, and falls into the Linth near Schwanden.

RIVULETS.—The Filzbach, the Löntsch, formed by the water issuing from lake Klön, the Diesbach, the Durnagelbach, the Fetschbach, the Schreyenbach, the Staffel, the Limmernbach, and a number of others whose names are almost unknown.

PRODUCTIONS AND INDUSTRY. — The Canton of Glarus has a fine breed of horned cattle, some horses, an improved breed of sheep, some goats and pigs. The streams and lakes are fairly stocked with fish, and there is a considerable quantity of game. Among the wild animals may be noticed the chamois, the fox, the badger, the martin, the marmot, the eagle, the vulture.

The grass of its pastures is generally excellent, especially the aromatic clover (ziegel klee), *melilotus coerulea*, or blue

Durna, and the Linth. The Freiberge were formerly a well known chamois preserve, but they are not now preserved so strictly as formerly, and, unless care be taken, will soon become extinct.—" *Peaks, Passes*," &c., 1*st Series*, *p.* 2o8—9.

* The Ober Sand Alp, a little green plain, 6,000 feet above the sea, at the very foot of the Tödl, is watered by streams which flow from the glaciers of Sand, Spitzälpeli, Geispützl, and Becki. These rivulets unite with the Röthebach and the Biferten-bach, near the foot of the Biferten Glacier, and form the Sandbach, which takes the name of Linth after its junction with the Limmern, a mile above the Pantenbrücke.—" *Peaks, Passes*," &c., 1*st Series*, *p.* 263.

melilot, which is an essential element in the manufacture of the green cheese, known as *schabzieger*, constituting an article of great commercial value, particularly in the north of the Canton. The yield of wine and cereals is small, but good crops of potatoes, hemp, and flax are raised, and fruit as well as vegetables generally succeed well in the valleys, being rapidly ripened by the " sweet south " winds that prevail in them in summer. There are fine forests and good quarries of sandstone, gypsum, and a superior kind of slate, which is converted into the article used in schools, and exported largely to distant countries. Good mineral springs occur in this Canton, which has manufactures of muslin, linen, and cotton stuffs, utensils and other objects in wood, &c., &c.

HOT SPRINGS AND BATHS. — Among these may be noticed the Baths of the Niedercrurnen at the foot of the Rothenberg, the sulphurous Baths of the Luchsengen, and the baths of Wichlen; the latter situated at the foot of the mountain of the same name, on the road leading by Mount Segnes, into the Canton of Grisons. But the most important spring occurs at the Stachelberg, in the Linththal, of which a fuller description is given at page 232.

POPULATION AND RELIGION.—The population of the Canton amounts to 30,400 inhabitants, all speaking a patois of the German, and the greater portion Protestants, the Catholics amounting to less than 4,000.

ABBEYS AND CONVENTS.—On the hill of Naefels, where formerly stood the castle of the Austrian governor, there is now a Capuchin Convent, called Marienbourg. It was built in 1075.

ESTABLISHMENTS FOR PUBLIC INSTRUCTION AND SCIENCE, AND CHARITABLE INSTITUTIONS.—Since 1820, the elementary schools of this Canton have been well developed, but nothing has hitherto been done for a collegiate education in higher branches. Accordingly, the Protestant youth who wish to advance beyond the first elements, attend courses of lectures, in Germany, at Göttingen, Jena, or in Switzerland, at Bâle. The Catholics are in the habit of frequenting schools attached to the convents in Einsiedeln and Pfëffers, or the Gymnasium of Lucerne, from which they commonly proceed to Milan and Turin, to finish their studies there. Considerable bursaries were provided in these cities for the special education of Swiss students.

LIBRARY.—A library belonging to the Protestant inhabitants of the Canton, and called the Landesbibliothek, has been established at Glarus, since 1758.

The hospital of Glarus is the only general hospitable institution in the Canton; but, as is usual in the democratic states of Switzerland, each parish is obliged to provide for its own poor.

SURVEY OF THE CANTON OF GLARUS.

Bourg (The), is a hill near Glarus, commanding a charming view of the valley.

Elm, a village in the Sernft Valley, where it opens to meet the Ramina Furke Pass from the Unter Thal. Elm is surrouded by fine scenery, and has a nice, clean little inn, kept in 1861, by Jacob Elmer, a very kind and careful landlord.

The Segnes Pass (over the Sardona Glacier), leads from Elm to Reichenau in Grisons. Another pass leads from Elm, the Panixer Pass, S.W. of the Martinsloch, into the Grisons.

Enneda is a fine village, situated opposite the town of Glarus, at the foot of the Schilt. The road leading to it, is bordered with fine fruit trees, and follows the Linth, which it crosses by a handsome wooden bridge. Enneda is inhabited by several wealthy commercial men, who have manufactures in the village, exporting their produce to the capital cities *of Europe, and even beyond the seas.*

Glarus.—The small town of Glarus i properly the capital of the whole Canton It is rebuilt on the banks of the Linth on the site of the former town, most o which was destroyed by the great fire o 1861, and stands beneath a rock whicl gives birth to many springs, and closes i the valley very much in this place.

Its population is now 6,000, havinj increased by 2,000 in 30 years; it contains important manufactures of muslin and cotton, and carries on a considerable trade. Its principal hotel is the Glärnerhof. Before the fire, the Golden Eagle, and the Crow had some repute.

Murray gives it 4,826 inhabitants. Page 231, 1863.

Of old Glarus, before the fire, a popular autho gives the foll wing description:—"The town, which contains some five or six thousand souls, lies alon the Linth, principally in one extended street. The pecular smell of the (Schabzieger) cheese, was quite strong on approaching the town. Glarus has som manufactures that are conducted in a pastoral and pleasing manner. and in a way to obviate the vice and broken constitutions of a crowded population

The town is principally built of stone rough cast. The houses have projecting roofs, but, in other respects, are more like the buildings near the Rhine, than those we are accustomed to in Switzerland. Many are painted externally in designs."

Principal hotels, Glärnerhof, new, good; Schweizerhof; Ross; Raben. Room, 1*fr.*; breakfast, 1*fr* Guides, Andrew Fordermann, well known.

Rail.—Four trains a-day to Wesen (for Zurich) Fares, Glarus to Nestal, 1st class, 1*fr.* 30c.; 2nd 70c.; 3rd, 65c. Nestal to Näfels 1st class 1*fr.*; 2nd 70c.; 3rd, 50c. Näfels to Wesen, 1st class, 50c 2nd, 35c.; 3rd, 25c. Post car twice a-day, from Glarus to Linththal (Stachelberg), in 2 hours, 2*fr.* 30c

PUBLIC BUILDINGS.—The Cathedral which is a building in a fine style of architecture, in which both Protestants and Catholics attend Divine Worship at different times of the day, happily escaped the fire. The Hotel de Ville, and the Hospital as well as the Free School House of the Protestants were less fortunate. Glarus possessed several other fine buildings, all of which fell before the destructive element.

MANUFACTURING INDUSTRY.—Both in Glarus, and its vicinity, there are several manufactures of calico prints (one of the most noted of which, used to be that of M. Egidius Trumpy); also manufactures of cloth, and of hats; besides bleaching grounds, and mills for the manufacture of schabzieger cheese made of cow's milk, and the melilotus (honigklee), a large quantity of it being exported even as far as America. Six fairs are held annually at Glarus, and add considerably to its commercial activity.

Klönthal (The), is worth a visit, both on account of the delightful scenery enjoyed on the road, and because it possesses the monument of Solomon Gesner, a noted Swiss poet. You reach it by Riden, and ascending the course of the Loentsch, you arrive at the charming lake of Klön. This spot has some of the enchanting scenery peculiar to the Alps. rendering all attempts at description hopeless. From hence, the path leads across beautiful pastures, to the Teufen Winkel, and thence to the Glarnisch 2 l. (6 miles.) The foot of this mountain is strewed with blocks and fragments of rock, and one of these blocks has been selected by his admirers, as a tablet for an inscription in honour of Gesner; the site is well chosen, and the monument in good taste. Seated under the trees that overshadow it, the visitor hears the murmers of a neighbouring cascade, and the sound of the cows' bells, scattered over the meadows near him, helping to raise gentle emotions, akin to those described in the idyls of the poet, and which are heightened if the distant echo of the Alpine horn comes to add to the magical effect of the surrounding scenery. The spot and scenery near the monument, and the charming lake of Klön, are so sweetly pastoral, that it is a realization of our ideals of Alpine beauty, a region of romantic illusions, and amply will the traveller be repaid for his toil in visiting this real choice bit of Swiss scenery.

"Nowhere," says J. Fenimore Cooper, "is the contrast between the mild verdure of the valleys and the savage aspect of the mountains, more marked than in Glarus; still the latter nourish vast herds of cattle. which constitute a principal part of the wealth of the Canton." Page 56, v. 2, "Excursions in Switzerland."

Linth (The Valley of the) is specially deserving of a visit, as the main artery, and leading up to the sublimest scenery in the Canton. This valley presents a multitude of changing scenes and of striking views, delighting the mind but defying description. All that can be attempted here is to point out rapidly the choicest spots and most remarkable points on the road leading up to the Panten-Brucke, distant 5 l. (15 miles) from Glarus, and present its itinerary as follows:—

Glarus to Mittlödi: To the right of this village appears Mount Glarnisch, and to its left Mount Fäsis.

Schwanden.—Before reaching this fine village, and near the junction of the Sernft with the Linth, the Hohe-Guppen meets the eye. At Luchsingen there occur springs and baths of sulphurous waters; and at this place the Linth is crossed by a bridge, and the road continues through Häzigen, Diesbach, and Dornhaus, as far as Betschwanden and Ruti, where the gigantic pics and glaciers of the Selbstsanft, the Tödi, the Hammerstock, the Clariden, and others come into view. At length, after passing the village of Linththal, you reach the Panten Bridge, which is built of stone, ana consisting of one arch, has been thrown over a fearful abyss, resting on two pointed rocks.* Turn ng to the left, after passing the Panten, you arrive at the Limmern Alp; but if you continue along the road that leads straight forward, after climbing four hours up a very steep ascent you attain to the highest terrace of the Sand-Alp,† and

* The Pantenbrucke is 20 feet wide, 140 feet above the torrent, and (the old bridge being destroyed by the avalanche in 1852) has been rebuilt.

† Upper Sand Alp, or Oberstaffel. The highest point of the Sand Grat Pass between the Catscharauls and Kleiner Todi is 9,272 feet above the sea. The descent to Dissentis, by the Rosein Alp, takes three hours. From Kavrein a path strikes off into the Maderaner Thal well worth visiting.

thence by the glacier covering the base of the Tödi, in three hours, to Dissentis, in the Canton of Grisons.

Naefels (Mollis) is the capital of the Catholic part of the Canton, contains 2,000 inhabitants, and stands on the banks of the Rautibach, at the celebrated spot where the men of Glarus defeated, in 1388, an Austrian force of six times their number. Naefels is situated in a level but very fertile country, and its population are exclusively engaged in the tending of cattle. Its distance from Glarus is 1¼ L. (3¾ miles). Above the town the Rauti forms a fine cascade, but the torrent is a frequent cause of devastation in the valley. From the Convent of Marienburg, built on an eminence, a delightful view is enjoyed. Inns: the Hirsch and Schwerdt.

The battle of Naefels was fought in the fields of Rauti on the 11th April, 1388, and eleven stones were placed there to commemorate the number of attacks by the enemy, who was obliged at length to fly the field with the loss of 183 horse and 2,500 foot. The anniversary of this victory (500 Swiss to 6,000 Austrians), so glorious to the Swiss, is celebrated every year, on the 1st of April, by a procession of Catholics to the field, and by Divine Service in the Protesant churches. A handsome church has been erected on the site of the chapel that once stood here.

A path leads from Naefels, in four or five hours, to the Valley of Wiggis; it passes by the lower and upper pastures of See Alp (Nieder and Ober-See-Alpen). Another road, adapted to carriages and built on piles, crosses the marshes of the Linth to Wesen. Beyond the Linth, and opposite Naefels, is Mollis (see above).

Schilt (The).—Four hours are required to scale this mountain from Glarus, the road to it leading over the Ennetberg, the Henboden, and the Frohnalp. The view from the Schilt is extremely beautiful, embracing the entire Canton of Glarus.

Segnes Pass (The), 8,612 feet above the sea. The road to this pass leads from Glarus to Mittlödi and Sol, where is held the yearly assembly of the people (Landsgemeinde). Thence it passes up the valley of Sernft, by the villages of E gi, of Matt, of Elm, of Schwendi, and of Obermoos, to reach the baths of Wichlen, and soon after the Pass of Segnes, 8 L. (24 m.) from Glarus. To the east of Elm appears the rock of Segnes (Tschingel, or Tschinglenspitz, rising 800 or 900 feet above the ridge or screen, which runs along the summit of the Segnes Pass, and containing the Martinsloch, which is about 30 feet in diameter), elevated about 9,000 feet above the Mediterranean, and in it a remarkable cavern, attributed in legendary lore to St. Martin in conflict with the evil one, and called the Martin's Loch. At the time of the equinox, that is, on the 3rd, 4th, and 5th of March, and the 14th and 15th of September, the rays of the sun shining through this hole fall on the spire of Elm Church; but during six months of the year the inhabitants of that village are deprived of his cheering face. The top of the pass is four hours from Elm. Elm is about seven hours from Stachelberg, and on reaching the top of Segnes Pass you cross the Flimser Fohn, a sort of glacier or nevé, and the shoulder of the Flimserstein, commanding a glorious view of the Tödi, Hausstock, and Bifertenstock, 10,779 feet high, with the Grisons and St. Gothard Alps. Soon after you descend to the Vorder-Rhein, and in two hours to Reichenau, in the Grisons.

Stachelberg (Baths and Hotel of), situated in the Linththal, close to the village of that name, and on the right bank of the river. This place has risen into some repute of late years. The mineral spring which drips from a rent in the Braunberg consists of alkaline sulphureous water; it enjoys a high reputation, and is said to effect cures after a course of 20 or 24 days.

The hotel and baths of Stachelberg, a tolerably well-managed house, stands on a hill on the west of the Linth, and is an excellent centre for visiting the surrounding glaciers and peaks, and delightful ex

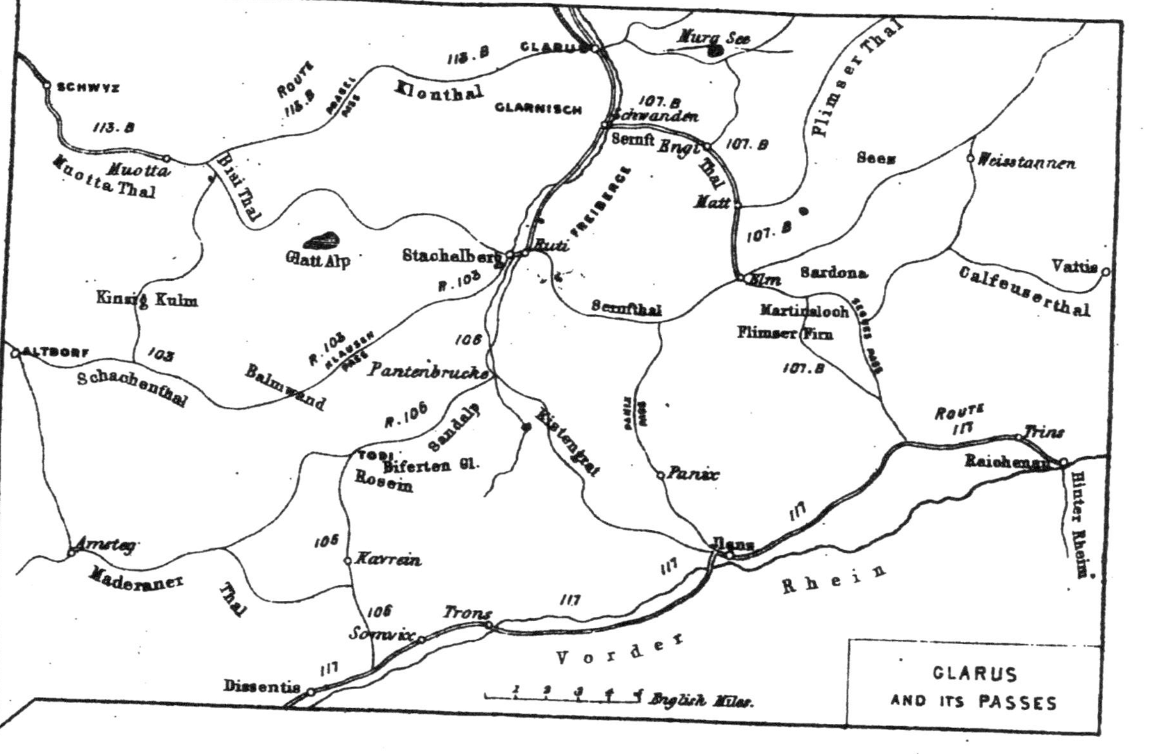

SCHWYZ
113.8
ROUTE 113.8
MASEL PASS
Klonthal
113.8
GLARUS
Murg See
Plimser Thal
GLARNISCH
107.8
Schwanden
Sernft Engt
107.8
Thal
Sees
Weisstannen
Muotta
Muotta Thal
Biai Thal
Matt
107.8
FREIBERGE
Glatt Alp
Stachelberg
Ruti
Elm
Sardona
Calfeuserthal
Vattis
R.103
Kinsig Kulm
Sernthal
Martinsloch
Flimser Firn
107.8
ALTDORF
103
R.103 KLAUSEN PASS
106
Pantenbrucke
Schachenthal
Balmwand
PANIX PASS
ROUTE 117
Trins
R.106
Sandalp
Kistengrat
Panix
Reichenau
Hinter Rheim
TODI
Biferten Gl.
Rosein
105
Amsteg
Kavrein
Ilanz
117
Rhein
Maderaner
Thal
106
Trons
117
Sorwix
Vorder
Dissentis
117
1 2 3 4 5 English Miles.
GLARUS
AND ITS PASSES

' the exceeding beauty of its situation.
ming waterfalls—the Fatschbach (⅓ m.),
Schreyenbach, 1 l. (3 m.)—are close at
Peaks, Passes, and Glaciers," 1st Series.)
nmer the Bath Hotel is so full,
rellers have often to sleep at the
Hotel, at Linththal, and come up
.t the Baths.

excursions round Stachelberg are
to the capacity of travellers of
1; and range from a promenade
r three to a day's work of 10 or
or more." The Scheyenstock is a
.k rising immediately above Sta-
, and does not appear difficult.
Passes," &c., 1st S., p. 265.

oun..ry round the hotel is en-
., offering delightful walks, and
ns to the Sassberg, the Bisithal,
:enbrucke, &c., &c. More adven-
olrits have here the opportunity
:ing the dangers and terrors of
er world in ascending the Tödi,
ausstock, the Glarnisch and other
ling giants.*

s (The), is a mountain 4 l. from
and reached by passing through
, ¾ l. (2¼ m.), thence over the
lp, on to the Gaumen from which
nd to the Scheye or Schien, the
point of the Wiggis. The view
from this spot is magnificent, not
nmanding the lakes and moun-
north-eastern Switzerland but
g even to the Tyrol.

'δdi is 11,383 feet above the sea, the
oint being called Piz Rosein by the people
It is surrounded by a mass of snow and
d difficult as well as dangerous to ascend.
r Ulrich made the ascent from the Sand
by a small turn on the Röthe, crossed the
and advancing east passed under the
.k, descended to the Biforten Glacier,
ne red snow, went round by the Glacier
the south of the summit, and got up be-
d the Piz Rosein.
ascent from Disentis leads by the Gin-
ns or Hems and the Stokgrön, thence to
extremity of the Tödi Glacier, and you
highest point by passing over the Piz
his latter route is said to be dangerous on
large crevasses that have to be crossed.
Passes," &c., 1st S., p. 264—5.

For the convenience of travellers we
shall add here the passes that lead from
Glarus and Stachelberg to the neighbouring cantons.

From *Glarus*—
1. To *Schwyz.*—By the Pragel Pass and
Klönthal through a charming valley 10½ l.
To the Grisons and Vorder-rhein.
2. The Panixer Pass, 11h. to 11h. 30m.
3. The Segnes Pass, 12h. 30m.
4. To *St. Gallen.*—The Flimser Pass,
from the railway between Wallenstadt
and Sargans.
5. The Riseten Pass, from Matt to Sargans 8h. 30m., to 9h. 30m. Guide needed.
6. The Ramina Pass, from Elm to
Sargans, 9h. 30m. to 11h. Guide required.
7. To *Wallenstadt* (Lake).—One mountain path by the Kerenzenberg, 3 l. from
Mollis (Bear Hotel) to Mühlehorn Station.
(Hotel Seegarten.)
8. The other to Murg by E. shoulder
of the Murtschenstock, 6h. Foot path.

From *Stachelberg*
To—
9. *Altdorf,* by the Klausen Pass. Guide
unnecessary. Horse, 25fr. 11h.
To—
10. Dissentis, by the Sand Grat and
Kisten Grat at the foot of the Tödi.
From Stachelberg to Dissentis, 15 hours.
Over ice (Sandfirn). G. Zweifelg of Linththal, good Guide.
To—
11. Reichenau, by the Segnes Pass, 15½
hours from Elm.

ITINERARY FROM GLARUS.

ROUTE 103.

ALTDORF, 12½ l. (37½ m.)

	Leagues.	Miles.
Schwanden	1½	4½
Diesbach	1½	4½
Bettschwanden	½	1½
Linthal (5 l.)	1½	4½
Over the Klausenberg—		
To Klus	3	9
Esch	1	3
St. Ann	½	1½
Unter Schächen	½	1½
Spiringen	1	3
Wetterschwand	½	1½
Burglen	½	1½
Altdorf	½	1½
	12½	37½

Or by Schwyz (Nos. 113 and 207).

ROUTE 104.

ALTSTAETTEN, 13 l. (39 m.)

	Leagues.	Miles.
Nettstal	¾	2¼
Molis	½	1½
Wesen (2¼)	1	3
Old St. John (rough mountain road)	2	6
Wildhaus	1¼	3¾
Gambo	1	3
Salez	1½	4½
Sennwald	1½	4½
Reuti	1	3
Oberried	½	1½
Altstäetten	2	6
	13	39

Another and a more frequented road is through—

ROUTE 105.

APPENZELL, 15 l. (45 m.), and thence to Alstäetten, 3 l. (9 m.), total, 18 l.

	Leagues.	Miles.
Nettstal	¾	2¼
Näfels	½	1½
Urnen (1¾ l.)	½	1½
Ziegelbruck	½	1½
Schännis	1½	4½
Kaltbrunn	¾	2¼
Ermetschwyl	1¼	3¾
Bildhaus	½	1½
Hummelwald	½	1½
Wattwyl	1	3
Lichtensteig	½	1½
Brunnadern	1½	4½
Degersheim	1¼	3¾
Herisau	2	6
Hundwyl	1	3
Appenzell (15 l.)	1	3
Altstäetten	3	9
	18	54

Art, by Schwyz (Nos. 113 and 207).

Baden (in Switzerland), by Zurich (Nos. 116 and 18).

Bâle, by Zurich (Nos. 116 and 44).

ROUTE 106.

BELLINZONA, 33 l. (99 m.)

	Leagues.	Miles.
Linththal No. 103)	5	15
Au	½	1½
Panten Bridge	1½	4½
Upper Sand Alp	4	12
Tödi Glacier to Dissentis	1½	3¾
Mont Permedels	1½	3¾
Piatta	¾	2¼
S. Rocco	½	1½
S. Giacomo	1½	4½
S. Gallo	½	1½
S. Marie	1	3
Casaccia	1½	4½
Campier	1	3
Olivone	1¾	5¼
Biasca	4¾	14¼
Osogna	1½	4½
Ciaciano	1¾	5¼
Bellinzona	1¼	3¾
	31¼	93¾

Or by Schwyz (Nos. 113 and 207), and Altdorf (No. 229), or by Altdorf (Nos. 103 and 229).

Berne, by Zurich (Nos. 116 and 79).

Bex, by Zurich (Nos. 116 and 79), and Berne (No. 58), or by Lucerne, Thun, and the Simmenthal Nos. (113, 161, 76, and 72).

Bienne, by Zurich (Nos. 116 and 79), and Berne (No. 59), or by Zurich (Nos. 16 and 18), Aarau (No. 16), and Solothurn (No. 218).

Brougg, by Zurich (Nos. 116 and 298).

Bulle, by Zurich (Nos. 116 and 79), and Berne (No. 54).

Burgdorf, by Zurich (Nos. 116 and 302, as far as Morgenthal); thence by route No. 6 to Kirchberg, and thence to Burgdorf.

Chamouni, by Zurich (Nos. 116 and 79), Berne (No. 63), Lausanne (No. 96), and Geneva (No. 95), or by Zurich (Nos. 116 and 18), Aarau (No. 16), Solothurn (No. 223), Lausanne (No. 96) and Geneva (No. 95).

Champery, by Altdorf (No. 103), Susten Pass (Nos. 229 and 55), and the Simmenthal to Bex (No. 72).

Chaux de Fonds, by Zurich (Nos. 16 and 79), Berne (No. 70), and Neuchâtel (No. 169); or by Zurich (Nos. 116 and 18), Aarau (No. 16), and Solothurn (No. 220).

Chiavenna, by Coire (Nos. 107 and 121, 122, or 123)

ROUTE 107 (a).

To Chur or Coire, 14½ l. (42¾ m.)

	Leagues.	Miles.
Wesen (No. 104)	2½	6¾
Crossing the Lake to Walenstadt	4	12
Berschis	¾	2½
Halbmeil	¾	2½
Sargans	1½	4½
Ragatz (10½ l.)	1	3
Zizers	2½	6½
Coire	1½	5½
	14½	42½

ROUTE 107 (b).

By the Martinsloch, 14½ l. (42½ m.)

	Leagues.	Miles.
Elm	4½	13½
Martinsloch	2½	7½
Over the Tschingel to Fliins.	3	9
Trinser Mühle	1	3
Trins	½	1½
Tamins	½	2½
Reichenau	½	
Eins	½	1½
Coire	1½	3½
	14½	42½

Constance, by Frauenfeld (Nos. 107 and 240).

ROUTE 108.

Einsiedeln, 8½ l. (24¾ m.)

	Leagues.	Miles.
Urnen (No. 105)	1½	5½
Bilten	½	1½
Richenbourg	½	½
Schubelbach	1	3
Galgenen	½	1½
Lacken	½	1½
Altendorf (4½ l.)	½	½
Over the Esel	2½	6½
Einsiedeln	1½	3½
	8½	24½

Engelberg, by Schwyz (Nos. 113 and 213) and Stanz (No. 252).

ROUTE 109.

Frauenfeld, 15 l. (45 m.)

	Leagues.	Miles.
Lichstensteig (No 105)	8½	24½
Dietfurt		1½
Bütschwyl		1½
Thierhag		2½
Gonzenbach		½
Carried forward	10½	30½

ROUTE 109—*(Continued.)*

	Leagues.	Miles.
Brought forward	10½	30½
Lutisbourg	½	
Oberhazenheid	½	1½
Unterhazenheid	½	
Rikenbach	½	2½
Wyl (12½ l.)	½	
Munchwyl	½	2½
Mazingen	1	3
Frauenfeld	1	3
	15	45

Fribonrg, by Zurich (No. 116 and 79) and Berne (No. 54).

Gais, by St. Gallen (Nos. 112 and 116).

Geneva, by Zurich (Nos 116 and 79), Berne (No.63), and Lausanne (No. 96) ; or by Zurich (Nos. 116 and 16), Aarau (No. 16), Solothurn (No. 223), and Lausanne (No. 96).

	Leagues.	Miles.
Grimsel to Altdorf (103)	12½	37½
By Wasen and Susten Pass to Gadmen (55) and Im Hof	14	42
Im Hof to Grimsel Hospice..	6½	20½
	33½	99½

Grindelwald, by the Klausen Pass to Altdorf Canton of Uri, No. 103), or over the Sand Alp, and down the Maderaner Thal, to Amstag Nos. 103 and 229), thence to Altdorf, and by the Engelberg (Nos. 257 or 258) to Meyringen, or by Wasen, Canton of Berne, No. 55, and Canton of Uri, Nos. 257 and 258) over the Susten Pass to do. (1 ½ hours) From Meyringen over Great Schiedeck to Grindelwald, 27½ and 23½ l. (82½ and 70½ m.)

Hasli and Meyringen, Cantons of Uri and Berne (Nos. 103, 229, and 55) also the last No. Grindelwald.

ROUTE 110.

Herisau, 13 l. (39 m.)

	Leagues.	Miles.
Lichtensteig (No. 105)	8½	24½
Brunnadern	1½	4½
Degersheim	1½	3½
Herisau	2	6
	13	39

Hofwyl, by Zurich (Nos. 116 and 302).

Interlaken, see Grindelwald and Hasli and (No. 55) Canton of Berne.

Lauffenbourg, by Zurich (Nos. 116 and 302).

Lauterbrunnen, see Grindelwald.

Lausanne, by Zurich (Nos. 116 and 79) and Berne (No. 63), or by Zurich (Nos. 116 and 16), Aarau (No. 16), and Solothurn (223).

Locarno, by Schwyz (Nos. 113 and 207), or by Altdorf (Nos. 103 and 229) and Bellinzona (No. 232).

Locle, by Zurich (No 116 and 18), Aarau (No. 16), and Solothurn (No. 24), or by Zurich (Nos. 116 and 79), Berne (No. 70), and Neuchâtel (No.175).

Loesch (baths), by Schwyz (Nos. 113 and 227) and Altdorf (No 260), or by Altdorf (Nos. 103 and 260), or by Zurich (Nos. 116 and 79) and Berne (No. 65), or by Zurich (Nos. 116 and 18), Aarau (No. 16), Solothurn (No. 227), and Sion (No. 268).

Lucerne, by Zug (Nos. 115 and 165), or by Schwyz (No. 113 and 161).

Lugano, by Schwyz (Nos.113 and 207), Altdorf (No. 229), and Bellinzona (No 233), or by Altdorf (Nos. 103 and 229) and Bellinzona (No. 233).

Mendrisio, the same routes and from Bellinzona (No. 235).

Meyringen, see Haßli (No. 55) and Grindelwald (No. 55).

Morat, by Zurich (Nos. 116 and 79) and Berne (No. 77), or by Zurich (Nos. 116 and 18), Aarau (No. 16), and Solothurn (No. 221).

Morges, by Zurich (Nos. 116 and 79), Berne (No. 63), and Lausanne (No. 96), if by rail, Fribourg or by Zurich (Nos. 116 and 18), Aarau (No. 16), Solothurn (No. 223), and Lausanne (No. 96).

Moudon, by Zurich (Nos. 116 and 79) and Berne (No. 68), or by Zurich (No. 116 and 18), Aarau (No. 16), and Solothurn (No. 245).

Neuchâtel, by Zurich (Nos. 116 and 79) and Berne (No. 70), or by Zurich (No. 116 and 18), Aarau (No. 16), and Solothurn (No. 178).

Orbe, by Zurich (Nos. 116 and 79) and Berne (No. 71), or by Zurich (Nos. 116 and 18), Aarau (No. 16), Solothurn (No. 178).

Oria, by Bellinzona (No. 106), and Bellinzona to Oria (No. 235).

Payerne, by Zurich (Nos. 116 and 79) and Berne (No. 77), or by Zurich (Nos. 116 and 18), Aarau (No. 16), and Solothurn (No. 223).

ROUTE 111.

Pfäffers (Baths), 12¼ L. (36¾ m.)

	Leagues.	Miles.
Ragatz (No. 107 A)	10¼	30¾
Valens	1¼	4¾
Pfäffers	¾	1¾
	12¼	36¾

Pilatus, by Lucerne (Nos. 131 and 161), or rail.

Pontresina, by Chur (107 A and B)

Chur to Pontresina (Nos. 123 and 139).

Rigi, by Schwyz (Nos. 87, 113, and 212).

ROUTE 112.

Saint Gallen, 15 L. (45 m.)

	Leagues.	Miles.
Herisau (No. 116)	13	39
Brugg en	1	3
St. Gallen	1	3
	15	45

Saint Moritz, by Chur (No. 107 A and B).

Chur to St. Moritz (No. 123).

Schaffhausen, by Zurich (Nos. 116 and 200).

ROUTE 113 (a).

Schwyz, 13¼ L. (40¼ m.)

	Leagues.	Miles.
Urnen (No. 105)	1¾	5¼
Bilten	¼	1¼
Richenbourg	¼	
Schubelbach	1	3
Siebenen	¼	
Galgenen	¼	
Lachen	¼	1¼
Altendorf	¼	
Pfäffikon	1¼	3¾
Richtenschwyl	1¼	4¼
Schindellegi	1	3
Altmatt	1¼	4¼
Rothenthurm	1	3
Sattel	½	1½
Steinen	1	3
Seewen	¼	1¼
Schwyz	¼	1¼
	13¼	40¼

ROUTE 114 (b).

Schwyz, by the Pragel, 10 L. (30 m.)

	Leagues.	Miles.
Seegen	1¼	4¼
Klöuthal	1	3
Schwellaui	1	3
Over the Pragel	1¼	3¾
La Croix	1	3
Stalden	1	3
Muttathal	½	1½
Au Riedt	1	3
Ober-Schönenbuch	1	3
Schwyz	¾	2¼
	10	30

Sion, by Schwyz (Nos 113 and 207) and Altdorf (No. 201), or by Altdorf (No. 103 and 261), or by Zurich (Nos. 116 and 79) and Berne (No. 72 or 74), or by Zurich (Nos 116 and 18), Aarau (No 16), and Solothurn (No. 227).

Solothurn, by Zurich (Nos. 116 and 18) and Aarau (No. 16).

Stanz, see Unterwalden.

Thun, by Zurich (Nos. 116 and 79) and Berne (No. 5).

Trogen, by St. Gallen (Nos. 112 and 193).

Unterwalden, by Schwyz (Nos 113 and 213).

Vevay, by Zurich (Nos 116 and 79) and Berne (No. 54), or by Zurich (Nos. 116 and 18), Aarau (No. 16), and Solothurn (No. 227).

ROUTE 115.

WINTERTHUR.

	Leagues.	Miles.
Manchwyl	¾	2¼
Duttwyl	1	3
Aderf	½	1¼
Elgg	½	1½
Reterschen	1¼	3¾
Winterthur	½	1¼

Yverdun, by Zurich (Nos. 116 and 118), Aarau (No. 16), and Solothurn (No. 227), or by Zurich (Nos. 116 and 79) and Berne (No. 77).

ROUTE 116.

ZUG, 12¼ l. (36¾ m.)

	Leagues.	Miles.
Horgen (No. 116)	9	27
Sihlbrücke	1¾	5¼
Baar	¾	2¼
Zug	¾	2¼
	12¼	36¾

ROUTE 117 (a).

ZURICH, 12½ l. (37½ m.)

	Leagues.	Miles.
Altendorf (No. 108)	4¾	14¼
Pfeffikon	1¼	3¾
Richtenschwyl	1½	4½
Wadenschwyl	¾	2¼
Horgen (9¼ L)	1	3
Oberrieden	½	1½
Thalwyl	½	
Ruschlikon	½	1½
Kilchberg	½	
Wollishofen	¾	2¼
Zurich	1	3
	12¼	37¼

ROUTE 118 (b).

To ZURICH, by Uznach, 15 l. (45 m.)

	Leagues.	Miles.
Urnen (No. 105)	1¾	5¼
Ziegelbruck	½	1½
Schännis	1½	4½
Kaltbrunn	¾	2¼
Carried forward	4½	13½

ROUTE 118 (b).—(Continued.)

	Leagues.	Miles.
Brought forward	4½	13½
Uznach	¾	2¼
Schmerikon	1¼	3¾
Wurmspach	1½	4½
Rapperswyl	1	3
Feldbach	1	3
Stäfa	½	½
Männedorf	½	2¼
Uetikon	½	1½
Meilen	½	1½
Herrliberg	½	2¼
Ehrlibach	½	1½
Kussnacht	½	1½
Zollikon	½	1½
Zurich	¾	2¼
	15	45

Zurzach, by Zurich (Nos. 116, 305. or 306).

To Bavaria, Austria, and all Upper Germany, by St. Gallen.

To Suabia, Saxony, and Franconia, by Frauenfeld and Schaffhausen.

The traveller who approaches Switzerland from Austria, Bavaria, or the Rhine, by Friedrichshafen, and the Lake of Constance, will be frequently disposed to make a little deviation in order to see the Falls of the Rhine in the contiguous Canton of Schaffhausen, which can easily be reached from N. W. Switzerland by rail on both sides of the Rhine from Bâle. Before the introduction of railroads, travellers used occasionally to approach Switzerland through the fine scenery of the Black Forest, and after viewing the falls of the Rhine at Schaffhausen, to follow down the river to Bâle, on the German side, and pass from Bâle to Berne, through the beautiful Münsterthal, an expedition that may still be recommended to those who have time at their disposal.

CANTON OF SCHAFFHAUSEN.

LIMITS.—This is the only Swiss Canton entirely on the right bank of the Rhine, which forms its S. limit, separating it from the Cantons of Zurich and Thurgau. On all other points, it is surrounded by the Grand Duchy of Baden.

AREA, SOIL, AND CLIMATE.—The area

of the Canton of Schaffhausen [illegible] ... [several lines largely illegible] ... [the scenery] ... the [illegible] very much diversified ... great [illegible].

Mountains. — Schaffhausen contains no mountains of considerable elevation; [illegible] in the Canton [does not rise more] than 2000 feet above the sea.

Rivers and Brooks. — The only river in this Canton is the Rhine; it flows along part of its southern frontier, and quits it 4 1/2 l. (2 g. m.) below Schaffhausen, near the Château of Laufen. This Canton contains several [brooks and] unimportant rivulets; the principal are the Mühlenbach, the Biberach, and the Klosbach.

Agricultural and Manufacturing Industry. — Some cattle, horses, and sheep, are bred in this Canton. Game is abundant, and fish is plentiful in the Rhine and other streams; the salmon fishery carried on near the Rhine Falls is even of considerable importance. Vines, cereals, and orchard fruit, are cultivated to a considerable extent; the Canton has also fine meadow land and forests. In minerals, it yields good iron ore, very fine white clay, limestone, gypsum, &c. There are also springs of mineral water. Manufactures are not very numerous or extensive, but at the capital there exist steel works, print and silk mills, manufactures of cotton and worsted stockings, &c.

Thermal Waters. — There are springs of mineral water containing alum and sulphur at Osterfingen, but they are only frequented by local patients.

Population and Religion. — The population of this Canton is now 35,000; 30 years ago it was 30,000. They are mostly Protestants, only a few Catholics inhabiting chiefly the village of Ramsen.

Public Instruction, Charities, &c. — Elementary education is generally very

fair in this Canton, and in the capital there are schools of a superior class, as well as several scientific societies and [illegible] institutions. The people are [illegible] and enterprising, but the [illegible] welcome and much of the old simplicity of manner [illegible] are giving way to Parisian finery and frivolity. The only trace of the earlier and more primitive times is seen in the long tresses of hair still worn by the girls down their back.

SURVEY OF THE CANTON.

Eglisau — See Schaffhausen.
Laufen — See Schaffhausen.
Finthen — See Schaffhausen.
Rheinau — See Schaffhausen.

Schaffhausen, the capital and the centre of all [interest in the] Canton. Hotels: Hôtel du Laufen, very near the fall, good, clean, and moderate charges. Hôtel de la Couronne, delightfully situated; recommended to English travellers; the nearest to the landing-place. Belle Vue, close to Railway. Schweizerhof: excellent first-class hotel, deservedly recommended; splendid views. Opposite the town, at Feuerthalen, is a very good hotel, The Stag or Hirsch). At Mühlethal is a Café d'Été.

Railways: every day 5 trains. (Routes 196—201)

Fares in Francs and Centimes.

TO	1st cl. fr. c.	2nd cl. fr. c.	3rd cl. fr. c.
A[illegible]	15 70	13 35	12 25
Express	26 55	19 45	—
B[illegible]	27 0	18 70	13 30
Express	29 50	20 75	—
[illegible] by C[illegible]	11 70	8 35	6 70
[illegible] by W[illegible]	11 65	8 20	6 55
[illegible]rne	16 75	13 80	9 55
C[arlsru]he	29 15	20 20	14 15
Do. Express	32 55	22 55	—
C[illegible] by W[aldshut]	71 30	53 15	—
Dachsen	0 50	0 35	0 25
Rhine Falls — there and back	0 80	0 60	0 40
Francfort by Wald-ht	41 60	28 50	19 00
Do. Express	47 45	32 60	—
Friedrichshafen	10 30	7 60	5 [?]
Geneva	35 35	24 95	17 [?]
Heidelberg	31 95	23 50	16 [?]
Do. Express	38 85	26 50	—
Lausanne	30 85	21 45	15 40
Lindau	11 50	8 50	6 [?]
Lucerne	12 50	8 75	6 [?]
Mayence	52 40	30 90	—
Munich	30 70	21 90	14 [?]
Do. Express	33 25	23 60	—
Paris	71 30	53 25	—

	1st cl. fr. c.	2nd cl. fr. c.	3rd cl. fr. c.
Ragatz by Wallisellen	15 50	10 85	7 75
Romanshorn	6 45	4 95	3 25
Rorschach	11 15	7 60	5 55
St. Gallen	9 35	6 55	4 65
Stuttgart	27 45	18 85	—
Do. Express	29 5	19 95	—
Thun	22 90	16 0	11 45
Zurich	6 0	4 20	3 0

Schaffhausen has a population of 9,000, and still retains the aspect of an old Suabian city with tortuous, ill-paved streets and houses adorned with quaint turrets. The town though frequented in connection with the Rhine or lake navigation at a very early date, rose into superior importance chiefly through the foundation of all Saints' Convent in the year 1052. It is built on the right bank of the Rhine, and is united with the opposite bank belonging to the Canton of Zurich, by a bridge. It is the birthplace of the noted historian, John Muller, and of an able sculptor, Trippel.

PUBLIC EDIFICES.—The Cathedral and the Church of St. John are of the 12th century. The great bell has this inscription, "*Vivos voco, mortuos plango, fulgura frango.*" The Munoth, an old fortress above the town (with bomb-proof walls 18 feet thick, built from 1564 to 1590, to shelter the citizens during war) deserves a visit. Other public buildings are the Stadthaus, Salzhof and College.

EDUCATIONAL AND CHARITABLE INSTITUTIONS.—In the College, courses of lectures are delivered on theology, philosophy, the classics, mathematics, physical science, and history. The town has also a gymnasium, a commercial school, &c. The town Library is in the old Convent, and has been enriched in 1809, by acquiring the library of John Muller, the historian. There are also theological and medical libraries, and private collections of fauna and flora, &c., belonging to the M. Laffon Seiler, Stierlin, &c.

WALKS near Schaffhausen. — To the Hohenfluh and Enge; to Herblingen 1 l. (3 m.); to the Convent of Paradies 1 l. (3 m.); to Kluss; to the Monastery of Rheinau; but for fine views especially to Lohn 2 l. (6 m.); to the Randenberg; to the five conical summits of the Hohen-Krähen; Hohen-Staffeln and Hohentwiel 2 l. (6 m.); and to the Saeckelamshüsli, with a panoramic view of the Alps from Austria (Vorarlberg) to the Blumlis Alp, near Thun. The great attraction is found in the

Falls of the Rhine.—For the mass of water the most remarkable in Europe (if we except Iceland), but otherwise inferior to the Handeck, Tosa, and other falls, situated between the Château of Worth, and Lauffen 1 l. (3 m.) from Schaffhausen. The stream is broken by rocks before it reaches the principal falls, down which it rushes to the depth of 70 or 80 feet. The roar of waters is heard at some distance, but is not so deafening as that of the Nile cataracts, described by Herodotus. Finest point of view is from the Fischenz, Pavilion, standing out above the fall at Lauffen Hotel.

Two roads lead from Schaffhausen to the Falls. Right Bank. Carriage Road. (45 minutes). You can proceed by the regular omnibus plying to the station from the Schweizerhof and Bellevue Hotels. Fare, 1*fr.*; or by the Bâle Railway to the Neuhausen Station. At Neuhausen, with 1,286 inhabitants, (elevation, 413 metres), close to the Fall, is an inn, Zum Rheinfall. Not the best resting place. Proceed to Schweizerhof or Bellevue Hotels. Then descend to Château of Worth, where is another hotel, in which you pay 75c. for a dark room. Worth is opposite the Falls, on a protruding rock.

A boat takes you under the Falls to the Château of Lauffen. Under the railway bridge the Rhine takes its leap of 20 metres, with a breadth of 100, between the hill of Bolhuenberg and that of Kohlfirst, N.E. of Lauffen. Reckoning all its rapids the Rhine descends 33 metres at this place. The chief rock bisecting the Fall and surmounted with a colossal statue of Tell, can be ascended. 5 fr. for one or two persons; 1 *fr.* 5*c.* each if the party be larger. Boats cross under the Falls for 90*c.*; or, if several persons, for 30*c.* each.

Left Bank.—45 minutes, rail or carriage. By rail to Dachsen Station, 10 minutes. Fare, 50*c.*, 35*c.*, or 25*c.* Hotel Witzig, is very fair. From this you go on foot or in carriage to Château of Lauffen, 15 minutes from Dachsen. The Hotel of Lauffen is held in the old château. The balcony of the first story (1 *fr.*) has a fine view of the Fall.

Stein, though beyond its territory, belongs to the Canton, 4 l. (12 m.) from Schaffhausen, up the stream and on the Rhine. It is on the site of Ganodurum, a Roman fort, destroyed by the Germans, and is in a picturesque situation, on the right bank, at a spot where the Rhine issues from the part of the Lake of Constance, named Zeller See. In the middle-ages the town of Stein was under the rule of the house of Hohenklingen, the ruins of whose ancient castles of Klingen and Steinerklingen may still be seen; the former on a hill above the town, the latter on the left bank of the Rhine opposite. Population, 1,800. Inns, Schwan, Krone. A bridge of 44 metres crosses the Rhine at this place, which derives much animation from the lake navigation. Near Stein (45 minutes), at Oehningen, on the Schienerberg, are quarries, containing petrifactions of plants, amphibiæ, &c. Fine view from ruins of Château of Hohentwiel, 2 l. (6 m.) from Stein.

Most interesting excursions from Schaffhausen are to Constance, the Island of Reichenau, and the Château of Arenenberg. Steamer every day to Constance, 4 hours up the stream, 2 down; fare, 4 *fr.* Landing place, Unnoth Château. For rail, see below.

Constance, in the Duchy of Baden, is connected by steamer with all parts of the lake, as follows:

Three times a-day to Bregenz, 1st cl., 2 *fl.* 12*kr.*; 2nd, 1 *fl.* 27*kr.* To Friedrichshafen, three times, 1st cl., 1 *fl.* 6*kr.*; 2nd, 42*kr.* To Lindau, three times, 1st cl., 1 *fl.* 57*kr*; 2nd, 1 *fl.* 18*kr.* To Meersberg four times, 1st cl., 24*kr.*; 2nd, 16*kr.* T[o] Romanshorn, three times, 1st cl., 54*kr.* 2nd, 36*kr.* To Rorschach, three time[s] 1st class, 1 *fl.* 30*kr.*; 2nd, 1 *fl.* To Uber lingen, twice, 1st cl., 36*kr.*; 2nd, 24*kr.*

RAILROADS.—The Baden Line joins th[e] North East Swiss at Schaffhausen an[d] Waldshut. Fares from Constance t[o] Schaffhausen, 1st cl., 2 *fl.* 6*kr.*; 2nd, 1 *fl.* 24*kr.* 3rd, 54*kr.* To Waldshut, 1st cl., 3 *fl.* 30*kr.* 2nd, 2 *fl.* 30*kr.*; 3rd, 1 *fl.* 36*kr.* To Bâl[e] 1st cl., 5 *fl.* 57*kr*; 2nd, 4 *fl.* 3*kr.*; 3rd 2 *fl.* 36*kr.* Posts every day to Donau-eschingen, 10 l. (30 m.), in 9½ hours, 4 *fl.* Frauenfeld, 11 l. (33 m.), in 3½ hours, 3 *fr.* 30*c.* Romanshorn, 2½ l. (7½ m.), i[n] 2 hours, 2 *fr.* 15*c.*. To Rorschach, twi[ce] a-day, 7½ l. (23½ m.), in 5 hours, 3 *fr.* 95[c.] To St. Gallen, 8½ l. (24¼ m.), by Amvisw[yl] 3 *fr.* 90*c.*; by Romanshorn, 4 *fr.* 20*c.*

HOTELS.—Hecht, a first-class establishment, most situate opposite the harbour and the lake. Krone Adler; Badischer Hof; Café Leo, with a swimming school on the lake. Population, 7,819 or [illegible] inhabitants; in the middle ages, 40,000. Unite[d to] Petershausen and the main land by a wood[en] bridge. The Douane (date, 1348) is a [illegible] ancient pile.

HISTORY.—Built 304, by the Roman Emperor, Constantius Chlorus; mad[e a] Bishopric, 553; it was the residence [of] Charlemagne, Charles le Gros, Fred[erick] Barbarossa, and other worthies. Gr[eat] persecutions of the Jews took place h[ere] 1348, 1425. Constance was the place wh[ere] the great Church Council of 1414 to [1]4 met, which deposed three rival P[opes] John XXIII., Gregory XII., and Ben[edict] XII., and elected Martin V., after demning and burning John Huss Jerome of Prague. The Council attended by 25 cardinals, 4 patriar[chs] electors, 23 dukes, 5 princes, 19 bishops, 300 bishops, 100 prelate[s] 1,800 priests. The Douane contai[ns nu] merous curiosities, including a co[py of] the 15th century. In a salle in the[se] story were held the sittings of the C[ouncil.] It contains pretended or real reli[cs] as the arm chairs of Pope Martin and of the Emperor Sigismund; the prison of John Huss, a missal, pictures of value, &c. At the Faubourg of Bruhl they shew in a meadow the spot where John Huss and Jerome of Prague were burnt, 1414 and 1415.

The greatest curiosity is the Cathedral, founded 1052, finished about the 16th century. A modern steeple has been built 1857, for one of the towers burnt in 1511. Wood sculpture at the entrance doors (1470). The organ, built 1250, was restored 1680. To visit the interior the fee, out of service hours, in 24 kreutzers. There are several good pieces of sculpture and monuments in the interior, including the Entombment by Hans Moring, the Death of the Virgin, sculpture of the 15th century, the choir stalls, &c. The treasury contains a missal of 1426, an old painting of 1524, &c. In the cloisters there is also some good statuary. The Cathedral, or Dom, contains also a Roman inscription and an ancient crypt. In the Old Domschule are some fine stained glass and antiquities: fee, 1*fr.* The church of St. Stephen contains other good stained glass windows. The church is of the 8th century, but was rebuilt in the 13th. It contains sculptures of Hans Moring (1560 to 1610). Other objects deserving notice are the Dominican Convent, now a cotton factory, with picturesque ruins and Roman remains; the house of Huss, Paul's Strasse, near the Schnetzthor. Curious works, and a globe of 1493, in the Lyceum, formerly the Jesuits' College. The Leo coffee-house is called Curia Pacis, because Frederic Barbarossa concluded peace with the Lombards there in 1183. The harbour and lighthouse are good; and the bridge over the Rhine is adorned with four colossal statues, of 12 feet—two bishops, a grand duke (Leopold of Baden), and Duke Berchtold I. of Zähringen. Among the walks or sails in the neighbourhood of Constance, two deserve notice:—

1. Isle Meinau (1 hour 33 min.), in the north bay of the Lake Uberlingersee, the property of the Grand Duke of Baden, with palaces, terraces, and gardens.

2. The Isle of Reichenau (1 hour), in the Untersee, 1½ league long, ½ a league broad, and having 1,440 inhabitants. It was formerly a very rich Benedictine Abbey, founded by Charles Martel, 724. Some of its monks were distinguished men of learning, which they helped greatly to promote. Among them may be noticed Walafried, Strabo, Berno, Henry of Klingenberg, &c.

3. The Chateau of Arenenberg was the residence of Queen Hortense and of Louis Napoleon, who has purchased it.

4. The Chateau of Eugensberg, once belonging to Lady Temple (1843), and to Prince Eugene Beauharnais, has some fine paintings of Raphael, Murillo, &c. It is to sell.

The greatest lake fishery is at Ermatingen. Inns: the Eagle, the Crown. Near are the chateaux of Wolfberg and Hard, with a fine park.

A direct line of rail brings us from Schaffhausen to Zurich.

CANTON OF ZURICH.

LIMITS.—Its limits to the north are the Grand Duchy of Baden and the Cantons of Schaffhausen and Thurgau; to the east, Thurgau and St. Gallen; to the south, St. Gallen, Schwyz, and Zug; to the west, the latter Canton and Aargau.

AREA, SOIL, AND CLIMATE.—The area of the Canton of Zurich is 90½ leagues (1,723 kils.), of which only one-third is fit for agriculture; accordingly it does not yield enough to support the inhabitants. It has only a few mountains, none of which reach 4,000 feet. The rest of the surface consists of undulating ground, which becomes even flat and somewhat marshy in the centre of the Canton, but in the vicinity of Zurich and Winterthur it is superiorly cultivated and very productive. The climate is generally rather mild throughout the Canton, though subject to rather sudden changes.

MOUNTAINS.—Three chains of mountains traverse the southern part of the Canton of Zurich, the first, called the Allmanns, is the highest; it runs along the east frontier of the Canton, and its most remarkable summits are the Hörnli, (3,589 feet), the highest point in the Canton, commanding a most magnificient view; the Schnäbelihorn, the Hulftegg, the Scheidegg, and the Allmann, properly so called. This chain is prolonged by ramifications to the north-west as far as the Rhine. The second chain of mountains extends from near Rapperschwyl to the east of the lake, as far as beyond Zurich; and the third chain, or *Albis*, runs along the west bank of the lake, reaching from the Sihlbrücke to beyond the village of Albisrieden, where it melts into the plain. The Läger Mountains, which are in reality nothing more than the eastern prolongations of the Jura, forming a fourth, but very small chain, running only 2 l. (3 m.) along the Limmat.

LAKES, RIVERS, AND RIVULETS.

(a) LAKES. — 1. The Lake of Zurich waters, the territory of three cantons (Zurich, St. Gallen, and Schwyz), is 9 l. (27 m.) long, and at its greatest breadth, between Richterswyl, or Richtenschwyl, and Stäfa, 1½ l. (4½ m.) wide. It does not belong exclusively to the Canton of Zurich, which only retains possession of its northern portion, extending 6 l. (18 m.), as far as Rapperswyl on the north-east, and Richterswyl on the south-west bank. An uncovered bridge, 1,800 feet in length, crosses at Rapperswyl, the narrowest part of the lake, and joins a narrow tongue of land advancing from the other bank to meet it. The lake is supplied chiefly by the Linth, which enters its upper extremity at Uznach, and issues from it in a clear dark blue rapid current at the town of Zurich, where it takes the name of Limmat. Thirty different kinds of fish are caught in this lake, the most esteemed being the salmon, *the trout, and the eel.*

2. The Lake of Greiffen (Greiffensee), situated two leagues east of Zurich, is ¾ l. (2¼ m.) long, ½ l. (1½ m.) wide, and very fully stocked with fish. It is supplied by the Aa and other streams, and it discharges its waters by the Glatt into the Rhine.

3. The Lake of Pfëffikon (Pfeffikensee) is 1½ l. (4½ m.) to the east of the town of Zurich. Its length is 1¼ l. (3¾ m.), and its width only ¼ l. (¼ m.) It is very deep, and contains a great multitude of fish. It communicates with the Greiffensee by means of the Aa.

The Canton of Zurich contains other lakelets, such as the Durlersee, to the south of the Albis, and discharging its waters into the Limmat by the Rappisch; the Bergsee and the Katzenzee, but they are insignificant.

(b.) RIVERS. — 1. The *Rhine* borders most of the N. frontier of the Canton and at the Castle of Lauffen forms the celebrated falls described under Schaffhausen.

2. The *Reuss* separates Zurich for a short distance on its W. border from Aargau.

3. The *Limmat* issues from the lake of Zurich, and is in fact the continuation of the Linth coming from the uplands of Glarus. It receives near the town of Zurich the Sihl and enters the Canton of Aargau, between Dietikon and Oetwyl, after which it passes by Baden and falls into the Aar near Vogelsang.

4. The *Sihl* rises in the Canton of Schwyz and enters that of Zurich near Schindellegi; immediately below the town of Zurich, it falls into the Limmat, as stated before.

5. The *Thur* comes from the Canton of Thur, crosses running E. and W., part of the Canton of Zurich, and falls into the Rhine below Ellikon.

5. The *Töss* has its source on the borders of the Toggenburg, flows through the marshy valley called Turbenthal, or turf valley, and also falls into the Rhine near the hamlet of Teuffen.

7. The Glatt is formed by the waters

discharged by the Greiffensee and carries them off by a subterranean channel that has been cut through the rock near the hamlet.

(c.) RIVULETS.—The most remarkable streams in the Canton are the Rappisch, the Aa, the Erlibach, which makes a fall of 40 feet situated on the N.W. bank of the lake; the Eulach and many others.

AGRICULTURAL AND INDUSTRIAL PRODUCTIONS.—A large number of horned cattle, and a fair number of swine are bred in the Canton, but few horses, and its waters are alive with fish. It has a great number of fine meadows, and yields a tolerably large crop of corn, but not enough for the consumption. The slopes are not unfrequently planted with vines, especially near Zurich, Winterthur, and on the banks of the Rhine, where they make a very fair wine. The Canton yields moreover colza, hemp, flax, potatoes., &c., and plenty of fruit. The woods have been so much cleared that fuel is wanting, but there are coal mines, and turf is plentiful: there are also quarries of gypsum, limestone, marl, &c., and the Canton contains several mineral springs. Commerce and industry are very lively and thriving in Zurich. The cotton trade has assumed importance of late years, and there are many print, leather, and tobacco manufactories, potteries and distilleries of Kirschenwasser (cherry brandy). Beside these branches of industry the Canton has some good glass and dyeing works, the latter being quite noted for their fine red dye called Turkish.

HOT SPRINGS, BATHS, &c.—Several mineral springs occur in this Canton, one even in the town of Zurich, near the Wasserkirche, but the waters are mostly deficient in strength and efficacy, and accordingly little used. The best baths are the Nydelbad, Wannenbad | near Stäfa, the aussere and innere (outer and inner) Gyrenbad, the Rösslibad on the Rietli near Zurich, all mostly used by the poor. The Wenzibad is behind the Albis.

POPULATION AND RELIGION.—The Canton is peopled by 266,000 inhabitants, of whom 11,000 are Roman Catholics, the rest being Protestants.

ABBEYS AND CONVENTS.—There is a Chapter of Canons at Zurich, the prebendaries acting as professors to the Lyceum, Gymnasium, &c. There is also a Catholic Abbey of the order of St. Benedict at Rheinau.

SCIENTIFIC, EDUCATIONAL, AND CHARITABLE INSTITUTIONS.—Public education has long received much attention at Zurich, the birth-place of Pestalozzi and Lavater. Educational matters are placed under the direction of a council probably less governed by Red Tape than the committee in Downing Street, and directs the instruction of the Canton, which for that purpose is divided into 15 circles, each of which is placed under an inspector with two assistants. The village schools are generally well managed, and improvements are being continually introduced. Zurich and Winterthur have Gymnasiums, and at Zurich there is a University with chairs of Theology, Law and Medicine. See under Zurich.

The Canton has nine libraries, seven at Zurich, one at Winterthur, and one in the Convent at Rheinau. There are five cabinets of Natural History, many other collections (antiquarian especially), and its Federal Polytechnicum, forming a kind of great exhibition, with a chemical laboratory, and the University which has been transferred to it.

SURVEY OF THE CANTON.

Albis (The). See Zurich.

Cappel.—A village 4 l. (12 m.) from Zurich, on the road to Zug and near the border of the Canton, on the spot where the reformers were beaten in battle, 1531, and where Ulrich Zwingli lost his life.

Forche.—Two leagues (6 m.) from Zurich, presents a fine view over a great part of East Switzerland.

Richtenschwyl and Rapperswyl, may be reached by steamboat, sailing boat, rail, or post road; whichever mode of progress you adopt, the excursion is most pleasing. If you go by land you can proceed on one side and return by the other bank of the lake; both banks presenting a series of pretty views and graceful scenery, amid thriving villages and verdant slopes, backed by the snowy Alps of Glarus and Schwyz, which seen afar off, offer a delightful and striking contrast to the more immediate home view near the water side. At the widest part of the lake is the Island of Uffnau or Affnau, 5½ l. (16½ m.) from Zurich, ¼ l. (1½ m.) from Rapperswyl, and 1 l. (3 m.) from Richtenswyl. This little spot is most picturesque in appearance; it belongs to the Abbey of Einsiedeln and contains besides the rustic abode of the former, a church (date 973), a little chapel and a summer-house. The ashes of the German poet and hero, Ulrich von Hutten, repose on this island. Driven from his native land he came to pass the last fortnight of his life on this isolated spot, died there August 30th, 1523, and was buried in the chapel. A sepulchral stone, on which the inscription is almost effaced, points out the place where his body lies. (For a description of Rapperswyl, see Canton of St. Gallen, to which it belongs).

Regensberg is a little town situated on the east slope of the Läger Mountains, 3 l. (9 m.) from Zurich, and only deserves notice on account of the splendid view you enjoy from its château.

Richtenschwil or *Richterswyl* has a good Inn and pension, the Angel; Three Kings, another old-established house; ¼ l. (2½ m.) from Wadenschwyl, 5 l. (15 m.) from Zurich, 3,500 inhabitants, is on the frontier of the Canton. A post-car runs twice a-day hence to Einsiedeln, Schwyz and Brunnen; and once a-day to Lachen and Glarus. 1½ l. (4½ m.) hence, rising to the foot of the hill Hohe Rhone, is the *much frequented* pension Hütten.

Schnabelberg, see *Albis*.

Stäfa (Hotels, the Sun, and Crown.) is one of the largest and richest villages in Switzerland. It stands on the E. bank of the lake opposite Richterschwyl, 4¼ l. (14¼ m.) from Zurich. Both commercial industry and agriculture are thriving and well developed and a source of the wealth and comfort of the inhabitants who have played an active part in the political history of the Canton. The population of Stäfa is 3,800. Near the Crown Inn is the Wannenbad, with sulphur springs, and near the church, which stands on an eminence, you command a delightful view.

Utliberg. See Zurich (town).

Waedenschwyl or *Waedenschweil*.—Hotels, the Angel, said to be good; Crown; Stag; Eagle. Population, 6,000. An active thriving place on the W. bank of the lake, ¾ l. from Richterschwyl, 4¼ l. (12¾ m.) from Zurich. The town has a pleasant aspect, with many handsome houses, rising out of a bower of fruit trees. It has a fine church, town house, schools, good cotton mills, and the largest tannery in Switzerland. It has a château, belonging to M. Dollfus, reading room, and a society of musical amateurs (Verein.) The inhabitants are industrious and enterprising. The tannery belonged a few years ago to M. Hauser. Excursions to the old castle and fine ruins of Richtenschwyl Castle, in a splendid situation. A fine view near it from a spot called Burghalden.

Winterthur, the second town in the Canton, and a great railway centre; in fact the Olten of East Switzerland. The four lines which meet here lead to Zurich, Schaffhausen, Romanshorn, and Rorschach. Most passengers have to change carriages. Train stops ten minutes. Restaurant at the station. Travellers from Zurich to Romanshorn stay in their carriages. Those to Schaffhausen and St. Gallen change. As four lines meet, take care not to mistake the train. Seven times a-day to Zurich, 1st cl., 2fr. 75c.; 2nd, 1fr. 95c.; 3rd, 1fr. 40c. Five times a-day to Schaffhausen, 1st cl. 3fr. 25c.; 2nd, 2fr. 25c.; 3rd, 1fr. 60c. Four times a-day to Rorschach.

1st cl. 7*fr.* 90*c.*; 2nd, 5*fr.* 55*c.*; 3rd, 3*fr.* 95*c.* Hotels: The Sun, Lion, Eagle, Casino. Café Ritter, near the station, good. Population, 6,500. A very industrious town, consists of two long parallel streets, crossed by six smaller ones. Winterthur stands on the Eulach rivulet, and contains several respectable buildings, as, 1. The parish church, the town house, and the hospital. 2. A superior school, a commercial school, and a ladies' school. 3. A library fairly supplied with good books, and containing Roman medals and antiquities found in the neighbourhood. Collections: in ornithology, M. Ziegler's. Arts and sciences: MM. Kuster, Hegner, and Sulzer.

Winterthur is an active industrious little town, with cotton mills, muslin and print manufactories, large dyeing works, and Messrs. Ziegler manufacture vitriol, alum, Glauber-salts, and mineral waters of all kinds.

The town is in a very pretty country, presenting pleasing walks in all directions, on the neighbouring heights. Veltheim, Wiesendangen, Bruderheaus, and the Château of Kyburg, with a fine panoramic view, are the points best worth visiting.

M. Pfau's gallery of pictures is open every day at Winterthur, from 10 to 12; and from 2 to 4 p.m.

Zurich (City).—Hotels: Hotel de Belle Vue au Lac, one of the best situated hotels in Switzerland; kept by C. Guyer. Hotel Baur (en ville), Bahnhofstrasse. Hotel de l'Epee, well situated, view on the lake and environs; recommended. Hotel Bauer au Lac.

Pension Swan at Muhlbach; pension Rinderknecht, at Fluntern, ¼ l. (¾ m.) above the Cantonal School; pension Palmhof near the Polytechnic School. Of the numerous restaurants and cafés, the best are the cafés Safran, Schutzenhaus, café Litteraire, Schmidstube, Zurcherhof. The Kronenhalle is a café Chantant. There are cafés with gardens out of the town, at Drathschmiedli, Riedli, ¼ l. (1½ m.); Carolinenburg: Burgli (30 min.), summer concerts and fine view. Sonnenberg ½ l. Tiefenbrunnen by the lake, &c. Baugarten is a pleasure garden by the lake. Entrance free to foreigners. Printsellers: Meyer and Zeller, Fussli and Co. Photographs at Cramer and Luthery, &c.

Railroads. Zurich to	1st cl. *fr. c.*		2nd cl. *fr. c.*		3rd *fr.*
Antwerp	98	10	80	5	—
Augsburg Express	2"	15	20	60	—
Baden Baden Express	28	95	19	90	—
Bâle by Olten	10	20	7	5	4 80
Bâle by Waldshut	10	75	7	45	5 25
Berlin by Waldshut	130	70	89	95	—
Berlin by Friedrichshafen	137	65	94	60	—
Berne	13	75	9	65	6 90
Brussels	96	90	78	85	—
Curlsruhe Express	31	65	21	70	—
Chur	13	90	8	80	6 0
Cologne Express	69	60	51	45	—
Darmstadt Express	43	75	29	85	—
Frankfort by Waldshut Express	46	50	31	80	—
Frankfort by Friedrichshafen	51	30	34	65	—
Fribourg Swiss	17	25	12	10	8 65
Friedrichshafen	9	95	7	80	5 10
Geneva	29	70	20	95	15 15
Glarus	8	80	5	10	3 55
Heidelberg Express	33	0	22	70	15 0
Lausanne	24	0	16	85	12 5
Lindau	11	25	8	60	6 5
London by Ostend	152	55	134	50	—
Lucerne	6	50	4	55	3 25
Montreux	26	85	19	5"	13 70
Munich	33	"	23	5	15 70
Neuchâtel	16	75	11	90	8 85
Paris	71	0	53	10	—
Ragatz	11	50	7	35	4 55
Romanshorn	8	75	6	10	4 35
Rorschach	10	65	7	50	5 35
Schaffhausen	6	0	4	20	3 0
Solothurn	11	5	7	75	5 55
St. Gallen	8	85	6	25	4 45
Stuttgart Express	30	55	20	80	—
Thun	16	0	11	85	8 50
Vienna	103	50	76	5	—

Stations at N. of the town ½ l. (1½ m.) from the landing place of the steamers.

STEAMERS.—Eight times a-day to Rapperschwyl and back. Four times a-day by each bank: the other voyages following only one side of the lake, but the boat calls every journey at Horgen and Stäfa.

[illegible] is a [illegible]. Theatre [illegible].

[illegible].—Zurich to Meilen [illegible] ½d. [illegible] 2d. [illegible] 2d. [illegible] 2d. 4d. [illegible] 2d. 1d. [illegible] 2d. 4d. [illegible] 2d. [illegible] 4d. [illegible] 2d. [illegible] 4d. [illegible] for children. Return tickets [illegible] fares.

Conveyance.—Inside the town, one or two persons, fare, above two persons, 1/. [illegible], two persons [illegible] above two persons, 3/. A day, [illegible] more two persons [illegible]. To the Albis Grütli, to the [illegible] of the Uetli, 2/; three persons and more, 3/.

Baths by the lake. Great bathing establishment at Hotel Baur, open 5 [illegible] a.m. [illegible] cabinet, about three persons in the same cabinet. [illegible] and [illegible]. Hot baths, Koch, Baur and Zimmermann.

The history of Zurich has presented many changes. The Romans had established Castrum Turicense, on the Linden-hof. Subsequently, an imperial palace rose on the spot, honoured by visits of Henry I., Henry II., and Conrad the Salic. An Abbey at Grossmünster was founded by Louis the Germanic, whose two daughters were the abbesses. Zurich was subject to the abbey, to imperial bailiffs, and dukes of Zähringen. It was declared an Imperial City by Henry III., But at the time of Albert and his rival, Adolph of Nassau, it was a powerful commercial city, and in 1327, it allied itself with the three Forest Cantons. Many conflicts took place after this time, between the nobles and the citizens, and much bloodshed was occasioned by secret plots of the aristocracy. In 1353, Zurich made an eternal alliance with the Forest [Cant]ons. It increased in power, and at [last it] became so covetous and ambitious, [that it] engaged in wars, like Prussia, with

its brothers and confederates. It had a glorious share in the wars against Burgundy, its troops being led by a hero called Hans Waldmann, who, like the great and good of all times, perished a victim of base intrigues, low calumnies, and mutual jealousies. The Reformation headed by Zwingli took a great development at Zurich, which was enriched by the arrival of industrious refugees, persecuted elsewhere. In 1799, at the time of the French revolution, Zurich was the scene of bloody struggles between the Russians, and the French, and in one of these, the eminent Christian philosopher, Lavater, was shot by a French grenadier, in the name no doubt, of liberty, fraternity, &c. A revolutionary government was [illegible] on the Canton, in 1836, and endeavoured to bring David Strauss into the chair of theology, at Zurich, but the country people opposed this as a risk, thinking it inappropriate that religion should be taught by a man who considered God an abstract idea, and Christianity a theme of fables.

The town, which is not large, stands at the extremity of the lake, and on both banks of the Limmat, united by five bridges. The faubourgs are numerous, with handsome streets. They are separate parishes, such as Oberstrass, Enge, Fluntern, Hottingen, Riesbach, &c. The principal part of the old town, which is hilly and full of old narrow streets, is the Grossmünster, or large town.

PUBLIC EDIFICES.—The Cathedral or Grossmünster, on an eminence on the right bank of the Limmat, referred to Otho the Great, and even Charlemagne. The two handsome, but unfinished towers, are of more recent date. The interior has nothing remarkable. In the girls' school, formerly a canonry and cloister, are some curious sculptures. The Fraumünster Church is not remarkable. The Augustinian Church, restored to the Catholics since 1848, has some paintings by Deschwanden. The Hotel de Ville, or Stadthaus, is in the centre of the town. The

town library situated in the Wasser
Kirche, is of great interest (open Monday,
Tuesday, or Thursday, from 10 a.m. to
noon; and on Wednesday, Friday, and
Saturday, from 1 to 2 p.m.; and on Monday and Thursday, from 3 to 4 p.m. This
library, which has 8,000 volumes, and
3,000 MS., some of great value, is an
object of much interest. Among its treasures observe a Greek Psalter, on purple
parchment, in gold letters; a Code of
Birman Laws, on palm leaves; an excellent
MS. of Quintilian; the Greek Bible of
Zwingli; three Latin letters written from
the Tower, to Bullinger, by Lady Jane
Grey; various autographs; a bust of
Lavater, by Daneker; another of Pestalozzi, by Imhoff; portraits of eminent
magistrates; a fine plan of Switzerland
in relief, by Muller, on a scale of 1-40,000.
A plan of Engelberg; a collection of
2,000 models, &c. (Fee 1f., or if a party,
2fr.) On the Upper story is the Archæological Society's collection, containing
especially, arms, instruments, relics, &c., of
Lacustrine Swiss habitations, and of the
stone age. Also, Roman remains, cameos
and MS. The transactions of the Society
are published. There are many other collections and libraries at Zurich, particularly
the Natural History collection, transferred to the Polytechnicum. The collection of insects of Escher, his minerals and
shells, and the Anatomical collection by
the New Hospital, are good. Among
other collections may be noticed, the
Zoological Museum, the Botanic Garden
and the Polytechnicum, previously noticed,
&c., &c. The Great Hospital is a fine
charity.

Zurich has several manufactories, especially of prints and cotton, paper mills,
silk mills, carpet manufactories, &c.

WALKS.—To the Lindenhof, the Bau-
schänzli, the great bridge and the quay
with a fine lake view, the Hohe promenade
with a monument to the composer, Nageli
(+ 1836). The Katz Bastion has a very
fine view, embracing the Alps of Glarus,
Schwyz and Uri, including the Glarnisch

and the Tödi (11,153 feet high); the Hufi
Stock, the Mythen above Schwyz, the
Ruchi and Oberalpstock (borders of Uri
and the Grisons), the Bristenstock, the
Uri Rothstock, and the Titlis (Unterwalden). From both banks of the lake
delightful views are enjoyed, especially
from Weid (1 hour), and from a point
called Schlössli, Burgli, Sihlholzli, Hockler
by the Sihl at the foot of the Albis, &c.

EXCURSIONS.—The Uetliberg 1 l. (3 m.)
464 metres (2,400 feet) above the lake,
873 metres (1,100 feet) above the sea,
forming the summit of the Albis, with a
very fine view. A good inn on the top.
1 hour 25 minutes from Zurich. Fair
sleeping accommodation. Fare in carriage
to Albisguti (30 minutes from top) 4fr.,
there and back 6fr. One of the finest
views in Switzerland, from Engadin in
Grisons to the Oberland. You can dis-
tinguish Piz Linard, the Santis in Appenzell, the Titlis, Schreckhorn, Jungfrau,
Monch, &c.

2. To the Forche by Kreuz and Zu-
mickon 2 l. (6 m.) with a fine view over
East Switzerland.

3. The Schnabelberg above the Albis
Inn is a still finer view.

Zurich is on the direct line to the Canton of Glarus, which can be reached either
by rail or steamboat.

The tourist may also return from the
Grisons by Glarus to Zurich if he prefer
it. In either case he will visit the beautiful neighbourhood of Stachelberg and the
Tödi, which are amongst the finest scenery
in the Alps.

ROUTES OF ZURICH.

Aarau (No. 18).

Aarberg, by Berne (Nos. 79 and 53), or by Aarau
(No. 18), and Solothurn (Nos. 16 and 216).

Aarbourg, by Aarau Nos. 18 and 1).

Aeggischhorn, by Altdorf and Grimsel (Nos. 215,
207 and 55), or by Furka (No. 130).

Aigle, by Berne (Nos. 79 and 59) or by Thun (Rail
to Lucerne, No. 76), and the Simmenthal (No.
72), over Col de Pillon, and on by the Ormond
Valley.

Altdorf, by Schwyz (Nos. 215 and 207).

Altstätten, by St. Gallen (Nos. 196 and 180).

Appenzell (No. 28).

Art, by Zug (Nos. 295 or 296 and 281).

Baden (No. 18).

Bâle (No. 44).

Bellinzona, by Schwyz (Nos. 215 and 207), and Altdorf (No. 229).

Berne (No. 79).

Bex, by Berne (Nos. 79 and 58), or by Thun and the Simmenthal (No. 72).

Bienne, by Aarau (No. 18), and Solothurn (No. 218), or by Berne (Nos. 79 and 59).

ROUTE 298.

BRUGG, 6 L. (18 m.)

	Leagues.	Miles.
Baden (No. 18)	4	12
Wyl		1¾
Unterwyl		¾
Gebistorf		1½
Königsfelden		1½
Brugg		¾
	6	18

Bulle, by Berne (Nos. 79 and 54).

Burgdorf (No. 302) as far as Morgenthal, (No. 6) as far as Kirchberg, and thence to Burgdorf.

Chamouni, by Berne (No. 79 and 63), Lausanne (No. 96), and Geneva (No. 95), or by Thun and the Simmenthal (Nos. 76 and 55), Martigny (No. 263), and Tête Noire (No. 265.)

Champery in the Val d' Illiez (Nos. 215 and 207), to Schwyz, by Altdorf and Furka (Nos. 229 and 130), to Sion (No. 266), and Bex (No. 74), or by Thun (No. 76), and Simmenthal to Bex (No. 72.) [From Sion to Bex instead of 74 take Rail.]

Chiavenna, by Chur (No. 142 and 121, 122, 123).

Chur (No. 142).

ROUTE 299.

EINSIEDELN, 7¼ L. (21¾ m.)

	Leagues.	Miles.
Wollishofen	1	3
Kilchberg		2¼
Rueschlikon		
Thalwyl		1½
Oberrieden		
Horgen		1½
Bockenbad		1½
Löblismuhle	1	3
Schindellegi	1	3
Einsiedeln	1½	4½
	7¼	21¾

ROUTE 300.

OZ, 7½ L. (22½ m.)

	Leagues.	Miles.
By the Lake to Richtenschwyl	5	15
Einsiedeln	2½	7½
	7½	22½

Engelberg, by Lucerne (Nos. 160 and 153

Frauenfeld (No. 245).

Fribourg, by Berne (Nos. 79 and 54).

Gais, by St. Gallen (Nos. 196 and 186).

Geneva, by Berne (Nos. 79 and 63), and Lausanne (No. 96), or by Thun (No. 76), and the Simmenthal (No. 72).

Glarus (No. 116), or Rail.

ROUTE 301.

HERISAU, 13 L. (39 m.)

	Leagues.	Miles.
Schwammendingen	1	3
Wollisellen		
Rieden		
Bassersdorf		2¼
Breite		2¼
Tös		2
Winterthur 4 L. (12 m.)		
Raterschen		2¼
Elg	1¼	3¾
Aadorf		1½
Dutwyl		1½
Munchwyl	1	3
Wyl		2¼
Burenbrucke	1½	4½
Niederwyl		2¼
Gossau		2¼
Herisau	1¼	3¾
	13	39

ROUTE 303.

LAUFFENBURG, 13 L. (39 m.)

	Leagues.	Miles.
Baden (No. 18)	4	12
Frick (No. 31)	6	18
Einken		1½
Stein		1½
Lauffenburg	2	6
	13	39

Lausanne, by Berne (Nos. 79 and 63), or by Thun (No. 76), and the Simmenthal (No. 72).

Locarno, by Chur (Nos. 142, 119 or 120), and Bellinzona (No. 232), or by Schwyz (Nos. 215 and 207), Altdorf (No. 229), and Bellinzona (No. 232),

Loesch (Baths), by Berne (Nos. 79 and 65), or by Thun (No. 76), the Simmenthal (No. 72), and Lenk, the Ravil Pass (No. 73), or by Thun (No. 72) and the Gemmi (No. 65).

Lucerne (No. 160).

Lugano, by Chur (No. 142, and 119 or 120) and Bellinzona (No. 233), or by Schwyz (Nos. 215 and 207), Altdorf (No. 229), and Bellinzona (No. 233).

Mendrisio, by Chur (Nos. 142, and 119 or 120) and Bellinzona (No. 235), or by Schwyz (Nos. 215 and 207), Altdorf (No. 229), and Bellinzona (No. 235).

Morat, Morges, and Moudon, by Berne (Nos. 79 and 63), or by Aarau (Nos. 18 and 16), and Solothurn (No. 223).

Neuchâtel, by Berne (Nos. 79 and 70), or by Aarau (Nos. 18 or 16) and Solothurn (No. 178), and Neuchâtel (No. 97).

Orbe, by Berne (Nos. 79 and 71), or by Aarau (Nos. 18 and 16), Solothurn (No. 178), and Neuchâtel (No. 97).

Ormond Valley, near Bex. By Schwyz and Altdorf (Nos. 215 and 207), Altdorf and Furka (Nos. 229 and 130), to Sion (No. 266), and Bex (No. 74), or by Thun (No. 76), Simmenthal (No. 72), and over Col de Pillon to Sepey.

Orta, by Chur and Bellinzona (Nos. 142, 119, or 120, and 232), or by Schwyz (Nos. 215 and 207), Altdorf (No. 229), and Bellinzona (No. 232). Pallanza and Omegna (No. 235—4).

Pallanza, see last Route.

ROUTE 304.

Pfäffers (Baths), 23¼ l. (69¾ m.)

	Leagues.	Mile .
Zollikon	¼	2½
Kusnacht	¼	1½
Erlibach	¼	1½
Herrliberg	¼	1½
Meilen	¼	2½
Uetikon	¼	1½
Stäfa	1¼	3½
Feldbach	¼	¾
Rapperswyl	1	3
Wurmspach	1	3
Schmerikon	1½	4½
Uznach	1½	3½
Kaltenbaum	¼	2½
Schännis	¼	2½
Ziegelbruck	1½	4½
Wesen	¼	1½
Wallenstadt	4	12
Berschis	¼	2¼
Halbmeil	¼	2¼
Sargans	1½	4½
Ragatz	1	3
Valens	1½	4½
Pfäffers	¼	1½
	23¼	69¾

The rail can be taken from Zurich to Ragatz (108 kilometres).

Pilatus (Mount), by rail to Lucerne, or by boat to Horgen, road to Zug; lake to Immensee, and road or lake to Lucerne (295, 296, 294, 165, or 148).

Pontresina, by Chur (142 A, B, and 139).

Righi (Mount), by Zug (295, 296, and 294).

Saas, by Schwyz, Altdorf, Andermatt, and Visp (Nos. 215, 207, 57, 130, and 266).

Saint Moritz (Grisons), by Chur (Nos. 142 A, B, and 123).

Saint Gallen (196).

Schaffhausen (No 200).

Schwyz (No. 215 .

Sion, by Berne (Nos. 79, 73, or 74) or Thun (Nos. 55, 153, and 76), the Simmenthal (No. 72) and the Ravil Pass (No. 73).

Sixt, by Schwyz, Altdorf, the Furka, and Sion, to Monthey (Nos. 215, 207, 229, 130, and 226), [from Sion by rail to Monthey] up to Champery, and over the Col de Coux. (See Routes of Valais.)

Solothurn, by Aarau (Nos. 18 and 16).

Stachelberg, rail to Glarus, and (No. 103).

Stanz, see Unterwalden.

Stein am Rhein, by Winterthur Railway Junction, and road to Andelfingen.

Thun, by Berne (No. 79), or rail to Lucerne, and over the Brunig (Nos. 153 and 76).

Trogen, by Saint Gallen (Nos. 196 and 193).

Unterwalden, by Lucerne (Nos. 160 and 153).

Varallo, by Chur (Nos. 142, 119, and 120) or Bellinzona (No. 232), or by Schwyz (Nos. 215 and 207), Altdorf (No. 229), Bellinzona (No. 232,) and Orta (No. 237—2), or by Pallanza and Omegna (Nos. 235—4).

Vevay, by Berne (Nos. 79 and 54), or by Thun (Nos. 153 and 76) and the Simmenthal (No 72), to Col de Jaman, Winterthur, rail, and (No. 331).

Yverdun, by Berne (Nos. 79 and 77), or by Thun (Nos. 153, 76, and 77), or by rail to Olten, Solothurn, and through Neuchâtel.

Zermatt, by Schwyz to Altdorf (Nos. 215 and 207), Andermatt (No. 57), Visp (No. 130), and the Visp Valley (No. 130 and 266).

Zug (No. 295 or 296).

Suabia and Central Germany, by rail to Romanshorn and Friedrichshafen.

Bavaria, Austria, and East Germany, by ditto or Lindau.

Tyrol, by Chur (Nos. 144 and 146).

Heidelberg, Frankfort, and the Rhineland, by Bâle.

Paris, by Bâle or Neuchâtel (rail throughout).

Piedmont, by Berne, Lausanne, Geneva, rail to St. Jean de Maurienne, and over the Cenis to Susa.

Italy (in general), by Altdorf and Bellinzona to Milan (No. 238).

MAIN ROUTE (F).

(F) The last main approach to Switzerland that we have to follow is that by the Canton of Tessin, on the side of Italy. This Canton may be reached in several ways; either, 1st, from Milan by rail to Arona, and thence up the lake to Locarno; or, 2nd, by road from Como to Mendrisio, on the Lake of Como; or, 3rd, from Bergamo, by Lecco, Bellaggio, and Bellinzona.

The approach from Italy to Switzerland by the Simplon and St. Bernard has been noticed under the Canton of Valais. Having reached Locarno, Lugano, and Bellinzona, from Italy, the tourist wishing to penetrate into German Switzerland has the choice of several routes, the principal being that by the St. Gothard to Altdorf. (See Cantons of Lucerne and Uri.) Three other routes conduct him by the Lukmanier, Bernhardin, and Splugen, into the Grisons; and if he wishes to reach the Valais, he can pass up Val Formazza, over the Gries, to Viesch, and up to the Aeggischhorn, taking the finest falls in the Alps, those of the Tosa, *en route.*— (See Canton of Valais.)

CANTON OF TESSIN.

Its northern limits are Uri and the Grisons; to the east it has the Grisons again, besides Lombardy, which forms also its southern boundary, and together with Piedmont, its western.

AREA, SOIL, AND CLIMATE.—The surface of Tessin (Italicè Ticino) is 146⅔ square Swiss leagues (2,836 square kiloms., 1,304 square English miles), and consists essentially of mountains and valleys, the latter being in most cases formed by the south slopes of the High Alps, and discharging their waters either into the Lago Maggiore (Lange see) or into that of Lugano. It is only in the vicinity of the latter lake that you find an expanse of beautiful green prairies and plains, where the climate, as is the case generally at the southern entrance of all the valleys, is

quite Italian. As you advance higher, and more north, it becomes naturally colder and ruder, and ultimately resists the growth of all vegetation.

MOUNTAINS.—Several branch chains of the High Alps, linked on to the main Pennine and Lepontine Chain, near St. Gothard, intersect especially the northern part of the Tessin. These branch chains, running mostly south, and sending out numerous tertiary offshoots, form a multitude of valleys, of different size. The highest ridge of the Canton, at the extreme north, forms a part of the main chain of Lepontine Alps, and comprising among other passes the Gries (7,336 feet), the Furka (7,795 feet), the Lukmanier (5,740 feet), the St. Gothard (6,357 feet), the Centovalli, and the Greina. In the north-east may be remarked the Piz Moscheles and Camoghé, the Lenta and the St. Giori. In the interior of the Canton Mount Cenere deserves a special attention.

LAKES, RIVERS, AND RIVULETS.

(a) 1. LAKES.—Lago Maggiore (Langeses, Lacus Verbanus), perhaps the most beautiful sheet of water in the Alps. The Canton of Tessin only possesses a small portion of this lake, namely, the reach extending from the small town of Brissago, situated on the right bank, and from the village of Zenna, on the left or Lombard bank, opposite Brissago, to the north end of the lake. This reach only comprises about one-fifth of the area of the lake, which is 8½ German geographical miles in length, 14 to 15 hours, covering a surface of 3¼ German square miles (190 square Italian miles). Its height above the sea is 195 metres, or 643 feet; its depth, 800 metres (2,465 feet), being the deepest of all the Alpine lakes, with a higher temperature than that of all the others. Its greatest width, near Laveno, is nearly 3L (9 m.) It is particularly well stocked with a great variety of fish, and therefore very attractive to fishermen. It contains several islands, especially the Borromea

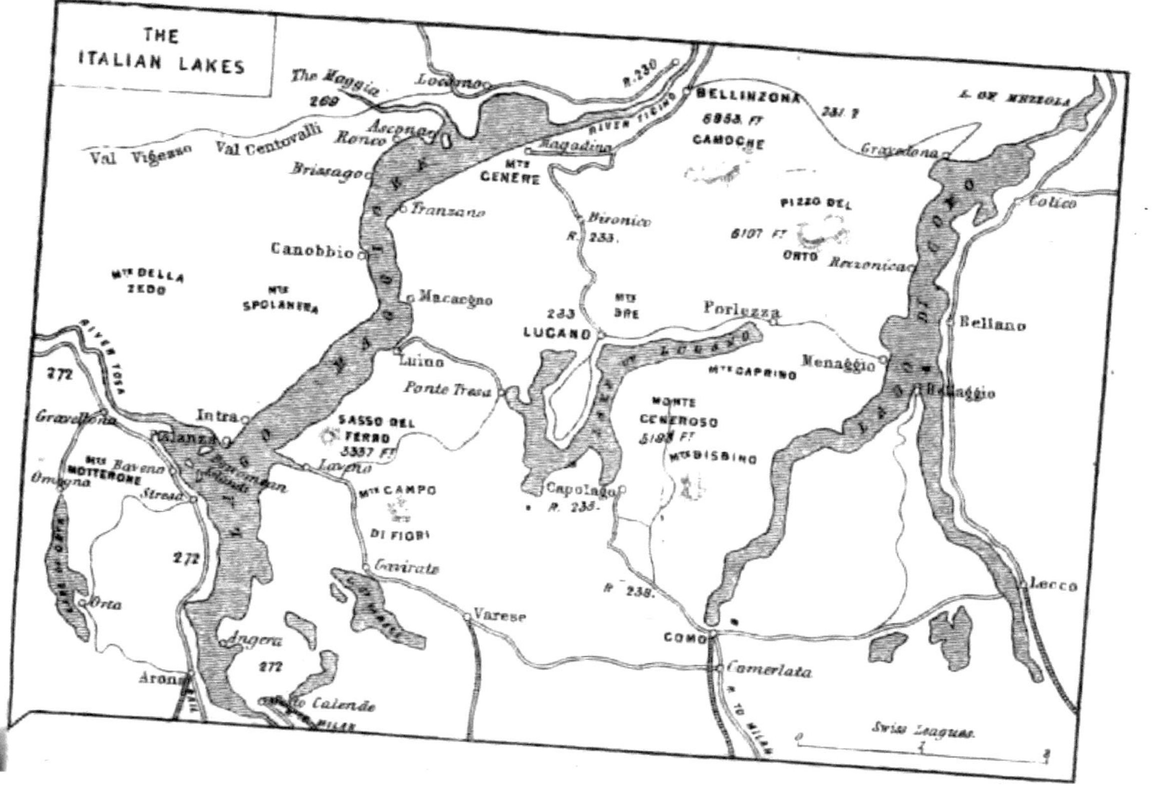

THE ITALIAN LAKES
The Maggia
269
Val Vigezzo
Val Centovalli
Ronco
Ascona
Locarno
R. 230
RIVER TICINO
Magadina
BELLINZONA
6953 FT
231.?
CAMOGHE
L. DI MEZZOLA
Gravedona
Colico
Brissago
MTE CENERE
Franzano
Bironico
R. 233.
PIZZO DEL
6107 FT
ORTO
Rezzonico
Canobbio
MTE DELLA ZEDO
MTE SPOLANERA
Macagno
233
LUGANO
MTE
ORE
Porlezza
LAGO DI LUGANO
MTE CAPRINO
Menaggio
Bellano
272
RIVER TOSA
Luino
Ponte Tresa
MONTE CENEROSO
5188 FT
MTE BISBINO
LAGO DI COMO
Bellaggio
Gravellona
Intra
Pallanza
SASSO DEL FERRO
3387 FT
Capolago
R. 235.
MTE Baveno
MOTTERONE
Omegna
Stresa
Isola Bella
Laveno
MTE CAMPO
DI FIORI
LAGO D'ORTA
272
Orta
Gavirate
R. 238.
Lecco
Varese
Angera
272
COMO
Arona
to Calende
MILAN
Camerlata
R. TO MILAN
Swiss Leagues.
0
1
2

of world-wide reputation. Six steamboats furrow the waters of the lake from end to end — the Helvetia, the Simplon, the Tessin, the Lukmanier, the Gothard, and the Bernhardin, the three latter of 64, the Helvetia of 100-horse power. There are moreover two small steamers of 32-horse power. For fares, &c., see further on.

2. Lago di Lugano (Ceresio), a charming sheet of water, with varied scenery, belongs almost entirely to the Canton of Tessin; only at the south and east extremities small portions of this winding lake enter the Italian territory of Lombardy. Length, 8 l. (24 m.); mean width, ½ l. (1½ m.); depth, 540 feet. Since 1856 it has a small steamer. The banks of the lake are enchanting. A long bridge spans it near Melide. It is connected with the Lago Maggiore, which lies 230 feet lower, by the Tresa, which issues from the lake near Agno.

Other lakes in this Canton are the Lago di Luzendro (the source of the Reuss), the Lago della Stella (one of the sources of the Ticino); these two lakes flank the St. Gothard road. Two other lakelets occur on Monte Piora, and another in a lateral valley of Val de Vedretto; the remaining waters of the Canton being nothing more than montain tarns.

(b) 1. Rivers.—The Tessin, or Ticino, derives its water partly from the Lake Della Stella, and from the lakes of St. Gothard, which have been mentioned above; and also from other sources at the top of Val Vedretto, which unite their currents near Airolo. From that point it runs through the Val Leventina, where it receives first the Piora, and subsequently all the other streams that pour into the valley; it is eventually increased by the accession of the Blegno (between Poleggio and Biasca). of the Moesa, near Gorduno, and of the Marobia, near Giubasco, and ultimately falls into the Lago Maggiore, near Magadino.

2. The Maggia descends from the highest and remotest part of the Val Lavizzara, receives the accession of a number of streams as far as Cevio, where it receives the Bovana. It proceeds thence towards Ponte Brolla, where it rushes impetuously through a narrow rocky gorge, and after entering the plains it is joined by the Melezzo after its confluence with the Onsernone, near Intragna. The Maggia empties itself eventually into Lago Maggiore, near Locarno.

3. The Blegno rises at the foot of the Greina, waters the Val Blegno, from which it derives all its waters, and runs into the Ticino, below Biasca.

4. The Agno receives its waters partly from Monte Cenere, partly from the Carmoghè, flows through the Val d'Agno, and reaches the Lake of Lugano not far from the village of Agno.

5. The Moesa issues from the Misocco and Calanca valleys, in the Grisons, runs through a small portion of the Valley of Bellinzona, and joins the Ticino near Gorduno.

6. The Verzasca proceeds from the head of the valley of that name, and enters Lago Maggiore to the east of the valley of Minusio.

7. The Tresa issues from the Lake of Lugano, near Ponte di Tresa, from the frontier of the Canton towards Italy, and enters the Lago Maggiore, thus forming a communication between the Lakes of Lugano and Maggiore.

(c) Rivulets. — The principal small streams of Tessin are the Piora, the Marobia, the Bovana, the Melezzo, and the Onsernone, already mentioned. To these may be added the Fallonia, the Breggia, and the Isone. There are a multitude of other streams in the Canton, but they do not need to be specified more minutely.

Agricultural and Industrial Productions. — A considerable number of cattle are bred in this Canton, but they are not of so fine a race as those in the other Cantons. Horses are not so numerous as mules and asses. Sheep, goats, and pigs are numerous. Game is very abundant, including the chamois, white and grey hares, pheasants, partridges woodcocks, quails, waterfowl, &c. The higher regions are frequented by wolves, eagles, and vultures. The lakes and streams literally teem with fish, but pike do much havoc among them. Much care is given by the inhabitants to bees and the silkworm. The Canton yields good crops of cereals, especially maize, a good deal of wine, fine forests, and offers magnificent meadow land, besides a fair quantity of tobacco, &c. Beside the fruit trees common to other parts of Switzerland, Tessin has a number of others peculiar to Italy or more southern climate, such as the chesnut, mulberry, laurel, olive, fig trees, &c. The mineral kingdom is very rich. At Arzo, on the frontiers of Lombardy, are quarries of a splendid marble, and in Val Lavizzara, are quarries of pot-stone and lavezza. At Abiasco occur a good many garnets, and crystals are numerous on the mountains bordering on the Valais. Gypsum, limestone, sandstone, and coal are tolerably plentiful in the Canton, which has also some iron mines and mineral springs.

Among the manufactured productions of Tessin may be specified cherry brandy, olive and nut oil, tar, wooden and stone carved implements, and pottery, glass, paper, straw hats, and silk. There are a good many iron and copper forges, and furnaces in the Canton.

MINERAL SPRINGS. — These are numerous, but are not of much note or much frequented.

POPULATION AND RELIGION. — The population is now 130,000 (30 years ago it was 88,793), all Roman Catholics, and speaking a very corrupt Italian patois. The character of the people is Italian, quick, clever, and hasty. The mode of life in the town is quite Italian.

ABBEYS AND CONVENTS.—Besides the seven chapters of Canons, at Bellinzona, Lugano, Locarno, Agno, Biasca, Abiasco, Riva, and Balerna, there were in the Canton of Tessin nearly twenty monasteries of men and women, till 1848, most of them been closed since then.

EDUCATIONAL, SCIENTIFIC, AND CHARITABLE INSTITUTIONS.—Education is generally neglected in Tessin, and only a few villages have public schools. In the three principal towns, Bellinzona, Lugano, and Locarno, as well as at Poleggio and Ascona, elementary education, and the seminaries were till lately taught by religious orders, but they generally admit of considerable improvement.

As regards charities, they consist chiefly in the distribution of alms, for the Canton does not possess any charitable institution of a secular nature. The people are very Italian in character. Ignorant, superstitious, and indolent, they are not easily led to work, and no means are employed to diminish pauperism and mendicity, which amount to real scourges. It would be very desirable that some means should be devised to improve the condition of this Italian republic. The people are easily excited to anger, but they shew the usual vivacity and dexterity of southerns.

A B C GUIDE OF TESSIN.

Airolo. —(Hotels: Post, chez Motta; room 1½fr. to 2fr.; breakfast, 1½fr.; telegraph; Three Kings, same proprietor; horses provided). A village, 3,692 feet above the sea, and 2,880 feet below the top of the Pass of St. Gothard. Airolo is in the Val Leventina, 3 hours from the top of the pass, ascending, 1½ hour descending. The views enjoyed on descent are among the most delightful in the Alps. Issuing from the savage gorge of the Reuss and the sombre horrors of St. Gothard, the eye is soothed and greeted by the soft and charming vegetation of the south. You descend first by the Val Tremola (so called from its avalanches), having to the right the steep slopes of the Fibbia, the cascades at the source of the Tessin, and to the left the high Alp of Sorescia. On a rock at the entrance of Val Tremola is seen the inscription "Suwarov victor," in commemoration of a battle gained over the

French, September 25th, 1797. After passing the refuges of St. Anthony and St. John, you issue from the gorge, and the pedestrian can shorten his route by cutting off the zig-zags of the carriage descent. The view is splendid. At your feet is Airolo, to the right Val Bedretto, and above it the Poncione di Vespero and the mountains of Campolungo.

Val Leventina, 13 l. (39 m.) in length, is watered by the Tessin, and forms the ascent from Bellinzona to the St. Gothard Pass. It is the principal valley of the Canton of Tessin, and is divided into the Upper, Middle, and Lower Val Leventina, down to the entrance of Val Blegno, and thence to Bellinzona; the Valley is called the Riviera. It abounds in the finest scenery, including several picturesque cascades. The population, amounting to 25,000, speak an Italian patois, and professes Catholic religion; all their characteristics, like those of the valley, with its habitations and culture, bespeak an Italian nature. The valley was governed down till the French Revolution by the bailiffs of Uri, Schwyz, and Unterwalden, and treated as a conquered country, for the sturdy republicans showed in this instance the usual defects of a stronger race lording it over a weaker one.

Val Bedretto, 4 l. (12 m.) in ascent, opens opposite Airolo, leading at its upper end over the Col de Novena, and Eginenthal to Obergestelen in the Canton de Valais, 8 hours (see Obergestelen under Canton de Valais). It derives its name from the birches which grow there to 5,780 feet above the sea. Surrounded by snowy summits, it is a grand centre for avalanches in winter. Many of its villages, such as Albinasca, Fontana, Osasco, Villa, and Ronco having been partially destroyed by avalanches, especially in January 1863. Further up the valley is a communication by the Col St. Giacomo, 7,100 feet, and the Alpe Formazzova into Val Toccia and Formazza in 3½ hours.

Arbedo, at the junction of Val Misocco with Leventina, ¼ l. (2¼ m.) from Bellinzona, is remarkable as the scene of one of the most gallant actions in Swiss history. It was an engagement, June 30th, 1422, between 3,000 Swiss and 24,000 Milanese. The Duke of Milan had been irritated by some recent events, consisting of real or imaginary grievances occasioned by the Swiss of Uri in their encroachments on the south side of St. Gothard. Accordingly he armed secretly and surprised the Swiss garrisons of Ossola and Bellizona. The confederates prepared to resist when it was too late, and being divided by factions could only collect a small force. At Arbedo they encountered the whole Milanese army, led by Carmagnola, who attacked them at once, and before they could receive reinforcements. Yet the sturdy Swiss resisted from morning till night. Many heroes perished in the fray, including John Roth, landamman of Uri, and the aged Peter Kolin, landamman and banneret of Zug. The latter fell at the head of his battalion, banner in hand; one of his sons drew it from beneath the bleeding corpse of his father and waved it in the air, he soon fell too, but the flag never fell into the hands of the enemy; it was saved by John Landwing. The banneret of Lucerne, seeing his banner in danger, furled it, placed it under his feet and defended it like a hero. The foe fell under his blows like corn before the sickle, and soon he actually seized the great banner of St. Ambrose, the principal standard of the Italians. At length this handful of heroes was overwhelmed. Their remains are covered by three mounds near the Chiesa Rossa. The Swiss took their revenge at Giornico, where only 600 of them put to flight 15,000 Italians.

Bellinzona, one of the three capitals of Tessin, 729 ft. above the sea. Hotels:— Hotel de Ville, hot and cold baths; carriages to Lugano. Angelo, post and pension, 60 rooms. Cervo, said to be clean and well kept.

RATE OF POSTING FROM BELLINZONA

TO	Distance.		Interior.			Coupé.	
	Lgs.	Mls.	Hrs.	*fr.*	*c.*	*fr.*	*c.*
Airolo..................	12	36	7	11	95	10	10
Andermatt	18	54	9¼	18	85	16	10
Arona, by Maga- dino	15½	46½	6½	7	30	6	80
Chur	25½	76½	17½	28	...	24	10
Faido..................	8½	25½	4¾	7	90	6	60
Fluelen	26½	78¾	15	27	20	23	20
Genoa, by Arona...	52¼	156¼	12	24	45	18	60
Locarno..............	4	12	2½	2	50	2	...
Lugano	6½	19½	3¾	5	20	4	20
Lucerne..............	35½	105¾	18½	31	20	27	20
Magadino	3½	9½	1½	2	50	2	...
Milano	17	51	11	17	95	14	60
Misocco	6½	19½	4½	6	65	5	65
Olivone	9	29	8	...	...	5	70
Rorschach, by Chur	46½	139½	12	37	80	30	95
Splugen..............	15	45	10½	16	60	14	30
Bernhardin	9¾	28½	7¼	10	10	8	65
Turin, by Arona ...	42½	127½	12	39	50	35	50
Zurich, by Wallen- stadt	47¾=142¼		23	41	90	36	10

Bellinzona, contains 2,330 inhabitants, and stands 230 metres above the sea. It is built on the left bank of the Tessin, in the valley of the Riviera. The principal buildings in the town are, the parish Church of St. Peter and St. Stephen, an edifice of the 16th century, containing several basso-relievos; the very ancient Church of San Biaggio, near the Gate of Lugano, the Palace of the Government, built in 1850: a bridge of 714 feet built of granite, by Poccobelli; a dyke 2,400 feet long to protect the town from the inundations of the Tessin. and the three ancient châteaux, formerly the stronghold of the bailiffs of Uri, and now forming the cantonal prison and arsenal and part of the fortifications of the town, for Bellinzona is a federal fortress. These castles are respectively named the Castello di Mezzo and the Castello Corbario, and the one containing the arsenal and commanding a fine view is the Castello Grande. Fee for admission, 1 *fr.*

EXCURSIONS NEAR BELLINZONA.—The Church of Artore, called La Madonna della Salute (fine view); Madonna della Nevé and especially Le Motte, near Giubasco, *are* points worth visiting.

From Mount Camoghè. 6 l. (18 m.) *from Bellinzona,* the whole southern chain of Alps can be seen, as well as the three neighbouring Italian lakes, Maggiore, Lugano, and Como, and the great plain of Lombardy as far as Milan. This view is one of the most magnificent in Switzerland.

Another expedition may be made from Bellinzona to the Gorge of Sementina where local legends represent that the spectres and spirits of misers and deceivers are doomed to wander.

Biasca.—(The Unione, a decent Inn). A large village, containing 2,200 inhabitants (many of these cretins), a posting house and telegraph station at the entrance of Val Blegno into the Riviera, 3½ l. (10½ m.) from Bellinzona. Interesting objects here are an ancient church, and on a neighbouring eminence a noted calvary and pilgrimage of St. Petronilla, commanding a fine view. Not far off is the Cascade of La Froda. The village of Biasca was destroyed by inundations of the Brenno in 1514 and 1745. The Val Blegno leads up to the Luckmanier Pass (see Grisons), under the shining snowy peaks of the Rheinwaldhorn. Passing over the Col de Greina this route takes you to the Vorder-Rhein valley in the Grisons.

Val Blegno (Bolizenthal) watered by the Blegno which joins the Tessin at Biasca, runs between a ridge separating it from Val Leventina to W. (2,000 to 3,000 metres high), and another ridge which separates it to the E. from the Hinter-Rhein and Calancasca (height. 2,500 to 3,000 metres.

Distance from Olivone at foot of Luckmanier Pass to Bellinzona, 9h. 30min. Carriage road, diligences; at Acqua Rossa an inn, and mineral water, 530 metres high. Olivone, dear inn, chez Stefani, 911 inhabitants, 892 metres high.

For Route over the Lukmanier, see Grisons Route 119.

Biasca is on the high road from Bellinzona to St. Gothard.

Bironico.—In the pretty Val d'Agno surrounded by high mountains, 3½ l. (9¾ m.) from Bellinzona, on the road from thence to Como and Milan. Bironico is at the entrance (to left) of Val Isone by which you ascend Mount Camoghè. (See Bellinzona).

The following directions will aid in the ascent:—A guide desirable. Route to left at Val Isone, by Medeglia ¼ l. (2¼ m.) to Isone ¾ l. (2¼ m.) You may ride to the top through forests and pasturages. Elevation, 6,853 Vienna feet.* Best plan to sleep at Isone and start at 2 a.m. to see the sun rise from top. Provisions needed. View extends from Ortlerspitz, Tyrol to Monte Rosa, embracing the Bernina Groupe, almost all the Tessin valley, and other features previously noticed.

Bodio.—Inns : Adler or Post. In the Livine Inferieure, 5½ l. (16½ m.) from Bellinzona, on the road to the St. Gothard is a post station situated at the foot of black rocky precipices, and surrounded by rich vegetation, including splendid specimens of mulberry, and fig trees. Tradition relates that this village has been entirely demolished by a landslip.

Camoghè (Monte).—See Bironico.

Capolago (Inn on the lake).—A small, poor village, at the south end of the Lake of Lugano, being the landing place from the steamers, and on the direct route from Lugano to Como, by Mendrisio. Capo Lago was once noted as containing a great propaganda press of revolutionary books, prohibited in the neighbouring Italian provinces.

Cenere (Monte).—On the road from Bellinzona to Lugano, commanding a very fine view (30 minutes) from Bironico. Height, 553 metres (1718·3 feet). There is an inn near the Corps de Garde.

Centovalli (Val).—See Locarno.

Chiasso (Hotel, the Angelo), 1,406 inhabitants. 3½ kilometrès, 2¼ m. from Como, is the last Swiss village, and not far from Monte Olimpino, with a fine view of the Lake of Como. Passports and the customs are no longer any cause of trouble to travellers entering Italy.

Dazio Grande (has an Inn), 2,870 feet above the sea, at the head of the Upper Livinthal, which was formerly blocked up by the Monte Piottino; but a convulsion

of nature threw down and rent the rock, breaking a passage for the Tessin, which rushes furiously through this gap. On issuing from the savage crevasse, the traveller passes down to the romantic and lovely Middle Livinthal.

Faido, a post station, (Inns, the Sole and the Angelo, chez Bullo) in the Middle Livinthal. This is a pretty place, presenting a mixture of Italian manners with German Alpine ways. The first vines occur here on the descent from St. Gothard. Near the Capuchin Convent is a shady walk, with a fine view. This spot was the scene of bloody executions inflicted by the Swiss bailiffs of Uri, when they oppressed these valleys.

Two fine waterfalls (the principal is called la Piugmegna) descend from the rocks near this place.

Giornico (Cervo and Corona Inns), the largest village in the Middle Livinthal, with 750 inhabitants, stands on both banks of the Tessin, near classical ground in Swiss history, of which more anon. The position of Giornico is charming. The first fig trees are seen here. The Church of San Nicolo da Myra, said to be on the site of a Pagan temple, is an object of special interest. Some remains of old walls are seen by Santa Maria di Castello. Near Giornico are two fine waterfalls, Baroglia and la Cremosina. Behind the village are some piles of stone, *Sassi grossi*, forming the monument of Stanga, a captain of the Livinthal, who, after contributing in gaining the battle of Giornico, fell dead as he reached his house.

The battle was fought ¾ l. (2¼ m.) from the village, by the St. Gothard road, and occurred December 28th, 1478. It was provoked by some subjects of the Duke of Milan making border forays on Swiss ground, leading to retaliations. War ensued, and the Duke of Milan sent considerable forces, under Count Borelli, up the Tessin valley. The Swiss vanguard, consisting of 600 men of Uri, Schwyz,

<hr>

* One Vienna foot=1 English and 5 lines.

Lucerne, and Zurich, were posted near Giornico, and the mass of their army, 10,000 strong, was a long way behind. Borelli advanced to engage the vanguard with his picked troops, in mid-winter. The Swiss inundated the meadows with the waters of the Tessin which soon froze; they then put on crampons (or shoe irons), and while the Milanese were painfully toiling up the slippery slopes, they dashed upon them and overthrew the large host of their unsteady enemies, whom they drove in a shameful flight before them; 15,000 flying before 600 Swiss. The snow was tinged with Italian blood the whole way down to Bellinzona, the number of slain alone amounting only to 1,500! This almost incredible action spread the fame of Swiss valour far and wide.

Il Caprino.—See *Lugano.*

Intregna.—A village of 1,656 inhabitants. (Hotel chez Bustelli. Good guides.) Fine view at the confluence of the Melezza and Onsernone. This village comprises three places: Intragna proper, Golino, and Verdacio; stands on the road from Locarno to Domo D'Ossola, 1 hour 25 minutes from the former, in the val Centovalli.

Locarno (Hotels: Angelo, Corona, Albergo Svizzero, Gallo, Aquila), 2,969 inhabitants, built on the right bank of Lago Maggiore, near the mouth of the Maggia. Climate, almost too relaxing. Has a port on the lake. The town covers more ground than Bellinzona; but the population in 1830 was only 1,200. The principal business of the town relates to cereals, agriculture, and the transit of goods. Locarno is fairly built, and it presents a theatrical appearance seen from the Lake. The principal buildings are the Collegiate Church of St. Francis, with five altar-pieces, and a colossal statue of St. Christopher bearing the Christ, the Capuchin Convent, and the old Castle built by the Lombards.

A curious market is held every fortnight, presenting specimens of the various types and costumes of the neighbouring peasantry. The neighbourhood is full of objects of interest, especially two convents, first, Madonna del Sasso, a pilgrimage built against a rock, and a Minorite monastery ½ l. (1½ m.) above the town, commanding a delightful view. The altar-piece of the high altar is a very fine Madonna. Another point worth visiting, is Madonna della Trinita. The village of Tenero 1½ l. (4½ m.) N. of the town, commands splendid views, which are enjoyed also from the following points: Ponte Brolla 1½ l. (4½ m.) W. of Locarno, the inn of Belvedere at Intragna 1 l. (3 m.) from the town, a further delightful excursion can be made to Ronco d'Ascona, by Solduno, Losone, and the Molino Dei Siseri (with a fine view), returning by the carriage road that passes Ascona.

Two routes lead from Locarno to Bellinzona, one by land, the other partly by water. For the former, see table of routes at the end of this Canton. The water route brings you over the Lago Maggiore. Distance 3⅜ l. (9½ m.) Swiss posts, 1¼ l. Time, 2h. 35m. Boat with rower from Locarno to Magadino, 1fr. 50c.; two rowers, 3fr. Passage, 1 hour in quiet weather; with a fair wind, in half an hour. Omnibus every day, in 1h. 35m. from Magadino to Bellinzona. Fares, 2fr. 50c. and 2fr. Magadino is a village of 714 inhabitants, on the N.E. bank of Lago Maggiore. Hotels: Belvedere, moderate, horses for St. Gothard; Poste; Vapour. Situation unhealthy and marshy. Avoid staying a night there. From Magadino, the route takes you to Quart (20 min.) at foot of Monte Cenere, thence to Contone in (20 min.), thence again to Cadezzo (20 min.) more, and finally to Bellinzona (1h. 15m.)

The most interesting excursion from Locarno, is that down the Lake to the Borromean Islands, and the enchanting scenery surrounding the

Lago Maggiore, called Langensee in German, the Verbanus lacus of the Romans. This the largest of the Italian lakes, after that of Garda, is the deepest of all the Alpine waters, descending even below the level of the Mediterranean. Its surface comprises 190 square Italian miles, its elevation is 195 metres or 643 feet above the sea, its length is in time from 14 to 15 hours' walking, or 345 geographical miles (8½ German), its greatest width from Mergozzo to Cerro, near Laveno, is 2h. 15m., or about 8 miles, and its depth varies from 800 metres (2,465 feet) to 63 (230 feet.) Its temperature is higher than that of any other Alpine lake, and it is seldom the cause of inundations. Its principal tributaries are to the north, the Tessin, the Verzasca, the Maggia, and the Tosa; to the west, the Canobbina; to the east, the Gioena and the Tresa, which unite it with the Lake of Lugano. It discharges its waters by the Tessin at Sesto Calende. The steamers that ply upon it have been already noticed.

The only carriage roads that are carried along the banks of the lake, are those, 1st: from Locarno to Ronco d'Ascona; 2nd: from Magadino to Scajano; 3rd: from Canobbio to Ghiffa; 4th: from Pallanza to Fariolo; 5th: from Fariolo to Sesto Calende; 6th: from Luino to Porto; 7th: from Laveno to Sesto Calende. The railroad from Novara to Arona follows the eastern bank of the lake from the mouth of the Rezza to Arona. Mule paths connect the other places along the lake.

Proceeding down the lake by steamer from Magadino to Sesto Calende, you pass the following places on the two banks of the lake.

RIGHT BANK.

Ascona, 1,026 inhabitants, has an old Hotel de Ville, a seminary, date 1584; ruins of two castles, a bridge of 11 arches over the Maggia.

Ronco d'Ascona, opposite the Brissago or rabbit islands. Good wine.

Brissago (Hotel, Albergo Antico), 1,237 inhabitants. Near Monte Limidario, 2,184 metres high.

Loro, San Bartolomeo, Cinzago, and St. Agata.

Canobbio—Hotel Bissone, good. Capital of the Val Canobbina, opening N. E., and forming an access to Val Vigezza. Has famous tanneries, dating from the 15th century. Fine frescoes in the Church of La Pieta.

Viggiona, Canero, (Albergo dei Tre Re). Opposite two islands, with ruins of the 15th century. Sasso, Oggabbio, Ronco, Ghiffa, Succello.

Intra—(Hotel, Leone d'Oro), manufacturing town. Villa Prina, near it, very handsome. Fine view of Cima di Jazzi, Mischabelhorner, and other snowy peaks from here. Promontory of San Remigio.

Pallanza (Hotel l'Universo, good, moderate; l'Italie); 8,000 inhabitants. Superb views from the port and precincts. Good point whence to visit the Borromean Islands. Boat with two rowers, 4*fr.* Coming to Pallanza from either end of Lake by early steamer, there is time to visit the islands before the arrival of the second boat. On bank of Lake, statue of San Stefano.

Good painting in Church of Madonna di Campagna. Diligence to Fariolo, on Simplon Road, way to Orta and Domo d' Ossola.

Fariolo, Baveno, Stresa, Belgirate, and Arona.

Rail hence to Milan and Turin.

LEFT BANK.

Vira,
Gera.
Simiana.
Ranzo and St. Abbondio. Brissago and the latter are the last Swiss villages.

Pino, at the foot of Sasso di Pino, Bassano, and Tronzano.

On the left as far as Luino, are Musignano, Campagnano, Macagno superiore, Macagno inferiore, at the issue of Val Vedasca (with the Girona river) and Colmegna.

Luino (Hotel Beccacia Posta) commanded by the Castle of Grivelli. This is the landing-place for Lugano, by Ponte Tresa.

Germignaga, San Pietro, Castello di Calde, Valdinacca.

Laveno (Hotels, Posta Moro; Stella); widest part of Lake, opposite Baveno. Fortified town at foot of Sasso di Ferro, 1,084 metres, (3,240 ft.) near the mouth of the Boesio, and at the entrance of Val Cuvio. Splendid view of the lake, and of the Borromean Islands.

Arolo, Ispra, Ronco, Angera (with old castle), Lisanza.

Sesto Calende, at south end of Lake. Hotel Posta. Rail to Milan, 59 kilometres; time, 2h. 20m.

BORROMEAN ISLANDS. — Enchanting spots, notwithstanding grumbling critics, who would probably object to the seventh heaven. Formerly arid rocks, the Milanese prince, Vitalino Borromeo, undertook in 1671 to cover them with mould, and succeeded at length in producing a magical change. Three in number, only two have been honoured with this artificial adornment, these are the Isola Bella and the Isola Madre, separated by an interval of 1½ l. (4½ m.)

Isola Bella is remarkable for its ten terraces, forming a pyramid, and built on arches, rising 120 feet above the lake, with a colossal statue of Pegasus at the top. The palace on the west side of the island is adorned with mosaics. statues, and pictures, and has deliciously cool recesses. A splendid vegetation adds to the charm of the spot. The gardens, though stiff, present a pleasing mixture of local and exotic plants, orange and lemon trees, bouquets of laurels and various rare shrubs, frequented by pheasants, pintados, and other birds of gay plumage. In the flowering season the sweet south bears the perfume of these enchanted bowers far and wide over the lake. Fee required to see it, 3*fr.* in all. Hotel of the Delfino on the island. (See Hotel Guide.)

Isola Madre is smaller but more natural than Isola Bella. It has seven terraces, the highest crowned by a palace. The climate being milder than on the Bella, it yields a most luxuriant growth of exotic plants, with many aloes, &c., and frequented by curious birds. and so arranged as to have a wilder and less uniform appearance than the sister isle.

The third island, Isella, or dei Pescatori, scarcely ½ mile in circuit, is covered with a fishing village, very picturesque, and very dirty, containing 200 inhabitants.

A little islet, called Isolino, has nothing remarkable about it.

Fare per boat, with 2 rowers, from Baveno, 5*fr.* for 2 first hours, subsequent hours, 50c. for each rower. 3 to 4 hours wanted to make the tour of the islands.

Starting from Magadino the whole Lake can be viewed in one day, much of it in from 3 to 4 hours. Leave Locarno or Magadino for Pallanza in the morning, thence visit Borromean Islands in boat. Take the afternoon steamer, without returning to Pallanza, descend to Arona, and on by rail to Turin and Geneva, or return in the evening up the lake to Magadino and Bellinzona.

FARES FROM LOCARNO AND MAGADINO.

TO	1st cl. fr. c.	2nd cl. fr. c.	3rd cl.
Luino	2 10	1 20	—
Pallanza	3 30	1 85	—
Isola Bella	3 60	2 0	—
Baveno	4 5	2 25	—
Stresa	3 60	2 0	—
Arona	4 80	2 65	—
Sesto Calende	5 30	2 95	—

Return Tickets, available for 3 days, 20 per cent. reduction. Luggage free, except 30c.

Rail from Arona.

TO	1st cl. fr. c.	2nd cl. fr. c.	3rd cl. fr. c.
Milan, in 3 hours	13 15	10 40	4 40
Turin, in 6 hours	21 30	14 95	10 70

Four departures a-day for Geneva.

Twice a-day post from Sesto Calende to Gallerate on the rail to Milan.

While engaged with Lago Maggiore we have to notice Baveno, and the excursions thence to the Italian valleys.

Baveno is a village on the right bank, at the widest part of the Lake, under the vine-clad smiling slopes of Monte Motterone. It is the usual spot whence people visit the Borromean Islands, but its boatmen have become extortionate, and Pallanza is a better place for that purpose. The scenery about Baveno is lovely and dreamy, and the character of the opposite mountains above Laveno is very fine. (Hotel, Bellevue.) Stresa, another place, 1 l. (3 m.) from Baveno, on the same bank of the lake, has an excellent hotel, Des Iles Borromées, rather dear, with fine views. Excursions on horseback or in carriages can be made hence to Orta and Monte Motterone.

Distance from Sesia to Monte Motterone, 4½ l. (13 m.) Time from Baveno, 3 hours. Guides, not essential, but useful. Height, 1,491 metres (4,905 feet). Fee of guide, 5*fr.* This mountain is the watershed summit, between the lakes Maggiore and Orta. The panoramic view from summit extends from Monte Rosa to the Tyrol, and includes the Bernina, six lakes, Milan, the Lombard plains, and the silver streams of the Tosa and Sesia. The descent from the summit is by Chegino, 1 l. (3 m.); Masino, 1 l. (3 m.); Orta, ¾ l. (2¼ m.); Albergo dei lione d'Oro on the banks of the lake; Albergo Ronchetti, or San Giulio, smaller, but good; (exquisite view from balcony.) The Sacro Monte, a kind of calvary, with 20 chapels, deserves a visit. The figures as large as life, in terra cotta, do not represent the Passion, but the life of St. Francis of Assisi. The chapels have also frescoes. A good road leads from Orta to Omegna and the Simplon route. Omnibus to Arona, 3 hours, 2*fr.* 50c.

The Lago d'Orta is described by a competent judge as a perfect gem, and nothing can exceed the enchantment of a row on its glassy, dreamy waters. It supplies trout of a large size and excellent flavour, the hotels receive en pension at Orta, and in the beautiful island of St. Giulio, crowned with a convent and church, and this spot is altogether one of the choice centres on the South side of the Alps. Mr. King's description of it represents it as an Eden of peace and poetry.

The island of San Giulio contains a very ancient Church (with frescoes of Ferrari and Tibaldi, and relics of Saint Julius). It is reached in 15 minutes. Boat, 1*fr.*

Three roads strike out from Orta: 1st. Three hours to Gignese, whence in one hour you reach Stresa or Baveno. 2nd. By Lake of Orta to Buccione, Gozzano, Borgomanero, and the stations of Arona, Novara and Biella. 3rd. By lake to Pella, thence by road to Varallo, Riva, and Alagna, or to Ponte Grande by Val Mastalone. An omnibus runs every day in 3 hours, 3*fr.* 50c. from Orta to Arona.

Length of the Lake of Orta 15 kilometres; mean width 1,500 metres; 312 metres above the sea; 185 metres above Lago Maggiore. English measure, length 9 miles; breadth 1,641 yards; height 1,026 feet, and 609·6 above Lake Maggiore.

Omegna at the north end of the Lake (Hotel Posta, middling and dear), 22 kilometres from Pallanza, and 13 from Orta; can be reached from Orta by lake or road.

Having given an account of the upper Italian valleys, we can only briefly notice their lower parts and the passes connecting them.

(*A*) Orta to Ponte Grande by Val Mastalone 55 or 60 kilometres (34 to 37 English miles). The first part of the route brings you from Orta to Varallo, which may be reached by three paths.

(*a*) By the Colma. From Orta to Pella in boat 1 to 2 *fr.*; from Pella to Varallo mule track, guide not required. Time by this route 6 hours. At Pella, asses can be procured. At 3 kilometres to the S. of it, Madonnadel Sasso, fine view. Hence to Arta 1 hour. A little further on Cascade of the Pellino. 2 hours 30 minutes from Pella is the Col de Colma, with view of Lombardy, Lakes Orta and Varese, the Combin, Monte Rosa, and Monte Vi

Steep descent into Val Sesia. 2 hours from Col to Rocca.

(b) From Orta to Varallo by Borgomanero 51 kilometres; carriage road. Omnibuses from Varallo to Novara Station pass twice a-day by Romagnano. Borgomanero is 13 kilometres from Orta, and can be reached from the Lake by Gozzano. Romagnano is 23 kilometres from Orta (Hotel Posta), 2,452 inhabitants on the Sesia. Near this place Bayard fell in battle in 1524. Ascending the Sesia amidst fine views of a soft character, and passing the villages Prato Grignasco (noted for its wines) and Ara, you cross the Strona near Montrigone.

Borgosesia with 3,070 inhabitants is 38 kilometres, and Quarena at the foot of Cima de Turri 44 kilometres, Rocca on the Pascone 51 kilometres from Orta.

Varallo (Albergo d'Italia, good but dear; Posta; Falcone Nero), 3,270 inhabitants, 462 metres above the sea at the confluence of the Sesia and Mastalone. Noted for sculpture in wood. In the Church of San Gaudenzio is a painting of Gaudenzio Ferrari. In the Church of Santa Maria delle Grazie, belonging to the Minorite Observantines is a Pieta in the early style of Ferrari, and the Chapel of Saint Marguerite contains frescoes and paintings of the same artist (date 1507).

The Sacro Monte or Nuova Gerusalemme Sacro Monte di Varallo, a much frequented place of pilgrimage was founded in 1486 by Bernardino Caimo, a noble. Milanese. It is 604 metres high (1987·16 feet) and 150 metres (493·5 feet) above the junction of the two rivers. A good road, abounding in charming views leads to the summit (in 15 minutes) marked by a chapel and crucifix. Besides a large church and many fountains, the hill has 46 chapels containing terra cotta groupes, dressed and painted. representing the principal events in the life of our Lord, and in Sacred History. *The most remarkable chapels are Nos. 5, 11, 17, and 38. The frescoes are chiefly from the brush* of Tibaldi and

Ferrari. The cloisters command the most glorious views. The staircase venerated by the faithful is an exact imitation of the Scala Santa at Rome.

At Varallo, it well repays the stranger to visit the market which presents interesting types and costumes of the handsome and classical population of the Italian valleys.[*]

From Varallo you reach Ponte Grande by two routes, 1st by Val Mastalone, 2nd by the Val Strona. 1. By Val Mastalone, following the lovely emerald[†] stream, by a new road presenting enchanting views, combining the perfection of the sublime and beautiful, you pass several hamlets and the Ponte della Gula. The Valbella joins the Mastalone at Ferrara. At Fobello (has an Inn) the Rimella and Fobello torrents join to form the Mastalone. Ascending the Val Fobello to Agazzo you reach Barranca, pass the Col de Barranca, 1752 metres high (5764·08 feet) with a fine view, pass on by a difficult mule track, commanding fine views of Monte Rosa to the Val d'Olloccia, and descending amidst superb primeval forests near its torrents you reach Bannio, a village 682 metres high, and at length Ponte Grande on the Anza (Hotel di Ponte Grande, vast rooms).

From Col Barranca, you can pass to the Col d'Eguia Carcoforo, Rimasco, and Varallo.

The 2nd Route from Orta to Ponte Grande, is by the Val Strona. First sail over lake to Omegna, 2 hours. Omegna to Campello, by a mule track, 5 hours. Campello to Ponte Grande, by two footpaths.

From Varallo, the distance to Alagna, is 42 kil. (26 1-11th miles), 7 or 8 hours. Carriage road to Piode. Car road to Mollia. Mule path from Mollia to Alagna.

[*] King's Italian Valleys, 1887.

[†] Lady's Tour round Monte Rosa.
Die Deutschen in Piedmont.

This road follows the Val Sesia, passing Valmaggia, 30 minutes; Vocca, 1 hour; Balmuccia, 2 hours 30 minutes, at junction of Sarmenta with Sesia. From Balmuccia, a path leads to Ponte Grande and Quarazza, in Val Anzasca, by Rimasco and Carcoforo, 11 hours; Scopa, 2 hours 50 minutes. Good inn, of Giuseppe Typino, 3 hours 30 minutes, 17 kilometres; Scopello, dear inn. Copper mines. Pita, 3 hours 40 minutes; Piode, 4 hours, 20 kilometres; Campertogno, 4 hours 45 minutes; Mollia, 5 hours 15 minutes, 31 kilometres; good inn, Albergo Valesiano. Boccorio, 6 hours 15 minutes. Riva, 7 hours, 38 kilometres; middling inn; last Italian village, 1,152 metres high, confluence of Sesia and Vogna. On façade of church, fresco of Tanzio d'Alagna (16th century.) Riva to Gressonay, by Val Dobbia, 6 to 7 hours.

Alagna, 8 hours, 42 kilometres (26 1-11 miles); Hotel du Monte Rosa, clean, obliging people. Exorbitant charges for guides.

Before quitting these delicious Italian valleys, it is right to add that, in some respects, they appear the choicest spots on our globe. The extreme beauty of the rocks, porphyry, serpentine, and granite, and of the vegetation, including many charming southern plants and rare ferns, the coerulian and emerald tints of the exquisite streams, the classical beauty, graceful dress, and noble, honest, and intelligent character of the German colonies inhabiting the upper part of these valleys, contribute in giving those features of exceptional interest and attraction. The description of the beauties and glories of these valleys, from the pen of competent judges, reads like a scene of Oberon, or the Loves of the Angels; and yet, it is sober truth. There, if anywhere is the happy valley of Rasselas! May the curse of gold and fashionable vulgarity, long spare the interesting people inhabiting the south slopes of Monte Rosa.

Lugano—Hotel et Belvedere du Parc, kept by M. Beha, first-class hotel, with 150 sleeping rooms and saloons, all elegantly furnished; the hotel is very conveniently situated for the two seasons. Hotel Suisse; good, cheaper; English church service in summer

POST CARS.—Three time a-day, to Bellinzona, 6½ l. (19¼ m.), in 3½ hours, 5fr 20c., 4fr. 20c.; to Airolo, 18½ l. (55½ m.). in 11 hours, 17fr. 15c., 14fr. 30c.; to Fluelen, three times a-day, 32¾ l. (98¼ m.), 20 hours, 32fr. 40c., 27fr. 40c.; Lucerne, three times a-day, 41¼ l. (125¼ m.), in 24 hours, 36fr. 40c., 31fr. 40c.; Chur once a-day, 32½ l. (96¼ m.), in 21 hours, 32fr. 20c., 28fr. 30c.; Luino, once a-day, 4¼ l.(16¼ m.), in 2¼ hours, 3fr. 60c., 2fr. 90c.; Camerlata, three times a-day, 6 l (18 m.), in 3¼ hours, 5fr. 40c., 4fr. 50c. Milan, three times a-day, 15¼ l. (45¾ m.), in 6 hours, 12fr. 75c., 10fr. 40c.

STEAMERS.—From Lugano to Bissone, 1st class, 55c.; 2nd, 35c.; Capolago, 1st class, 1fr.; 2nd, 60c.; Oria, 1st class, 1fr.; 2nd, 50c.; Osteno, 1st class, 1fr.; 2nd, 60c.; Porlezza, 1st class, 2fr.; 2nd, 1fr. Goods to Capolago, 1 *quintal*, 10 *centimes*.

CARRIAGES.—Two horses, buona mano included, one hour, 5fr.; every hour after, 3fr.; without a driver, one hour, 3fr. 50c.; each hour after, 2½fr.

ROW OR SAIL ON THE LAKE.—One waterman, first hour, 2fr.; each hour after, 1½fr.; two rowers, 3fr. first hour; each hour after, 2fr.; boat to Porlezza, one rower, all included, 7fr.; two rowers, 12fr.; three rowers, 16½fr.; four rowers, 20fr.; boat without rowers, 1fr. per hour. Horses to Monte Salvatore, 9fr.; to Pazzolo and back, 5fr.; to Monte Brè, 11fr.; guide to Salvatore, 4fr.

Lugano, forms like Bellinzona and Locarno, one of the three capitals of the Canton. It is the largest and most industrious town of Tessin, numbering 5,200 inhabitants, and owing to its delightful position and enchanting scenery, is one of the most favoured centres on the south slope of the Alps. The town stands on the N. bank of the lake, on the slope of a hill between Monte Salvatore, and Monte Brè, and presents a southern and stately appearance, with the white walls of convents and church towers, and cupolas rising above the clear blue waters. Its interior is neat and clean, and presents all the animation of an Italian town.

PRINCIPAL BUILDINGS.—San Lorenzo, Cathedral, fine view ; richly sculptured portico, façade of Bramante, curious ossuary or bone house ; Church of Santa Maria degli Angeli (Convent suppressed, 1853); frescoes and paintings by Luini ; Government Palace (post and telegraph office); monument of architect Canonica di Tesserete, and bust of General Dufour; Hospital of 13th century ; handsome Theatre. All the convents except two, were closed 1848 to 1853. Colossal statue of William Tell, by Vincenzo Vela (1856), facing l'Hotel du Parc. Many manufactures, silk, powder and paper mills, tanneries, hat manufactures, &c. A noted fair from October 8th to 14th, ever since 1513.

Five minutes from l'Hotel du Parc, Villa Tanzina (lodgings), with bust of Washington.

Lugano is surrounded by fine villages, beautiful villas, and charming gardens, yielding oranges, lemons, figs, olives, and other southern fruits. The vicinity is reckoned among the most beautiful scenery in Switzerland.

Excursions: Park of M. Ciani, 10 minutes from the town; fee to gardener ; family monument, by Vela, 1850. Villa Vasali, fine view. Pambio, 30 minutes, southwest, in front of church of St. Peter, monument, by Vela, of Captain Carloni, killed 1848. Cemetery of Saint Abbondio, with another monument of the Torrionis, by Vela. Excursions on the lake to Agno and Ponte Tresa, to the Convent of Bigorio, 2 hours 30 minutes, containing a Madonna, attributed to Guercino, and swing gardens with charming views.

Lake of Lugano, or Ceresio, belongs almost entirely to this Canton, and is supposed to be of recent formation, as it is not noticed by writers of the sixth centery. Its sinuous shape, like that of a fishing hook, has some resemblance to the Lake of Lucerne. Length, 8 l. (24 m.); mean width, ½ l. (1½ m.) ; greatest depth, 540 feet. Since 1856 has a small steamer. Scenery of banks quite enchanting, combining the softness of Maggiore and Como with a sterner and more Alpine character, especially at the Porlezza end. A bridge, connects its two banks at Melide. Height above the sea, 271 metres. The first points of view are at Lugano, Melide, Agno, Morcote, Caprino, and Gandria. Carriage roads connect Lugano and Morcote, Bissone and Capolago, Agno and Ponte Tresa. Other points on the lake banks are connected by foot paths. Lugano Lake is connected with Lago Maggiore by the Tresa, issuing from the former at Ponte Tresa.

The Lake of Lugano, beginning at Porlezza, runs from north-east to south-west to Lugano (town), 3 hours ; thence south to Melide, 1 hour, where it forks. South-east branch runs, 1 hour 30 min., to Capo Lago ; south-west branch runs to Porto, 2 hours, then turning north-west and north, 1 hour 30 min., it forms two other branches, the largest, 1 hour, going up to Agno, and the other, 30 min., to Ponte Tresa.

Longer expeditions by and over the lake from Lugano :—

Caves of Caprino (The).—Passage in boat, with two rowers, 1 hour, 2 to 3fr. there and back. Caprino is a mountain facing Lugano, full of caves, where the inhabitants keep their wine cool, and the visitors can drink iced Asti. Fine views. Cascade Cavallini.

Monte Brè, 3 l. (9 m.) on foot, 930 metres high, 2 hours or 2 hours 30 min. from Lugano. Take provisions with you, as nothing but cheese, inferior wine, and hard bread can be got at Brè. Road passes by village of Desago, where it forks. Take right-hand path. View splendid.

Monte Salvatore.—Interesting excursion to this dolomite mountain, passing curious varieties of strata. Rises like a rounded pyramid surrounded by the lake, belted by villages, hamlets, villas, chesnut groves and fruit trees. Two hours from Lugano, 1 hour 10 min. to descend; 2 hours from Morcote, 2 hours 30 min. from Agno, 1 hour 30 min. from Melide. Guide, 4*fr.*; 9*fr.* horse and driver; 8*fr.* for a mule. Monte Salvatore forms with Arbostora a promontory of the lake, 2 l. (6 m.) long, bearing at its extremity Morcote, 10 kils. from Lugano. Its base swarms with vipers. Follow road to Melide, 15 min., along the lake, then turn to right, passing Villa Marchino, 25 min., and Parzallo, 5 min., turn to left, and reach top by direct path, 1 hour 30 min., 909 metres. The little Chapel of San Salvatore is a place of pilgrimage, commanding a magnificent panoramic view. You can return to Lugano by Corona and Melide.

Camoghè (Mount).—See Camoghè.

Monte Generoso, the Italian Righi, can be approached by four different roads:— 1. From Lugano, in carriage, by post or on horseback, as far as Bissone; also by the steam boat. Then on foot to Melano, passing the Sovaglia. Ascend Val Sovaglia, by a zig-zag. Rovio in a fertile district; dirty inn. Guide may be engaged here. By a ravine, and over grassy slopes to top, 5,219 feet, 3 leagues (18 m.), from Rovio. 2. Another gentler ascent by pastures from Melano; guide and provisions wanted. 3. From Mendrisio by Somazza to the ridge, thence by steep ascent to top. 4. Finest views are by Balerna, good plain inn; fair food, cheap. By carriage or horse to Muggio. Then steep ascent to Scudelatte, ½ l. (1½ m.) Hence over meadows, 1½ l. (4½ m.) to top. From this you descry an immense horizon of Alps, from Savoy to the Bernina. Monte Rosa presents itself admirably, part of Lago Maggiore is visible, with Isola Bella. Lake Lugano is at your feet,

except the Morcote branch, hid by Monte Giorgio. The ascent from Lugano takes 5 or 6 hours. Two inns stand 2 hours from the summit, where the traveller can pass the night.

Lugano to Como.—1st, by lake, 5 hours. 2 h. 15 m. from Lugano to Capolago (1*fr.* 60c.); 2 h. 45 m. in omnibus from Capolago to Como (2*fr.* 10c.); to Camerlata (2*fr.* 40c.) 2nd, by land, 6 l. (18 miles or 28 kilometres to Camerlata) 2 diligences daily, in 3 h. 35 m., for 5*fr.* 40c. and 4*fr.* 50c. Principal places passed on land route:—Melide, 6 kilometres from Lugano; 308 inhabitants. Bissone, with long causeway of 753 metres. (7 metres wide) across lakes. Capolago, 13 kilometres, Mendrisio. Hotel, Angelo, 18 kilometres. Chiasso, 24 kilometres. Hotel, Angelo. Como, 28 kilometres. Hotels: d'Italia, good, civil people; Angelo; Magazino di Gastronomia, di Franconi; Il Monte di Brianza. See *Bradshaw's Illustrated Hand-book to Italy*, p. 34.

Lugano to Menaggio on the lake of Como. Steamboat from Lugano to Porlezza, 1st class, 1*fr.* 50c.; 2nd class, 80c. Thence to Menaggio by a bad road. One horse car, 5 or 6*fr.*; two horses, 10*fr.* Good walkers can do the distance in three hours. Guide useless. Walk, to Porlezza delightful, by north bank; 4 hours to Gandria. The botanist has full occupation throughout. On by Val Cavargna to Lago di Piano. On heights of Croce grand view of Lake of Como above Bellaggio. Road forks at Croce, left to Menaggio, ½ l. (2¼ m.), right to Cadenobbio. Stop at neither but go on direct to Bellaggio, a place noted for glorious scenery and every comfort. Porlezza has an inn and Douane. At Bellaggio, best inns are Grande Bretagne and Genazzini, rooms, 2½*fr.*; dinner, 3½*fr.* Hotel Grandi is in the Italian style. Boats to Cadenobbio, 3*fr.*, to Menaggio, 4*fr.*, to Melzi and Carlotta, 4*fr.* At Cadenobbio, are the Bellevue Hotel, room, 2*fr.*, dinner, 4*fr.*, pension, 7*fr.*; Belle Ile, moderate; Ville de Milan. This place is held to from Como to Colico. At Menaggio, (principal inn, Corona), is a large silk manufactory, and near it Villa Vigoni, with fine marble statues and reliefs of Italian sculptors and Thorwaldsen (especially Eve, Ruth, Nemesis, &c.)

Mendrisio (Hotel: Angelo), is capital of a district of that name, the last Swiss village on this side, rather badly built and dirty, but it stands in the mildest climate of the republic, and its neighbourhood is a perfect Eden. The people give much care to the breeding of silk worms, and the country near yields wheat, tobacco, and excellent wine. The vine is cultivated not only on the slopes, but even in the corn fields, where it is trained in festoons, forming garlands from tree to tree. These fields called campi vignati, give a delightful festive character to the country, which abounds in charming views and walks, especially to Balerna 1 l. (3 m.), with a splendid Church, to the hill of Padrinate, near Chiasso, to Val Muggia or Mara, the only valley of an Alpine character, in this district; the hill of Stabio South of Mendrisio, &c.

The road from Bellinzona to Milan passes by Capo di Lago, to Mendrisio, 1 l. (3 m.), and continues thence by Balerna, 1 l. (3 m.), Chiasso 1 l. (3 m.), Como 1 l. (3 m.) to Camerlata, and on by rail to Milan. (See *Bradshaw's Hand-book to Italy and Continental Railway Guide*).

The rest of the surface and routes of Tessin may be classified under the head of the following valleys:—
Val Centovalli, Val Maggia, Val Onsernone, Val Verzasca, Val Vegezza or Vigezza, and their embranchments. These valleys form the principal modes of communication between Locarno and the neighbouring districts.

Val Blegno. See *Biasca.*

Val Centovalli and Val Vigezza lead from Locarno to Domo d'Ossola, a journey of 9½ or 10 hours. The former, Centovalli, opens West of Locarno, and follows a north-west south-east direction,

watered by the Melezzo. It has 800 inhabitants. The Tessin part of it extends to Carnet or Comedo. The Ribellasca forms the frontier. Principal town Intragna (see that place), which may be reached by two carriage roads from Locarno. The prettiest is by the Cascade of San Remo and that of Richnisa. After crossing the Ribellasca you enter Val Vigezza, in Italy, forking near Riva. Passing the pilgrimage of Re, much frequented April 30th, route takes you to Finero, whence a route branches in 4 hrs. to Cannobbio, on Lago Maggiore, advancing to Santa Maria Maggiore (Hotels: Lion d'Oro, Croce di Malta), and passing the picturesque Cascade of Melezzo you come to Masera near Crevola, and soon after reach Domo d'Ossola.

Val Maggia.—13 hours 15 minutes from Locarno to Airolo. To Peccia, carriage road. Peccia to Airolo, mule path. Diligence every day, from Locarno to Bignasco 5¾ l. (17¼ m.) 3 hrs. 30 min., fare, 2fr. 90c. Val Maggia is 12 l. (36 m.) long, ½ l. (1½ m.) wide. Fine view from Ponte Brolla. Old gnarled chesnut trees. Val Onsernone opens to the left, and Centovalli, communicating with Domo d'Ossola. Road through rocky woody scenery. Maggia, principal village, 2¼ l. (8¼ m.) from Locarno. At Coglio a cascade of the Giumaglio. Near Boschetto, cascade of the Soladino. Valley now forks. Left Val Bovana; right Val Lavizzara. Clay of that name brought from here and used for pottery and vases. Left of Bignasco, descent to Val Bavona. At head of Val Lavizzara, Col de Narret, leads to Val Bedretto. From Bignasco to Menzonio pass a narrow, rocky defile. Val Lavizzara at north end has a wild Alpine character. At Peccia it forks again. Left Val Peccia (or of pines), straight on is Val Fusio, with Fusio, last inhabited village, well built, and occupied by a rich population who bring home their gains from the plains. Good inn. Near it Cascade Masnaro, crescent shaped, Val Bavona, branching near Cevio, is rich in picturesque scenery. Contains Bosco, the only Tessin village where German is spoken. By Col de Bosco you reach Stafelwald in the Val Formazza (6 hrs. 40 min.) Col de Bosco is also called Furca del Bosco and Criner Furca; height (2,326 metres). At village of Corin in Val di Campo the sun is not seen during three months in the winter. A path by south branch of Val di Campo leads in (6 hours) to Val Formazza and Domo d'Ossola.

Val Onsernone, or Lusernone, watered by the Isorgno, opens 2 hours, N.W. of Locarno, near Intragna. Length, 4 l. (12 m.) between Val Maggia and Val Centovalli. It runs E. and W. to Russo, where it forks, it contains 8 parishes and 3,000 inhabitants. It has numerous villages and hamlets. By N. branch you can reach Val di Campo, from Vergeletto; the W. branch reaches the foot of Pizzo Ruscata 2,007 metres (7,500 feet) and to Italy. Near Bagni di Craveggia (with mineral springs) paths lead (6 hours) to Domo d'Ossola by the Campo Latte and Val d'Isorgno.

Val Verzasca (5 parishes, 3,458 inhabitants) opens on right bank of Tessin, below Tenero, stretching north (7 or 8 hours) between Val Leventina to east, and Val Maggia to west, so narrow that the path along the precipices is dangerous in rough weather. Carriage road finished in lower part of valley, which forks at Lavertezzo. North branch is uninhabited. North-west (1 hr. 30 min.) has Brione, 761 metres, where it forks again. North-west branch is the Val d'Ossola, terminating at Monte Zucchero, 2,737 metres. North-east branch (2 hours) leads to Sonogno 909 metres high, where valley forks the third time. East fork takes the name of Val Redorta; North fork Val di Cabione. These valleys are little known and visited. From Lavertezza you can pass to Val Leventina by the ridge of Ambra, also to Personico and Bodio. From Sonogno to Prato by the Pass of Redorta, and to Chironico by a Col at base of Cima Bianca, where you descend by the Alps del Lago (1,782 mètres) to the valleys of Chironico and Lavizzara.

The route from Bellinzona to Chur passing up the Misocco has been described under the Grisons (which see). But a lateral valley called Val Calanca deserves a particular notice here. It opens between Grono and Roveredo, extending 5 l. (15 m.) to the Pizzo di Muccia 2,963 metres, and to the Adula Groupe. Near Santa Maria, are seen the fine ruins of the Château of Calanca. Four hours from Roveredo is Augio, where paths lead to Misocco (3 hours) or to Soazzo (3½ hours) by the Buffalora. From Valbella (1,336 metres) the last hamlet of Val Calanca you can pass in 3 hours to Misocco by the Col de Tresculmene (2,153 metres). Again from the Châlets of Alogna (1,419 metres) a path leads in 3 hours to San Bernardino by the Col de Passeti (2,075 metres).

ROUTES OF TESSIN.

From Bellinzona to:—

Aarau, by Altdorf (Nos. 229 and 147), and Lucerne (Nos. 11, 12, or 13).

Aarberg, same routes and No. 11, you can also reach it by Wesen and the Bernese Oberland.

Aarberg, by Berne (Nos. 57 and 53) or by Sion (Nos. 236 and 262).

Aigle, by Sion (Nos. 236 and 74), and Bex (No. 53)

ROUTE 229.

ALTDORF, 22½ l. (67½ m.)

	Leagues.	Miles.
Wesen (No. 57)	17½	52½
Weiler		2½
Meitschlingen		2½
Im Ried		
Amsteg		
Silinen		
Clus	1	3
Erstfeld, 21 l. (63 m.)	1½	1½
Altdorf	1½	4½
	22½	67½

Altstätten, by Chur (Nos. 119, or 120, and 118).

Appenzell (same routes, and from Chur, No. 2'), or by Altdorf (Nos. 229 and 207), and Schwyz (No. 26).

Art, by Altdorf (Nos. 229 and 207), Schwyz (No. 214), and Zug (No. 231).

Baden, by Altdorf (Nos. 229 and 147), and Lucerne (Nos. 149 or 150).

Bâle, by Sion (Nos. 236 and 227), and Solothurn (No. 32), or by Altdorf (Nos. 229 and 147), and Lucerne (No. 39).

Berne (No. 57), or by high road to Sion (Nos. 236, 73, or 74), or by Altdorf (Nos. 229 and 147), and Lucerne (Nos. 66, 67, or 68).

Bex, by Sion (Nos. 236 and 74).

Bienne, by Berne (Nos. 57 and 59), or by Sion (Nos. 236 and 262), and Aarberg (No. 59).

Brougg, by Altdorf (Nos. 229 and 147), and Lucerne (No. 151).

Bulle, by Sion (Nos. 236 and 74), and Bex (Nos. 53 and 54).

Burgdorf, by Berne (Nos. 57 and 60), or by Sion (Nos. 236 and 74), and Berne (No. 60).

Chamouni, by Sion (Nos. 236 and 98), and Geneva, or by Sion (No. 236), Martigny and Tête Noire.

Chaux de Fonds, by Sion (Nos. 236 and 267), Lausanne (Nos. 173 and 174), and Neuchâtel (No. 169).

ROUTE 230.

CHIAVENNA, 14⅔ l. (44¼ m.)

	Leagues.	Miles.
Soazza (No. 120)	7¼	22½
Pass of Furcola	3¼	10⅓
Santa Maria, in the valley of San Giacomo	2	6
Chiavenna	1¼	5¼
	14⅔	44¼

Chur (Nos. 119, or 120).

Einsiedeln, by Altdorf (Nos. 229 and 207), and Schwyz (No. 209).

ROUTE 231.

ENGELBERG, 30 l. (90 m.)

	Leagues.	Miles.
Erstfeld (No. 229)	21	63
Surenen Pass and Valley to Engelberg	9	27
	30	90

Frauenfeld, by Chur (Nos. 119, or 120, and 127), or by Altdorf (Nos. 229 and 207), Schwyz (No. 215), and Zurich (No. 245).

Fribourg, by Sion (Nos. 236 and 89, or 90).

Gais, by Chur (Nos. 119, or 120 and 128).

Geneva, by Sion (Nos. 236 and 98).

Glarus (No. 106), or by Altdorf (Nos. 229 and 207), and Schwyz (No. 113).

ROUTE 231 (D).

GRAVEDONA, on the Lake of Como, 8 hours.

	h.	m.
Giubasco	0	35
Pianezzo	0	35
Carmena	0	50
Carenna	0	30
Val Morobbia to l'Alpe Giorio and Col di San Osorio (1,956 metres)	1	30
Brencio (Church with good paintings	0	30
Gavedona	3	30
	8	0

Herisau, by Glarus (Nos. 106 and 110), or by Altdorf (Nos. 229 and 207), and Schwyz (No. 210).

Lauffenburg, by Altdorf (Nos. 229 and 147), Lucerne (Nos. 11, 12, and 13), and Aarau, by rail or road (No. 10).

Lausanne, by Sion (Nos. 236 and 267).

Locarno (No. 232).

Locle, by Sion (Nos. 236 and 267), Lausanne (Nos. 173 or 174), and Neuchâtel (No. 175).

ROUTE 232.

LOESCH (Baths), 34 l. (102 m.)

	Leagues.	Miles.
Sementina	1¼	3¾
Gudo	¼	¾
Cegnasco	¼	2¼
Gordola	¼	2¼
Tenero	¼	¾
Locarno, 4¼ l. (16¼ m.)	1	3
Losona	1¼	4¼
Rosa	1	3
Verdasia	¾	2¼
Borgnone	¾	2¼
Cancet	½	1½
Olgia	½	1½
Malesco	1	3
Masera	2	6
Domo d'Ossola	1	3
Crevola	1	3
Divedro	2	6
Ruden	2¼	6¾
Simplon	2	6
Hospiz	1½	4½
Persel	2¼	6¼
Ried	2	6
Brieg	1¼	3¾
Glys	¼	¾
Gambsen	½	2¼
Visp or Viege	¾	2¼
Brunk	1	3
Turtmana	½	2¼
Loesch (Town)	½	1½
Varen	1	3
Loesch (Baths)	1½	4½
	34	102

ROUTE 233.

LUGANO, 5¾ l. (17½ m.)

	Leagues.	Miles.
Giubasco	¼	¾
Cadenazzo	1¼	3¾
Bironico	1¼	3¾
Taverna Sotto	1	3
Mesagua	1¼	4¼
Lugano	½	1½
	5¾	17½

ROUTE 234.

LUCERNE, 32 L. (96 m.)

	Leagues.	Miles.
Altdorf (No. 229)	22½	67½
Lucerne (No. 147)	9½	28½
	32	96

ROUTE 234 (2).

	Leagues.	Miles.
Macugnaga, by Locarno and Domo d'Ossola (No. 232)	14½	43¼
Villa	1¼	3¼
Valauzano or Pallanzeno	1	3
Masone	1	3
Vogogna	½	1½
Ponte Grande	3	9
Vanzone	¾	2¼
Ceppo Morelli	1	3
Prequantero	½	1½
Pestarena	1	3
Borgo	½	1½
Macugnaga from Vogogna, 7½ L. (22½ m.)	½	1½
	25¼	76¼

ROUTE 235.

MENDRISIO, 9¼ l. (27¾ m.)

	Leagues.	Miles.
Lugano (No. 23)	5¾	17¾
Over the lake to Capo di Lago	2½	7½
Mendrisio	1	3
		27¾

Morat, by Zion (No. 236 and 263)

Morges, by Sion (No. 236 and 267), and Lausanne (No 96).

Neuchâtel, by Sion (No. 236 and 267), and Lausanne (No. 173 or 174).

Olivone (No. 119).

Orbe, by Sion (No. 236 and 267), and Lausanne (No. 174).

ROUTE 235 (2).

OBERGESTELEN.

	Leagues.	Miles.
By Domo d'Ossola (No. 232)	14½	43½
Crevola	1	3
Crodo (Leone d'Oro Inn)	1½	4½
By Val Antigorio to Premia	2	6
Foppiano (Unterwald)	½	½
Staffelwald (San Michele) } Andermatten (Alla Chiesa) }	3½	9½
Zum Steg (Al pont)	1	3
Frutwald (in Camscha)		1½
Sulla Frutta (Tosa Falls)		2½
Kehrbüchi		1½
Morass Châlets		1½
Bettehmatten Châlets		2½
Punta di Pasodan	1	3
Gries Col. 3 l. (9 m.) to Obergestelen } Altstafel Châlets }	½	2½
Im loch	1½	4½
Obergestelen	½	2½
	30½	91½

ROUTE 235 (3).

OBERGESTELEN, by Nufenenthal and Val Bedretto.

	Leagues.	Miles.
Airolo (No. 57)	10½	32½
Fontana	1	3
Ossasco	½	1½
Villa	½	1½
Bedretto	½	1½
Hospice All' Acqua (4,880 ft.)	1½	4½
Nufenen Pass	1½	4½
Obergestelen by Gries Glacier	3½	10½
	19	57

ROUTE 235 (4).

ORTA.

	Leagues.	Miles.
Locarno (No. 232)	4½	13½
Steamers to Pallanza, 3 fr. 30c.; 1 fr. 35c.		
Omnibus to Omegna, 1½ fr. 6 30 a.m.		
Gravellona	3	9
Omegna	1½	4½
Orta	2½	7½
Journey exclusive of water passage	11¼	33¼
Journey with water passage	12¼	67½

Pallanza. See last route.

Payerne, by Sion (No. 236 and 262).

Pfeffers Baths, by Chur (Nos. 119 or 120, and 141).

ROUTE 235 (5).

PONTRESINA, by Sondrio and Tirano.

	Leagues.	Miles.
Bellinzona to Gravedona	8	24
Over Lake of Como to Colico	1	3
Morbegno.—Hotel de la Reine d'Angleterre, room, 1 fr. 70c.	3¼	9¾
Bassella	3¾	11¼
Sondrio	¼	¾
Chiaro	1½	4½
San Giacomo	1	3
Tresenda	1	3
Bianzone, Madonna di Tirano to Tirano	2	6
From Tirano to Pontresina, (No. 139)	10¼	30¾
	32	96

Righi (The), by Altdorf (No. 229 and 207), and Schwyz (No. 212).

St. Gallen, by Chur (No. 119 or 120, and 132).

ROUTE 235 (6).

	Leagues.	Miles.
St. Moritz, (No. 235—5), or by Chiavenna (No. 230)	14¾	44¼
St. Croce	1	3
Castasegna (Restaurant)	1	3
By Premontogno (with inn) and Stampa to Vicosoprano	3¾	11¼
Casania	1½	4½
Maloja Pass (inn)	1½	4½
Lake of Sils	1½	4½
Silva-plana	1	3
St. Moritz	1	3
	27	81

Schaffhausen, by Altdorf (Nos. 229 and 207), Schwyz (No. 215), and Zurich (No. 200), or by Sion (Nos. 286 and 74), and Berne (No. 197).

Schwyz, by Altdorf (Nos. 229 and 207).

ROUTE 236.

SION, 35¾ l. (117½ m.)

	Leagues.	Miles.
Leesch—town (No. 232)	31¼	94¼
Sierre	1¼	3¾
St. Leonard	2	6
Sion	1	3
	35¾	107½

Solothurn, by Altdorf (Nos. 229 and 147), and *Lucerne* (No. 162), or by Sion (Nos. 236 and 237), Stanz, see Unterwalden.

ROUTE 237.

THUN, 45¾ L (137½ m.)

	Leagues.	Miles.
Wesen (No. 57)	17¼	52½
Thun (No. 55)	28¼	84½
	45¾	137½

Trogen, by Chur (Nos. 119 or 120, and 133).

Unterwalden, by Altdorf (Nos. 229 and 231).

ROUTE 237 (2).

VARALLO.

	Leagues.	Miles.
Bellinzona to Orta (No. 235—4), exclusive of water passage	11¼	33¾
Pella	¼	¾
Col di Colma	¾	2¼
Val Duggia to Civiasco	1	3
Varallo	1	3
Total exclusive of water passage	14¼	42¾

Vevay, by Sion (Nos. 236 and 263).

ROUTE 237 (3).

VOGOGNA.

	Leagues.	Miles.
Bellinzona to Gravellona (No. 235—4)	10½	32¾
Ornavasso (Auberge d'Italie, Croce Bianca)	1½	4½
Migiandone	2¼	7
Premosello	1¼	4¾
Vogogna (Corona Inn)	¾	1¾
	16¼	48¾

Winterthur, by Altdorf (Nos. 229 and 207), Schwyz, (No. 215), and Zurich (No. 160).

Yverdun, by Sion (Nos. 236 and 237), and Lausanne (Nos. 173 or 174).

ROUTE 237 (4).

ZERMATT, by Macugnaga (No. 234—2, or 237—3), 25¾ L (77¼ m.) and 23¾ l. (71¼ m.,

Macugnaga to Zermatt, by Alt Weissthor, 14 hours.

Macugnaga to Zermatt, by New Weissthor, 11 to 12 hours. (See Canton of Valais at the end).

Zug, by Altdorf, (Nos. 229 and 207), and Schwyz (No. 214),

APPENDIX.

ELEVATION OF SOME OF THE PRINCIPAL SWISS TOWNS AND VILLAGES ABOVE THE SEA.

Name.	Trigonometrical Measurement.	Barometrical Measurement.
Aarau	1,140 Paris feet.	
Aeggischhorn Hotel	7,228 English feet.	
Airolo	3.540	3,608·6
Altdorf	1,410	
Alveneu Baths Grisons	3,120	
Amsteg	1,579	
Appenzell	2,135	
Bâle	890	854
Bell Alp	6,909	
Bellinzona	711	845
Bernard St.	7,548 Paris feet.	7,793
Cor...ett	8,200 English feet.	
Berne	1,708 Paris feet.	1,691
Bernina Inn and Pass	6,514	
Bevers (Grisons)		5,151
Bex	1,328	
Burgdorf	1,798	
Chamouni	3,144 or 3,150	
Chaux de Fonds	3,075	
Chur	2,035	
Einsiedeln	2,974 or 2,938	
Engelberg	3,180 or 3,065	
Gadmen	4,146	3,691 (Church yard of Gadmen.)
Geneva	1,152	1,252·5
Geschenen (St. Gothard Pass)	3,396 or 3,450	
Gessenay (Saanen)	3,108 or 3,090	
Gestelen (Haut Chatillon Valais)	4,100	
Grimsel Hospice	6,570 or 6,604	
Grindelwald	3,150	3,302
Hacken (Canton of Schwyz)	4,470	
Hasli (Village)	2,030	
Hospice of St. Gothard	6,422	6,421
Hospital, Village in Uri	4,542 or 4,566	4,661·2
Lausanne	1,570 or 1,560	
Lauterbrunnen	2,450	2,522

Name.	Trigonometrical Measurement.	Barometrical Measurement.
Lax (Valais)		3.284·2
Liechtensteig (St. Gallen)	1,979	
Loesch (Baths)	4,404	
Lucerne	1,368	1,383
Lugano	882	
Martigny	1,480	
Meyringen	1,935	1,904
Morat	1,344	
Münster (Valais)		4,236·2
Obergestelen (Valais)		4,262
Pantenbrücke (Glarus)	3,012	
Pfeffers (Baths)	2,110	
Pontresina	5,915	
Realp	4,733	4,772·2
Rosenlauibad	4,094 Vienna feet	
Simplon (Village)	4,548	4,159·6
Saint Moritz (Grisons)	5,629	
Saint Gallen	2,086	
Septimer (Hospice)	7,359	
Sion	1,746	
Solothurn	1,284	1,347
Steinberg Cottage Thun	1,738 or 1,730	1,911
Trachsellauinen (Lauterbrunnen Valley)	3,079	
Unterseen	1,803	
Urseren (Uri)	4,446 or 4,356	,506·0
Valens (St. Gallen)	2,872	
Vœgelisegg (Appenzell)	2,963	
Wallenstadt	1,364	
Wesen (Uri)	2,847	2.852
Weissbad Baths (Appenzell)	2,542	
Wildhaus (St. Gallen)	3,360 or 3,420	
Wildkirchlein (Appenzell)	4,615	
Worms or Bormio (Valtellina)	4,611	
Yverdun	1,278	
Zurich	1,270 or 1,240	1,258

3. From Pile Alpe to Macugnaga, by Col della Loccia. One day of 14 to 15 hours, hard climb, best taken from Macugnaga side.

(B) Intermediary Passes.

1. Val Tournanche to Ayas, by Col de Portola. One day. Guide required.

2. Champoluc to Gressoney St. Jean, by Col de Pinta, 6 hours. (Ascend Grenhaupt.)

3. Gressoney St. Jean to Allagna, by Col d'Ollen, 9 hours with mule; 7 hours on foot. Guide wanted.

4. Allagna to Macugnaga and Pestarena, by Turlo Pass, 8 to 10 hours. Guide.

(C) Lower Passes.

1. Chatillon to Brusson, by Col de Joux, 4 hours to 4 hours 30 min. Mule path.

2. Brusson to Gressoney St. Jean, by Col de Ranzola, 4 hours to 4 hours 30 min. Mule path.

3. Gressoney to Riva, by Col de Val Dobbia, 6 to 7 hours. Mule path. Guide unnecessary.

4. Riva to Rimasco, by Col de Mend, 6 hours 30 min. to 7 hours. Mule path.

5. Riva to Rimasco, by Vals Sesia and Sermenta, 8 hours. Car road.

6. Rimasco to Ponte Grande, 8 hours. Mule path.

APPENDIX.

Name.	Trigonometrical Measurement.	Barometrical Measurement.	Name.	Trigonometrical Measurement.	Barometrical Measurement.
Aarau	1,140 Paris feet.		Lax (Valais)		3.284·2
Aeggischhorn Hotel	7,228 English feet.		Liechtensteig (St. Gal-		
Airolo	3,540	3,608·6	len)	1,979	
Altdorf	1,410		Loesch (Baths)	4,404	
Alveneu Baths	3,120		Lucerne	1,368	1,383
Grisons			Lugano	882	
Amsteg	1,579		Martigny	1,480	
Appenzell	2,135		Meyringen	1,935	1,904
Bâle	890	854	Morat	1,844	
Bell Alp	6,909		Münster (Valais)		4,236·2
Bellinzona	711	845	Obergestelen (Valais)		4,263
Bernard St.	7,548 Paris feet.	7,793	Pantenbrücke (Glarus)	3,012	
Corvehl	8,200 English feet.		Pfeffers (Baths)	2,110	
Berne	1,708 Paris feet.	1,691	Pontresina	5,915	
Bernina Inn and Pass	6,514		Realp	4,733	4,772·2
Bevers (Grisons)		5,151	Rosenlauibad	4,094 Vienna feet	
Bex	1,323		Simplon (Village)	4,548	4,159·6
Burgdorf	1,798		Saint Moritz (Grisons)	5,629	
Chamouni	3,144 or 3,150		Saint Gallen	2,086	
Chaux de Fonds	3,075		Septimer (Hospice)	7,359	
Chur	2,035		Sion	1,746	
Einsiedeln	2,974 or 2,938		Solothurn	1,284	1,347
Engelberg	3,180 or 3,055		Steinberg Cottage Thun	1,788 or 1,780	1,911
Gadmen	4,146	3,691 (Church and of Gadmen.)	Trachsellauinen (Lau- terbrunnen Valley)	3,079	
Geneva	1,152	1,252·5	Unterseen	1,803	
Geschenen (St. Gothard Pass)	3,396 or 3,450		Urseren (Uri)	4,446 or 4,356	,506·6
Gessenay (Saanen)	3,108 or 3,090		Valens (St. Gallen)	2,872	
Gestelen (Haut Chatil- lon Valais)	4,100		Vœgelisegg (Appenzell)	2,963	
Grimsel Hospice	6,570 or 6,604		Wallenstadt	1,364	
Grindelwald	3,150	3,303	Wesen (Uri)	2,847	2.852
Hacken (Canton of Schwyz)	4,470		Weissbad Baths (Ap- penzell)	2,542	
Hasli (Village)	2,030		Wildhaus (St. Gallen)	3,360 or 3,420	
Hospice of St. Gothard	6,422	6,421	Wildkirchlein (Appen- zell)	4,615	
Hospital, Village in Uri	4,542 or 4,566	4,661·2	Worms or Bormio (Val- tellina)	4,611	
Lausanne	1,570 or 1,560		Yverdun	2,278	
Lauterbrunnen	2,450	2,522	Zurich	1,379 or 1,240	1,246

HEIGHT OF PEAKS AND ALPS—(Continued.)

Name.	Triangulation.	Barometrical Measurement.
Mönch (Schwarz)	8,075	
Mönch	13,438	
Mont Blanc	14,700 or 14,793 Paris ft.	
Mont Brevent	7,836 Paris ft.	
Mont Cervin.—See Matterhorn.		
Montendre	5,202 or 5,170	
Monte Rosa (Höchste Spitze)	14,580, 14,429, and 14,284 Paris ft.	
Mont Velan	10,327, or by Saussure, 10,391 Paris ft.	
Morcles (Dent de)	9,689	
Morteratsch	11,556	
Motterone (Monte)	2,518	
Mürtschenstock		
Mutterhorn (Uri and Urserenthal)	8,450	
Napf (Lucerne)	4,950 or 4,845	
Naye (Dent de) above Montreux	6,693	
Nesthorn (Gross)	12,533	
Niesen	7,763	
Nivollet (Dent de)	4,597	
Nona (Becca di)	10,384	
Nüffenenjoch		7,745·2
Oberaarhorn	11,928	
Oberlauinenhütte		6,971·6
Oche (Dent d')	8,010	
Oberlauinenhüte (Oberland)		8,553·8
Œschinenhorn	11,457	
Oldenhorn	10,250 or 9,630	
Ott (Piz)	10,660	
Pain de Sucre		
Palu (Piz)	12,835	
Panixer Alp	7,419	
Parrot Spitze	14,577 English feet.	
Petersgrat		9,958·4
Pilatus	7,080 or 6,562 Paris ft. / 7,290 English ft. (The Esel on Pilatus.)	6608·1
Pleureur (Monte)	12,159	
Pollux	13,432	
Rhätikon (Grisons) (Sulzfluh)	8,750	
Righi (Kulm)	5,905 English ft / 5,555 Paris ft.	5,327·0
Righi (Staffel)	4,866 Paris ft. / 5,210 English ft.	4932.0
At Schwesterhorn	4,404 Paris ft.	
At Klösterli	4,035 Paris ft.	
Righi Scheidegg	5,206 English ft.	
Rosa (Monte)	See Monte Rosa	
Rosenhorn	12,107	
Rossboden	13,084	
Rothhorn	11,644	
Rothstock Uri	9,620	
Roththal Sattel	12,119	
Roththal Entrance		8,266·3

Name.	Triangulation.	Barometrical Measurement.
Roththal Top		8,923·3
Rouges (Aiguilles)		
Ruffi or Rossberg	4,870 Paris ft.	
Rympfischhorn	13,790 English ft.	
Saint Gothard	6,443 Paris ft.	
Point of Fibbia	8,410 Paris ft.	
Do. Fiando	8,150 Paris ft.	
Do. Prosa	7,850 Paris ft.	
Saleve (Monte) Savoy	4,235 Paris ft.	
Salontore (Monte)	8,051	
Seesa Plana	9,738	
Scheidegg Grosse	6,910	6,029·3 Vienna ft.
Schilthorn	9,728	
Schwarzhorn	14,092	
Schreckhorn	13,394	
Segneshorn	10,870	
Sentis	7,670	
Sidelhorn	9,449	8,524·3 Vienna ft.
Silberhorn		
Silvio (Monte)	See Cervin.	
Sonnenhorn	9,147	
Staffelberg		
Steinberg		8,283·0
Stockhorn	7,195	
Stuffstein Alp		4,873·4
Studerhorn	11,878	
Sustenhorn	11,529	
Sustenjoch		6,860·3
Tacul (Aiguille du)	10,013	
Tambohorn	10,748	
Täschhorn	14,758	
Thierberg	10,410	
Tiarms (Piz)	10,338	
Titlis	10,620	
Tödi	11,887	
Tödi (Klein)	10,072	
Tola (Bella)	9,929	
Torrenthorn	9,679	
Tour d'Ai (Vaud) near Aigle	7,188 or 6,818	
Tour de Mayen (Vaud)	7,198	
Trelatête (Aiguille de)	13,845	
Trifthorn	12,261	
Tschingelhorn	11,746	
Uertsch (Piz)	10,738	
Ulrichshorn	12,891	
Umbrail (Piz)	9,954	
Uri Rothstock	9,621	
Urlaun (Piz)	11,063	
Vadred (Piz)	10,010	
Valrhein (Piz)	11,148	
Vaulon (Dent de)	4,877	
Velan (Monte)		
Verte (Aiguille)	13,432	
Vesulspitz	10,154	
Viul (Piz)	10,347	
Viescherhorn (Grosser)	12,747	
Wesenhorn	10,628	

HEIGHT OF PEAKS AND ALPS—(*Continued.*)

Name.	Triangulation.	Barometrical Measurement.	Name.	Triangulation.	Barometrical Measurement.
Wasserfluh	2 680		Weissthor (New)	11,139	
Weisse Frau	12 011		Weithorn	10,186	
Weissnorn	13 400	Paris ft.	Wildstrubel	10,715	
Weissenstein (Jura)	3,946		Windgeile (Grosse)	10,468	
Wetterhorn	11,412 or 11,453	Vienna ft.	Zwurgi or Twirgi	3,049	
Weissernhorn (a Peak of the Brunig	5,895				

SWISS HOTEL GUIDE.

Larger and more frequented Towns.

The Hotels de l'Ecu, des Bergues and the Couronne, at Geneva; the Hotel Gibbon, at Lausanne; the Schweizerhoff, at Lucerne; the Trois Couronnes, at Vevey; the Hotel Baur, at Zürich; and Hotel Bellevue, at Thun, are as good as any in Germany, France, or England.

Alphabetical List of the favourite Centres with their Hotels.

Æggischhorn.—The Hotel de la Jungfrau. In 1856, the landlord of this hotel, then just established, was an Italian, and the accommodation was imperfect. Since that date the hotel has been greatly improved by its proprietor, Wellig, and it is described as deserving of the highest praise in works written by members of the Alpine Club (Peaks, Passes, and Glaciers, 1st series, p. 200), who say that "the excellent Hotel de la Jungfrau on the east slope of the Æggischhorn, has afforded travellers facilities for exploring the great Aletsch Glacier, second only to those furnished by the hotel on the Riffel" (ditto p. 316, chap. xii). The only complaint here has been that the proprietor seeks to induce travellers to employ guides, favoured by him, and to take more food with them, on ascensions, than is necessary. The path up to Æggischhorn Hotel from Viesch is excellent. It has been made mainly by M. Wellig, the landlord of the Jungfrau Hotel. He is altogether the most enterprising, thoughtful man I ever met among Swiss innkeepers. Symptoms of Herr Wellig's concern for his coming guests are seen directly you begin to mount the Æggischhorn from Viesch. Wellig's path is carried carefully up by well graduated zig-zags, and kept in good walking order.

The hotel on the Æggischhorn has become the chief starting place for the ascent of the Jungfrau, Mönch, Eiger, &c. The hotel has 25 beds; lodging, 2 fr.; dinner, 3½ fr.; supper, 3 fr., without wine. The Æggischhorn Hotel commands a magnificent view, and above it (1½ hours) is the Æggischhorn

(9,054 ft.), with one of the finest panoramic views in Switzerland.

Alagna, in the Val Sesia, has an inn which is said to be good, clean, and kept by obliging people. Its name is the Monte Rosa. But complaints are made of attempts at extortion in the prices demanded for guides and mules.

Aosta, has an hotel kept by an old Chamouni guide, Jean Tairraz, and described as comfortable in the 2nd Series of Peaks, Passes, and Glaciers (Vol. I., p. 309). Indeed in the 2nd Volume, the positive has passed into a superlative, for we find the hotel of Tairraz described as excellent (Vol. 2, p. 397). The Alpine Guide, for 1865, calls the Mont Blanc, kept by Tairraz, good, and adds that the Couronne in new hands, newly fitted up, may deserve a trial. The Ecu is called pretty good, and the Italie tolerable.

Bell Alp Hotel, is four to five leagues from the Æggischhorn, stands in a fine situation near the end of the Aletsch Glacier, 3 hours from Brieg descending (4 hours up), 6,000 feet above the sea. Bell Alp is recently established, and is described by Tyndale, as follows:—From the windows of the hotel upon the Bell Alp, noble views are commanded, and you may sit upon the bilberry slopes adjacent, in the presence of some of the noblest of the Alps. Berlepsch describes the view as superior to that from the Jungfrau Hotel on the Æggischhorn. The establishment has been enlarged latterly, and its prices are the same as at Herr Wellig's. A climb of 1½ hour takes you from Bell Alp to the Sparrhorn or Bellhorn (9,278 ft.), with a panoramic view comparable to that from the Æggischhorn.

Breuil, on the ascent to Col St. Theodule, and thence to Zermatt, at the head of Val Tournanche is said to have a comfortable inn in the 2nd series of Peaks, Passes, and Glaciers (Vol. I, p. 109). It is named the Hotel du Mont Cervin, and has been a favourite starting place for attacks on the Matterhorn. The Alpine Guide describes this as one of the most comfortable of Alpine inns, and adds that its cuisine is said to be particularly good. This in-used formerly to bear the name of *Jomont* or *Giomen*. It is two hours from the St Theodule Col, from Zermatt, 7; from Val Tournanche, 3; from Chatillon, 5 hours.

Brienz (Bernese Oberland), has the Bear, described as large, good, and dear; and the Weissenkreuz at the landing place (Tracht) post-office, and telegraph office. The hotel and pension of Bellevue is at Kienholz, one mile from Brienz on the road to Meyringen. Of the two former inns the Alpine Guide says, that the Bear is noisy, with first-rate prices; and the Weissenkreuz cheaper, with better attendance. Murray describes the innkeeper of the Bear as quite a linguist.

Brussone (Val d'Ayas), South of Monte Rosa, is one of the most picturesque villages in the Italian valleys. The principal auberge of the place is now the well-known Lion d'Or. I recommend both it and its proprietor, Jean Alexandre Vuillermet, prince of cuisiniers, to the patronage of the members of the Alpine Club (2nd series, Peaks and Passes, Vol. 1, p. 39). It is called a good mountain inn, in the Alpine Guide.

Chamouni.—The Union Hotel of M. Eisenkramer is described as excellent, in Peaks and Passes (2nd series, p. 199, Vol. 1). Berlepsch says of it, that it is dear, but very good, and comfortable. At Hotel du Mont Blanc, which is clean and comfortable, visitors are taken, en pension for a week, at 6fr. per day.

Champery.—Joanne, Berlepsch, and the Alpine Guide, agree in describing the Hotel of the Dent du Midi, as good. The Alpine Guide says it is reasonable. The Diamond Guide tells us that it has 92 rooms, and a whey cure, M. Lonfats, proprietor. Pension, 4fr. 50c. per day, without wine.

The Federal Cross is at the foot of Dent du Midi. Inn, beautifully situated, second rate, but not bad. One hour below Champery is the Hotel du Repos, at Val d'Illiez. Pension, 4fr. 50c.

Val d'Illiez is well known to geologists, on account of its erratic blocks, to which attention was first directed by M. Charpentier.

Chatillon, in Piedmont.—The Hotel du Palais Royal is mentioned in the 2nd series of Peaks and Passes. The Alpine Guide calls it tolerably good. Joanne describes it as *bon*. Murray does not specify its character. The Rev. H. Jones says of it "the inn was thoroughly Italian; the shape of the loaves, the taste of the wine, and the voice of the waiter, were all different."—The Regular Swiss Round, p. 123.

Chur or Coire.—The Rev. H. Jones describes the Steinbock Hotel as excellent, in 1855. Cotta, in his Geological Letters, writes in 1850—"If ever you go to Chur, I recommend the Steinbock." An hotel like a man that retains a good character for 15 years may be regarded as trustworthy and successful.

Comballaz.—The highest pension in the world, not in price, but in situation. Its elevation is 1,345 metres or 5,000 feet. Its name, the Pension Lys. Pension, 5fr. per day. Situated in the fine scenery above Sepey in the Ormond Valley, near the Col de Pillon and the Upper Sho[men]-

thal. Murray calls it a rustic, but comfortable inn and boarding-house, much frequented in summer on account of the fine air, and its mineral spring. Berlepsch speaks of the excellent Pension de la Roche at Comballaz. The Alpine Guide gives Comballaz an elevation of 4,416 feet. The prices at Pension Roche, which are described as very reasonable, are 5fr a-day, without wine; children, 2½fr.; servants, including wine, 4fr. The landlord has ponies for expeditions in the mountains. Alpine Guide, Central Alps, p 7. See also Alpine Journal, Vol 1., No 2 June, 1863, p 96.

Diablerets (Hotel)—On the same pass, and in the same charming scenery near Les Iles, at a place called Plan des Isles, amidst charming meadows, aged forests, glaciers, streams, and beetling rocks capped with everlasting snows, 2¼ l. (7½ m) from Sepey. Murray calls it a very good hotel and pension. The Alpine Guide uses the same words, and adds that near it is a small, very cheap inn, Au Chamois. Though at times rather hot, it is stated that this is the best head-quarters for exploring the Alps west of the Diablerets. It also affords fine air, and beautiful walks without number (3,837 feet above the sea). Les Iles is described as a delightful idyllic spot beyond Gstoig in the Valley of Ormond dessus and as presenting the most perfect scene an artist could dream of. A beautiful walk leads hence to the Châlet de Villard, with a good pension kept by M Roux (4½fr) near Bex (see Grionne).

Evolena, in the Val d Herens Canton of Valais, the centre for countless excursions and ascensions in the sublimest scenery. The Alpine Guide says a good inn has been lately opened there, very favourably reported of by travellers. This inn is the Hotel de la Dent Blanche, mentioned by Berlepsch, described by Joanne as having 18 rooms and a good guide, Veignet: proprietor's name, Favre. Murray simply says, Hotel de la Dent Blanche is very good, but he gives no list of prices. Mr R W E Forster, of the Alpine Club, describes the rooms at this inn as good, but adds that the party should write beforehand, as the supply of provisions is liable to run short. It is not strictly a pension, but arrangements of that kind can be made, if you stay, as at most Swiss inns. (Page 96, Vol. 1. No. 2 Alp. Journal).

Faulhorn.—A good inn (Joanne's words) is on the top, inhabited from July to September 25th. Elevation, 2,683 metres (8,799 feet); 4½ hours from Grindelwald, 5 hours from Giessbach, 8 hours from Schienige Platte. One of the finest panoramas in Switzerland. "A tolerable inn" (Alpine Guide, Central Alps, p. 69). bedrooms mere closets, two beds in each. In settled weather house over full. Cold at night, and plenty of wraps wanted. Murray gives it 24 beds, not very soft; 9fr. or 10fr. have been asked for a bed, when the house is full, we presume. Berlepsch gives the prices as 3fr. bed; 3½fr., a very frugal supper; coffee, 2fr.; attendance, 1fr., &c.

Giessbach.—Hotel kept by M. Ed. Schmidlin, close to the noted falls, Lake of Brienz. Attached to the hotel is a restaurant, one of the best cuisines in Switzerland. Hotel also excellent, 170 beds, 12,000 visitors per annum. Yet life at the hotel is quiet and comfortable. Falls lighted up at night with Bengal lights, 1fr. Walks and seats all about the Falls. Price of pension, 6fr. to 1·fr. per day. Newspapers and reviews, three times a-day. Steamboats to and from Interlaken and Brienz.

Gressonay.—St. Jean, in the Val de Lys, forming one of the enchanting valleys south of Monte Rosa. The Alpine Club says, "We found the Pension De la Pierre, at Gressonay, a most agreeable resting place, and it was not without reluctance we quitted that charming spot." Mr. King takes the same view, and speaks highly of De la Pierre's obliging ways and excellent cookery. The Alpine Guide says that the Hotel De la Pierre is very good, considering its remote position, and that the landlord is very attentive. Joanne describes everything as bon at the Hotel De la Pierre.

Grimsel.—Hospice and Hotel, retains its grim character. But it is visited by fashionable tourists, and retains its high prices since the time of old Vater Zybach, who made a fortune there, insured the house largely, and then set fire to it: an act for which he was banished to America. The hospice was re-built, and contains a vast number of half furnished rooms, warmed by a vast stove, which insists on smoking sometimes. Room, 2fr.: supper, without wine, 2fr. Bad coffee, 1½fr. Indifferent attendance.

Gruben.—In the Upper Turtmann Thal, near the Zmeiden Pass, and the centre of many excursions, is the little inn of Grüben, small, good, and clean. The landlord is described as a good cook, and reliable guide. We presume that this is the same place as the nice, clean little inn that has been built at Zmeiden, in the Turtmann Thal, though Gruben and Zmeiden are described as adjoining hamlets, in the Alpine Guide.

Grindelwald.—The Bär and Adler are old and noted houses, rather dear, with pensions. Hotel du Glacier is more economical. Hotel Eiger, recently built.

Grionne.—A valley above Bex, near les Ormonds, full of charming pastoral scenery, and of cheap pensions. The largest is the Chålet of Villard, kept by M. Roux, a retired officer. It commands a splendid view, and is in the midst of delightful excursions. Accommodation rather rustic, but good. Fare, en pension, 4½fr.

Grion is a village in a fine pastoral country, 1 hour above Montreux, with several large pensions. The largest, Righi Vaudois, now said to be fallen off. Pension, E. Dufour Delarottaz, at Breu, is said to be good.

Interlaken.—The town or village consists of hotels and pensions. At Unterseen, the Bellevue Hotel, Pont and Cerf, receive at 4fr. to 6fr. per day. The cheapest plan is to take a lodging in the cot of a family.

Joch (on the), between Engelberg and Meyringen, at the Engstlen Alp, 5 hours 45 minutes from Hof, in the Haslithal, is a good hotel, pension, 4fr. per day, at an elevation of 1,839 metres, amid the pastures, and scenery, and a good centre for the ascension of the Titlis, 6 hours, &c.

Isola Bella in Lago Maggiore, near Baveno, has an hotel with 20 rooms to hold 30 or 35 persons. The attendance is good, but as the hotel is small another has been opened by the proprietor at Stresa, near the island. This is a good centre for fishing.

Kandersteg, on the Gemmi Pass, 26½ miles from Thun. The Hotel Victoria is not in great favour with Berlepsch, who prefers the Bear at Æggischwand, burnt in 1867, re-built since, and said to be more comfortable. This is an excellent centre for numberless excursions and ascensions. Of the former may be recommended the Œschinen See, 1½ l., the Gasteren Thal, the Kienthal, &c. Of the ascensions, the Altels, Balmhorn, Doldenhorn, Schilihorn, &c. At Kandergrund 1½ l. (4½ m.) from Kandersteg; a new hotel has been opened quite recently, said to be well kept (Hotel Altels).

Lenk, 2½ l. (8½ m.) from Zweisimmen in the Simmenthal, is an excellent centre amidst the rare beauties of a pastoral district. It has three inns, said to be fair, the Crown, Star, and Bear.

Luc, St. in the Val d'Anniviers is considered a charming spot, with a view of Monte Cervin. The landlord, Pons, is represented as a good guide.

Lucerne is full of good hotels and pensions, with different charges. Pension Æschmann, 6fr. a day if you stay above two days. The Balance (Waage) is an hotel with moderate prices. (See Lucerne).

Lugano.—Hotel du Parc is a fine establishment and centre of delightful excursions. Dear in summer, 8 to 9fr. Moderate in winter, 5 or 6fr. pension. Lodgings at Villa Tanzina. Other hotels Posta, Corona.

Macugnaga.—Hotel du Monte Moro, kept by Gaspard Delmonte, good. Zum Monte Rosa is considered rather disorderly, but held by the best guide of the district, Franz Lochmatter. The Alpine Guide describes Macugnaga as situated in the most wonderful scenery in the Alps. Mr. King and Professor Tyndale agree in this view.

Matmark See Hotel, 2,133 metres, 6,714 feet on the Telli or Vispback, and on the road from Saas to Macugnaga. It is in the centre of fine cascades, and a good spot from which to reach Zermatt by the Gorner Glacier, and make various ascensions. The hotel was built in 1856. 7 l. (21 m.) to Macugnaga.

Ormond.—See Diablerets and Comballaz.

Orta.—Hotel Sun Giulio is said to be very satisfactory. Landlord speaks English and does everything to make the residence agreeable to English guests. At a short distance from the hotel he has a Hotel Garni, in which he receives persons en pension. Families stay here for weeks. A reading-room with newspapers is attached. Orta is one of the most delightful centres in the Alps. For exploring the Italian valleys it is unrivalled.

Ouchy.—Hotel Beau Rivage, one of the most sumptuous in Europe. Superb situation. Fashionable company. Telegraph station at hotel.

Pallanza on Lago Maggiore, opposite the Borromean Islands. Hotel l'Univers, good and moderate. Charming country.

Pontresina.—Best centre for Bernina district. 2 hours 45 minutes from St. Moritz in the Engadin. Hotel, the Krone, chez Gredig: good, moderate. Also Weisser Kreuz Guides: Jenul, Fiüri, Cobani, Walthur, Enderlin, Arnbühl. Topp; tariff too dear.

Poschiavo.—La Croce and Bernina Hotels, near Lake of Poschiavo. Baths of La Prese. Excellent hotel. Sulphur springs. Charming water parties. A vapour bath, 1fr. 20c.

Riffelberg.—Hotel at head of Zermatt Valley amidst the finest scenery of Monte Rosa and the Matterhorn. Elevation, 7,600 feet. Grand view even lying in bed. Best point for ascension of many of the highest peaks.

Righi.—This celebrated mountain has many hotels, some of which are pleasant stations as summer pensions Among these hotels may be named the Unten Dächli. Superb view on the Goldau path, the Schwert and Sonne at Klosterli, and the Kaltbad and Scheidegg. The Righi Scheidegg Hotel can hold 150 persons. Height, 5,073 feet. Ferruginous source. Temperature, 6 centigrade. This is also a place for whey cure, it commands very fine views and is much frequented, especially by Swiss.

Rosenlaui (Baths.)—A charming centre for exploring the Oberland: kept by M. Brunner, a noted botanist. Good fare; moderate prices. Lovely position. Rooms, 1½ to 2fr.; breakfast, 1½fr.; dinner, 2½ to 3fr. Pension (without wine) 5fr. per day if engaged for a week.

Saas.—Good centre for ascensions. Hotel, Monte Rosa and Monte Moro. Good guides. Imseng the old Curé will give every information about excursions.

Saint Gervais (Baths of).—Near Chamouni mineral spring. Temperature, 20 to 60 centigrade. There are two hotels: Hotel du Mont Joli and Hotel de Geneve. Sulphur springs. 100 rooms; moderate prices.

Saint Moritz in the Upper Engadin. Pensions: Fuller or Zum Engadiner Kulm, now Hotel Badrutt and Pension Bairer, 1,856 metres above the sea, one of the highest spots in Europe, amidst numberless charming excursions. At the ferruginous springs splendid bath-house, 150 rooms, called Curhaus. A bath 1fr. 50c. Warm clothing required.

Samoens, in the valley of the Giffre, below Sixt. Croix d'Or, good inn; Couronne, Ville du Lyons, inferior. Surrounding country glorious.

Sixt, higher up same valley. Admirable centre for finest excursions. Hotel du Fer a Cheval. Landlady well meaning, but house ill kept, noisy, and not clean. Other inns, Etoile and Couronne. The Hotel and Pension des Cascades has superseded the Fer a Cheval; in the same building a Convent of 12th Century.

Schienige Platte.—Charming centre, near Lauterbrunnen. View equal to Faulhorn. Alpenrose Hotel, 2,070 metres high.

Stachelberg.—Baths and hotel in the Linththal (1½ m.) from Glarus. Carriage there and back, 1fr. One of the best centres in East Switzerland.

Very fine walks, far and near. Expenses of patients, moderate. For others, room, 1½fr.; bed, 1fr.; dinner, 3fr.; attendance, 75c. Often overcrowded, so that visitors have to sleep at Seggen, the winter hotel on the other side of the Linth. Waters are strong, sulphureous, and alkaline.

Stoss (The).—A mountain 2,971 feet above the lake of Uri (Urner See), near Tellenplatte, has a small very healthily situated pension, 3½fr. per day, called Frohnalp. An excellent centre for much fine scenery.

Tarasp. (Bad.)—A new bath establishment with mineral waters in the Lower Innthal on left bank of Nairs. Many pleasant excursions around.

Uetliberg (The).—An inn stands on this, the highest point of the Albis, near Zurich, and affords fair accommodation for the night to enable the traveller to see sun rise.

Villeneuve.—Hotels: Byron, slightly fallen off, in a delicious position, close to Chillon: moderate; 7fr. per day, if you stay a week; 5 or 6fr. in winter. Veytaux, a station for Chillon, has a Hotel Bonivard. Pension Masson, 4fr. and l'Abri, 5fr. One of the most beautiful centres in the world.

Varallo.—Albergo d'Italia, is good, but dear. Posta, Falcone Nero. Fine centre for the Italian valleys.

Visp, or Viége, not a very healthy position, but heavy luggage may be left here by those going up to the Rosa Cervin district. The Soleil and Post are both good houses.

Weissbad, in Appenzell. A great place for whey cure, and a fine centre for many excursions. Plain, but respectable accommodation for 120 persons. Room, 1½fr.; breakfast, 75c.; dinner, 2fr.; attendance, 1½fr.

Weissenstein, near Solothurn: charming summer station with one of the finest panoramic views in the world. Pension, 4fr.; room, 1½fr.; breakfast, 1fr.; supper, 2fr.; whey cure. Crowded on Saturdays.

Wengern Alp—Jungfrau Hotel: room, 2fr.; breakfast, 1½fr.; dinner, without wine, 3fr.; attendance, 75c. Wengen or Little Scheideck: Hotel Bellevue: room, 2fr.; breakfast, 1½fr., supper, 2fr.; attendance, 75c. Best spots in Switzerland to see avalanches.

Zermatt.—Has good well kept inns, Hotel du Monte Cervin: Hotel du Monte Rosa. The first kept by Seiler Brothers, who also keep the Riffelberg hotel higher up, near the grand panoramic view of the Rosa Cervin chain. Hotel du Monte Cervin belongs to Clemens.

Zug.—Above the town, and on the Zugerberg, the landlord of the Bellevue, at Zug, keeps a hydropathic establishment, commanding a magnificent view.

Zurich, has a legion of pensions and hotels. Hotel Bauer, is one of the first in Europe. On the Lake of Zurich, near Richterschwyl. (1fr. 80c. by steamer from the capital). is a Pension Hütten, at the foot of Hühe Rohne, most frequented in summer. Distance from Richterschwyl, 1½ L. (4½ m.)

GUIDE TO THE RECENTLY DISCOVERED LAKE HABITATIONS
OF THE ANCIENT POPULATION.

Within the last 15 or 20 years, various highly interesting discoveries have been made in France, Switzerland, and Italy, corresponding to similar discoveries in Ireland, Scotland, and Denmark, and all relating to the early population of Europe in what is called the age of stone.

The Museums in London, Zurich, Berne, Geneva, Paris, and elsewhere, present considerable collections of stone, bronze, and iron instruments, and ornaments, of the food and clothing, mostly carbonized by fire, of these ancient people.

The age to which they are to be referred is uncertain. Geologists suppose from the nature of the formations overlying the French remains at Abbeville, Aurignac, &c.) that they belong to a very remote age, not only antediluvian, but pre-Adamite, and even 100,000 years have been assigned to them. The Swiss lake dwellings though representing a duration of more than a 1,000 years, are not thought to reach upwards more than 2,000 or 3,000 years before Christ. But it must be admitted that with our present imperfect knowledge of the whole question any very decided opinion on this point would be premature.

Our present purpose is to offer a practical guide for the visitors to these highly interesting remains of a remote fore world.

The first ancient lake dwelling at Mei'en was systematically explored by the Zurich Antiquarian Society in 1854, since which date the number of pile works has increased to 2 0. some situated on the lakes, and others on peat beds deserted by the waters.

The most numerous lake dwellings have been discovered on the lakes of Neuchâtel, Bienne, Morat, Constance, Pfaffikon, Zurich, and Geneva.

Of the various pile works discovered, some are referred (from the relics found there) to the age of stone, or the older period, others to the age of bronze, in the time of Homer and David, 1,000 years B.C., and others to the iron age reaching down to the Christian era, and shewing evidences of Roman workmanship. It should be added that great similarity, shewing intimate connection, is found between the Swiss lake habitations and those of North Italy, at Lago Maggiore, the Lake of Garda, and elsewhere.

Before we pass to a list of the localities of the pile works it will be useful to state that those at Moossedorf (a little lake two hours from Berne), afford the most perfect example of a regular lake dwelling of the stone period. Amongst all the peat moor pile works that at Robenhausen on Lake Pfaffikon, takes the first rank. It appears to be chiefly of the stone age. The greater portion of the pile works on the lake of Constance are thought to have reached back to the stone age. The pile works on the Lake of Neuchâtel (especially on the E. side), amount to fifty, and appear to have lasted longer than most others, even after the Roman occupation

of Helvetia. Twenty-one settlements (some of the Roman period) have been found on the Lake of Bienne; the settlements on the lake of Morat are in many cases of the stone age, while others afford evidence of a high pre-historic civilisation. The pile works discovered on the Lake of Geneva are mostly of more recent date than those mentioned above.

The animal remains of the relic beds of the pile works, shew the existence of the *Bos urus* (a large extinct species of ox), the bison, and the elk, with varieties of species still existing in Switzerland. The remains of plants, shew the presence of barley and beans of an archaic type, of flax, cherries, apples, and existing wild fruit. The people were mostly clad in flax dresses, used canoes made out of a single log, as is still done on certain lakes, such as Zug, &c., and lived in the earliest times, chiefly by hunting with bows, and fishing with bone fish-hooks. Flint and horn instruments were largely used in the oldest period for carpentry, &c., but moulds for copper of a later date have been found in many places.

A succession of pile works one above the other have been found as at Robenhausen, each generally showing an advance on the older dwelling. But we must now give a list of the localities.

Many of the lake habitations can be visited by rail, and in steamer. Others as the peat pile works must be reached in carriage, or on foot, from the nearest station. The following instructions will be of use.

1. For the pile works west bank of Lake of Neuchâtel, take rail [Neuchâtel and Geneva (west Swiss) line to nearest Station]. See Special Edition of *Bradshaw's Continental Guide,*

For east bank, cross lake in steamer and proceed by carriage, row boat, or on foot.—*Bradshaw's Special,*

2. For Lake of Bienne, take rail from Neuchâtel to Bâle, stop at Bienne or any nearer station on the lake: a row boat will be the pleasantest access to most of these pile works.—*Bradshaw's Continental Guide,*

3. Morat is best reached by diligence or post from Berne, or steamer from Neuchâtel to Cudrefin and post on. Take boat on lake. See *Bradshaw's Continental Railway Guide,*

4. Visit pile works of Lake of Constance by steamer or by rail to nearest station, and then walk or take row boat. See *Bradshaw's Special Guide,* p. 94, and steamer daily to Meersburg.

5. Pfaffikon is reached by lake or rail from Zurich and in carriage.

6. Geneva pile works. Rail, north bank. Steamer, south bank, and then a row boat. See *Bradshaw's Special,*

The annexed lists will guide the traveller to any of the pile works, from some known and accessible centre.

LAKE OF NEUCHÂTEL.

The principal settlements on this Lake are:
1. At N.W. end Pré Farg er. and Marin.
2. Cret, half-a-mile N. of Neuchâtel (town.)
3. Auvernier, 3 miles S. of Neuchâtel.
4. Cortaillod, 3 miles S. of Auvernier.
5. St. Aubin, 5 miles S. of Cortaillod.
6. Concise, the richest piles work of the lake, 4½ miles N. of Grandson.
7. Corcelettes, a mile N. of Grandson. On the E. bank of the lake, the most interesting pile works are at
8. Estavayer, age of stone and bronze, reached by steamer from Neuchâtel.
9. La Crazaz, ¼ a league N.W. of Estavayer
10. Yvouand, 6 mi'es N.E of Yverdun.
11. Clendy, 1 mile from Yverdun.
12. Chevroux, 4 miles N. of Estavayer.
13. Port Alban, 4 miles N. of Chevroux.
14. Cudrefin, near N.E. end of the Lake.

LAKE OF BIENNE.

1. Nidau, stone and bronze, N.E. end of lake; a vary interesting settlement.
2. Sütz, half an hour's walk from Nidau.
3. Lattringen, 10 minutes' walk from Sütz.
4. Meringen, ¼ of an hou 's walk f om Lattringen.
5. Peter's Island, where Rousseau lived, probably called in ancient times, Ubinowa, has a large pile wo k.
6. Vinelz, W. bank of lake, near Nidau.

LAKE OF MORAT.

1. Richest place on the lake for these relics is Guévaux, W. bank, 4 miles from Morat (town), by water,
2. Greng, a large pile work. 2 miles S. of Morat. Has yielded specimens of the Urus and the Elk.
3. Montellier, half-a-mile north of Morat, has yielded specimens of the potter's art, like those in Italian lakes and Etruscan sepulchres.

LAKE OF CONSTANCE.

Mostly of the early age of stone.
Ueberlinger See. Branch of the lake N. of Constance (town).
1. Unter Uhldingen.
2. Maurach.
3. Nassdorf.
4. Sipplingen.
5. Bodman.
6. Wallhausen.
7. Lützelstetten.
8 Mainau.
Five pile works, on the east shore of this branch of the lake, are within the limits of a short three hours' work, viz.:—Stone age settlements, at Nussdorf; and Maurach; bronze age settlements, at Unter Uhldingen and Sipplingen.

N.B. The antiquities at Nussdorf are of special interest; distance from Constance about nine miles. *The settlements on this branch of the lake are most tempting.*

UNTER SE

Or branch of the lake below Constance.
1. Ermatingen, below and opposite Constance.
2. Allensbach.
3 Markeltingen.
4. Iznang.
5. Hornstad.
} On the bay called Zeller Zee.
6. Gaienhofen.
7. Hemmenhofen.
8 Wangen. E. of the village. No pile work has yielded so many implements as this.
9. Oberstaad in the bay between Wangen and Kattenhorn.
10. Stein, just where the Rhine runs out of the Unter See.
11. Neuenburger Horn, above Mammern, close to the Taubmühle, stone celts or spuds have been found here by hundreds.
12. Felabach
13. Above town of Steckborn.

LAKE OF PFÄFFIKON.

1. Irgenhausen.
2. Robenhausen.

LAKE OF ZURICH.

1. Bauschanz, near Hotel Baur au Lac.
2. Mänedorf.

LAKE OF SEMPACH.

1. Eich.
2. Schenken.
3. Mariazell.

LAKE OF ZUG.

1. Zug.
2. Koller.
3. St. Andreas, near Cham.
4. Derschbach.
5. Zweirn.

LAKE OF GENEVA.

1. Cully
2. Lu'ry
3. Pully
} Between Vevay and Lausanne; reached by rail from either place.
4. Cour.
5. St. Sulpice.
7. Morges – Railway station. The most important pile work on the lake.
8. St. Prex.
9. Rolle.—Railway station.
10. Nyon, opposite the anchoring ground between the harbour and the point of Promenthou. Railway station.
11. Versoix.
12. Paquio.
13. Rive.
14. Opposite Geneva. The piles are to be seen in different l calities of the lesser or smaller part of Lake Leman.
15. La Belotte.
16. La Gabiule.
17. Bssy.

OUTLINE TOURS IN SWITZERLAND.

Tour of Eight Days.

I.

DAYS

To Paris by Calais, Boulogne, or Dieppe see Bradshaw's Continental Railway Guide — 1

From Paris by express train ... Lyons Railway ... to ... Lyons, arriving at Geneva ... — A day's rest at Geneva — 1

Geneva to Chamouni by diligence ... Mont Anvert on foot or mule. Cross Mer de Glacier and descend by the Chapeau, proceed to Head de la Barberine, Tête Noire, or not made — 1

From Head de la Barberine by Tête Noire to Martigny on foot or mule. Martigny to Lausanne or Terry by rail, or from Villeneuve by steamer — 1

Visit ... lake habitations near Morges (Lake of Geneva) ... proceed to Fribourg by rail, staying there to see the Cathedral, Suspension Bridges &c., and on by rail to Berne, where sleep — 1

From Berne to Thun by rail. Thun to Interlaken, steamer or carriage; Interlaken to Giessbach, steamer on lake of Brienz, sleep at Giessbach Hotel — 1

From Giessbach to Brienz, steamer; and from Brienz over the Brünig to Stanzstad, in carriage; Stanzstad to Waggis, steamer or row boat; Ascend Righi on foot or mule — 1

From Righi to Lucerne, on foot or mule to Kussnacht, and thence by steamer; Lucerne to Bâle, by rail. Bâle to Paris by night train — 1

— 8

II.

DAYS

From London to Paris, as before — 1
From Paris to Bâle, by night train (express), stoppage at Bâle; on by rail to sleep at Zurich. 1
Zurich to Horgen, steamer; Horgen to Art, carriage or by steamer; Art to Righi, on foot or mule, sleep at Righi — 1

Descend Righi to Waggis, on foot or mule; Waggis to Fluelen; Fluelen to Lucerne.—Tour on the lake, Tell's chapel, &c., steamer; sleep at Lucerne — 1

Lucerne to Alpnach or Sarnstad, steamer; Alpnach or Sarnstad to Brienz, carriage— ... Giessbach where sleep — 1

Brienz to Rosenlaui, carriage, thence to Grindelwald by Rosenlaui and Great Scheidegg on foot or mule — 1

Grindelwald to Lauterbrunnen by Wengern Alp on foot or mule, Lauterbrunnen to Interlaken, on foot or carriage; and on to Neuhaus, thence by steamer to Thun, where sleep — 1

Thun to Berne, rail, where stay; Berne to Lausanne, via Fribourg, rail.—Lake dwellings at Morges — 1

Lausanne to Geneva, stoppage at Geneva; (night train to Paris) — 1
Paris to London — 1

— 10

Or, deducting to and from London to Paris, 2

— 8

From Paris, Bâle, or London, Ten Days.

Return Tickets, Billets Circulaires, at Reduced Prices issued at Paris from May to October.

III.

DAYS

London to Paris, as before — 1
Paris to Bâle (night train); from Bâle at 5.30 a.m. train to Lucerne arrives at 10 a.m.; in the afternoon, steamer to Waggis.—Ascend Righi on foot or mule — 1

Descend to Waggis, at 10 a.m.; steamer to Fluelen; Post or other conveyance to St. Gothard; Andermatt and Hospenthal — 1

DAYS.

On foot or mule over the Furka to the Rhone Glacier, and up by the Malenwand to the Grimsel Hospice 1

Down Haali Valley, by Handeck Falls to Meyringen, by mule or on foot; to Reichenbach Falls, and on to Rosenlaui Baths, where sleep... 1

Over Great Scheidegg to Grindelwald; and in the afternoon up the Wengeren Alp, where sleep 1

Descend on foot to Lauterbrunnen and Staubbach; carriage to Interlaken; afternoon by steamer to Gies-bach Hotel, where sleep...... 1

Steamer to Interlaken; walk or omnibus to Neuhaus; steamer to Thun; rail to Berne, where sleep 1

Rail from Berne to Bâle 1

Night train from Bâle to Paris; Paris to London 1

—
10

Or, deducting to and fro, Journey from Paris to London 2

—
8

IV.
DAYS

The last tour may be varied by taking from Bâle the Baden rail through Waldshut to Neuhausen and the Rhine Falls at Schaffhausen (stop 4 hours); rail from Neuhausen to Schaffhausen and Constance, 1½ hours; on direct by steamer over Lake of Constance to Romanshorn; from Romanshorn by rail to Zurich 1

From Zurich proceed as in Tour, No. II.

V.

By adding two other days to Tours Nos. I and II, you can take in the Bernese Oberland: Interlaken to Brienz, by Lauterbrunnen, Grindelwald, Rosenlaui, and Reichenbach in No. I; and in No. II, you can include the Chamouni round: from Lausanne to Geneva, by Villeneuve, Bex, Martigny, the Col de Balme, Chamouni, Sallenches, &c.

Fortnight Tours.

VI.
DAYS

London to Paris, as before 1

Paris to Geneva (as in No. I) 1

Geneva to Chamouni 1

Visit Glacier des Bossons and la Flegere 1

Chamouni to Martigny, by Col de Balme or Tête Noire, on foot or mule 1

Martigny to Bad Leuk, rail and carriage.—Excursion to the Echelles...... 1

Gemmi Pass, foot or mule, to Kandersteg, and thence to Frutigen or Thun, carriage, (pass the night at Thun or at Frutigen) 1

Thun to Interlaken, steamer; or from Frutigen to Interlaken, on foot or in carriage; from Interlaken to Lauterbrunnen, in carriage; Lauterbrunnen to Wengeren Alp, mule or foot, there sleep 1

DAYS.

Wengeren Alp to Grindelwald.—Visit Lower Glacier; ascend Faulhorn...... 1

Faulhorn to Reichenbach, by Rosenlaui, foot or mule; carriage to Brienz; excursion to Giessbach; sleep there 1

Brienz to Beckenried, in carriage; Beckenried to Fluelen, foot, mule, or steamer 1

Fluelen to Wäggis, steamer; Wäggis to Righi, foot or mule 1

Righi to Lucerne, foot or mule; and steamer from Küssnacht 1

Lucerne to Bâle, rail (night train Bâle to Paris) 1

—
14

VII.
DAYS

London to Paris 1

Paris to Bâle, rail; stoppage at Bâle; Bâle to Zurich, rail; sleep 1

Zurich to Schaffhausen, rail, stoppage; Rhine Fall; Schaffhausen to St. Gallen, rail; Excursion to the Freudenberg...... 1

St. Gallen to Ragatz, rail; visit Pfeffers Baths; Ragatz to Rapperschwyl, rail 1

Rapperschwyl to Horgen, steamer; Horgen to Art, carriage or steamer; Art to Righi, foot or mule 1

Righi to Wäggis, foot or mule; Wäggis to Fluelen, steamer; Fluelen to Andermatt, foot or carriage 1

Andermatt to the Grimsel, by the Furka and Rhone Glacier, foot or mule 1

Ascend Sidelhorn, on foot; Grimsel to Guttannen, foot or mule 1

Guttannen to Reichenbach, and on to Grindelwand, by Rosenlaui 1

Grindelwald to Lauterbrunnen by Wengeren Alp, foot or mule; Lauterbrunnen to Interlaken, foot or carriage 1

Interlaken to Thun, steamer; Thun to Berne, rail; sleep at Berne 1

Berne to Lausanne, rail 1

Lausanne to Geneva, steamer or rail (stop at Geneva); Geneva to Paris, night train 1

Paris to London 1

—
14

Tour of Seventeen Days.

VIII.
DAYS

London to Paris 1

Paris to Geneva, rail (stop at Geneva) 1

Geneva to Chamouni, carriage 1

Visit Glacier des Bossons, Mont Anvers, La Flegerè, foot or mule 1

Chamouni to Martigny, by Col de Balme, or Tête Noire, foot or mule 1

Martigny to Villeneuve, rail; visit castle of Chillon, foot or carriage; Villeneuve to Lausanne, per rail or steamer 1

Lausanne to Berne, rail; stopping at Fribourg 1

Berne to Thun, rail; Thun to Interlaken, steamer; Interlaken to Lauterbrunnen, carriage 1

DAYS.

Lauterbrunnen to Grindelwald, by the Wengeren Alp, foot or mule; visit Grindelwald Glacier 1

Grindelwald to Reichenbach, foot or mule; on to Brienz, carriage; Brienz to Giessbach; sleep there 1

Giessbach to Brienz, boat; Brienz to Alpnach or Stanzstad, carriage; on to Lucerne, steamer or carriage 1

Lucerne to Fluelen, steamer, and back to Waggis; ascend Righi foot or mule 1

Righi, foot or mule; Art to Horgen, steamer or carriage; Horgen to Rapperschwyl, steamer; Rapperschwyl to Ragatz, rail 1

To Pfeffers Baths foot or carriage; Ragatz to St Gallen rail; on to Rhine Fall (Schuffhausen), by rail 1

Schaffhausen to Zurich, rail; visit Uetliberg, foot or mule; or ancient lake habitations at Meilen, boat 1

Zurich to Bâle, rail; stay at Bâle; on to Paris by night train 1

Paris to London 1

——

17

Tour of the Grisons and Italian Lakes, (Seventeen Days).

IX.

DAYS

London to Paris 1

Paris to Bâle, night train; Bâle by Olten to Berne; on by afternoon train to Lausanne 1

Rail from Lausanne, by lake of Geneva, and up Rhone valley to Sierre; thence by carriage to Brieg 1

Diligence (6 a.m.), over Simplon to Stresa ... 1

Row boat or steamer to the Borromean Islands and Pallanza; sleep there 1

Steamer by Lago Maggiore to Luino; carriage to Lugano ascend Mount Salvatore, on foot or horse 1

Steamer to Capolago; carriage to Como; steamer to Bellagio 1

To Villas Frizzoni, Serbelloni, Melzi, and Somariva 1

Steamer to Colico; carriage to Chiavenna ... 1

In carriage or on foot by the Bergell, over the Maloja to Upper Engadin, St. Moritz, or Samaden 1

Excursions to Piz Ott, the Glacier of Morteratsch, or Piz Languard 2

Post (Diligence), over the Julier Pass, and by Oberhalbstein Valley, to Chur 1

Rail to Ragatz; in carriage or on foot in the Tamina Valley, and back to Ragatz; rail along the Lake of Wallenstadt, to Zurich 1

Visit Town of Zurich, and ancient lake habitations; afternoon, rail to Schaffhausen Rhine Falls 1

Rail to Bâle (night train to Paris) 1

Paris to London 1

——

17

X.

DAYS

London to Paris 1

Paris to Bâle, night train; Bâle to Lucerne 1

Lucerne to Fuelen, in steamer; return to Waggis; ascend the Righi on foot or by mule; 1

Righi to Art, foot or mule; Art to Horgen, steamer or carriage: Horgen to Zurich, steamer 1

Zurich to Ragatz; visit Pfeffers Baths, and Calfenserthal, foot, and part in carriage; Ragatz to Chur, rail 1

Chur to Splugen, carriage 1

Splugen to Colico, carriage; Colico to Bellaggio, steamer 1

Bellaggio to Como, steamer; visit ancient lake habitations at the Pliniana 1

Como to Milan, rail; stay at Milan 1

Milan to Arona, rail; visit ancient lake habitations; on by steamer to Baveno; excursion to the Borromean islands 1

Baveno to Domo d'Ossola, carriage; Domo d'Ossola, carriage; Domo d'Ossola to the Simplon village, carriage or foot 1

Simplon to Brieg, carriage or foot; Brieg to Sion, carriage 1

Sion to Martigny, rail; Martigny to Chamouni, foot or mule 1

Up Flegeré and Montanvers, or to Glacier des Bossons, foot or mule 1

Chamouni to Geneva, carriage 1

Stay at Geneva; on to Paris by night train 1

Paris to London 1

——

17

Three Weeks' Tours.

XI.

DAYS

London to Paris 1

Night train, Paris to Neuchâtel; on next day to Lausanne, and Vevay, or Montreux, where stop 1

Stay a day at Neuchâtel to visit the numerous ancient lake dwellings on that lake, or on the Lakes of Morat and Bienne, near it. All accessible by rail and boat. See Appendix.

Rail by Martigny and Sion, to Sierre, carriage on to Viège 1

Viège to Zermatt, on foot or horse 1

Ascend to Riffelberg and Gorner Grat; sleep at Riffel or Zermatt 1

Excursions hence, if wished, to Cima de Jazzi, Pass of St. Theodule, &c. 1

Down Valley of Visp, to Visp, horse or foot; on by carriage to Brieg 1

Carriage to Viesch, up to the Ægglschhorn, foot or horse; sleep at Jungfrau Hotel or Bell Alp 1

Back to Viesch; thence to Rhone Glacier ... 1

Over Furka to Hospenthal, carriage by St. Gothard to Fluelen 1

Steamer to Waggis, up Righi 1

Down to Lucerne, afternoon steamer to Alpnach; thence by carriage or dilligence over Brunig to Brienz; boat to Giessbach; back by Brienz to Meyringen, on foot or horse, to Rei-

DAYS.

chembach Falls; up to Rosenlaui, and sleep there, or at Grindelwald 1

From Rosenlaui and Grindelwald, over Wengeren Alp to Lauterbrunnen 1

Carriage to Interlaken, stay there 1

Carriage or foot, to Neuhaus, steamer to Thun; rail to Berne; visit lake habitations of Moosseedorf 1

Berne to Zurich, rail 1

Steam from Zurich to Rapperschwyl; rail to Ragatz; visit Pfäffers 1

Rail to Chur; carriage to Thusis; foot or carriage to Via Mala; back to Thusis 1

Carriage back to Chur; rail to Rorschach; steamer over Lake of Constance; rail, Constance to Bâle, stopping at Schaffhausen Falls 1

To Bâle, and the night train to Paris............ 1

Paris to London 1
———
21

From Rorschach, the tourist can cross the Lake of Constance to Friederichshafen, and take rail by Stuttgardt, Baden, and the Rhine, to Belgium and England. This would add about two days to the journey.

XII. DAYS

London to Paris 1

Paris to Geneva 1

Geneva to Chamouni 1

Visit la Flégère, the Brevent, the Jardin on the Mer de Glace, or the Grand Mulets 1

Chamouni to Martigny, by Col de Balme or Tête Noire 1

Martigny to Bad Lenk, rail and foot; visit Torrenthorn 1

Bad Lenk to Kandersteg, by Gemmi, mule or foot; on by Oeschinen Lake, back to Interlaken 1

Interlaken to Grindelwald, by Lauterbrunnen and Wengeren Alp, foot, or mule and carriage, as far as Lauterbrunnen............ 1

Grindelwald to Reichenbach, by Rosenlaui or Faulhorn; on to Brienz, carriage from Meyringen 1

Brienz by Brunig to Alpnach, and over lake to Wäggis; then up Righi 1

Righi to Art; Art to Brunnen, by Goldau Landslip and Schwyz; Brunnen to Fluelen, boat............ 1

Fluelen to Andermatt 1

Andermatt to Bellinzona 1

Bellinzona to Como, by Lugano, visiting Mount Salvatore 1

Como to Chiavenna, steamer and carriage; and up to village of Splugen, carriage 1

Splugen to Chur, by Via Mala 1

Chur to Ragatz, rail; visit Pfäffers (baths); foot, Ragatz to St. Gallen, rail 1

St. Gallen to Schaffhausen, rail; From Rhine to Zurich, rail 1

Zurich to Berne 1

DAYS.

Berne to Neuchâtel; visit ancient lake habitations on Lakes of Bienne, Neuchâtel, and Morat 1

Neuchâtel to Paris, night train.

Paris to London 1
———
22

XIII. DAYS

London to Paris 1

Paris to Geneva, night train; rest at Geneva; visit ancient lake dwellings 1

Geneva to Sixt............ 1

Ascension of the Buet, foot; Buet to châlets of Villy 1

Villy to Chamouni, by the Brevent 1

Chamouni to Nant Borant 1

Nant Borant to the Motets, by the Cols of Bonhomme and Fours, foot or mule 1

Motets to Cormajeur, by the Col de la Seigne and the Allée Blanche, foot or mule 1

Cormajeur to Aosta, carriage; Aosta to Chatillon, Carriage; Chatillon to Breuil, foot... 1

Breuil to Riffellberg, by the Col de St. Theodule, foot 1

Ascend Gorner Grat, or Cima de Jazzi, or, if possi-ble, Monte Rosa............ 1

Descend to Zermatt. Zermatt to Mattmark See by Saas and Adler Pass, foot 1

Mattmark See to Vogogna, by Mont Moro and Macugnaga 1

Vogogna to Baveno, in carriage. To the Borromean Islands, and on to Locarno by steamer. Thence to Bellinzona in carriage... 2

Bellinzona to Airolo, carriage; Airolo to Andermatt, by St. Gothard, foot or carriage ... 1

Andermatt to Fluelen, carriage; Fluelen to Wäggis, steamer; Waggis to Righi, foot or mule 1

Righi to Lucerne, by Küssnacht, foot and steamer; Lucerne to Alpnach, steamer; Apnach to Sarnen, steamer, or Lungern, or over Brunig to Brienz or Meyringen............ 1

Brienz or Meyringen to Faulhorn, by Giessbach, foot 1

Faulhorn to Grindenwald, foot; Grindelwald to Lauterbrunnen by Wengeren Alp 1

Lauterbrunnen to Interlaken, foot or carriage; on to Thun, steamer; Thun to Berne, rail; Berne to Neuchâtel (see ancient lake dwellings) 1

Night Train from Neuchâtel to Paris; stoppage at Paris 1

Paris to London 1
———
23

Four Weeks' Tour to Swiss and Italian Lakes—Chamouni.

XIV. DAYS

London to Paris 1

Paris to Bâle, night train; Bâle to Zurich ... 1

Steamboat to Rapperschwyl (visit ancient lake dwellings at Meilen); rail by Wesen to Ragatz 1

DAYS.

Rail to Chūr, carriage to Thusis, by the Viâ Mala, and the valley of Schams to the Splügen 1

Start from Splugen (village), 6 a.m. by diligence for Chiavenna and Colico; steamer on Lake Como to Bellaggio 1

Row on lake in gondola; in the afternoon steamer to Como; omnibus to Camerlata: rail to Milan 1

Stay and visit Milan; if time allows, excursions may be made to Peschiera. Lake of Garda, to the Lake Varese and Terramare, district of Modena, to see ancient lake habitations 1

Rail to Sesto Calende; visit lake habitation at Arona: on by steamer up Lago Maggiore to the Borromean Islands; sleep at the Isola Bella or Stresa 1

Steamer to Luino; carriage or diligence to Lugano; ascend Mont Salvatore 1

Diligence to Bellinzona, and up the Val Levantina to Airolo 1

Carriage or dilligence by St. Gothard to Altdorf; walk into the Schächenthal; visit Tell's house, at Bürglen 1

Omnibus to Fluelen; at 7 a.m., steamer over Lake of Lucerne to Brunnen; take a row boat to visit the Grütli and back; afternoon, steamer to Wäggis, ascend Righi 1

From Righi to Lucerne, on by steamer to Meyringen (1st day); to Grindelwald, by Rosenlaui (2nd day); to Lauterbrunnen, by Wengeren Alp (3rd day); to Interlaken and Giessbach or Thun (4th day) 4

Rail to Berne; visit ancient lake habitations, Mosseedorf and Bienne (Nydau) 1

Rail from Berne to Thun 1

Carriage to Kandersteg, on foot or mule, over Gemmi to Bad Lenk 1

Ascend Torrenthorn, on to Visp, up Visp Valley to Zermatt 1

Ascend Gornergrat or Monte Rosa; return to Visp; on to Sierre or Sion 1

Rail to Martigny; over Col de Balme or Tête Noire to Chamouni 1

Excursions to Breven, Jardin, or La Flegere 1

Carriage by Arve Valley to Geneva 1

Stay at Geneva 1

Rail by Neuchâtel (viewing ancient lake habitations) to Weissenstein by Soleure 1

To Bâle (night train to Paris) 1

Paris to London 1

———
28

Month's Tour.

XV.

DAYS

London to Paris 1

Paris to Geneva 1

Geneva, by steamer to Chillon or Montreux; excursion to Dent de Jaman; En Avant or Sepey, and the Val des Ormonds 1

Return to Geneva, visiting old lake habitations at Morges 1

Geneva to Sixt 1

DAYS.

Ascend the Vandruz by the Buet to the Châlet of Villy 1

To Chamouni by the Brevent 1

To Chamouni, to the Jardin (or ascend to the Grands Mulets) 1

Chamouni to Nant Borant, by the Pavillon de Bellevue; ascend Mont Joli 1

Nant Borant to Motets, by the Cols du Bonhomme and des Foure 1

Motets to Cormajeur, by the Col de la Seigne and Allée Blanche; ascend the Cramont 1

Cormajeur through Aosta and Chatillon to Val Tournanche 1

Val Tourmanche to Gressonay, by Cimes Blanches and Betta Furke 1

Gressonay to Alagna, by Col d'Ollen 1

Alagna to Macugnaga, by the Col delle Loccie 1

Macugnaga to Zermatt (for good walkers 12 to 14 hours) 1

Excursions from Zermatt to Riffelberg, Gorner Grat or Evolena: Zermatt to Saas, by Adler Pass 1

Saas to Pestarena, by Monte Moro (excursion to Pizzo Bianco) 1

Pestarena to Baveno (visit Borromean Islands) 1

Baveno to Milan, by Arona (viewing the ancient lake habitations) 1

Stay at Milan

Milan to Como, rail; Como to Colico, steamer; Colico to Chiavenna, carriage. Excursion to Lugano and Mounts Camoghe and Salvatore. Ascend Monte Generoso 1

Chiavenna to St. Moritz or Pontresina. Ascend Piz Longuard; visit Bernina and Rosegg Glaciers 1

From Pontresina to Alveneu, by the Albula 1

From Alveneu to Chur, carriage; Chur to Ragatz, rail; visit Pfeffers Baths 1

Ragatz to St. Gallen; St. Gallen to Schauffhausen, rail; visit Rhine Fall; Schauffhausen to Zurich, rail 1

From Rorschach or St. Gallen to Appenzell, by Heiden and Gais. Ascend Guebris, Kamor, and Saentis 1

Zurich to Horgen, steamer; Horgen to Art, carriage or foot and boat; Art to Righi. Ascend Pilatus 1

Righi to Wäggis, on to Fluelen, steamer; Fluelen to Andermatt; ascend Frohnalp or Bristentock; visit Engelberg; Titlis the Surenen Pass, &c. 1

Andermatt to Grimsel, by Furka. Excursion to Bell Alp or Æggischhorn; ascension of Sidelhorn. Visit Pommatt and Tosa Falls 1

Grimsel to Reichenbach 1

Reichenbach to Grindelwald; ascend Faulhorn or Schienige Platte 1

Grindelwald to Lauterbrunnen, by Wengeren Alp, and on to Interlaken. Excursions from Lauterbrunnen to the Schmadribach, by the Tschingel Glacier to Kandersteg and round to Interlaken 1

From Kandersteg to Bad Lenk, by Gemmi

DAYS

back to Thun, by the Ravil or by Bex les Iles, Col de Pillon and the Simmenthal. Excursion from Interlaken to the Giessbach 1

Interlaken to Berne, by Thun. Ascend Niesen or Stockhorn... 0

Berne to Paris, by Bâle or Neuchâtel. Excursions to ancient pile works, Lakes of Bienne, Morat, and Neuchâtel 1

Paris to London 1

———

35

XVI.

DAYS

London to Paris 1

Paris to Bâle, night train; Bâle, by Munsterthal. Ascend Weissenstein. Visit ancient lake habitations near Bienne: rail to Lucerne.......... 1

Lucerne to Zurich and Schaffhausen, Rhine Fall, rail 1

Schaffhausen to St. Gallen, rail, or to Weissbad, by Appenzell, carriage. Excursion by Weissbad to Wildkirchli. Ascend Saentis 1

Weissbad to Kamor. Kamor to the Rheinthal, Ragatz, Pfeffers, and the Calfeuserthal. Ascend Scesa Plana 1

Ragatz to Klosters, by Davos 1

Davos to Süss, by Fluela 1

Süss to Pontresina or St. Moritz. Ascend Piz Languard. Excursion to Rosegg and Berina Glaciers; Pontresina to Tiefenkasten 1

Tiefenkasten to Thusis; Thusis to Splugen . Splugen to Hinter Rhein, by Valserberg .... Excursion to Hinter Rhein Glacier; Ilanz Stachelberg, by Kistengrat; ascend Tödi ... Stachelberg to Schwyz, by Pragel .... Schwyz to Alpnach; ascend Pilatus.......... Pilatus to Engelberg; ascend Titlis .... Over Joch, to Rosenlaui .... Over Faulhorn to Giessbach; or by Gui horn to Interlaken .... To Kandersteg by Mürren .... From Kandersteg to Wildstrubel and Leni Over Rawil Pass or Saanetsch to Sion ...... Rail to Sierre, up Val Anniviers to Evolena Excursion to Bella Tola; over Col de Torre and Col d'Herens to Zermatt; Evolena to St Monthey and Champery .... Ascend Dent di Midi; Champery to Sixt ... Champery to Sixt .... Ascend Fer a Cheval; visit Falls; Sixt Sallenches, by Portellas............................ Sallenches to Geneva .... Geneva to Vevay.................................... Vevay to Col de Jaman to Fribourg .... Fribourg to Neuchâtel; Ancient lake habitations .... Night train to Paris................................. Paris to London ....